TALIBANISTAN

EDITED BY

PETER BERGEN

WITH

KATHERINE TIEDEMANN

TALIBANISTAN

Negotiating the Borders Between
Terror, Politics, and Religion

OXFORD
UNIVERSITY PRESS

OXFORD
UNIVERSITY PRESS

Oxford University Press is a department of the University of Oxford.
It furthers the University's objective of excellence in research, scholarship,
and education by publishing worldwide.

Oxford   New York
Auckland   Cape Town   Dar es Salaam   Hong Kong   Karachi
Kuala Lumpur   Madrid   Melbourne   Mexico City   Nairobi
New Delhi   Shanghai   Taipei   Toronto

With offices in
Argentina   Austria   Brazil   Chile   Czech Republic   France   Greece
Guatemala   Hungary   Italy   Japan   Poland   Portugal   Singapore
South Korea   Switzerland   Thailand   Turkey   Ukraine   Vietnam

Oxford is a registered trademark of Oxford University Press in the UK and certain other
countries.

Published in the United States of America by
Oxford University Press
198 Madison Avenue, New York, NY 10016

Library of Congress Cataloging-in-Publication Data
Talibanistan : negotiating the borders between terror, politics and religion / edited by
Peter Bergen ; with Katherine Tiedemann.
pages ; cm
Includes bibliographical references and index.
ISBN 978-0-19-989309-6—ISBN 978-0-19-989307-2   1. Taliban.   2. Insurgency—
Pakistan.   3. Insurgency—Afghanistan.   4. Religious militants—Pakistan.   5. Religious militants—
Afghanistan.   6. Afghan War, 2001–   7. Qaida (Organization)   I. Bergen, Peter L., 1962– editor of
compilation.   II. Tiedemann, Katherine, editor of compilation.
DS389.T355 2013
958.104'71—dc23
2012017447

ISBN 978-0-19-989309-6 (pbk); 978-0-19-989307-2 (cloth)

1 3 5 7 9 8 6 4 2
Printed in the United States of America
on acid-free paper

Contents

Acknowledgments

FIRST, THANKS TO my coeditor Katherine Tiedemann, who spent countless hours working with the researchers in this book to help shape their work and make a complex subject as accessible as feasible. (After Katherine left the New America Foundation in May 2011 she was not involved further in preparing this volume.) Thanks also to Andrew Lebovich and Jennifer Rowland of New America, who helped to finalize the book as it went into production.

Thanks to Brian Fishman and Patrick Doherty at New America, who helped to shape this project in myriad ways. And thanks to Steve Coll, the president of New America, who provided critical intellectual and moral support to this project. Thanks to Simone Frank of New America, who handled the many contractual issues that arose while working with more than a dozen authors, many of whom are based in Pakistan or Afghanistan.

Thanks also to all of the researchers in this book who worked long and hard to make their chapters as authoritative as possible while writing on a subject that is simultaneously often obscure—and in some cases, quite risky.

Thanks to Marin Strmecki of the Smith Richardson Foundation, who was instrumental in making this book happen by giving both critical financial and intellectual support to this project. Barmak Pazhwak of the United States Institute of Peace also provided funding and intellectual support for the poll we conducted in Pakistan's tribal regions. Thanks to Troy Schneider of New America and Development Seed for conceptualizing and creating the data visualization for that poll, which can be found at www.pakistansurvey.org. Thanks also to our partner on the ground who conducted that poll, the Community Appraisal and Motivation Programme.

The Pashtun journalist Imtiaz Ali was very helpful throughout this project, as was copy editor Keith Sinzinger. Thanks to Gene Thorp for the handsome maps that can be found throughout this book.

Thanks to editor Timothy Bent at Oxford University Press, who believed in this project from its inception and who has been an unfailingly helpful and thoughtful collaborator; and to his colleague Keely Latcham, who helped to bring the book through the production process. And thanks also to Thomas Finnegan for his copyediting, as well as Jashnie Jabson at Newgen and Maria Pucci at Oxford for their help with production.

Finally, thanks to my wife, Tresha Mabile, who has spent time on the ground in both Afghanistan and Pakistan reporting on the Taliban for National Geographic Television and who has been, as always, supportive of this project.

Peter Bergen, Washington DC, August 2012.

Contributors

Hassan Abbas was Quaid-i-Azam chair professor at Columbia University and is now professor at National Defense University. He previously held high-ranking positions in the Pakistani police.

Ken Ballen is the author of *Terrorists in Love* and the president of Terror Free Tomorrow, a nonpartisan organization that studies extremism around the world.

Peter Bergen, CNN's national security analyst and author of four books on al-Qaeda, is a director at the New America Foundation.

Martine van Bijlert is the co-director of the Afghanistan Analysts Network and is based in Kabul.

Patrick Doherty is the director of the Smart Strategy Program at the New America Foundation.

Brian Fishman is a counterterrorism research fellow at the New America Foundation.

Anand Gopal is a fellow at the New America Foundation and a journalist who has reported for the *Wall Street Journal*, the *Christian Science Monitor*, and other outlets on Afghanistan. He is writing a history of Afghanistan after September 11, 2001.

Daud Khan Khattak is a Pashtun journalist currently working with Radio Mashal, a project of Radio Free Europe/Radio Liberty in Prague.

Khattak has worked with Pakistan's English dailies *The News* and *Daily Times* and Afghanistan's Pajhwok Afghan News, and he has also written for the *Christian Science Monitor* and London's *Sunday Times*.

Sameer Lalwani, a research fellow at the New America Foundation, is pursuing a Ph.D. in political science at the Massachusetts Institute of Technology.

Thomas F. Lynch III is Distinguished Research Fellow for South Asia and the Near East at the Center for Strategic Research, part of the National Defense University's Institute for National Strategic Studies (NDU-INSS).

Mansur Khan Mahsud is the research coordinator for the FATA Research Center, an Islamabad-based think tank. He is from the Mahsud tribe of South Waziristan and has worked with several NGOs and news outlets as a researcher. He holds a master's degree in Pakistani studies from the University of Peshawar.

Rahmanullah is a Pashtun journalist working with the BBC in Peshawar. Previously, he worked with Pajhwok Afghan News and has written for numerous local and foreign publications. He uses one name.

Jennifer Rowland is a program associate at the New America Foundation.

Thomas Ruttig is the co-director of the Afghanistan Analysts Network. He speaks Pashtu and Dari.

Pir Zubair Shah, a journalist hailing from Waziristan, is the Edward Murrow fellow at the Council on Foreign Relations and is one of a small group of *New York Times* journalists who won the Pulitzer Prize for their coverage of Afghanistan and Pakistan in 2009.

Anne Stenersen is a research fellow at the Norwegian Defence Research Establishment (FFI) in Oslo. She has an M.Phil. in Asian and African studies from the University of Oslo, majoring in Arabic language. She is pursuing a doctorate about the relationship between al-Qaeda and the Taliban.

Katherine Tiedemann is a former research fellow at the New America Foundation.

Introduction

Peter Bergen

Not since the Khmer Rouge, wearing their distinctive black pajamas, emerged out of the forests of Cambodia in the mid-1970s and seized Phnom Penh, and then dragged their country back to the "Year Zero," has so much mystery surrounded an armed group as that which attended the Taliban movement when it burst onto the world stage in the mid-1990s. Turbaned religious warriors swept seemingly out of nowhere in fleets of Toyota pickup trucks to take over much of Afghanistan, where they imposed by force their ultrapurist and unforgiving version of Islam—only to fall from power following the September 11, 2001, attacks because they refused to hand over Osama bin Laden to the United States.

At the core of the Taliban mystery is the movement's leader, Mullah Omar. He has been photographed on only a couple of occasions, and when he ran Afghanistan he rarely traveled to the capital, Kabul, preferring instead the southern city of Kandahar, long the traditional center of power for the Pashtuns. At his residence in Kandahar Mullah Omar assiduously avoided meeting non-Muslims and most journalists. He ruled like a medieval lord, dispensing wads of cash to his acolytes from a wooden box, while using his interpretations of his dreams to guide his decisions. A man often described as humble and undereducated, Mullah Omar allowed himself in 1996 to be anointed the "Commander of the Faithful," a rarely invoked religious title used at the time of the immediate successors of the Prophet Mohammed and implying that he sees himself as the leader not only of the Taliban but of all Muslims everywhere.

This suggests that Mullah Omar is a religious fanatic with significant delusions of grandeur. Otherworldly he may be, but his movement, consisting of tens of thousands of religious warriors, has for more than a decade remained undefeated by the world's greatest military power.

Mystery continues to swirl around Mullah Omar today. He makes rare, opaque public statements that are released via Taliban websites and is believed to have spent the past decade in or around the southwestern Pakistani city of Quetta, as well as in Karachi, the Pakistani megalopolis on the southern coast, though no one seems to know for certain. Likewise, the degree of operational control that he exercises over his movement remains a matter of debate. Most Taliban groups continue to regard him as Commander of the Faithful, but what this means in practice is hard to decipher. That is because the Taliban movement—as this book will make clear—is both fractious and localized, composed of many, sometimes competing, factions. Some factions are close to al-Qaeda, while others disdain it; some attack the Pakistani government, while others have a modus vivendi with the Pakistani state and instead attack NATO forces in Afghanistan as well as the Afghan government.

Even many years after the September 11 attacks a profound murkiness surrounds the Taliban. As a measure of its impenetrability, in 2010 someone claiming to be Mullah Akhtar Muhammad Mansour, one of the senior leaders of the Taliban movement, spent months in "peace negotiations" with NATO officials, and even met with Afghan president Hamid Karzai, only later to be revealed as an impostor who was conning NATO for considerable sums of money.

Welcome to Talibanistan.

This volume seeks to clarify some of the murkiness. It begins, appropriately, in Kandahar with a chapter by journalist Anand Gopal that explains how the Taliban insurgency was first spawned in early 2002, and how it consolidated over time. The nub of Gopal's findings, which are based on dozens of interviews with members of the Taliban, including leaders of the movement, is that it was far from certain that the Taliban would form an insurgency after the fall of their regime. Gopal explains:

> The Taliban's resurgence in Kandahar post-2001 was not inevitable or preordained. The Taliban—from senior leadership levels down to the rank and file—by and large surrendered to the new government and retired to their homes. But in the early years after 2001, there was a lack of a genuine, broad-based reconciliation process in which the Taliban leadership would be allowed to surrender in exchange for amnesty and protection from persecution. Rather, foreign forces and their proxies pursued an unrelenting drive against former regime members, driving many of them to flee to Pakistan and launch an insurgency.

Gopal then describes how the Taliban over time developed in many Afghan provinces

> an intricate shadow government apparatus. At the top is the shadow governor, who works closely with a body called the Military Commission. In theory, the governor directs strategy, coordinates with leadership in Pakistan, and carries out liaison with other actors in the province, while the Military Commission adjudicates disputes and serves in an advisory role. There is also a detailed district-level apparatus, including shadow district governors and, in some districts, police chiefs.

From Kandahar we move to the area on Afghanistan's eastern border with Pakistan, where the Taliban and al-Qaeda have sporadically worked together tactically for the past decade. (This is not the case in southern Afghanistan in the traditional Taliban strongholds of Kandahar and Helmand, where there is no al-Qaeda presence to speak of.) In her piece, Anne Sternsen, a Norwegian researcher, analyzes the relations between the Taliban and al-Qaeda. She bases her findings on a close reading of Arabic- language biographies of "martyred" al-Qaeda fighters in Afghanistan as well as al-Qaeda propaganda videos focusing on the Afghan war.

We then move to central Afghanistan, where Martine van Bijlert, a Kabul-based researcher who has spent more than a decade working in Afghanistan, Pakistan, and Iran, and the co-director of the Afghanistan Analyst Network—by far the best think tank involving

Afghanistan—delves into the tribal dynamics that helped fuel the Taliban in Uruzgan and Zabul. Her conclusions stem from some three hundred interviews that she conducted with a variety of local officials, Taliban commanders, and NGO workers. Van Bijlert warns that NATO's reliance on local militias to help police the two provinces may backfire.

From central Afghanistan we cross the Pakistani border into the tribal agency of North Waziristan, home to arguably the most effective of all the Taliban militias, the Haqqani Network, which has provided shelter to foreign militants, including al-Qaeda, for many years. Anand Gopal was able to interview Sirajuddin Haqqani, the reclusive and de facto leader of the Haqqani network. Together with the Waziri researcher Mansur Khan Mahsud, and aided by the New America Foundation's Brian Fishman, Gopal traces the history of the Haqqanis and the precise nature of their alliances with other Taliban groups, including Mullah Omar's "Quetta Shura."

From there we move southward to South Waziristan with Mansur Khan Mahsud as our guide. Mahsud, a member of the Mahsud tribe from South Waziristan, leads us through the labyrinth of Waziri tribal politics that has produced the leadership of the "Pakistani Taliban," which has focused much of its energies on attacking the Pakistan state. In retaliation, the Pakistani military has launched operations against the Taliban, with moderate success.

Those operations and similar ones in the northern region of Swat are detailed in the essay by Sameer Lalwani, who is studying political science at MIT. He explains how the Pakistani military has not adopted a classic "population-centric" counterinsurgency (COIN) doctrine, as outlined in the US military's 2006 COIN manual (written under the direction of David Petraeus, then an Army lieutenant general and now director of the CIA) but rather has taken its own distinctive approach to defeating the Taliban, with some degree of success. For instance, when the Pakistani army was planning its attack on the Taliban in the northern region of Swat in 2009 it ordered some two million residents of the region to leave the area, a tactic that worked fairly well.

Another approach is the CIA-directed drone war in Pakistan. Although the drone campaign is generally understood as being aimed at al-Qaeda, in fact many of the strikes have targeted various factions of the Taliban. Pulitzer prize–winning journalist Pir Zubair Shah, himself from Waziristan, provides a summary of his six years of reporting on the ground about the drone strikes. (Thanks to Susan Glasser, the editor-in-chief of *Foreign Policy*, where this essay first appeared, for permission to reprint it.)

New America Foundation's Jennifer Rowland and I then analyze the toll that drone strikes have taken on Taliban leaders and foot soldiers. All told, the 307 strikes launched by the United States in Pakistan between June 2004 and June 2012 have killed, according to some news accounts, roughly 1,600–2,400 suspected militants. Of those strikes, 70 percent have struck North Waziristan, and more than a third have reportedly targeted members of the Taliban, with at least ten of the strikes killing senior Taliban commanders as well as hundreds of lower-level fighters.

Our analysis is followed by an assessment of an opinion poll in Pakistan's tribal regions, conducted by the New America Foundation in 2010 under the direction of Ken Ballen, Patrick Doherty, and me, and in collaboration with a local NGO called the Community Appraisal and Motivation Programme. This was the first scientific poll in the tribal regions taken to probe sensitive political issues. It found that more than three-quarters of the residents of the tribal regions oppose American drone strikes.

Opposition to American policies in the region does not mean, however, that the people of the Federally Administered Tribal Areas (FATA) embrace either al-Qaeda or the Taliban. More than three-quarters of FATA residents oppose the presence of al-Qaeda and more than two-thirds oppose the local Taliban groups. Indeed, according to the poll, were al-Qaeda or the Taliban on the ballot in an election, fewer than 1 percent of the residents of FATA said they would vote for either group.

Hassan Abbas, a leading Pakistani political scientist and former high-ranking police officer, explains the larger political context in which the Taliban functions in northwestern Pakistan, and in particular the support it receives from a coalition of hard-line religious parties known as the MMA. The MMA's unwillingness to confront the Taliban when it controlled the North-West Frontier Province (now renamed Khyber Pakhtunkhwa) between 2002 and 2008 enabled the Taliban to attack at will in the provincial capital city, Peshawar.

It also helped set the stage for the Taliban seizure of much of Swat in 2009, the history of which is recounted by Pashtun journalist Daud Khan Khattak, who spent considerable time on the ground in Swat while the Taliban advanced toward the Pakistani capital, Islamabad, and were then repelled by the Pakistani military. In his chapter, Rahmanullah, a Pashtun journalist who goes by only one name, describes the structure of the Taliban factions in Bajaur, one of the seven tribal agencies along the Afghan border, and a region that has also hosted members of al-Qaeda.

Brian Fishman of the New America Foundation then analyzes all of the Taliban groups in northwest Pakistan and their various alliances and target sets. In the process Fishman points out that the practice, so common in certain circles, of separating the "Afghan Taliban" and the "Pakistani Taliban" tends to obscure as much as it clarifies.

Thomas F. Lynch III of the National Defense University was an active-duty U.S. Army officer for three decades and served as a special assistant to the chairman of the Joint Chiefs of Staff. In his essay Lynch makes the case that in the wake of bin Laden's death in 2011 al-Qaeda has been strategically defeated. He considers what that means for U.S. policy in South Asia and argues that the United States should shift its focus from killing off every last al-Qaeda-affiliated leader or midlevel Haqqani Network operative in Pakistan to preventing a proxy war in Afghanistan between Pakistan and India, one in which Pakistan would back the Taliban in a civil war that pits them against elements of the former Northern Alliance supported by India.

Part of heading off such a proxy war must involve some kind of peace process with the Taliban, or at least with those elements of the Taliban that are "reconcilable." Thomas Ruttig, a co-director of the Afghanistan Analysts Network who has spent decades working in Afghanistan, examines the history of Taliban "reconciliation" and the additional momentum that the process gained in 2010. Ruttig warns, however, that the contacts with the Taliban remain preliminary and exploratory, and that the discussions have not yet reached the "nego-tiations" stage. This means that even though all parties to the conflict are open to exploring a political solution they continue to fight each other. That reality lies at the heart of Talibanistan.

After more than three decades of various kinds of wars, one can only hope that the Taliban as well as other Afghan factions will tire of the end-less conflict that has gripped their country and find common ground.

TALIBANISTAN

ONE

The Taliban in Kandahar

Anand Gopal

EXECUTIVE SUMMARY

As Afghanistan's cultural and political heartland, Kandahar is a province of key strategic importance for foreign forces, the Afghan government, and the insurgency. A sizable chunk of the Taliban's senior leadership hails from the province, and the cultural and political dynamics of rural Kandahar shape aspects of the movement's character to this day. This study attempts to understand the Taliban of Kandahar by looking at the factors that spurred their rise and the networks and structures through which they operate. Among the findings:

- The Taliban's resurgence in Kandahar post-2001 was not inevitable or preordained. The Taliban—from senior leadership levels down to the rank and file—by and large surrendered to the new government and retired to their homes. But in the early years after 2001, there was a lack of a genuine, broad-based reconciliation process in which the Taliban leadership would be allowed to surrender in exchange for amnesty and protection from persecution. Rather, foreign forces and their proxies pursued an unrelenting drive against former regime members,

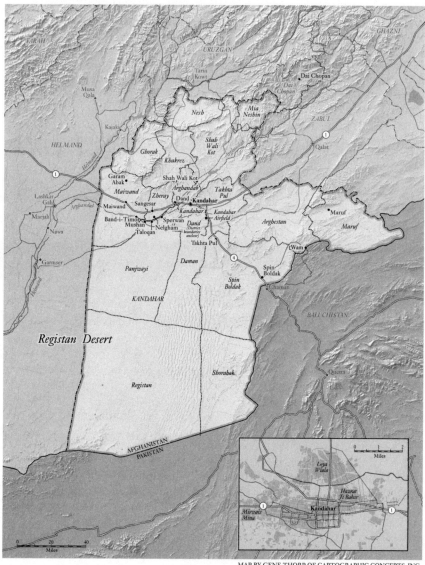

MAP BY GENE THORP OF CARTOGRAPHIC CONCEPTS, INC.

driving many of them to flee to Pakistan and launch an insurgency.

- Once the Taliban leadership decided to stand against the Afghan government and its foreign backers, they were able to take advantage of growing disillusionment in the countryside. In particular, the dominance of one particular set of tribes caused members of other, marginalized tribes to look to the insurgency as a source of protection and access to resources. The weakness of the judiciary and police forced many to turn to the Taliban's provision of law and order, while widespread torture and abuse at the hands of pro-government strongmen eroded government support. At the same time, the heavy-handed tactics of U.S. forces turned many against the foreign presence.

- Despite popular belief, the Taliban in Kandahar cannot easily be divided into an "ideological core" and rank-and-file fighters motivated mainly by material concerns. After 2001, most senior Taliban leaders in the province accepted the new government, or at least rejected it but declined to fight against it. Most did not invoke the notion of *jihad* as an immediate reaction to the new government. Rather, only after a protracted campaign against former Taliban did many of them feel they had no place in the new state of affairs and begin to see the presence of the government and foreign fighters as necessitating jihad. And after the emergence of the insurgency, there were a number of attempts by senior leaders to come to terms with the Afghan government, yet at the same time there were very few attempts to do so on the part of rank-and-file field commanders.

- The Taliban have developed an intricate shadow government apparatus. At the top is the shadow governor, who works closely with a body called the Military Commission. In theory, the governor directs strategy, coordinates with leadership in Pakistan, and liaises with other actors in the province, while the Military Commission adjudicates disputes and serves in an advisory role. There is also a detailed district-level apparatus, including shadow district governors and, in some districts, police chiefs and district shuras.

- Parallel to this formal structure are numerous informal networks through which the Taliban make decisions and propagate influence. Although there are detailed mechanisms in place, involving the provincial shadow apparatus, to deal with battlefield strategy or intra-Taliban disputes, many times strategic decisions or punitive actions are taken through informal means. These include cases where senior leaders in Pakistan direct operations through their network of commanders in Kandahar.

- Contrary to popular perception, the Taliban in Kandahar do not appear to receive regular salaries. Rather, each commander is responsible for raising funds for his group, which is typically done through capturing spoils in operations or collecting (sometimes forcefully) local taxes. Some funding also comes from external sources, such as merchants in Pakistan and wealthy donors in the Persian Gulf states.

- In addition to winning support from marginalized communities and offering law and order, the Taliban were able to gain influence through severe intimidation and widespread human rights abuses. Moreover, a brutal assassination campaign against anyone even remotely connected to the government—tribal elders, government officials, aid workers, religious clerics, and others— succeeded in widening the gap between the local communities and the government.
- The Taliban's rise in Kandahar after 2001 can be divided into four periods. From 2001 to 2004, the group was involved in reorganizing itself, resuscitating old networks, and forging new connections. Between 2004 and 2006, the burgeoning movement was focused on consolidating itself, while winning rank-and-file recruits outside those who had worked with the Taliban in the 1990s; it began to amass members in large numbers. A turning point came in the western part of the province in 2006, when the Taliban suffered a major battlefield loss against foreign forces in Operation Medusa. This was one factor that spurred the next phase, asymmetric warfare, between 2006 and 2009. These years were marked by the increased use of suicide bombings and roadside attacks. The year 2010 marked a new phase in the struggle. While the insurgents were still relying heavily on suicide attacks and roadside bombs, foreign troops were giving unprecedented attention to the province, and violence escalated to a level not previously seen in this war.

METHODOLOGY

The information in this study is drawn from interviews with Taliban members at all levels (including the senior leadership), Afghan government officials (including, but not limited to, district and provincial officials, lawmakers, and intelligence officials), and U.S. and NATO military personnel (including, but not limited to, officers and enlisted soldiers in the field, and intelligence officers). This reporting is supplemented by a variety of publicly available written sources, including news articles, research monographs, and books. Some of the interviews were conducted during my work as a journalist in Afghanistan for more than two years, in which time I visited Kandahar (and many of its districts) multiple times. This reporting includes many occasions when I traveled with Taliban forces or U.S. troops in the districts, and other cases when I traveled on my own. In particular, many of the interviews were conducted during trips I made to the province in the summer of 2010.

In many instances, sources spoke on the condition of anonymity due to the sensitive nature of the topic and the tense security situation in Kandahar. Every story or anecdote from a source was cross-checked with at least one other independent source. I list the names and positions of Taliban commanders only when this information is widely known in Kandahar, or the commanders themselves gave permission to include it, or U.S. personnel indicated that they had knowledge of it.

INTRODUCTION

In the early morning hours of July 20, 2010, a group of armed men approached a home in the Mahalajat area of Kandahar city. They asked to speak to Ghulam, an employee of a nongovernmental organization. When he appeared, they declared that he was under arrest by the Islamic Emirate of Afghanistan for working with foreigners. They tied him and his cousin to a nearby electric pole, shot them, and left their bodies there under the moonlight for all to see.[1]

It was a move as audacious as it was indicative of the Taliban's growing reach. Unlike in many other urban centers in Afghanistan, the Taliban have been able to penetrate deep into Kandahar city. In 2009 they even set up checkpoints in the heart of the provincial capital, close to the attorney general's office.[2] The Taliban's growing power—indeed, by 2010 they controlled most of Kandahar's districts and parts of the city—prompted plans for a major U.S. offensive in the province sometime in 2010.

Such plans were also an admission of the province's position as the country's political and cultural crucible, a role it has played for centuries.

The majority of Afghanistan's rulers in its history—including the current president, Hamid Karzai—have hailed from the sunbaked province. And in 1994, from the dusty riverbeds west of Kandahar city, came a group of religious students bringing a strict version of Islamic justice to the then-warring country. The Taliban, a group of mullahs largely from greater Kandahar, went on to capture most of Afghanistan. When the movement collapsed following the U.S.-led invasion of 2001, in the wake of al-Qaeda's September 11, 2001, attacks on New York and Washington, the insurgency that eventually emerged was led predominantly by these same mullahs. Today, in many ways, Kandahar is the heart of the insurgency, and many believe that progress there is the key to the entire war.

The insurgency in Kandahar can be understood only by examining the factors that motivate it and the structures through which it operates. This study aims to do both, and in the process illustrate that the Taliban's resurgence in Kandahar was not at all inevitable; nor was it simply due to a lack of resources or will on the part of the international community.

PART 1: THE TALIBAN IN KANDAHAR: CAUSES AND MOTIVATIONS

- The resurgence of the Taliban in Kandahar was not preordained simply because the province was their "spiritual home." Nor was it merely a result of a lack of troop presence in the early years. Rather, it was due to specific policies pursued by the Kandahar government and its American backers. A significant part of the senior Taliban leadership in Kandahar had surrendered or attempted to surrender to the Afghan government. But intense harassment left many of them with the feeling that there was no option but to flee to Pakistan and reorganize their movement. Increased troop presence would not likely have changed the dynamic, since the problem was political—the lack of a reconciliation process—rather than military.
- Once the Taliban's leadership fled to Pakistan and decided to fight against the Afghan government and foreign forces in the country, they were able to build support in disaffected

communities that were excluded from power and resources in the post-2001 world. These include, but are not limited to, second- and third-tier tribal communities such as Panjpai Durranis, victims of government abuse, victims of mistreatment by the foreign forces, the unemployed, and opium poppy cultivators (who were the target of antidrug campaigns).

ORIGINS

The leaders of today's insurgency were born into a rural, conservative, and isolated world.[3] Almost all of those living outside of Kandahar city were engaged in either subsistence farming or various forms of sharecropping. There was little access to news or other media outside of the city. In village life, most locals followed the practice of *purdah*, the strict segregation of the sexes. Social mobility was limited and education offered little value to those working the land.[4]

At the time, the central government was strongest in the city, with traditional notables—*maleks*, khans, and tribal elders—holding the most authority in the rural areas. Tribal politics was deeply entwined with governance, and tribal membership often influenced one's ability to access resources and state services. Pashtun tribes such as the Popalzais, Alikozais, and Barakzais formed a sort of tribal aristocracy, with deep ties to the ruling apparatus in Kabul and Kandahar.[5] These tribes were often given choice land, and their members usually filled the high ranks of government. In chronically underdeveloped areas such as Panjwayi, Zheray, and Maiwand, to the west of Kandahar city, the majority of the wealthiest landowners were Alikozais and Barakzais, while members of the many other less-favored tribes worked their land.

State services were limited and many Kandahari families—especially those in neglected areas like Panjwayi—sent their sons to study in *madrassas*, the religious schools that offered free room and board and the possibility of employment. This trend accelerated in the late 1970s as Pakistan financed a boom in madrassa construction throughout the border areas. After the rise of the Communists in Afghanistan in the late 1970s, the government's targeting of tribal elders and the resulting call to jihad precipitated a shift in power and prestige toward religious clergy.[6]

It is partly for these reasons that when the countryside exploded in resistance against the Soviet occupation in 1980, southern Afghanistan—and western Kandahar in particular—saw the emergence of semiautonomous mullah-led mujahideen groups. These "*taliban* fronts" typically consisted of a mullah and madrassa students and were usually nominally linked to one of the seven major mujahideen parties.[7] Many (but certainly not all) of these mullah-commanders came from underserved regions such as Panjwayi and marginalized tribes such as the Noorzais. Some hailed from a long line of mullahs, and some were orphans. As Mullah Abdul Salaam Zaeef, a 1990s-era Taliban official who fought in these fronts against the Russians, explains, the taliban fronts were often more religiously strict than other mujahideen factions:

> Fighting alongside the taliban meant more than just being a *mujahed*. The Taliban followed a strict routine in which everyone who fought alongside us had to participate, without exception. We woke before sunrise to perform the *fajr* or morning prayer in the mosque… we would recite *Surat Yasin Sharif* every morning in case we were martyred that day.… Apart from dire emergencies during operations or enemy assaults, the mujahedeen were engaged in [religious] study. Senior Taliban members would teach younger seekers, and the senior *mawlawis* would instruct other older taliban members.… Not all the fronts worked in this manner, but we were taliban and this was our way. We wanted to stay clean, to avoid sinning, and to regulate our behavior.[8]

Associated with some taliban fronts were taliban judges, religious clerics who would adjudicate disputes on the basis of their interpretation of Islamic law, or *sharia*. Given the frequent squabbles between commanders over spoils, the fractious nature of tribal society, and the failure of the state to deliver judicial services to the countryside, the need for an effective justice system was paramount. The taliban courts were extremely popular for this reason, and they remain so even today.

From the embers of the anti-Soviet insurgency emerged the core leadership of today's insurgency. Many of those who later served on the Quetta Shura, the movement's senior leadership body based in Quetta, Pakistan, served in the Taliban fronts, as Table 1.1 shows.[9] Upon the Soviet exodus, Kandahar fell into chaos as mujahideen commanders from the seven major parties carved up the province for themselves. By

TABLE I.I A Sample of Commanders of Taliban Fronts in
Kandahar in the 1980s and Their Positions in the Post-
2001 Insurgency

Commander	Tribe	Origin	Position in insurgency
Mullah Muhammad Omar	Hotak	Kandahar and Deh Rawud, Uruzgan	Supreme leader/ figurehead
Mullah Beradar	Popalzai	Deh Rawud, Uruzgan	Leader of the Quetta Shura, 2006–2010
Mullah Hassan Akhund	Babar	Soonzi, Arghandab	On-and-off member of the Quetta Shura and military shuras
Mullah Akhtar Muhammad Mansour	Ishaqzai	Band-i-Timor, Maiwand	Leader of the Quetta Shura, 2010
Tayeb Agha	Sayed	Jelahor, Arghandab	On-and-off member of the Quetta Shura and financial committee, envoy of Mullah Omar
Mullah Dadullah	Kakar	Char Chino, Uruzgan	Member of the Quetta Shura and military shuras, frontline commander as well, killed in 2007
Hafiz Majid	Noorzai	Sperwan, Panjwayi	Member of the Quetta Shura, 2010

1994, tales of rape and plunder became widespread, prompting Taliban commanders, who had been sitting aside during this civil war, to rise up against these warlords. These Taliban commanders saw their role as restorative (rescuing jihad from the hands of rapacious commanders who were using it for their own ends) and judicial (halting the conflict-fueled breakdown of society by installing their interpretation of Islamic law).

Kandaharis and Afghans from neighboring provinces dominated the resulting Taliban movement and government. To this day, greater Kandahar has provided the bulk of the Taliban's leadership.

2001–2006: CAUSES FOR THE TALIBAN'S RESURGENCE IN KANDAHAR

The Taliban were initially greeted with enthusiasm by the Pashtun-dominated war-torn south. The Taliban mullahs were already well respected in rural Kandahari society, as described above. Once the Taliban were in power, some of their strictures went against the grain of traditional rural Pashtun society, such as the banning of music, but others fit neatly with the prevailing culture, such as their approach toward women.

By the close of the 1990s, however, unending war, joblessness, and underdevelopment had eroded the Taliban's support in rural Kandahar. When U.S.-led forces invaded in 2001, the Taliban were little match for the overwhelming American firepower, and the population seemed unwilling to side with the failing government against the foreigners. Kandahar city fell on Dec. 7, 2001, prompting Mullah Omar and other senior Taliban leaders to flee to Pakistan. The former mujahideen commanders Gul Agha Sherzai, of the Barakzai tribe, and Mullah Naqib, a leader of the Alikozais, feuded for control of the city (much as they had in the early 1990s, before the Taliban's emergence).[10] The U.S. forces backed Sherzai, and within two days of Kandahar's fall he was appointed governor. Over the next few years, Sherzai and his network of commanders would do much to alienate the population and spark the Taliban's resurgence.

THE VICTORS' HUBRIS AND FAILURE OF RECONCILIATION

Just as Kandahar was falling, fissures appeared in the Taliban movement. As most of the government was crumbling—Kabul and other major cities had fallen, leaving just Kandahar, Helmand, and Zabul provinces still under Taliban control—some of Mullah Omar's chief lieutenants secretly gathered and decided to surrender to the forces of Hamid Karzai.[11] This group included Tayeb Agha, at one point Mullah Omar's top aide; Mullah Beradar, a former governor and key military commander; Sayed Muhammad Haqqani, the former ambassador to Pakistan; Mullah Obaidullah, the defense minister; Mullah Abdul Razzaq, the interior minister; and many others.

The group, represented by Obaidullah, delivered a letter to Karzai— then en route from Uruzgan to Kandahar city, one of the Taliban's last-standing urban strongholds.[12] The letter accepted Karzai's recent selection at the Bonn Conference as the country's interim leader and acknowledged that the Islamic Emirate (the official name of the Taliban government) had no chance of surviving. The Taliban officials also told Karzai that the senior leaders who signed the letter had permission from Mullah Omar to surrender. That same day, Taliban officials agreed to relinquish Kandahar city, and opposition forces successfully entered the city forty-eight hours later. The surrendered Taliban leaders continued to exchange a number of messages with the new government to work out the terms of their abdication.

The main request of the Taliban officials in this group was to be given immunity from arrest in exchange for agreeing to abstain from political life.[13] At this juncture, these leading Taliban members (as well as the rank and file) did not appear to view the government and its foreign backers as necessitating a 1980s-type jihad. Some members even saw the new government as Islamic and legitimate.[14] Indeed, Mullah Obaidullah and other former Taliban officials even surrendered to Afghan authorities in early 2002.[15] But Karzai and other government officials ignored the overtures—largely due to pressures from the United States and the Northern Alliance, the Taliban's erstwhile enemy.[16] Moreover, some Pashtun commanders who had been ousted by the Taliban seven years earlier were eager for revenge and were opposed to allowing former Taliban officials to go unpunished.[17] Widespread intimidation and harassment of these former Taliban ensued. Sympathetic figures in the government told Haqqani and others in the group that they should flee the country, for they would not be safe in Afghanistan. So the men eventually vanished across the border into Pakistan's Baluchistan province. Many of the signatories of the letter were to become leading figures in the insurgency. Mullah Obaidullah became a key deputy of Mullah Omar and one of the insurgency's leading strategists, playing an important role in rallying the scattered Taliban remnants to rebel against the Americans.[18] Sayed Muhammad Haqqani is an important participant in the Taliban's political activities. Tayeb Agha has been a leading member of the Taliban's financial committee and has served on the Quetta Shura, in addition to being one of Mullah Omar's envoys. Mullah Beradar became the day-to-day leader of the entire movement. Mullah Abdul Razzaq, based in Chaman, Pakistan (across the border from Spin Boldak), is an important weapons and cash facilitator for the Taliban and has ties to the Kandahar insurgency.[19]

The alienation of leading former Taliban commanders in Kandahar would become a key motivating factor in sparking the insurgency there. Kandahar's governor, Gul Agha Sherzai, had initially taken a conciliatory attitude toward former Taliban figures. But his close ties with U.S. special forces, who often posted rewards for top Taliban leaders, as well as isolated attacks against the government and the possibility of exploiting his position for financial gain, eventually led to a retaliatory approach. The provincial government began to harass former Taliban commanders, usually midlevel military figures, who had remained behind in Kandahar. A group of Sherzai's commanders—Khalid Pashtun, Zhed Gulalai, Karam, Agha Shah, and others—became synonymous with abuse. Some of these men had a role in provincial government: Khalid Pashtun was Sherzai's spokesman, for example, and Karam was an official of Afghanistan's intelligence agency, the National Directorate of Security (NDS).

These commanders targeted men formerly associated with the Taliban, often torturing them in secret prisons, according to numerous tribal elders, government officials, and Taliban members. Famous in the Mushan village cluster of Panjwayi district, for instance, is the case of Mullah Ahmad Shah. Shah, a former Taliban official and military commander who had surrendered, was at home in the early months of the Sherzai government. Karam and his men arrested Shah and some others on charges of having weapons, took them to a Kandahar city NDS prison and tortured them. Hajji Fazel Muhammad, who led a group of tribal elders from Panjwayi to the city to try to secure their release, recalled the scene at the prison:

> We met them in jail and saw that their feet were swollen. Their hands and feet had been tied for days, and they told us that the

prison guards would roll them around on the ground. They also beat them with cables. [The prisoners] were begging us to tell the guards to just kill them so that they could be put out of their misery.[20]

Shah was kept in custody for about three weeks, until his family members purchased weapons simply to hand over to the authorities to get him freed. But the men were arrested again and Shah's family was forced to sell all of their livestock so they could pay a bribe to the authorities. A short while later, Shah and others were arrested for a third time and held for forty-four days, until immense pressure from tribal elders brought about their release. Shah and his brothers soon fled to Pakistan, joined the burgeoning Taliban insurgency, and returned to Panjwayi as Taliban fighters. Today Shah is the head of the Taliban's main court in Mushan. His brothers Qari Allahuddin and Qari Muhammad Sadiq, along with two other siblings, are also Taliban commanders active in Panjwayi.[21]

Similar stories across Kandahar's districts abound. Hajji Lala, a prominent Taliban-era commander who went into retirement after 2001, was repeatedly harassed by Zhed Gulalai, Habibullah Jan (a Zheray strongman), and other government forces for nearly a year. He eventually decided to flee to Pakistan and join the insurgency, then served as a key commander in Kandahar province until he was killed in action.[22] In some areas this trend was particularly grievous. Elders in Panjwayi district, for instance, estimate that nearly every former midlevel Taliban commander, along with their relatives and friends, fled Afghanistan in the first years of the Sherzai government and are now in the insurgency. Table 1.2 lists some of the most prominent insurgent commanders in Kandahar who are in this category.

In some cases, former Taliban members did not survive to be able to fight again. The NDS prison chief Karam arrested Mullah Abdul Razziq Baluch, an imam of a prominent mosque in the Sperwan area of Panjwayi district, and took him in for questioning. Baluch held Taliban sympathies during the previous regime but had accepted the new government. A delegation of tribal elders went to Kandahar city to negotiate his release, but they were simply shown Baluch's discolored, badly bruised body. The prison officials told them that he had committed suicide.[23]

TABLE 1.2 Taliban Commanders in Kandahar Who Rejoined After Harassment by Afghan Officials or U.S. Forces

Commander	Area of Retirement	Current Area of Operation	Reason for Rejoining Taliban
Malim Feda Muhammad	Panjwayi	Panjwayi-Zheray and Pakistan	Abused by Americans
Hajji Lala	Kandahar city	Dand, Kandahar city, Maiwand	Harassed by Zheray strongman Habibullah Jan; Lala is believed to have been killed
Mullah Ahmad Shah	Panjwayi	Panjwayi	Tortured by Sherzai's forces
Qari Allahuddin	Panjwayi	Panjwayi-Zheray	Brother of Ahmad Shah
Mullah Saleh Muhammad Akhund	Panjwayi	Panjwayi-Zheray	Harassed by Sherzai's forces
Kaka Abdul Khaliq	Panjwayi	Panjwayi-Zheray	Harassed by Sherzai's forces
Mullah Akhtar Muhammad Mansur	Maiwand	National	Harassment of other former Taliban
Mullah Muhammad Akhundzada	Panjwayi	Panjwayi-Zheray	Harassed by Sherzai's forces
Mullah Rashid	Panjwayi	Panjwayi-Zheray	Harassed by Sherzai's forces
Mullah Abdul Khaliq	Zheray	Panjwayi-Zheray	Harassed by Sherzai's forces
Khalifa	Zheray	Panjwayi-Zheray	Harassed by Sherzai's forces

The failure to grant amnesty to Taliban figures who had abandoned the movement and accepted the new Afghan government had repercussions far beyond the specific individuals targeted. Soon a sense began to develop among those formerly connected to the regime, from senior officials to rank-and-file fighters, that there was no place for them in the post-2001 society.[24] In the Band-i-Timor area of Maiwand, for instance, former civil aviation minister and leading Taliban official Mullah Akhtar Muhammad Mansour had accepted the new government and was living at home.[25] But the violent drive against former Taliban by Sherzai's network and U.S. special forces led Mansur to realize it would be foolish to stay in Afghanistan. "He said that this government wouldn't let him live in peace," recalled lawmaker Ahmad Shah Achekzai, who had met him during that time. "It wasn't a surprise to us when he finally fled to Pakistan and rejoined the Taliban."[26] Today Mansur is a leading figure in the movement and one of the replacements for captured Taliban leader Mullah Beradar.[27]

Even after fleeing to Pakistan, large segments of the leadership were still open to returning to Afghanistan and abandoning the fight. In 2002, for instance, the entire senior leadership except for Mullah Omar gathered in Karachi, Pakistan, for a meeting organized by former Taliban officials Mawlawi Arsala Rahmani and Mawlawi Abdul Sattar Siddiqi.[28] The group agreed in principle to find a way for them to return to Afghanistan and abandon the fight, but lack of political will on the part of the central government in Kabul and opposition from some sections of the U.S. leadership meant that such approaches were ultimately ignored.[29] In each of the following two years another delegation representing large sections of the Taliban leadership traveled to Kabul and met with senior government officials, but again nothing came of these overtures because of the lack of will from the government side.[30]

INEFFECTIVE AND DIVISIVE GOVERNANCE

By 2005, much of the Taliban's old guard—at the leadership and field commander levels—had decided to stand against the Afghan government. During those years, a concomitant process of systematic marginalization of broad sections of Kandahari society led to widespread disillusionment with the government and foreign forces, giving the Taliban leadership a rank-and-file force. Government institutions were predatory and divisive, corrupt to the core, and completely ineffective in meeting basic needs.

Tribes

One of the biggest social changes following the fall of the Taliban was a reversion to the rule of the traditional tribal leadership.[31] Pashtun tribes are generally divided into hundreds of subtribes and clans, with many of the classifications and groupings varying in different parts of the country. The scores of tribes and clans in southern Afghanistan are roughly grouped into two confederations, the Ghilzais and the Durranis, with the latter subdivided into the Zirak and Panjpai confederations.[32] In traditional Kandahari society, the Zirak tribes, which include the Barakzais and Popalzais, formed a sort of tribal aristocracy. The years of Soviet occupation and the subsequent Taliban rule had upset this trend—the Taliban included many Panjpai Durranis and Ghilzais in the ranks of leadership.

After 2001, Gul Agha Sherzai's governorship brought many of his fellow Barakzai tribesmen into positions of power. Similarly, the presence in the presidential palace of Hamid Karzai and in Kandahar of his half brother Ahmed Wali Karzai, who in the early years formed a second locus of power in the province, led to the promotion of the Popalzais. In certain regions or government functions, particular tribes would dominate. The Alikozais had early influence over the security apparatus, for instance, while certain Achekzais held key positions in Spin Boldak district.[33] The Barakzais were heavily involved in the business sector in Kandahar city and neighboring Dand district, a historical trend that was amplified by security and logistics contracts coming from the International Security Assistance Force (ISAF) to Sherzai's network.[34]

Meanwhile, other tribes were largely excluded from positions of power and resources. Table 1.3 shows that Panjpai Durranis (Noorzais, Ishaqzais, Alizais, Khogiyanis, and the Mako) make up about 27 percent of the population but account for only 10 percent of the government positions. The numbers are rough, considering the immense challenges in surveying populations in Afghanistan. Regardless of exact figures,

TABLE 1.3 Tribal Percentages in Government and Population at Large

Tribe	Percentage of Government Positions	Percentage of Kandahar Population
Zirak Durrani	69	61
Other	13	8
Panjpai Durrani	10	27
Ghilzai	8	2
Popalzai	24	20
Achekzai	19	9

Note: numbers are rounded.

Source: Interview with a tribal elder from Panjwayi, Kabul, July 2010.

there is an acute sense among the Panjpai Durranis that they are being excluded in the post-2001 arrangements. "Show me a single Barakzai in jail," said one Noorzai elder from Panjwayi. "It's only our people who get arrested."[35] This may not necessarily be true, but it is born from an observation that Barakzais and Popalzais have more government connections and are able to use these networks to free their arrested relatives.

The numbers in Table 1.3 obscure the district- or village-level differences that are most important in understanding the relationship between tribal dynamics and the insurgency. In Panjwayi district, where Noorzais and Ishaqzais make up the bulk of the population, before 2008 every single district governor was a Zirak Durrani. The majority of the chiefs of police were Alikozais. Similar imbalances characterize other key districts, even today.

Although tribal structure has eroded significantly thanks to thirty years of war, with tribes or clans rarely acting as cohesive units any longer (if ever), tribal identity is still an important mechanism through which individual interests are negotiated. In southern Afghanistan's system of largely informal networks, a shared tribal or clan background with the holders of power means access to state services, resources, and more. Thus the privileging of Zirak Durranis at the expense of the rest of the population was a major factor in alienating Panjpai Durranis and others from the center.[36]

A disproportionate number of Panjpai Durranis and other alienated groups formed the recruiting base for the Taliban. This continued a historical trend that was briefly described above; Zirak Durranis dominated the governance structures, held access to the state's services and business channels, and made up a huge share of the landowning class, while second-tier tribes disproportionately produced mullahs and lower-rung jihadi commanders who later become the backbone of the Taliban movement. After the Taliban's defeat, the Zirak Durrani–dominated government viewed entire tribes, such as the Noorzais and Ishaqzais, with suspicion, which partly fueled their exclusion from power and their harassment by authorities. This in turn led large numbers of individuals from these tribes back to the Taliban.

The population of Spin Boldak, for instance, is split nearly evenly between Achekzais and Noorzais, but Achekzais have control over key parts of the border trade and count among their number the influential Border Police commander Abdul Razziq, one of the most powerful men in the province.[37] Although Noorzais in the district are not nearly as disadvantaged as they are elsewhere in Kandahar, their weakness in regard to control over the border trade and their second-tier status in relation to the center means that they contribute far greater numbers to the insurgency in the district than the Achekzais. Table 1.4 lists the key Taliban commanders active in Spin Boldak district today; nearly all are Noorzais.[38]

At times, government policies actively exacerbated tribal tensions and imbalances. In 2006, the provincial government ordered Commander Abdul Razziq's largely Achekzai militia and police force into the Noorzai-dominated Panjwayi district to quell a growing number of insurgents. The Noorzais and Achekzais have a historical rivalry, probably originating in attempts to control the lucrative border crossing of Spin Boldak.[39] News spread quickly of Razziq's arrival. "People began to say that Razziq was here to kill every Noorzai he could find," said one Noorzai elder from the district. Noorzai tribesmen rallied to fight against their invading rival; some accounts say that Noorzais from neighboring districts and even Helmand province came for backup. The Taliban quickly amassed a force of their own, portraying their moves as a defense of the Noorzais. The combined force ambushed Razziq's men as they crossed from the Panjwayi district center toward Sperwan, inflicting many casualties. Razziq's forces eventually retreated, and the ranks of the Taliban swelled with fresh recruits

TABLE 1.4 Prominent Taliban Commanders Active in Spin Boldak

Commander	Tribe	Role
Mullah Abdul Razzaq	Achekzai	Quetta Shura member
Mullah Ataullah	Noorzai	Commander
Mullah Amin Kamin	Noorzai	Commander
Mullah Jabbar	Noorzai	Former shadow district governor
Mullah Hayat Khan	Noorzai	Commander
Mullah Muhammad Amin	Noorzai	Shadow district governor
Mullah Muhammad Hashim	Noorzai	Commander
Mullah Raouf	Noorzai	Shorabak district governor, Spin Boldak commander
Mullah Muhammad Issa Akhund	Noorzai	Influential commander in a number of districts

eager to defend the Noorzais against further government oppression. "In our area, the Taliban went from 40 people to 400 in just days," recalled Neda Muhammad, a Noorzai elder.[40]

Similar tales made the rounds in local communities. In an interview with journalist Graeme Smith in Quetta, one insurgent explained that "In Kabul, all of the government officials are northerners or Popalzai... that is why there are problems. There is no justice." He added: "These tribes took Kandahar by force.... This is the main reason we fight."[41]

Other factors contribute to the Taliban's tribal makeup. Traditionally second-tier tribes such as the Noorzais and Ishaqzais have turned to smuggling and illicit trade because opportunities in the legal realm were meager. Criminality and insurgencies often have a symbiotic relationship, and in the post-2001 years many prominent smugglers developed ties with the Taliban. Also, over the years a large number of clerics and spiritual healers have populated the ranks of the Ishaqzai tribe in western Kandahar, leading them to develop close ties to the traditional religious clergy. These bonds persisted through the anti-Soviet insurgency and strengthened with the emergence of the Taliban. Finally, Sayeds, patrilineal descendants of the Prophet Muhammad, are considered by Afghans a separate tribe, and in southern Afghanistan they have historically played a role in conflict mediation. The role of the Taliban in conflict mediation in the 1980s and 1990s led to a natural alliance and overlap between these groups, and today in Panjwayi and Zheray districts a disproportionate number of Taliban commanders are Sayeds.

It is important to mention that despite these trends, the Taliban is not a tribal movement as such. Some commentators have called the Taliban a "Ghilzai insurgency" or tribal rebellion, but the reality is far more complicated.[42] The movement seeks to win recruits from all tribes and plays upon whichever grievances are relevant in a particular area or moment. Thus in Panjwayi it supported Noorzais against the marauding Achekzai militia, but in Maiwand it supported Khogiyanis against Noorzais when a dispute over land rights emerged and the local government backed the latter group.[43] And there are a number of important Zirak Durrani Taliban commanders, such as Kandahar's current shadow governor, Mawlawi Muhammad Issa (a Popalzai).

Moreover, tribal identity itself is quite complicated: locals rarely use the names of confederations such as "Ghilzai" or "Zirak Durrani" in self-identification.[44] Rather, the operational unit of identity is the tribe, as with Noorzai, or more often the subtribe, such as Gurg.[45] Clashes or rivalries between subtribes can be just as frequent as those between tribes. The Taliban deftly plays on such rivalries, often to its advantage. Indeed, the Taliban in Kandahar should more properly be seen as a nationalist Islamist insurgency that feeds on and manipulates tribal imbalances and rivalries to its own ends.[46]

Governance

From the examples of torture and extrajudicial killing given above, it should be clear that governance was a major problem in the post-2001 years. A series of corrupt and predatory government officials, from district governors and police chiefs all the way up to the provincial governor, regularly robbed or imprisoned locals. Asadullah Khaled, who served as Kandahar governor from 2005 to 2008, kept a secret prison and even personally tortured and administered electric shocks to captives.[47] Mullah Maqsud, a district governor of Maiwand, joined with U.S. forces in a series of disastrous raids that killed many civilians and is blamed for the deaths of key figures in the community. Hajji Saifullah, also at one time a district governor of Maiwand and later of Panjwayi, is widely accused of stealing aid funds and destroying the poppy fields of rivals to boost the profitability of his own fields.[48]

As mentioned above, security officials were notorious for abuse. One Kandahar city resident recalls a scene he witnessed involving Karam, the NDS prisons chief:

> Once we were walking on this road [near the center of Kandahar city] when a man on a motorcycle bumped into Commander Karam's vehicle. Karam's men jumped out of the car and started beating this man. He was almost killed, in front of everyone, and then they took him and threw him into the NDS prison. The elders came and tried to convince Karam to release the man but he refused. He spent the night in jail just for bumping his car.[49]

One Noorzai tribal elder in Maiwand recounted the following story:

> Hajji Gul Ahmad, one of my brothers-in-law, was taken by Akhundzada and Manay [two of Sherzai's commanders]. They had arrested him and I went to Kandahar city and met Hajji Niamat[50] [formerly a Sherzai associate now connected to Ahmed Wali Karzai] and he took me to my brother-in-law. He opened the door and I saw him sitting on the ground. His hands and feet were tied together and he was bruised. He had barely eaten in six days. I went crazy! I said what is this? What crime did he commit? Hajji Niamat said that if I wanted him to be released, I would have to pay. In the evening I paid 2 million Pakistani rupees (roughly $20,000) and they released him.[51]

Many Kandahar residents say that the government became even more pernicious after Sherzai left and Ahmed Wali Karzai, President Hamid Karzai's half brother, consolidated his hold over the province. Many locals accused him of running Kandahar like a mafia don, saying he vetted nearly all government appointees, dominated the licit and illicit trade networks, and ruthlessly sidelined opponents.[52]

Poor governance also meant a plodding bureaucracy, riddled with corruption. Even simple administrative tasks would be fraught with difficulty, and many Kandaharis sought to avoid dealing with the government whenever possible. In some cases, fraud and mismanagement had dire consequences. In the southern district of Shorabak, for instance, repeated fraud in the various national elections since 2004 pushed many away from the government. In 2005, one of the most respected leaders of the Bareetz tribe (which dominates the district[53]), Hajji Muhammad Bareetz, ran for parliament. He recalls that:

> I won more than 40,000 votes here and even the media announced me as the winner, but Karzai and his family here—I mean his brother—stopped me from going to parliament by using fraud. After this many of my tribesmen got disgusted with the government and joined the Taliban. They even told me to join the Taliban, but I'm too old. I can't live that kind of lifestyle anymore.[54]

The experience left a bitter taste in their mouths, and in 2009 the tribal leadership decided to oppose Karzai and support his opponent, Dr. Abdullah. But on election day, provincial officials shut down the polling centers, detained the district governor, and used Abdul Razziq's forces to stuff ballots, robbing the Bareetz tribe of their vote.[55] Since the election, locals report, provincial officials have not been treating them well, largely because of their attempted betrayal of Karzai in favor of his rival. "So many more people have fled the area or joined the Taliban since then," Hajji Bareetz said.

Policing

Hand in hand with broken government was a notoriously corrupt police force. International actors and the Afghan government generally paid little attention to coordinating efforts to build a viable police force in Kandahar in the early years after 2001. Although some international agencies and governments did focus on police development, the CIA, U.S. Special Forces, and others were backing militias (such as Sherzai's). Furthermore, lucrative contracts to Sherzai and Karzai, or their associates, funded militias and delegitimized police institutions. An ISAF study estimated in 2010 that only about half of the police forces in Kandahar are under the command of the provincial police chief: "The rest are influenced by Kandahar's power brokers and tribal leaders. When the provincial governor recently instructed him to replace a district police chief in Panjwayi, the Provincial Chief of Police's orders were countermanded after local power brokers intervened."[56]

Another study found that police in Kandahar were typically paid less than private security forces, and what resources they did receive were meager:

> On 31 January 2004, 300 ANP [Afghan National Police] were deployed to Kandahar in one of the first deployments of centrally trained police to a province. Within the unit, high levels of optimism about their training and pride for their symbolic representation of the central government were reported. The arrival of the ANP in Kandahar led to considerable disappointment— they were accommodated in the remains of the Kandahar Hotel, given little ammunition and sent to guard UN compounds, rather than engage in policing. The 260 deployed were also undersupplied in terms of weapons, vehicles and accommodation, which prompted 100 to desert.[57]

Under such conditions, police corruption and predation became endemic. There are many legendary tales of police brutality in Kandahar, from simply shaking down motorists at checkpoints to much worse. In one well-known incident in Panjwayi, a police officer demanded goods from a shopkeeper in the district center. When the shopkeeper refused, the policeman shot and killed him and absconded with the goods.[58]

The Taliban would begin to position themselves as protectors of the population against the police. At the same time, they cultivated ties with certain police officials, which they exploited to purchase weapons or cooperate in smuggling.

Judiciary

The role of dispute resolution in Pashtun society cannot be emphasized enough. Rural Afghan society is largely informal, meaning that there are few records of land holdings, particularly after decades of war in which documents were destroyed and many people fled, leaving their land behind. Disagreements over land ownership, water access, grazing rights, and other issues are very common, usually between tribes, clans, or family members (such as second cousins). Moreover, under the current circumstances, in which the state is extremely weak, corrupt, or nonexistent (as in much of Kandahar), criminality often goes unpunished. Historically, this has led large segments of the population to support the implementation of sharia, particularly those sections of Islamic law that can be applied punitively or to resolve conflicts.[59] The popularity of the Taliban courts of the anti-Soviet insurgency is a good example in this regard. Researchers Alex Strick van Linschoten and Felix Kuehn, in their study of the relationship between al-Qaeda and the Taliban, cite one appraisal of the courts:

> [T]he Islamic courts were very strict and would even sentence commanders or field leaders if they did something wrong. One time, a battle took place between two commanders so they went to court and asked for its ruling. The judge decided to arrest them both and beat them up before throwing them in jail. This judge and his court gained great respect in the Kandahar area because of that.[60]

In post-2001 Kandahar, the Taliban's judicial services (discussed in more detail in the next section) became one of the key advantages the movement had over the state. In some instances, the problem is simply a paucity of judges: In Kandahar city, for instance, there are only nine judges out of eighty-seven possible slots.[61] Where there are judges, the system is laboriously slow, ineffective, and very susceptible to bribery. Moreover, Taliban threats in recent years have forced many judges to flee to Kandahar city, further eroding judicial services in the districts and increasing reliance on the insurgents.

COALITION FORCES ACTIVITY

Many Kandaharis insist that the foreign coalition forces have been a source of insecurity. The perceptions of the government mentioned above also fall upon the foreign troops, since foreigners are largely seen as being the real power in the country. Sections of the military, such as the U.S. Special Forces, actively supported strongmen and militias, undermining state-building efforts. Men like Ahmed Wali Karzai and Gul Agha Sherzai were largely made through the support—financial and political—of the United States. U.S. forces also worked closely with strongmen such as Karam, one of Sherzai's commanders, to hunt down former Taliban, and they helped create a perverse incentive system in which such commanders would hand over suspects on dubious grounds or simply arrest people to extract money.[62] The foreigners were caught in a complex system that they didn't fully understand and often fell prey to local rivalries. They frequently failed to distinguish between friend and foe, in the process creating many enemies.

In Panjwayi and Zheray districts, the heartland of today's insurgency, the case of Malim Feda Muhammad is seared into the consciousness of many Taliban fighters. Muhammad, a schoolteacher when the Russians invaded, joined the mujahideen and became a famous commander in the greater Panjwayi area. He joined the Taliban movement in its early days and later became a frontline commander in the north. After the Taliban's fall, he retired from political life back to Panjwayi. But U.S. forces captured him and sent him to their detention facility at Kandahar Airfield, and he was released only after intensive intervention by tribal elders. One NDS official who visited him after his release recalled that:

> I went to his home. For weeks he had been hiding in the house, too ashamed to come out and talk to people. Finally I convinced his son to let me see him. He looked like a disaster. He hadn't been sleeping well. He started to tell his story of how he was humiliated, stripped naked, beaten, and how they put dogs on him while he was in that state. He was crying and asked how he could possibly live in Afghanistan with any dignity.[63]

It is difficult to verify Muhammad's claims, although they fit with other testimonies of abuse at the Kandahar prison from that time. Still, for our purposes—to understand the motivations and ideology of the insurgency—the fact that other Taliban and the community in general *believe* his story is what is important. Many of the Taliban and tribal elders interviewed in Panjwayi repeated his tale as an example of why people were standing against the Americans. Muhammad eventually fled with his family to Quetta, where he rejoined the Taliban and today commands a number of fighters in the Panjwayi and Zheray areas.[64]

In the northern district of Shah Wali Kot, Taliban fighters, locals, and elders tell the story of Mullah Sattar Akhund, a former Taliban official who was living at home during the early years after the movement was ousted. One Taliban commander recalled that:

> In that first year of the Karzai government Mullah Sattar was in retirement. But the government kept coming to his house and questioning him or searching his house. Sometimes he was going out during the day and would come home at night to sleep. One of those days the Americans came and searched his house. They came again and again and searched his house, and it turned out to be a big shame for him. The people in his village started to gossip about his family. Finally his mother got very angry and told him, "You are bringing shame upon our family! Either defend us from this or run away. She gave him the family weapon, a Sakeel[65] from the old days, and told him to use it. The next time the Americans came he started firing at them, and he got many people in the village to fire at them. The Americans called for an airplane, which finally came and bombed the house. Later on they arrested all of the surviving adult male family members and many were taken to Bagram. They took the heart out of the village. We knew that we had to fight them and so we joined the Taliban.[66]

Along with the arbitrary arrests and abuse, night raids by special forces and targeted assassinations played a significant role in turning many against the foreign presence. The case of Hajji Burget Khan in particular had lasting negative effects. Khan was one of the best-known leaders of the Ishaqzai tribe, which has hundreds of thousands of members in Kandahar, Helmand, and elsewhere.[67] In 2002, U.S. forces raided his home in the Band-i-Timor area of Maiwand, killing him and leaving his son a paraplegic. "They took the women and children and put them in a *bawaray*," a type of shallow well, recalled one prominent Noorzai elder from the area. "It was a shock to us. We had lost our leader and even the women were mocking us, saying that despite our big turbans we could not protect our community. The Americans also arrested a number of relatives of Hajji Burget Khan and shaved their beards and cut their hair," a humiliating act for a Pashtun man.

The killing of Hajji Burget Khan is often cited as the single most important destabilizing factor in Maiwand district and other Ishaqzai areas. Three Taliban commanders from the region interviewed for this report all mentioned the killing as one of the main factors that led them to join the insurgency. Afghan government officials concede that it had disastrous effects in the area. It is unclear why Khan was targeted; he was very old at the time—most put his age over seventy—and was not a member of the insurgency. He had a son who was with the Taliban during the 1990s but had since retired. And like many other Ishaqzai and Noorzai elders in the area, he may have had ties to drug traffickers. But the most likely explanation is that the commanders with whom U.S. forces had allied had seen Khan as a rival.

News of his death even had effects on other tribes and districts. "We heard about Hajji Burget Khan's murder," said one elder in Shorabak district. "It was enough to convince many people the foreigners and the government were our enemy." Khan's paraplegic son moved to Quetta, where he became a Taliban facilitator, while his brother became a leading commander in Helmand.[68]

The killing was notorious throughout Kandahar province, but nearly every district had similar stories. In Zheray, for instance, foreign forces killed two influential religious scholars, Mullahs Abidullah and Janan, causing many of their followers to join the insurgency.[69]

One Taliban commander in Zheray gave his reasons for joining.

There were so many examples in the last nine years of the foreigners' methods. During last Ramadan, it was 12:15 a.m. and the Americans invaded a house of my relatives in Hazaruji Baba.[70] They killed an innocent 18-year-old boy named Janan who was sleeping under a net. They left his body there while they searched the house, and dogs began to gnaw at him. In the same month, in the Nar-i-pul area, they raided the house of Mawlawi Ahmadullah. They killed him, took one of his brothers with them, and tied the wives to each other and left them as they searched the house. When we arrived later, we could not untie the women with our hands and we had to use a stick [because of Pashtun customs that forbid contact between members of the opposite sex who are not relatives or married]. What were we to do after these sorts of things? So I joined the Taliban.[71]

Furthermore, there were a number of high-profile incidents in which airstrikes killed a sizable number of civilians, such as the 2008 bombing of a wedding party in Shah Wali Kot.

JOBLESSNESS, POPPIES, AND OTHER CAUSES

A number of studies have found a positive correlation between low income level and insecurity.[72] "Insecurity" here generally means Taliban presence, although areas with just the Taliban (or just pro-government forces) are generally much more secure than areas with both. With few jobs, occasional drought, and landlessness, many rank-and-file insurgents are at least partially motivated by money.[73]

As the government began to eradicate the opium poppy fields of poor farmers, the Taliban portrayed themselves as these farmers' protectors. Poppy eradication has played a significant role in pushing locals in Maiwand district, for instance, into the insurgency in order to safeguard their lands and income.[74] During cultivation season, the Taliban often join with local farmers to expel government agencies such as the Poppy Eradication Force, and in areas under Taliban control locals are usually free to pursue the activity.[75] In Graeme Smith's landmark study of the Taliban for the Canadian *Globe and Mail* newspaper, one insurgent explained that previously "they were cutting them [poppies] down, but now those areas are controlled by mujahideen and now they cannot cut them down."[76]

Sometimes the motivations to join the insurgency are subtler than those outlined above. As the Taliban grew during the period 2004 to 2007, communities that were not aligned with the insurgents would join the movement simply to protect themselves from insurgents. These communities would then exert pressure on neighboring areas, until they too joined.

In some cases, joining the Taliban allows disaffected young men to step outside of traditional roles in society. Rural Pashtun culture places extraordinary emphasis on age and experience, so that even thirty-year-olds can be considered "youth" and have little or no part in decision making. But a twenty-five-year-old Taliban commander wields far more power and authority than any elder in the community, which can be intoxicating in such a society.

Finally, some individuals or communities join or temporarily align with the Taliban simply as a means to project power and influence in personal disputes. A family feuding with another might throw its support to the insurgents as a way to gain leverage. In a number of cases, communities have sought an alliance with the Taliban to give them an upper hand in disputes over such issues as land or water rights.[77] Similarly, communities have been known to use the insurgents to side against Kuchis (Pashtun nomads), whose migration to or settlement in an area typically causes tensions.[78] Others use Taliban membership as a means to carry out criminal activity. By no means is all of the violence in Kandahar province due to actual antigovernment insurgents; drug mafias, feuding commanders, rival families, and key government power brokers are also sources of instability, although their actions are usually attributed to the Taliban. In short, in a militarized society with a nearly complete breakdown of the rule of law and the absence of the state, the Taliban movement is a potent weapon for individuals and communities looking to settle scores and further personal agendas.

TALIBAN IDEOLOGY

A number of commentators have divided the Taliban into an "ideological core" and a rank and file motivated primarily by material concerns. The actual role of ideology is much more complicated, however, as the recent history of Kandahar shows. Initially, much of the Taliban in the province—from the senior leadership to the rank and file—fell into two categories: they either accepted the legitimacy of the new government or they rejected it but did not feel that fighting against it was appropriate or possible. Senior leaders such as Mullah Akhtar Mansur, who today has a leading role in the Quetta Shura, had made peace with the government in the early years. Scores of others were in similar positions. This indicates that many Taliban did not take up arms simply as an exercise of the principle of jihad or expulsion of foreigners, as many Taliban would later try to portray it, but rather because it was the only viable alternative for individuals and groups left without a place in the new state of affairs. In other words, initially it was not the existence of a new government per se that drove these former Taliban back, but the *behavior* of that government. Likewise, initially it was not the presence of foreign troops as such that spawned opposition from these former Taliban, but the *behavior* of those troops. This is in contrast to groups such as al-Qaeda, which viewed the presence of foreign troops on Afghan soil ipso facto as justification for jihad. For these reasons, it took some time for the Taliban to regroup, for former leaders to grow disaffected and flee to Pakistan, and for the various factors that alienated communities to play out. Sizable opposition did not emerge until 2003, and the insurgency did not gain significant momentum until after 2004, when community after community began falling to the Taliban.

This is not to say that ideology does not play a role—only to call attention to cause and effect. After finding themselves on the wrong side of the new regime, former Taliban leaders and affected individuals understood their misfortunes by viewing the government as un-Islamic.[79] They explained the actions of foreign troops by viewing them as an occupying force, bent on robbing Afghanistan of its sovereignty, culture, and religion. And many among the rank and file were attracted to the movement because it provided the most viable means of protecting themselves or accessing resources and power. Indeed, a study of insurgents and insurgency-affected areas commissioned by Britain's Department for International Development (DFID) found that radicalization (i.e., viewing the conflict in jihadist or religious terms) often took place *after* an individual joined the insurgency.[80] Therefore it is not accurate or helpful to divide the Taliban into "moderates" and "ideological," as motivations are a complex interplay of structural causes (social, political, and economic) and ideology. Very few field commanders in Kandahar have reconciled with the government despite growing opportunities to do so in recent years, yet at the same time a number of senior leaders have made approaches to the government.[81]

Finally, it is worth emphasizing that the ideological justifications— Islamic culture under attack, foreigners' desire to convert Afghans, the loss of sovereignty and the desire for self-determination, and so on—have little to do with those of transnational jihadist movements. In interviews with Taliban commanders and senior leaders for this study, not a single person made an appeal to international jihad or pan-Islamism. This reinforces the finding of the DFID survey of Taliban fighters, in which the report's author writes that opposition to foreign troops is "due to a perceived attack on Islam but it is an attack that is perceived to be happening within the country by foreign forces. There was little evidence of common cause being made with Islamist movements outside Afghanistan."[82]

PART 2: THE TALIBAN IN KANDAHAR: STRUCTURE AND TACTICS

- The Taliban's chain of command and decision-making processes are neither simple nor straightforward. A formal network exists in Kandahar, from the shadow governor and Military Commission down to district governors and local judges. In theory, provincial and district political leaders direct military efforts in their respective areas, although actual decisions to carry out small-scale attacks, involving one or a few groups, are left to field commanders. Larger-scale efforts fall under the supposed control of prominent regional commanders and the provincial leadership. In reality, however, most attacks take place with little input from higher levels. Moreover, the Taliban's formal structure in Kandahar sits in parallel with informal networks that tie commanders back to specific leaders in Quetta. Prominent leaders over the border there have networks of commanders that extend throughout Kandahar province. Many decisions are made through these informal channels, bypassing the formal structures.

- The Taliban's response to increased Western attention to Kandahar province was to do the same themselves. Assassinations, roadside bombings, and complex attacks have hit record highs in Kandahar in 2010. The insurgent strategy of targeting anyone even remotely associated with the government, and the foreign forces' strategy of reaching out to tribal leaders and their incipient militia programs, have made it very difficult for locals to remain neutral in this conflict. Many tribal leaders today are left with only two choices: flee to a government stronghold like Kandahar city or Kabul, or align completely with the insurgents.

STRUCTURE OF THE KANDAHAR TALIBAN

Although initially accepting the legitimacy of the new Kabul government, or at the very least viewing it as an entity that they could not oppose, Taliban members eventually came to view the actions of the

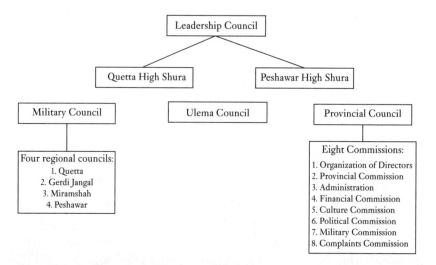

FIGURE 1.1 Taliban Leadership Structure
Note: The material for this section is based on dozens of interviews with Taliban in Kandahar, 2008–2010, unless otherwise noted.

government and the foreigners as necessitating jihad. By 2003, the majority of the old-guard senior leadership had relocated to Quetta or Peshawar, Pakistan, and launched a formal body to oversee the nascent insurgency. That body, which came to be known as the Quetta Shura, would closely direct strategy on the ground, as well as facilitate the transfer of funds, persuade erstwhile comrades to rejoin, and direct propaganda efforts. Over the years, the leadership developed an elaborate structure of sub-shuras and committees to meet the growing organization's needs, as depicted in Figure 1.1.[83] Like other Afghan groups, however, the Taliban operates as much through informal networks as it does through formal ones. It is important to realize the limits of looking at the organization through a purely Western understanding of command and control.

THE SHADOW GOVERNMENT

The Taliban's initial antigovernment organizing was done entirely through informal networks, but as the insurgency grew it began to develop a formal shadow administration alongside these networks. Today, every province in the country has a centrally appointed shadow

governor, although in some areas (such as Panjshir) this is purely a titular role. In theory, the provincial council (see Figure 1.1) together with
the leadership council makes appointments, but often the reality is
more blurred. Senior leader Mullah Abdul Qayum Zakir, who is mostly
involved with military affairs, has also made political appointments, for
instance.[84] The shadow governor's role is to oversee all activities in the
province, act as liaison with Quetta, manage conflicts between commanders, and interact with non-Taliban actors, such as international
agencies, government officials, and construction companies. As in the
era of the Taliban government, governors are rotated often, and it is
rare to find one who has been in his post for more than a year. This is
likely done for security reasons, but also to ensure that these governors
do not develop an independent power base.

As of August 2010, Kandahar's shadow governor is Muhammad
Issa, a Popalzai from the Gawarai area of Arghestan district. During
the anti-Soviet insurgency, he fought in a Taliban front under Mullah
Muhammad Ghaus, who would later become the Taliban's foreign
minister.[85] In the Taliban government, Issa worked as a finance officer
under deputy leader Mullah Muhammad Rabbani. In the post-2001
years, before being promoted to shadow provincial governor, he
worked closely with Mullah Beradar and was at one point the district
governor of Arghestan.[86]

Working with the shadow governor is the Military Commission, a
council of four to six members that helps direct provincial affairs. In
theory the governor and Military Commission plan operations, but
in practice lower-level commanders often take their own initiative
and the leadership bodies have more of a ceremonial role. In some
areas the provincial leadership wields considerable authority; when
two commanders in Wardak province sparred recently, for example,
the Military Commission and shadow governor were able to banish
them from the province. But Kandahar's proximity to Quetta, and the
long-standing ties between its commanders and the senior leadership
across the border, mean that most important decisions are made outside of the province.

A number of mawlawis (religious clerics) are supposed to be associated with the Military Commission, which doubles as the supreme
judicial body for a province. "Ideally, the Military Commission should
not also do court activities," explained one Taliban commander from

Zheray, "but right now it is not possible to separate the two functions." The commission functions as a sort of mobile supreme court, hearing cases that cannot be settled in the lower courts. It also is the likely adjudicator for intra-Taliban disputes. In practice, the commission is often staffed with mullahs or commanders who have not undertaken religious studies, rather than mawlawis, and has a high turnover rate.[87]

Most districts in Kandahar also have a shadow district governor, and those districts in which the Taliban have complete or nearly complete control also have a "chief of police" and a district shura.[88] The district governor helps manage the forces in his area and in some cases organizes tax collection and even directs expenditures.[89] In theory the chief of police is supposed to enforce the decisions of the district governor and provincial leadership, but in practice the role is largely ceremonial. "They hand out posts like chief of police to please those commanders who didn't get a good title like district governor," explained one Taliban commander who used to have the lesser title.[90] The district shura includes the police chief as well as at least one leading cleric, who functions as the head of the judiciary in the district.

THE JUDICIARY

The judicial system forms the backbone of Taliban governance and generally appears to be superior to the official government alternative. In most areas, mawlawis or experienced mullahs run mobile courts that are attached to Taliban groups. A Taliban commander from Zheray explained the process:

> They are not at a fixed or given location. When a person wants to solve their problem and he enters a Taliban area, we will stop him and ask him what is he doing. If he says that he has a problem that needs to be solved by the court, we will let him know where the court is at that moment. For instance, we will say go to this fruit farm or that field and you will find the judges there who will solve your problem.

Typical cases taken before these courts include disputes over land rights, water access, and debts. The judges rule on the basis of their interpretation of sharia, or Islamic law, and the verdicts are usually thought of as fair, transparent, and binding, unlike those of government courts.[91] Even residents in government-controlled areas, such as Kandahar city or district centers, often travel to Taliban territory to use the courts.[92] In those areas where Taliban control is extensive, such as the Mushan area of Panjwayi or the Garamabak area of Maiwand, there have been fixed courts that move from village to village in the region. In parts where insurgent control is more contested, the courts come at certain points in the week or month, and commanders usually give advance notice to the community.

The local courts handle most small disputes, but if the disagreement is more substantial or is between Taliban groups, the case is referred to the Military Commission. This body then orders the local district governor to investigate the matter. The district governor relays his findings back to the Commission, which then delivers a verdict. Thus the Taliban system has its own bureaucracy, with disputants required to collect signatures from officials and move between various courts and authorities. If a disputant ignores the ruling, the Commission orders the chief of police to "arrest" him. There are a number of makeshift prisons throughout western and northern Kandahar for this purpose.

Of course, the reality strays from this model. Commanders often detain people without ever referring their cases to higher bodies, and Taliban court rulings are rarely if ever ignored (for fear of the consequences). Moreover, it appears that a main role of these higher judicial bodies is to adjudicate disputes between the Taliban themselves, as most civilian cases are resolved in the lower courts.[93] And like any institution, the Taliban courts have their weaknesses. Some residents have complained that the courts sometimes favor those connected to the insurgency, mullahs, or others. However, in comparison with the government system, the Taliban courts appear to be far superior.

In recent years, a system of checks and balances has developed in which civilians and Taliban members can appeal to higher authorities when insurgents abuse their power. Most provinces have a Civilian Commission, which acts as an appeals court for civilian complaints against the Taliban. A secret NATO report on the Taliban also discusses a higher-level system to curb malfeasance:

A shura-level commission system, based in Quetta, Pakistan, maintains teams of specifically-designated personnel who travel throughout Afghanistan speaking to locals, eliciting complaints against the Taliban leadership, and mediating any disagreements between the Taliban themselves. This is designed to ensure that the provincial governor does not intentionally manipulate the system for the benefit of himself or his subordinate commanders.[94]

MILITARY STRUCTURE

The Taliban's smallest operating unit is the *delgai* (diminutive form of *dala*, or group), which in theory consists of ten men but in reality can have from five to twenty fighters.[95] The delgai leader typically collects the men under him by way of kinship ties, informal bonds forged through years of war (known as *andiwal* networks), and sometimes charisma.[96] In Kandahar, delgais are usually confined to a specific area, although they are becoming more mobile. Associated with these delgais are various facilitators, such as smugglers and bomb makers. The delgai leader plans assaults, and the group conducts most of the attacks in its area of operation. The majority of such attacks are planned without input from higher levels.[97] The andiwal ties between a delgai commander and his men mean that when a commander decides to stop fighting, all of his men usually do so as well. Similarly, it is rare that individual fighters will leave the Taliban without their commander doing so. Still, at times the commander has to cajole his men into an attack, particularly if it is a dangerous mission. One commander recalled this story:

> We wanted to attack the government headquarters [of an area]. It was a dangerous thing to do because the government would call for the foreigners to help them with airpower very quickly. I convinced another delgai leader, a friend of mine, to join us in the attack. But my men were too scared. I had to spend a lot of time convincing them, and even I had to promise them more rewards if we were successful. Finally they agreed, but they were not happy.[98]

A group of delgais—sometimes ten or more—fall under a regional commander. In Kandahar, these influential men are the real power in most areas, rather than district governors or clerics. They plan

ambitious assaults, coordinate strategy with other regional commanders, and carry out close liaison with the leadership in Pakistan. The
commanders themselves are usually very mobile, particularly after the
U.S. military has stepped up its campaign against field commanders.
The relationships between the regional commander and his delgai
commanders are not always as close as those between the delgai leader
and his men; much of this varies from case to case. In one instance in
Uruzgan in 2007, for instance, a regional commander defected and
brought about ten delgais with him. But such defections at this level are
rare, so it is difficult to assess the strength of the vertical ties between
delgai and regional leaders. In any event, organizing coordinated
attacks at the regional level is not always straightforward. Sometimes a
commander will go from group to group to raise volunteers; in other
cases he will rely on a small subset of the delgais available in a region.

A large number of regional commanders form a front, or *mahaz*.
The modern Taliban structure is not organized into fronts per se, as
most regional commanders operate individually or are tied directly to
the leadership. However, there have been some famous fronts in recent
years—for instance, Mullah Dadullah headed a front of thousands of
fighters throughout Kandahar, Helmand, and beyond.[99] More recently,
Mullah Abdul Qayum Zakir and Mullah Abdul Raouf Khadem are said
to have also commanded fronts in southern Afghanistan.[100] Fronts are
large and varied enough geographically that they do not act as a coordinated unit. Dadullah, however, was able to introduce certain techniques, such as suicide bombing, and disseminate them through his
subordinate commanders.

When a delgai leader is killed or captured, his group usually dis-
bands or is absorbed into other groups. But sometimes a brother or
cousin will fill his shoes. Regional commanders have deputies, who
fill in when the commanders travel to Pakistan or are in hiding. When
these commanders are killed, the deputy or a brother usually assumes
charge.

Decision making within the insurgency depends on the context.
Local commanders, at the delgai and regional levels, carry out the
majority of their attacks without any input from above. Attacks are
often undertaken for strategic purposes, but as in any organization
there may be other reasons as well. One insurgent commander admitted in an interview that his main motivation for planning a particularly

daring raid on a government installation was to increase his standing in the eyes of his superiors, which could one day lead to a promotion.[101]

THE INFORMAL STRUCTURE

The Taliban's informal networks are likely far more important than anything discussed above. The most important decision making happens through personal connections between commanders and the leadership in Pakistan. As of August 2010, three senior Taliban figures from the Quetta Shura—Hafiz Majid, Mawlawi Gul Agha, and Mawlawi Salaam—were responsible for directing the insurgency in Kandahar.

Majid, a Noorzai tribal elder from Sperwan, Panjwayi, was the Kandahar chief of police during the Taliban government. Unlike most of his comrades, he resisted the U.S. invasion until the very end and fled to Pakistan shortly after Mullah Omar did. He is said to have considerable business interests in Quetta, much of which he sold off recently to raise funds for the movement. He is well respected in parts of his native Panjwayi, where he still maintains ties with the community.[102]

Gul Agha, an Ishaqzai from Band-i-Timor, Maiwand, is a childhood friend of Mullah Omar, having studied in the same madrassa with him. He fought in the anti-Soviet jihad in Helmand and Kandahar and later served as Mullah Omar's personal assistant and finance officer during the Taliban government. Considered Omar's most trusted ally, Gul Agha disappeared into Baluchistan just as Kandahar was falling to Sherzai and the U.S. forces. He later played a key role (along with Mullah Obaidullah) in resurrecting old Taliban networks by persuading former commanders to rejoin the movement. He also was an important fundraiser during the early years. After Mullah Beradar's arrest, he stepped to the forefront for the first time to take an active day-to-day role in the insurgency and has even pushed to be recognized as Beradar's successor.[103]

Mawlawi Salaam, a Kakar from Taloqan, is from a newer generation of Taliban leaders. He is the younger brother of Mullah Baqi, a well-known Taliban commander who was involved in the northern front during the pre–September 11 Taliban government, including the siege of Mazar-i-Sharif. In the post-2001 years, Baqi fought under the Dadullah front in Zheray and was an early advocate for use of suicide bombers. When Baqi was killed during Operation Medusa in 2006 in Panjwayi, Salaam took over his network. Having graduated to the Pakistan-based leadership, Salaam is responsible today for directing suicide attacks in Kandahar province.

These and other political leaders wield influence in a number of ways: through the formal Taliban leadership at the provincial and district levels, directly to field commanders by virtue of their position on the Quetta Shura and their stature in the movement, and through informal networks of allies and subcommanders. The Majid network is an example of influence and command traveling through informal links. A number of commanders in Panjwayi, Zheray, and Maiwand answer directly to Majid, such as Pahlawan Gul Muhammad, Pawlawan Ainudeen, Mawlawi Abdul Sattar, and Hafiz Sharif (Majid's brother). They operate side by side with other commanders who answer to other leaders, either in Kandahar or in Quetta and Chaman, across the border from Spin Boldak.

Further complicating issues is the fact that sometimes the provincial or district leadership is in name only. In some cases, the shadow district governors are themselves powerful commanders. In other cases, district governors do not even reside in the district they "govern." This is particularly the case for areas such as Spin Boldak and Dand, where the Taliban's roots are much weaker. Much of this depends on the personality of the district governor, his roots in the local community, his ties to senior leadership, and the extent of Taliban control in the district. These shadow district governors are also changed quite frequently, making it difficult for them to assert effective command. Thus the stablest links are usually between field commanders and senior leaders based in Pakistan. One Taliban commander in Kandahar city admitted that:

> In some places the commander is a battlefield person and the district chief has civil concerns, but in other cases this isn't true. [The battlefield commanders] are supposed to respect the order of the district governor, but in some places they don't. They are too powerful, they have 15 or 30 men or more, and they will only listen to senior leaders.[104]

Sometimes these senior leaders in Pakistan even handle disputes between commanders, especially when the disputants are connected to them or the case is too complicated for provincial figures. Other times the leadership will discipline commanders for acting out of line. This can be done through senior provincial commanders and the Military Commission, but leaders in Quetta often do this directly. Mullah Adam of Maiwand, a notoriously brutal commander, led the killing of nearly two dozen Afghan migrant workers en route to Iran in 2008. The leadership immediately summoned him to Quetta, where he was disarmed and his followers disbanded. It is unclear whether he has been able to rejoin the insurgency.[105] (Interestingly, in this case a Taliban spokesman defended and took credit for the deadly assault, saying that those targeted were Afghan National Army soldiers, even though the attack was not sanctioned by the leadership and indeed was frowned upon. This suggests that one method the Taliban uses in its media strategy is to immediately assert responsibility for certain actions and spin them favorably, even if leaders are opposed to them internally.)[106]

One Taliban commander active in Mahalajat, a restive region in the southwestern part of Kandahar city, recalls another case:

> In Kandahar city lived the sons of Hamid Agha and Fazluddin Agha [former government officials in Spin Boldak]. The Taliban had gotten military uniforms and they entered these people's houses and kidnapped six members of their family. This was in Mahalajat and the whole raid was done by the head commander of Mahalajat. Later this commander asked his captives for 50 guns and some money, but the captives refused. An argument ensued and the commander killed one of these six people. When Quetta found out, they were furious. They summoned him to Quetta and demanded to know why he had killed the person. "Who told you to kidnap these people?" they asked. "If you were going to kill one person, you should have killed them all. Or you should have not touched any of them and let everyone go. But you shouldn't have done this—you are making people hate us." They were also angry that he asked for money. He was given a warning. He now has no choice but to obey, because if he continues, it would mean death.[107]

FUNDING

Each commander is responsible for raising funds for his group. This arrangement allows for maximum flexibility and adaptability for the movement, but at the same time it fosters criminality and freelancing. One former Taliban commander, who until 2007 led about a hundred men, explained how the process works:

> I was always trying to figure out how to raise money for my men. We sometimes got money from our leaders, but it was usually for weapons and it was very intermittent. And the commanders above us would usually keep the money or spend it on weapons and ammunition. We would raise money from the village. Villagers would give us donations sometimes, but they were poor so this was also irregular. Then one day we found a list of NGOs in the area and we told some people [working there] that they had to pay us money. Other times we would capture vehicles and try to sell them. Once in a while a rich person from the village would come and give us money. They believed that this was a holy jihad and is just for God. They would come and tell us, "Please take this, it is 50,000 Pakistani rupees,[108] or 100,000 Pakistani rupees. This is our assistance, done in the way of God."[109]

Despite popular conception, it does not appear that the Taliban in Kandahar (or elsewhere) receive a regular "salary" as such. Funds are irregular but appear to average the equivalent of at least fifty to a few hundred dollars a month per fighter. The Taliban commander active in the Mahalajat part of Kandahar city gave an example of how this works:

> Sometimes people—usually, rich people—would come and say, "Who is the leader of your group? I want to give *zakat* or *ushr*."[110] Or after attacks we would capture spoils and then sell them. Either way, we divide the money with our men and tell them that this is for your expenses for the coming month. You can use this to survive. We never call it a salary.[111]

Although none of the Taliban commanders interviewed admitted to this, some locals report that insurgents forcibly collected money in the form of zakat or ushr from the community. Another source of revenue in Taliban areas is the "taxation" of businesses and associated smuggling activities. This includes protection money from construction companies, private security firms, and others.[112] Opium poppy cultivation falls under this category, as it is a significant source of income for the local population (particularly in areas like Maiwand) and contributes a major portion of funds to the Taliban's coffers in Kandahar. The insurgents either tax opium production and smuggling or partake in it themselves. Many rank-and-file insurgents, particularly from the western part of the province, are poppy farmers. Moreover, some commanders have links to prominent drug smugglers or are involved in smuggling themselves.

In parallel with bottom-up efforts to raise money, the Taliban headquarters in Quetta also actively procures funds. Its financial commission (see Figure 1.1) is involved in raising money from wealthy traders in the Spin Boldak-Chaman-Quetta corridor, other parts of Pakistan, and the Persian Gulf states. At the same time, individuals such as Mawlawi Gul Agha, who have not always had a formal role, have been involved in the effort. Quetta also levies "taxes" on major projects in Kandahar. There is reportedly even a Taliban engineer who examines contracts and taxes the holder 10 percent of the appraised value.[113]

It is unclear what proportion of funds at the battlefield level comes from Quetta and what proportion is locally raised. Almost all of the current and former Taliban figures interviewed for this report gave the impression that the majority was locally raised, but it is possible that they have reasons to play down external funding sources. Without more visibility in this area, it will difficult to draw definitive conclusions.

DISTRIBUTION

Only Kandahar's rugged northern district Mia Neshin is completely under Taliban control—meaning the insurgents occupy the district center. But most other districts are under de facto insurgent control; that is, the government occupies the center and little else, and movements by officials outside of the center are severely curtailed if not impossible without a sizable military escort. The exceptions are areas with strong tribal or patronage ties to government power brokers, such as parts of Dand and Daman districts.

Mia Neshin, Shah Wali Kot, Nesh, Ghorak, and Khakrez Districts

Kandahar's rugged, remote mountainous northern districts are very disconnected from Kandahar city, and the government has limited influence. In fact, areas such as Shah Wali Kot were the first to fall to the Taliban in the post-2001 years. The Taliban are firmly entrenched in this region, which functions as a staging ground for pushes into Arghandab as well as a transit corridor between Helmand and the rest of Afghanistan (via Zabul and Ghazni). Indeed, the ring of districts from Kajaki and Baghran in the west, through northern Kandahar to Dai Chopan in Zabul, forms the largest continuous stretch of Afghan territory that is almost completely under Taliban rule.

Zirak Durrani tribes make up the majority in these areas, but the Taliban has still been able to build significant roots in these communities, largely because of their disconnection from Kandahar city. Moreover, as elsewhere, the insurgents used a combination of appeals to disaffected minority groups (such as Ishaqzais, Ghilzais, and even a small number of Wazirs) and threats against possible government sympathizers. They have also promoted a number of Barakzai and Alikozai commanders in an attempt to make inroads with the majority populations. In Nesh, the main force arrayed against the insurgents is the militia of Matiullah Khan of Uruzgan, which protects convoys en route to Tirin Kot and facilitates the movements of government officials within the district.

Among the prominent commanders in the area is Mullah Mohebullah, the Taliban-era governor of Takhar province and a former Bagram detainee who has since returned to the front lines in Shah Wali Kot. Other influential figures there include Mullah Azzam and Mullah Sardar. In Khakrez, Mullah Saif is a regional commander who is also active in Ghorak and Arghandab.

Maiwand, Zheray, and Panjwayi

This region of western Kandahar is the birthplace of the Taliban, the heartland of the insurgency, and one of the key contested geographic areas over the last few years. The Taliban exert almost complete control outside of district centers. In particular, the regions of Mushan in

Panjwayi, Sangesar in Zheray, and Garamabak in Maiwand are strongholds, each with standing courts. Although foreign fighters are negligible in the insurgency overall, these three areas are believed to host groups of foreigners, usually Pakistanis.[114]

The dynamics fueling the conflict in this area were described above: harassment of former Taliban, marginalization of certain tribes, poor governance, and so on. Moreover, this region has the special distinction of playing a central part in the Taliban's history. In addition to the role of Taliban fronts here in the 1980s, one of the movement's founding meetings took place in Sangesar, where Mullah Omar was preaching at a mosque at the time.

In Maiwand, important commanders include Mawlawi Khatib, a respected cleric from the Ishaqzai tribe who has served as a Taliban judge, and Mullah Noor Muhammad, a Noorzai from Garamabak. Muhammad is the area's most significant regional commander.[115]

Zheray boasts more than thirty delgai commanders and almost a dozen regional commanders, which gives a sense of the Taliban's sizable manpower in the region.[116] One of the most prominent regional commanders is Mullah Obaidullah (not to be confused with the former defense minister), a Kakar from Nelgham who had worked in the Taliban's interior ministry. Believed to be a major player in the drug trade, he is quite unpopular and cruel, many say. Locals give an opposite assessment of one of his colorful subcommanders, Kaka Abdul Khaliq. A Baluch who has been an active fighter for almost thirty years, Khaliq was one of those driven back to the Taliban because of harassment by government officials and foreign forces. He appears to have substantial support from the community, partly because of the ties he forged over three decades of activity in the area. He is famous for taking his small son with him on attacks; the son carries rocket-propelled grenade rounds and dutifully feeds his father ammo during battle. Both Obaidullah and Khaliq were among the first group that infiltrated Panjwayi and Zheray in 2004 and worked to reestablish the old Taliban networks.[117]

Another prominent figure is Mullah Zhedgay, one of the four commanders in charge of Kandahar city, overseeing the western part. An Alizai from Zheray, he was a foot soldier during the Taliban government and has risen in recent years to become a powerful regional commander, with at least four delgais under him. U.S. forces claimed to have killed him and another prominent Alizai commander, Mullah Amir, in 2010, but Zhedgay is said to be still alive.[118]

Taliban fighters move freely between Panjwayi and Zheray, and to a lesser extent Maiwand.[119] Malim Feda Muhammad, whose case was discussed above, is a well-known commander in Panjwayi and neighboring areas, but he spends most of his time in Pakistan and has deputies who lead his groups on the ground in battle. Muhammad and his men appear to have support from the community. As mentioned above, members of the Hafiz Majid network are also active here, alongside Mullah Akhtar Mansour's network. One key commander in the latter group is Mawlawi Matee, a Noorzai from Spin Boldak who had worked with Mansur in the civil aviation ministry during the Taliban government. Many Taliban figures from Spin Boldak operate in the more amenable climate of western Kandahar, where there is a large Noorzai population and a weak government.

As explained earlier, Sayeds are overrepresented in the Taliban here compared to their overall numbers, and they make up one of the most significant non-Pashtun Taliban populations (along with Baluchis). Important commanders from this group include Mullah Jabbar Agha, a relative of Akbar Agha, who had attempted to launch a Taliban splinter group in 2004 and kidnapped U.N. workers to finance the operation, and Sediq Agha, who is notorious for his brutality and led the infamous attack on Saraposa prison in 2008 that freed hundreds of inmates.[120] Mullah Janan Agha commands a number of groups in the region and is an example of the new breed of field leadership, having risen through the ranks after serving as a foot soldier during the Taliban government.

Although the commanders in this area are predominantly from the majority Panjpai tribes, there are notable exceptions. Mullah Bacha, for example, is a powerful Alikozai commander known for his skill in making roadside bombs.

Kandahar City, Dand, and Daman

In recent years, the insurgents have been steadily increasing their hold over parts of Kandahar city. To date they have managed to assert a degree of control in the southwest (Mahalajat area), west (Mirwais Mina area), and north (Loya Wiala area). Indeed, many parts of these areas are now completely no-go at night for those connected to the government, tribal elders, or foreign organizations. Taliban commanders spend one or two months in the city and then rotate to a district or to Pakistan to help ensure their safety. The aforementioned Mullah Zhedgay is a prominent commander here, along with Sheikh Mawlawi Nazar Muhammad and Mawlawi Feda Muhammad (different from the Feda Muhammad profiled above).

The unofficial district of Dand has been one of the most successful areas outside of the city in resisting Taliban takeover, largely due to close patronage links between segments of the local population and President Karzai and Gul Agha Sherzai.[121] The Barakzai-majority area is home to many Sherzai-backed militias and some Popalzai strongmen, both of which have resisted Taliban encroachments in recent years. The Taliban therefore lacks a natural base in the population of the sort it enjoys in neighboring Panjwayi. Indeed, Dand's shadow district governor, Mullah Ahmadullah "Mubarak," is based outside of the district, in Panjwayi. Nonetheless, the insurgents appear to have made Dand a strategic priority in 2010; attacks and instances of intimidation have skyrocketed. A key commander is Qari Khairullah Munib, a Noorzai from Spin Boldak who is an expert in roadside bombs and is connected to the Majid network.[122]

Maruf and Arghestan

The Barakzai majority in Maruf has ties to the government, and the Taliban initially recruited among the marginalized minority communities, including the Alizais and Ishaqzais (who make up about 30 percent of the district's population).[123] Maruf's long border with Pakistan and Zabul makes it a key transit corridor for insurgents, and the Samaai mountains along the border serve as an important Taliban redoubt. Unlike in most other parts of the province, here a number of tribal elders and maliks became Taliban commanders during the early post-2001 years. By 2006, the Taliban had saturated the non-Zirak areas and begun to move into Barakzai strongholds. It promoted a number of Barakzai commanders to leading positions, including Hafiz Hekmatullah, Mullah Bismullah, and Mullah Abdul Sattar, who also serves as the chief judge of the district. The most important commander, who doubles as the shadow district governor, is Mullah Muhammad Nabi, a Barakzai from

Arghestan. Despite his duties in Maruf, he is known to operate as far afield as Panjwayi. The leading commander from the minority communities is known as Commander Akhtar, an Alizai.[124]

The insurgents' rise in Maruf was aided by the relatively weak ties between Maruf Barakzais and major pro-government Barakzai power brokers such as Gul Agha Sherzai. During the anti-Soviet war, the Barakzai communities in Maruf and other outlying districts developed stronger connections to Hizb-i-Islami than to Sherzai. Today, the Taliban have been able to take advantage of this dynamic, giving them better links with these communities than with those in the Barakzai stronghold in Dand, which is strongly pro-Sherzai.[125]

Neighboring Arghestan also has a sizable Zirak population with whom the Taliban have made inroads. The most prominent commander is Hafiz Dost Muhammad, an Alikozai from the district. The shadow district governor is Mullah Burjan, a Kuchi. In addition to the Taliban, there are a few small, autonomous militias that are opposed to both the insurgents and government forces. Locals say that these militias, which operate in the Wam area, are tied to Abdul Razziq, a well-known mujahideen and later Taliban commander (this Razziq, a Popalzai, is not to be confused with the Border Police commander Abdul Razziq in Spin Boldak).[126]

Arghandab

Like Dand, Arghandab has been a key strategic focus for the Taliban, as it provides a second route into Kandahar city after the westerly approach. The Alikozai tribe and the legacy of its late senior figure, Mullah Naqib, dominate the politics of Arghandab. Naqib, the most important commander of Jamiat-e-Islami in Kandahar during the anti-Soviet insurgency, was a key player during the civil war in the 1990s, when he controlled parts of the city. Upon the Taliban's emergence, he stood down, allowing them to take Kandahar. After the 2001 invasion, the Taliban surrendered and gave Kandahar city back to Naqib, but U.S. forces backed Gul Agha Sherzai (who in their eyes was not tainted by accommodation to the Taliban). Naqib's men were partially absorbed into the Afghan security forces, and his stature and relationship with the Taliban meant that the insurgents made few gains in the district. When he died of a heart attack in October

2007, however, the insurgents were quick to seize the opportunity and invaded Arghandab from Shah Wali Kot and Khakrez, led by Mullah Shukoor.

The Alikozais, already weakened by a number of assassinations of key leaders and internally split between a pro-Jamiat faction and a pro-Karzai faction, were not able to resist the Taliban's pressure. Mullah Naqib's successor was his twentysomething son Karimullah Naqibi, who was seen as weak and lacking his father's force of personality. When the Taliban fighters invaded, they ransacked Naqib's house and even danced on the roof, openly showing contempt for the old order and signaling the shifting currents. Foreign forces were able to temporarily beat the insurgents back.

The Taliban's approach was aided by the marginalization of the non-Alikozai tribes in the district, including Kakars and Ghilzais. The insurgents were able to develop a support network in these communities just as the Alikozai leadership was weakening. Following the Sarposa prison break in the summer of 2008, fighters amassed again in Arghandab. Foreign forces killed Mullah Shukoor and were able to repel the attack once more. A third Taliban offensive, in the spring of 2009, was also eventually repelled. However, locals and Western officials report that the insurgents are now making inroads with the Alikozai community, in particular by forging connections with important leaders and government officials.[127] At the same time, the Taliban have given key positions to some Alikozais, such as Qari Shafiqullah, the current shadow governor for the district. Because a significant number of older field commanders such as Mullah Shukoor have been killed in various engagements over the last few years, insurgent ranks in Arghandab are increasingly led by men from Khakrez and Shah Wali Kot and by younger commanders with much less experience, like "Channa" Mullah Asadullah and Agha Wali.

Spin Boldak, Takhta Pul, Shorabak, and Registan

Like Dand and Daman, Spin Boldak is a relatively government-controlled district. Border Police commander Abdul Razziq's hold on the district and the importance of cross-border trade to both the government and the insurgency appear to have muted the Taliban's activity. The insurgency here is drawn almost entirely from the Noorzai tribe, as shown in Table 1.4. Most of the Spin Boldak Taliban spend at least some time in other districts, perhaps because of the difficult operating conditions in their home area. Across the border, Chaman is a vitally important hub for Taliban activities in Kandahar, as Quetta is for Afghanistan overall. The Achekzai-dominated Takhta Pul district is also under Razziq's influence, and the Taliban have less of a presence than elsewhere.[128]

As described above, government corruption and attempts to influence the elections were key destabilizing factors in Shorabak district. This extremely underdeveloped, income-depressed area is home to the Bareetz tribe, and many locals feel they have been neglected by the central government. Unsurprisingly, the majority of the Taliban here are Bareetz. Key commanders include Mawlawi Wali Jan, Mawlawi Abdul Halim, and Hafiz Sayed Muhammad. Interestingly, however, the shadow district governor is Mullah Raouf, a Noorzai from the neighboring Spin Boldak district.[129]

Finally, the barren district of Registan is home mostly to Baluchis. This desert area bordering Pakistan is a major smuggling and transit corridor for the Taliban.

FORCE SIZE

Estimating the size of the Taliban forces is fraught with difficulties. Fighters often move between Pakistan and their district of operation, and there are a number of facilitators and part-time fighters who may generally tend to their fields or do other work and pick up the gun only during bigger operations or missions with a chance of sizable spoils. Districts such as Dand, Zheray, and Panjwayi are especially difficult to study because fighters there are very mobile.

Maruf, however, affords a good opportunity to make a guess at force size: the majority of the fighters are based in or near their home villages, while their commanders travel back and forth between Kandahar and Pakistan. Moreover, the natural defenses of the Samaai mountains enable a relatively static insurgent population. According to Taliban members, local officials, and local residents, there are twelve major delgai commanders in Maruf. District officials and Taliban fighters put the number of fighters in each delgai at between 10 and 22, with the exception that Mullahs Mirza Muhammad and Muhammad Nabi and

TABLE 1.5 Approximate Force Ratios in Maruf District

	Afghan National Police	Afghan National Army	NDS	Taliban
Force Size	80	0	40	200
Force-to-population ratio	1 for every 380 people	Not applicable	1 for every 765 people	1 for every 153 people
Force-to-male-population ratio	1 for every 190 males	Not applicable	1 for every 380 males	1 for every 75 males
Force-to-family ratio	1 for every 55 families	Not applicable	1 for every 110 families	1 for every 22 families

Note: Based on a population estimate of 30,600 and a family size of seven, from United Nations Development Program, *Kandahar Anzor*, 2009. Force sizes of ANP and NDS are official figures from Maruf district government and are likely to be exaggerated, since in many districts officials report higher numbers in order to get more resources from the central government. NDS size includes assistants and paid agents.

Commander Akhtar appear to have larger groups. If these fluctuations are ignored and an average of 16 fighters per group is used, this means there are close to 200 Taliban fighters in the district. This is likely to be an underestimate, since a number of smaller groups are not included in the count; nor are part-timers or facilitators. Table 1.5 gives estimated force ratios for three armed groups in the area. The numbers of Afghan National Police and National Directorate of Security personnel are almost certainly overestimates, as they are based on the number officially on payroll rather than the number who may actually be present in the district. Still, the table gives the best-case scenario from the perspective of the pro-government forces. Of course, this doesn't give nearly the full picture, because the police and NDS are concentrated in the district center while the Taliban are dispersed throughout the district (including the district center). Moreover, in terms of effectiveness, many ANP officers are nonnative, unlike the Taliban, who are rooted in the communities in which they operate.

FOREIGN FIGHTERS

In the early years of the insurgency in eastern Afghanistan, and to a much lesser extent in the southern region, foreign fighters—al-Qaeda, Central Asian militants, Pakistanis, unaffiliated Arabs, and others—played a training and facilitation role. These groups, particularly the Arabs, were also a likely funding channel for the Taliban. But in recent years, the importance and relevance of such fighters appear to have diminished greatly. The insurgents are now largely self-sufficient in funding, raising money locally or through their own networks in Pakistan and the Persian Gulf region. Also, the insurgents have developed their own expertise in the technical aspects of warfare, such as building improvised explosive devices (IEDs).[130]

Today, areas such as Mushan (Panjwayi), Sangesar (Zheray), Garamabak (Maiwand), the Samaai mountains (Maruf), and the remote northern districts such as Nesh have some foreign fighter presence.[131] There do not appear to be any independent foreign commanders as there are in Kunduz or Nuristan; rather, small numbers of fighters are attached to Afghan groups. However, locals and the Taliban do speak of one independent, largely Pakistani group linked to certain Taliban commanders called "the Zarqawis," presumably in homage to the late insurgent Abu Musab al-Zarqawi, a Jordanian known for his activities in Iraq. A detailed list of ninety-one IED attacks since April provided by Taliban commander Qari Khairullah Munib, the Dand in-charge for IEDs, included a couple that were carried out by the Zarqawis.[132] The group appears to have emerged in the second half of 2010. There are other fleeting references to this enigmatic group, but for the most part it appears to stay away from the spotlight and does not contribute significantly to the insurgency.

TACTICS AND STRATEGY

The Taliban's approach to retaking Kandahar can be divided roughly into four periods.

When the Taliban leadership first disappeared across the border, they maintained contact with key facilitators in their home villages. These people would usually be mullahs or tribal elders, who would do much to formulate the Taliban's message of jihad in the coming years. In particular, there existed throughout the province an informal network of mullahs who offered ready condemnations of malfeasance by the government and foreign forces. One Taliban commander recalled those days: "We would meet every week with the mullah. We would talk about the situation, especially about the government and the foreign forces. We had long discussions and the mullah would try to convince us to fight against these people."[133]

At the same time, key leading figures such as Mullah Obaidullah and Mawlawi Gul Agha would call their former commanders or associates. "Gul Agha called me one day," recalled one former Taliban commander. "He told me that this is the time to do jihad. He invited me to Quetta so that we could discuss our options."[134] Some Taliban interviewed for this report said that they were initially reluctant to rejoin the movement but the state of affairs eventually forced them back.

In this early period of reorganization, it was vital to bring religious legitimacy to the incipient Taliban project. While the sympathetic mullah networks preached against the foreign occupation, the insurgents also launched an assassination campaign against pro-government religious clerics. In 2003, a number of influential clerics were killed, including Mawlawi Jenab, who was gunned down in Panjwayi.[135]

In these early years, the Taliban's message resonated with many in rural communities. The insurgents also realized early that the best way to ensure that locals would be completely dependent on them was to enforce a strict separation between the population and the government. Thus one of the first acts of many newly formed Taliban groups in Kandahar was to demand that all locals cut ties with the government. The commander quoted above (about mullahs) said:

> After some time and a lot of discussion we decided that we should join the Taliban. We formed a small group, and the mullahs advised us. The first thing we did was find those people who

were working for the government and tell them that they had one chance to quit. If they did not, we would kill them.[136]

Together with this intimidation, the Taliban began to issue "night letters." The first came in 2002 in the form of leaflets left overnight at various schools, urging Afghans not to cooperate with the foreign forces. By 2003, they were a regular occurrence.[137]

The first of the revived Taliban groups appear to have been based in Shah Wali Kot and nearby, perhaps because these areas north of Kandahar city were the most rugged, remote, and cut off from the center. Moreover, these areas were connected to Zabul and Uruzgan, other sites of early Taliban resurgence. The insurgents targeted those areas where locals were most disaffected; in some cases the locals themselves reached out to the Taliban or formed their own groups and allied with the insurgents.

Consolidation: 2004–2006

From Shah Wali Kot and northern Kandahar, the insurgents were able to reconnect with old networks in the Panjwayi-Zheray-Maiwand area, the birthplace of the Taliban. By 2006 most of these areas had fallen completely to the insurgents. Taliban courts were established in western and northern Kandahar, and other elements of the shadow apparatus, such as governorships, began to be assigned.

The insurgents' ranks swelled during this period, as disaffected former Taliban returned and communities sought protection from predatory officials or the foreigners. However, it is important to also note the limits of Taliban support. The movement enjoyed greater backing among rural, uneducated, low-stature populations who were thoroughly disconnected from the central government. But urban dwellers, the traditional elite, educated individuals, and those connected through tribal, kinship, or experiential ties to power brokers tended to have little sympathy for the insurgents. It appears that the Taliban's support in Kandahar was greater during these early years of revival and consolidation than it is now, as heavy-handed tactics have disillusioned some of their erstwhile supporters. Moreover, the issue of Taliban support itself is complicated by the insurgency's diverse nature. Some commanders are quite popular, whereas others are reviled. Some people support certain Taliban functions—such as their courts or attacks on foreign troops—but oppose others, such as attacks on schools or government workers. Finally, some communities join with the Taliban simply to protect themselves *from* the Taliban.

As the movement consolidated during this period, the insurgents began to launch more ambitious and coordinated assaults, moving away from reliance on the "pinpricks"—hit-and-run attacks, rocket and grenade assaults, and the occasional car bomb—that had characterized the previous period. In 2006, mimicking moves from the Soviet war, large numbers of fighters began to assemble in the vineyards of Zheray and Panjwayi, possibly for an assault on Kandahar city. Coalition forces, led by the Canadians, responded with Operation Medusa, a massive siege of Taliban positions in the river valley of the two districts. It was the closest thing to a conventional battle in Afghanistan since Operation Anaconda in Paktia province in 2002. The Taliban were little match for the foreigners' overwhelming firepower; more than two hundred insurgents were killed and scores were captured. Operation Medusa (and similar battles around that time, such as the Battle of Baluchi Pass in Uruzgan) forced the Taliban to rethink their strategy. Instead of preparing for a final push into the main urban centers of Kandahar, which implied taking on the military forces directly, they transformed their approach.[138]

Asymmetry: 2006–2009

Under pressure from airstrikes and unable to challenge the foreign forces directly, the Taliban shifted to more small-scale tactics. Previously, dozens of fighters would be associated with an insurgent base, or *otaq*, but now they began to opt for more and smaller groups.[139] Mullah Dadullah, who was leading a major front at that time, pioneered the use of suicide bombs in southern Afghanistan, a tactic that some claim he borrowed from Iraqi insurgents.[140] The devastating weapon had the advantage of being able to penetrate the enemy's defenses in ways conventional weapons could not, but it also carried the risk of civilian casualties. Many religious scholars insisted that such methods were proscribed in Islam. The use of such weapons sparked debates in the Quetta Shura, with Mullah Omar reportedly opposed to their use.[141] The realities on the ground eventually won out, however, and today the leadership appears to have made a virtue of necessity. The number of suicide attacks skyrocketed after 2006. Bombers attacked district centers, like Dand, and targeted key government institutions, such as the provincial council in Kandahar city. In 2009 the campaign accelerated: suicide attackers struck the governor's palace, the NDS headquarters, and other sites in Kandahar. Some attacks killed a large number of civilians as well. A bombing at a dog-fighting match in early 2008 killed Alikozai strongman Abdul Hakim Jan and more than a hundred others in the bloodiest suicide strike in Afghan history. The following day, an attack on an ISAF convoy in Spin Boldak killed scores more.

In this period, insurgents also began to employ another deadly weapon: the roadside bomb. Stuffed in culverts and ditches along roads frequented by military convoys, these mines proved to be the most effective killer of foreign troops. The threat became so pervasive that avoiding such bombs became a main preoccupation for foreign troops outside the relative safety of their bases. Though usually cruder than their Iraqi counterparts, these weapons were still capable of considerable destruction. Their use encouraged secondary insurgent groups, whose main focus would be to procure bomb-making materials and help in assembly.

Assassinations of tribal elders and government officials continued to increase in this period. The decisive factor in these targeted killings was whether the target had some connection to the government. The victims included civilians who worked closely with the government, as well as district shura members. One organization found that, from 2001 through July 2010, more than 515 tribal elders had been assassinated in Kandahar.[142] In some districts, entire sections of the tribal leadership were either killed or driven away. The killings often followed a pattern: in areas where a particular tribe was seen as closer to the government, that tribe was predominantly targeted. In Spin Boldak, with roughly a fifty-fifty split between Achekzais and Noorzais and where the former is seen to be much closer to the government, thirty-six out of forty-nine assassinations were of Achekzais. In Arghandab, where the insurgents have positioned themselves as protectors of the Ghilzai tribes vis-à-vis the Alikozai majority, twelve of the sixteen killed were Alikozais. (In addition, a number of prominent Alikozai figures around the province have been killed.) But in Panjwayi, with Noorzai and Ishaqzai predominant, most of those killed were also from these tribes.[143]

In Maiwand, the Taliban were essentially able to shut down the district shura by intimidation. Insurgent threats in 2006 forced all but five of the shura's twenty-two members to resign. Some who quit joined the Taliban, while the remaining members fled to Kandahar city.[144]

The insurgents also devised other ways to pressure and isolate the government. Attacks on schools began to intensify by 2005. At the same time, the Taliban issued oral or written warnings to residents not to send their children to school. By 2009, most of the schools operating outside firmly held government territory had been shuttered. This should not be seen, however, as opposition to education as such. (Indeed, the Taliban have spoken of opening their own schools, and when they captured Musa Qala in Helmand, they allowed schools to function.) Rather, this was an effort to block one of the few services that the state had attempted to provide to rural communities, and in doing so further the separation between the population and the government. For the same reason, there was a discreet but concerted campaign to attack or force the closure of clinics.[145] In the case of both schools and clinics, however, the Taliban (particularly the older generation) appeared willing to negotiate their existence with the community, so long as the inviolable principle of independence from the government and foreigners was upheld.

In cases where the carrot did not work, the insurgents used the stick. In addition to assassination campaigns and intimidation, the Taliban marked its rise with regular human rights abuses targeting those who stood in their way. These abuses included arbitrary imprisonment, collective punishment, summary execution, beheadings, extortion, and kidnapping for ransom. Because of this, as mentioned above, individuals or communities joined the Taliban simply to protect themselves from the Taliban.

Escalation: 2009 to Present

Two factors led to a shift in Taliban tactics in 2010. First, an increased foreign focus on Kandahar, especially the growing talk of a major offensive there, prompted a renewed Taliban emphasis on the province. This was marked by an effort to pressure the Afghan government via a brutal assassination campaign. The targeting of tribal elders, civil servants, low-level officials, and NGO workers proceeded at an unprecedented pace. In the first four months of 2010, there were at least sixty-four assassinations in the province—about one every two days.[146] The pace increased to almost one per day in the summer of 2010. Some of the killings were truly chilling: one Afghan employee of an American contractor received a call while he was visiting relatives in Mahalajat. He was told that it was the neighbors and that they needed to speak to him urgently. When he walked out of the house, Taliban fighters abducted him, took him to another area, bludgeoned him, stabbed him in the eyes, and left him for dead.[147]

The insurgents also continued to make a push into Kandahar city, just as foreign forces and the Afghan government made plans to consolidate their presence there by increasing patrols and troop strength, and erecting a security cordon around the city. In the first hundred days or so of 2010 there were 135 security incidents in the city alone, more than one a day. Thirty-three of these were assaults with small-arms fire, and five involved multiple attack methods. Consider a typical one-week stretch in early March: on that Monday around 2:00 p.m., a suicide car bomber attacked the Afghan National Police headquarters, killing a policeman and wounding seventeen other people, including eight civilians. At 10:00 p.m., in District 4, a man on a motorcycle shot and killed a civilian and escaped into the night. The next day, at 5:00 a.m. in District 9, a private security vehicle struck an IED, injuring one person. An hour later, an IED went off in front of the house of an owner of a private security company in District 9, but it failed to harm anyone. The next day, Wednesday, a civilian was found shot and hanging from a tree in District 2. That morning a police vehicle hit a roadside bomb in District 9, wounding one civilian. At 7:30 the next morning, gunmen opened fire at a road construction company, killing five workers. Later that day, gunmen raided a civilian's house in broad daylight in District 3, prompting the Afghan National Police to respond. The following day, Friday, the day of rest in Afghanistan, saw no incidents. But on Saturday morning, gunmen attacked a police patrol in District 3, killing one policeman and wounding four civilians. That evening a pair of IEDs went off under police vehicles parked in front of an officer's home, but there were no casualties. Early Sunday morning, gunmen entered the compound of a local NGO, tied up the staff, and set fire to many vehicles before leaving. Insurgents capped off the week by attacking a police foot patrol in District 3 later that morning, killing two policemen but losing one of their own in the process.[148]

It is very likely that not all of these incidents were due to the Taliban. With entrenched drug mafias, pernicious government officials, family rivalries, and other factors, there are many possible sources of violence. Nonetheless, if even some of these attacks were conducted by the insurgents, they indicate that the Taliban's campaign to force a separation between the government and the population in the city is taking root.

The focus on Kandahar city is part of a general upward trend of insurgent-initiated attacks in the province, as Figures 1.2 and 1.3 show. The foreign forces met the growing violence with a series of troop increases, but this escalation was unable to halt the Taliban's growth. In large part this was because key elements of the Taliban operations were outside the traditional military scope: the insurgents' control over an area was dependent not on their ability to physically hold territory, but on their ability to influence the inhabitants of that territory. This influence has been spread largely through informal means: mosques, family ties, tribal ties, connections from the 1990s, and so on. These channels are generally not available to foreign troops. Thus, although coalition forces easily swept through Marjah in Helmand province, displacing many insurgents and forcing others to melt back into the population, they still have not been able to compete effectively with the insurgents for influence over the population.

Nonetheless, one military approach appears to have forced the second major shift in Taliban tactics in 2010: the concerted U.S. Special Forces assassination campaign targeting insurgent field commanders. A number of commanders have been killed or captured, placing unprecedented pressure on the Taliban. As Figures 1.2 and 1.3 illustrate, however, this has not diminished the insurgents' capability to attack or dampened the levels of violence.[149] What it has done is force major demographic shifts in the makeup of the insurgency and a concomitant shift in insurgent operating procedures. Until this year, almost the entire field leadership of the insurgency had been active in some capacity during the Taliban government era; when asked, tribal elders, officials, and insurgents could not identify a single pre-2009 commander who was not active himself or connected to someone (such as a brother) who was active during the Taliban era.[150] Today, however, a number of younger commanders have risen to replace those killed or captured, and some have no personal ties with the senior leadership. The result has been a steady fragmentation of the insurgency, with smaller and more numerous groups in operation, some of which have

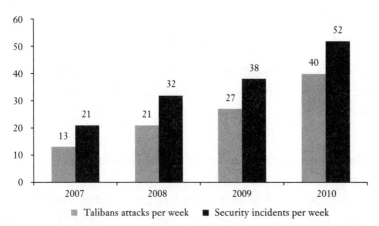

FIGURE I.2 Taliban-Initiated Attacks and Total Security Incidents Per Week in Kandahar Province.

Note: The latter category includes incidents related to foreign forces' operations as well as crime. Data from Sami Kovanen of Indicium Consulting, inclusive through the end of August. The term "Taliban attacks" refers to all cases in which insurgents initiated an attack, as opposed to assaults initiated by foreign forces. The incidents in both sets of data include discovered IEDs. It is possible that some attacks attributed to the insurgents were conducted by other actors (such as pro-government forces).

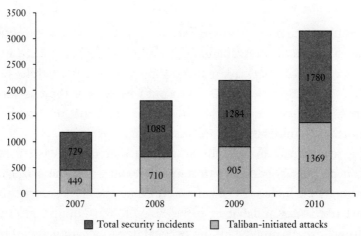

FIGURE I.3 Taliban-Initiated Attacks and Total Security Incidents in Kandahar Province.

Note: the latter includes incidents due to foreign forces' operations.

only a tenuous connection to Quetta. Insurgents are moving in smaller groups now for safety, as one elder from Panjwayi describes:

> These people keep getting killed, but they keep getting replaced. They used to stay in otaqs of 15 or 30 people, but now there are only three or four people per an otaq. They focus more on placing mines, since that is safer.[151]

It's too early to say what long-term effects these changes will have on the insurgency. It appears that the pressure is forcing Taliban groups to be more mobile than ever. This has the potential to spark more inter-insurgent conflicts as groups vie for territory. For the time being, it appears that the ability of foreign forces to kill or capture commanders is matched by the insurgents' ability to replace them. In Panjwayi, for instance, where before there were a dozen or so strong commanders, now there are two dozen or three dozen group leaders. Mullah Amir (the former shadow governor of Dand) and Ikram "Khadem" are prominent examples of those killed in 2010, and in their place are now a number of lesser-known commanders: Mullah Agha, "Gud" Ahmadullah, Haidari, Misteri, Baghawan, and others.

CONCLUSION

In the fall of 2010, the foreign forces launched a major offensive in Taliban strongholds in Arghandab, Panjwayi, and Zheray. U.S. authorities hope this will mark a key turning point in the war, while Taliban members insist they will simply wait out this push as they have previous ones. To gauge the possible outcomes of the battle for Kandahar, it is important to understand Kandahar's recent history.

The resurgence of the Taliban was not inevitable. A failed reconciliation process, together with perceived abuses by the government and foreigners, fueled the insurgency. Once the Taliban was able to reassert itself in Kandahar, it expertly exploited popular grievances, operating with an understanding of local dynamics unmatched by the foreign forces. The Coalition Forces have difficulty competing with the insurgents even when they have a distinct military advantage: the Taliban use networks that were not available to the foreigners, such as kinship ties, mullah networks, and so on. The Taliban's structure in Kandahar is a potent mixture of formal, top-down command and informal, bottom-up initiative. The movement is not so tightly structured that the arrest or killing of top leaders affects its activities, but at the same time it is not so decentralized that coordinated action cannot be taken.

Yet the insurgents have weaknesses. What they cannot achieve through appealing to local sentiment, they do so through force. So just as they position themselves as protectors of marginalized communities, their harsh rule can also breed resentment. And their informal structure, which has proven so hardy, relies on bonds between fighters that have persisted for decades. As a newer generation of fighters emerges to replace slain commanders, this informal structure could become an impediment and the leadership's ability to control its charges could weaken. The Taliban in Kandahar has proven itself resilient, however, and it is too soon to say for sure whether such trends will materialize. But what is certain is that so long as the war continues Kandahar province will remain one of its key fronts, and the Taliban there will continue to be the heart of the insurgency.

Notes

1. Interviews in Kandahar city, July 2010. "Ghulam" is a pseudonym.
2. Alex Strick van Linschoten, "Kandahar Timeline," www.alexstrick.com/timeline.
3. This study focuses exclusively on the Taliban. Hizb-i-Islami, another major Afghan insurgent group, has today a minimal presence in Kandahar.
4. Interviews, Kandahar, 2008–2010; Gilles Dorronsoro, *Revolution Unending: Afghanistan 1979 to Present* (London, C. Hurst, 2005).
5. In particular, the Muhammadzai tribe—sometimes thought of as a clan of the Barakzais, sometimes as an independent tribe—provided a number of rulers.
6. Alex Strick van Linschoten and Felix Kuehn, *An Enemy We Created* (C. Hurst, 2012).
7. Nationally, these seven parties were made up of four "fundamentalist" groups: Jamiat-i-Islami, led by Burhanuddin Rabbani, Hizb-i-Islami Gulbuddin, led by Gulbuddin Hekmatyar, Hizb-i-Islami Khalis, led by Mawlawi Younis Khalis, and Ittihad-i-Islami, led by Abdul Rasoul Sayyaf; one traditionalist party, Herakat-i-Inqalabi Islami, led by Mullah Muhammad Nabi; and two royalist groups, Mahaz-i-Mill Islami (led by Pir Gailani) and Jabha-e-Najat-e-Milli (by Sibghatullah Mujaddeddi). In Kandahar there was another group, Fedayeen-i-Islam, that eventually broke from the mujahideen ranks and allied with the Afghan government.

8. Abdul Salaam Zaeef, *My Life with the Taliban* (New York, Columbia University Press, 2010), 26–27.

9. Information from interviews in Kandahar and Kabul with former mujahideen, 2009–10. It should be noted that these commanders were not very important in the 1980s *jihad*.

10. See, for instance, Sarah Chayes, *The Punishment of Virtue: Inside Afghanistan After the Taliban*, Penguin Press, 2006.

11. Details of these events are from interviews with Mullah Abdul Hakim Mujahed, Mawlawi Arsala Rahmani, Mullah Abdul Salaam, Abdul Wahed, officials in Hamid Karzai's office, and officials and Taliban figures in Kandahar province who spoke on condition of anonymity, 2010. See also Hamid Karzai's speech at the Afghanistan Consultative Peace Jirga, June 2, 2010.

12. This event took place on December 5, when Karzai was near the Dahla Dam in Shah Wali Kot district. In addition to receiving the letter, he was also actively negotiating with the Taliban officials about the surrender of Kandahar city.

13. Interview with Afghan government officials, August 2010.

14. Interviews with current and former Taliban and Afghan officials in Kandahar and Kabul, 2010.

15. Bradley Graham and Alan Sipress, "Reports That Taliban Leaders Were Freed Shock, Alarm U.S.," *Washington Post*, Jan. 10, 2002. Obaidullah and others were freed by the government but came under criticism from the United States.

16. Interview with Afghan government officials, August 2010.

17. In Kandahar, they included the commanders of Gul Agha Sherzai. In Uruzgan, Jan Muhammad Khan (who had been imprisoned by the Taliban) and, in Helmand, strongman and eventual governor Sher Muhammad Akhundzada are in this category.

18. Pakistan arrested Obaidullah in late 2007. He died in 2012 in Pakistani custody.

19. Interviews with Afghan government officials and Taliban figures, 2008–2010. From 2010 on, Tayeb Agha served as Mullah Omar's representative in talks with the United States.

20. Interview with Fazel Muhammad, Kabul, August 2010.

21. Interviews with Kandahar government officials and tribal elders, August 2010.

22. Interviews with Kandahar government officials and tribal elders, July 2010.

23. Ibid.

24. Interviews with residents and officials in Maiwand and Kandahar city, 2008–2010.

25. Interviews with Kandahar government officials and tribal elders, 2010.

26. Interview with MP Ahmed Shah Achekzai, April 2010.

27. Interviews with Taliban commander and Taliban fighter, Kandahar, July 2010.

28. Interviews with Rahmani, Siddiqi, Abdul Hakim Mujahed, Ali Jalali, Felix Kuehn, 2010.

29. In particular, there was opposition from the Northern Alliance.

30. Interviews with Arsala Rahmani, Abdul Hakim Mujahed, Abdul Sattar Siddiqi, and Ali Jalali.

31. We will follow the mainstream English spelling of the tribes (with English plural markings) as opposed to the Latinized Pashto variants.

32. There are other confederations in addition to these in the south, among them the Gharghusht (which includes the Kakar tribes). Also, tribal affiliations are not always fixed; individuals and areas have their own notions of tribal taxonomy. Thus the Noorzais are considered by most as part of the Panjpai Durrani group, but by some as part of the Ghilzai confederation.

33. Historically the Alikozais have played a role in administering security, including through the use of tribal militias.

34. See, for instance, Carl Forsberg, "Politics and Power in Kandahar," *The Institute for the Study of War*, April 2010.

35. Interview with Noorzai elder, Kandahar city, August 2010.

36. As mentioned above, historically the Zirak Durranis held the leadership at the expense of other tribes, but the Soviet experience, the civil war, and the Taliban government led to an inversion of these roles. Many previously second-class citizens joined the Communists, the mujahideen, or later the Taliban, while many of the traditional leaders tied to the center fled or were killed.

37. For more on Razzik and his role in cross-border trade and smuggling, see Matthieu Aikins, "The Master of Spin Boldak," *Harper's*, December 2009.

38. Interviews with government officials, intelligence officials, and tribal elders in Spin Boldak, April 2010.

39. Another largely Achekzai militia has historical importance in Kandahar. Commander Ismat Muslim led a group in the 1980s that broke ranks with the mujahideen after receiving payments from the Communist government and frequently feuded with the more Noorzai-friendly mujahideen parties such as Hizb-i-Islami. Abdul Razzik's uncle was a key commander in Ismat Muslim's militia and was publicly killed by the Taliban in 1994 during the birth of that movement. Source: interviews in Spin Boldak, April 2010.

40. Interview with Neda Muhammad, in Kabul, and elders from Panjwayi, in Kandahar city, August 2010.

41. Graeme Smith, "The Canadians Try to Kill Everybody," *Globe and Mail*, Nov. 27, 2006.

42. See, for example, Thomas Johnson and M. Chris Mason, "Understanding the Taliban and Insurgency," Naval Postgraduate School, 2006.

43. Interviews with Maiwand elders and government officials, Keshk-i-Nakhud, 2008.

44. Moreover, locals sometimes dispute tribal affiliations. Some consider the Noorzais as part of the Panjpai Durrani confederation, whereas others insist it belongs to the Ghilzai confederation. Also, in Kandahar today many don't like to openly discuss tribal affiliations, which is a sensitive subject.

45. For instance, the Noorzai tribe in Kandahar is divided into two branches, the Durzai and the Daudzai, each of which is further divided into another series of tribes.

46. Here "nationalist Islamist" means an Islamist movement with national aspirations—in this case to evict foreign forces and capture power throughout the country.

47. See Graeme Smith, "House of Pain: Canada's Connection with Kandahar's Ruthless Palace Guard," *Globe and Mail*, Apr. 10, 2010.

48. Interviews with locals, elders, and government officials in Kandahar, 2008–2010.

49. Interview with Kandahar resident in Kandahar city, July 2010.

50. Niamat is now head of Kandahar's Peace and Reconciliation Commission, a body tasked with persuading Taliban fighters to lay down their weapons and reconcile with the government.

51. Interview with Maiwand tribal elder, Kabul, August 2010.

52. Interviews with Kandahar residents, 2008–2010.

53. The Bareetz are neither Durranis nor Ghilzais. Their members are mostly in Shorabak, Baluchistan, Nimroz, Helmand, and Sindh.

54. Interview with Hajji Muhammad Bareetz, Kandahar, May 2010.

55. See Dexter Filkins, "Tribal Leaders Say Karzai's Team Forged 23,900 Votes," *New York Times*, Sept. 1, 2009.

56. Kandahar City Municipality and Dand District: District Narrative Analysis, Mar. 30, 2010, from the Stability Operations Information Center, Kabul.

57. Michael V. Bhatia and Mark Sedra, *Afghanistan, Arms and Conflict: Armed Groups, Disarmament and Security in a Post-War Society* (Routledge, 2008), Kindle Electronic Edition.

58. Interviews with tribal elders and locals, Panjwayi, 2010.

59. There are other mechanisms of dispute resolution in traditional society, such as those based on tribal customs. The weakening of tribal structures over the years has helped the Taliban in this regard. Indeed, in those areas where stronger tribal structures exist side by side with weaker ones, such as Paktia province, one can argue that the Taliban have been able to penetrate areas with weaker structures more deeply, in part because they offer judicial services that the tribes cannot compete with. Historically, influential or respected individuals in society have also played a role in dispute resolution; they include Sayeds and, in some cases, khans. Today, some people are said to take their disputes directly to Ahmed Wali Karzai, for instance.

60. Alex Strick van Linschoten and Felix Kuehn, *An Enemy We Created* (C. Hurst, 2012).

61. Kandahar City Municipality and Dand District: District Narrative Analysis, Mar. 30, 2010, from the Stability Operations Information Center, Kabul. The shortage is likely due to a dearth of qualified individuals and to Taliban threats, which keep people away.

62. For examples of special forces working with Sherzai's commanders, see Anonymous, *Hunting Al Qaeda: A Take-No-Prisoners Account of Terror, Adventure and Disillusionment* (Zenith Press, 2005).

63. Interview with NDS agent, Kabul, August 2010.

64. Interviews with Taliban fighters, tribal elders, and government officials, Kandahar, 2010.

65. A type of PK machine gun.

66. Interview with Taliban commander and elders from Shah Wali Kot, 2009.

67. Interviews with Ishaqzai elders in Helmand, Kandahar, and Kabul, 2009–10, and Malalai Ishaqzai, lawmaker, 2010.

68. In this chapter, "Taliban facilitator" means someone who is not an active military commander but works in other spheres—political, financial, or logistics—to aid the movement.

69. Interviews with Zheray elders, Kandahar, April 2010. Janan was preaching against the foreign forces but was not a fighter himself. Despite his preaching (or maybe because of it), he was very popular and influential in the area.
70. *Ramazan* is the Persian and Afghan term for Ramadan.
71. Interview with Taliban commander in Kandahar city, July 2010.
72. See, for example, U.K. Department for International Development, Understanding Afghanistan: Poverty, Gender and Social Exclusion Analysis, November 2008. Of course, Taliban presence itself, or insecurity, could also cause joblessness and depressed income levels.
73. This does not mean, however, that the Taliban pay a regular "salary" to their fighters. See the section below on Taliban financing.
74. Interviews with locals, Keshk-i-Nakhud, Maiwand, April 2008.
75. Ibid.
76. Graeme Smith, "Talking to the Taliban," *Globe and Mail*, Mar. 22, 2008.
77. One example of this is the Khogiyanis in Maiwand (against the Noorzais, for land rights).
78. And vice versa, where Kuchis use the Taliban against local settled communities.
79. Interviews with Quetta Shura leaders, Taliban commanders, and tribal elders, 2008–2010.
80. Sarah Ladbury in collaboration with Cooperation for Peace and Unity, Kabul, "Testing Hypothesis for Radicalization in Afghanistan: Why Do Men Join the Taliban and Hizb-i-Islami? How Much Do Local Communities Support Them?" Independent report for DFID, Aug. 14, 2009.
81. They include Mullah Beradar and at least six other senior leaders, who were at various times on the Quetta Shura. They made approaches to the Afghan government at various times in the last four years. The others cannot be named here in order to protect their security.
82. Ladbury et al.
83. Interviews with Quetta Shura members, 2010.
84. Ibid.
85. According to Alex Strick van Linschoten, a Kandahar-based researcher (interview, August 2010), Mullah Ghaus served under Abdul Razziq, a Popalzai commander with Hizb-i-Islami Khalis (not to be confused with the other Abdul Razziqs mentioned previously in this chapter).
86. Interviews with locals from Arghestan, officials, and Taliban figures.
87. Moreover, the term *mullah* is used very loosely by the Taliban. Typically most Taliban commanders take the title even if they have not attended a religious school or are not qualified to lead Friday prayers.
88. These include Panjwayi, Zheray, Mia Neshin, Maiwand, Khakrez, Ghorak, and Arghestan.
89. In Taliban areas where there is electricity, residents pay electric bills to the district governor. In a few cases (such as near Muhsan in Panjwayi), insurgents have even paved or graveled some roads with tax money. Foreign forces bombed the Muhsan road in 2009.
90. Interview, Kabul, March 2010.

91. It is important to note, however, that even the Taliban courts sometimes have their biases. Some locals complain that the courts unjustly favor its members when in disputes with civilians. However, overall the courts appear to be much fairer than government ones.

92. See, for instance, Dan Murphy, "Dent in Afghanistan War Strategy: Why Kandahar Locals Turn to the Taliban," *Christian Science Monitor*, July 6, 2010.

93. Beginning in 2006, the Taliban also published a code of conduct, meant to govern the behavior of its fighters. Though it was distributed in parts of southern Afghanistan, it does not appear to play a prominent role in day-to-day activities or in the leadership's attempts to police rank-and-file behavior.

94. "State of the Taliban," ISAF Secret Report, TF 3-10, Bagram, Afghanistan, Jan. 6, 2012.

95. *Otaq* is also used. This means either a "cell" or a physical base, depending on the speaker and the context. Taliban members in Kandahar tend to use the term *delgai* more frequently.

96. Andiwal means "friend" in Pashto and Dari.

97. Interviews with Afghan intelligence officials, 2008–2010, and a U.S. intelligence official, 2008.

98. Interview with Taliban commander, April 2010. By "rewards" he means spoils, such as weapons.

99. Dadullah's front fell apart after his death in 2007 and the expulsion of his brother from the Taliban.

100. "Zakir" and "Khadem" originated as radio names and have since stuck. Zakir used to be the deputy of Abdul Raouf during the Taliban era, but now the two have switched roles. Both Zakir and Raouf are former Guantánamo detainees. For more on them, see Anand Gopal, "Qayum Zakir, The Afghanistan Taliban's Rising New Mastermind," *Christian Science Monitor*, Apr. 30, 2010.

101. Interview with Taliban commander, June 2010.

102. Interviews with Afghan intelligence officials, tribal elders, and Taliban commanders in Panjwayi, Zheray, Kandahar city, and Kabul, 2009–10.

103. Interviews with Afghan intelligence officials, tribal elders, and Taliban commanders in Kandahar city and Kabul, 2010. For more on Gul Agha's moves for leadership, see Sami Yousufzai and Ron Moreau, "Taliban in Turmoil," *Newsweek*, May 28, 2010.

104. Interview with Taliban commander, Kandahar city, July 2010.

105. Adam was part of Mullah Abdul Manan's network. Manan was a prominent commander who is believed to have been killed by an air strike in 2007 or 2008. Adam is Ishaqzai by tribe.

106. See Fisnik Abrashi, "More Than 1,000 Afghans Protest Taliban Killings," *Associated Press*, Oct. 24, 2008.

107. Interview, Kandahar, July 2010.

108. The Pakistani rupee is a commonly used currency in Afghanistan, especially for large transactions.

109. Interview, Kandahar, July 2010.

110. *Zakat* is the practice, obligatory for Muslims, of giving a small portion of one's wealth or income to charity, generally to help the poor and needy. *Ushr* is less standard in the Muslim world and refers to the custom of sharing 10 percent

of one's earnings with the community. In practice this appears to be limited to earnings on land and as such can be seen as a sort of land tax. In traditional rural society in southern Afghanistan, the religious clergy survives on zakat and ushr.

111. Interview, Kandahar, July 2010.
112. See, for example, Aram Roston, "How the U.S. Funds the Taliban," *Nation*, Nov. 11, 2009.
113. In addition, 10–20 percent can go to the local commander. Interview with Felix Kuehn, Kabul, July 2010.
114. Interview with U.S. Army officer, near Sangesar, April 2010, and interviews with locals in Zheray, Maiwand, and Kandahar city, 2010.
115. Interviews with locals, officials, and Taliban fighters, Maiwand, 2008–2010.
116. Interviews with locals, officials, and Taliban fighters, Zheray, 2008–2010.
117. Interviews with tribal elders, Taliban commanders, locals, and Afghan officials in Zheray, Maiwand, and Panjwayi, 2009–10. Obaidullah is injured and his deputies are now taking the leading role. One news report claimed that Kaka Abdul Khaliq was killed in the October 2010 Kandahar offensive, but this has not been independently confirmed. See Heidi Vogt and Amir Shah, "Afghan: Consult System on Military Ops Not Working," *Associated Press*, Oct. 17, 2010.
118. Interviews with local officials and Taliban, 2010.
119. Zheray was created in 2005 out of parts of Panjwayi and Maiwand districts to establish an Alizai-dominated district, and therefore its boundaries may seem less than natural to Taliban fighters.
120. Akbar Agha's short-lived group was called Jeish ul-Muslimeen. He was imprisoned for his role and was released on a pardon from President Karzai in 2010.
121. The Karzai family hails from Karz, a village in Dand, and the Sherzai family is also from the district.
122. Interviews with Taliban commanders and Afghan intelligence officials, 2010. Munib is also active in Zheray and Panjwayi and is associated with Muhammad Issa, the Noorzai commander from Spin Boldak (not to be confused with the shadow governor).
123. United Nations Development Program, Afghanistan, *Kandahar Anzor*, 2009.
124. Interviews with locals, elders, government officials, and Taliban from Maruf, 2010.
125. Interview with international observer in Kabul and locals in Maruf, 2010.
126. Interviews with locals and elders from Arghestan, 2010.
127. Interviews with locals, elders, Taliban, and government officials in Arghandab, July 2010, and interview with U.S. Army officer, August 2010.
128. Interviews with government officials, Taliban, and U.S. military officials, Spin Boldak, 2008–2010. Takhta Pul is an unofficial district.
129. Interviews with government officials, elders, and locals from Shorabak, 2010.
130. Interviews with Afghan intelligence officials and U.S. military officers, 2009–10. The expertise appears to have been shared among members, and training appears to take place both within Kandahar and in Pakistan.
131. Interviews with locals, government officials, and U.S. military personnel, 2010. The foreign fighters appear to be mostly Pakistanis, although there are some Arabs and fighters from the Central Asian Republics as well.

132. The list was provided to me in August 2010.

133. Interview with Taliban commander, Kandahar city, July 2010.

134. Interview with former Taliban commander, Kabul, August 2010.

135. Alex Strick van Linschoten, "Kandahar Timeline," www.alexstrick.com/timeline.

136. Interview with Taliban commander, Kandahar city, July 2010.

137. Linschoten, "Kandahar Timeline."

138. Antonio Giustozzi, *Koran, Kalashnikov, and Laptop: The Neo-Taliban Insurgency in Afghanistan* (New York: Columbia University Press, 2007), pp. 125–29.

139. *Otaq* literally means "room," but it appears that insurgents use it to mean a base, either physical or conceptual (as in a "cell"). See also note 95.

140. There were sporadic suicide attacks before this period, but it appears that Dadullah put them into regular use. From interviews with Quetta Shura members, 2008–2010.

141. Interviews with Quetta Shura members and associates, 2008–2010. See also Sean M. Maloney, "A Violent Impediment: Evolution of Insurgent Operations in Kandahar Province 2003–2007," *Small Wars and Insurgencies*, 19: 2, 201–220.

142. Suleiman Shah Durrani, "Since 2002 Kandahar Has Witnessed the Assassinations of More Than 515 Tribal Elders in Only 13 Districts," *Surghar Weekly*, Aug. 1, 2010.

143. Ibid.

144. Interviews with government officials in Keshk-i-Nakhud, April 2008, and tribal elders in Kandahar city, 2010.

145. Giustozzi, *Koran, Kalashnikov, and Laptop*, 102–7.

146. Statistics from Sami Kovanen of Indicium Consulting.

147. Interview with locals from Kandahar city, August 2010.

148. Incident reporting from Sami Kovanen of Indicium Consulting.

149. It could be argued that the level of violence would be even higher absent this campaign, but the effort still has not been able to reverse the trend of worsening violence every year.

150. The same does not hold true for foot soldiers, however.

151. Interview with a tribal elder from Panjwayi, Kabul, July 2010.

TWO

The Relationship Between al-Qaeda and the Taliban

Anne Stenersen

EXECUTIVE SUMMARY

Fragmented alliances. This chapter examines the nature of the relationship between al-Qaeda and the Taliban after 2001, which is complex because neither the Taliban nor al-Qaeda is homogeneous. Rather, each is a network of like-minded groups and individuals that answer, to some degree or other, to a centralized leadership.

al-Qaeda operations in Afghanistan. al-Qaeda's contribution to the Afghan insurgency since 2001 has been highly localized, taking place mostly in the southeastern and eastern provinces of the country. This concentration is due to both geographic factors and al-Qaeda's long-standing ties to local militants in these regions.

al-Qaeda and the Quetta Shura. Although al-Qaeda fighters continue to cooperate with the Taliban on a tactical level, al-Qaeda and the Quetta Shura have diverged strategically since 2001. This development can be ascribed to al-Qaeda's relocation to the Federally Administered Tribal Areas (FATA) in 2001–2002—hundreds of miles from the Quetta Shura's base in Baluchistan—and its alignment with Pakistani tribal militants.

Fighting on two fronts. Initially, the alliance between al-Qaeda and its tribal hosts in FATA was based on a shared desire to fight U.S. and NATO forces in Afghanistan. However, 2004 saw the rise of a violent campaign against the Pakistani state, which was intensified after the Lal Masjid (Red Mosque) siege in Islamabad in July 2007. Militants in the FATA, such as the network of Baitullah Mehsud, participated in the campaign, while the Afghan Taliban opposed it. al-Qaeda decided to lend vocal support to the campaign, although it essentially contradicted the Quetta Shura's policy of fighting inside Afghanistan only.

Pakistan as a likely recruiting ground for al-Qaeda. In a fundamental shift in al-Qaeda's strategy, al-Qaeda's leaders are seeking to be more influential in the Pakistani militant environment. This is probably not a conscious change, but the result of the network's development over time after being relocated to Pakistan in 2001–02. Though the jihad in Afghanistan is still a core theme in al-Qaeda's propaganda, Pakistan is emerging as a likely recruiting ground in the future.

INTRODUCTION

The nature of al-Qaeda's relationship with the Taliban after 2001 remains a contentious issue in the West. Some analysts argue that the bonds are as strong as ever, others that the Taliban is ready to abandon al-Qaeda if given enough incentive to do so.[1] In reality, both theories are gross simplifications. There is no single way to characterize "the al-Qaeda–Taliban" relationship after 2001, because neither al-Qaeda nor the Taliban is a homogeneous and centrally controlled organization. Rather, they consist of networks of like-minded groups and individuals that answer, to some degree or other, to a centralized leadership but at the same time have autonomy to act on their own.

To present a more nuanced understanding of the al-Qaeda–Taliban relationship, this chapter focuses on two questions: Why was al-Qaeda able to establish a safe haven in FATA after 2001? And what is the nature of the relationship between al-Qaeda and various Taliban factions in Afghanistan and Pakistan today?

Most articles that discuss al-Qaeda's relationship with the Taliban tend to focus on the role and influence of al-Qaeda in the local militant environment.[2] The general finding is that al-Qaeda functions as a "force multiplier" for local groups, supporting them with manpower, specialist knowledge, and propaganda, and acting as an adviser and negotiator. Moreover, al-Qaeda's presence in the area is said to have strengthened the link between local insurgencies in Afghanistan and Pakistan and the global jihadist current. However, these observations do little to clarify why certain factions of the Taliban movement seem to be more closely aligned with al-Qaeda than others. The greatest challenge to conducting such a study is the lack of accurate and detailed information on the groups in question. This chapter seeks to fill the information gap by examining original sources from the al-Qaeda network, including "martyr biographies" (short, biographical stories published by al-Qaeda after a militant's death), battle footage, and official and unofficial statements from al-Qaeda militants who were based in Afghanistan and Pakistan after 2001.[3]

HISTORICAL BACKGROUND

From 1996 to 2001, various groups of foreign militants (primarily from the Middle East, North Africa, Central Asia, and Pakistan) enjoyed sanctuary in Afghanistan under the Taliban regime. They included bin Laden's al-Qaeda network but also a host of other groups that cooperated with al-Qaeda while pursuing separate agendas. al-Qaeda's terrorist attacks on New York and Washington on September 11, 2001, received mixed reactions from the Arab and Central Asian militants in Afghanistan and the Taliban. Although many of al-Qaeda's allies did not oppose the idea of attacking Americans, there were fears that the attacks would provoke the United States to invade Afghanistan and destroy the sanctuary the foreign fighters enjoyed there. The Taliban shared this fear, though many of the leaders were reluctant to believe that bin Laden was responsible for the attacks.

Despite the controversy of September 11, there was no fundamental split between the major foreign fighter groups in Afghanistan and the Taliban leadership at that point. Instead, they joined hands to confront the U.S.-led invasion of the country, which started on October 7, 2001.

From the outset, the al-Qaeda leadership was involved in organizing the foreign fighters. High-ranking al-Qaeda commanders such as Sayf al-Adl and Abd al-Hadi al-Iraqi stayed in Afghanistan and fought the U.S.-led invasion, until the Taliban decided to withdraw from the major cities and start a guerrilla war. In the words of Abd al-Hadi al-Iraqi, who was interviewed by the jihadist website al-Neda in 2002: "The order to withdraw came from Mullah Omar.... A regular war would not harm the enemy, so that's why there was a decision to switch to guerrilla warfare, which hurts the enemy much more than when we were holding on to the cities."[4] This indicates that there was a relatively high degree of coordination between al-Qaeda and the Taliban at the time.

The Taliban's fighters and commanders would either quietly return to their villages and blend in with the Afghan population, or withdraw across the border to Pakistan, where they had extensive networks of supporters. Arabs, Uzbeks, and other foreigners who could not blend in so easily had no choice but to leave the country. The evacuation of foreign fighters and their families from Afghanistan to Pakistan took place over several months, in cooperation with Taliban commanders and locals in southeastern and eastern parts of the country.

It was hardly a coincidence that the main withdrawal routes of the foreign fighters went from eastern Afghanistan through FATA. Ever since the 1980s, al-Qaeda militants have had ties to militant networks in this region. Bin Laden's first base on Afghan soil was established in Jaji, in southeastern Afghanistan, at the height of the Afghan-Soviet war. When bin Laden returned to Afghanistan from Sudan in 1996, he did so at the invitation of Yunus Khalis, an old ally from the mujahideen period based in Nangarhar, in eastern Afghanistan.[5]

After the Taliban came to power, al-Qaeda's headquarters moved to Kandahar at the request of Mullah Omar, but al-Qaeda continued to operate training camps in the southeastern and eastern parts of the country. After the U.S.-led campaign against Afghanistan in late 2001, al-Qaeda's last battles were staged in the same regions—the battle of Tora Bora in Nangarhar (December 2001), and the battle of Shah-i-Kot in Khost, also known as Operation Anaconda (March 2002). Militants connected with eastern Afghan Taliban factions (including Jalaluddin Haqqani, Yunus Khalis, and others) appear to have helped the Arabs flee across the border to FATA.[6]

FATA did not immediately emerge as the new headquarters of al-Qaeda's leadership. In the years following 2001, al-Qaeda was geographically dispersed. Although most foreign militants fled to FATA, others settled in safe houses in Pakistani cities such as Karachi and Rawalpindi where they continued their activities. A group of high-ranking al-Qaeda leaders also took refuge in Iran.[7] From 2003, the sanctuary in FATA increased in importance as it became harder for al-Qaeda operatives to hide elsewhere in the region. Around 2003, there was a crackdown on al-Qaeda members based in Iran, and the same year several high-ranking al-Qaeda members were arrested in Pakistani cities, including the September 11 mastermind, Khalid Sheikh Mohammed. After this, al-Qaeda's operational headquarters effectively moved to FATA.[8] In subsequent years, FATA would become known as a staging ground for a number of al-Qaeda–linked terrorist plots and attacks in the West, including the terrorist attacks in London on July 7, 2005.

The focus on al-Qaeda's international terrorist activities tends to overshadow the fact that after 2001, the main concern for foreign fighters who consolidated their base in this area was to regroup and prepare for guerrilla war in Afghanistan, in cooperation with local insurgents on both sides of the border. This is an important backdrop for understanding how al-Qaeda managed to establish and sustain its ties with the local militants in this area.

DEVELOPING THE FRONT LINES

In mid-2002, Abu al-Laith al-Libi was speaking on a scratchy phone line from the borderlands between Afghanistan and Pakistan: "We are now developing the fronts along all lines to make it a large-scale war—the war of ambushes, assassinations, and operations that take place in the most unexpected places for the enemy," he confidently declared.[9] The phone interview with al-Libi was recorded and published as an audio file on jehad.net, al-Qaeda's main media outlet at the time. Few outside observers had heard of al-Libi back then, but he would turn out to be one of the most influential Arab commanders in the Waziristan area, until his death in an air strike in North Waziristan on January 29, 2008.[10]

Al-Libi's declaration of a guerrilla war against U.S. troops in Afghanistan in the summer of 2002 illustrates the priorities of many of the Arab fighters who had settled in Waziristan after 2001. Al-Libi— who was associated with the Libyan Islamic Fighting Group (LIFG) before he "officially" joined al-Qaeda in 2007—belonged to a network of experienced foreign militants who were disappointed by the rapid fall of the Taliban regime in Afghanistan and determined to continue the war against U.S. "occupation" of the country. According to local militants, the foreigners who came to the area soon started organizing training camps for volunteers, preached to the local population, and carried out cross-border attacks on U.S. forces in Afghanistan.[11]

A reading of martyr biographies of 120 (mostly Arab) fighters who were killed in Afghanistan or Pakistan in 2002–2006 confirms this picture. After they settled in the tribal areas, 60 percent of the militants reportedly were involved in guerrilla warfare (rocket attacks, ambushes, and planting roadside bombs), 14 percent were involved in training and instruction, 14 percent were involved in administrative/media work, and 11 percent were involved in organizing or executing suicide attacks in Afghanistan. However, only 4 percent were involved in activities related to international terrorism.[12] The overall activities of the foreign fighters in Waziristan, therefore, seemed to be centered on fighting U.S. troops in Afghanistan, corresponding with the al-Qaeda leadership's ambitions at the time.

The Arab foreign fighters were united by the fight in Afghanistan rather than by affiliation with any particular group. For example, al-Libi was a veteran of the LIFG, who, like many militant Islamists facing persecution in the Arab world, moved to Afghanistan and found refuge under the Taliban regime in the 1990s. After the withdrawal to Waziristan, he worked as an independent commander supporting the war against U.S. forces in Afghanistan. Some sources have indicated that his relationship with the al-Qaeda leadership was strained at times and that he preferred to work directly with the Taliban.[13] However, this did not prevent him from cooperating with the other Arab commanders in Waziristan.

In 2003, al-Libi was reported to have shared headquarters with several al-Qaeda commanders in Wana, among them Abu Khabab al-Masri and Hamza Rabia al-Masri.[14] He also had a close relationship with Abu Yahya al-Libi, appearing with him in several propaganda videos.[15] His alliance with al-Qaeda became "formalized" in early 2007, when al-Qaeda's official media arm, al-Sahab, started presenting him as an "al-Qaeda commander" in its productions.[16] An official "merger" between Afghan-based LIFG and al-Qaeda took place in 2007, though it had few practical ramifications for al-Qaeda's global jihadist campaign. After his death, Abu al-Layth al-Libi was eulogized by several high-ranking al-Qaeda leaders, including Ayman al-Zawahiri, Mustafa Abu al-Yazid, and Abu Yahya al-Libi, as well as various regional al-Qaeda branches and media outlets,[17] indicative of the high stature he had in the al-Qaeda network by then.

Among militants on the ground, Abu al-Layth al-Libi's soldiers were known as "majmu'at Abu al-Layth" (Abu al-Layth's group). This was not uncommon; there were other commanders also described as having their own "groups" of fighters, such as the Egyptian Abu Abd al-Rahman al-Misri.[18] Though the most prominent Arab commanders were often Egyptian, Libyan, or Saudi, the membership of their groups appeared to be mixed. Abu al-Layth al-Libi's group consisted of a number of nationalities, including Afghans and Pakistanis.[19] It is likely that other Arab-led groups also had mixed composition, among them Pakistanis and Afghans who had trained in their camps. A local militant explained what happened after he graduated from an Arab training camp in Waziristan along with around 160 Pakistani tribal members and 40 Afghans: "We were divided into 10 groups. Each had two or three Arabs assigned to it as commanders and instructors. We split up: Some groups went to Khost and Paktiya provinces, and others to Ghazni and Kandahar."[20]

Non-Arab militant groups established themselves in FATA as well, in particular the Uzbek-led groups Islamic Movement of Uzbekistan (IMU) and the Islamic Jihad Union (IJU). During the Taliban regime, the IMU had a base in Northern Afghanistan and supported the Taliban's fight against the Northern Alliance. After 2001 the IMU—like the Arab volunteers—fled to Pakistan and established new sanctuaries in FATA. The IJU was created as an offshoot of the IMU in 2002.

The Arabs in FATA worked together with the Uzbeks and other Central Asians in IMU and IJU whenever their goals coincided. For example, during the Battle of Shah-i-Kot in 2002, the IMU played a prominent role in the fighting alongside the Arabs. Moreover, Arabs and Uzbeks cooperated in running militant training camps. But there were also frictions. In 2007 some IMU militants were accused of killing an Arab al-Qaeda member in South Waziristan.[21] Such episodes are not necessarily indicative of a general split or competition between al-Qaeda and IMU; the 2007 incident was the result of a local power struggle that also included local tribal militants.[22] When analyzing their ties and activities, it is important that neither the Arabs nor Central Asians or local militants be treated as one single category.

AL-QAEDA'S TRIBAL HOSTS

A madrassa student from Wana, in South Waziristan, witnessed the changes in his district after the fall of the Taliban:

> I watched as wounded, disabled, and defeated Taliban fighters straggled into Wana and the surrounding villages, along with Arabs, Chechens, and Uzbeks. Every morning as I went to school I could see them wandering around town, almost like homeless beggars. Little by little, the tribal people started helping them, giving them food.[23]

Little is known about how the foreign fighters came to be hosted by local tribesmen and militants in the tribal areas of Pakistan. Some accounts, like the one above, indicate that the relocation to Pakistan was by no means smooth and that the foreign "guests" were not guaranteed sanctuary in the places they came to. Instead, they had to rely on the charity of the local population, while gradually establishing ties with local authority figures. If this is indeed the case, it means that the relationship with locals was determined by geography, rather than by existing ties and networks. Since Waziristan was on one of the main withdrawal routes of the Arabs from Afghanistan, it also became the place where foreigners would establish ties with locals. However, other militants may have relocated to Waziristan because they already had ties with local militants there, dating back to the period before 2001.

Nek Muhammad

The story of Nek Muhammad seems to illustrate that there were indeed historical ties between foreign fighters and the Pakistani tribesmen who hosted them in FATA after 2001. Nek Muhammad, an Ahmadzai Wazir from South Waziristan, was one of the first tribes-men to host foreign militants in Waziristan after their withdrawal in 2001–02. He controlled areas around Wana, the administrative center of South Waziristan. According to jihadist sources, Nek Muhammad joined the Taliban regime in Afghanistan in the 1990s and fought alongside Afghan and foreign fighters against the Northern Alliance around Kabul. During this experience, he befriended several of the Arab militants in the area. After the fall of the Taliban, he went back to Waziristan and, according to one unconfirmed account, personally oversaw the Arabs' flight from Afghanistan to more secure areas.[24] Another account says that once in South Waziristan, he "gave the Arabs places to train and access to weapons and other supplies," and in the spring of 2003 he became involved in coordinating cross-border attacks with Arab commanders.[25]

Nek Muhammad was killed in a drone attack in 2004. After his death, some Arabs and Uzbeks continued to stay with his relatives in Wana.[26] But in 2007 Mullah Nazir, a rival militant leader from the same tribe as Nek Muhammad, decided to oust the Uzbeks from the area. According to one source the Uzbeks lost two hundred fighters in the battles; the rest were forced to flee to Mehsud-controlled South Waziristan.[27] The conflict appeared to be rooted in the Central Asians' "interference in the local affairs of the region," rather than arising from broad-based local opposition to all foreign militants in the area.[28] Moreover, the conflict can be seen as part of a local power struggle between various Wazir tribesmen.[29]

It is not clear what happened to the Arab militants and al-Qaeda during Mullah Nazir's conflict with the Uzbeks. Some Arabs most likely continued to stay with local protectors in Wana, as they were not directly involved in the conflict. Mullah Nazir himself continued to have relations with Arab militants.[30] However, some Arabs—including high-ranking al-Qaeda—followed the Uzbeks' example and started cooperating with Baitullah Mehsud in the Mehsud area of South Waziristan.

Baitullah and Abdullah Mehsud

Little is known about Baitullah Mehsud's previous ties to the Taliban regime, or to the Arabs. Mustafa Abu Al-Yazid indicated that Mehsud joined the Taliban movement "early on" after the Islamic Emirate of

Afghanistan was established [in 1996], and assisted the group in its war against its enemies in northern Afghanistan.[31] Another source stated that during the reign of the Taliban regime, Mehsud "frequently went to Afghanistan as a volunteer to join in the Taliban's enforcement of sharia and to offer his services."[32] There is probably some truth to this. After 2001, Mehsud was said to have close ties with the Afghan Taliban movement and allegedly was appointed as Mullah Omar's "special representative" for the Mehsud tribe in Waziristan.[33]

Mehsud himself stated in an interview with al-Jazeera in 2008 that he had yet to meet either bin Laden or al-Zawahiri. However, he did claim to have had a "strong relationship" with Abu Musab al-Zarqawi before the latter went to Iraq sometime in 2001–02.[34] Al-Zawahiri, who spoke at length about Mehsud after the latter's death in 2009, did not mention any previous ties between Mehsud and Arab militants. Instead, he described Mehsud as a madrassa student who interrupted his studies to join the jihad after the U.S. invasion of Afghanistan in 2001. Al-Zawahiri credited him with gathering a large group of followers to fight "the Crusaders and their apostate agents in Afghanistan and Pakistan," and for working actively for the unity of Pakistani mujahedin. He also referred to Mehsud's role in the establishment in 2007 of the Tehrik-i-Taliban Pakistan (TTP), an umbrella organization for Pakistani militant groups, and said that a good relationship was established between the TTP and foreign mujahedin.[35] The relationship between Mehsud and al-Qaeda that emerged from 2004 onward was probably based on a common cause and ideology, more than long-standing personal friendships.

Another Mehsud tribesman with ties to foreign militants was Abdullah Mehsud, a relative of Baitullah. An unconfirmed account of Abdullah Mehsud's life states that he started his militant career as a trainee in a camp run by Emir Khattab (the Saudi-born Chechen rebel leader) in Kunduz province in Afghanistan in the early 1990s, together with Tajiks, Arabs, and some Afghans.[36] In 1995 he joined the Taliban movement, and right before September 11, 2001, he was said to have fought with some Arab fighters in Northern Afghanistan. According to the biography, he developed a deep respect for the Arabs and the other foreign fighters in Afghanistan during this period. In 2001–2004 he was imprisoned in Guantánamo, where he apparently continued to develop relations with fellow Arab inmates. In 2004 he returned to South Waziristan and continued his militant activities until he was killed in

July 2007. Little is known about his actual activities and ties in this period. Because of a personal conflict with Baitullah Mehsud, he gradually became isolated from the Mehsud tribe, and he allegedly went to North Waziristan to cooperate directly with the Afghan Taliban. Again, the biography seems to describe an individual who was committed to supporting the Taliban in Afghanistan, and who had developed an admiration and respect (but not necessarily direct personal ties) with the Arabs and other foreign militants who settled in Waziristan after 2001.

The nature of the personal ties between FATA-based militant leaders and Arabs before 2001 remains opaque. However, the accounts of Nek Muhammad and Baitullah and Abdullah Mehsud illustrate that the foreign fighters and the tribesmen who initially supported them in Waziristan were tied together by a shared purpose, namely a desire to wage jihad in support of the Taliban in Afghanistan. This attitude was not in itself new. Reportedly, thousands of tribesmen from FATA fought in Afghanistan for shorter or longer periods, both in the Afghan-Soviet war in the 1980s and under the Taliban movement from 1994 through 2001. The Taliban continued to welcome the contribution of tribal allies after being deposed in 2001. According to one source, the Taliban shura led by Mullah Baradar worked actively to enlist tribal support from the Pakistani side from the early stages of the insurgency.[37]

On the other hand, it is a misconception that al-Qaeda found sanctuary in FATA thanks to Pashtun "tribal hospitality": neither Nek Muhammad nor Abdullah or Baitullah Mehsud were important tribal leaders prior to their ascendancy as Taliban commanders in South Waziristan. As demonstrated by Farhat Taj, the Pashtun militants who hosted al-Qaeda in FATA came to power after eradicating traditional Pashtun tribal leaders in their respective areas, replacing the tribal rule with Taliban-style government.[38] This particular local context made FATA a receptive environment for foreign fighters who came to the area after 2001, and who were intent on supporting the war in Afghanistan from the very beginning.

Bonds of Matrimony

In addition to historical and ideological ties, the "strategy" of marrying into local Pashtun tribes is another common explanation of why al-Qaeda managed to establish a sanctuary in FATA and adjoining areas after 2001.[39] Despite this being a popular claim, there are few studies that can tell us how widespread the phenomenon actually has been. Farhat Taj, who did extensive research among the tribes in FATA after 2001, found no evidence of the phenomenon at all.[40] This casts some serious doubt on the claim that intermarriages between foreign militants and local women helped to facilitate al-Qaeda's sanctuary in FATA after 2001.

It does not mean that the phenomenon was nonexistent. al-Qaeda's own sources give some hints about this: the author examined 103 biographies of foreign militants (excluding Afghan and Pakistani-born individuals) who were killed in Afghanistan or Pakistan between 2002 and 2006.[41] Thirty-one of these biographies state that the individual was married, while the rest contain no information on the individual's marital status. Of the thirty-one married individuals, eight were reported to have married Pashtun or Pakistani women, and at least five of these marriages took place after 2001. Although the numbers are small and probably incomplete, they indicate that the phenomenon of marriage into tribes was not uncommon: at least 8 percent of the foreign militants described in these biographies were presumably tied to Afghan or Pakistani families through intermarriage.

The biographies indicate that marriage into Afghan or Pakistani tribes or families was much less common before 2001. Of fifteen marriages taking place before 2001, only one was to an Afghan, while the majority were to Arab women (see Figure 2.1). This may be ascribed to greater mobility on the part of the foreign fighters in this period. Many of the marriages took place while the fighters resided in the Arab world or Central Asia. As for those who resided in Afghanistan under the Taliban regime (1996–2001), many probably took their families with them, as this was relatively common before 2001. This seems to be confirmed by general accounts of the al-Qaeda network's history in Afghanistan. Marriage of Arabs into Afghan families does not seem to have been a widespread phenomenon, at least not among those who migrated to Afghanistan under the Taliban regime. It might have been more common among those who settled in Afghanistan after the Soviet-Afghan war (al-Qaeda's headquarters moved to Sudan in this period, but some militants also remained in Afghanistan or Pakistan). However, this group is underrepresented in the biographies reviewed above.

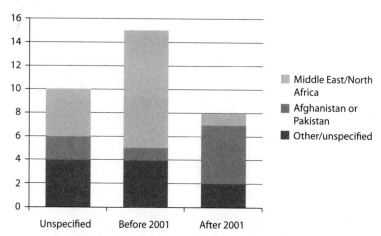

FIGURE 2.1 Marriages of Foreign Fighters Who Were Killed in Afghanistan or Pakistan 2002–2006: Year of Marriage and Wife's Country of Origin

Note: The total number of individuals is thirty-one, while the total number of marriages is thirty-three, because two individuals were reported to be married twice.

After 2001, the conditions for family life and travel abroad became much more restricted, and this may explain why a higher proportion of foreign fighters appear to have married Afghan and Pakistani women.

Even though marriage into local tribes indeed seems to have taken place, it is doubtable whether this has become a deliberate "strategy" of al-Qaeda since 2001. The most high-ranking al-Qaeda member alleged to have married into a local tribe is al-Zawahiri, who married a woman from the Mohmand tribe in Bajaur after 2001. In Bajaur, al-Zawahiri is said to have been protected by the local Taliban leader and Mohmand tribesman Maulana Faqir Muhammad.[42] The al-Qaeda commander Abu Ikhlas al-Misri, who operated in Kunar province for many years, has also been described as well entrenched in the local community. According to the BBC, he is "one of many of Bin Laden's Arab fighters who married a local woman, speaks the language and enjoys the protection of the local tribes against all outsiders."[43]

Anecdotal evidence suggests, at least, that intermarriage may have strengthened the ties between foreign and local militants. However, it is hard to say whether intermarriages are merely an expression of, rather than a cause of, strong relationships between al-Qaeda militants and their local Taliban hosts. In any case, it is a misconception that foreign fighters who married local women increased their personal security through earning the "protection of the local tribes." As discussed previously, tribal laws are fluid, and the relationship between foreign militants and local Taliban leaders is primarily guided not by Pashtun tribal code but by loyalty bonds based on common goal, ideology, and mutual interest.

Joined by a Common Cause... and U.S. Dollars?

The above accounts explain the relationships between Arabs and tribal militants in South Waziristan after 2001. The study is only partial and has a significant drawback in that it is not based on actual fieldwork in FATA. With these limitations in mind, the study nevertheless indicates that a shared desire to wage jihad in support of the Taliban in Afghanistan—i.e., shared ideology, rather than "tribal hospitality"—was an important reason for the foreign militants finding sanctuary in FATA. Personal ties between tribal militants in FATA and Arabs probably also existed prior to 2001, but there is very little verifiable information on these ties.

It is important to remember that on an individual level, there may have been a host of other reasons certain tribesmen in the FATA decided to support or oppose the presence of foreign fighters in their area. It has been argued, for example, that tribesmen who hosted al-Qaeda and Uzbeks in FATA were motivated by monetary incentives and the prospect of using foreign fighters to boost their own military standing. A journalistic source stated in 2004 that Nek Muhammad's motivation for hosting the foreign fighters was based on the monetary and material benefit the Arabs would give him.[44] Some of the foreign militants who trained in FATA after 2001 reported that they had to pay the local militants relatively large sums of money in order to gain access to transportation, lodging, food, and paramilitary training.[45] Yet, monetary incentives alone cannot explain why some of the Wazir and Mehsud tribesmen described above decided not only to support foreign fighters in their area but also to take an active role in the fighting in Afghanistan after 2001. This act appears to be motivated more by ideological and religious reasons than by purely material incentives.

In the alliance between foreign fighters and local militants in FATA, common cause seems a more important motivation than U.S. dollars. However, there are exceptions where individuals may be motivated more by pragmatic reasons, and the support is also not unconditional. In theory, therefore, it would be possible to drive a wedge between foreign fighters and their local allies. However, given the localized nature of these alliances, this would be an extremely challenging task. For one thing, experience has shown that peace agreements between the Pakistani government and tribal leaders have had little impact on their relationship with foreign fighters. And even if one succeeds in persuading a tribal faction to abandon the foreign fighters in their area, they can simply move to a different village in the same area. Despite highly publicized attempts by tribal leaders to evict the IMU from South Waziristan in 2007, Uzbek militants remain alive and active across Waziristan today. This has been demonstrated, for example, in recent video footage showing IMU members fighting for Mehsud's army in South Waziristan.[46] It seems, indeed, that the foreign fighters have come to FATA to stay.

This analysis illustrates the intertwined nature of the ties between Afghan Taliban, Pakistani Taliban, and al-Qaeda—which is one explanation for al-Qaeda's resilience in the area. Another important reason is al-Qaeda's strategy in dealing with the Afghan Taliban's leadership, which is outlined in the next section.

A MEETING BETWEEN BROTHERS

The meeting between the Egyptian al-Qaeda leader Mustafa Abu al-Yazid and the Afghan Taliban commander Mansour Dadullah in 2007 was carefully directed and filmed for propaganda purposes. Surrounded by gunmen, the two leaders are seen greeting each other like old friends. The movie title, *A Meeting Between Brothers*, flashes over the screen. Later, they are seen seated together outside, speaking of the brotherly relations between al-Qaeda and the Taliban. "The ties between the brothers in al-Qaeda and brothers in the Taliban have increased. The affection between them has increased. The Iman [faith]-based brotherhood has increased," al-Yazid states. To date, it is the highest-level meeting between al-Qaeda and the Taliban captured on tape.

Yet, the significance of the meeting is hard to gauge. Mansour Dadullah and his brother, Mullah Dadullah, were two of the most vocal supporters of al-Qaeda within the Taliban's leadership ranks. At the same time, they were known to have differences with other Taliban leaders, including Mullah Muhammad Omar himself. These differences were clearly shown when Mansour Dadullah was dismissed from the Taliban in December 2007, reportedly because he had refused to follow Mullah Omar's orders. In light of these internal disagreements, the Dadullah brothers' view of al-Qaeda is not necessarily representative of the relationship between al-Qaeda and other factions of the Taliban leadership.

In general, the relationship between the organizations' leaders is said to be cordial but superficial owing to geographic distances and the security risks involved in meeting. The Taliban leadership is believed to be based in Quetta, in the Baluchistan province of Pakistan, while al-Qaeda's headquarters is based in or around FATA. This means that the leaders of the two networks meet only on rare occasions and otherwise communicate via messengers and representatives.

Formally, al-Qaeda's leaders have sworn an oath of allegiance (bay'a) to Mullah Omar. Osama bin Laden first swore allegiance to him in 1998, and al-Yazid renewed the pledge in a videotaped speech in 2007.[47] This means, in essence, that al-Qaeda's leaders recognize Mullah Omar as the supreme commander of the jihad in Afghanistan. Ayman al-Zawahiri put it like this in 2008: "Mullah Muhammad Omar, may God preserve him, is the Emir of the Islamic Emirate in Afghanistan and those among the mujahedin who joined it. Sheikh Osama bin Laden… is one of his soldiers."[48] Al-Zawahiri continued the same policy of submission to Mullah Omar after bin Laden's death in 2011.

However, in practice the relationship between al-Qaeda and the Quetta Shura is not necessarily one of command and control. Rather, it is a political relationship, where al-Qaeda has agreed not to establish a competing organization to Mullah Omar's. This aspect of the relationship has also been emphasized by Mullah Baradar. When asked why the Taliban allowed foreigners to fight in its ranks, he said that they were volunteers who had come to fight for the sake of Islam; they had not come to Afghanistan "to establish political parties and organizations."[49]

By submitting to the authority of Mullah Omar, the al-Qaeda leadership in Pakistan is avoiding some of the mistakes of Abu Musab al-Zarqawi in Iraq, where the local al-Qaeda branch he was leading tried to compete for power with other Iraqi insurgent groups. Arguably, this was in part why al-Qaeda in Iraq became increasingly unpopular with other insurgent factions and in the end failed to maintain a strong presence in the country.

The strategy of submitting to Mullah Omar may partly explain al-Qaeda's resilience in the Afghanistan-Pakistan border areas. This does not necessarily mean that al-Qaeda and the Quetta Shura have become more closely aligned since 2001. On the contrary, they seem to have moved farther apart. One indication of this is that there is relatively little tactical cooperation between al-Qaeda fighters and Taliban groups in southern Afghanistan, where the Quetta Shura is believed to exercise most influence over the insurgency. Another indication is that since 2001, al-Qaeda has become more closely aligned with Pakistani militant leaders, which is due to its dependence on a sanctuary in FATA.

TACTICAL COOPERATION

Among rank-and-file Taliban members, the attitude toward al-Qaeda ranges from admiration and praise to outright hostility. A local Taliban commander interviewed in *Newsweek* in 2009 expressed a rather derogatory attitude toward Arabs and other "foreigners": "As far as I know, Al Qaeda is weak, and they are few in numbers. Now that we control large amounts of territory, we should have a strict code of conduct for any foreigners working with us.... We cannot allow them to roam freely."[50] According to a U.S. intelligence report published in 2009, captured Taliban fighters told interrogators that Taliban leaders "see al-Qaeda as a handicap."[51] This view was reinforced in a leaked NATO report from 2012, which concluded, "In most regions of Afghanistan, Taliban leaders have no interest in associating with Al Qaeda. Working with Al Qaeda invites targeting, and Al Qaeda personnel are no longer the adept and versatile fighters and commanders they once were."[52]

On the other hand, al-Qaeda's cooperation with the Taliban groups in Afghanistan on a tactical level seems to continue.[53] This is not a contradiction, but it reflects the fact that ever since 2001 al-Qaeda's contribution to the Afghan insurgency has been highly localized, taking place mostly in the southeastern and eastern provinces of the country.

An indication of the geographical spread of al-Qaeda's activity can be found by looking at battle footage produced by the al-Qaeda-affiliated media institute al-Sahab. From 2005 to March 2012, al-Sahab issued at least 117 films in its series *Hell of the Americans in the Land of Khurasan* (Afghanistan) and 6 films in a new series started in 2011 called *Diaries of a Mujahid*. Both film series show groups of fighters carrying out rocket attacks, ambushes, and attacks with IEDs, mainly on Afghan territory. The films do not necessarily mean that Arab or other foreign fighters took part in the attacks, but they do imply a connection between the fighting group and al-Qaeda's media operation, which disseminates the footage through al-Qaeda–affiliated discussion forums on the Internet.

Al-Sahab began producing these films in 2005, when the insurgency started picking up speed. The year 2006 saw the largest production, with 38 films in total. The production decreased in subsequent years, and only 6 were released in 2009. In 2010, 18 were released, but the following year production dropped to 9. Since nearly all the films contain information on where the film was shot (and if we assume this is accurate), we can assemble a distribution by province (see Figure 2.2).

The high concentration of films from Khost and neighboring Paktika (53 in total) and Kunar (18) is worth noting. These areas border the agencies in FATA where Arabs are believed to have their main sanctuaries: Waziristan and Bajaur. It suggests that al-Qaeda has established few bases deep inside Afghan territory itself, and that cross-border raids seem to be the preferred type of activity. Moreover, there is a disproportionate number of films from southeastern Afghanistan, given the high level of insurgency-related violence in this area. In other words, al-Sahab's coverage of the insurgency seems to be biased toward certain areas. It is interesting to note that al-Sahab's coverage of certain provinces appears to have changed over time. Neither Helmand nor Kandahar has been covered since 2008, while production of films from Wardak and from Pakistani territory has increased.

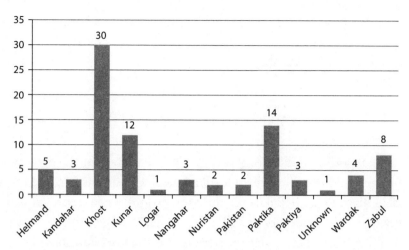

FIGURE 2.2 Province Distribution of al-Sahab's Operational Films, January 2005–March 2012

Notes: The twelve Afghan provinces were the only ones mentioned in al-Sahab's operational films. Additionally, seven films were shot in Pakistan; four other films were shot in unclear locations.

* = As of March 25, 2012.

The preference for border areas is confirmed by other jihadist sources, such as martyr biographies of foreign fighters. The most common type of operation mentioned in these biographies is cross-border raids from Waziristan into southeastern Afghanistan. However, the biographies also describe teams of Arabs who were sent into eastern Afghanistan to support insurgent activities. For example, a Syrian fighter went to Jalalabad around 2004 to establish a jihadi cell in the area. Allegedly, he took part in constructing the bomb that killed the city's security chief, Ajab Shah, on June 1, 2004.[54] Foreign fighters were also active in the networks that organized and executed suicide attacks in various parts of the country, including Kabul and northern Afghanistan. In contrast, foreign fighters appear to have been much less active in the Taliban's heartland, the southern provinces of Afghanistan.

The jihadist sources seem to confirm that since 2001 al-Qaeda's contributions to the insurgency in Afghanistan have been highly localized: Arabs have mostly fought in certain provinces and for certain commanders. This implies that tactical cooperation between al-Qaeda fighters and local insurgent groups in Afghanistan is based on geography and historical, personal ties, rather than on a close relationship with the Taliban leadership in Quetta.

A PAKISTANI AL-QAEDA?

There are other indications that al-Qaeda is moving farther away from the "traditional" Taliban leadership. al-Qaeda has become more closely aligned with Pakistani militant groups since 2001, from its dependence on sanctuary in FATA. In the beginning of the insurgency this did not present much of a problem, because Pakistani groups operated in a subservient role to the Mullah Omar–led insurgency in Afghanistan.

However, 2004 saw the rise of a violent campaign against the Pakistani state, which intensified after the Lal Masjid (Red Mosque) siege in Islamabad in July 2007. The campaign was carried out by various Pakistani groups based mainly in FATA and the North-West Frontier Province. Some of them, such as the Baitullah Mehsud Group, had by that time built a close relationship to al-Qaeda by acting as al-Qaeda's "hosts" in South Waziristan.

In 2007, al-Qaeda's leaders became increasingly vocal in their support of violence against the Pakistani state.[55] al-Qaeda's hostility toward the Pakistani regime is not in itself new, but before 2007 it was mostly limited to carrying out terrorist attacks on Western targets and making assassination attempts on Pakistani leaders. The new focus is therefore interesting, as it essentially contradicts the Quetta Shura's strategy of fighting inside Afghanistan only.

A fundamental shift in al-Qaeda's strategy also seems to have occurred with al-Qaeda's leaders seeking to be more influential in the Pakistani militant environment. This is probably not a conscious change of priorities, but the result of the al-Qaeda network's development over time after being relocated to Pakistan in 2001–02.

In the FATA, al-Qaeda seems to have found a more receptive environment for its global jihadi ideology. The Afghan Taliban strives to recover power lost in Afghanistan; al-Qaeda's tribal allies in the FATA have never run a state. However, similar to al-Qaeda, they have a long tradition of fighting other people's wars, especially in neighboring

Kashmir and Afghanistan. Although the jihad in Afghanistan is still a core theme in al-Qaeda's propaganda, Pakistan is emerging as a likely recruiting ground in the future.

CONCLUSION

al-Qaeda's presence in the Taliban's ranks is sanctioned by the Taliban leadership, mainly because the Arabs do not pose a threat to Mullah Omar's political leadership. On the tactical level there is ambivalence toward "foreigners," but al-Qaeda seems to have remained active on a tactical level in Afghanistan. To achieve this, al-Qaeda appears to have relied mainly on its historical and personal networks with militants in southeastern and eastern Afghanistan—the Haqqanis, the Yunus Khalis faction, Salafi groups in Kunar, and elements of Gulbuddin Hekmatyar's Hizb-i-Islami (HIG). al-Qaeda's involvement in the Taliban insurgency is localized, reflecting the fragmented nature of the insurgent movement itself.

This implies that al-Qaeda would be able to operate in Afghanistan with or without the support of the Quetta Shura. However, as long as NATO forces are present in Afghanistan, there is little incentive for the Taliban leadership to abandon al-Qaeda. Besides, this might jeopardize the unity of the insurgent movement, as al-Qaeda remains popular with some of the Taliban's eastern Afghan factions.

At the moment, Gulbuddin Hekmatyar is more likely to sever his ties with al-Qaeda through a power-sharing agreement with the Afghan government, because he is in a weak position relative to the Taliban. This would not necessarily affect the cooperation between al-Qaeda and HIG elements at a tactical level. If the local HIG elements desire to continue the fight, they may simply switch sides and join the Taliban's caravan, as happened in the 1990s when the Taliban movement was on the rise.

In the future, al-Qaeda's alliances with local militant groups in Afghanistan and Pakistan may develop in one of two possible directions. The al-Qaeda militants could dissolve into the local militant environment and adapt to the agenda of local groups. If such a development takes place, al-Qaeda would gradually become irrelevant as an international terrorist organization.

Alternatively, and of more concern, al-Qaeda could succeed in inserting its ideology into the local militant environment. al-Qaeda's alliance with the late Baitullah Mehsud and the TTP may be seen as a development in this direction. (In 2010, the TTP was involved in a failed attempt to bomb Times Square in New York City.[56]) If this development continues, it will make the Afghanistan-Pakistan region a hub for anti-American Islamist militancy for years to come. This is the primary reason the United States and its allies should continue the effort to build stable regimes in the region.

Notes

1. See, for example, Thomas Joscelyn and Bill Roggio, "Analysis: Al Qaeda is the Tip of the Jihadist Spear," *Long War Journal*, Oct. 8, 2009, http://www.longwarjournal.org/archives/2009/10/analysis_al_qaeda_is.php; Stephen M. Walt, "The 'Safe Haven' Myth," *Foreign Policy*, Aug. 18, 2009, http://walt.foreignpolicy.com/posts/2009/08/18/the_safe_haven_myth.

2. Some recent articles include Jeremy Binnie and Joanna Wright, "Conflict of Interest: The Taliban's Relationship with al-Qaeda," *Jane's Intelligence Review* 22, no. 1 (January 2010); Barbara Sude, "Al-Qaeda Central: An Assessment of the Threat Posed by the Terrorist Group Headquartered on the Afghanistan-Pakistan Border," Counterterrorism Strategy Initiative Policy Paper, *New America Foundation* (December 2009); Don Rassler, "Securing Sanctuary: Understanding Al-Qaeda's Strategy in Pakistan," in "Al-Qaeda's Senior Leadership (AQSL)," *Jane's Strategic Advisory Services* (November 2009); Peter Bergen, "The Front: The Taliban-Al Qaeda Merger," *New Republic*, Oct. 19, 2009, http://www.tnr.com; Sami Yousafzai and Ron Moreau, "The Taliban in Their Own Words," *Newsweek*, Sept. 26, 2009.

3. The sources have been accessed via al-Qaeda-affiliated websites on the Internet and were downloaded between 2003 and the present.

4. "Interview with the Field Commander Abd al-Hadi al-Iraqi, May God Protect Him," *Al-Neda*, July 28, 2002 (stored electronically by author).

5. "Commander Abu al-Hasan... Jihad and Martyrdom," al-Sahab (1429 h./2008), downloaded via *al-Ikhlas, www.al-ekhlaas.net* (accessed 9 July 2008).

6. For the role of Jalaluddin Haqqani, see Ahmed Rashid, *Descent into Chaos: The United States and the Failure of Nation Building in Pakistan, Afghanistan, and Central Asia* (London: Viking Books, 2008): 99. For the role of Yunus Khalis, see Philip Smucker, *Al Qaeda's Great Escape: The Military and the Media on Terror's Trail* (New Delhi: Manas, 2005).

7. Rohan Gunaratna and Anders Nielsen, "Al Qaeda in the Tribal Areas of Pakistan and Beyond," *Studies in Conflict and Terrorism* 31, no. 9 (September 2008): 781–82.

8. Ibid., 782.

9. Abu al-Laith al-Libi, in *"liqa' ba'd suqut taliban*," audio file, downloaded via al-Ikhlas, http://www.alekhlaas.net/forum/showthread.php?t=120370 (accessed Feb. 2, 2008). An English translation can be found at Mario's Cyberspace Station, http://mprofaca.cro.net/abu-laith.html (accessed Mar. 11, 2010).

10. "Top al-Qaeda Commander 'Killed,'" *BBC*, Feb. 1, 2008, http://news.bbc.co.uk/2/hi/south_asia/7220823.stm (accessed Mar. 11, 2010).

11. Sami Yousafzai and Ron Moreau, "The Taliban in Their Own Words," *Newsweek*, Sept. 26, 2009, www.newsweek.com/id/216235 (accessed Mar. 11, 2010).

12. Anne Stenersen, "'Al-Qaida's Foot Soldiers': A Study of the Biographies of Foreign Fighters Killed in Afghanistan and Pakistan Between 2002 and 2006," *Studies in Conflict and Terrorism* 34, no. 3 (March 2011): 171–98. The study is based on a collection of biographies: Abu 'Ubayda al-Maqdisi, "shuhada' fi zaman al-ghurba," Al-Fajr Media Center, accessed via al-Ekhlas http://www.alekhlaas.net/forum/showthread.php?t=120223 (Feb. 2, 2008).

13. Guido Steinberg, "The Return of al-Qaeda," *SWP Comments* 22 (December 2007) http://www.swp-berlin.org/en/common/get_document.php?asset_id=4610 (accessed Mar. 11, 2010).

14. Yousafzai and Moreau, "The Taliban in Their Own Words."

15. Jarret Brachman, "Retaining Relevance: Assessing Al-Qaeda's Generational Evolution," in "Al-Qaeda's Senior Leadership (AQSL)," *Jane's Strategic Advisory Services* (November 2009): 28.

16. "Interview with Sheikh Abu al-Layth, One of the Leaders of al-Qaeda in Khurasan," al-Sahab (Rabia' al-Akhar 1428 h./April 2007), downloaded via al-Firdaws, www.alfirdaws.org/vb (accessed Apr. 30, 2007).

17. These included al-Qaeda in the Islamic Maghreb, Ansar al-Islam (Iraq) Young Mujahidin Movement (Somalia), Naser Salahuddin Brigades (Palestine), Jaysh al-Islam (Palestine), al-Fajr Media Center, and Global Islamic Media Front.

18. See, for example, the biography of Abu Bakr al-Iraqi, in Abu 'Ubayda al-Maqdisi, "shuhada' fi zaman al-ghurba," 65–66.

19. See, for example, the biographies of Ahmed al-Hassan Dawir (pp. 27–28) and Abdallah Jan al-Afghani (pp. 175–78), in Abu 'Ubayda al-Maqdisi, "shuhada' fi zaman al-ghurba."

20. Yousafzai and Moreau, "The Taliban in Their Own Words."

21. Farhat Taj, *Taliban and Anti-Taliban* (Newcastle: Cambridge Scholars, 2011): 77.

22. Ibid.

23. Yousafzai and Moreau, "The Taliban in Their Own Words."

24. Abu 'Ubayda al-Maqdisi, "shuhada' fi zaman al-ghurba," 324–26.

25. Yousafzai and Moreau, "The Taliban in Their Own Words."

26. Other foreign fighters, including Arabs and Central Asians, went to North Waziristan in this period to establish new sanctuaries there. These events are not discussed in detail in this chapter.

27. Hassan Abbas, "South Waziristan's Maulvi Nazir: The New Face of the Taliban," *Terrorism Monitor* 5, No. 9 (May 14, 2007), http://www.jamestown.org/single/?no_cache=1&tx_ttnews%5Btt_news%5D=4147.

28. Sadia Sulaiman and Syed Adnan Ali Shah Bukhari, "Hafiz Gul Bahadur: A Profile of the Leader of the North Waziristan Taliban," *Terrorism Monitor* 7, no. 9 (Apr. 10, 2009).

29. Taj, *Taliban and Anti-Taliban*, 77.

30. Syed Saleem Shahzad, "Taliban and al-Qaeda: Friends in Arms," *Asia Times*, May 5, 2011, http://www.atimes.com/atimes/South_Asia/ME05Df02.html.

31. Mustafa Abu al-Yazid, "Condolences and Congratulations to the Islamic Ummah for the Martyrdom of the Emir, Baitullah Mehsud, May Allah Have Mercy on Him," Al-Sahab (September 2009).

32. Sohail Abdul Nasir, "Baitullah Mehsud: South Waziristan's Unofficial Amir," *Terrorism Focus* 3, no. 26 (July 9, 2006), www.jamestown.org/programs/gta/single/?tx_ttnews[tt_news]=829&tx_ttnews[backPid]= 239&no_cache=1 (accessed Feb. 22, 2010).

33. Ibid.

34. Ahmed Zaidan, "Interview of the Day," *al-Jazeera* 25 Jan 2008, downloaded via al-Ikhlas, www.ekhlaas.org/forum (accessed 28 Jan 2008).

35. Ayman al-Zawahiri, "Eulogy for the Model Young Emir, the Martyr, Baitullah Mehsud, May Allah Have Mercy on Him," Al-Sahab (September 2009).

36. "Kabul … Guantanamo … Waziristan … Steps on the Way of Jihad for the Martyr Abdullah Mehsud," *Ma'arik Islamic Network*, Mar. 21, 2009, http://m3-f.com/forum/showthread.php?t=14234 (accessed 4 February 2010).

37. Mustafa Hamid, "*ikhtitaf mulla Baradar: 'amaliyya istikhbariyya najiha tatahawwal ila fashal istratiji*" (in Arabic), *Mawqi'a adab al-matarid*, http://mafa.maktoobblog.com/750453/kidnapping-mullah-berader-mostafa-hamed/ (accessed Mar. 11, 2010).

38. Taj, *Taliban and Anti-Taliban*, 1–4.

39. See, for example, Barbara Sude, "Al-Qaeda Central: An Assessment of the Threat Posed by the Terrorist Group Headquartered on the Afghanistan-Pakistan Border," Counterterrorism Strategy Initiative Policy Paper, *New America Foundation* (December 2009).

40. Taj, *Taliban and Anti-Taliban*, 8–11.

41. Stenersen, "Al-Qaeda's Foot Soldiers."

42. Gunaratna and Nielsen, "Al Qaeda in the Tribal Areas of Pakistan and Beyond," 779.

43. Paul Danahar, "Afghanistan Five Years After 9/11," *BBC*, Sept. 11, 2006, http://news.bbc.co.uk/2/hi/south_asia/5335060.stm (accessed Feb. 24, 2010).

44. M. Ilyas Khan, "Profile of Nek Mohammad," *Dawn*, June 19, 2004, http://www.dawn.com/2004/06/19/latest.htm (accessed Mar. 11, 2010).

45. Paul Cruickshank, "The Militant Pipeline: Between the Afghanistan-Pakistan Border Region and the West," *New America Foundation*, February 2010, http://counterterrorism.newamerica.net/sites/newamerica.net/files/policydocs/cruickshank.pdf (accessed Mar. 11, 2010): 14.

46. "Soldiers of Allah 2," Jundullah Studio (January 2010), downloaded via Ansar al-Jihad Network, http://as-ansar.com/vb (accessed Jan. 19, 2010).

47. "A Meeting Between Brothers," al-Sahab (2007).

48. "Open Meeting with Sheikh Ayman al-Zawahiri, Part 2," al-Sahab (1429 h./2008).

49. "Interview with Mullah Baradar," *al-Sumud* (2008).

50. Yousafzai and Moreau, "The Taliban in Their Own Words."

51. Peter Bergen, "U.S. Intelligence Briefing: Taliban Increasingly Effective," *CNN*, Jan. 25, 2010.

52. "State of the Taliban," ISAF, Jan. 6, 2012, accessed via *New York Times*, http://www.nytimes.com/interactive/world/asia/23atwar-taliban-report-docviewer.html.

53. Ibid.

54. Abu 'Ubayda al-Maqdisi, "*shuhada' fi zaman al-ghurba*," 88–90.

55. Don Rassler, "Securing Sanctuary: Understanding Al-Qaeda's Strategy in Pakistan," in "Al-Qaeda's Senior Leadership (AQSL)," *Jane's Strategic Advisory Services* (November 2009): 31–35.

56. Charlie Savage, "Holder Backs a Miranda Limit for Terror Suspects," *New York Times*, May 9, 2010, http://www.nytimes.com/2010/05/10/us/politics/10holder.html?_r=1 (accessed Mar. 25, 2012).

THREE

The Taliban in Zabul and Uruzgan

Martine van Bijlert

EXECUTIVE SUMMARY

The relatively early resurgence of the Taliban in Afghanistan's Uruzgan and Zabul provinces is linked to a combination of factors, including (1) the historical links of the Taliban movement to the area, which provided a robust and revivable network of fighters and supporters; (2) the behavior of local Karzai-era strongmen who used their links to the government and the U.S.-led war to target and marginalize their rivals; (3) the general backwardness of the area and the near-total lack of attention on the part of the government; and (4) the existence and expansion of cross-border resourcing and militant command-and-control networks in Pakistan.

The Taliban in Uruzgan and Zabul have their roots in the anti-Soviet resistance, in particular the early fronts based on local religious networks. Although the movement fractured early on, more sharply in Uruzgan than in Zabul, it retained a certain cohesion that was strong enough to allow for it to be revived twice: first in response to the chaos under the mujahideen government of the early 1990s, and second under the Karzai regime when former Taliban fighters and margin-alized tribes were targeted and mistreated by the pro-government strongmen and their international allies.

The insurgency in Zabul and Uruzgan is dominated by the "Kandahari Taliban," roughly spread across two networks in the west and the east. This insurgency is a rather unruly collection of local com-mander networks that alternatively cooperate with, coexist with, and fight each other. It is directed and monitored from Pakistan by what is known as the Quetta Shura, but clearly has a dynamic of its own. The Taliban shadow administration in the two provinces is often domi-nated by local strongmen, who may or may not have formal positions within the insurgency. The Taliban collect taxes locally, and command-ers receive regular payments, although foot soldiers probably do not.

Heavy losses on the Taliban side due to air raids and military con-frontations in the early post-2001 years have changed the nature and tactics of the movement; the core of the network retreated from the battlefield, and the remaining fighters increasingly relied on guerrilla tactics. The targeting of middle- and high-level commanders seems to have had only limited impact on the operational capabilities of the movement, although it has affected morale, while night raids and bomb-ings breed resentment and fear and often exacerbate local tensions.

There is a strong belief among large parts of the Afghan population that the international military alliance is in reality commanding and equip-ping at least parts of the Taliban insurgency. Changes in international military tactics, such as the shift from heavy reliance on capture-and-kill operations to an approach focused more on tribal balance and inclusion, has had some positive results, although there are also examples where this has exposed the local population and made them vulnerable to retribu-tion, as happened in Khas Uruzgan and may happen in Gizab.

An analysis of the origin and spread of the insurgency in Zabul and Uruzgan demonstrates certain patterns in terms of where and why the Taliban resurgence has been particularly strong or effective. Important factors include tribal targeting and marginalization; key events involv-ing grave human rights abuses and other forms of oppression; weakness or absence of government; the existence of local conflicts and griev-ances that can be used and manipulated to the movement's advantage; tribal and other links to prominent Taliban leaders; local competition over resources; and a history of insurgency in the provinces.

It is clear that the violence in southern Afghanistan cannot be properly understood without taking into account the role and impact of tribal affiliations and feuds. However, there is a tendency among foreign observers to overstate the importance of tribal relations and ignore the fluidity of conflicts and relations between groups. There is in particular a tendency to simplify matters by presenting the insurgency in the south as a historical conflict between the Durrani and the Ghilzai and, within the Durrani, between the Zeerak and the Panjpai, with the Zeerak Durrani defending the current government. This, however, is not how many Afghans see the conflict, which they describe in terms of a confrontation between oppressors (*zalem*) and the oppressed (*mazlum*). The international intervention, both military and civilian, has provided local leaders with a wide array of opportunities to dominate and marginalize. Although important lessons have been learned over the last few years, they may well be overridden by the pervading sense of haste among American political leaders and the desire to return to the military's previous reliance on counterterrorism operations and local militias. Such a shift is likely to have disastrous consequences for places like Zabul and Uruzgan.

The southwestern provinces of Zabul and Uruzgan were among the first provinces to be affected by the post-2001 Taliban resurgence. Since then violence and instability have been endemic, and the presence of the Afghan government has been very limited. The situation has not, however, unraveled in the same way as in neighboring Helmand and Kandahar provinces, and much of the violence is highly localized. Zabul and Uruzgan have benefited from the fact that neither the Taliban leadership nor the international military and Afghan government consider the area a great priority, but this also leaves the population largely at the mercy of commander networks.

This chapter explores the roots and resurgence of the Taliban in Zabul and Uruzgan, and in doing so it teases out some of the recurring themes. The first section of the chapter discusses the area's main loyalties and fault lines, as well as the evolution of the Taliban movement in the two provinces, from the anti-Soviet resistance to the establishment and fall of the Islamic Emirate. The second section focuses on factors that facilitated the revival of the movement as a potent insurgency. The third section discusses the current nature and structure of the movement in Zabul and Uruzgan.[1] Finally, the fourth section discusses the impact of the international military operations on the situation in the provinces.

THE ROOTS AND RISE OF THE TALIBAN

The insurgency is shaped by tribal and subtribal networks, but other relationships such as those forged in religious orders and during combat against the Soviets have also played an important role in tying networks of insurgents together. In fact, although many current Taliban fighters and commanders fought the Soviets, many also reached accommodations with the communist Afghan government before and after Soviet forces withdrew.

Loyalties and Fault Lines

Uruzgan and Zabul were established as separate provinces in 1964 from what is now known as Loy Kandahar (greater Kandahar). The main tribal, political, and economic networks in the provinces continue to transcend administrative boundaries. Both provinces are among Afghanistan's most thinly populated, with more than 95 percent of the people living in rural areas.[2] Being remote, mountainous, and poor, Uruzgan and Zabul have traditionally had low levels of education, a limited government presence, and high levels of conservatism and violence, even by Afghan standards. The original inhabitants of large parts of southwestern Afghanistan, the Hazaras, were forced out by King Ahmad Shah Durrani in the mid-eighteenth century and by Amir Abdul Rahman Khan in the 1890s. Their lands were given to Pashtun leaders who had helped quell the Hazara uprisings. The area is, as a result, now populated by a wide variety of Pashtun tribes and subtribes, which has resulted in a tribal system that is traditionally less coherent than in the east and the southeast of the country. However, tribal affiliations continue to be an important factor in defining patterns of loyalty, conflict, obligation, and patronage. The importance of tribal affiliations and divisions has moreover increased since the collapse of the Taliban government that ruled Afghanistan from 1996 to 2001, mainly owing to the absence of functioning and credible government institutions and to local governmental policies that have encouraged tribal polarization.

The main tribal fault lines in greater Kandahar are first of all between the two main confederations, the Durrani and the Ghilzai[3]; second, within the Durrani, between the two branches the Zeerak and the Panjpai; and third, within the Zeerak, between the Popalzai and Barakzai/Achekzai tribes.[4] The fortunes of the various groups changed as regimes rose and fell. Under the current government the dominant force in Loy Kandahar is formed by the Durrani Zeerak (Popalzai, Barakzai, Achekzai, Mohammadzai, Alikozai), at the expense of the Durrani Panjpai (Noorzai, Ishaqzai, Kakar) and the Ghilzai. Within Kandahar and Uruzgan the Popalzai have disproportionate influence, because of their close links to Afghan President Hamid Karzai (until recently through his half brother Ahmad Wali Karzai and former Uruzgan governor Jan Mohammad—both were killed in 2011), while in Helmand the Barakzai and the Alizai dominate. In Zabul, which is predominantly inhabited by Ghilzai tribes, the main tensions are fed by the power struggle between the two largest tribes, the Tokhi and the Hotak; by tensions between the Hotak and Tokhi against the rest; and by the animosity between *kuchis* (nomadic herdsmen) and settlers.[5] The Tokhi, who are said to make up 40 percent of the province's population, have managed to link themselves closest to power and hold most of the local government positions. The main ongoing conflict in the province is a land dispute between the Nasser and the Shomalzai branch of the Tokhi in the border areas of Shomalzai district. There seems to be no conflict of any significance with the Durrani minority in the province.

Where Zabul mainly suffers from limited intra-Ghilzai tensions, Uruzgan has been the arena for a whole range of tribal power struggles and grievances. These historically have included the violent conflicts between Hazaras and Pashtuns in Gizab and Khas Uruzgan in the 1980s; the long-running struggle for power between the Popalzai and the Barakzai, which continues to shape local politics; the traditional Zeerak-Panjpai and Durrani-Ghilzai divides revisited under every regime, particularly the current one; and a multitude of bloody clashes between rival commanders, usually over resources or prominence within the (sub)tribe.

Outside observers often lose track of the fact that tribe and subtribe are not the only important solidarity groups. Other important affiliations include those based on the mujahideen political parties or *tanzims* (which can represent a shared political or religious outlook, shared battlefield experiences, or simply being part of a shared network with the access and resources that provides), area of origin, shared economic interests, ties through marriage, and the bonds between former brothers in arms, classmates, and colleagues (the *andiwali* or comrade networks). These ties help shape the nature of the insurgency and the complex webs of relationships that exist among government, Taliban, and everything in between.

Taliban Roots in the Anti-Soviet Resistance

The Taliban movement in Zabul and Uruzgan has its roots in the 1979–89 resistance against Soviet occupation.[6] Many of the well-known personalities from that time—or their relatives—continue to play prominent roles in either the current insurgency or the struggle against it, as is the case in many of the other provinces as well. The armed mobilization against the Soviet-backed Afghan communist regime in the south was initially very localized, with tribal and social leaders organizing themselves in local "fronts," the so-called *mahaz* or *jebha*.[7] These fronts were originally independent and self-sufficient, but as the struggle continued the Pakistan-based mujahideen parties, or tanzims, became increasingly important as the providers of weapons, money, and a place of refuge for the fighters' families. Local fronts united and fragmented, as conflicts over power and resources surfaced, and loyalties were fluid.

The Pakistan-based parties that managed to garner the largest following in both Zabul and Uruzgan included Harakat-e-Enqelab-e Islami, which was led by Maulvi Mohammad Nabi and was strongly linked to existing religious networks; and both factions of the Hizb-i-Islami party, led by respectively Gulbuddin Hekmatyar and Yunus Khales (the former presided over a party with a very centralized organization, while the latter headed a party closely linked to the local religious networks). Other parties with a more limited or localized following included the moderate Mahaz-e-Melli led by a sufi notable, Pir Seyyed Gailani; Jamiat-e-Islami, led by Professor Burhanuddin Rabbani, which was particularly strong in the north of Afghanistan but also had considerable pockets of support around greater Kandahar; and Ettehad-e-Islami, which was led by Ustad Sayyaf. For most local commanders, the choice of a particular party had little to do with ideological outlook and was largely determined by personal connections and what seemed to be the best offer of resources. Many commanders linked themselves to multiple parties over time.

The "Taliban Front" in Zabul and Fragmented Resistance in Uruzgan

In Zabul the religious networks and madrassas played a central role in the initial mobilization of the anti-Soviet armed resistance. As in many other provinces, religious leaders and madrassa students joined the armed resistance and established their own fronts, alongside other fronts led by local tribal leaders and newly surfaced commanders. In Zabul the taliban[8] front (*jebhe-ye taleban* or *de talebano jebha*) seems to have, at least initially, been the main vehicle to fight the Soviet-backed government, and most commanders and tribal leaders initially linked themselves to this front.[9] The taliban front in Zabul, like many other resistance groups based on religious networks, was initially most closely associated with the Harakat-e-Enqelab-e-Islami.

Over time many prominent commanders switched allegiance, which caused the front to fragment along tribal and party lines. The fragmentation was exacerbated by the deaths of the front's legendary leader, Mullah Musa Kalim, in 1979 and his deputy and successor, Mullah Madad, in 1988.[10] Several prominent Tokhi commanders joined Hizb-i-Islami, while others linked themselves to rival parties.[11] Some of the smaller tribes established their own fronts, which included the *jebhe-ye Hotak* led by Salam Khan Babozai and Noorullah, the *jebhe-ye Nasseri* led by Amer Abdul Qader, and the *jebhe-ye Shomalzai* led by Shah Khan Sarhadi.[12] But even though the original taliban front fragmented fairly soon and lost its single leadership, it did maintain a certain coherence. This may explain why the infighting in Zabul was never as bad as in some of the other provinces, such as Uruzgan.

The resistance in Uruzgan seems to have been more fragmented from the beginning, and the role of religious networks was much less pronounced. There were taliban fronts in Uruzgan, but they do not seem to have played as prominent a role as the one in Zabul, although they did produce many prominent Taliban figures. The early taliban front in the Dehrawud district, in the west of the province, included several currently active Taliban, notably Mullah Muhammad Omar, Mullah Mir Hamza, Haji Mullah Mohammad Rahim, Mullah Abdul Bari, and Alullah

Agha. The Chora/Tirin Kot area in central Uruzgan had a taliban front that was linked to Khales' Hizb-i-Islami. Current Taliban commanders Mullah Qaher and Mullah Shafiq were part of this front.[13]

Alliances in Uruzgan were fleeting and loose, with many commanders having multiple affiliations to the various mujahideen parties, depending on the availability of resources and the actions of their local rivals. Many of the commanders entered into "protocols" and nonaggression pacts with the local branches of the ruling communist People's Democratic Party of Afghanistan (PDPA) as the years went by. These protocols involved, for instance, the mujahideen agreeing not to attack the main bazaars or to engage in ambushes in exchange for the cessation of bombing in the area. In some cases salaries were offered, or local groups were encouraged to turn against other groups. Interviews suggest that almost all commanders in both provinces were involved in such deals and protocols.[14]

Although a few commanders managed to achieve a degree of prominence within their tribal group and managed to control larger areas, power was mainly dispersed among a large number of minor commanders and their support networks. Resistance infighting was fierce and usually over resources or power.[15] The conflicts resulted in a string of killings and counterkillings that continue until this day. Recent violent deaths include Mullah Khudainazar, Mohammad Ikhlas' brother Mohammad Payend, local commander Abdul Ali Aka in Dehrawud, and Hashem Khan Tokhi in Darafshan.[16]

From Resistance to Emirate and Back

After the Soviet withdrawal in 1989 and the collapse of the Afghan communist administration in 1992, government positions and territory were divided among the most assertive local mujahideen commanders, many of whom proceeded to fight each other over opportunities to plunder and extort. Not all commanders participated in the infighting and lawlessness, and many traditional tribal leaders and land owners disbanded their armed groups and returned home.

When the Taliban took Kandahar in 1994, they marched on to Uruzgan and Zabul province almost without a fight. As in most places, people were tired of the infighting and lawlessness under mujahideen commanders' rule and welcomed the new order. In Zabul the Taliban initially excluded all former mujahideen commanders, but later, when their skills were needed on the battlefield, several were absorbed into the movement. This included Mullah Salam Rakety, a former Ettehad-Islami commander; Amer Khan Haqqani, the brother of Mullah Madad; and Noorullah Hotak, a former Mahaz-e-Melli commander. Because they brought a large number of fighters, they quickly gained senior military positions.[17] Several of Uruzgan's local commanders landed positions in the Taliban military structure in a similar fashion. Prominent local figures who were from the "wrong" tribe or *tanzim* were marginalized and harassed—there are the usual reports of forced disarmament and extortion—but were otherwise largely left in peace. There were no reports of large-scale armed resistance, and it seems that practically all commanders and leaders either entered into some form of accommodation with the Taliban or left. Some of them went to Pakistan, while others joined the Northern Alliance in Panjshir or elsewhere.[18]

The lack of local open resistance against the Taliban rulers probably explains why it was initially so difficult for Hamid Karzai to mobilize Uruzgan's tribal leaders for his armed uprising against the Taliban in October 2001. It was only after it was clear that he had the backing of U.S. Special Forces that he managed to mobilize a significant following.[19] Once U.S.-led military operations in Afghanistan were well under way, it was clear to most commanders who had allied themselves to the Taliban that the regime's days were numbered, and many of them sought to contact the other side to negotiate a peaceful transfer of allegiance.[20] Afghan traditions of power struggle and regime change are characterized by the parallel dynamics of accommodation and abuse. Those who have been defeated risk being treated harshly by the victors, who will want to ensure that the losers are sufficiently weakened or punished (particularly if they abused power when they had it).[21] But there is also a tradition of approaching the victors and negotiating an honorable surrender, which usually includes handing over almost all weapons and promising to not engage in any form of resistance. Many Taliban commanders in Uruzgan and Zabul took part in such negotiations and returned home.

THE RESURGENCE OF THE TALIBAN

After the Karzai government took power, the appointment of many pre-Taliban commanders to government positions quickly engendered dissatisfaction among the population. Corruption and abuses perpetrated by these government officials fostered open grievances and resulted in a return to insurgency by some of the former Taliban fighters as well as growth in their ranks of those angered by the behavior of the Western-supported government. The history of insurgency in Zabul and Uruzgan, and the existence of strong ties dating to the anti-Soviet jihad, allowed insurgent networks to reassemble easily and quickly after the Taliban's fall.

The Karzai Government at the Local Level

After the fall of the Taliban regime in late 2001, many Afghans assumed that power would be either returned to the traditional elites—the landowners, tribal leaders, intellectuals, and possibly the king's family—or given to a new cadre of educated and enlightened administrators. In reality, however, the pre-Taliban mujahideen networks made a strong and largely unexpected comeback. Throughout the country, pre-Taliban commanders were reappointed as governors, police chiefs, corps commanders, and district administrators. According to scholar Antonio Giustozzi, at least twenty of the first group of thirty-two provincial governors appointed by the Karzai government were militia commanders, warlords, or strongmen, while smaller militia commanders populated the ranks of district governors.[22]

In Uruzgan, the province's main strongman, Jan Mohammad, was appointed governor in early 2002. He had held that position before the Taliban took over in 1994, and his reign was harsh and violent. A long stay in a Taliban prison had not made him any milder. In Zabul, Hamidullah Tokhi, a former militia commander linked to Hizb-i-Islami (Hekmatyar), was appointed as provincial governor. Hamidullah Tokhi had fought in the anti-Soviet resistance and served as provincial corps commander under the mujahideen government of Rabbani.

Both were implicated in the pre-Taliban time of plunder and chaos, and both were given virtual free rein under the Karzai regime to target rivals and appoint friends, thus bringing to power a network well known for brutality and involvement in the narcotics trade. Hamidullah Tokhi was replaced relatively swiftly, as were his successors.[23] Jan Mohammad, however, lasted until March 2006, when he was replaced by Abdul Hakim Munib, a Ghilzai (Alikhel) from Paktia, who had been deputy minister of Border Affairs in the Taliban government. In the meantime

Dilbar Jan Arman, a Shinwari from Khost and former Hizb-i-Islami (Hekmatyar) commander, was appointed governor of Zabul.

The relative neutrality of both new governors and their former links to the Taliban and Hizb-i-Islami respectively made them potentially well placed for outreach to disaffected tribes and leaders. Although some progress was made, both governors suffered from a lack of political (and financial) support from the Karzai government and soon seemed to be mainly concerned with their personal survival. Munib in particular suffered from having been appointed against the will of Jan Mohammad. He was replaced in September 2007 by Assadullah Hamdam, a Wardak from Zabul with army training and a background of working with non-governmental organizations (NGOs). Hamdam was appointed with the consent of Jan Mohammad, which came with strings attached and lasted until March 2010, when he was recalled to Kabul. He was replaced by Omar Sherzad, a Khogyani from Kandahar. Dilbar Jan Arman was moved to Badghis in February 2009 and replaced by Badghis governor Mohammad Ashraf Nasseri, a Nasser from Paktia.

Hamdam and Nasseri, with their NGO backgrounds and their command of English, represented a new professionalized type of governor that the Independent Directorate for Local Governance (IDLG), the government organ responsible for governor appointments, prefers to recruit.[24] Both governors have, however, been credibly accused of embezzlement; Hamdam was removed for this reason and may face prosecution.[25] The fact that they are not perceived as directly violent or overly predatory can be considered progress, but there are, on the other hand, no indications that appointment of nonviolent but probably corrupt officials will do much to repair the reputation of local government.

The Fall and Rise of the Taliban

Zabul was among the first provinces to see a resurgence of Taliban activity, with recruitment and mobilization taking place as early as 2002. The rapid remobilization was facilitated by the continued presence of strong religious networks and the continuity provided by ties forged during the mujahideen and Taliban eras. It was also, as in most provinces, fueled by local grievances.

The insurgency in Zabul restarted from Daichopan district in the north of the province (where the province's anti-Soviet resistance also started), and by summer 2003 the Taliban had reestablished its first major base in this area, harboring large numbers of fighters.[26] The district's rough terrain makes it particularly suitable for guerrilla warfare and as a base for training and recuperation, while its history of insurgency meant that the necessary physical and social infrastructure was in place (routes were known, networks were easy to revive, shelter and storage facilities were in place). Daichopan is largely inhabited by the Kakar tribe. Tribal links to prominent Taliban commanders, such as the late Mullah Dadullah Lang ("the Lame"), coupled with disaffection over the fact that the Kakar had been largely passed over in the distribution of government positions and spoils, played an important role in solidifying support for the movement as it regrouped.[27]

In Uruzgan, the Taliban took somewhat longer to reemerge. Although Uruzgan has its share of religious networks, their role was more limited and the resurgence of the Taliban movement was in particular linked to the behavior of the province's local power brokers. Uruzgan's post-Taliban governor Jan Mohammad had been close to President Karzai's family since the 1980s, which gave him great leverage to appoint his associates to positions in the provincial administration and security organs. Moreover, he used his relations with foreign military forces and his reputation as an effective Taliban hunter to target a wide range of potential rivals. These included local leaders who had been associated with the Taliban, as well as the (often pro-government) leaders of the weaker tribes, in particular the Ghilzai in Darafshan and Mirabad, near Tirin Kot, and the Noorzai and Babozai in Dehrawud and Charcheno, in the west of the province.

The return to power of the pre-Taliban mujahideen networks in the south had disastrous consequences for tribal relations and the reputation of the newly established government. Former Taliban commanders and notables who had agreed to lay down their weapons were violently targeted. Haji Pay Mohammad, a prominent Hotak commander from Mirabad who commanded the Kabul front under the Taliban regime, was taken from his house and killed, according to locals after he had sought permission from the new government to return home. His body was displayed at the town square for days, together with those of several of his men. The local command post in Mirabad, through which the Hotak tribe had restored security in the area after the fall of the Taliban, was forcibly dismantled and ransacked.

An important factor in these events was the competition, between Jan Mohammad and former Taliban commander Mullah Shafiq immediately after the Taliban collapse, over who should be the governor (Mullah Shafiq even established a separate *welayat*, or governor's compound, in his area in Mirabad) and accusations by Jan Mohammad that the Hotak commanders were responsible for his detention under the Taliban. Mullah Shafiq and Mullah Qaher left the area as a result of the targeting and soon joined the revived insurgency. They remain the key insurgent commanders in the area.[28]

Other examples of former Taliban being targeted despite having laid down their weapons included the detention and mistreatment of Haji Hodud, a Tokhi commander from Darafshan, and the detention and handover to U.S. forces of Mullah Rahmatullah Sangaryar (reportedly out of spite that he had surrendered his weapons to tribesman Gul Agha Sherzai and not to Jan Mohammad). Sangaryar was held in Guantánamo until the summer of 2007, after which he returned to Afghanistan. He has not joined either side. A former Taliban commander from Zabul, Mullah Jabbar, reportedly was badly beaten by governor Hamidullah Tokhi for not surrendering his vehicle. He joined the active resistance and was mentioned as the Taliban provincial governor as early as 2003. He remains one of the province's key insurgent commanders.[29]

But not only former Taliban commanders and officials were targeted. In several cases prominent tribal leaders who had demonstrated their neutrality or even support for the Karzai government were also detained or beaten, or saw their properties ransacked and bombed. Leaders targeted in this way included Hashem Khan Tokhi in Darafshan and Nassim Khan in Charcheno. Both were important tribal leaders with no links to the insurgency, and both departed their areas, leaving them highly vulnerable to insurgent infiltration and recruitment. Hashem Khan did not join the insurgency, but several of Nassim Khan's relatives did. At least two of his brothers died on the battlefield.[30]

This was a pattern that was repeated in varying degrees all over the country, where those newly back in power reverted to their pre-Taliban ways of asserting dominance, exacting revenge, and marginalizing rivals. District governors, police chiefs, and informal militia commanders who were involved in extortion and mistreatment of the population were not sanctioned for their behavior; on the contrary. An elder from Uruzgan once recounted how he felt that his public complaints against a particularly abusive district administrator might actually have consolidated the official's position.[31] A judge from Uruzgan told how he had once sentenced a local commander to twenty years' imprisonment for killing four people. The commander in question had wanted to take a piece of land forcibly, so he took a police car and several armed men and surrounded the house in question. In the ensuing firefight, four men died. Since his sentencing, the commander has escaped and now heads a government-linked militia in Zabul. The relatives of the men who were killed have fled and joined the Taliban.[32]

The reemergence of the Taliban in Zabul and Uruzgan was further facilitated by the fact that some of the most prominent figures within the Taliban leadership hailed from the area or were tribally linked. When the targeting of former Taliban commanders started, there was a strong network of people who had worked and fought together, which was easy to revive. This included the leaders of religious networks, the former mujahideen commanders who fought in the anti-Soviet resistance, and the generation of younger men who did not participate in the jihad but had strong ties to the commanders they fought under during the pre-Karzai Taliban regime. Important leaders included Mullah Omar himself (a Hotak—possibly a Babozai—who grew up in Dehrawud but whose family is said to be originally from Shinkay in Zabul), second-in-command—and currently in Pakistani custody—Mullah Baradar (Popalzai from Dehrawud), and Mullah Dadullah Lang, who was killed in 2007 (Kakar from Dehrawud), as well as a large number of former Taliban ministers, governors, and prominent frontline commanders.

THE STRUCTURE AND NATURE OF THE CURRENT TALIBAN MOVEMENT

Albeit loosely organized, much of the Taliban structure in the provinces falls under the auspices of the "Kandahari Taliban" commanded from Pakistan by the so-called Quetta Shura. This organization has created a fluid structure, complete with shadow administrators and attempts at reform through the removal of underperforming or abusive shadow officials, though the organization remains divided over proper treatment of civilians and the proper balance between fighting and governing. There continue to be scattered reports of small groups of foreign fighters operating with the Taliban.

The Insurgency Today

Over the years, the Quetta Shura's influence has expanded to include the crescent that runs from Faryab in the northwest, down into Badghis, Ghor, Herat, and Farah in the west, toward Nimruz and greater Kandahar in the south, as well as parts of Wardak, Logar, Kapisa, and Ghazni, and Baghlan and Kunduz in the northeast.[33] The movement has a hierarchical structure with delegated authority given to lower-level shuras in Pakistan and at the provincial and district level inside Afghanistan. There is a committee in Quetta that deals with operational matters relating to southern Afghanistan, as well as several committees responsible for the various provincial shadow administrations. Taliban provincial governors tend to spend much of their time in Quetta, from where they seek to coordinate and direct administrative matters in the province. Deliberations relating to the district level are often done in the Afghan border town of Chaman.[34]

The post-2001 Taliban movement was not recruited and trained from scratch. On the local level, it tends to be made up of an unruly collection of local commander networks that alternately cooperate, coexist, and fight with each other.[35] The Taliban leadership tries to regulate the actions of these networks through an administrative and military hierarchy and a system of mobile inspection teams that travel the areas and gather information about the behavior of their commanders and administrators. The frequent leadership shuffles on the provincial and district levels usually signify shifts in internal politics and sometimes attempts by the Quetta-based leadership toward internal reform.

For instance, in late 2008 and early 2009 a large number of the Taliban's shadow governors and district governors (including those in Uruzgan and Zabul) were replaced. So-called reform commissions were dispatched to the provinces to gather information on how "Taliban officials" were performing. Complaints about abusive behavior led to removal, replacement, and sometimes punishment of some of the commanders in question. Locals explained how, in addition to the delegations coming from Quetta, the reform commissions appointed representatives on the ground who reported back to the leadership. These measures seemed mainly aimed toward greater control over the commanders and their behavior. In other cases, however, shadow district governors and officials have been replaced or recalled to Quetta for not displaying enough appetite for war and for being "too soft" toward the local population. There seems to be no real agreement among the movement's leadership and its main commanders on how the population should be treated; pushes for greater internal accountability are often overridden by those who believe in more violent tactics.[36] The issuance of the *layha*, or code of conduct, agreed by the Quetta leadership and communicated to all field commanders, has so far not led to greater coherence.[37]

The Taliban in Zabul and Uruzgan

The core of the current Taliban movement in Zabul and Uruzgan is relatively stable and, as said before, has its roots in mujahideen and Taliban regime networks. The main commanders are a combination of old mujahideen fighters and those belonging to a younger generation who were given positions under the Taliban regime in the 1990s. There are increasing reports that a new and even younger generation of fighters is seeking to replace the senior leaders, whom they consider too soft.[38] Locals confirm that many current field commanders are young, but most of them still seem to have been involved with the Taliban since its rule or are related to long-standing commanders. The emergence of a younger generation does not seem to have fundamentally altered the core of the Taliban hierarchy or its fighting force in the two provinces—at least not yet.

The movement is further being fed by a pool of potential commanders, formed by local leaders, landowners, and entrepreneurs who can mobilize groups of armed young men. Some of them join under pressure, out of opportunism, or in search of revenge, and there are occasional shifts of allegiances from the government to the Taliban and vice versa.

An example of shifting allegiances took place in early 2010 in Khas Uruzgan, a district in the east of Uruzgan bordering Zabul and Ghazni. Several tribal elders contacted the local government and U.S. forces, indicating that they wished to make peace on behalf of the Taliban in their area. Most of them had relatives or tribesmen who played prominent roles in the insurgency, and several were themselves suspected of engaging in (occasional) active support. The local population was largely skeptical, arguing that the insurgents simply wanted to regroup during the winter and were seeking temporary protection from the night raids and bombardments. The Taliban district governor was apparently recalled to Quetta to explain the move. Although the tribal elders promised to introduce local fighters to man check posts, it didn't materialize and by the summer of 2010 the situation in Khas Uruzgan had deteriorated: there was no peace deal and local Taliban commanders closed the bazaar, beat teachers, and engaged in a series of killings targeting local council members and suspected informants. Several weeks later, the situation turned after one of the main Taliban commanders in the area was killed.[39] A Pashtun Afghan Local Police (ALP) unit was established but fragmented again when its commander Neda Mohammad was killed in July 2011—probably in revenge over brutality and killings by his unit.[40]

The Taliban in Uruzgan and Zabul have established a shadow administration, as in most other provinces, with a provincial governor (*wali*), district governors (*woleswali*), a host of security and military commanders, a court system linked to the religious networks, and an extensive and rather loose network of groups of fighters that are organized in so-called units (*delgai*) and cells (*otaq*).[41] The main "officials," such as the provincial governor and the provincial security commander (*qomandan-e amnia*),[42] tend to reside in Pakistan and only occasionally visit. The positions are somewhat fluid, and in practice key commanders are often interchangeably described by locals as security commander (*qomandan-e amniya*), front commander (*qomandan-e mahaz*), or responsible for operations (*massoul-e amaliyat*), guerrilla warfare (*massoul-e amaliyat-e cheriki*), or military matters (*massoul-e bakhsh-e nezami*). Most commanders have one or two deputies, who seem to be selected mainly on the basis of personal links or the commander's wish to broaden his base by having deputies from different tribes or subtribes, rather than through central appointments. The fluidity of the "administration" seems to reflect the fact that the Taliban in Uruzgan and Zabul remain primarily an armed insurgency. The officials, with the exception of judges, tend to be military commanders, whose main importance remains their role on the battlefield, as in the days of the Taliban regime when even ministers were sent to the front lines to fight.[43]

Almost a decade since the reemergence of the Taliban movement, even those living in or regularly traveling to Taliban-controlled areas continue to provide conflicting information on who holds the various key positions in their areas. In Zabul in early 2010, for instance, several local inhabitants said that Abdullah, a commander from the Tokhi tribe who had been part of the original taliban front during the anti-Soviet jihad, was still the shadow governor. Others, however, maintained that he had been succeeded by the lesser-known Qari Ismail, an Andar from Ghazni province with no reported track record in Zabul. It is likely that Qari Ismail was in fact the formal appointee but that he lacked the local links to establish his authority. Abdullah, who continued to have frontline responsibilities as a mahaz commander and probably a formal position as provincial military commander, is likely to still have informally outranked the appointed shadow provincial governor.[44]

Uruzgan has recently seen a succession of relatively weak Taliban shadow governors. Baz Mohammad, a Popalzai believed to be close to Mullah Baradar, was appointed just before the Taliban assault on Dehrawud in September 2007. He had some influence in western Uruzgan but relatively little in the eastern part. He was succeeded by Rohullah Amin in a general leadership shuffle in January 2009. Amin, who is from Helmand province, had no strong links to the local insurgent or tribal networks and was widely considered to be weak and ineffective. He was recalled to Quetta in early 2010, after which Baz Mohammad was temporarily reappointed. There were rumors that Amin had been detained or that he had fled the country with a large sum of money, but he was reappointed in April 2010—probably after having received the personal backing of one of the Quetta Shura members.[45] The back-and-forth surrounding his removal and appointment suggests that the Taliban suffer from patronage dynamics similar to those of the Afghan government.

The Taliban also have their local strongmen, who are difficult to replace or circumvent. An example is Mullah Qahar from Daichopan district in Zabul.[46] An Uruzgan elder described it this way: "It doesn't really matter who is the Taliban governor in Zabul, the real power lies in the hands of Mullah Qahar. He was already big during the *jihad*, but now he controls Daichopan and Khak-e-Afghan district [northern Zabul], he has people fighting in other districts in Zabul, and he has fronts in Khas Uruzgan [east Uruzgan] and

Ajiristan [southwest Ghazni]. Whenever there is a problem between the Taliban in Khas Uruzgan, people go to him. He has great influence. If he asks the leadership in Quetta to remove the district governor, they will listen."[47]

Most inhabitants in Taliban-controlled areas, and often even those who have left the area, are subject to some form of taxation. This particularly affects those who want to engage in projects or trade, or who have sought a kind of authorization for their involvement with the government or the international community. There seems to be a consensus that practically all government officials, businessmen, landowners, construction and transportation companies, and project implementers in Uruzgan and Zabul pay a percentage of their income, harvest, or budget to selected Taliban commanders. The Taliban leadership would like to see this as a formal and legitimate tax. In reality it is much messier, and it is often not clear whether this is a kind of revenue collection by a shadow administration, a form of extortion or protection money extracted by the local strongman, or establishment of patronage relations between the population and the friendly—or not so friendly—neighborhood commander (often a relative, tribesman, or former brother-in-arms). Interviews so far suggest it would be an exaggeration to say that the Taliban have set up a centralized and functioning revenue system. The system seems much closer to informal revenue collection by, for instance, the government police or the customs office, where officers gather money for themselves and pass up a percentage to their superiors.

Although there have been steady reports in the international press describing how the Taliban are paying individual soldiers regular monthly wages,[48] interviews with tribal elders from Uruzgan and Zabul suggest otherwise. In Uruzgan, for instance, locals described how the commanders received money for ammunition and other expenses, but the foot soldiers tended to be fed by the local population. They also described how locals sometimes joined voluntarily for reasons other than ideology, grievance, or pay: several local leaders linked themselves to the local Taliban with the intention of keeping out the "outsider" Taliban (those who are not from the area), as they can be more ruthless and exploitative, while families often sent their sons to join the Taliban ranks, preferably in noncombat duties, so they would have a representative within the movement. They also reported instances of forced conscription or pressure to join, often in areas where the local leaders have been weakened or forced to leave.[49]

The arrests of high-level Taliban commanders by Pakistan in early 2010, which included apprehension of Mullah Baradar and former Zabul shadow governor Mullah Yunus, a Tokhi from Zabul,[50] do not seem to have undermined the operational capabilities of the Taliban in the area, although they probably did lead to internal shifts in the relative strength of the various networks. There was some initial confusion over who succeeded Mullah Baradar as the movement's number two, but most reports pointed toward Mullah Qayum Zakir and Mullah Akhtar Muhammad Mansour, who are respectively from Helmand and Kandahar.[51] Neither had any specific links to Uruzgan or Zabul, and with the movement's attention mainly directed toward Helmand and Kandahar, partly in response to the focus of international military operations, Uruzgan and Zabul continued to be left largely to the upheavals of local politics and conflicts.

The Insurgency's Geographic Networks

There are several active insurgent networks in the area that are loosely connected to specific tribal groups, geographic areas, and supply routes. In the west of Uruzgan, there is a network covering the districts of Dehrawud and Charcheno and linked into northern Helmand (particularly the Zamindawar valley and Baghran), northwestern Kandahar (Nesh and Ghorak), and southern Daikondi (Kijran). The western network covers important drug-trading routes. It is closely linked to the now-detained Mullah Baradar and the late Mullah Dadullah, and it probably has roots in the early Dehrawud taliban front. Shortly after the arrest of Mullah Baradar in Pakistan, there were indications of a possible relative shift in power and influence within the Taliban ranks, in favor of the Kakar and Ishaqzai in Helmand and the Noorzai and Babozai in Dehrawud and Charcheno, but this does not seem to have led to any fundamental changes.[52]

A second network covers eastern and central Uruzgan (Khas Uruzgan, and the Darafshan and Mirabad valleys in Tirin Kot district), as well as northern Zabul (in particular Daichopan and Khak-e Afghan). It is linked into Kandahar (Shah Wali Kot and Mianeshin) and Ghazni (in particular Ajiristan, locally referred to as Daya). The network covers important supply and transit routes to and from Pakistan, with Daichopan featuring as a major supply base. A third network covers eastern Zabul and is linked into Paktia and Paktika.

The divide between the two Uruzgan networks is largely based on the tribal and geographic characteristics of the area. The eastern Uruzgan zone covers roughly the Ghilzai and Barakzai/Achekzai areas of the province, while the western zone more or less covers the Noorzai, Babozai, and Popalzai areas. The eastern and western Uruzgan zones are separated by mountain ranges with only a few passes connecting them. The divide also coincides with the administrative boundaries in place before 1964, when Khas Uruzgan still belonged to Ghazni (forming the *loya* woleswali Uruzgan, together with current-day Ajiristan and Daichopan) and the rest belonged to greater Kandahar province. Gizab district in northern Uruzgan is where the two networks meet. The area is connected to the eastern network through its Achekzai Pashtun population and the routes into Chora and Khas Uruzgan, and to the western network through the routes into northern Helmand, via Kijran and Charcheno.

Mobility among the networks is limited; commanders from one side seem only rarely to cross over to the other side for operations or consultation, which suggests that there is little direct coordination or cooperation. Rather, they seem to operate in parallel, reporting to the Taliban shadow governor or to their local military commanders—who in turn report to the Quetta leadership for operational matters—or, alternatively, directly to the Quetta leadership.

Locals have reported a limited presence of foreign fighters in both provinces, mainly Pakistanis, Arabs, and to a lesser extent Chechens and Uzbeks, who are possibly a holdover from the time of Taliban rule. They are mostly concentrated in a number of bases in outlying areas: in Daichopan and Khak-e Afghan in Zabul; and Charcheno, Gizab, and a valley in the far north of Chora in Uruzgan. During military operations, their numbers and spread are said to increase, suggesting some form of coordinated deployment. There have been reports of a kind of mentoring system, where foreign fighters are "seconded" to mobile Afghan combat groups to increase their effectiveness. In the summer of 2010 inhabitants of Zabul and eastern Uruzgan reported an increased presence of Arabs, which resulted in greater pressure on the population and, in some cases, the local Taliban commanders.[53]

THE IMPACT OF THE INTERNATIONAL MILITARY

Although air raids and direct military confrontation with coalition forces have led to a shift in Taliban tactics toward guerrilla warfare, killing Taliban leadership has had little appreciable effect on the insurgency's effectiveness. Focused counterinsurgency efforts in these provinces produced some positive results, but a reliance on tribal militias viewed as predatory by the population, as well as attempts to kill Taliban leaders, exacerbated tensions between local populations and international forces. Increased assassination campaigns against cooperative local leaders and the withdrawal of Dutch forces from southern Afghanistan throw into doubt even the limited advances that international forces have made in gaining the trust and support of the population in Uruzgan and Zabul.

The international military presence in Uruzgan and Zabul in the early years of the past decade was focused on waging the "war on terror," largely through kill-or-capture operations. It was only after the International Security Assistance Force (ISAF) expanded into the more volatile southern provinces in 2006 that the military started adopting a greater counterinsurgency approach. The international military presence in Zabul was relatively limited and focused mainly on securing the ring road that traverses the province,[54] but the Dutch and Australian military in Uruzgan sought to emphasize the importance of development as part of the military's counterinsurgency approach. What seems to have been more important, though, is the realization, particularly within the Dutch Task Force, that much of the insecurity in the province was related to local conflict and that ill-conceived military and development interventions can easily exacerbate the situation. Tribal tensions have somewhat subsided over the years as a result of this approach, although the situation remains volatile. The American and Australian military have shown an awareness of the importance of understanding local and tribal conflicts; they have also sought to expand their links with what are essentially viewed by large parts of the population as predatory tribal militias, thus threatening to exacerbate the situation.

Heavy casualties as a result of coalition air raids and military confrontations in the early post-2001 years changed the nature and tactics of the insurgency. The core of the resurgent Taliban network, particularly in Zabul and as well in the more ideological segments, decided to extract themselves from the fight and wait until coalition operations decreased or coalition forces left.[55] Their places were taken by other fighters, which may explain how a local movement that was known for its roots in the religious networks is now often mentioned as being involved in criminal activities and economic rackets. An Afghan analyst, who referred to the Taliban in Zabul as the "thief Taliban," maintained that they were less ideologically motivated than the Taliban in other areas and that many of them were motivated by personal economic gain. A young entrepreneur with close links to the Taliban suggested something similar when he described how in Zabul, more than in other areas, individual Taliban commanders were prepared to sell their services to the highest bidder. Such services could include allowing or disrupting local elections, agreeing to local cease-fires or nonattack pacts, or allowing vaccination or other aid programs.[56]

In response to the heavy losses inflicted by the overwhelming airpower of the international military, the Taliban shifted early on from large-scale frontal attacks to guerrilla operations and asymmetrical warfare: ambushes, assassinations, small-scale attacks, IEDs, suicide bombings. The coalition's targeting of high- and midlevel commanders, which has been going on for years and has taken out a large number of prominent fighters, kept the movement in flux but had relatively little impact on its operational capabilities. This specific targeting did, however, affect morale and result in a steady flow of midlevel commanders exploring their options for leaving the battlefield. Night raids, house searches, and military operations resulting in the killing of civilians, detention of allegedly innocent people, and destruction of property continue, in contrast, to breed resentment, particularly as the insurgency in many areas has not shown much sign of being defeated or weakened.[57]

In districts such as Charcheno and Khas Uruzgan, where government presence has been limited and the only permanent international military presence is a Special Forces base, the population is caught between fear of night raids and arrests, pressure to provide intelligence, and the necessity to maintain links with the insurgent commanders (or conversely, fear of Taliban punishment, pressure to pay taxes and provide sanctuary, and the necessity to link themselves to the international forces). Counterinsurgency interventions aimed at securing the support of key local leaders and recruiting local forces have shown very mixed results, and in some cases seriously exacerbated tensions. In particular, the recruitment of Hazara militias to guard the Special Forces bases in Khas Uruzgan and Charcheno and to partici-pate in local operations resulted in strained relations between Hazaras and Pashtuns—particularly in Khas Uruzgan with its partially mixed population. There have been a string of killings and attacks targeting Hazara fighters and notables over the years, while the Pashtun pop-ulation accuses the Hazara guards of engaging in false reporting and unnecessary targeting.[58]

Attempts by Special Forces to reach out to the Pashtun tribes in Khas Uruzgan resulted in targeting implicated leaders. In early 2010, several local elders brokered a peace agreement between the Taliban and the international forces and the local Afghan government. Although the military showed great optimism,[59] most of the popula-tion was highly skeptical and saw the move as an attempt to quietly regroup during winter. During June and July 2010, four Pashtun elders who were linked to the newly established shura and two sons of elders who were accused of working closely with the U.S. Special Forces were killed by the Taliban in targeted killings, as well as nine Hazaras in an act of revenge for a deadly night raid a few weeks before. Most of the killings were directly linked to military operations, with the victims being accused of having provided information.[60]

A tribal leader described the dilemma the population faces when dealing with the U.S. Special Forces in this way:

> My tribe asked me who we should introduce to the tribal *shura* for the Americans. I said you should send [this minor elder], so that it will be not such a big blow for the tribe if he is killed by the Taliban or arrested by the foreigners. I said don't send [that big elder], because the foreigners will want him to achieve results and that is impossible in the current situation. When there are no results, they will detain him and accuse him of being involved with the Taliban. Joining a *shura* like that is dangerous, and it destroys your reputation. It brands you as a collaborator, and when the air raids and the night raids continue, the Taliban accuse you of having provided the information.[61]

There is a widespread perception among the population that the Taliban mainly target Afghan national security forces and leave the international forces alone—which may be the result of fear of triggering air raids. This avoidance of engagement feeds the popular conviction that international forces have made deals with the Taliban or, as people increasingly believe, are actually commanding and equipping parts of the insurgency.[62] Whereas the presence of foreign forces did not seem to be an overriding reason to take up arms in the early years, it is now increasingly cited as a reason to fight. The sentiment has always seemed to be stronger in Zabul than in Uruzgan—possibly because of the greater influence of the religious networks—and this continues to be the case.[63]

Major military operations in Uruzgan—including Chora in summer 2007, Dehrawud in early 2008, Operation Spin Ghar in the Darafshan valley in late 2008, and the "liberation" of Gizab in April 2010—illustrate some of the dilemmas the international military faces.

What is now known in the Netherlands as the battle for Chora started when a large Taliban force attacked two auxiliary police posts close to the district center. The Taliban threatened to overrun the district capital, while the pro-government security forces—both the national police and the informal militia linked to strongman Mattiullah Khan—were nowhere to be found. The attack was repelled after the Dutch military, accompanied by a tribally affiliated local commander, came to their aid, but the accompanying artillery and air strikes resulted in a large number of civilian casualties.[64]

Dehrawud district was largely overrun by Taliban forces in September 2007 after several post commanders of the auxiliary police left their stations, probably after having made a deal with local Taliban commanders. Although the complete background to the events remains murky, it is clear that several groups conspired to create a situation conducive to acts of revenge. The population clearly expected the Taliban to be swiftly repelled by the international forces and expressed dismay—and suspicion that this was somehow intentional—when this didn't happen and large numbers of families remained displaced over the winter. A military operation in January 2008 retook most of the district, although there was some controversy when a planned Dutch operation was preempted by U.S. forces (accompanied by Mattiullah's militiamen).[65]

The "liberation" of Gizab in April 2010 was largely the result of a long-standing local feud. A local member of a *khan*, or landowning, family, who found himself under increasing pressure from particular Taliban commanders, saw his chance after he established contact with U.S. Special Forces in neighboring Daikondi province, who were keen to support what they saw as an indigenous anti-Taliban force. U.S. Special Forces, Australian military, and again Mattiullah's militiamen came to the aid of the local uprising, and a nominal government presence was established by appointing locals to government positions and mobilizing a local defense force. However, the lack of further attention from the central or provincial government and the failure so far to send additional army or police units to protect the province, has disappointed the population.[66]

CONCLUSION

There is a considerable reservoir of disaffected fighters in areas subjected to tribal targeting and marginalization, or where there have been instances of killings, grave human rights abuses, and other forms of oppression that warrant revenge, or where government has been weak, predatory, or nonexistent. Other important factors include a history of local conflict and grievances that can be used and manipulated by insurgents; local leaders who have tribal, tanzim, or other links to prominent Taliban leaders; local competition over resources; and a history of insurgency and military mobilization in the region.

It is clear that the violence in southern Afghanistan cannot be properly understood without taking into account the role and impact of tribal affiliations and feuds. However, there is a tendency among foreign observers to overstate and distort the importance of tribal relations by ignoring the fluidity of conflicts and alliances among local actors. This is often fed by the tendency of many Afghan interlocutors to paint rival tribes as historical troublemakers and themselves as the only true representatives of their own tribal constituencies. So although politics and power struggles in southern Afghanistan have traditionally been shaped by tribal fault lines with rather long histories, the reverse is even truer: tribal loyalties and conflicts, far from being static, are exacerbated or muted as the politics around them change. Historical alliances and conflicts, which are seldom straightforward, are constantly revisited, reinterpreted, and used.

The simplified representation of the insurgency in the south as a historical Durrani-Ghilzai and Zeerak-Panjpai conflict, with the Zeerak tribes defending the current government,[67] is not how many Afghans described the conflict to this author. Rather than viewing the current divides as feuds between whole tribes or subtribes, they tend to see them as violent conflicts between leaders who fight and kill each other for power (and who drag their followers with them), and in terms of intentional marginalization of weaker groups by stronger ones, in order to limit the number of competitors. Although local conflicts are often referred to as the continuation of old tribal enmities, they are in essence seen and described as confrontations between oppressors (zalem) and the oppressed (mazlum). Even members of the locally dominant tribes often describe the disruptive effect of their strongmen's behavior on tribal relations, sometimes indicating that they wished to be rid of them if only the situation allowed it (although they may at the same time still praise them for their ability to protect the tribe or the area, or rally around them in the event of an external threat).

The international intervention, both in military and civilian terms, has provided local leaders with a wide array of opportunities to dominate and marginalize. Important lessons have been learned over the last few years, but they may well be overridden by the current pervading sense of haste and a desire to return to the reliance, of the early days, on counterterrorism operations and local militias. This is likely to have disastrous consequences for places such as Zabul and Uruzgan.

Notes

1. The information and analysis in this chapter is based on more than three hundred in-depth interviews over several years with tribal elders and community leaders, NGO workers, teachers and doctors, local government and security officials, villagers, former and present Taliban commanders, local politicians, and to a lesser

extent international analysts. Most conversations took place between November 2005 and July 2010, although some are from an earlier date. The chapter builds on an earlier analysis of Taliban networks: Martine van Bijlert, "Unruly Commanders and Violent Power Struggles: Taliban Networks in Uruzgan," in *Decoding the New Taliban*, Antonio Giustozzi, ed. (Hurst, London, 2009).

2. Uruzgan has an estimated population of 395,00, while Zabul has an estimated population of 355,000. The two provinces rank thirty-second and thirty-third in terms of population density (only Panjshir ranks lower, while Nimruz's population density is comparable to Uruzgan). Source: Central Statistics Office's household listings of 2003–2005, Afghanistan Socio-economic and Demographic National and Provincial Profiles (UNFPA and Central Statistics Office, 2007). Gizab district is included in the Uruzgan estimate. Although it was initially added to the newly established province of Daikondi in 2004, it was returned to Uruzgan in 2006, after the district fell into Taliban hands. In terms of Taliban networks, Gizab is firmly part of Uruzgan.

3. The Ghilzai/Durrani (Panjpai) divide is somewhat fluid. The Babozai subtribe is a case in point. Originally a subtribe of the Hotak from Zabul, they joined the Noorzai after being persecuted under King Nader Shah. Nowadays there is confusion: in the Ghilzai environment of Zabul, the Babozai are still considered a Hotak subtribe, whereas in western Uruzgan, where they are surrounded by Durrani tribes, most view them as part of the Noorzai. Author's interviews with Babozai elders from Zabul and Uruzgan in January 2006.

4. The Achekzai is formally a subtribe of the Barakzai but operates as a separate tribe, due to its large size. The links, however, remain very close, and when under pressure the Achekzai and Barakzai tend to support each other (together with the Mohammadzai, another subtribe of the Barakzai). There have been signs of a convergence of the three related tribes in recent years, in an attempt to increase their political weight.

5. The Kuchis have an interesting position in Afghan politics. They are on one hand generally seen as close to the insurgency and are thus often targeted by the Afghan army at the local level. On the national level, however, their position tends to be supported by Pashtun nationalists within the government who are seeking greater Pashtun influence. This is illustrated by establishment of separate kuchi seats in both the Parliament and the provincial councils, as well as alleged support by people in government for the kuchis in the recurring and increasingly violent disputes with Hazaras over the use of grazing land.

6. The information in this section is based on a large number of author's interviews with elders, former commanders, and other well-informed sources from Zabul and Uruzgan, mainly between October 2005 and April 2010.

7. *Jebha* is often used for the actual front where the fight is taking place, while *mahaz* is generally used for a collection of armed groups under the loose command of a respected commander. There is, however, some crossing over in use of the terms.

8. This chapter distinguishes between the "Taliban," meaning Afghanistan's religious government in power from 1996 to 2001 and the current insurgency, and the "taliban," groups of religious students who fought Soviet forces during the 1980s.

9. Another example of single fronts around which much of the initial resistance activities coalesced was the leftist Teachers Front (*jebhe-ye moallemin*) in Farah province, which was established at roughly the same time (author's interviews with former commanders in Farah, February 2006).

10. Most accounts seem to agree that the leadership of the front was initially taken over by Qias ul-Haq, a Tokhi commander, but there were rival branches, including a Taraki branch led by Haji Ali Mohammad. Both Qias ul-Haq and Ali Mohammad are still alive; neither is formally linked to the government, nor openly supportive of the Taliban. Within the family and tribe, Mullah Madad was succeeded by his brother, Aziz Khan, who led the group when it joined the Taliban in 1994. He was killed in the north in 1997 and was succeeded by another brother, Amer Khan Haqqani, who became one of the main Taliban commanders in the area. Author's interviews in Kabul and Qalat, January 2007 and February 2010. See also Abdul Awwal Zabulwal, "Taliban in Zabul: A Witness' Account," in *Decoding the New Taliban*, 181–82.

11. Prominent Tokhi commanders who joined Hizb-i-Islami included taliban front leader Qias ul-Haq; Abdul Bari, who later established the separate *jebhe-ye markazi* (central front); and Hamidullah Tokhi, who became the Zabul governor under Karzai. Another Tokhi commander, Sardar Mohammad, joined Jamiat-e Islami, while current Zabul legislator Abdul Salam Raketi at the time joined Ettehad-e Islami, taking with him many of his Suleimankheil fighters. Author's interviews in February and April 2010.

12. Salam Khan Babozai has no formal position but is considered a prominent elder. Abdul Qader Nasseri has had several government positions under Karzai, including head of the provincial department of Borders and Tribes. Shah Khan Sarhadi, a Shomalzai Tokhi, was elected into the provincial council in 2005. Author's interviews in January 2006 and February and April 2010.

13. Author's interviews with tribal leaders from Dehrawud and Tirin Kot in April 2010.

14. Interviews with former mujahideen and PDPA government officials from Uruzgan and Zabul, September 2007 to May 2010. See also Antonio Giustozzi, *War, Politics and Society in Afghanistan, 1978–1992* (Georgetown University Press, Washington, DC, 2000)—for instance, p. 127.

15. Such infighting included power struggles between Mullah Khudainazar and Mohammad Ikhlas in Dehrawud district in the west of the province (Khudainazar and Ikhlas belonged to rival Hizb-i-Islami factions, but they fought mainly over prominence within their Noorzai Sultanzai subtribe); between Gholam Nabi and Khalifa Saadat in Dehrawud (over prominence within the Babozai); and between Haji Hodud and Haji Hashem Khan (both Tokhi) in the Darafshan valley, to the north of Tirin Kot—a feud that was reported to have started as a conflict over a rocket-propelled grenade and escalated from there.

16. Author's interviews with tribal leaders from Khas Uruzgan, Tirin Kot, Dehrawud, and Kandahar, August 2007–July 2010. Mullah Khudainazar disappeared after he was invited to meet the Dehrawud district governor in May 2008. His mutilated body was returned to the family weeks later. The

district governor was removed, but there has otherwise been no follow-up. Mohammad Ikhlas' brother Haji Payend was killed in a suicide attack in November 2009, while his rival Abdul Ali Aka was killed in an ambush a month earlier. These deaths are generally viewed as part of an intratribal conflict, rather than a targeting by the insurgency (see also Thomas Ruttig, "A Suicide Attack in Uruzgan," Afghanistan Analysts Network blog, Nov. 23, 2009, http:// aan-afghanistan.com/index.asp?id=470.) Haji Gholam Nabi has been in hiding since the Taliban briefly overran Dehrawud in September 2007, and he was accused of joining them. Haji Hodud was killed in April 2006, probably on the battlefield after he joined the Taliban. Several of his relatives are still part of the armed insurgency. Hashem Khan Tokhi was shot dead in his village in June 2010. The killers were local Taliban, but several Uruzganis believe they were hired to do the job.

17. Zabulwal, "Taliban in Zabul: A Witness' Account," in *Decoding the New Taliban*, 182.

18. Author's interviews with former mujahideen from Uruzgan, 2008–2010.

19. See Bette Dam, *Expeditie Uruzgan: de weg van Hamid Karzai naar het paleis* (Expedition Uruzgan: Hamid Karzai's Journey to the Palace; Arbeiderspers, Amsterdam, 2008). English translation is in preparation.

20. See, for instance, Michael Semple, *Reconciliation in Afghanistan* (United States Institute of Peace Press, Washington, 2009).

21. For a further discussion on inclusion and exclusion dynamics within Afghan society, see Martine van Bijlert, "Imaginary Institutions: State Building in Afghanistan. Patrons, Clients and Nation Builders," in *Doing Good or Doing Better? Development Policies in a Globalising World* (WRR/Dutch Scientific Council for Government Policy, The Hague, 2009). See also Semple, *Reconciliation in Afghanistan*.

22. Antonio Giustozzi, *Koran, Kalashnikov and Laptop: The Neo-Taliban Insurgency in Afghanistan* (Hurst, London, 2007), p. 16. The remaining two provinces— Panjshir and Daikondi—were established in 2004, in the run-up to the country's first presidential elections.

23. Hamidullah Tokhi was replaced in July 2003 by Hafizullah Hashemi, a Durrani (Popalzai or Barakzai) from Kandahar. Hashemi was replaced in January 2004 after troops loyal to him reportedly clashed with the local ANA (see, for instance, UNHCR Ankara COI Team, "Chronology of Events in Afghanistan January 2004," http://www.unhcr.org/refworld/pdfid/415191b74.pdf). His successor, Khyal Mohammad Hosseini, an Andar from Ghazni linked to Sayyaf's Ettehad, was widely accused of being closely involved in the narcotics trade (interviews with politicians and tribal leaders from southern Afghanistan, 2005) and was replaced in March 2006 by Dilbar Jan Arman. Various sources describing Zabul's recent history cite differing and conflicting dates for the governor replacements. The dates cited here have been checked with dated media reports quoting the governors in question.

24. Martine Van Bijlert, *Between Discipline and Discretion: Policies Surrounding Senior Subnational Appointments* (AREU Briefing Paper, Kabul, May 2009). Sherzad represented more of a hybrid appointment, having a limited command of the English language and close personal ties to the Karzai family.

25. Radio Netherlands Worldwide, "Governor of Uruzgan Confirms Dismissal," Mar. 25, 2010, http://www.rnw.nl/english/article/governor-uruzgan-confirms-dismissal.
26. Giustozzi, *Koran, Kalashnikov and Laptop*, 3.
27. Author's interviews with Kakar elder, 2008–2010.
28. Author's interviews with tribal elders, September 2007–May 2010.
29. Author's interviews with local leaders from Uruzgan and Zabul between August 2007 and May 2010.
30. Author's interviews, among others in September and December 2007. Hashem Khan relocated to Kandahar. He was persuaded to return to Uruzgan, where he was killed in June 2010.
31. Author's interview with elder from Uruzgan in May 2007.
32. Author's interview with judge from Uruzgan in April 2010.
33. For more details on the Taliban's expansion to the north, see Antonio Giustozzi and Christoph Reuter, *The Northern Front: The Afghan Insurgency Spreading Beyond Pashtuns* (Afghanistan Analysts Network, Kabul, June 24, 2010).
34. Author's interviews with inhabitants of Uruzgan, Zabul, Kandahar, and Helmand between May 2008 and April 2010.
35. For a more detailed discussion of what this looks like in Uruzgan province, see van Bijlert, "Unruly Commanders."
36. Author's interviews with inhabitants of Kandahar, Helmand, Zabul, and Uruzgan, May 2007–July 2010.
37. Thomas Ruttig, "The Other Side: Dimensions of the Afghan Insurgency" (Afghanistan Analysts Network, Thematic Report 01/2009, Kabul, July 2009), refers to the release of a layha as early as 2006. Newer versions were issued in May 2009 and recently in July 2010. See Kate Clark, "The Layha: Calling the Taleban to Account," Afghanistan Analysts Network, Kabul, July 2011.
38. See, for instance, Sami Yousafzai and Ron Moreau, "Not Your Father's Taliban," *Newsweek*, May 17, 2010.
39. Author's interviews with inhabitants and IDPs from Khas Uruzgan, January–September 2010.
40. For background, see Martine van Bijlert, "Khas Uruzgan Violence and ISAF Press Releases," Afghanistan Analysts Network blog, June 26, 2011, http://www.aan-afghanistan.com/index.asp?id=1846.
41. *Delgai* seems to be used mainly for the small mobile groups (ten to twelve people) that can be mobilized, while *otaq* is often used to refer to static places, for instance, houses that can serve as a logistic base. For a commander it is important to know how many *delgai* and *otaq* he can call on in a certain area.
42. This is often translated as police chief, since *qomandan-e amniya* is also the title given to a government police chief. Such a translation, however, suggests the presence of a parallel Taliban police force, for which there seems to be no evidence.
43. Author's communication with international aid workers, Kabul 1997–98.
44. Author's interviews with Zabul inhabitants in Qalat and Kabul, February, April, and July 2010.
45. Author's interviews with tribal leaders and other inhabitants from Uruzgan in Tirin Kot, Kandahar, Kabul, and by phone, 2007–2010.

46. For an interview with Mullah Qahar by Al Sumud, see "Taliban Military Commander in Zabul Province Discusses Tactics and Strategy," *Terrorism Monitor*, vol. 8, no. 2, Jan. 14, 2010, http://www.jamestown.org/uploads/media/TM_008_2_03.pdf.

47. Author's interview with local leader from Khas Uruzgan in April 2010.

48. See, for instance, Stanley McChrystal, "Coalition Forces Pay Afghan Soldiers Less Than Taliban," *Huffington Post*, Sept. 12, 2009, http://www.huffingtonpost.com/2009/12/09/mcchrystal-coalition-forc_n_385579.html.

49. Author's interviews with local leaders from Uruzgan and Zabul, 2007–2010. See also van Bijlert, "Unruly Commanders."

50. Some media reports maintained that Mullah Yunus is also known as Akhundzadah Popalzai (see, for instance, Anand Gopal, "Who's Who in the Taliban Leadership," *Christian Science Monitor*, Feb. 26, 2010), which may or may not be true. He is, however, definitely not a Popalzai by tribe.

51. The Taliban hierarchy, however, continued to be fluid and imprecise, as was illustrated by several local claims that in fact other, relatively unknown, commanders had been appointed as Mullah Omar's new deputies (author's interviews with local leader from Helmand, February and April 2010). This can point to several things, including the absence of clearly delineated positions, internal lack of consensus on who should be or has been appointed, limited ability or intention on the part of the leadership to communicate appointments, or lack of authority on the ground, as well as attempts by local interlocutors to increase the importance of commanders whom they are close to. But despite lack of clarity on their exact positions, there was broad consensus on the relative importance of Mullah Zaker and Mullah Akhtar Mohammad Mansour within the movement's leadership.

52. Locals, for instance, reported in March 2010 that commanders linked to Mullah Baradar were being disarmed by fellow Taliban in Helmand (where Mullah Baradar's influence is always likely to have been less than in western Uruzgan), while tribal leaders from Uruzgan commented that the Popalzai felt under increased pressure after the arrest of Mullah Baradar and as a result of the increased international scrutiny on Ahmad Wali Karzai (which later subsided). Author's interviews with inhabitants from Helmand and Uruzgan, February–June 2010.

53. The information on mentoring by foreign fighters comes from an interview with an international analyst, March 2010. The rest of the information is from author's interviews with inhabitants of Uruzgan and Zabul, January 2007–July 2010. Inhabitants reported how in Daichopan and surrounding areas the foreign fighters checked the phones of local Taliban commanders to see who they were in touch with, while in Khas Uruzgan there was a marked surge in beatings and threats.

54. This changed somewhat in 2009, when in August a Stryker brigade was deployed to the province and in autumn 2009 Special Forces operations were stepped up. See Sandra Jontz, "Arrival of Stryker Unit Shifts Attention to Zabul Province," *Stars and Stripes*, Sept. 9, 2009, http://www.stripes.com/news/arrival-of-stryker-unit-shifts-attention-to-zabul-province-1.94615; and Michael M. Phillips, "U.S. Steps up Missions Targeting Taliban Leaders," *New York Times*, Feb. 1, 2010. The

Stryker brigade was moved to Helmand in February 2010 but redeployed to Zabul in July 2010. Its activities, however, remained limited, compared to other provinces.

55. Author's interview with international analyst in March 2010.

56. Author's interviews January 2007 and August 2009. The descriptions of the Zabul Taliban may be partially informed by some of the prejudices against kuchis.

57. Author's interviews 2007–2010. See also Thomas Ruttig, "How Tribal Are the Taliban?" (Afghanistan Analysts Network, Thematic Report 04/2010, June 2010), http://www.aan-afghanistan.org/uploads/20100624TR-HowTribalAreth eTaliban-FINAL.pdf. Ruttig argues that the combination of vertical (religious/ideological) and horizontal (tribal) structures gives the movement "a high degree of cohesion while maintaining organisational elasticity."

58. Interviews with Pashtun and Hazara elders, 2007–2010.

59. See, for instance, Capt. Rebekka Lykins, "Change Comes to Khas Uruzgan" (Combined Special Operations Task Force—Afghanistan Media Operations Centre, Apr. 11 2010), an article that even identifies the cooperating "suspected Taliban facilitators" by name. http://www.dvidshub.net/?script=news/news_show. php&id=48318.

60. Interviews with Pashtun and Hazara leaders from Khas Uruzgan, April–July 2010. For information on some of the killings, see Alissa J. Rubin, "Taliban Kill 9 Members of Minority in Ambush," *New York Times*, July 25, 2010, http://www.nytimes.com/2010/06/26/world/asia/26kabul.html?_r=1&src=mv; "Insurgents Kidnap, Execute Two District Council Members in Khas Uruzgan" (US Army Special Operations Command, July 26, 2010), http://news.soc.mil/releases/News%20Archive/2010/July/100726-01.html; "NATO Says Mullah Omar Ordered Killing of Afghan Tribal Chief," loatay.com, July 15, 2010, http://loatay.com/nato-says-mullah-omar-ordered-killin g-of-afghan-tribal-chief.

61. Author's interview with a tribal elder from Khas Uruzgan, July 2010.

62. There is a firm belief across southwestern Afghanistan that the Taliban can be divided into *Taliban-e asli* (the real Taliban), *Taliban-e Pakistani* (the Pakistani Taliban), and the *Taliban-e Amrika'i* (the American Taliban or alternatively the British Taliban: *Taliban-e Engresi*). Author's interviews with inhabitants from Uruzgan, Zabul Helmand, and Kandahar between 2006 and April 2010. For a more extensive discussion of how the various Taliban categories are perceived, see van Bijlert, "Unruly Commanders."

63. Author's interviews in Zabul and Uruzgan during 2006–2010.

64. An AIHRC and UNAMA investigation estimated that between thirty and eighty-eight civilians were killed and eighty to one hundred wounded. AIHRC and UNAMA joint investigation into the civilian deaths caused by the ISAF operation in response to a Taliban attack in Chora district, Uruzgan, on June 16, 2007. AIHRC and UNAMA (undated).

65. Author's interviews with tribal elders, NGO workers, government officials, and international military in Kabul, Dehrawud, and Tirin Kot, September 2007–June 2008.

66. Author's interviews with tribal elders from Gizab and surrounding districts, April–July 2010. See also van Bijlert, "The Revolt of the Good Guys in Gizab," Afghanistan Analysts Network, June 24, 2010, http://www.aan-afghanistan.org/index.asp?id=852.

67. See, for instance, Kenneth Katzman, "Afghanistan: Post-War Governance, Security and U.S. Policy," Congressional Research Service report for Congress (updated July 11, 2008); and Thomas H. Johnson, "The Taliban Insurgency and an Analysis of Shabnamah (Night Letters)," *Small Wars and Insurgencies*, vol. 18, no. 3. September 2007.

FOUR

The Taliban in North Waziristan

Anand Gopal, Mansur Khan Mahsud, and Brian Fishman

EXECUTIVE SUMMARY

North Waziristan, the second-largest of Pakistan's Federally Administered Tribal Areas (FATA), is the most important springboard for violence in Afghanistan today, much as it has been for decades. The most important militant group in the agency is the Haqqani Network, led by the legendary Afghan mujahideen commander Jalaluddin Haqqani and his son Sirajuddin. The elder Haqqani left his native Khost province and settled in North Waziristan's capital, Miram Shah, in the mid-1970s; the younger was raised in the area.[1] Jalaluddin quickly became the most important mujahideen commander in eastern Afghanistan during the 1980s; Sirajuddin now manages the network his father built, employing it to support violence against U.S. and NATO forces. Like his father, Sirajuddin uses North Waziristan to recruit, as a safe haven, and for strategic depth. North Waziristan is well suited for all of these purposes because of its geographic isolation, difficult terrain, and relatively stable coalition of tribal militants.

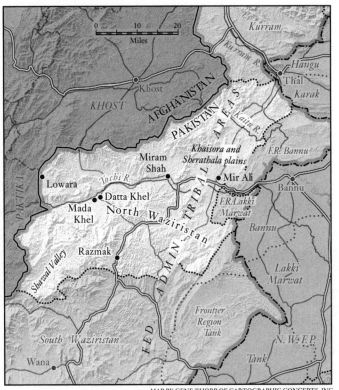

MAP BY GENE THORP OF CARTOGRAPHIC CONCEPTS, INC.

Besides the Haqqanis, the largest militant coalition in North Waziristan is headed by Hafiz Gul Bahadur, of the Mada Khel clan of the Uthmanzai Wazir. Bahadur does not have the record of militant accomplishment of his collaborators in the Haqqani clan, but he does have something they do not: a strong tribal base in the rugged mountains between Miram Shah and the Afghan border. This provides important strategic leverage over militants who must traverse his territory to reach Afghanistan. Bahadur's deputy, Maulana Sadiq Noor, is from the Daur tribe and leads a coalition of both Wazir and Daur tribesmen. Sadiq Noor is very close to the Haqqanis and Bahadur seems to follow Haqqani guidance on difficult questions, such as whether to attack Pakistani troops in the region.

North Waziristan has been a safe haven for successive waves of militants fleeing U.S. or Pakistani military operations. Shortly after the fall of the Taliban regime in Afghanistan in late 2001, thousands of Taliban members associated with the regime flooded into North Waziristan. Many took shelter in the agency's treacherous and heavily forested

Shawal Valley, which became a refuge for foreign militants, including those from al-Qaeda. Pakistani government forces subsequently targeted other Pakistani safe havens, including South Waziristan. In 2004, a wave of militants arrived in North Waziristan after being pushed out of South Waziristan's Shakai Valley. More recently, a variety of militants associated with the Mehsud tribe in South Waziristan sought safe haven in North Waziristan.

Militants in North Waziristan have tended to be less fractious than their cousins in South Waziristan, largely by avoiding divisive tribalism. But the divisions among North Waziristan militants are important. For example, Rasool Khan leads a group of fighters who chafe at Bahadur's prominent role in the agency. Khan's support for Uzbek fighters—who have angered many Pakistani militants—is one reason, but Khan's operation also seems to have a strong criminal element. Similarly, a contingent of foreign and local fighters led by Abu Kasha al-Iraqi has squabbled with Bahadur's chief commander, Sadiq Noor, who resents the Abu Kasha group's foreign leadership. As in other parts of the FATA, the most common strategic disagreements are over the role of Arab and Central Asian fighters and whether to attack Pakistani targets in addition to U.S. and NATO forces in Afghanistan.

Disputes between militants tend to be overlaid on tribal and geographical tensions. Bahadur's stronghold is west of Miram Shah; the militants opposed to his leadership tend to operate in and around Mir Ali, which is slightly farther from the border with Afghanistan. The Haqqani Network seems to have a powerful mediation role among militants in North Waziristan. Both Jalaluddin and Sirajuddin Haqqani are widely respected, and the younger man has intervened many times over the past five years to resolve disputes among militant groups in North Waziristan and other areas of the FATA. The Haqqanis' reputation of effective military action in Afghanistan gives them influence over North Waziristan militants who lack their own networks across the border. Moreover, the Haqqanis' long relationship with the Pakistani military and intelligence establishment makes them effective interlocutors between militants and the Pakistani state. And despite their differences, the militants know that internal squabbling weakens the effort in Afghanistan and makes each group susceptible to pressure from the Pakistani military.[2]

North Waziristan Facts

North Waziristan is a mountainous, 4,707-square-kilometer (1,817-square-mile) tribal agency that directly abuts Afghanistan to the west. Its capital and largest city is Miram Shah. North Waziristan was incorporated into Pakistan at its founding in 1947.

The major towns of North Waziristan are Miram Shah, Mir Ali, Datta Khel, and Razmak. The vast majority of North Waziristan residents are Pashtun, and the bulk of these hail from the Wazir and Daur tribes. Uthmanzai Wazirs dominate Datta Khel and Razmak along with most of the hilly regions, the Khaisora and Sherathala plains, the Kaitu valley, and lower stretches of the Kurram River valley. Daurs dominate Mir Ali, where they are known as Lower Daurs, as opposed to Upper Daurs, who live near Miram Shah.

North Waziristan consists of three subdivisions and nine tehsils. The Miram Shah subdivision comprises the Miram Shah, Ghulam Khan, and Datta Khel tehsils. The Mir Ali subdivision contains the Mir Ali, Spinwam, and Shawa tehsils. The Razmak subdivision consists of the Razmak, Dossali, and Garyum tehsils.

MILITARY OPERATIONS IN NORTH WAZIRISTAN

The Pakistani military has not conducted major military operations against militants in North Waziristan, though it clashed with fighters before signing peace agreements in 2006 and 2008. Indeed, the relationship between militants and the Pakistani military has been relatively cooperative in North Waziristan. Under the terms of a 2009 peace agreement, vehicles driven by Taliban members are exempt from rules stipulating that all vehicle occupants must be searched at Pakistani military checkpoints. Only the Taliban drivers are searched. The effect is that the Taliban can easily smuggle people and weapons around North Waziristan. The peace agreements have created other gaps for the Taliban to exploit. For example, a 2008 agreement seems to have stipulated that Pakistani security personnel manning checkpoints in North Waziristan must operate unarmed.[3]

But North Waziristan has been the primary location of U.S. drone strikes in the FATA, a clear indication of the importance that

U.S. officials place on the militants operating there. From 2004 to 2007, 6 of 9 U.S. drone strikes in the FATA were conducted in North Waziristan. In 2008, 20 of 34 drone strikes were conducted there. In 2009, 22 of 53 strikes took place in North Waziristan, but the pace accelerated dramatically after October 17, when drone attacks in South Waziristan were halted ahead of the Pakistani military offensive there.[4] The trend has continued since; from 2010 through the first three months of 2012, 154 of 200 drone strikes in Pakistan were conducted in North Waziristan.[5]

THE STRUCTURE OF THE INSURGENCY

The Haqqanis

The Haqqani Network, based in Miram Shah, is one of the most important militant groups operating in Afghanistan against U.S. and NATO troops. Operating primarily in Loya Paktiya—the Afghan provinces of Paktiya, Paktika and Khost, which border North and South Waziristan—the network also has a significant presence in Logar and Wardak provinces, and in the capital, Kabul.[6] Jalaluddin Haqqani, the aging former anti-Soviet insurgent leader, nominally leads the network, although in practice his son Sirajuddin has assumed day-to-day command. During the 1980s, Jalaluddin earned a reputation as one of the most effective and skillful mujahideen leaders fighting the Soviets. He built extensive links with Pakistan's Inter-Services Intelligence agency (ISI), the American CIA, and Arab fighters in the region, including Osama bin Laden.[7] Despite fighting in Afghanistan, Jalaluddin has always had a strong base in North Waziristan. Indeed, his decision to launch an uprising against Afghanistan's Soviet-backed communist government reportedly took place at a meeting of Afghan refugees at the Hay al-Muhajareen mosque in Miram Shah in the spring of 1978.[8] During the anti-Soviet jihad, Jalaluddin operated under the Yunus Khalis faction of the Hizb-i Islami mujahideen party, an arrangement that provided political cover and access to resources. Although Jalaluddin was well educated, he was primarily a military commander, earning his greatest victory in 1991 when he captured the city of Khost from the post-Soviet communist regime in Kabul.

After initially resisting them, Jalaluddin eventually ceded power to the Taliban when they arose in the mid-1990s. He was later awarded the relatively unimportant post of minister for borders and tribal affairs in the Taliban government. In practice, however, he and his fighters never fully accepted Taliban authority, especially over Loya Paktiya, and remained essentially an independent but allied force.[9] His forces played an instrumental role in the Taliban's military campaign against the Northern Alliance in the regions north of Kabul.

After the U.S.-led invasion of Afghanistan in 2001, Jalaluddin and his allies returned to Miram Shah, much as they had in the face of threats in the mid-1970s. Jalaluddin Haqqani's legacy in Miram Shah is apparent in many areas, but especially at Haqqani-run madrassas, which have provided food and lodging to a generation of religious students in the area. Although Jalaluddin is widely respected among militants in North Waziristan for his role in the anti-Soviet jihad, his relationship with tribal leaders in the agency is complex. The Haqqanis come from the Zadran tribe, which is based in Afghanistan's Khost province, and their lack of tribal roots in North Waziristan has occasionally prompted scorn from tribal leaders in the agency, even in the 1980s.[10] This weakness has likely empowered Hafiz Gul Bahadur, who does have tribal roots in North Waziristan.

By the time the Taliban began to reemerge, after 2003, Jalaluddin went into semiretirement and his son took over the movement's day-to-day leadership. Today Sirajuddin enjoys unparalleled prestige among the militant groups in North Waziristan, and as such he has often been called upon by the Taliban leadership to mediate between feuding guerrilla factions. Sirajuddin was born in 1979 but is the most senior Haqqani Network commander; even elders such as Jalaluddin's brothers—Haji Khalil and Ibrahim—serve under him.[11] Sirajuddin's leadership role at such a young age suggests that his father continues to exert power in the background on behalf of his son.[12]

Sirajuddin's ties in Pakistan are deep. He was raised in mujahideen camps around Miram Shah and, like his father, attended the Darul Uloom Haqqania madrassa in Akora Khattak, near Peshawar in Pakistan's North-West Frontier Province.[13] Despite lacking the religious credentials of his father, who is a mawlawi (high-ranking religious scholar), Sirajuddin is described by associates as more devout than Jalaluddin.[14]

Haqqani Network Structure in North Waziristan

The Haqqani Network's organizational base is Miram Shah, where it operates from at least three compounds: the Miram Shah bazaar camp, which contains a madrassa and computer facilities; a compound in the suburb of Sarai Darpa Khel; and another in the suburb of Danday Darpa Khel, where members of Jalaluddin's family reside.[15] Most major financial decisions, organization of weapons acquisition and delivery, and development of overall military strategy take place in Miram Shah.

As with other Afghan insurgent groups, the Haqqanis' funds come from a variety of sources. Some of Sirajuddin's brothers are believed to travel to the Persian Gulf region to raise money, relying on Jalaluddin's networks from the mujahideen years and more recently established contacts. Within Afghanistan, commanders receive some cash and weapons from the group's leaders in Miram Shah, but they are also expected to raise their own funds; methods include collection of donations through mosques, taxation of trade in areas under their control, extortion from trucking companies, and cross-border smuggling.[16] The Haqqanis have also been implicated in occasional kidnapping-for-ransom schemes, including the abduction of *New York Times* reporter David Rohde. One of Sirajuddin's brothers, Badruddin, demanded millions of dollars for the release of Rohde and two Afghan colleagues.[17]

The network broadly consists of four groups: those who had served under Jalaluddin during the Soviet era; those from Loya Paktiya who joined the movement after 2001; those from North Waziristan who have been associated with Haqqani or his madrassas over the years; and foreign (non-Pashtun) militants, including Arabs, Chechens, and Uzbeks. Although Haqqani Network fighters on the ground in Afghanistan belong to a number of tribes, the vast majority of the network's leaders in North Waziristan are from the Zadran tribe, and in particular from Haqqani's Mezi clan and its allies. This does not, however, mean that the Haqqani movement is simply tribal; rather, under the secretive conditions in which the group operates, only those bound closely by family or clan ties can win the leadership's trust. Those in the first group, who served under Jalaluddin, enjoy the most power. Newcomers from Loya Paktiya and foreign (non-Pashtun) commanders typically are not part of the inner leadership circle.[18]

The Haqqani Network's North Waziristan leadership—usually called the Miram Shah Shura—consists of a number of Haqqani family members and closely associated long-serving commanders. At the top of the network is Sirajuddin Haqqani, who oversees the group's political and military activities and is the main liaison to the Mullah Muhammad Omar–led Quetta Shura Taliban, the Taliban's leadership body (named for the capital of Pakistan's Baluchistan province). He is also one of the network's liaisons to Pakistani Taliban figures and al-Qaeda. Today, he rarely travels into Afghanistan and instead communicates with field commanders through intermediaries. He also occasionally travels to Peshawar and South Waziristan to connect with militants there.[19]

As of 2010, Sirajuddin's deputy commander was Bakhti Jan, a prominent figure in North Waziristan politics who has played an important liaison role with the Tehrik-e Taliban Pakistan (TTP) and other Taliban groups based in North Waziristan. Jan, who is considered Sirajuddin's closest adviser, comes from a family of Islamist rebels; eight of his brothers fought against the Soviets under Jalaluddin and Yunus Khalis. Today many of his brothers and uncles are Haqqani commanders active in Loya Paktiya. Bakhti Jan reportedly died in late 2009, at the age of fifty, while on pilgrimage to Mecca, but this has not been confirmed. His son Asmatullah, who is approximately thirty years old, reportedly now heads his group.[20]

As of 2010, Sirajuddin's top political deputy was Jan Baz Zadran. Unlike the rest of the Miram Shah Shura, Baz Zadran is not a military commander and does not have experience fighting under Jalaluddin. However, he hails from the Haqqanis' home village of Srani in the Garda Tseray district of Paktiya and is one of Sirajuddin's most trusted associates.[21] He is in charge of Haqqani Network finances and weapons and ammunition acquisitions, a position that gives him considerable authority in the movement.

A number of Haqqani family members also are involved in the Miram Shah Shura. These include the longtime commanders Haji Khalil and Ibrahim, two brothers of Jalaluddin, and Badruddin and Nasiruddin Haqqani, two of Jalaluddin's sons. Nasiruddin, who is Sirajuddin's half brother by way of Jalaluddin's Arab wife, can speak Arabic and has acted as a liaison with al-Qaeda figures. For instance, senior al-Qaeda commander Abu Laith al-Libi (who was killed in a drone attack in 2008) was close to Nasiruddin.[22] Before the September 11, 2001, attacks on the United States, Abu Laith worked for Ibn al-Shaykh al-Libi, head of the Khaldan training camp, which was located in Haqqani territory in Khost province. Nasiruddin was arrested by Pakistani forces in December 2010 but was reported released in May 2011, reflecting a pattern of intermittent Pakistan pressure on the Haqqani Network.[23] He has subsequently acted as an interlocutor between the Haqqani Network and Mullah Omar's team negotiating with the United States and the Afghan government.[24]

As of 2010, the remainder of the Miram Shah Shura was made up of Afghan and Pakistani commanders who split their time between North Waziristan and the front lines in Afghanistan. Among the prominent Afghan commanders are Nai Arsallah and Mawlawi Noor Kasim, both from the Sabari district in Khost; Mali Khan and Mawlawi Ahmed Jan, brothers who are related by marriage to the Haqqanis; and Muhammad Amin, Mira Jan, and Bahram Jan, from Khost's Ali Sher district. Most of the Pakistani commanders have been associated with the Haqqanis since Soviet times. The most prominent was Darim Sedgai, believed to have been behind some high-profile assaults in Kabul. Sedgai was killed by "unknown gunmen" in early 2008.[25]

Traveling frequently between Afghanistan and Pakistan, these commanders serve as the main link between Sirajuddin and the field commanders, although in 2009 Sirajuddin went to the front lines himself.[26] More recently, however, fear of the U.S. military has kept him in Pakistan. There are many field commanders in Afghanistan, but turnover is high because many get killed or captured. The most prominent are Mawlawi Sangin, who is believed to be holding Pfc. Bowe Bergdahl, a captured U.S. soldier, and Zakim Shah, the movement's shadow governor of Khost province.[27]

The field commanders typically recruit the group's rank and file, often from the commanders' home villages and districts. Unlike many Taliban members, who when not fighting work as farmers or do not work at all, a significant proportion of Haqqani fighters double as madrassa students. Many of them attend madrassas in North Waziristan, especially those built or funded by Jalaluddin's network. This may contribute to the more radicalized, ideological orientation of some Haqqani fighters relative to the Quetta Shura.

The Relationship Between the Haqqani Network and the Quetta Shura

The relationship between the Haqqani Network and the Quetta Shura Taliban movement, led by Mullah Omar, is complicated. The Haqqani movement has distinct historical and ideological roots from the Taliban. Jalaluddin Haqqani initially resisted the Taliban when they first entered Paktiya and Khost in the mid-1990s, but he was eventually persuaded by some of his associates (and possibly the Pakistani ISI) to accept Taliban rule. Thus he became the most prominent mujahideen commander to submit to the Taliban's authority. This created a unique situation in which Haqqani functioned as an independent commander within the Taliban government. Throughout the Taliban years, he maintained a group of fighters who worked directly for him in his role as a frontline commander against the anti-Taliban Northern Alliance or in his various ministerial positions.

The Palestinian journalist Abdel Bari Atwan has reported that Osama bin Laden claimed to have personally persuaded Jalaluddin to cooperate with the Taliban's final assault on Kabul in 1996.[28] This was "a huge favor," according to Atwan, though the report has never been verified.[29] Other sources suggest that Haqqani and the Taliban already had an accommodation in the spring of 1995, a year before bin Laden returned to Afghanistan.[30]

The Haqqanis and the Taliban did not see eye-to-eye on everything. Jalaluddin Haqqani was opposed to some Taliban measures such as banning music, enforcing beard length, and limiting women's access to education.[31] In fact, a U.S. State Department assessment found him to be "more socially moderate" than the Taliban.

The Haqqanis regrouped in North Waziristan after the U.S. invasion of Afghanistan because of their historical links to the area. Most of the early commanders and fighters for Haqqani after 2001 were men who had served directly under him during the Soviet and Taliban eras. Therefore, the Haqqanis were able to carry their organizational independence into the post–September 11 Afghan insurgency.

Today the Miram Shah Shura operates autonomously within the Taliban movement. It maintains a separate command-and-control apparatus, as outlined above, but the leadership is integrated into Mullah Omar's organization. Sirajuddin Haqqani holds a seat in the

Quetta Shura, likely a titular position that nonetheless serves to symbolize the Haqqanis' subordination to the Taliban. It is estimated that almost 90 percent of the militant fighters within Loya Paktiya are part of the Haqqani Network.[32] There are almost no "Taliban fighters," as distinct from Haqqani Network fighters, in this region; rather, these men are under the command of Sirajuddin, who acts as a representative of the Quetta Shura Taliban but with a high degree of autonomy.

The Haqqani Network issues statements only under the name of the Islamic Emirate of Afghanistan, the name of the ousted Taliban government. The Haqqanis prefer to avoid any reference to themselves as distinct from the Taliban, most likely because they recognize the Islamic Emirate wields far more national legitimacy than the parochial Haqqanis. For instance, Sirajuddin told one of the authors in an interview that "there is no such thing as the Haqqani Network. We are under the command of Mullah Muhammad Omar and the Islamic Emirate of Afghanistan."[33]

The Miram Shah Shura coordinates activities with the Quetta Shura Taliban in the areas of Loya Paktiya, Logar, and Kabul. Sirajuddin typically meets Quetta Shura leaders in South Waziristan or Peshawar but rarely travels to Quetta.[34] In Logar and Kabul, the Quetta Shura Taliban and the Haqqani Network operate side by side. In particular, the Haqqani Network has been authorized by the Quetta Shura to carry out attacks in Kabul and has installed a head of operations (Mawlawi Tajmeer) who is based there.[35]

This arrangement has enabled the Haqqani Network to expand into areas where it did not historically have influence, such as Kabul. In some cases, Sirajuddin has used tribal connections and his father's old mujahideen network to expand even further afield. As of 2010, one of the most important insurgent leaders in the northern Afghan province of Kunduz was a Haqqani-aligned commander named Mullah Inayatullah. Based in Chahar Dara district, Inayatullah is from Haqqani's Zadran tribe and has nearly a dozen subcommanders serving under him.[36]

The Haqqani Network's coexistence with the Quetta Shura Taliban sometimes causes tensions. For instance, a Haqqani Network attack on a U.N. guesthouse in Kabul in October 2009 was conducted without the sanction of the Quetta Shura. The incident strained relations between the groups, since the Quetta Shura has been keen to avoid attacks on the United Nations in order to promote an image that it is a respectable government-in-waiting.[37]

In other instances, the Haqqani Network and the Quetta Shura Taliban have even acted as competitors. The Quetta Shura Taliban largely controlled Logar province in the years before 2008.[38] But the Taliban treated locals with a heavy hand, sometimes harassing village elders and forcing civilians to give fighters food and shelter. Foreign fighters, mostly Pakistanis, frequented the area, which further alienated residents. Eventually, villagers forcibly evicted the Taliban from some areas and made it clear in others that the Taliban were not welcome. As a result, much of the province was left with a power vacuum, which neither the coalition forces nor the Afghan government filled.

The Haqqani Network moved into the vacuum. It reestablished networks with Logar-based commanders who had served under Jalaluddin in the 1980s (particularly in the province's southeast, which borders Paktiya) and built relations with local Quetta Shura commanders who had not alienated the local community. By 2009, the Haqqani Network was the main insurgent group in many parts of Logar.

The Relationship Between the Haqqani Network and the Taliban Groups in Pakistan

The Haqqanis have a similarly complex relationship with militants in North Waziristan. By many accounts, Sirajuddin Haqqani enjoys unparalleled prestige within the militant landscape of North and South Waziristan, which derives from his family legacy and his role in the Afghan insurgency. (Baitullah Mehsud, for instance, who went on to lead the TTP, fought under Jalaluddin Haqqani in Afghanistan during the 1990s).[39] The Quetta Shura and, by some accounts, Pakistan's ISI have asked Sirajuddin to intervene in the frequent internecine conflicts erupting between local Taliban commanders in the Waziristans, and in conflicts between Pakistani militants and the state.[40]

The Haqqani Network's post–September 11 relationship with Waziristan commanders was built when Haqqani paid North Waziristan tribal leaders to smuggle Afghan and Arab fighters out of Afghanistan in the face of U.S. attacks.[41] In North Waziristan, Sirajuddin developed links to Sadiq Noor, a key deputy of Hafiz Gul Bahadur, who supplied fighters and suicide bombers to the Haqqani Network in

Afghanistan. He similarly developed ties to Mullah Nazir in South Waziristan, who also trained and supplied suicide bombers for the network.[42] In some cases, the Haqqani Network has also drawn fighters from South Waziristan–based militant leaders, such as Qari Hussain, who have moved their training camps into North Waziristan when under Pakistani military pressure.[43] The Haqqani Network has relied on such connections because it generally has not run its own suicide training camps.[44]

The Haqqanis' first significant move into Pakistani militant politics was in the summer of 2006 in North Waziristan, when Sirajuddin and Taliban commander Mullah Dadullah arranged a cease-fire between Bahadur's forces and the Pakistani government, which had been fighting an on-again, off-again war for almost two years.[45] The two, carrying letters from Mullah Omar and Jalaluddin Haqqani, asked the Pakistani militants to direct their energies against the U.S. forces in Afghanistan and not the Pakistani government.[46]

Haqqani Network commander Bakhti Jan has played a pivotal role in such negotiations. In 2006 he acted as a Haqqani representative to the North Waziristan tribal communities and helped persuade key Pakistani militant commanders to consider a one-month cease-fire so talks could be initiated.[47] A document, signed by Jan and the late Taliban leader Mullah Akhtar Muhammad Osmani, was distributed. It said:

> The policy of the Emirate-i-Islami [Islamic Emirate of Afghanistan] is that we do not want to fight Pakistan. All those, whether ansaars [locals] or mohajirs [refugees] who are [sympathetic] with the [cause of the] Emirate-i-Islami are hereby informed that they should stop fighting Pakistan because fighting Pakistan benefits Americans.[48]

Sirajuddin and Bakhti Jan also regularly intervened in local politics in South Waziristan. They established Taliban councils in 2006 to help mitigate tensions between locals, Pakistani Taliban commanders, and foreign (especially Uzbek) militants. In early 2007, the two, together with the Taliban's Mullah Dadullah, established a Taliban council meant to govern South Waziristan and promoted Mullah Nazir as its leader.[49] When clashes erupted between Nazir and Uzbek militants in the spring of 2007, the Haqqanis interceded again to establish a "supreme council" that would be the final arbiter of all decisions made by other Taliban councils. Bakhti Jan served on this body.[50] Jan was also involved in the February 2008 peace deal between Baitullah Mehsud and the Pakistani government.

The Haqqanis played a role as well in the February 2009 agreement by Hafiz Gul Bahadur, Mullah Nazir, and Baitullah Mehsud that launched the Shura Ittihad-ul-Mujahideen, a united front among the three commanders. Sirajuddin and Bakhti Jan worked for months, meeting the commanders a number of times, to bring the three to an agreement.[51] Both Haqqani and Quetta Shura leaders pushed the unification in an effort to have the commanders work together and focus their fire on Afghanistan. The alliance appears to have broken down after the death of Baitullah Mehsud in August 2009.[52]

In 2010, Jalaluddin's brothers were involved in efforts to strike a cease-fire deal between extremist sectarian Sunni groups and Shia tribal elders in Kurram agency. Ostensibly, the move was done out of concern for intra-Muslim unity, although it is likely the cessation of hostilities would also greatly ease Haqqani fighter movements through the area, a key transit corridor into Afghanistan.[53]

The Relationship Between the Haqqani Network and Foreign Militants

Jalaluddin Haqqani established contact with Arab fighters very early in the anti-Soviet war. In 1981, American journalist Jere Van Dyk traveled with Haqqani in Afghanistan and was confronted by a fundamentalist Egyptian named Rashid Rochman.[54] Although Rochman was generally disliked by Jalaluddin's men, who were turned off by his ideological extremism, the mujahideen leader favored the man. Rochman gleefully questioned Van Dyk about the recent assassination of Egyptian President Anwar Sadat, an attack that landed future al-Qaeda second-in-command Ayman al-Zawahiri in an Egyptian prison. It seems likely that Jalaluddin understood that relationships with Arabs such as Rochman could be a fundraising boon for his movement. Jalaluddin still maintains ties through marriage to the Persian Gulf, and much of the Haqqani Network's funding comes through such relationships.[55] In addition, the movement maintains ties to al-Qaeda and the Uzbek Islamic Jihad Union, and has used its leverage with other militants to protect foreign fighters.[56]

Osama bin Laden built a relationship with the Haqqanis in the mid-1980s when he spent months along the front lines with Jalaluddin.[57] The relationship has paid dividends for both parties. In the 1980s, bin Laden's wealthy family and royal connections in Saudi Arabia would have been indispensable for a mujahideen leader like Jalaluddin, and the elder Haqqani's military success offered bin Laden the opportunity to exaggerate his own role in those operations. Indeed, bin Laden's ties to Haqqani were much deeper than those he had with Mullah Omar's Taliban government, which ultimately operated from Kandahar and Kabul.[58] Jalaluddin and bin Laden had much more in common than bin Laden and the illiterate leader of the Taliban. They had shared history from the anti-Soviet jihad. Jalaluddin spoke Arabic and had an Arab wife. Bin Laden may have even emulated some of Jalaluddin's leadership affectations. The Afghan commander toted a relatively rare AK-74 assault rifle in the early 1980s as a symbol of his leadership; bin Laden was given the same model by a top lieutenant, Abu Ubaidah al-Banshiri, after the Lion's Den battle in 1987 and subsequently carried it everywhere, including in Sudan.[59]

al-Qaeda and aligned groups have two main roles in the Haqqani Network: facilitating attacks and providing suicide bombers. Attack facilitation includes providing training, weapons expertise, and arms and funding procurement. Haqqani compounds in and around Miram Shah have housed a number of al-Qaeda weapons stashes.[60]

In recent years, however, as the Haqqani Network developed and al-Qaeda's operational reach declined, this facilitation role has diminished.[61] al-Qaeda, the Islamic Jihad Union, and other groups still provide suicide attackers, however.

Nonetheless, the Haqqani leadership's direct contact with al-Qaeda figures is minimal today, partly because drone attacks make communications difficult and risky.[62] Moreover, the relationship is reportedly strained because of the Haqqanis' ties to the Pakistani state—an enemy of al-Qaeda. Pakistani authorities have conducted a number of raids on Haqqani compounds that house al-Qaeda men and supplies, but Haqqani fighters are often left untouched. This prompted al-Qaeda to grow gradually closer to militants in South Waziristan, such as those led by Baitullah and later Hakimullah Mehsud, who are also at war with the Pakistani government.[63]

It is hard to determine exactly how the Haqqani Network fits ideologically with the al-Qaeda organization. Former and current Haqqani Network commanders say that their movement is closer to the Quetta Shura's nationalist rhetoric than al-Qaeda's vision of global jihad, but some members of the group espouse al-Qaeda-like language. The Haqqanis have avoided the anti-Pakistan rhetoric common to al-Qaeda and the TTP. In June 2006, Jalaluddin Haqqani's office released a letter arguing that attacking Pakistan "is not our policy. Those who agree with us are our friends and those who do not agree and [continue to wage] an undeclared war against Pakistan are neither our friends nor shall we allow them in our ranks."[64] Sirajuddin Haqqani has gone further, explaining in an interview that he opposed "any attempt by Muslims to launch attacks in non-Muslim countries."[65] In May 2009, he argued to two French journalists: "It is a mistake to think that al-Qaeda and the Taliban are pursuing the same aim. al-Qaeda is trying to spread its influence throughout the world. This does not interest us. The Taliban's aim is to liberate Afghanistan from foreign troops."[66]

However, former Haqqani Network commanders say the movement is unlikely to break ties with al-Qaeda unless it is forced to do so by military or diplomatic pressure.[67] It is unclear whether all Haqqani Network commanders agree with Sirajuddin's efforts to separate the group from al-Qaeda. Mullah Sangin, an important field commander, said in an interview with as-Sahab, al-Qaeda's media arm: "We do not see any difference between Taliban and al-Qaeda, for we all belong to the religion of Islam. Sheikh Usama has pledged allegiance to Amir Al-Mumineen [Mullah Muhammad Omar] and has reassured his leadership again and again. There is no difference between us."[68] (It should be noted, however, that in speaking to al-Qaeda's media, he is unlikely to go into details about differences in strategy.) Sangin has often played a diplomatic role among competing militants, attempting to broker conflicts between Baitullah Mehsud and Mullah Nazir and serving as an interlocutor between the Afghan Taliban led by Mullah Omar and militants in North Waziristan.[69]

New York Times journalist David Rohde, who was kidnapped by Haqqani supporters and held captive in North Waziristan for seven months before his escape, argued that he "did not fully understand how extreme many of the Taliban had become."

Before the kidnapping, I viewed the organization as a form of "Al Qaeda lite," a religiously motivated movement primarily focused on controlling Afghanistan.

Living side by side with the Haqqanis' followers, I learned that the goal of the hard-line Taliban was far more ambitious. Contact with foreign militants in the tribal areas appeared to have deeply affected many young Taliban fighters. They wanted to create a fundamentalist Islamic emirate with Al Qaeda that spanned the Muslim world.[70]

The Haqqani Network: Tactics and Strategy

The Haqqani Network has shown more sophistication and daring than other insurgent outfits in Afghanistan, most strikingly in a series of high-profile assaults in urban centers. The first such operation was a raid on the luxury Serena Hotel in Kabul in early 2008. In subsequent months the group undertook similar attacks, many of which were near-simultaneous assaults on multiple prominent targets. Other attacks in Kabul included an attempt to assassinate President Hamid Karzai, two separate car-bomb strikes against the Indian Embassy, and a simultaneous raid on various government offices. Typically, foreign militants participate in these assaults.[71] In particular, the Haqqani Network employs what it calls the "Hamza brigade," a team of operatives who organize and deploy suicide attackers.[72] Pakistani militants such as Mullah Nazir and Sadiq Noor, and occasionally Arab groups, do most of the recruiting and training of suicide bombers before passing them on to the Haqqanis.[73]

In 2009, the network began launching similar attacks in smaller, less well-guarded urban centers, including Gardez in Paktiya province, Khost city, and Pul-i-Alam in Logar province. In an interview with the Taliban's magazine *Al-Samoud*, Haqqani commander Mawlawi Noor Kasim explained that the purpose of such assaults was "to show the enemy the extent of the mujahideen's ability to operate and carry out military attacks in the heart of the city, and our ability to strike directly at the military and government command centers."[74]

In rural areas, the Haqqani Network relies on roadside bombs and hit-and-run tactics, much like the Taliban. Unlike the Taliban, however, it does not have an extensive shadow government apparatus in the areas it controls. In parts of Ghazni and Helmand provinces, for instance, the Taliban have full-blown administrations in place, with taxation, rudimentary development work, and a judiciary. Most areas of Haqqani control lack such institutions, but in parts of Loya Paktiya the group has been known to employ Islamic judges to adjudicate disputes.[75]

The Haqqanis and the Pakistani State

The Haqqanis have had a long relationship with the ISI, beginning during the anti-Soviet insurgency when Jalaluddin was a favored ISI (and CIA) commander. This relationship continues today; Pakistani intelligence officials reportedly see the Haqqanis as a valuable asset for promoting their interests in Afghanistan. For instance, a car bombing at the Indian Embassy in Kabul in the summer of 2008 was a joint operation between ISI operatives and Haqqani fighters, according to Afghan and U.S. intelligence officials. The attack specifically targeted two senior Indian officials, including the defense attaché, who was killed. ISI officials provided detailed intelligence to Haqqani operatives about the Indian officials' route and time of arrival. The suicide bomber reportedly timed his detonation precisely for the moment when the defense attaché arrived at the embassy gates.[76]

Jalaluddin Haqqani summed up Pakistan's motives for supporting militants in Afghanistan in an interview he gave just as the Taliban regime was falling in 2001:

> On Pakistan's Eastern border is India—Pakistan's perennial enemy. With the Taliban government in Afghanistan, Pakistan has an unbeatable 2,300 km strategic depth, which even President Pervez Musharraf has proudly proclaimed. Does Pakistan really want a new government, which will include pro-India people in it, thereby wiping out this strategic depth?[77]

Those associated with the Haqqani Network, and U.S. intelligence officials, say that ISI support of the Haqqanis is neither direct nor straightforward. Figures associated with Pakistani intelligence have provided small amounts of funding and training to Haqqani Network fighters, but their biggest role is providing a safe haven and intelligence.[78]

According to current and former Haqqani Network fighters, officials associated with the ISI tip off Sirajuddin before raids on Haqqani compounds in Miram Shah. Haqqani fighters then gather important documents and flee to mountain hideouts, where they wait until it is safe to return. The system is imperfect for some; the raids often net weapons and occasionally provide intelligence that leads to the capture or death of al-Qaeda figures, which has caused tensions between the Haqqani Network and al-Qaeda.[79] Nonetheless, the relationship allows the Haqqanis an invaluable safe haven that leaves the group's operational commanders sometimes seeming more amused than frightened by the Pakistani army.[80]

The Haqqani Network's safe haven in North Waziristan allows the leadership to avoid U.S. military operations in Afghanistan (excepting cross-border drone strikes), but it also creates complications. Former and current Haqqani Network fighters complain about Pakistan's power over the group—and the precarious state in which it leaves them.[81] The spate of arrests of Taliban leaders in Pakistan in the winter of 2010 illustrates this position. Pakistan has even arrested a number of high-ranking Haqqani commanders, including Bakhti Jan, over the years. Almost all of these figures were later released, but the arrests serve as a potent reminder of Pakistan's power over the movement. In an interview, a Haqqani commander claimed that "Pakistan can pull the rug out from under us at any moment."[82]

Hafiz Gul Bahadur and the Tribal Militants

Besides those in the Haqqani Networks, Hafiz Gul Bahadur is the most important Pakistani militant leader in North Waziristan. He is believed to be around forty-five years old and is from the Mada Khel clan of the Uthmanzai Wazir tribe, which is based in the mountains between Miram Shah and the border with Afghanistan. He is a resident of the village of Lowara and a descendant of the Faqir of Ipi, a legendary fighter known for his innovative insurrection against British occupation in the 1930s and 1940s.[83] Bahadur is a cleric and studied at a Deobandi madrassa in the Punjabi city of Multan. Bahadur fought in Afghanistan during the civil war that followed the Soviet withdrawal and upon returning to North Waziristan became a political activist in the Islamist party Jamiat Ulema-e-Islam (Fazel ur-Rahman), or JUI-F.[84]

He rose to prominence in 2004 following Pakistani military operations in North Waziristan and coordinates closely with the Haqqanis on both strategy and operations in Afghanistan.[85] Today, Bahadur has more than fifteen hundred armed men under his direct command.

Strategy and Relationships

Bahadur is a pragmatist, maintaining constructive relations with a host of militants in North Waziristan and beyond while avoiding confrontation with the Pakistani state that might initiate a powerful crackdown. He has entered alliances with Baitullah Mehsud and his successors—leaders of the anti-Pakistan TTP—but carefully refrained from provoking a harsh backlash from the government. Not surprisingly, Bahadur's tightrope walk parallels that of the Haqqanis, who are favorites of the ISI and with whom he is co-located. Like the Haqqanis, Bahadur focuses his military efforts on U.S. and NATO forces in Afghanistan.

Bahadur's relationship with Taliban militants in other FATA agencies is complex. Although he led North Waziristan fighters against Pakistani security forces in 2006 and 2008, he also signed two peace agreements with the Pakistani government, and then proceeded not to fully implement either.[86] Bahadur has moved in and out of coalitions with other Pakistani Taliban elements but always aimed to maintain productive relationships with them. Most recently, he left a coalition of anti-Pakistan militants in 2009 after the death of Baitullah Mehsud but still offered safe haven to Mehsud fighters fleeing Pakistani government operations in South Waziristan.

The TTP, commonly known as the Pakistani Taliban, was formed in December 2007 as a coalition to unite militant groups across the FATA and in settled areas of Khyber-Pukhtunkhwa (known previously as the North-West Frontier Province NWFP).[87] At its formation, Baitullah Mehsud of South Waziristan was named emir and Bahadur his deputy. The alliance was somewhat surprising because Bahadur maintained a strong relationship with Baitullah's most important rival from South Waziristan, Mullah Nazir. Moreover, Bahadur was frustrated with Uzbek militants backed by Baitullah, many of whom relocated to areas near Mir Ali in North Waziristan after being evicted from Nazir's territory in South Waziristan. In addition, although the TTP was founded as an explicitly anti-Pakistan alliance, Bahadur began negotiations with Pakistan almost as soon as the coalition was announced.[88] Not surprisingly, he did not stay in the TTP very long, leaving in July 2008, whereupon he and Nazir created a separate alliance opposed to Baitullah's insistence on fighting Pakistani government forces.[89] Some reports suggest that the Bahadur-Nazir coalition was backed by the Haqqanis as a way to mitigate the power of Baitullah Mehsud.[90] Yet even the new anti-Mehsud alliance did not last long. In February 2009—at the prodding of Sirajuddin Haqqani—Baitullah Mehsud, Mullah Nazir, and Hafiz Gul Bahadur announced the formation of the Shura Ittihad-ul-Mujahideen (SIM), or Council of United Mujahideen.[91] The SIM was designed to end hostilities among the factions, and it reportedly included an agreement that pardoned all parties for past wrongs.[92] The agreement was holding in June 2009 when forces loyal to Bahadur attacked a military convoy in North Waziristan that was supporting Pakistan's South Waziristan operations against Mehsud.[93] Such attacks on key logistical routes into South Waziristan severely threaten the viability of Pakistani operations against Mehsud-dominated TTP strongholds because there are very few roads in and out of Mehsud territory. Recent reports suggest, however, that the SIM became defunct after the death of Baitullah Mehsud in August 2009, and there have been no reports of major violence between Bahadur's forces and Pakistani troops since.[94]

Bahadur has hedged his bets since the June 2009 convoy attack and seems to have largely allowed Pakistani troops to pass through North Waziristan, while simultaneously offering anti-Pakistan South Waziristan militants safe haven in North Waziristan. It is unclear exactly how Baitullah Mehsud's death affected relations between Bahadur and the Mehsud elements led by Baitullah. Some sources suggest that the SIM alliance collapsed after Baitullah was killed, while others suggest that his death did not damage relations because Baitullah's successor and cousin, Hakimullah, is considered close to Bahadur.[95] (Hakimullah was believed killed in a January 2010 drone strike, though the Tehrik-i-Taliban Pakistan has denied that he is dead.)

Bahadur's most important commander is Maulana Sadiq Noor of the Daur tribe. Sadiq Noor is around forty-five years old and has had close contacts with the Afghan Taliban since 1996, when they formed the government in Afghanistan. Like Bahadur, Sadiq Noor is based near Miram Shah, where he directs the Mamba-ul-Uloom madrassa, originally built by Jalaluddin Haqqani to support the Afghan jihad against the Soviet occupation in the 1980s. The madrassa and a neighboring housing complex served as Sadiq Noor's headquarters until a U.S. drone strike in September 2008.[96] Although the strike did not kill Sadiq Noor, there were conflicting reports that either nine of his family members or nine members of the Haqqani family were killed in the attack.[97] Such confusion is understandable, considering Sadiq Noor's close connections with both Jalaluddin and Sirajuddin Haqqani and the shared legacy of the Mamba-ul-Uloom compound. Sadiq Noor has about eight hundred fighters in his group.

Sadiq Noor's right-hand man in North Waziristan is Saeed Khan Daur, who plays something of a *consigliere* role. Saeed Khan is also from Miram Shah. Although he is younger than either Sadiq Noor or Bahadur—he is thirty-three or thirty-four—Saeed Khan has a university degree and is known as a computer expert. Rumors suggest that his code name is Aryana, but he is rarely seen and avoids the media.[98]

Maulana Abdul Khaliq Haqqani is another of Bahadur's commanders, also of the Daur tribe. He is based in Miram Shah and is reported to have around five hundred armed men in his group. Abdul Khaliq follows Bahadur's delicate balancing act between TTP militants and the Pakistani government. Nonetheless, local actors expect that Abdul Khaliq would support militant resistance to the Pakistani army in the face of a full-scale incursion.[99]

Wahidullah Wazir leads a militant group of two hundred Wazir tribesmen around Miram Shah. The Wahidullah group is involved in cross-border attacks in Afghanistan but also conducted operations against the Pakistani military in 2006 and 2008. Similarly, Halim Khan Daur, a thirty-five-year-old militant based near Mir Ali who leads about 150 men, is primarily involved in cross-border attacks on NATO forces but also actively engaged the Pakistani army in 2006 and 2008.[100]

A man referred to locally as Buddah (old man) has been appointed by Gul Bahadur as the head of the Mir Ali area. Buddah, who reportedly has been a supporter of the Afghan Taliban since 1996, closely toes Gul Bahadur's political line. He avoids fighting the Pakistan Army and has clashed with Rasool Khan, a rival of Gul Bahadur's. Buddah has earned a local reputation as an enforcer as well and reportedly beheaded suspected American spies.[101]

Another Bahadur ally in North Waziristan is Saifullah Wazir, a local Uthmanzai Wazir based near Shawal, a notorious hideout for foreign militants in North Waziristan. He is very close to Bahadur and represented him for the 2006 peace agreement between militants and the Pakistani government. He reportedly has four hundred men in his militia, many of whom are active against U.S. and NATO forces in Afghanistan. He is also known to fight the Pakistani army.[102]

A variety of militant groups in North Waziristan do not operate under Bahadur's direct leadership, for either personal or political reasons. One is led by a Wazir tribesman from Miram Shah named Zanjir, who focuses attacks on U.S. and NATO forces in Afghanistan. Unlike Bahadur and most other militants in the region who trace their political roots to the JUI-F faction, Zanjir is politically affiliated with Jamaat-e-Islami (JI) and Gulbuddin Hekmatyar's Hizb-i Islami.[103]

Rasool Khan Daur runs an independent militia around Mir Ali, where he is a schoolteacher. Bahadur appointed Khan head of the Mir Ali bazaar area but removed him in 2009, after which Khan started his own militant group. It now has between 120 and 150 men. Khan's group is known for its extensive criminal activities, which may have prompted his dismissal by Bahadur. The group's militants do not strike U.S. and NATO forces in Afghanistan but are known to target Pakistani security forces and installations in North Waziristan.

One of the more important independent militant leaders is Maulana Manzoor Daur. His support base is Eidak, a village near Mir Ali on the Mir Ali-Miram Shah road. He reportedly has nearly three hundred fighters under his command and is widely believed to have a strong support base among foreign militants. This support created tension with Bahadur and Sadiq Noor after they tried to evict some foreign militants from North Waziristan in 2006. Manzoor's militia fights both in Afghanistan against U.S. and NATO forces and in Pakistan against the Pakistani army.[104]

One other independent militant group in North Waziristan is led by Haq Nawaz Daur, a forty-five-year-old religious scholar from the Daur tribe. He operates near Mir Ali, hails from the nearby village of Aisori, and has very good relations with foreign militants who have worked in the area, especially Uzbeks. This has similarly caused tension with Sadiq Noor and Bahadur. Haq Nawaz avoids fighting the Pakistani army and is reported to have about three hundred men under his command.

Jaish-e Muhammad (JeM) was established in 1999 by Mawlawi Masood Azhar, after splitting from the venerable Pakistani militant group Harakat-ul-Mujahideen (HUM). The traditionally Punjabi group has established an outpost in Miram Shah that is led by Asmatullah Mowia, who is in his early thirties. JeM is involved in fighting against the Pakistan state and has been implicated in several major terrorist attacks in the Pakistani heartland. The group reportedly has close links with the Qari Hussain faction of the anti-Pakistan militant TTP.[105]

The Formation of a Taliban Alliance

In January 2012, a pamphlet surfaced in North and South Waziristan announcing the formation of a "leadership council" comprising the leaders of four Pakistani insurgent groups—the TTP, Gul Bahadur's group, the Haqqani Network, and Mullah Nazir's faction—plus the Afghan Taliban. The aim of the alliance was reportedly to merge the Taliban forces so that they could effectively fight American and NATO forces in Afghanistan and Pakistan. Taliban militants have admitted that fighting against the American and NATO forces in Afghanistan and against the Pakistani Army in Pakistan separately and independently is difficult, and they have suffered major setbacks because of their divisions.

The militant leaders reportedly discussed forming the council for the first time at a November 27, 2011, meeting in Wana, South Waziristan. The confab was reportedly attended by more than a hundred militants, including notable figures such as Abu Yahya al-Libi of al-Qaeda, Sirajuddin Haqqani from the Haqqani Network, Wali ur Rehman, and Mullah Nazir.

The attendees decided that an alliance of the mujahideen groups active in South and North Waziristan was direly needed, and they agreed that Mullah Omar would be the supreme leader of the combined groups. The leaders also announced that the official aim of the combined Taliban is to fight the "infidels" in Afghanistan and other countries where Muslims are being brutalized. They urged local Taliban groups to solve their disputes with one another as soon as possible.

The new alliance does not have a formal name, but participants reportedly prefer the name Ittihad ul-Mujahideen al-Alami over Ittihad ul-Mujahideen Muslimeen because of its international connotations.

Local residents and militants reported that the second meeting of the Taliban groups took place in Datta Khel, North Waziristan, between December 11 and 13 and was attended by as many as three hundred militants.

Maulana Gul Nasib of Nifaz-e-Islam said during the second meeting that he had been designated by Hakimullah Mehsud to hold talks with the Pakistani government to bring peace back to North Waziristan. He said that Hakimullah Mehsud's demands include compensating people whose houses were destroyed in military operations in South Waziristan, the release of all Taliban militants in Pakistani custody, and the withdrawal of all charges against TTP militants.

There are still numerous disputes among militants. During the meeting, the TTP and Haqqani Network argued over the TTP's seizure of an old Haqqani base in Kurram Agency. And Haqqani leaders decided to hold a jirga to resolve the differences between the Tehrik-e-Islami Taliban and the TTP in Kurram Agency. That brokerage led to Tehrik-e-Islami Taliban chief Fazal Saeed Haqqani agreeing in November 2011 to open three roads that he had previously closed to TTP militants in exchange for being named the new TTP Emir in Kurram.

The second round of meetings between the Tehrik-e-Islami Taliban Pakistan and the Haqqani Jirga took place on December 5, 2011. At that meeting, Maulana Gul Nasib Shah, head of the Tehrik Nifaz-e-Islam Khyber Pakhtunkhwa (KPK), claimed that members of the Quetta Shura had deposited ten million rupees into a fund established for the new alliance. A senior commander of the TTP chapter in Karak District of KPK Province, Maulana Silah Jan, confirmed the fund's existence and expressed hope for a peace deal between the Pakistani government and TTP militants. Such a deal should be first confined to South Waziristan, he said, and could later be extended to other FATA agencies.

The alliance has not eliminated the fundamental disagreement with the Taliban movement in North Waziristan: whether or not to attack the Pakistani state. That debate continues to rage, even inside the traditionally anti-Pakistan TTP.[106]

Formation of the Shura Marakaba

In mid-December 2011, the four main militant groups in North and South Waziristan formed a five-member shura to look after the affairs of the local militant and civilian population in the two agencies of

Waziristan. Every group has one representative in the five-member Shura Marakaba, except the TTP, which has two members. One represents Wali Rehman Mehsud, and the other represents Hakimullah Mehsud. The names of the five members in the Shura Marakaba are:

1. Maulvi Azmatullah, representing the Wali Rehman group of the TTP
2. Noor Sayed, representing the Hakimullah Mehsud group of the TTP
3. Saeedullah, representing the Haqqani Network
4. Maulana Safdar Hayat, representing the Hafiz Gul Bahadur group
5. Amir Humza, who was representing Maulvi Nazir until he was killed in a U.S. drone strike on March 13, 2012, in the Birmal area of Wana, along with six other militants

Foreign Militants

In addition to his tribal troops, Haq Nawaz works closely with an Arab faction led by Abu Kasha, an Iraqi jihadist who has been based near Mir Ali since 2002. Abu Kasha, whose real name is Abdur Rehman, lives in Mir Ali with his wife and sons.

Abu Kasha is an interesting figure because he has not always cooperated with mainstream al-Qaeda. He left the group in 2005 after disagreeing with its increasingly Egyptian leadership, notably Ayman al-Zawahiri. Although Abu Kasha retains strong ties to the organization, he founded an independent group called Jaish al-Mahdi, which reportedly has 250 to 300 followers, including local Daur tribesmen, Uzbeks, Chechens, Tajiks, and Turkmen. Abu Kasha has very close links with members of the Islamic Movement of Uzbekistan (IMU) and its splinter group, the Islamic Jihad Union (IJU).[107]

Abu Kasha has worked hard to integrate himself into the local society and is now widely regarded as a local leader. He is known in the region for attending every funeral and marriage ceremony around Mir Ali. Some of Abu Kasha's local supporters even consider him a saint (*pir*) as a result of a 2006 incident in which he took shelter in the home of a local Pashtun during a Pakistani military operation. Upon leaving, he promised the owner that his house would not be destroyed, after which Pakistani troops tried repeatedly but failed to bring down the house with dynamite. Since then, locals in Mir Ali have approached Abu Kasha to purchase amulets in hopes of resolving their problems— with profits promised to be used for the jihad against U.S. and NATO forces in Afghanistan. Abu Kasha also serves as a local judge, mediating disputes for a substantial fee of between 20,000 and 500,000 rupees (up to almost $6,000).[108] Those reluctant to pay are compelled to do so by Abu Kasha's well-armed militiamen, who assert that the money is used for the fight in Afghanistan. Abu Kasha has recently played an important role supporting TTP militants fleeing the fighting in South Waziristan.[109]

Abu Kasha is not on good terms with Maulana Sadiq Noor, Hafiz Gul Bahadur's powerful commander. Sadiq Noor objects to Abu Kasha's prominent role in Mir Ali, particularly his intercession in tribal customs and dispute resolution. Like many militants in the FATA, Abu Kasha has become very security-conscious, especially after an October 31, 2008, drone strike in which he was almost killed. He now moves at the sound of a drone and does not stay in any one place for more than a few days.[110]

al-Qaeda

Foreign militants in North Waziristan are based mostly in Mir Ali and Miram Shah, near the border with Afghanistan. Abu Kasha is in Mir Ali, as is Najmiddin Jalolov, leader of the Islamic Jihad Union. U.S. drone strokes have targeted al-Qaeda figures in North Waziristan and killed a number of senior leaders, such as Abu Laith al-Libi and Abu Jihad al-Masri. On December 8, 2009, a U.S. drone targeted Saleh al-Somali, an al-Qaeda member charged with planning attacks abroad.[111] The Arabs of al-Qaeda are said to live in the Shawal mountains, Mir Ali, and the Miram Shah area.

al-Qaeda's propaganda also illustrates the importance of North Waziristan to its operations in Afghanistan and Pakistan. In the eighty-nine al-Qaeda propaganda videos released from 2004 to 2009 illustrating al-Qaeda "attacks" in Afghanistan, forty-seven incidents occurred in Loya Paktiya, the Haqqani heartland just across the border from North Waziristan.[112] Although al-Qaeda fighters may not have conducted the violence portrayed, the geographic focus demonstrates the group's relationship with the Haqqani Network and its ability to operate in the region.

Islamic Jihad Union

The Islamic Jihad Union's most important base in North Waziristan is in Mir Ali, where it receives local support from a variety of Pakistani tribal commanders. The IJU's stated purpose is to overthrow the secular government of Islam Karimov in Uzbekistan. In the past five years, however, it has organized a variety of attacks and provided training for the so-called Sauerland cell, which planned to attack U.S. military bases and other targets in Germany in 2007. The IJU is led by Najmiddin Kamolitdinovich Jalolov (emir), Suhayl Fatilloevich Buranov (deputy emir), and Muhammad Fatih.[113]

The IJU was founded in Pakistan in 2002 as a splinter of the Islamic Movement of Uzbekistan. Today the group has 150 to 200 members, most of whom are Uzbek, but it includes Tajik, Kyrgyz, and Kazakh fighters. The group is known to have strong relationships with Chechen fighters in the FATA and has produced a host of propaganda material in Turkish.[114]

Several German citizens were recently killed operating with the IJU in the FATA.

Eric Breininger was killed by Pakistani security forces in April 2010 after a firefight with troops at a checkpoint.[115] A month later, Pakistani police arrested a German national named Rami Mackenzie, who was reportedly an expert bombmaker.[116] On October 4, 2010, American drones targeted a house containing as many as eight German citizens who were reportedly planning Mumbai-style attacks in France, Britain, and Germany.[117]

Tehrik Islami Britain Group

In March 2010, at a meeting of Punjabi Taliban in the Khider Khel village of Mir Ali tehsil (*tehsil* is analogous to the word *county*), a man named Jabbar from Sargodha district was chosen as amir of a new group, known as the Tehrik Islami Britain (TIB). Long active in jihadi movements, Jabbar and his wife are reportedly both British citizens. Jabbar was first affiliated with Lashkar-e-Taiba, but later Jaish-e-Muhammad, before quitting it as well. He then rallied his own group, known as al-Furqan, from disillusioned members of Jaish-e-Muhammad, Harakat ul-Mujahedeen, Lashkar-e-Taiba, and Lashkar-i-Jhangvi.

Jabbar reportedly has worked with the Afghan Taliban since 1994, when they first appeared in Afghanistan and fought against American and NATO forces when they invaded Afghanistan in October 2001.

The TIB reportedly has several other British citizens in leadership roles. Azam Mir is a close childhood friend of Jabbar's from Punjab Province, who often travels with a friend named Adam. Another Briton named Abdullah resides in Punjab and is responsible for training forces to fight in Afghanistan. A fifth, named Mujahid Ahmad, focuses on outreach with other militants and recruitment.

Jabbar was killed in an American drone attack on July 8, 2010, in Mir Ali, which has dramatically weakened and divided the group.[118]

CONCLUSION

North Waziristan is the most important center of jihadist militancy in the FATA today, in large measure because of the impunity with which militants in the agency have operated. Even as the Pakistani government confronted anti-Pakistan militant coalitions in other regions, it largely ignored fighters in North Waziristan. The Haqqani Network and Hafiz Gul Bahadur have been politically sensitive and very careful to avoid upsetting the Pakistani authorities but nonetheless occasionally clashed with the Pakistani government. Both the Haqqanis and Bahadur have worked closely with TTP elements from South Waziristan. In late 2009 and into 2010, they sheltered fighters from the Mehsud group fleeing the Pakistani military in South Waziristan. The Haqqanis clearly have strong ties with al-Qaeda militants operating in and around North Waziristan, and they likely support al-Qaeda's goal of reestablishing a caliphate. Nonetheless, the network's leaders seem firmly focused on Afghanistan. Although they tolerate and may tacitly support al-Qaeda's attacks elsewhere, the Haqqanis are unlikely to expand their field of operations as long as the current leadership is in charge.

Drone strikes have been a compelling tool against militants in North Waziristan, though their impact on local public opinion is difficult to discern. The current campaign of drone attacks frightens North Waziristan's militants and perhaps presages more aggressive Pakistani military action in the region. The United States promptly halted drone strikes in South Waziristan when the Pakistani military began major operations there in October 2009, but intensified drone attacks farther north. These hints of coordination raise the possibility that the uptick in drone strikes in North Waziristan is designed to lay the groundwork for future Pakistani operations.

Whatever the signs of a more aggressive approach toward militants, it is unlikely that Pakistan will take decisive action to crush the Haqqani Network. The Haqqanis understand Pakistan's strategic thinking—including its extreme focus on India—and will continue efforts to forestall a Pakistani crackdown by illustrating the group's usefulness against that enemy. The arrests of Mullah Baradar, the Quetta Shura's second-in-command, and other Afghan Taliban leaders in the first months of 2010 suggest that Pakistani state policy toward militant networks may be changing, but it is unclear by how much or whether the Haqqanis would even be included in a Pakistani crackdown on Mullah Omar and the Quetta Shura. Indeed, the North Waziristan militants remain enigmas precisely because they are so powerful militarily but creative politically. They show deep pragmatism and yet have clearly been influenced by al-Qaeda's ideology. They are likely to negotiate with the Afghan government, but there are no indications they are in the mood to cut a deal. The combination of military power, strategic utility to Pakistan, and political savvy suggests that North Waziristan's militant groups will be Pakistan's most difficult to dismantle.

Notes

1. Ruttig, Thomas, "Loya Paktiya's Insurgency: The Haqqani Network as an Autonomous Entity," in Antonio Giustozzi, ed., *Decoding the New Taliban* (Columbia University Press, New York, 2009), pp. 66, 75.

2. Safdar Daur (local journalist in Miram Shah), SKM Interview, July 12, 2009, Peshawar.

3. David Rohde, "You Have Atomic Bombs, But We Have Suicide Bombers," *New York Times*, Oct. 20, 2009, http://www.nytimes.com/glogin?URI=http://www.nytimes.com/2009/10/20/world/asia/20hostage.html&OQ=_rQ3D1&OP=14cba970Q2FQ24ut_Q24d8ToL88sVQ24VIIQ5DQ24qIQ24VIQ24u8LQ7DdQ24JoXJQ24VIy8osJQ5EtSysQ3AQ7D.

4. Scott Shane and Eric Schmitt, "C.I.A. Deaths Prompt Surge in U.S. Drone Strikes," *New York Times*, Jan. 22, 2010, http://www.nytimes.com/2010/01/23/world/asia/23drone.html.

5. Peter Bergen and Katherine Tiedemann, "The Year of the Drone," New America Foundation, http://counterterrorism.newamerica.net/drones (as of Mar. 22, 2010).

6. Numerous Afghan intelligence officials and Haqqani Network operatives, AG Interviews.

7. Steve Coll, *Ghost Wars* (Penguin Books, New York, 2004), p. 157.

8. Mustafa Hamid (Abu Walid al-Masri), "Jalal al-Din Haqqani, a Legend in the History of the Afghanistan Jihad," *Al-Sumud* magazine in English, http://www.ansar1.info/showthread.php?t=20201.

9. Former Haqqani associates Hanif Shah Hosseini, Malim Jan, Madde Khan Hajji Zadran, Arsala Rahmani, interviews with author AG.

10. Jere Van Dyk, author BF interview, Mar. 17, 2010.

11. Sirajuddin Haqqani, interview with AfPax Insider, April 7, 2009, http://www.afpax.com/index.php/post/7478/Talibans_Siraj_Haqqani_Shrugs_Off_5m_Bounty. Malim Jan and Ghani Muhammad, commanders who were close to Sirajuddin in Miram Shah, gave similar information, saying he is under thirty years old.

12. Jere Van Dyk, BF interview, Mar. 17, 2010.

13. Sirajuddin Haqqani, AG interview, October 2009.

14. Ghani Muhammad (Haqqani commander), AG interview, February 2010.

15. Former Haqqani commander, AG interview, May 2009, Paktiya province; Farhat Taj, "Target: Terror Secretariat," *News International*, Apr. 4, 2009, http://www.thenews.com.pk/editorial_detail.asp?id=170708.

16. Former Haqqani commanders, AG interviews, May 2009, Paktiya province; February 2010, Kabul.

17. Rohde, "You Have Atomic Bombs."

18. This typology is based on numerous interviews with current and former Haqqani Network figures.

19. Former Haqqani commanders, AG interviews, May 2009, Paktiya province; February 2010, Kabul.

20. Adnan Daur and Inam Wazir, Gul Bahadur Group, May 2011, Bannu, Pakistan, MKM interview.

21. Haqqani commanders Ghani Muhammad, Malim Jan, AG interviews, February 2010. Jan Baz Zadran is believed to have been killed in a drone strike in 2011.

22. Former Haqqani commander, AG interview, May 2009, Paktiya province.

23. Chris Lawrence, "Son of Notorious Insurgent Leader Arrested," *CNN*, Dec. 24, 2010, http://articles.cnn.com/2010-12-24/world/pakistan.haqqani.arrest_1_haqqani-network-miram-shah-north-waziristan?_s=PM:WORLD.

24. Tahir Khan, "Dialogue with the US: Afghan Taliban Share 'Peace' Blueprint with Pakistan," *Express Tribune*, Jan. 25, 2012.

25. Combined Joint Task Force-82 Press Release, "Coalition Forces Confirm Darim Sedgai Death," CJTF-82 Jan. 26, 2008, www.cjtf.com/press-releases-manmenu-326/272-coalition-forces-confirm-darim-sedgai-death.html. U.S. forces captured Mali Khan in 2012.

26. Author AG has sent Afghan associates to interview Sirajuddin, and they have reported that he spends considerable time in Loya Paktiya, and particularly Paktika. This might be partly explained by the CIA drone campaign in the tribal areas, which makes it dangerous for Haqqani to spend too much time there.

27. Sangin is likely now living in Karachi.

28. Abdel Bari Atwan, *The Secret History of al-Qaeda* (University of California Press, Berkeley, CA, 2006).

29. Del Bari Atwan, in Peter Bergen, *The Osama bin Laden I Know* (Free Press, New York, 2006), p. 236.

30. For Jalaluddin "declared for the Taliban," see Coll, *Ghost Wars*, p. 293.

31. Former Jalaluddin associates Arsala Rahmani, Hanif Shah Hosseini, Khan Jaji, interviews, March–May 2009.

32. ISAF intelligence official, AG interview, October 2008.

33. Sirajuddin Haqqani, AG interview, October 2009.

34. Ghani Muhammad, AG interview, February 2009.

35. Maulavi Tajmeer, AG interview, February 2010.

36. Muhammad Razaq Yaqubi (Kunduz province chief of police), AG interview, March 2010. There are reports indicating that Inayatullah was killed in a drone strike in 2011.

37. Mullah Beradar (second in command of the Quetta Shura Taliban), AG interview, January 2010; ICRC, AG interview, December 2009; security official from the NGO community who declined to be named, AG interview, February 2010.

38. This description of the Haqqani Network's rise in Logar is based on an interview (AG) with an official from the Afghan security agency NDS, an international security expert based in Kabul, and residents of Logar province, all of whom spoke on the condition of anonymity.

39. Imtiaz Ali, "Baitullah Mehsud—the Taliban's New Leader in Pakistan," Jamestown Terrorism Focus, Jan. 9, 2008, http://www.jamestown.org/single/?no_cache=1&tx_ttnews[tt_news]=4637.

40. Ahmed Rashid, *Descent into Chaos* (Penguin Books, New York, 2008).

41. Ibid., p. 268.

42. Former Haqqani commander, AG interview, May 2009, Paktiya; "Ahmad Noor" (failed suicide bomber), AG interview, May 2009, Kabul.

43. Jane Perlez, "Taliban Leader Flaunts Power Inside Pakistan," *New York Times*, June 2, 2008, http://www.nytimes.com/2008/06/02/world/asia/02pstan.html.

44. Former Haqqani commander, AG interview, May 2009, Paktiya; current commander Ghani Muhammad, AG interview, February 2010.

45. Sirajuddin may have also played a part in the February 2005 cease-fire between Baitullah Mehsud and the Pakistani military, but Haqqani Network associates disagree on the extent of his role.

46. Haqqani commanders Ghani Muhammad, Malim Jan, AG interviews, February 2010, Kabul.

47. Ibid.

48. Ismail Khan, "Islamabad Announces Setting Up of Tribal Council," Dawn.com, July 17, 2006.

49. Ibid.

50. Iqbal Khattak, "Who Is Maulvi Nazeer," *Friday Times*, Mar. 30, 2007.

51. Haqqani commander Ghani Muhammad and a current Haqqani commander who declined to be named, AG interviews, February 2010, Kabul.

52. Journalist Mudassar Shah, interview, February 2010, Peshawar.

53. Zulfiqar Ali, "Taliban Trying to End Tribal Clashes in Kurram," Dawn.com, Sept. 16, 2010.

54. Jere Van Dyk, *In Afghanistan* (Authors' Choice Press, New York, 1983).

55. U.S. military intelligence official, AG interview, October 2008.

56. Ghani Muhammad, AG interview, February 2010.

57. Jamal Ismail, in Bergen, *The Osama bin Laden I Know*, p. 47.

58. For more on the Haqqani relationship with al-Qaeda, see Don Rassler and Vahid Brown, *The Haqqani Nexus and the Evolution of al-Qaeda* (Combating Terrorism Center at West Point, New York, 2011).

59. For Jalaluddin, see Van Dyk, *In Afghanistan*; for bin Laden, see Lawrence Wright, *The Looming Tower* (Knopf, New York, 2006).

60. Ibid.; "Pakistan Busts Tribal Region's Biggest al-Qaeda Base" AFP, Sept. 15, 2005.

61. Ibid.

62. Ghani Muhammad, Malim Jan, AG interviews, February 2010.

63. Ibid.

64. Ismail Khan, "Forces, Militants Heading for Truce," Dawn.com, June 23, 2006, http://www.dawn.com/2006/06/23/top2.htm.

65. Sirajuddin Haqqani, AG interview, May 2009.

66. Nadia Bletry and Eric de Lavarne, "Obama and Bush Are Two Ears of the Same Donkey," *Le Journal du Dimanche*, May 3, 2009.

67. Malim Jan and another former commander who asked to remain anonymous for safety reasons, AG interview, February 2010.

68. Mullah Sangin, interview with As-Sahab, Sept. 17, 2009, http://theunjustmedia. com/Islamic%20Perspectives/sept09/An%20Interview%20with%20 the%20Director%20of%20Military%20Affairs%20of%20Islamic%20 Emirate%20of%20Afghanistan%20for%20Paktika%20province%20Mawlawi- %20Sangeen%20(May%20Allah%20protect%20ohim).htm.

69. Adnan Daur and Inam Wazir, Gul Bahadur Group, May 2011, Bannu, Pakistan, MKM interview.

70. David Rohde, "7 Months 10 Days in Captivity," *New York Times*, Oct. 18, 2009, http://www.nytimes.com/2009/10/18/world/asia/18hostage.html.

71. Official from NDS, the Afghan security agency, AG interview, and author observations of these fighters.

72. Ghani Muhammad, AG interview, February 2010.

73. Ibid.
74. *Al-Sumud* magazine, author (AG) translation.
75. Hanif Shah Hosseini (Khost MP) and Madde Khan Hajji Zadran, AG interviews, May 2009, Paktiya; UNAMA official who declined to be named, AG interview, May 2009, Paktiya.
76. Mark Mazetti and Eric Schmitt, "Pakistanis Aided Attack in Kabul, U.S. Officials Say," *New York Times*, August 1, 2008, http://www.nytimes.com/2008/08/01/world/asia/01pstan.html; Afghan intelligence official, interview with NDS, July 2008.
77. Aslam Khan, "Taliban Warn of Long Guerrilla War," *The News*, Oct. 20, 2001.
78. Haqqani commander, who spoke on condition of anonymity, AG interview, May 2008, Paktiya.
79. Ibid.
80. Rohde, "You Have Atomic Bombs."
81. This has been the case in numerous interviews the author (AG) has conducted with current and former Haqqani Network fighters.
82. Haqqani commander, who spoke on the condition of anonymity, AG interview, May 2008, Paktiya.
83. Sadi Suleiman, "Hafez Gul Bahadur: A Profile of the Leader of the North Waziristan Militants," Jamestown Terrorism Monitor, Apr. 10, 2009, http://www.jamestown.org/programs/gta/single/?tx_ttnews%5Btt_news%5D=34839&tx_ttnews%5BbackPid%5D=412&no_cache=1.
84. Nadeem Yaqoub, "Islamists Cut Cable TV," *Asia Times*, June 27, 2000.
85. Imtiaz Gul, *The Most Dangerous Place* (Viking, New York, 2011).
86. Charlie Szrom, "The Survivalist of North Waziristan: Hafez Gul Bahadur Biography and Analysis," August 6, 2009, http://www.criticalthreats.org/pakistan/survivalist-north-waziristan-Hafez-gul-bahadur-biography-and-analysis#_Edn5.
87. Amir Mir, "The Swelling Force of Extremism," *News International*, Mar. 22, 2009, http://jang.com.pk/thenews/mar2009-weekly/nos-22-03-2009/enc.htm#1.
88. Abbas, Hassan, "A Profile of Tehrik-e Taliban Pakistan," CTC Sentinel 1, no. 2 (January 2008): 1–4, http://belfercenter.ksg.harvard.edu/files/CTC%20Sentinel%20-%20Profile%20of%20Tehrik-i-Taliban%20Pakistan.pdf.
89. "Mehsud Challenged by New Militant Bloc," *Daily Times*, July 2, 2008, http://www.dailytimes.com.pk/default.asp?page=2008/07/02/story_2-7-2008_pg1_4.
90. Gul, *The Most Dangerous Place.*
91. Yousaf Ali, "Taliban Form New Alliance in Waziristan," *News International*, Feb. 23, 2009, http://www.thenews.com.pk/top_story_detail.asp?Id=20512.
92. Mushtaq Yusufzai, "Top Militant Commanders Resolve Rift," *News International*, Feb. 21, 2009, http://www.thenews.com.pk/top_story_detail.asp?Id=20477.
93. Rahimullah Yusufzai, "Army Facing Tough Choice After NWA Ambush," *News International*, June 30, 2009.
94. Sailab Mehsud, "Army Embarks on Rah-i-Nijat Finally," Dawn.com, Oct. 18, 2009, http://www.dawn.com/wps/wcm/connect/dawn-content-library/dawn/news/pakistan/07-curfew-imposed-in-south-waziristan-ahead-of-operation-ha-01.

95. Sailab Mahsud (researcher with the FATA Research Center), interview, Nov. 22, 2009, Dera Ismail Khan.

96. Shamim Shadid, "US Drones Bomb Madrassa in NW," *Nation*, Sept. 9, 2008, http://www.nation.com.pk/pakistan-news-newspaper-daily-english-online/ Politics/09-Sep-2008/US-drones-bomb-madrassa-in-NW.

97. Ibid.

98. Sailab Mahsud (researcher with the Fata Research Center), interview, November 22, 2009, Dera Ismail Khan.

99. Ibid.

100. Ibid.

101. Tahir Wazir, Gul Bahadur Group, October 2011, Bannu, Pakistan, MKM interview.

102. Sailab Mahsud (researcher with the FATA Research Center), interview, Nov. 22, 2009, Dera Ismail Khan.

103. Safdar Daur (local researcher in Miram Shah North Waziristan agency), interview, Dec. 7, 2009, Peshawar.

104. Ibid.

105. Tahir Wazir, Gul Bahadur Group, October 2011, Bannu, Pakistan, MKM interview.

106. Author interview with Associated Press reporter Ishtiaq Mahsud, and Sailab Mahsud, correspondent for the FATA Research Center for South Waziristan Agency in Dera Ismail Khan.

107. Asif Khan Daur (local researcher and resident of MirAli area in North Waziristan Agency), interview, Dec. 8, 2009, Peshawar.

108. Ibid.

109. Ibid.

110. Ibid.

111. Mark Mazetti and Souad Mekhennet, "Qaeda Planner in Pakistan Killed by Drone," *New York Times*, Dec. 11, 2009, http://query.nytimes.com/gst/fullpage. html?res=9C0CE7D81630F931A25751C1A96F9C8B63.

112. Anne Stenersen, "Al-Qaeda's Allies: Explaining the Relationship Between al-Qaeda and Various Factions of the Taliban After 2001," New America Foundation, Apr. 19, 2010.

113. Ronald Sandee, "The Islamic Jihad Union (IJU)," NEFA Foundation, Oct. 14, 2008, http://www.nefafoundation.org/miscellaneous/FeaturedDocs/ nefaijuocto8.pdf.

114. "Islamic Jihad Group of Uzbekistan," Global Security, http://www. globalsecurity.org/security/profiles/islamic_jihad_group_of_uzbekistan. htm.

115. Yassin Musharbash, "German Jihadist Eric Breininger Killed in Pakistan," *Spiegel*, May 3, 2010, http://www.spiegel.de/international/ world/0,1518,692673,00.html.

116. "German al-Qaeda Suspect Nabbed in Pakistan," *United Press International*, June 22, 2010, http://www.upi.com/Top_News/Special/2010/06/22/ German-al-Qaida-suspect-nabbed-in-Pakistan/UPI-10681277226434/.

117. Issam Ahmed, "Pakistan Drone Strike Kills Germans in Response to Europe Terror Plot," *Christian Science Monitor*, Oct. 5, 2010, http://www.csmonitor.

com/World/Asia-South-Central/2010/1005/Pakistan-drone-attacks-kill-Germans-in-response-to-Europe-terror-plot.

118. Interviews with Safdar Hayat Daur, president of Tribal Union of Journalists; Sailab Mahsud, FRC correspondent; and Ishtiaq Mahsud, Associated Press reporter, Dera Ismail Khan, August 2010.

FIVE

The Taliban in South Waziristan

Mansur Khan Mahsud

O F ALL THE tribal agencies and districts of the Federally Administered Tribal Areas (FATA) of northwest Pakistan, few have assumed as much importance for the United States since September 11, 2001, as South Waziristan. Comprising 6,619 square kilometers, or about 2,555 square miles, South Waziristan is the country's southernmost tribal agency and the largest by area.

Following the establishment of Pakistan in 1947, peace largely prevailed in South Waziristan, with the exception of a revolt by a mullah named Noor Mohammad Wazir in the years 1975–76 that was crushed by a military operation. However, the 1978 revolt against the communist coup in neighboring Afghanistan and the subsequent Afghan jihad against invading Soviet occupation forces heavily affected the broader Waziristan region. Tens of thousands of Afghans flooded into refugee camps in Waziristan, some of them training camps for the Afghan mujahideen, or holy warriors.[1] These refugees told the local people about how the Soviets and their Afghan allies insulted and brutalized the Muslim Afghan population, sowing hatred for the Russians and their puppet government in Kabul. Many young men from Waziristan went to Afghanistan to fight against the Soviets, a tendency supported by

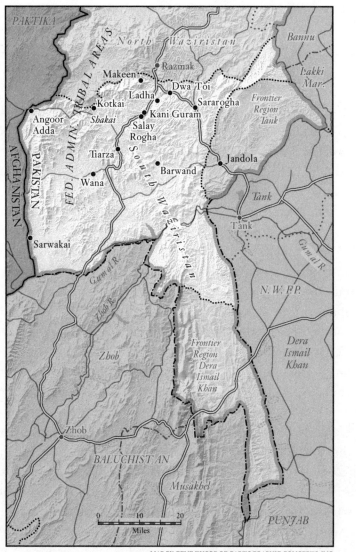

MAP BY GENE THORP OF CARTOGRAPHIC CONCEPTS, INC.

both the Pakistani and American intelligence services, which launched a propaganda program against the Soviet Union to recruit fighters.

The people of South Waziristan are almost all orthodox Sunni Muslims, and the great majority of them are illiterate. Many follow the teachings of clerics who were financially supported by the Pakistani government during the anti-Soviet war.[2] In this period, these religious leaders in Pakistan's tribal regions opened dozens of madrassas, or Islamic schools, where young Mehsud and Wazir tribesmen were indoctrinated to participate in jihad. The madrassas were supported financially by the governments of Persian Gulf countries, especially Saudi Arabia, boosting the stature and authority of the clerics in South Waziristan.[3] Most of these madrassas were connected to Jamiat Ulema-e-Islam (JUI-F), an Islamist political party founded in the 1950s that is popular in the tribal areas.[4] After the Soviet Union withdrew its troops from Afghanistan in 1989, many of the FATA tribesmen who took part in the fight brought the jihadist ideology back to their hometowns in Pakistan. Some of them traveled to Kashmir to fight against the Indian occupation in the predominantly Muslim state. As the Taliban began gaining strength in Afghanistan in 1994, many of the FATA jihadists joined the Afghan movement.[5]

When the Taliban formed a government in Afghanistan in 1996, it was initially somewhat popular in South Waziristan. Tribesmen were impressed with the movement's ability to enforce strict Islamic rule over Afghanistan and to ensure security in the areas it controlled.[6] Some veterans of the anti-Soviet jihad maintained links with the Afghan Taliban, slowly introducing the Taliban's ideology to South Waziristan, but in general between 1996 and fall 2001 residents of the agency didn't have much contact with Afghanistan's Taliban rulers.

The security situation in South Waziristan took a drastic turn when U.S. and NATO forces invaded Afghanistan in October 2001, in the wake of the September 11 terrorist attacks on New York and Washington and the subsequent refusal by the Taliban government to hand over the al-Qaeda leader behind the attacks, Osama bin Laden. Thousands from the Afghan Taliban, the Arab al-Qaeda, and their foreign affiliates—such as groups of Uzbeks, Chechens, and Tajiks—came to South Waziristan looking for refuge and bases to continue their fight against the American and NATO forces occupying Afghanistan.[7] The local tribes, sympathetic to the cause, provided shelter and assistance to the fighters, while local militants who were affiliated with the Afghan Taliban government before September 11—such as Abdullah Mehsud, Baitullah Mehsud, Nek Muhammad, Haji Sharif, and Haji Omar—began to organize local Taliban groups across South Waziristan.[8]

Nek Muhammad, a member of the Ahmadzai Wazir tribe who had joined the Taliban movement in 1993 when he was just 18, was the first head of the Taliban in South Waziristan. He later fought against the Northern Alliance and fought near Bagram air base outside Kabul after the U.S. invasion of Afghanistan.[9] After the fall of the Taliban government in Kabul, Nek Muhammad returned to Wana, South Waziristan, in

December 2001, where he began to organize local Taliban fighters. Having gathered several hundred local Wazirs, he began to launch cross-border attacks in 2003 on American and NATO forces in Afghanistan with the support of veteran mujahideen commanders such as Haji Omar, Haji Sharif, and Maulvi Abbas.[10] Nek Muhammad also provided refuge for fleeing members of the Afghan Taliban, Arab al-Qaeda fighters, and the Uzbeks of the Islamic Movement of Uzbekistan (IMU) led by Tahir Yuldashev.

Under pressure from the U.S. government to act against the mix of militants proliferating in Waziristan and attacking U.S. forces in Afghanistan,[11] the Pakistani military launched its first major operation in Wana in 2004, putting seven thousand troops against the local Taliban fighters and their foreign allies. Nek Muhammad led the militants, assisted by Baitullah Mehsud, Abdullah Mehsud, and their supporters. After several weeks of intense fighting, the Pakistani government was forced to make a peace deal with Nek Muhammad's forces. Under the so-called Shakai agreement, Nek Muhammad agreed to lay down his arms and "register" foreign militants living in the area, while the government promised funding to the local Taliban so the fighters could pay their debts to al-Qaeda.[12] The deal promptly broke down, and Nek Muhammad was killed a few weeks later by a suspected U.S. drone missile while giving an interview by satellite phone to a foreign news organization.[13] The charismatic Nek Muhammad became something of a hero in South Waziristan, the one who defeated the mighty Pakistani army, and thousands from the Mehsud and Wazir tribes alike flocked to South Waziristan to join the Taliban fighters who were already there.

After the death of Nek Muhammad, Haji Omar became the leader of the Wana Taliban in South Waziristan, and he continued to support the presence of Uzbeks and other foreign fighters there.[14] The Uzbeks believed it was more important to fight against the Pakistani government and military than to attack U.S. and NATO targets across the border in Afghanistan. This put them in conflict with the Taliban commander Mullah Nazir, who expelled them and their supporters, Haji Omar and Haji Sharif, by April 2007. The Uzbeks then sought refuge in the Mehsud-dominated areas of South Waziristan, where Abdullah Mehsud and Baitullah Mehsud had organized their own anti-Pakistan, anti-Western Taliban movements.[15] These groups also began to take part in cross-border attacks on U.S. and NATO forces and their Afghan allies from inside Pakistan.[16]

GRIEVANCES OF THE LOCAL POPULATION: THE RISE AND FALL OF THE TALIBAN

Before 2003, tribesmen across South Waziristan were growing frustrated with the inefficient and allegedly corrupt local political administration. Job opportunities were scarce, as were functioning roads, schools, and hospitals. The local political agents and tribal leaders reportedly used schoolhouses and hospitals in Makeen, Ladha, Sararogha, Sarwakai, and Dwa Toi as personal guesthouses for their friends. Tribal elders and their family members received the salaries of the teachers or hospital staff as gifts or bribes. Teachers were paid without performing their duties, hospitals went unstaffed, and doctors and administrators reputedly drove ambulances for personal use.[17] Corruption and bribery were seen as commonplace.

In this atmosphere of frustration, the Taliban swept fully into South Waziristan in 2003. Local tribesmen believed that the Taliban would force doctors and teachers to provide services and would eliminate—or at least reduce—corruption in the agency's political system.[18] For the first year or so, the Taliban put pressure on professionals to improve services. It also dispensed rapid justice, killing or expelling criminals and deterring others who knew that if caught they would face severe punishment, often death.[19] In addition, the Taliban implemented a system of taxing the population to fund the fight against U.S. and NATO forces, and Pakistan's military, in the region. The people of South Waziristan, as orthodox Sunni Muslims, were apparently receptive to the militants' simple message of jihad against Western forces.

However, the Pakistani Taliban factions in South Waziristan made what appears to be a critical strategic error: they attacked tribal structures within the agency, which had held up the pillars of tribal society for generations. About two hundred of the maliks, or leaders, of the Mehsud and Ahmadzai Wazir tribes, who had acted as bridges between the Pakistani government and the tribes, were killed, forced to leave the area, or made to keep silent.[20] Taliban leaders apparently feared that in the event of conflict between the militants and the Pakistani government tribal elders could form anti-Taliban lashkars and turn the local populations against the militants. Thus, even though the Taliban consolidated power in the first half of the 2000s, it was in fact contributing to its own unpopularity.

As the Taliban's strength grew in South Waziristan, local militant leaders reputedly became arrogant and brutal in their dealings with the tribes; they did not punish Taliban members who committed crimes yet were quick to hand out harsh sentences to others, and they allowed petty thieves to join the movement.[21] In an ironic twist, Taliban commanders were also accused of taking bribes and bribing local political administrators. Additionally, because the movement prompted a crackdown by Pakistan's military, hundreds of thousands were forced to evacuate the area to escape the fighting, creating hostility among the population.[22]

EMERGENCE OF TEHRIK-I-TALIBAN PAKISTAN (TTP)

Over the years, these local Taliban militant groups became so powerful that in December 2007 they formed the Tehrik-i-Taliban Pakistan (TTP), an umbrella organization of dozens of Taliban groups throughout Pakistan, under the initial leadership of Baitullah Mehsud. Maulana Hafiz Gul Bahadur, a North Waziristan–based commander, was elected the first deputy chief, or amir, of the TTP, while Maulana Fazlullah, head of the Taliban in the Swat region of North-West Frontier Province (NWFP, now Khyber-Pukhtunkhwa), was elected general secretary (a position that was created to appease him but has no real function). Bahadur separated from the TTP in 2008 and allied himself with the like-minded Mullah Nazir, because he was not in favor of fighting against the Pakistani government; Baitullah Mehsud wanted to stage major attacks against Pakistani military, government, and civilian targets.[23] In the spring of 2009, however, Bahadur, Nazir, and Baitullah Mehsud formed the Shura Ittihad ul-Mujahideen, or Council of United Mujahideen, an alliance of their three groups, and claimed to have resolved their previous issues.[24] But by the fall of 2009, this union began to splinter after eleven of Nazir's men were killed by Uzbek fighters in Salay Rogha in South Waziristan, and the Baitullah faction, a protector of the Uzbeks, refused to hand over the militants and four Mehsuds involved in the killing.[25]

According to Taliban sources in South Waziristan and the Tank district of NWFP, nearly forty Taliban groups have joined the TTP, popularly known as the Pakistani Taliban. These groups are represented in a TTP shura, or council, based in Miram Shah, the administrative headquarters of North Waziristan. The TTP was created to conduct a coordinated jihad in Afghanistan and to put maximum pressure on U.S. and NATO forces and the Pakistani army; in a bizarre borrowing of NATO's Article 5, the shura decided that if the Pakistani army took action against one of the Taliban groups, it would be considered an attack on all. The TTP has spread its network in all seven agencies of the FATA and in the settled districts of the NWFP: Bannu, Karak, Hangu, Kulachi, Dera Ismail Khan (D.I. Khan), Lakki Marwat, Doaba, Kohat, Dir, Buner, and to some extent Mardan, the Swat Valley, and Shangla district.[26]

The Taliban virtually took over South Waziristan, running their own courts in the agency and collecting taxes from the local population. The Taliban militants also fostered the anti-Shiite ideology of al-Qaeda among Mehsuds and Wazirs—who had not previously engaged in sectarian violence. The TTP has carried out several suicide attacks against Shiites, targeting the Muslim minority sect in D.I. Khan, Hangu, Tank, and the Kurram tribal agency. For example, on February 20, 2009, a suicide bomber affiliated with the TTP killed at least thirty-two Shiites and wounded one hundred others attending the funeral of a slain Shiite leader in D.I. Khan.[27] Qari Hussain, the notoriously anti-Shiite Mehsud Taliban commander and trainer of suicide bombers, is a staunch supporter of the banned anti-Shiite group Sipah-e-Sahaba Pakistan (SSP) in South Waziristan. Another notorious terrorist, Qari Zafar, reputedly a close friend of Qari Hussain, was involved in the suicide attack on the U.S. consulate in Karachi in 2006 and took refuge in South Waziristan.[28] One U.S. diplomat and three Pakistanis were killed in that attack.[29] (Zafar was reportedly killed in a February 2010 drone missile strike in North Waziristan.)

THE STRUCTURE OF THE INSURGENCIES IN SOUTH WAZIRISTAN

The Taliban in South Waziristan draws its members primarily from three Pashtun tribes in the agency: the Ahmadzai Wazirs, the Mehsuds, and the Bhittanis. The presence of foreign fighters has proved controversial within the militant movements, as has the question of whether to target the Pakistani state in addition to U.S. and NATO forces in Afghanistan. The late Baitullah Mehsud and his ideological heirs were generally in favor of attacking Pakistani government and military targets, and offered shelter to Uzbek militants in the region. Mullah Nazir, on the other hand, focuses his Wana-based Taliban forces on fighting Western troops in Afghanistan, and he forcibly expelled Uzbek jihadists in 2007.

AL-QAEDA AND THE ISLAMIC MOVEMENT OF UZBEKISTAN

At the beginning of 2002, shortly after U.S. and NATO forces over-threw the Taliban government in Afghanistan, thousands of Uzbeks from the IMU, led by Tahir Yuldashev, and hundreds of Arabs affiliated with al-Qaeda went to South Waziristan. The Uzbeks and Arabs first settled in the area of Wana, historically inhabited by the Ahmadzai Wazir tribe. The Uzbeks and Arabs were fluent Pashto speakers who wore the native *shalwar kameez*, making them somewhat diffi-cult to recognize immediately as outsiders. They bought properties and agricultural lands in the Angoor Adda, Azam Warsak, and Shin Warsak areas around Wana near the Pakistan-Afghanistan border, as did smaller groups of Tajiks, Turkmen, and Chechens.[30] During the Pakistani military operations of 2004 in Wana, there were reports that Ayman al-Zawahiri, the deputy head of al-Qaeda, was living in or around Wana.[31]

Because of frequent U.S. drone strikes in 2008 and 2009, many of the Wana-based Arabs affiliated with al-Qaeda shifted to other, Mehsud-controlled areas of South Waziristan, namely Barwand, Makeen, Ladha, Sam, Darga, Sararogha, and Dwa Toi. IMU leader Tahir Yuldashev reportedly died from injuries suffered in a U.S. drone strike in a Mehsud-controlled area of South Waziristan in late August 2009, though some reports suggest he may have survived.[32] Repelled by recent Pakistani military operations in South Waziristan, the majority of Uzbek fighters, about twenty-five hundred men, retreated to the Pir Ghar, a mountainous region near Ladha. The hundreds of Arab mili-tants, meanwhile, relocated to areas inhabited by the Shobi Khel (*Khel* is analogous to *clan*) of the Mehsuds, in and around Makeen, Tiarza, Shaga, Zadrona, and Jhangra, near the border with North Waziristan.

The Mehsud Taliban, which had great expectations from the Uzbek fighters residing in South Waziristan, wanted to use them to counter the Pakistani military's fall 2009 operations. However, the results were very disappointing. The Uzbeks put up poor resistance against the Pakistani army in Spinkai Raghzai, Barwand, Makeen, Ladha, and Sararogha; they were chased out from all the major villages and towns in South Waziristan, and most of them were forced to retreat to North Waziristan. However, the remaining IMU Uzbeks continue to carry out attacks against Pakistani army check posts in the towns of Ladha, Makeen, Kani Guram, and Dwa Toi, and sometimes as far as Sararogha, South Waziristan. They travel by horse over the Pir Ghar mountains between North and South Waziristan, stopping overnight at the villages of Borakai and Koch Pandai, and returning to Miram Shah and Mir Ali.[33]

The majority of the al-Qaeda-affiliated Arabs in South Waziristan have also shifted across the border into North Waziristan because of frequent drone strikes in and around the main towns of the South. According to Sailab Mehsud, South Waziristan correspondent for the FATA Research Center, and Ishtiaq Mahsud, a reporter for the Associated Press, more than thirty-two senior or midlevel al-Qaeda militants were killed in late 2009 and early 2010 in conflict with the Pakistani military and in suspected U.S. drone strikes.[34]

QUETTA SHURA TALIBAN

The relationship between the TTP's leadership in South Waziristan and the Quetta Shura is unclear; the organizations are both very secretive, but the TTP considers Mullah Omar its amir. The Quetta Shura Taliban's "code of conduct" released in the summer of 2009 has had little effect on the TTP's operations in South Waziristan, however. Siraj Haqqani and one of his important commanders, Mullah Sangin, have in the past acted as liaisons between the Quetta Shura Taliban and the TTP's local leaders.[35]

The boxes shown here provide a brief outline of the structure of the TTP in South Waziristan; details follow.

Tehrik-i-Taliban Pakistan

Head, or amir	Hakimullah Mehsud*
Deputy amir	Maulvi Faqir Muhammad (removed from this post in March 2012 and not immediately replaced)
General secretary	Maulana Fazlullah (also head of Swat Taliban)
Head in South Waziristan	Wali ur-Rehman Mehsud
Deputy head in South Waziristan	Khan Saeed alias Sajna**
Head of suicide bombers and main military planner of TTP in South Waziristan	Latif Mahsud
Head of criminal gangs in South Waziristan***	Shamim Mehsud (also head of TTP in Ladha)
Chief spokesman	Ahsanullah Ahsan
Head of logistics in South Waziristan	Noor Muhammad
Head of coordination with other FATA-based TTP groups	Sher Azam Aka

Note: * Hakimullah Mehsud is believed to have been killed in a drone strike in North Waziristan in mid-January 2010, but the TTP has denied this and not publicly announced a replacement. ** Sohail Mahsud, midlevel Taliban commander in Ladha and a close friend of Khan Saeed alias Sajna, interview conducted in Ladha on Sept. 13, 2009. *** These gangs generate money for the TTP through crime in the settled districts of Pakistan.

Wana Taliban	
Head of Wana Taliban	Mullah Nazir
Deputies of Nazir	Malang Wazir and Halim Khan Wazir
Coordination with subtribes of the Ahmadzai Wazir in Wana area	Mettha Khan Wazir

Abdullah Mehsud Group	
Patron(s)-in-chief of Abdullah group	Banut Khan Mehsud and Sher Muhammad Mehsud*
Head of Abdullah group, in charge of military activities	Misbahuddin Mehsud**
Deputy head of Abdullah group	Turkistan Bhittani

Note: * These two men deal with the Pakistani government and intelligence agencies and keep contacts with the Mehsud tribal elders in Tank and Dera Ismail Khan. ** Deals with day-to-day logistical issues of the Abdullah group in Tank and D.I. Khan; responsible for keeping those districts free of TTP Taliban.

Turkistan Bhittani Group	
Head of Turkistan group	Turkistan Bhittani
Deputy head of Turkistan group	Ikhlas Khan, alias Waziristan Baba

WAR OF THE WAZIRISTANS: THE POST-BAITULLAH TRANSITION

The first leader of the Tehrik-i-Taliban Pakistan, Baitullah Mehsud, was a charismatic veteran of the Afghan jihad against the Soviets in the 1980s. A Mehsud from the Shobi Khel subtribe who lived in Dwa

Toi, he returned from Afghanistan to become something akin to a gym teacher at a boys' primary school in Landi Dhok near Bannu in the NWFP. He developed close ties to the Afghan Taliban in the late 1990s by keeping in touch with mujahideen friends and occasionally visiting the country. When the Taliban government in Afghanistan was overthrown in 2001, Baitullah began organizing a local Taliban movement in South Waziristan. It provided support for thousands of fleeing Afghan Taliban and al-Qaeda fighters, with whom he formed strong links, as well as Uzbek militants traveling to the region.[36] Baitullah was reputed to be intelligent, cool-minded, and accessible to his followers, in whom he inspired extreme loyalty. His profile rose when he officially formed the TTP in December 2007, uniting various factions of Pakistani Taliban groups under one umbrella organization. Two of his more notable plots include masterminding the 2007 assassination of Pakistani politician Benazir Bhutto and dispatching a team of Pakistanis to Barcelona to attack the city's public transit in 2008.[37] He was the frequent target of U.S. drone strikes before he was finally killed on August 5, 2009, by a drone.

After Baitullah Mehsud's death, his onetime personal driver and spokesman, Hakimullah Mehsud, was a top contender for the TTP leadership, along with Qari Hussain, Wali ur-Rehman Mehsud, Noor Saeed, Maulvi Azmatullah Mehsud, and Rais Khan Mehsud alias Azam Tariq. Intervention by Sirajuddin Haqqani, son of the legendary Afghan mujahideen fighter Jalaluddin Haqqani, apparently prevented an armed confrontation between the various factions of would-be Taliban chiefs, telling them they "must follow the path of a great leader… [and] save your bullets for your true enemies."[38] Hakimullah and Wali ur-Rehman also sought to avoid violent conflict, aware that it could splinter the entire movement, not just in South Waziristan but across the FATA and NWFP. Wali ur-Rehman is believed to have had knowledge of the impending Pakistani military operations across the tribal regions and thus wanted to avoid disunity within the TTP.[39]

The top three candidates for amir, or leader, of the Tehrik-i-Taliban Pakistan—Hakimullah Mehsud, Qari Hussain, and Azam Tariq (see profiles below)—belonged to the Bahlolzai branch of the Mehsud tribe, whereas Wali ur-Rehman Mehsud, Maulvi Azmatullah Mehsud, and Noor Saeed came from the Manzai branch, which historically had been at the forefront of power politics in Mehsud territory.[40] Furthermore, the Mehsud Taliban in South Waziristan reportedly favored the accession of Wali ur-Rehman because he had been a deputy of Baitullah.

After several weeks of reported infighting and deliberations during the late summer of 2009,[41] the Manzai finally lost to the Bahlolzai in the succession battle, as Hakimullah's support included not only the Bahlolzais but also Taliban fighters in the tribal agencies of Khyber, Bajaur, Kurram, and Orakzai. During these tense weeks, there were reports that Hakimullah was killed in conflict with Wali ur-Rehman,[42] but the militant group's leadership later invited local journalists to South Waziristan and put on a show of unity by sitting side by side.[43] After Hakimullah sidelined the rest of the contenders, the forty-member Taliban shura was left with no option but to choose him as head of the TTP. As a consolation, Wali ur-Rehman was made the head of Mehsud Taliban in South Waziristan, where he commands some seven to ten thousand men.[44]

According to local sources, Hakimullah, Hussain, and Azam Tariq consolidated power over the Mehsud Taliban based in South Waziristan and are now fighting against the Pakistani army. Taliban sources in South Waziristan also have said Hakimullah shifted his family to Miram Shah, in North Waziristan, where they are supported by Hafiz Gul Bahadur, the current head of the Taliban in North Waziristan. Wali ur-Rehman is reported to be living there with his family as well.[45]

SIGNIFICANT MILITANT COMMANDERS IN SOUTH WAZIRISTAN

Mehsuds

Hakimullah Mehsud

The most recent chief of the TTP, Hakimullah Mehsud (now believed to be dead; his successor is unclear), was around thirty and of the Woji Khel clan of the Ishangi branch of the Mehsud tribe. He was the son of Abdullah Din Mehsud and had at least four brothers—two of whom, Ijaz and Kalimullah, died while fighting Pakistani forces in South Waziristan in 2008—and four sisters.[46] Hakimullah was originally from the Kotkai area, in the Spinkai Raghzai region in South Waziristan. The TTP leader had two wives, one from his natal Ishangi tribe and one from the Afridi tribe in Orakzai.

Hakimullah received his early education from age five at the madrassa of Dar-ul Aloom Sharia in the Sarwakai Tehsil (or administrative subdivision) of South Waziristan. He also passed his middle school exams in Kotkai. However, he left his religious education incomplete as he joined the local Taliban organization in South Waziristan in the fall of 2003 and went to fight U.S. forces in Afghanistan, where he spent approximately four months. Hakimullah's first combat experience was under the leadership of Baitullah Mehsud in Afghanistan; the two were extremely close, and Hakimullah served as Baitullah's official spokesman for a time in 2006. Along with Maulana Sangeen, a Taliban commander in Afghanistan's Paktika province with links with Sirajuddin Haqqani's militant network, he was part of a force that attacked the Masha Kund military check post in Khost province in 2004. During his time in Afghanistan, Hakimullah also spent many weeks fighting coalition forces in the southern province of Helmand in the district of Sangeen, on the border with Kandahar. He is believed to have been involved in recent cross-border attacks into Afghanistan and has targeted NATO convoys and hundreds of trucks taking supplies there. In a December 2008 attack orchestrated by Hakimullah, dozens of Humvees were burned near Peshawar, the capital of the NWFP.[47]

After his return from Afghanistan in early 2004, Hakimullah turned his attention to the Pakistani forces in the Kalosha area of Wana, where the army had recently launched an operation against Nek Muhammad, then head of the Taliban in South Waziristan. Hakimullah also fought against Pakistani forces in 2006 and again in 2008, when the army launched operations against the local Taliban movements. Hakimullah was by then a commander, leading between 100 and 150 Mehsud Taliban fighters. Both times the Pakistani army was forced to sign peace treaties with the Taliban militants. Hakimullah also provided shelter and bases for members of al-Qaeda and the Afghan Taliban in South Waziristan, and he is said to be still doing so.[48]

Hakimullah was twenty-three when he joined the South Waziristan Taliban; within a year and a half the group was fully organized in the agency.[49] The TTP shura first made him head of the Mehsud Taliban in the Kurram agency and then added Orakzai and Khyber agencies to his portfolio. Hakimullah, a very active leader and the only one to be in charge of three agencies at once, strengthened the TTP in these areas while they were under his control. The militant chief also headed up the

Mehsud Taliban in Mohmand and Bajaur agencies for a short time but had to focus on building the Taliban in Kurram, Orakzai, and Khyber.

Hakimullah, who hated Shiites and considered them heretics, also had close links with the pro-Taliban, anti-Shiite SSP militant organization. As the head of the Taliban in Kurram, he fought against the Shiites and took part in sectarian clashes in Hangu district in early 2007.[50]

Temperamentally, Hakimullah was a hothead; he angered very easily, did not tolerate opposition, and was reputed to be arrogant and prone to emotional outbursts. He was rumored to have shot several men (including some in the Taliban) who disagreed with his orders.[51] He was also more media-friendly than his predecessor Baitullah and appeared in several videos and audiotapes released to the public, including a video with the Jordanian suicide bomber who attacked a CIA base in Khost, Afghanistan, on December 30, 2009.[52]

Hakimullah's ascension to the TTP's leadership came at a time when the umbrella group had lost support from local tribes across South Waziristan and the rest of the FATA, having been weakened by Pakistani military operations. This makes it unlikely that the TTP will be able to open more fronts against the Pakistani government in the near future. The organization may also be reluctant to attack local Mehsud Taliban opponents, for fear of starting "blood feuds" among area tribes.

The Khost attack may have been a turning point, however. Hakimullah asserted responsibility for the suicide bombing, in which seven CIA officers and a Jordanian intelligence agent were killed and others were injured.[53] The TTP released a video of Hakimullah and the bomber, Humam al-Balawi, sitting side by side; al-Balawi claimed the strike was to avenge the death of Baitullah Mehsud in an August 2009 drone attack (some of these drones are reportedly controlled by CIA teams in Khost).[54]

In the following weeks, an unprecedented number of drone-fired missiles slammed into various locations in North Waziristan, one of which reportedly injured Hakimullah. U.S. and other officials say they are almost certain he succumbed to his wounds, but the TTP continues to issue denials.[55] Hakimullah put out audiotapes on January 16 and 17, 2010, in a bid to quell rumors of his death, and he has since been confirmed alive.[56] He is said to be keeping a low profile in the Angoor Adda area of Wana near the border with Afghanistan to avoid being targeted again by U.S. drones.

Wali ur-Rehman Mehsud

Wali ur-Rehman, around forty years old and the son of Asmatullah, is from a middle-class family in the Mal Khel branch of the Mehsud tribe in South Waziristan. His family lives in Miram Shah, but he moves around Waziristan quite a bit; he is currently believed to reside in the Momi Karam area. He studied in the Jamia Islamia Imdadia madrassa in Faisalabad.[57] After graduating in 1996, he returned to South Waziristan to teach in a madrassa in Kani Guram. Before joining the Taliban movement in 2004, Wali ur-Rehman was affiliated with the Islamist JUI-F political party, with which he still maintains contacts.[58]

Wali ur-Rehman is reputed to be humble, cool-minded, intelligent, and polite. Despite earlier disagreements over the TTP's line of succession, he is now believed to be a close ally of the fiery Hakimullah and currently serves as chief of the TTP in South Waziristan, as well as the organization's primary military strategist. In 2007 he was given responsibility for looking after the movement's financial matters. Wali ur-Rehman has also participated in cross-border attacks in Afghanistan against U.S. and NATO forces, and against Pakistani security forces in 2005 and 2008. His brother, Qareeb-ur-Rehman, was killed by Pakistani forces when the militants attacked the Splitoi fort in South Waziristan in July 2008.[59]

Sailab Mehsud, a South Waziristan correspondent for the FATA Research Center, assesses tension between Hakimullah and Wali ur-Rehman as on the rise because Wali ur-Rehman wants to end the TTP's war with the Pakistani government, saying it has destroyed the Mehsud tribe. Wali ur-Rehman is reportedly in secret negotiations with elements of the Pakistani government in Peshawar or Khyber, but Hakimullah and Qari Hussain wanted to carry on fighting the Pakistani military.[60]

Qari Hussain

Another of the top contenders for the TTP leadership after the death of Baitullah Mehsud, Qari Hussain is around thirty-six years old and from the Ishangi subtribe of the Bahlolzai tribe in South Waziristan. He was originally based in the Spinkai Raghzai area of South Waziristan, a close aide of Baitullah Mehsud. Hussain graduated from the Jamia Binoria madrassa in Karachi in 1994 and became a member of the anti-Shiite SSP, before joining the Taliban movement in 2004.[61] Hussain's reputation—ruthless, anti-Shiite, and a powerful orator— lent itself to his spearheading a brutal campaign of suicide attacks across Pakistan, beginning around 2006. He trained hundreds of suicide bombers, some as young as eleven years old, to target Pakistani military and government installations as well as markets, funerals, hospitals, and other "soft" targets.[62] In 2008 alone, 965 people were reported killed in sixty-six suicide bombings across Pakistan, including police and army officials along with many innocent civilians.[63] In 2009, more than 1,200 people were killed and another 2,300 were injured in at least eighty suicide bombings across the country.[64]

Pakistani intelligence officials say that 70 percent of suicide bombers in Pakistan were trained at camps run by Qari Hussain, and the Pakistani government has a reward of 50 million Pakistani rupees (about $600,000) for information leading to his capture or death.[65] His influence is not limited to Pakistan: a 2007 U.N. report claimed that 80 percent of suicide attackers in Afghanistan came from camps in Pakistan.[66]

Hussain's virulent anti-Shiism is worth emphasizing: he reportedly used to abduct Shiites from Tank and Dera Ismail Khan and take them to his base in Spinkai Raghzai, where he would tie them up with barn animals, torturing and beheading some of the captives.[67] Hussain has also worked to strengthen the presence of the anti-Shiite SSP in South Waziristan, involving Mehsud and Wazir tribesmen in sectarian clashes in the frontier regions.

Once the head of the Pakistani Taliban in Kotkai, South Waziristan, Hussain has threatened to deploy even more suicide bombers against the Pakistani government, citing the recent military operations as provocation. One of Hussain's brothers carried out a suicide attack in Peshawar in November 2009, the first close relative of a local Taliban commander to carry out such an attack.[68] Hussain is now believed to be in Mir Ali, North Waziristan, having fled the Pakistani military operations in South Waziristan in the fall of 2009, and there he has strong support from the Daur tribe, a small group in and around central South Waziristan, mainly Miram Shah, Mir Ali, Datta Khel, and Dos Ali.

According to local tribal and Taliban sources in South Waziristan, Qari Hussain has refused to become head of the TTP since the reported death of Hakimullah Mehsud because he wanted to keep a low profile, presumably to avoid being killed himself. Thus he stays in Mir Ali most of the time.[69]

Qari Hussain was reported killed in an American drone strike in Mir Ali on November 8, 2010, as he drove three important al-Qaeda members to Miram Shah. However, the TTP still denies his death and claims he is busily supporting the jihad in Afghanistan and Pakistan.[70]

Azam Tariq

The current spokesman of the TTP in South Waziristan, forty-year-old Azam Tariq belongs to the Kie Khel subtribe of the Mehsuds and hails from the Delay area of South Waziristan. His real name is Rais Khan Mehsud, though the onetime schoolteacher in Tank city is well known by his alias, "Teacher."[71] In 2008 and 2009, Tariq was the TTP chief in Tank city, in the NWFP near the border of South Waziristan, an area populated overwhelmingly by the Mehsud tribe. He is also affiliated with Sipah-e-Sahaba, Pakistan (SSP). Because he is known as an intelligent man with expertise in local Mehsud traditions and politics, locals used to bring their disputes to him for settlement rather than engage the Pakistani judicial system. Tariq was appointed TTP spokesman in September 2009 after the arrest of Maulvi Omar of Bajaur in mid-August.[72] He is reputedly very close to Hakimullah and Qari Hussain.[73]

Noor Saeed

Noor Saeed, a thirty-year-old from the Shobi Khel clan of the Mehsuds, is a member of the TTP shura and very popular among the Mehsud Taliban, having been Baitullah Mehsud's deputy and part-time spokesman. He was a farmer before joining the Mehsud Taliban movement in South Waziristan in 2004. Noor Saeed is reportedly very religious and humble in his dealings with others.[74]

Shamim Mehsud

At the head of the TTP's network of criminals is Shamim, a thirty-five-year-old from the Shaman Khel tribe of the Mehsuds from Tangi in Ladha, South Waziristan. Shamim, from a very poor family in Ladha, worked as a waiter in Spinkai Raghzai before he was made head of the TTP of Ladha in 2007. He now serves as chief of a Taliban commando group of about thirty men—professional criminals—who collect millions of rupees every year through robberies, kidnapping for ransom, and bank lootings to fund the insurgency. The group has informants in all of Pakistan's major cities who provide intelligence about where to strike and the likely value of the targets.[75]

Latif Mahsud

Latif Mahsud, a TTP member in his midthirties from the Ishangi clan of the Mahsud tribe, worked alongside Hakimullah Mahsud and Qari Hussain in the Kotkai area of South Waziristan. Latif was educated only through the tenth grade, and he joined the TTP in 2008, becoming a close aide of Qari Hussain. Latif succeeded Hussain after his death in an American drone attack and now trains suicide bombers in South Waziristan. He is said to be running training camps for suicide bombers at several locations in the agency. Latif Mahsud is a brutal man and is involved in criminal activities such as kidnapping foreigners, government officials, and security forces for ransom to generate money for the TTP. Latif Mahsud is also considered by TTP militants to be Hakimullah Mahsud's deputy.[76]

Ahmad Hussain Alias Haji Hussain

At just twenty-eight years of age, Ahmad Hussain is one of Hakimullah Mahsud's top commanders. He comes from the Machi Khel clan of the Mahsud tribe and lives in the Woospass area of South Waziristan. In late 2011, Hakimullah Mahsud appointed him head of operations in the Tank, Dera Ismail Khan, and Lakki Districts of KPK Province. Like Latif Mahsud, Hussain is also involved in kidnapping government officials and NGO workers in both KPK and Balochistan provinces.

Differences Between Hakimullah Mahsud and Wali Rehman Mahsud

Soon after Baitullah Mahsud was killed in a drone strike in August 2009, old disputes between Hakimullah and Wali Rehman resurfaced. Wali Rehman had been Baitullah Mahsud's deputy, and Baitullah Mahsud had hinted that Wali Rehman would replace him in case of his death. Wali Rehman agreed, of course, but Qari Hussain and Hakimullah threatened that if Hakimullah Mahsud was not appointed as the head of the TTP, they would break away to form their own group. Presented with the group's fragmentation, Wali Rehman relented and gave up his claim to the leadership of the TTP.

In 2010, Qari Hussain kidnapped Colonel Imam, Khalid Khawaja, and the Pakistani-born British filmmaker Asad Qureshi, who had traveled to Miram Shah on the invitation of Wali Rehman Mahsud. The three were kidnapped in Mir Ali on their way back to Bannu. Wali Rehman worked to negotiate their release, but Hakimullah and Qari

Hussain refused. Qureshi was released after seven months in TTP captivity, while Khalid Khawaja and Colonel Imam were eventually killed.

As tensions between the two militant leaders escalated in 2010, they began targeting each other's key commanders. In November 2010, the Haqqanis mediated a TTP jirga in Miram Shah to settle the dispute between Hakimullah and Wali Rehman. The jirga ended with announcements from both TTP commanders that they had solved all disputes with one another.

However, tensions were ignited once again in mid-2011 by disagreements over whether to sign a peace agreement with the Pakistani government. Wali Rehman was in favor of a peace agreement, but Hakimullah held the Pakistani government responsible for dividing the TTP into two groups, one led by himself, and the other by Wali Rehman. The division was apparent in the two separate representatives each militant leader had in the newly formed Shura Marakaba in North Waziristan. Since its inception, Shura Marakaba members worked to resolve the dispute, but as of early 2012 they hadn't had any success.

Smaller Mehsud Militant Groups in South Waziristan

Abdullah Mehsud Group (Pro-government)

Abdullah Mehsud, the leader of a splinter group of militants first based in Nano village in South Waziristan and Miram Shah in North Waziristan, spent about two years at the U.S. military prison at Guantánamo Bay, and after his release in March 2004 he began organizing the local Mehsud Taliban in South Waziristan to fight U.S. and NATO troops in Afghanistan.[77] In October 2004 he was involved in the kidnapping of two Chinese engineers, one of whom was killed during a rescue mission by Pakistani security forces. Abdullah died in Zhob, Baluchistan, during a confrontation with military forces in July 2007 (by blowing himself up with a hand grenade, Pakistani officials say).[78]

After Abdullah's death, his followers coalesced around Saif Rehman Mehsud and later Abdullah's cousin, Qari Zainuddin Mehsud, also known as Qari Zain. Zainuddin developed serious differences with Baitullah Mehsud over whether to target Pakistan's security apparatus or focus on Western forces in Afghanistan—the TTP was in favor of targeting Pakistan—and was forced out of South Waziristan after open hostilities began in 2008.[79] Zainuddin was killed in June 2009 by one of his own bodyguards.[80] Zainuddin's younger brother, Misbahuddin Mehsud, now leads the group and is considered relatively pro-government for two reasons: first, the Abdullah group has split from the TTP over whether to fight the Pakistani army in the FATA and NWFP, and second, Misbahuddin's forces are no match for the TTP, so he needs government protection.

The Abdullah Mehsud group, which has about two thousand fighters, is now based in Tank and D.I. Khan in NWFP and has the support of the Pakistani government. Its fighters are allied with Turkistan Bhittani, another anti-TTP commander, causing concern for the TTP. The Abdullah group and its allies have forced the majority of TTP-affiliated militants from Tank and D.I. Khan back into South Waziristan. Many on both sides have been killed.[81]

Sheryar Mehsud Group (Antigovernment)

Sheryar Mehsud, a thirty-five-year-old of the Shobi Khel branch of the Mehsud tribe from the village of Jhangra in South Waziristan, was not on good terms with the late Baitullah Mehsud. Sheryar believed that his family, which is well off and respected in his region, put him in a stronger position to run the Mehsud Taliban in South Waziristan. Sheryar commands a small group of about 150 men who conduct cross-border attacks into Afghanistan and some criminal activities, such as car snatching and kidnapping for ransom in cities such as Tank and D.I. Khan. His enmity with Baitullah continued with Hakimullah, and Sheryar is considered antigovernment because of his focus on targeting Pakistani police and government.[82]

Wazirs

Mullah Nazir, Wana Taliban (Pro-government)

Mullah Nazir is a prominent Taliban commander from the Ahmadzai Wazir tribe of Wana, the administrative headquarters of South Waziristan. He had madrassa training, has dual citizenship in Afghanistan and Pakistan, and was a close aide to Gulbuddin Hekmatyar, the chief of Hizb-i Islami Afghanistan. He became the head of the Wana Taliban in late 2006 after challenging Haji Sharif and Haji Omar and their allies over the presence of thousands of militants from the IMU then living in South Waziristan. Nazir accused the Uzbeks of complicity in the assassination of dozens of Ahmadzai Wazir tribal elders in Wana. After ten days of fighting in April 2007, Mullah Nazir's forces—supported by the local Ahmadzai Wazir tribe and its militiamen, as well as the Pakistani government—succeeded in expelling about two thousand Uzbeks from Wana.[83] Baitullah Mehsud then offered the fleeing Uzbeks shelter in the Mehsud-controlled areas of South Waziristan, namely Darga, Sararogha, and Barwand, angering Nazir.[84] Baitullah was apparently ordered by Sirajuddin Haqqani, a leader of the Haqqani network, to give the Uzbeks temporary refuge because they had nowhere else to go.[85]

Mullah Nazir currently controls at least fourteen Taliban groups in Wana, comprising about four thousand fighters, and is involved in cross-border attacks on U.S. and NATO forces in Afghanistan.[86] He has been targeted at least twice by U.S. drones and suffered a leg wound in one attack.[87] He is considered "pro-government" Taliban because he primarily targets Western troops fighting in Afghanistan, although he maintains close ties with the Arab al-Qaeda movement.[88]

As discussed earlier, Mullah Nazir has been at loggerheads with the TTP leadership over a September 2009 incident in which Mullah Nazir alleges that eleven of his men were killed in Mehsud territory in Salay Rogha, South Waziristan, as they were returning to Wana. The TTP so far has refused to hand over the four Mehsuds and four Uzbeks implicated in the attack, straining relations between the Mehsuds and the Ahmadzai Wazirs. The Shura Ittihad ul-Mujahideen—formed by Baitullah Mehsud, Mullah Nazir, and Hafiz Gul Bahadur of North Waziristan in early 2009—has broken down.[89] Nazir is now considered the commander of all the Wana Taliban.

Anti-Mullah Nazir Waziri Groups

Haji Sharif Group (Antigovernment)

An Ahmadzai Wazir from Wana, Haji Sharif is around fifty years old and commands about five hundred men. He has fought against government forces in both Afghanistan and Pakistan and supported the Uzbek militants when they were being expelled from Wana by Mullah Nazir's fighters. After the Uzbeks were expelled, Haji Sharif shifted to Miram Shah, in North Waziristan, and allied himself with the late Baitullah Mehsud. However, Haji Sharif reconciled with Mullah Nazir in September 2007 after developing differences with members of the IMU over whether to target locals in Wana and the Pakistani government. After this reconciliation, Haji Sharif mostly stopped targeting local tribal elders and government officials in South Waziristan. He then returned to Wana, where he now resides.[90]

Haji Omar Group (Antigovernment)

Haji Omar, who is about fifty-eight and a veteran of the anti-Soviet jihad in the 1980s and member of the Yargul Khel subtribe of the Ahmadzai Wazirs,[91] was head of the Wana Taliban in 2004 when the Pakistani military launched operations there to flush out foreign militants and their local supporters after the death of Nek Muhammad. Reputed to have close ties to al-Qaeda fighters in the region, he was involved in the killing of tribal elders in Wana and was a strong supporter of Uzbek militants in Waziristan. He fought on behalf of the Uzbeks against Mullah Nazir and, like his brother Haji Sharif, was later forced to take refuge in Miram Shah in North Waziristan, where he allied himself with Baitullah Mehsud. Haji Omar was reportedly killed by a U.S. drone strike in North Waziristan in December 2009,[92] though earlier reports indicated he was killed in October 2008.[93] His group of several hundred men is now said to be relatively ineffective.

Abbas Group (Antigovernment)

Maulvi Abbas Wazir is a cousin of Haji Sharif and Haji Omar, against whom he fought in April 2007 while they were allied against archrival Mullah Nazir and the Ahmadzai Wazir militiamen in the dispute over the Uzbeks. He is about forty-two years old and from the Ahmadzai branch of the Wazir tribe. He is also involved in cross-border attacks on U.S. and NATO forces in Afghanistan and is said to have some 150 to 200 fighters under his command.[94]

Noor Islam Group (Antigovernment)

Noor Islam, another member of the Ahmadzai Wazirs, veteran of the anti-Soviet jihad, and a brother of Haji Sharif and Haji Omar, fought on behalf of the Uzbeks in April 2007 and was subsequently forced to leave Wana, after which he took refuge with Baitullah Mehsud. He is the sworn enemy of Mullah Nazir, and his associates killed Nazir's deputy, Malik Khanan, in May 2008 in South Waziristan. Noor Islam is reported to have about 250 to 300 fighters under his command; he directs them in cross-border attacks against U.S. and NATO forces in Afghanistan and also mounted attacks on the Pakistani army in 2004.[95]

Bhittani Groups in South Waziristan

Turkistan Bhittani Group (Pro-government)

The first of the three prominent Bhittani commanders operating in South Waziristan is Malik Turkistan Bhittani, a retired corporal of the Frontier Corps. He is from the Naimat Khel subtribe of the Bhittani tribe from the Sro Ghar area of Jandola, in South Waziristan, where he is the head of a peace committee whose goal is to keep the TTP away from Jandola and Tank. Turkistan Bhittani is considered pro-government and has allied himself with the Abdullah Mehsud group against the TTP. The Turkistan group has been attacked several times by TTP militants; in 2008 members of the TTP overran Jandola and killed about thirty peace committee members. In September 2009, TTP fighters and other Bhittani militants attacked Turkistan's forces in Tank, Jandola, and Sro Ghar, killing dozens. Turkistan himself survived and is now keeping a low profile in Tank and Dera Ismail Khan to avoid TTP threats.[96] The Bhittani tribe, though numerically smaller than the Mehsuds and the Wazirs, lives along the strategically important road from the settled district of Tank into South Waziristan and thus has outsize political sway. Turkistan Bhittani is also a deputy of the Abdullah Mehsud group, because on his own he is no match for the TTP.

During 2011, Turkistan Bhittani kept a low profile in Tank District, KPK Province. According to some reports, Bhittani was arrested by Tank police after a dispute he had with the government. Pakistan's government has the ability to use Bhittani against the TTP in Jundola and Tank districts at any time if the need arises.[97]

Asmatullah Shaheen Group (Antigovernment)

The second prominent Bhittani commander active in the Jandola area of South Waziristan is Asmatullah Shaheen, from the Khichi subtribe of the Bhittanis and Khichi village. Asmatullah was initially affiliated with the Islamic militant group Harkat-ul-Mujahideen of Maulana Fazal-ur-Rehman, but later he joined the TTP under Baitullah Mehsud. He is involved in kidnapping for ransom, vehicle hijacking, and cross-border attacks on U.S. and NATO forces in Afghanistan. Asmatullah is currently in conflict with Turkistan Bhittani, who expelled him from Jandola in July 2009 to the Mehsud areas of South Waziristan. Asmatullah controls between 200 and 250 men.[98]

Awal Khan Bhittani Group (Antigovernment)

Awal Khan Bhittani is the third important Taliban commander active in the Jandola area of South Waziristan. He is also involved in cross-border attacks into Afghanistan. Like Asmatullah Shaheen, Awal Khan is not on good terms with Turkistan Bhittani, though he maintains a decent relationship with the TTP around Jandola.[99]

Punjabi Taliban Group of Wana (Pro-government)

Lastly, the Punjabi Taliban, a relatively new phenomenon, used to operate out of Wana. It is affiliated with a variety of banned sectarian and militant groups such as Harkat-ul-Jihad-al-Islami, Lashkar-e-Jhangvi or LeJ, Jamiat ul-Ansar, Jamiat ul-Furqan, and SSP. Led by the Punjabi Abdur Rehman,[100] the Punjabi Taliban is allied with Mullah Nazir against the Uzbeks and is believed to number around three thousand men. Members generally live among the Ahmadzai Wazirs, as well as in the Mehsud-inhabited areas of Sararogha, Makeen, and Ladha, and in Angoor Adda and Azam Warsak. They focus their attacks on American and NATO forces in Afghanistan.

However, most members of the Punjabi Taliban have shifted from South to North Waziristan because it was difficult for them to blend in among the locals because of their complexion, and because as newcomers they were not well connected in the area. According to Safder Daur, a journalist in North Waziristan, these fighters are more inclined to fit in with North Waziristan because some of them were based there during the anti-Soviet jihad during the 1980s and have close links with the local Uthmanzai and Daur tribes.[101]

Peace Agreement Between Mullah Nazir and Hakimullah Mahsud

In November 2011, Hakimullah Mahsud and Mullah Nazir announced that the two leaders had solved their disputes with each other and agreed to a peace deal. According to the terms of the peace agreement,

Mullah Nazir would allow TTP militants, as well as the Ahmadzai Wazir Taliban affiliated with the TTP, such as Noor Islam, Abbas, Javeed Karamaz Khel, and Wali Muhammad (the younger brother of the late Nek Muhammad), to reside in Wana.

The peace agreement between Hakimullah and Mullah Nazir in Wana riled the Pakistani government and army, which considered it to be a breach of the 2007 peace agreement made between the Pakistani government and Ahmadzai Wazir of Wana. Pakistan sees the TTP as enemy number one, and by allowing the insurgent group to settle in Wana Mullah Nazir might have created serious problems for the government in Wana, which had been generally peaceful for the past several years. The Pakistani government fears that if the TTP and Mullah Nazir join forces in South Waziristan, it could seriously hinder the ongoing Rah Nijad military operation against TTP militants in the Mahsud-inhabited areas of South Waziristan. It would open a new front in Wana between the militants and the government, which would be very difficult for the army to control and defeat. The Pakistani government is putting pressure on Mullah Nazir to scrap his peace agreement with Hakimullah and disallow the TTP and their Ahmadzai Wazir allies from living in Wana. But Mullah Nazir has so far been adamant about sticking to his peace deal with Hakimullah Mahsud.[102]

A SHORT HISTORY OF PAKISTANI ARMY OPERATIONS AND PEACE DEALS IN SOUTH WAZIRISTAN, 2004–2008

There have been four major Pakistani-led military operations against factions of the Taliban in South Waziristan since 2004, the most recent of which was Operation Path to Salvation, or Rah-e-Nijat. The first major campaign, during the spring and summer of 2004, pitted the young and charismatic Taliban commander Nek Muhammad Wazir and thousands of his supporters—including militant leaders Noor Islam and Haji Sharif—against as many as seven thousand Pakistani soldiers in the area west of Wana. By the end of the nearly two-week-long operation, sixteen Pakistani soldiers had been killed in fierce fighting.[103] Several months later, some ten thousand Pakistani army troops attacked an area north of Wana, going up against more than two hundred Chechens and Uzbeks, a few Arabs, and several hundred local militants. As its casualties increased, however, the Pakistani government pursued a series of "peace deals" with the local militants.

The first of these deals, called the Shakai agreement, was signed in a madrassa in Shakai in spring 2004 by Nek Muhammad, some of his allies, and the commander of the Pakistani forces battling the militants in South Waziristan, Lt. Gen. Safdar Hussain.[104] The army agreed to remove troops from Nek Muhammad's territory and compensate the militants for losses, while Nek Muhammad promised to lay down arms and "register" foreign militants living in the area.[105] The peace deal was short-lived; Nek Muhammad soon violated the terms of the pact and in June 2004 was killed by a U.S. drone strike near Wana.[106]

The second military operation was carried out in early 2005, in the Mehsud-controlled areas of South Waziristan, against four thousand fighters led by Baitullah Mehsud and Abdullah Mehsud. As in the previous campaign, the Pakistani military suffered casualties and eventually negotiated a settlement with the militants. It was signed in early February in Sararogha by Baitullah, three tribal elders, and a representative of the Pakistani government; Sirajuddin Haqqani is reported to have played a role in the negotiations.[107] Baitullah promised he would stop sheltering foreign militants, attacking security forces in the area, and targeting government installations, while the army again agreed to remove troops and compensate for losses.[108] This peace arrangement also did not last long; Baitullah soon oversaw a suicide bombing campaign targeting the Pakistani government, which lasted until his death in August 2009.[109] The peace deal, however, emboldened the Mehsud Taliban, which began to virtually rule South Waziristan as thousands of local fighters joined the movement and the writ of the Pakistani government faded away.

The third major operation in South Waziristan was launched in January 2008 with the aim of clearing the area of Baitullah Mehsud's supporters and capturing or killing key leaders of the Taliban faction, including Baitullah and the suicide bomb campaign chief, Qari Hussain.[110] About two hundred thousand residents of South Waziristan were displaced during this conflict.[111] After around six weeks of harsh fighting, talks began toward a peace agreement with conditions similar to those of previous arrangements,[112] and the Pakistani army started to withdraw in May. A Pakistani military commander commented, "We are not moving out, and are only re-adjusting our positions."[113] Underscoring the freedom of movement given to Baitullah Mehsud in the spring 2008 peace agreement was his famed press conference in June, for which he invited local journalists to his base in South Waziristan.[114] Sirajuddin Haqqani was again rumored to play a role in negotiations between the Pakistani military and the Mehsud Taliban, reportedly traveling in an eleven-vehicle convoy to mediate the fighting.[115] The peace agreement broke down shortly, however, as the suicide bombing campaign continued, Qari Hussain rebuilt a suicide training camp in Spinkai Raghzai, and Baitullah's network continued to target Pakistani forces.[116] The Taliban's strength was demonstrated in two ambushes of military targets in South Waziristan in August 2007 and January 2008; in the first ambush, more than a hundred Pakistani troops were taken hostage, and in the second hundreds of Mehsud fighters captured a key fort at Sararogha.[117]

Some have argued that negotiating directly with militants rather than tribal leaders legitimized the extremist movement at the expense of the tribes.[118] Pakistani analyst Shuja Nawaz has also pointed out that the military campaigns relied heavily on Pakistan's Frontier Corps, which was not up to the job of "aggressively patrolling or fighting the well-armed and well-trained militants," suggesting a change in tactics was needed.[119]

Operation Rah-e-Nijat ("Path to Salvation"), October 2009–Present

After months of buildup,[120] around thirty thousand Pakistani soldiers pushed into South Waziristan on October 17, 2009, to face off against thousands of Taliban militants.[121] Over the next several weeks, both sides claimed an early lead, though information coming out of the war zone was nearly impossible to verify because the military prohibited journalists and aid workers from entering the region. Hundreds of thousands of residents fled the area ahead of the operations.[122] During the first two weeks of the fighting, the Taliban put up stiff resistance, but many of the fighters melted away into other tribal areas such as Orakzai and North Waziristan. They also have used guerrilla tactics such as raiding Pakistani army check posts at night and planting improvised bombs along roads in South Waziristan.[123]

The Pakistani forces appear to have the militant movement on the run with this campaign. In early November 2009, about three weeks into the offensive, Hakimullah Mehsud warned his followers that cowards "will go to hell... a very bad place," signaling that all was not well within the TTP ranks.[124] The Abdullah Mehsud group and fighters led by Turkistan Bhittani—both anti-TTP factions—also set out to South Waziristan to fight alongside the Pakistani military. This was a key benefit for the government, as the tribesmen are familiar with the area and its challenging terrain. The two groups have also attempted to keep the peace in Tank and D.I. Khan as the TTP fighters retreated deeper into the mountains of Waziristan.[125] Additionally, the many thousands of refugees fleeing South Waziristan have largely turned against the TTP, blaming it for the ongoing fighting.[126]

The idea of anti-TTP tribal militias, or *lashkars*, being formed by Mehsud tribesmen in South Waziristan is gaining traction. The move is supported by the Pakistani government, which has reportedly pressured Mehsud tribal elders to form such militias, assuring them of security and financial support if they do, while threatening a cessation of current benefits if they resist.[127] Humayun Khan, the son of Shahzada Waziristan Fazal Din Mehsud, the famed anti-British fighter in South Waziristan, is one possible chief for the South Waziristan lashkar. However, he does not have the full support of the community, as leaders are reluctant to trust the Pakistani government's promises. If the government cuts another peace deal with the tribes (as seems likely[128]) and the militants return to their South Waziristan strongholds, the lashkar fighters could face severe retribution from the Taliban.[129]

As Operation Rah-e-Nijat forces the TTP to take refuge in North Waziristan, the fighters have established thirteen bases across the agency in Spalga, Miram Shah, Mir Ali, Deegan, and Datta Khel. Mehsud Taliban militants regularly move from these bases to carry out sporadic attacks against Pakistani army camps and check posts in South Waziristan and across the FATA. The TTP leadership—Hakimullah (if he survived the drone strike), Wali ur-Rehman, Qari Hussain, and Azam Tariq—are presently believed to be living with their families under the protection of Hafiz Gul Bahadur in North Waziristan.[130]

According to Siraj Mehsud, deputy to Shamin Mehsud, the Taliban chief in Ladha, South Waziristan, Wazir, and Daur tribesmen are coming in groups of thirty to fifty to carry out guerrilla attacks against the

Pakistani army, staying for ten days or so before returning to North Waziristan, at which point fresh groups of fighters are sent into South Waziristan to carry on the cycle.[131]

APPENDIX A: A QUICK OVERVIEW OF MAJOR PASHTUN TRIBES IN SOUTH WAZIRISTAN

Like the other tribal agencies in the FATA, South Waziristan is home to a diverse collection of Pashtun tribes, the most prominent of which are the Mehsuds, Ahmadzai Wazirs, Bhittanis, Urmur-Burkis, Suleiman Khel, and Dottanis. The Mehsuds are the largest in population and have the most historical significance, followed by the Ahmadzai Wazirs and the Bhittanis. Tribal elders play an important dominant role in FATA society, although this role has been significantly weakened since the 1979 Soviet invasion of Afghanistan and the growing importance of the clergy associated with the rise of Islamism in the FATA. In recent years, Taliban commanders have even begun to act as tribal elders within their respective tribes and clans. However, original tribal leaders still maintain some influence over their followers and their traditional role has not been completely eradicated.

The box below lists major administrative units, or tehsils, in South Waziristan and the subtribes that inhabit them.

Mehsud Tribe

The Mehsud tribe mainly inhabits the central region of South Waziristan, concentrated in villages such as Makeen, Ladha, Sararogha, Spinkai Raghzai, and Kotkai. The three main subtribes of the Mehsuds are the Dre Masid, a branch of which is the Alizai, which splits into the Shobi Khel and Manzai; the Bahlolzai, which contains the Ishangi clan; and Shaman Khel. The Manzai are the largest in number, followed by the Bahlolzai and Shaman Khel. There are an estimated 650,000 to 700,000 Mehsuds in South Waziristan.

Much if not all of the TTP's current leadership is drawn from the Mehsud tribe: Baitullah Mehsud was from the Shobi Khel subtribe, while Hakimullah Mehsud and Qari Hussain come from the Ishangi clan of the Bahlolzai subtribe. Other subtribes active in the TTP are the Abdulai, Kie Khel, Langer Khel, and Haibat Khel.

Subtribes of the Major Districts in South Waziristan	
Ladha Tehsil	Shaman Khel, Langer Khel, Garri, Ishangi, Mal Khel, Shamiri, Sayyeds, Shobi Khel, Urmur-Burki tribe, Baba Khel, Bodenzai, Slamoni, Galishai, Malikdinai
Makeen Tehsil	Abdulai, Imar Khel, Malikshi, Ishangi, Shobi Khel, Band Khel, Nazar Khel
Sararogha Tehsil	Shaman Khel, Galishai, Shamiri, Langer Khel, Habiat Khel, Jalal Khel, Shobi Khel, Gory Khel, Abdulai, Ishangi, Malikshai, Faridi, Kikari, Paray Khel, Kie Khel
Tiarza Tehsil	Machi Khel, Nikzan Khel, Abdur Rehman Khel, Paray Khel, Langer Khel, Baand Khel
Shawal Tehsil	Jalal Khel, Shobi Khel, Habiat Khel, Abdulai
Sarwakai Tehsil	Jalal Khel, Machi Khel, Abdur Rehman Khel, Nikzan Khel, Faridi, Kikari
Wana (Ahmadzai Wazirs)	Zali Khel, Yargul Khel, Kaka Khel, Khoni Khel, Khojal Khel, Sarki Khel, Ganji Khel, Toji Khel, Moghal Khel

Ahmadzai Wazir Tribe of Wana

The Ahmadzai Wazirs, who are the cousins of Mehsuds, inhabit the western and southern parts of South Waziristan. Although they are smaller in number—around 150,000 to 200,000—than the Mehsuds, they control Wana, the administrative headquarters of South Waziristan. There are nine subtribes of Ahmadzai Wazirs, the largest of which is the Zali Khel. Most of the Pakistani Taliban leadership from 2003 to 2007 was derived from Yargul Khel, the largest clan of the Zali Khel.[132] Mullah Nazir, the supreme commander of the Ahmadzai Wazir Taliban, belongs to Kaka Khel, the smallest clan of the Zali Khel subtribe.[133] Malik Hanan and Malang are the most significant elders of Ahmadzai Wazir tribe.

Bhittani Tribe of Jandola

The Bhittani tribe is the third-largest tribe in South Waziristan, and its members mainly live in the western areas of the agency, along and over the border near Tank and D.I. Khan. Though relatively small, with about seventy to eighty thousand people, the tribe controls the main gateway into South Waziristan from the settled districts and provides passage to Mehsuds and Ahmadzai Wazirs. Asmatullah Shaheen, Turkistan Bhittani, and Sher Rehman are the elders of the Bhittani tribe.

Urmur-Burki Tribe of Kani Guram

The Urmur-Burki is a small tribe of about seven to ten thousand people who live in Kani Guram, a historic town that lies at the bottom of the Ladha subdivision, encircled by the much larger Mehsud tribe. Members of the Urmur-Burki tribe speak their own language, Ormuri.

Dottani Tribe

The Dottani tribe numbers about ten thousand people who live near the southern border of South Waziristan, across from the Zhob district of Baluchistan.

Notes

1. Steve Coll, *Ghost Wars: The Secret History of the CIA, Afghanistan, and bin Laden, from the Soviet Invasion to September 10, 2001* (New York: Penguin Press, 2004), p. 62.
2. Interview with Saif ul Islam Saifi, reporter for Al Jazeera, Oct. 14, 2009, in Peshawar, North-West Frontier Province, Pakistan.
3. Congressional Research Service, "Islamic Religious Schools, *Madrasas*: Background," http://www.investigativeproject.org/documents/testimony/335.pdf.
4. Interview with Maulana Mairaj u Din Mahsud, member of the National Assembly elected from South Waziristan on the JUI-F ticket in the 2002 election, Nov. 7, 2009.
5. Interview with Sailab Mehsud, correspondent for the FATA Research Center in South Waziristan, Oct. 17, 2009, in Tank city.
6. Ibid.

7. Saeed Shah, "Pakistani Insurgents Join Forces on Afghan Border," *Globe and Mail*, Dec. 17, 2007.

8. Sailab Mehsud interview.

9. Interview with Alamgir Wazir, Taliban commander for Mullah Nazir, Oct. 12, 2009, in Wana, South Waziristan.

10. Ibid.

11. Ibid.; Rahimullah Yusufzai, "Profile: Nek Mohammed," BBC, June 18, 2004, http://news.bbc.co.uk/2/hi/south_asia/3819871.stm.

12. "Pakistan's Tribal Areas: Appeasing the Militants: Crisis Group Asia Report," No.125, Dec. 11, 2006.

13. http://www.pbs.org/wgbh/pages/frontline/taliban/militants/mohammed.html; David Rohde and Mohammed Khan, "Ex-Fighter for Taliban Dies in Strike in Pakistan," *New York Times*, June 19, 2004, http://www.nytimes.com/2004/06/19/international/asia/19STAN.html; Alamgir Wazir interview.

14. Rahimullah Yusufzai, "Who's Who on the Insurgency in Pakistan's NWFP," Terrorism Monitor, Jamestown Foundation, Sept. 22, 2008, http://www.jamestown.org/programs/gta/single/?tx_ttnews[tt_news]=5169&tx_ttnews[backPid]=167&no_cache=1.

15. Alamgir Wazir interview.

16. Ibid.

17. Interview with Allah u Din Mehsud, head of a madrassa in Ladha, Oct. 6, 2009.

18. Allah u Din Mehsud interview, Oct. 6, 2009.

19. Sailab Mehsud interview, Oct. 10, 2009.

20. Interview with Malik Rafique u Din, a tribal elder of the Manzais, Oct. 5, 2009.

21. Ibid.

22. Ibid.

23. Sailab Mehsud interview.

24. Saeed Shah, "Taliban Rivals Unite to Fight US Troop Surge," *Guardian*, Mar. 3, 2009, http://www.guardian.co.uk/world/2009/mar/03/taliban-pakistan-afghanistan-us-surge.

25. Interview with Sailab Mehsud, Oct. 15, 2009, in Dera Ismail Khan, North-West Frontier Province.

26. Interview with Sailab Mehsud, Oct. 28, 2009, in D.I. Khan.

27. http://www.guardian.co.uk/world/2009/feb/20/suicide-bomb-pakistan.

28. Interview with Sailab Mehsud, Oct. 28, 2009.

29. "Pakistan Bomb Kills US Diplomat," BBC, Mar. 2, 2006, http://news.bbc.co.uk/2/hi/4765170.stm.

30. Interview with Sailab Mehsud, Oct. 10, 2009, Dera Ismail Khan.

31. "High Value Target in Wana," *Daily Times*, Aug. 22, 2006.

32. *The News*, Sept. 13, 2009, http://www.dailytimes.com.pk/default.asp?page=2010\01\22\story_22-1-2010_pg7_4.

33. Interview with Sailab Mehsud, Feb. 3, 2010, in Tank city.

34. Interview with Ishtiaq Mahsud, Associated Press reporter, and Sailab Mehsud, Jan. 19, 2010, in Tank city.

35. Ahmed Rashid, *Descent into Chaos* (Penguin Books, New York, 2008).

36. Interview with Abid Shaman Khel, TTP commander in Kani Guram, South Waziristan, Jan. 22, 2010, in Frontier Region Jandola.

37. Michael Evans, "Taliban Warlord Baitullah Mehsud Is New Public Enemy Number 1," *Times of London*, Feb. 6, 2008, http://www.timesonline.co.uk/tol/news/world/asia/article3315612.ece.

38. Matthew Rosenberg, "New Wave of Warlords Bedevils U.S.," *Wall Street Journal*, Jan. 20, 2010, http://online.wsj.com/article/SB10001424052748704561004575012703221192966.html.

39. Interview with Sailab Mehsud, Nov. 22, 2009, in D.I. Khan; interview with Sailab Mehsud, Oct. 28, 2009.

40. Alamgir Bitani, "Waziristan Power Politics," Dawn.com, Sept. 13, 2009.

41. Ibid.; Daud Khattak, "The New Face of the TTP," *Foreign Policy*, Aug. 24, 2009, http://afpak.foreignpolicy.com/posts/2009/08/24/the_new_face_of_the_ttp.

42. Interview with Malik Sadat Khan, Mehsud tribal elder with Manzai branch, Nov. 6, 2009; Sailab Mehsud, Sept. 7, 2009, Tank City.

43. Sailab Mehsud interview; interview with Alamgir Bitani, reporter, Dawn.com, Sept. 9, 2009.

44. Abid Shaman Khel interview; Sailab Mehsud interview, Nov. 30, 2009, in Islamabad, Pakistan; "Obituary: Baitullah Mehsud," BBC, Aug. 25, 2009, http://news.bbc.co.uk/2/hi/south_asia/7163626.stm.

45. Interview with Shah Swar Mehsud, TTP commander in Ladha, Nov. 24, 2009, in Gomal, South Waziristan.

46. Hakimullah, handwritten profile of himself, given to Sailab Mehsud of the FATA Research Center.

47. Jeremy Page, "US and Nato Humvees Destroyed as Islamists Attack Afghan Supply Bases," *Times* (London), Dec. 8, 2009.

48. Interview with Sairaj Mehsud, deputy of Shamim Mehsud, TTP leader in Ladha, Jan. 20, 2010, in Frontier Region Jandola.

49. Hakimullah, handwritten profile.

50. "Violence Mars Shiite Procession in Pakistan," *International Herald Tribune*, Jan. 30, 2007, http://www.nytimes.com/2007/01/30/world/asia/30iht-pakistan.4403718.html.

51. Sailab Mehsud interview, Nov. 22, 2009, in D.I. Khan.

52. Zahid Hussain, "Attacker of CIA Is Linked to Taliban," *Wall Street Journal*, Jan. 11, 2010, http://online.wsj.com/article/SB126305287870523271.html?mod=WSJ_hpp_MIDDLTopStories.

53. Saeed Shah, "CIA Suicide Bomber Appears in Video with Pakistani Taliban Leader," McClatchy Newspapers, Jan. 9, 2010.

54. Steven Farrell, "Video Links Taliban in Pakistan to C.I.A. Attack," *New York Times*, Jan. 9, 2010, http://www.nytimes.com/2010/01/10/world/middleeast/10balawi.html; Joby Warrick and Pamela Constable, "CIA Base Attacked in Afghanistan Supported Airstrikes Against al-Qaeda, Taliban," *Washington Post*, Jan. 1, 2010, http://www.washingtonpost.com/wp-dyn/content/article/2009/12/31/AR2009123100541_pf.html.

55. Katherine Tiedemann, "Daily Brief: Rumors Fly over Fate of Pakistani Taliban Chief," *Foreign Policy*, Feb. 1, 2010, http://afpak.foreignpolicy.com/posts/2010/02/01/daily_brief_rumors_fly_over_fate_of_pakistani_taliban_chief; Andrew Lebovich and Katherine Tiedemann, "Daily Brief:

Pakistani Taliban Chief Reported 'Wounded' in Drone Strike," *Foreign Policy*, Jan. 15, 2010, http://afpak.foreignpolicy.com/posts/2010/01/15/daily_brief_pakistani_taliban_chief_reported_wounded_in_drone_strike.

56. Alamgir Bitani, "U.S. Drone Attack Kills 15 in Pakistan's Waziristan," Reuters, Jan. 17, 2010.

57. Interview with Shah Sawar Mehsud, TTP commander in Ladha, Nov. 24, 2009, in Gomal, South Waziristan.

58. Bitani, "Waziristan Power Politics."

59. Interview with Ishtiaq Mahsud, Associated Press reporter, Oct. 14, 2009, in D.I. Khan.

60. Interview with Sailab Mehsud, Jan. 19, 2010, in Frontier Region Jandola.

61. Shah Sawar Mehsud interview.

62. Ibid.; Zahid Hussain, "Teenage Bombers Are Rescued from Taleban Suicide Training Camps," *Times* (London), July 27, 2009.

63. Amir Mir, "2009 Bloodiest Year for Pakistan Since 9/11," Middle East Transparent, Dec. 30, 2009, http://www.metransparent.com/spip.php?page=article&id_article=8889&lang=en.

64. Ibid.

65. Hussain, "Teenage Bombers"; interview with Allah u Din Mehsud, head of a madrassa in Ladha, Nov. 6, 2009.

66. Ed Johnson, "Most Afghanistan Suicide Bombers Trained in Pakistan," Bloomberg News, Sept. 8, 2007, http://www.bloomberg.com/apps/news?pid=20601087&sid=ap5SFbBoUT6c&refer=home; "Suicide Attacks in Afghanistan (2001–2007)," United Nations Assistance Mission in Afghanistan, Sept. 9, 2007, http://www.foreignpolicy.com/files/fp_uploaded_images/UNAMAsuicideattacks2007.pdf.

67. Allah u Din Mehsud interview.

68. Saliab Mahsud interview conducted on Dec. 10, 2009, via telephone.

69. Interview with Sohail Mahsud, midlevel Taliban commander, conducted on Feb. 17, 2010, in Gomal village in Tank district.

70. Interview with Associated Press reporter Ishtiaq Mahsud, Tank, Pakistan, Sept. 16, 2011.

71. "Pakistan's Most Wanted," November 2009: Qari Hussain no. 3, Azam Tariq, no. 4; AFP/Getty.

72. "Pakistani Taliban Spokesman 'Held,'" BBC, Aug. 18, 2009, http://news.bbc.co.uk/2/hi/south_asia/8206489.stm.

73. Interview with Sohail Mehsud, TTP military commander, Jan. 20, 2010, in Frontier Region Jandola.

74. Ihsanullah Mahsud, a close friend of Noor Saeed, interview conducted on Jan. 18, 2010, in Gomal village.

75. Interview with Malik Rafique u Din, a tribal elder of the Manzais, Oct. 5, 2009, in South Waziristan.

76. Interviews with Associated Press reporters Ishtiaq Mahsud and Saood Rehman, Tank, Pakistan, September 2011.

77. "The Guantanamo Docket," *New York Times*, n.d., http://projects.nytimes.com/guantanamo/detainees/92-abdullah-mehsud.

78. "Former Guantanamo Inmate Blows Himself up in Pakistan," Agence France Presse, July 25, 2007.

79. Shah Sarwar interview, Oct. 3, 2009, and Sailab Mehsud interview, Oct. 28, 2009.

80. Sailab Mehsud interview, Oct. 28, 2009.

81. Shah Sarwar interview, Oct. 3, 2009, and Sailab Mehsud interview, Oct. 28, 2009.

82. Interview with Abid Khan, member of Dera Ismail Khan peace committee, Jan. 13, 2010, in Dera Ismail Khan.

83. Interview with Sailab Mehsud, Oct. 15, 2009, in Tank city; Ismail Khan, "The Game Is Up for Uzbeks," Dawn.com, Apr. 5, 2007, http://www.dawn.com/2007/04/05/top9.htm; Interview with Gulab Wazir, a tribal elder from Wana, Oct. 11, 2009.

84. Interview with Essa Khan, former TTP amir of Bannu, Nov. 23, 2009.

85. Ibid.

86. Alamgir Wazir interview, Aug. 21, 2009, Wana, South Waziristan.

87. Interview with Alamgir Wazir, Taliban commander in Wana, Oct. 12, 2009, in Wana; "'US Strikes' on Pakistan Village," BBC, Oct. 31, 2008, http://news.bbc.co.uk/2/hi/in_depth/7702679.stm; "Five Killed in S Waziristan Drone Attack," GEO Pakistan, June 18, 2009, http://www.geo.tv/6-18-2009/44382.htm.

88. Sailab Mehsud interview, Oct. 28, 2009.

89. Shah Sarwar interview; Sailab Mehsud interview, Oct. 28, 2009.

90. Interview with Gulab Wazir, tribal elder of Ahmadzai Wazir in Wana, Oct. 13, 2009.

91. Sohail Abdul Nasir, "South Waziristan's Veteran Jihadi Leader: A Profile of Haji Omar," Terrorism Focus, Jamestown Foundation, Aug. 8, 2006, http://www.jamestown.org/programs/gta/single/?tx_ttnews[tt_news]=868&tx_ttnews[backPid]=239&no_cache=1.

92. Bill Roggio, "Senior Taliban Leader Reported Killed in New Year's Eve Strike," Long War Journal, Jan. 2, 2010, http://www.http://www.longwarjournal.org/archives/2010/01/senior_taliban_leade_1.php.

93. "Pakistan Taliban 'Commander Killed,'" Al Jazeera, Oct. 27, 2008, http://english.aljazeera.net/news/asia/2008/10/2008102751020664704.html.

94. Interview with Gulab Wazir, Oct. 7, 2009, in Wana.

95. Interview with Gulab Wazir, Oct. 11, 2009, in Wana.

96. Interview with Sohail Khan Mehsud, TTP military commander in Ladha and a close aide of Shamim Mehsud, Oct. 9, 2009, in Ladha.

97. Interview with FRC correspondent Sailab Mahsud, Dera Ismail Khan, May 2011.

98. Interview with Gul Muhammad, a commander of Asmatullah Shaheen group, Oct. 4, 2009, in Jandola.

99. Sailab Mehsud interview, Oct. 28, 2009.

100. Ibid.

101. Interview with Safder Daur, Nov. 24, 2009, in Dera Ismail Khan.

102. Interviews with TTP affiliates Altaf Mahsud and Sarwar Shah Mahsud Tank, Pakistan, Dec. 5, 2011.

103. C. Christine Fair and Seth G. Jones, "Pakistan's War Within," Survival: Global Politics and Strategy, December 2009.

104. Rahimullah Yusufzai, "Profile: Nek Mohammed," BBC, June 18, 2004, http://news.bbc.co.uk/2/hi/south_asia/3819871.stm; "Return of the Taliban: Nek Mohammed," PBS "Frontline," http://www.pbs.org/wgbh/pages/frontline/taliban/militants/mohammed.html.

105. "Return of the Taliban: Nek Mohammed."

106. David Rohde and Mohammed Khan, "Militant's Defiance Puts Pakistan's Resolve in Doubt," New York Times, June 10, 2004, http://www.nytimes.com/2004/06/10/world/militant-s-defiance-puts-pakistan-s-resolve-in-doubt.html?pagewanted=all; Rohde and Khan, "Ex-Fighter for Taliban Dies in Strike in Pakistan," New York Times, June 19, 2004, http://www.nytimes.com/2004/06/19/international/asia/19STAN.html.

107. Fair and Jones, "Pakistan's War Within"; Dilawar Khan Wazir, "Amnesty Granted to Militant Leader," Dawn.com, Feb. 8, 2005; "Pakistani militants 'call truce,'" BBC, Feb. 7, 2008, http://news.bbc.co.uk/2/hi/south_asia/7232203.stm.

108. Dilawar Khan Wazir, "Amnesty Granted to Militant Leader"; Fair and Jones, "Pakistan's War Within."

109. Fair and Jones, "Pakistan's War Within."

110. Ibid.; Zafar Abbas, "Taliban Ousted, But Spinkai Is Now a Ghost Town," Dawn.com, May 19, 2008.

111. Abbas, "Taliban Ousted."

112. "Pakistani Militants 'Call Truce,'" BBC; Philip Reeves, "Pakistan Holds Peace Talks with Tribal Leaders," NPR, May 2, 2008, http://www.npr.org/templates/story/story.php?storyId=90127353.

113. Abbas, "Taliban Ousted."

114. Jane Perlez, "Taliban Leader Flaunts Power Inside Pakistan," New York Times, June 2, 2008, http://www.nytimes.com/2008/06/02/world/asia/02pstan.html.

115. Interview with Essa Khan, former TTP chief in Bannu, former Guantánamo detainee, and close friend of Baitullah Mehsud, Oct. 12, 2009.

116. Fair and Jones, "Pakistan's War Within."

117. Griff Witte and Imtiaz Ali, "Taliban Ambushes Pakistani Convoy, Seizes 100 Troops," Washington Post, Aug. 31, 2007; Witte and Ali, "47 Killed as Insurgents Take Key Fort in NW Pakistan," Washington Post, Jan. 17, 2008.

118. Sameer Lalwani, "The Pakistan Military's Adaptation to Counterinsurgency in 2009," CTC Sentinel, January 2010, http://www.ctc.usma.edu/sentinel/CTCSentinel-Vol3Iss1.pdf.

119. Shuja Nawaz, "FATA—A Most Dangerous Place," Center for Strategic and International Studies, January 2009, http://csis.org/files/media/csis/pubs/081218_nawaz_fata_web.pdf.

120. Salman Mahsood, "Pakistan Braces for Taliban Attacks as It Prepares Offensive," New York Times, Oct. 6, 2009, http://www.nytimes.com/2009/10/07/world/asia/07pstan.html.

121. Katherine Tiedemann, "Daily Brief: Pakistan Pounds Taliban Militants in Ground Offensive," Foreign Policy, Oct. 19, 2009, http://afpak.foreignpolicy.com/posts/2009/10/19/daily_brief_pakistan_pounds_taliban_militants_in_ground_offensive.

122. Ibid.

123. Interview with Malik Sadat Khan, Mehsud tribal elder with Manzai branch, Nov. 9, 2009.
124. "Pakistani Taliban: Cowards Go to Hell," Associated Press, Nov. 5, 2009, http://www.cbsnews.com/stories/2009/11/05/world/main5535679.shtml.
125. Interview with Yasir Mehsud, military commander of the Abdullah Mehsud group, Dec. 13, 2009, in Tank.
126. Ibid.
127. Interview with Malik Mustafa Mahsud, tribal elder in Ladha, South Waziristan, Jan. 12, 2010, in Dera Ismail Khan.
128. Anwar Shakir and James Rupert, "Pakistan Sets Security Deal with Tribesmen in Taliban War Zone," Bloomberg News, Jan. 21, 2010.
129. Sailab Mehsud interview, Nov. 30, 2009.
130. Interview with Sailab Mehsud, Jan. 11, 2010, Dera Ismail Khan.
131. Interview with Siraj Mehsud, Jan. 7, 2010, in Jandola.
132. Mushtaq Yusufzai, "Maulvi Nazeer Group Ends Differences with Ahmadzai Wazirs," *News International*, Sept. 5, 2009, www.http://www.thenews.com.pk/daily_detail.asp?id=196707.
133. Malik Rafique u Din interview.

SIX

Pakistan's Counterinsurgency Strategy

Sameer Lalwani

EXECUTIVE SUMMARY

Although Pakistan has not completely adopted the models, tactics, and best practices of counterinsurgency (COIN) doctrine advocated by Western strategists, there is considerable evidence of movement in recent years toward a hybrid approach. Pakistan's security forces have historically employed a variety of tactics that include cooptation of militias, raiding, attrition, and sometimes population security, but they experienced repeated failures from 2001 to 2008. Though results of the more recent approach seem promising, prospects for long-term success remain unclear. A full conversion to "population-centric" COIN is unlikely—even with American assistance—because of its sheer difficulty, the prohibitive costs in money and manpower, organizational lags, and substantial trade-offs with Pakistani grand strategy and military doctrine. Triumphant expectations in late 2009 that Pakistan was turning a corner toward greater strategic cooperation with the West, based on its military campaigns in the tribal areas, should have been tempered by a closer analysis of Pakistani public opinion. These data painted a more nuanced picture, in which increased support for efforts to combat some extremist militant groups were matched by rising anti-Americanism and opposition to U.S.-Pakistan cooperation. Thus Pakistan appears to be constrained to a "learning by doing" process, with incremental rather than revolutionary improvements in its approach to counterinsurgency.

INTRODUCTION

Though often recognized for its role in supporting insurgencies against its neighbors in the 1980s and 1990s, the Pakistani military is also no stranger to fighting insurgencies. Since the birth of the nation in 1947, Pakistan has faced insurgencies in nearly all of its provinces and conducted counterinsurgency campaigns varying in scale, strategy, tactics, and outcomes. And even though counterinsurgency is not part of official doctrine, military publications have regularly engaged in sustained analysis and reviews of counterinsurgency tactics and strategy.[1] The 1970–71 campaign in East Pakistan, which employed brutal tactics of collective punishment,[2] failed miserably to quell the insurgency and, coupled with Indian intervention, resulted in the new, independent state of Bangladesh. By contrast, the response to the separatist movement in Baluchistan in 1973–1977 (under the democratically elected government of Zulfikar Ali Bhutto) used similar methods[3] but appeared to achieve moderate success. The Baluchi insurgency flares up every so often, most recently in 2005; the central government has answered with coercive force, heavy artillery, and airpower, compelling the insurgents into submission.

Pakistan's military has employed a variety of tactics in counterinsurgency campaigns. Operations against the most recent Baluchi uprising were best characterized as raiding—targeting insurgent strength and killing off militants. Significant firepower was employed with little regard for the collateral damage. By contrast, during the 1992–1995 campaign in Karachi to quell the urban insurgency led by the ethnic mobilization of the Mohajir Qaumi Movement (MQM) against Sindhis, Pashtuns, and the Pakistani army,[4] illiberal methods of sorting the population were commonly used. Through "cordon and search" operations, security forces attempted to coercively flush out and separate militants (who were embedded within the population) from noncombatants. This approach—though costlier in time, resources, and manpower—improved targeting of militants with less harm to civilians. The crude sorting practices, however, still provoked hostile responses from the host population. An improvement on these methods was developed amid rising violence in Punjab in the early 1990s. The Pakistani government employed a new approach of community policing to generate human intelligence, in which militants were gradually separated out and eliminated from the population with far less collateral damage.[5] Even though successful, the scale of this experiment was small and never achieved standing in military doctrine.

Since 2001, Pakistan has experienced a steady rise in militancy and insurgency in its Federally Administered Tribal Areas (FATA), with substantial infiltration into the adjacent settled areas of Khyber Pakhtunkhwa (KP), formerly the North-West Frontier Province. During this time, Pakistan's established approaches to managing, countering, and containing insurgency—especially the military actions—have come under heavy criticism from within Pakistan[6] as well as from outside observers[7] for their apparent failure.

This chapter reviews the recent history of Pakistani COIN operations, its divergence from Western doctrine and criticisms leveled against it, and adaptations that emerged during the campaigns in 2008–09. It also considers the role of public opinion in shaping and constraining these strategic choices. It concludes by evaluating the costs Pakistan has suffered despite these adaptations and the probability of further convergence to Western doctrine.

COUNTERING INSURGENCY SINCE 2002

Unrest in Pakistan's tribal areas began rising soon after the 2001 U.S. invasion of Afghanistan. The remnants of the Taliban and al-Qaeda leadership had been pushed up against the mountains of Tora Bora, but because of a shortage of forces[8] and insufficient coordination between the U.S. and Pakistani militaries[9] the insurgents narrowly escaped, bribing local guides to lead them through the mountains and harbor them in Pakistan's tribal areas.[10] The militants soon began reconstituting and consolidating their power in those areas. Pakistan helped to target and capture a number of al-Qaeda operatives, but it did not pursue most militant groups; it had dealt with and largely supported the Taliban for many years and believed it could work with local leaders in FATA to manage and contain the insurgents, while flushing out foreign fighters.[11] However, a combination of U.S. pressure and assassination attempts against Pakistan's president, General Pervez Musharraf, eventually propelled the Pakistani military to move against the militants.

For the first time in its fifty-five-year history, the regular Pakistani army (as opposed to local or paramilitary forces) was deployed into the tribal areas.[12] This was controversial, and certain actions, such as attempts to seal the border, actually generated local resistance.[13] From 2002 to 2006, the military conducted roughly two dozen counterinsurgency operations in the tribal areas under the broad auspices of Operation Al-Mizan.[14] The early operations were limited in scope and heavily dependent on Special Services Group (SSG)—Pakistan's special forces—to lead the operations mostly to target foreign fighters, including Operation Kazha Punga in June 2002, Operation Angoor Adda in October 2003, and the raid on Shin Warsak in January 2004.[15]

In March 2004, a section of the paramilitary Frontier Corps (FC) was dispatched to South Waziristan, where nearly all the tribes, but particularly the Ahmedzai Wazir, were actively or passively supporting displaced al-Qaeda members and their allies such as the Islamic Movement of Uzbekistan (IMU). While FC soldiers were attempting to cordon off and search a Taliban stronghold, the outer cordon was besieged by Waziri tribal fighters led by Pakistani Taliban commander Nek Muhammad. The military responded with Operation Kalosha, sending in seven to eight thousand troops to take on two thousand dug-in and heavily armed militants.[16] Pakistan mounted a conventional offensive, deploying heavy artillery, helicopter gunships, and fighter-bombers to blanket the area with firepower. The result was a disaster. Poor planning and a lack of intelligence led to the deaths of about two hundred Pakistani security personnel and more than four hundred civilians, numerous FC desertions, and the displacement of fifty thousand locals, while the operation largely failed to damage the militants' power or capabilities.[17] Moreover, the Pashtun honor code (*Pashtunwali*), which calls for the deaths of kinsmen to be avenged, compromised public support for the government and created more insurgents.[18] Even before the Taliban's political assassination campaign against local maliks, or leaders, the military deployment and the government's decision to replace knowledgeable local political agents, who historically had been helpful in influencing the tribes, contributed to a lack of intelligence on the ground.[19] Meanwhile, Taliban militants were lionized for seeming to have forced the military to negotiate peace, in the Shakai Valley agreement, by the end of March 2004.

The Pakistani military followed this debacle by sending eighty thousand troops into the tribal areas in June 2004 to continue pursuing the fight in a similar "enemy-centric" fashion. During Operation Shakai Valley, the army employed a variety of tactics but particularly the use of heavy firepower—including the Pakistan Air Force's bombers and helicopter gunships—causing considerable collateral damage affecting civilians and their towns.[20] None of these operations sought population security or used enduring small units to patrol and gather intelligence. Nor did the military refrain from extensive use of airpower. It attempted to contain the militants in the tribal areas, but their cross-border raids into Afghanistan and infiltration into the NWFP continued unabated.[21]

Each high-intensity Pakistani military campaign was followed by a cease-fire and a short-lived peace agreement (in 2004, 2005, 2006, and 2008), rather than a sustainable political solution. This further empowered militant groups. The insurgents and the army simply regrouped after each cycle and prepared for the next fight. During these lulls in conflict, Taliban militants were able to install parallel governments[22] in the tribal areas, enhancing their local credibility and authority.[23] The Pakistani military, after repeated failures and roughly seven hundred security force fatalities by the fall of 2006,[24] signed an agreement with the militants that it hoped would endure. But after the deadly raid on Islamabad's Lal Masjid (Red Mosque) in the summer of 2007—when Pakistani special forces commandos removed radical Islamist leaders calling for sharia (Islamic law) and the overthrow of the Pakistani government, while inciting local violence—Taliban leaders abandoned the cease-fire and violence escalated.

Although initially concentrated in the Waziristan agencies, militant attacks spread to other agencies in FATA and parts of KP, and suicide bombings escalated. Besides the Red Mosque incident, the other major trigger for this contagion and escalation was the perceived civilian casualties and uptick in U.S. drone strikes.[25] The

Pakistani military launched a second round of operations beginning in September 2007 in the South Waziristan and Bajaur agencies of the FATA and the Swat Valley of NWFP, intending to rid the area of Taliban militants who had taken root there. But these operations seemed to only exacerbate violence, as combined terrorist, insurgent, and sectarian attacks rose to 2,148 incidents in 2009, an increase of 746 percent from 2005.[26] One analyst estimates that by early 2009 the Pakistani military had lost 70 percent of its battles with the Taliban.[27] This might be corroborated by the extremely high soldier-to-insurgent loss ratios that Army Chief of Staff General Ashfaq Kayani acknowledged.[28]

The spread of militant violence from the Swat Valley through other parts of the Malakand Division of NWFP in spring 2009 revealed to both the Pakistani public and international audiences the continued failure of Pakistani counterinsurgency efforts. Although some tactical adaptations were beginning to emerge, army troops were still reported to be hunkering down in large encampments and lobbing heavy, destructive artillery shells from afar,[29] which appeared to harm the remaining civilians more than the militants.[30] In addition, the force deployed to the area did not appear to be of sufficient size for population security; this is generally believed to require a force-to-population ratio of 20:1,000.[31] As the Pakistani approach to insurgency appeared to be floundering, however, a new intellectual movement on counterinsurgency—based on the U.S. military's lessons in Iraq and lengthy studies of past Western occupation campaigns—was gathering force and adherents.

THE RISE OF COIN AND ITS PRESCRIPTIONS

The U.S. lessons and change of strategy in Iraq—stemming from and emerging alongside a doctrinal review (U.S. Army Field Manual 3–24) and new intellectual movement based around counterinsurgency theory—produced a set of best practices now generally referred to as COIN doctrine.[32] The goal of COIN, according to the U.S. government, is to achieve control by "build[ing] popular support for a government while marginalizing the insurgents: It is therefore fundamentally an armed political competition with the insurgents."[33]

Western COIN doctrine calls for political solutions over military, population security over enemy targeting, ground forces over airpower, and small-unit rather than large-unit force deployments for missions (such as patrols, intelligence gathering, and development assistance). In essence, these practices expose troops to greater vulnerability to achieve more discriminatory use of force.[34] Beyond these tactics, a successful COIN campaign requires certain "best practices," including unification of civilian and military structures; effective use of amnesty and rewards; construction and enforcement of border security; and development of local, perhaps indigenous, pacification capacities, which in the case of Pakistan would mean local militias, or lashkars.[35]

Given the successes of this population-security model of counterinsurgency touted by such scholars as David Kilcullen and James Dobbins,[36] theories of international relations would generally predict that, in the interest of survival, other countries would emulate and adopt these best practices as they have other successful strategies of warfare.[37] As an ally of the United States, not only recently but also during the Cold War during which the United States closely studied and identified these best practices in COIN, Pakistan should have been most likely to adopt a Western model of population-security COIN.[38] And yet it has rarely done so, if ever.

PAKISTAN'S DISTINCTIVE APPROACH TO COUNTERINSURGENCY

The Pakistani military has thus far mostly conducted campaigns that run counter to all these prescriptions of Western COIN doctrine. This is primarily attributable to military doctrine rooted in persistent fear of a numerically superior Indian army threatening the Pakistani core. Most operations since 2002 relied nearly exclusively on overwhelming force with heavy artillery and aerial bombing to break the enemy.[39] In some instances, the military deliberately used heavy-handed tactics to "out-terrorize the terrorist,"[40] but pure coercion and collective punishment achieved little.

Though several Pakistan experts and analysts have articulated the various failures of the Pakistani military approach,[41] Kilcullen neatly summarizes the several interlinking shortfalls since 2002: (1) a nearly exclusive focus on enemy targeting and "high-value targets"; (2) overdependence on large-scale, multiunit forces rather than small, lithe patrol units dispersed among the population; (3) frequent defensive deployment of forces to static garrisons, check points, or asset tasks, inhibiting proactive missions; (4) the absence of maneuver room and a shortage of resources such as quick-reaction forces for flexible responses to contingencies; (5) overreliance on kinetic "direct-action" operations; and (6) underuse of the capacity and knowledge of local forces (i.e., the Frontier Corps and tribal lashkars).[42]

The net result was rapid disappearance of whatever tactical gains the military had achieved. Fair and Jones write, "Pakistani operations were not sustained over time, but rather were marked by sweeps, searches and occasional bloody battles. None of these operations employed sufficient forces to hold territory."[43]

One might contend that the Pakistani military has in recent years modified its approach from outright raiding on insurgent positions, with little regard for civilians, to a more targeted strategy of clearing out the population to separate them from insurgents; this approach, however, still yields coercive dislocation, refugees, and simmering resentment. Moreover, raiding and coercive sorting can potentially exacerbate local grievances and in turn lead to more passive or active support of insurgents. Reports of insurgent infiltration and militant recruitment in refugee camps after the Swat and Bajaur campaigns suggest that coercive sorting operations designed to crudely separate the population and reduce collateral damage can still alienate the local people and thus be undermined by their unintended consequences.

Meanwhile, the nature of kinetic, "phase one," enemy-centric operations that disregard the "hold" and "build" phases of counterinsurgency—combined with historically poor civil-military relations, weak civilian capacity, and a historical absence of governance in this region—has limited the role of civilians in the counterinsurgency campaigns of the past eight years. Even with signs of a shift toward greater civilian participation in Swat, there is little evidence that this is balanced with the military's role or that it can be applied elsewhere, particularly in the FATA.

REASONS FOR DIVERGENCE: DIFFICULTIES, DRAWBACKS, AND COSTS

Pakistani deviation from COIN prescriptions can be attributed in large part to the great challenges involved in counterinsurgency. Manpower requirements notwithstanding, COIN is considered one of the most difficult operations to execute; it is extremely costly and time-intensive, and it can bog down even the most capable and sophisticated militaries in the world.[44] The tactical and organizational barriers are quite high for most modern militaries, particularly those in the developing world, where the relatively democratic and egalitarian social and political structures necessary for the success of a "hearts and minds" counterinsurgency are largely absent.[45]

Meanwhile, the process of transitioning to a COIN force can take years. Even after the U.S. military made doctrinal changes in response to the insurgency in Iraq, there was still a substantial time lag in actually adopting these practices. This organizational lag results in part from the need for a professional military to effectively "unlearn" what it has been trained to do, so it can then adopt the best practices of COIN.[46] It is therefore possible that the more professionally the military has trained for conventional warfare, the longer it takes to adapt. Not factoring in this organizational lag, should the Pakistani military exclusively dedicate itself to this purpose, one estimate of the time frame for retraining the Pakistani army and some irregular units for a population-security counterinsurgency campaign would still be two to five years.[47]

The downside of focusing on COIN, however, is that it can force strategic trade-offs, such as weakening the conventional capabilities for which the military is primarily trained. Recent studies suggest that the Israel Defense Forces, after decades of counterinsurgency in the occupied territories, were underprepared for the partially conventional fight against Hezbollah in the 2006 Lebanon war.[48]

The circumstances in Pakistan also provide explanations for its different approach. The Taliban insurgents have proved to be a much more formidable and committed opponent than either the Pakistani military or Western observers anticipated. The size of the insurgency—ranging from twenty to forty thousand, depending on the degree of Taliban unification—is quite large, and the diffusion of training and skills through field manuals has enabled the militants to punch above the weight of simply the battle-hardened fighters. Taliban affiliates are most unified when fighting U.S. and Western forces, but they can also unite around Pakistani military incursions. They have sought greater institutionalization in recent years, adapted to counter new Pakistani tactics, and managed to weather a succession process following the death of Baitullah Mehsud, leader of the umbrella group Tehrik-i-Taliban Pakistan (TTP). Among other factors that make any type of counterinsurgency campaign in Pakistan especially difficult: a high level of militant commitment, a long history of tribal autonomy and resistance to perceived efforts at centralized control (even those intended to improve development and governance), and the immensely challenging terrain of the tribal areas.[49]

Because of the insurgency's size and capacity, the Pakistani military is stretched thin in resources and manpower.[50] Even with sixty thousand troops stationed at a thousand posts along the border, the government has trouble controlling the area—that is, subduing militant training, cross-border raids into Afghanistan, and use of safe havens. The difficult mountainous terrain favors the insurgents,[51] with more than twenty "frequented" passes and some three hundred "unfrequented" passes that the fighters can use.[52] Though Pakistani forces can, in theory, be dispersed and deployed locally within the tribal areas in accordance with Western COIN doctrine, they remain surrounded by tribal networks and forces, and their lines of communication and supply depend on the goodwill of these groups.[53] Pakistan has often supplemented its regular army troops with local irregular forces, but their usefulness is constrained by limited skills and equipment.[54] Moreover, improving the abilities of these paramilitary fighters, or embedding them with regular troops, risks undermining the central government's control, embroiling the troops in tribal battles, and potentially weakening the regular forces.

Finally, a Western-style COIN campaign would present Pakistan with a Catch-22. Because of its limited resources, Pakistan would require substantial U.S. and other Western assistance—military aid, training, and economic support—for a successful and enduring COIN campaign. However, as the U.S. role expanded and became more visible, Pakistan would face a stiffer public backlash, a steeper decline in the morale of its regular and irregular forces, and a more cohesive insurgency.[55]

These obstacles to a purely "population-centric" COIN strategy helps explain why Pakistan has so far pursued low-intensity war with ample use of heavy firepower. After the many failures of this approach from 2001 to 2008, the most recent operations, which incorporated some new tactics, show promising signs of improvement and moderate success even without fully adhering to classical COIN doctrine.

"LEARNING BY DOING": RECENT ADAPTATIONS IN SWAT AND SOUTH WAZIRISTAN

Though the Pakistani military's approach diverges from Western COIN prescriptions, this has not inhibited learning, improvement, and adaptation to a hybrid model that combines some of the COIN practices with refined indigenous methods. Through a process of "learning by doing," the army addressed its failures of earlier years by raising troop levels, improving training, and "inoculating" troops for a very different type of battlefield.[56] The result has been dynamic incorporation of lessons learned from the field[57] and adoption of some U.S. military practices (some effective, but some counterproductive).[58] The COIN practices include deploying smaller and more dispersed units, patrolling to protect the population, and raising local police forces to sustain operational gains. And in recent years, more formal and advanced preparation for COIN has been incorporated into the curriculum of Pakistan military academies and training centers.[59]

The Pakistani military still uses substantial airpower to soften up militant targets, but it has begun to combine this with more follow-on ground forces to disperse militants and secure the area for the local population. Likewise, the hybrid strategy accepts the need for a political solution rather than a purely coercive military one, employing both a "hearts and minds" campaign and a "divide and rule" approach. These innovations and adaptations were displayed in the recent campaigns in the Swat Valley and South Waziristan.

SWAT: OPERATION RAH-E-RAST (RIGHTEOUS PATH)

In Swat, beginning in April 2009, the deliberate innovation of the military was to actively clear out the population in order to better target insurgents and reduce collateral damage.[60] This allowed freer targeting of insurgents, but it also risked a backlash from locals and a potential breeding ground for militant recruitment in refugee camps.[61] However, in follow-on operations, the military, combined with some civilian efforts, shifted to a more population-centric approach by working to quickly resettle the internally displaced persons (IDPs), reestablish the writ of governance, and help people restart their lives with injections of economic support.[62] The success of the operation and support for the central government's jurisdiction will depend heavily on the success of IDP resettlement and substantive changes in governance and the justice system in the Swat Valley.

At the tactical level, the military began to further incorporate advice from junior officers, which led to innovative use of forces and equipment on the battlefield. Before this, shifts in strategy and tactics had been promulgated from the top down, but with little positive effect. In the absence of established counterinsurgency doctrine or manuals, captains through colonels, who had drawn lessons from successful bottom-up experimentation in the Bajaur campaign (late 2008 to early 2009), were brought into the decision-making process.[63] Higher troop levels in Swat and use of combined air and ground maneuvers allowed the military to pursue and encircle insurgent forces, particularly foreign militants.[64] However, blocking forces made major blunders, failing to constrain local Taliban militants and to restrict outside combatants from entering Swat to join the fight. The military is reported to have made great use of dispersed forces,[65] including the SSG.[66] It also began building small bases within populated areas, enforcing curfews through small-unit patrols, and assisting with local aid.[67] After the "clear" phase (phase one), the military retained two divisions in Swat for the "hold" phase.[68] However, it is unclear how the troops are presently performing this role—whether they are patrolling and building confidence in the local communities, as they were doing immediately after phase one,[69] or remaining in close proximity for future punitive actions against a Taliban resurgence. As one of these divisions is mechanized, it is unlikely to be trained for the population-centric, risk-intensive missions of counterinsurgency.[70]

The sustainability of the gains in Swat remains uncertain, especially with reports that Taliban strength was merely displaced, and that reinfiltration and attacks continue.[71] After all, the Pakistani military declared victory in Swat once before, at the beginning of 2008, but the insurgents were able to return and regain their power in the region.[72] Consolidating success in Swat will remain contingent on the holding and building phases—reincorporating the two million IDPs while maintaining security, preventing Taliban reinfiltration, and working with civilian bureaucracies to "build" on the gains by addressing the economic and governance grievances that had provided openings for the Taliban takeover. This will be a challenge, given Pakistan's limited resources, the attention focused on subsequent operations in South Waziristan, and the fallout from that campaign in neighboring tribal areas. Consolidation of gains will also be hampered by the Pakistani state's structural problems, among them historically poor civil-military relations, cycles of political instability, and weak social and economic institutions.[73]

Additionally, in the bigger picture, only cautious optimism for the approach employed in Swat is warranted because Swat may present more of an exception than a model for future operations. Success in the "more settled" Swat Valley may not be replicable in the tribal areas because of pronounced differences in environmental and structural conditions. Swat's higher levels of development and infrastructure, population density, formal incorporation into the Pakistani state with political representation, and acceptance of central governance may better facilitate the consolidation of gains in Swat. This includes resettlement of IDPs, resumption of governance, reconstruction, establishment of local security forces, and demobilization of militants.[74]

SOUTH WAZIRISTAN: OPERATION RAH-E-NIJAT (PATH TO DELIVERANCE)

During the fall 2009 South Waziristan operation to dislodge the stronghold of TTP founded by Baitullah Mehsud, the Pakistani military followed on its successful maneuvers in Swat. It employed higher ratios of Peshawar-based regular army infantry in comparison to previous campaigns in the FATA, which relied heavily on the Frontier Corps. Though official military statements reported the deployment at thirty thousand troops, including two regular infantry divisions, some estimates inclusive of supporting troops placed the figure as high as sixty thousand.[75]

Before the actual operation, the military took several steps to effectively shape the environment and target the region. In a major tactical maneuver, it sidelined powerful tribal-based militant groups led by Mullah Nazir and Hafiz Gul Bahadur, whose resistance to previous operations in the FATA had foiled the Pakistani military's ability to concentrate power against a specific set of targets.[76] Second, the military experimented with psychological operations, distributing leaflets supposedly from religious authorities and local tribes warning youths of "false jihad" and blaming foreign militants for bringing destruction to the tribal areas.[77] Third, Pakistani Special Forces began targeting known commanders and suspected militant bases in the spring of 2009 with airpower and helicopter strikes to soften them.[78]

These steps all indicated a more sophisticated understanding of the enemy, but they remained part of a phase one "clear" operation. This approach did not necessarily bear much resemblance to COIN except in force-to-population ratios, but because it formed only the front end of what is expected to be a long campaign, the jury is still out on whether lessons of COIN are being incorporated into Pakistani military doctrine and practice.

After significant pummeling of suspected Mehsud encampments with artillery and airpower,[79] army ground forces advanced slowly and methodically toward Taliban strongholds along three axes in a section of South Waziristan.[80] Further tactical adjustments in the operation included seizing the high ground to control valleys and employing effective route clearance to limit damage from improvised explosive devices (IEDs).[81] The military also received operational intelligence support, with data collected by unmanned U.S. aerial vehicles, to help with navigation and targeting.[82] After seven weeks of ground fighting, the Pakistani government declared a tactical success but quickly added that the campaign would continue in other parts of the tribal areas where violence had resurfaced.[83]

As in the case with Swat, the outcome in Waziristan will depend heavily on the operation's material impact on the militants and the population (something still being examined), as well as future actions by the Pakistani military and government to consolidate these tactical gains. Analysts believe the Mehsud camp of the Pakistani Taliban, which has been targeting the Pakistani state, may have been dislodged from its bases and disrupted, but it may be far from being dismantled. (Baitullah Mehsud was killed by a reported U.S. drone strike in August 2009; his successor, Hakimullah Mehsud, is believed to have died following a January 2010 air strike, though the TTP has denied it.) It was estimated that the TTP had ten to fifteen thousand militants, including a thousand to fifteen hundred foreign (primarily Uzbek) fighters,[84] but the army offensive encountered only a few isolated pockets of intense resistance early, even in the Uzbek stronghold of Kaniguram.[85] With resistance melting away and only six hundred Taliban militants having been reported killed, this suggests that most TTP fighters dispersed early or during the fighting, or that they relocated to maintain operational capabilities. The rash of suicide bombings throughout Pakistan that claimed a thousand lives in 2009, the continued bombings—thirty-seven were conducted in the five months since the operations in South Waziristan began—and the flare-up of violence in neighboring tribal agencies seem to support the theory of continuing capability.[86]

The conclusion then is that the Mehsud camp may have been dealt a blow and lost its operational base, but the displaced militants have already resumed operations against soft targets. One retired Pakistani brigadier general has voiced his belief that the TTP will be able to regroup and resume hit-and-run tactics in South Waziristan.[87] And some former Pakistani generals and analysts contend that military operations in the tribal region are far from over, and that other agencies, once deemed stable in early 2009, might fall again to Taliban control.[88]

Meanwhile, a number of factors that remain unknown could unfavorably tip the balance and, in combination, determine the outcome in South Waziristan. One is the Taliban's ability to retreat into neighboring Afghan or Pakistani provinces or districts, avoiding immediate battle so the militants can return to fight again. In fact, raids launched from Eastern Afghanistan into Bajaur Agency and upper Dir became a major concern for Pakistan in 2011. Another concern is the limits of the Pakistani military presence in the tribal areas during the "hold" phase, due to scarce resources,[89] as well as possible tribal backlash that could collapse the fragile treaties that have kept other TTP affiliates neutral. A big question is the impact of South Waziristan's IDPs on the region in terms of resettlement, resentments and potential militant recruitment, and pathways for militant reinfiltration; this also applies to IDPs from Bajaur and Swat, an issue that has not been fully addressed.[90] Another unknown is the impact of retaliatory suicide bombings on the willingness of the government, the military, and the public to press the South Waziristan campaign further.[91] Finally, there is the choice of endgame for the tribal region, in part dependent on the previous factor of political will. Should there be a return to tribal autonomy managed by political agents, as Pakistani analysts seem to prefer,[92] or the much more difficult project of development, new governance, and greater political enfranchisement, which for historical and cultural reasons could engender even more resistance?[93]

THE ROLE OF PUBLIC OPINION

Though the Pakistani military seems to have adapted during its confrontations with militants in 2009, Pakistani public opinion has not demonstrably shifted in tandem, as some have claimed, and may force the state and military in different directions. Even with increasing popular support for combating certain militant extremists who threaten Pakistan's security, there has not been a substantial, corresponding shift in attitudes toward cooperation with the United States or alignment with its strategic vision for the region. The trends and role of public opinion need to be examined to assess potential support for or constraints on future counterinsurgency campaigns.

Before 2007, little publicized polling work was done in Pakistan outside of the Pew Global Attitudes survey and domestic Pakistani polls. Although public opinion from 2002 to 2006 was trending toward greater moderation in beliefs[94] and support for the United States— including a spike in favorability after U.S. relief efforts in response to the October 2005 earthquake—views were still extremely negative. U.S. favorability only once crossed the 25 percent threshold, while unfavorable opinions trumped favorables by approximately a 3:1 ratio. In 2004, 41 percent of those surveyed said they believed suicide bombing was at least sometimes justified, and in 2005 52 percent of the sample reported confidence in al-Qaeda leader Osama bin Laden.[95]

More recent polling by a variety of outlets has analyzed a broader range of Pakistani public opinion on more focused subjects. From late 2006 to 2009, the Pakistani public had largely dismissed the Taliban threat and opposed the military's cooperation with and participation in the U.S.-led war on terrorism.[96] Threat perceptions of extremist groups, particularly the Taliban, steadily grew and hardened over the decade, but Pakistanis were divided on the best course of action and remained "at best ambivalent about armed responses against the militants ravaging the country."[97] From mid-2007 until the spring of 2009, public support for peace deals with militants rose to a majority of Pakistanis, declining only after the operations in Swat Valley. During this same time span, perhaps owing to the repeated failures of military campaigns in 2002–2006, a majority of Pakistanis also opposed army operations against militants. But as the peace deals were broken and Taliban militants encroached into more settled areas such as Swat, public opinion began to turn.

Polls in the spring and summer of 2009 appeared to reveal a marked shift in public attitudes, with greater support for military action and declining support for peace deals. But it remained uncertain whether this shift would endure, given the potential consequences of unfolding military operations. After the operations in Swat, a poll by Al Jazeera and Gallup Pakistan revealed yet another turn, with renewed support for dialogue with militants over military action (43 percent versus 41 percent). However, this directly conflicted with the findings of an International Republican Institute poll from around the same time that suggested rising support for military operations in Malakand Division (i.e., Swat and its surrounding areas) and declining support for peace deals.

Additionally, these polls found escalating hostility toward the United States. Not only did support for cooperation drop sharply (from 37 percent in March 2009 to 18 percent in July 2009),[98] but more worrisome, a perception was emerging that the United States posed the greatest threat to Pakistan. At a staggering 59 percent, the figure for the United States more than doubled those of India (18 percent) and the Pakistani Taliban (11 percent) combined.[99]

As the South Waziristan operation was in its first few weeks, another Gallup Pakistan poll revealed even more mixed results. A slim majority in late October 2009 supported military action, but slightly more believed it would worsen the situation (37 percent) than bring peace (36 percent). Blame for the deteriorating situation in Waziristan was attributed somewhat evenly among the Taliban (25 percent), the Pakistani government

(31 percent), and the United States (36 percent). Similarly, opinions on ownership of the war were divided, with 37 percent believing it to be Pakistan's war, 39 percent saying it was America's war, and 22 percent believing both had a shared stake in the outcome.[100]

Recent statistical analysis of Pakistani public opinion reveals something more striking: public sentiment in support of militant groups cannot be explained simply by poverty, religion, or democracy. Rather, it depends on a more sophisticated strategic calculation of the usefulness of particular militant groups in different theaters for different objectives.[101] Though greatly in need of further study and replication, the implication of this evidence is that support for militants may not be easily sapped by a single social policy agenda, and that it could take years to change the perceived costs and benefits of these strategic choices.

The Pakistani military deftly navigated public opinion by waiting for a proximate cause—the militant assault on the army's general headquarters in October 2009—before publicly launching its ground offensive in South Waziristan.[102] In this instance, it was able to marshal public support and cast the offensive as one in defense of the Pakistani state rather than on behalf of the United States. But the Pakistani government will not always have such a public relations opportunity. Presently, Pakistani military operations are opposed by a plurality of residents in North and South Waziristan,[103] which means they would encounter resistance from the population in mobilizing support and collecting human intelligence, thus contributing to the government's hesitation to expand operations here. Moreover, increased popular support for the Pakistani state does not translate to more support for the United States, or change the tide of anti-U.S. public opinion in Pakistan. For instance, a 2011 survey in FATA shows continued support for Pakistani military presence and offensives, but not if combined with or supported by the United States or other external actors.[104] Even if a structural turn in Pakistani public opinion on counterterrorism issues emerges,[105] rising anti-American sentiment could prevent the Pakistani military from adopting a shared set of counterinsurgency practices, an improved training program,[106] and a broader strategic outlook on combating both the Pakistani and Afghan Taliban networks—all of which may be necessary to consolidate its gains against militants in the region.

CONCLUSIONS

Though the Pakistani military has a mixed record of success and failure, its approach to counterinsurgency has generally diverged from the recently ascendant set of prescriptions and best practices. Commonly referred to by Western analysts as COIN doctrine, these prescriptions emphasize population security and political solutions, winning the hearts and minds of the people with more controlled and discriminatory use of force. Pakistan's departure from this approach stems from strategic and doctrinal priorities, resource constraints, level of difficulty, and potential drawbacks and trade-offs, all of which make COIN a less attractive option.

Despite this divergence, the Pakistani military has demonstrated substantial learning and adaptation, and its approach to countering insurgency in the tribal areas has changed over the past decade. After establishing mechanisms and practices to learn from previous mistakes, the military has modified a number of its tactics against the Taliban, both on and off the battlefield, to improve its chances of success. Some of these lessons and adaptations were drawn from elements of COIN doctrine, particularly during the Swat operation, resulting in a hybrid model incorporating Western prescriptions and the military's own approach.

It is important to note that Pakistan's adaptations during the 2009 military operations were not a full-fledged doctrinal shift, but modifications in low-intensity conflict.[107] Whether due to constraints or by choice, the Pakistani approach to counterinsurgency retains many vestiges of conventional warfare. The nature of the military's equipment and force structure often yields tactical choices such as heavy use of airpower.[108] Moreover, until a formal institution or counterinsurgency training school is created, this approach to warfare will not fully change among the junior or senior officer corps. Since tactics derive from strategy, so long as Pakistan diverges from U.S. strategic aims in the region it will likely employ a different set of political tactics such as "divide and rule" in the tribal areas, much to the frustration of Western leaders and analysts.[109]

Pakistan's caution at fully converting to Western COIN—or quickly turning to take on militants in North Waziristan, as many analysts hoped—stems from the heavy cost since 2002, including thirty thousand people killed in the last four years[110] and an estimated net loss of $28 billion to Pakistan's economy during the war on terrorism.[111] Since beginning these operations, the Pakistan army has suffered nearly thirteen thousand casualties, which includes more than three thousand killed and more than seven hundred permanently wounded—the equivalent of two brigades of personnel. However, owing to the unusually high ratio of officers killed in this fight (one for every sixteen enlisted men), this is perceived to be tantamount to the loss of two divisions' worth of operational capacity.[112]

The neutrality agreements with some militant groups in the region (particularly those of Nazir and Gul Bahadur), created specifically to prevent them from opposing military operations in South Waziristan, do not constitute an enduring alignment or effective cooptation, but rather a sequenced strategic choice by both sides. Whereas the agreements will likely prove untenable in the medium to long run, given their incongruence with other Pakistani state objectives in the region, the government has shown no signs of foreclosing on these side deals in the near term. Meanwhile, the government hesitates to confront the militant networks that remain active in Afghanistan but seem to pose less of an immediate threat to the Pakistani state.[113] Overall, Pakistan's reluctance to confront the entire stock of radical militant networks within its borders is not uniquely a function of capabilities (both military and governance) or political will, but a mix of both that cannot be neatly separated.[114]

The Pakistani military has long experience contending with insurgencies throughout the country, as well as managing militant and insurgent groups on its borders since the 1980s. This vast indigenous knowledge, coupled with the military's doctrinal and strategic preferences, seems to inform Pakistan's path of counterinsurgency—an approach that is improving, absorbing lessons, and adapting, and one that ultimately may achieve degrees of success even as it departs from Western formulas.

Notes

1. These debates dating back to at least the 1990s are prominent in a number of Pakistan's service and strategic journals, including *Pakistan Army Journal*, *Pakistan Defence Review*, *National Defence University Journal*. Additionally, the *Pakistan Army Green Book* from 2002 specifically focused on "Low-Intensity Conflict."

2. "Pakistan: The Ravaging of Golden Bengal," *Time*, Aug. 2, 1971.

3. See Thomas H. Johnson and M. Chris Mason, "No Sign Until the Burst of Fire: Understanding the Pakistan-Afghanistan Frontier," *International Security*, Vol. 32, No. 4, Spring 2008, p. 76.

4. See Paul Staniland, "Cities on Fire: Social Mobilization, State Policy, and Urban Insurgency," *Comparative Political Studies*, Vol. 43, No. 12, December 2010.

5. C. Christine Fair, *Urban Battle Fields of South Asia: Lessons Learned from Sri Lanka, India and Pakistan* (RAND, Santa Monica, CA, 2004).

6. See Khalid Aziz, "Need for a Counterinsurgency Strategy," *News International*, June 15, 2008; Muhammad Khurshid Khan, "Analyzing Domestic Terrorism as a Threat to Pakistan's Security and the Policy Response," *Islamabad Policy Research Institute Journal*, Vol. 9, No. 2, Summer 2009, p. 61; Ahmed Rashid, "Pakistan's Continued Failure to Adopt a Counterinsurgency Strategy," *CTC Sentinel*, Vol. 2, No. 3, March 2009.

7. David J. Kilcullen, "Terrain, Tribes, and Terrorists: Pakistan, 2006–2008," Brookings Counterinsurgency and Pakistan Paper Series, No. 3, Sept. 10, 2009; Seth G. Jones, "Pakistan's Dangerous Game," *Survival*, Vol. 49, No. 1, Spring 2007.

8. Peter Krause, "The Last Good Chance: A Reassessment of U.S. Operations at Tora Bora," Security Studies, Vol. 17, No. 4, October 2008, pp. 644–84.

9. Fair and Jones argue that there was a convergence of interests over targeting al-Qaeda and meaningful cooperation between the U.S. and Pakistani forces. See C. Christine Fair and Seth G. Jones, "Pakistan's War Within," *Survival*, Vol. 51, No. 6, December 2009, pp. 161–88. However, Cloughley argues that the Tora Bora operation was not coordinated with the Pakistani military, despite U.S. claims, so it could not seal the border. Upon hearing about the operation through the press, the army deployed five thousand troops from the XI Corps within three days, although they could hardly seal such a long border. The failure of strategies on both sides of the Afghanistan-Pakistan border over the past few years has been partly attributed to this continued lack of coordination. Brian Cloughley, *War, Coups, and Terror: Pakistan's Army in Years of Turmoil* (Skyhorse, New York, 2009), pp. 187–88. This charge of failure to coordinate is echoed in Carey Schofield, *Inside the Pakistan Army* (Biteback, London, 2011), pp. 132–33.

10. Shuja Nawaz, "FATA—A Most Dangerous Place: Meeting the Challenge of Militancy and Terror in the Federally Administered Tribal Areas of Pakistan," Washington, D.C.: Center for Strategic and International Studies Press, January 2009.

11. Fair and Jones, December 2009, pp. 167–68; Imtiaz Gul, *The Most Dangerous Place: Pakistan's Lawless Frontier* (Penguin Books, New York, 2011), p. 13; Schofield, 2011, p. 134.

12. Kilcullen, 2009, p. 9.

13. Schofield, 2011, p. 143.

14. Fair and Jones, December 2009, p. 168.

15. Schofield, 2011, pp. 138–51.

16. Ahmed Rashid, *Descent into Chaos: The United States and the Failure of Nation Building in Pakistan, Afghanistan, and Central Asia* (Penguin, New York, 2008). Schofield, 2011, pp. 152–56; Gul, 2011, pp. 21–31.

17. This account is largely drawn from Nawaz, "FATA—A Most Dangerous Place,"
    p. 25; Fair and Jones, "Pakistan's War Within," pp. 168–69; and Rashid, *Descent
    into Chaos*. Fatality figures are from South Asia Terrorism Portal.
18. Nicholas Schmidle, *To Live or to Perish Forever* (Holt, New York, 2009), pp.
    50–51; Johnson and Mason, *International Security*, Spring 2008.
19. Nawaz, "FATA—A Most Dangerous Place," pp. 9–11.
20. For greater descriptions of these operations, see Fair and Jones, December 2009;
    Schofield, 2011, 156–60.
21. Rashid, 2008.
22. These governance institutions may not have filled every role of the state, but
    they included a degree of legitimate force, dispute arbitration, taxation, and
    conscription.
23. Fair and Jones, December 2009, p. 172.
24. This unofficial figure was reported by Shaun Gregory, "Pakistan on Edge,"
    OpenDemocracy.net, Sept. 24, 2006. This corresponds closely with data reported
    by South Asia Terrorism Portal, http://www.satp.org/satporgtp/countries/
    pakistan/database/casualties.htm.
25. Gul, 2011, pp. 96, 135–37.
26. Fair and Jones, December 2009, p. 174.
27. An anonymous American analyst is cited. "Pakistan and the Taliban: A Real
    Offensive or a Phony War?" *Economist*, Apr. 30, 2009.
28. Gul, 2011, p. 127.
29. Rashid, "Pakistan's Continued Failure to Adopt a Counterinsurgency Strategy,"
    March 2009.
30. Richard A. Oppel Jr. and Pir Zubair Shah, "In Pakistan, Radio Amplifies Terror
    of Taliban," *New York Times*, Jan. 25, 2009.
31. See quote from Gen. David Petraeus and FM 3–24 in Peter Krause, "Troop
    Levels in Stability Operations: What We Don't Know," MIT Audit of
    the Conventional Wisdom, February 2007; James T. Quinlivan, "Force
    Requirements in Stability Operations," *Parameters*, Vol. 25, Winter 1995–96, pp.
    59–69.
32. For evidence of this intellectual movement, see John Nagl, *Learning to Eat
    Soup with a Knife: Counterinsurgency Lessons from Malaya and Vietnam* (Praeger,
    Westport, CT, 2002); David Kilcullen, *The Accidental Guerrilla: Fighting Small
    Wars in the Midst of a Big One* (Oxford University Press, 2009); Stephen Biddle,
    "The New U.S. Army/Marine Corps Counterinsurgency Field Manual as
    Political Science and Political Praxis," *Perspectives on Politics*, Vol. 6, No. 2, June
    2008; Thomas Ricks, *The Gamble: General David Petraeus and the American
    Military Adventure in Iraq, 2006–2008* (Penguin, New York, 2009); U.S. Army
    Field Manual 3–24.
33. U.S. Government Counterinsurgency Guide, 2009.
34. Biddle, "The New U.S. Army/Marine Corps Counterinsurgency Field Manual."
    The dominant counterinsurgency approach—"clear-hold-build"—is described in
    Army Field Manual 3–24, pp. 5–18.
35. A report prepared for the U.S. defense secretary by RAND, drawing on the
    lessons of COIN from British, French, and U.S. experiences during the past fifty
    years, offers several practices and techniques that have been proposed for the

U.S. campaigns in Iraq and Afghanistan. Austin Long, *On "Other War": Lessons from Five Decades of RAND Counterinsurgency Research* (RAND, Santa Monica, CA, 2006).

36. David Kilcullen, *Counterinsurgency* (Oxford University Press, 2010), p. 7; James Dobbins, "Your COIN Is No Good Here," *Foreign Affairs*, Oct. 26, 2010, http://www.foreignaffairs.com/articles/66949/james-dobbins/your-coin-is-no-good-here.

37. See Kenneth Waltz, *A Theory of International Politics* (McGraw-Hill, New York, 1979), p. 127.

38. One retired Lt. General in the Pakistan Army acknowledged that Pakistan had access to and reviewed U.S. Army COIN doctrine in the 1970s but did not find it useful or applicable. Author interview, Rawalpindi, Pakistan, Oct. 22, 2011.

39. Rashid, 2009; Rashid, 2008.

40. Haider Ali Hussein Mullick, *Pakistan's Security Paradox: Countering and Fomenting Insurgencies* (Joint Special Operations University Press, Hurlburt Field, FL, 2009).

41. See Fair and Jones, December 2009; Rashid, 2009; Moeed Yusuf and Anit Mukherjee, "Counterinsurgency in Pakistan: Learning from India," *AEI National Security Outlook*, September 2007; Stephen P. Cohen and Shuja Nawaz, "Mastering Counterinsurgency: A Workshop Report," Brookings Counterinsurgency and Pakistan Paper Series, July 7, 2009; and Haider Ali Hussein Mullick, *Helping Pakistan Defeat the Taliban: A Joint Action Agenda for the United States & Pakistan*, Institute for Social Policy and Understanding, August 2009.

42. Kilcullen, 2009.

43. Fair and Jones, "Pakistan's War Within," December 2009, p. 172.

44. Biddle, 2008.

45. Daniel Byman, "Friends Like These," *International Security*, Vol. 31, No. 2, Fall 2006.

46. Austin Long, "Doctrine of Eternal Recurrence: The U.S. Military and Counterinsurgency Doctrine, 1960–1970 and 2003–2006," RAND Counterinsurgency Study, No. 6, 2008.

47. Sameer Lalwani, *Pakistani Capabilities for a Counterinsurgency Campaign: A Net Assessment*, Counterterrorism Strategy Initiative Publication, New America Foundation, September 2009.

48. Avi Kober, "The Israel Defense Forces in the Second Lebanon War: Why the Poor Performance?" *Journal of Strategic Studies*, Vol. 31, No. 1, 2008; Matt M. Mathews, "We Were Caught Unprepared: The 2006 Hezbollah-Israeli War," Long War Series Occasional Paper 26, Fort Leavenworth, KS: Combat Studies Institute Press, 2008.

49. See Kilcullen, 2009; Johnson and Mason, 2008; Nawaz, 2009; Lalwani, 2009.

50. Lalwani, 2009.

51. James D. Fearon and David D. Laitin, "Ethnicity, Insurgency and Civil War," *American Political Science Review*, Vol. 97, No. 1, February 2003.

52. Johnson and Mason, 2008.

53. "Afghanistan, Pakistan: The Battlespace of the Border," Stratfor Intelligence, 2008.

54. However, this is beginning to change in recent years.

55. Lalwani, 2009.

56. Stephen P. Cohen and Shuja Nawaz, "Mastering Counterinsurgency: A Workshop Report," Brookings Counterinsurgency and Pakistan Paper Series, July 7, 2009. The cumulative "learning by doing" process was also confirmed by a personal interview with Major General (Ret.) Mahmud Durrani, former Pakistani ambassador to the United States, December 2009.

57. Mullick, August 2009; Durrani, 2009.

58. Kilcullen, 2009, p. 13. For instance, Kilcullen explains how Pakistan began to model some U.S. techniques in Iraq and Afghanistan using high-value targeting, "sting" operations, and air-assault raids based on intelligence rather than patrolling and population security.

59. Shuja Nawaz, "Learning by Doing: The Pakistan Army's Experience with Counterinsurgency," *Atlantic Council*, February 2011.

60. Durrani, 2009.

61. "Taliban Finds Fertile Recruiting Ground in Pakistan's Tribal Refugee Camps," *U.S. News & World Report*, Feb. 9, 2009.

62. Durrani, 2009.

63. Mullick describes how commanders bucked field manuals by using soldiers to help local people escape before the use of heavy artillery, combining intelligence sources to improve targeting, and deploying tanks in urban areas to target snipers. See Mullick, August 2009, pp. 21–22.

64. Mullick, August 2009.

65. Durrani, 2009.

66. Brian Cloughley, "Insurrection, Terrorism, and the Pakistan Army," Pakistan Security Research Unit Brief, No. 53, Dec. 10, 2009.

67. Mullick, August 2009.

68. Frederick Kagan, "The Two-Front War," *Weekly Standard*, Nov. 9, 2009.

69. Mullick argues that they established small bases within the population, enforced curfews, and supported local government, but it is not clear this has endured. See Mullick, August 2009, p. 21.

70. Though by no means conclusive, recent quantitative analysis of counterinsurgency has suggested that a higher level of mechanization leads to a lower rate of counterinsurgency success. See Jason Lyall and Isaiah Wilson III, "Rage Against the Machines: Explaining Outcomes in Counterinsurgency Wars," *International Organization*, Vol. 63, Winter 2009, pp. 67–106.

71. Jane Perlez and Pir Zubair Shah, "Landowners Still in Exile from Unstable Pakistan Area," *New York Times*, July 28, 2009; Salman Masood, "Provincial Politician Is Slain in Pakistan," *New York Times*, Dec. 1, 2009.

72. Amin Ahmed, "Army Claims Success in Swat Operation: Militancy Almost Wiped Out," *Dawn*, Jan. 17, 2008.

73. On civil-military relations, see Ayesha Jalal, *The State of Martial Rule: The Origins of Pakistan's Political Economy of Defence* (Cambridge University Press, 1990); Ayesha Siddiqa, *Military Inc.: Inside Pakistan's Military Economy* (Pluto Press, London, 2007). On political instability cycles, see Paul Staniland, "The Poisoned Chalice: Military Culture, Contentious Politics, and Cycles of Regime Change in Pakistan," MIT Working Paper, 2009. On economic institutions, see Omar Noman, *Economic and Social Progress in Asia: Why Pakistan Did Not Become a Tiger*

(Oxford University Press, 1997); John R. Schmidt, "The Unraveling of Pakistan," *Survival*, Vol. 51, No. 3, June–July 2009.

74. Durrani, 2009.
75. Rahimullah Yusufzai, "Assessing the Progress of Pakistan's South Waziristan Offensive," *CTC Sentinel*, Vol. 2, No. 12, December 2009.
76. Durrani, 2009; Cloughley, 2009, p. 19.
77. Cloughley, 2009, p. 20.
78. Ibid., p. 16.
79. Yusufzai, 2009; Syed Adnan Ali Shah Bukhari, "New Strategies in Pakistan's Counter-Insurgency Operation in South Waziristan," *Terrorism Monitor* (Jamestown Foundation), Vol. 7, No. 37, Dec. 3, 2009; one analyst in close contact with Pakistani military general headquarters estimated there were initially more than 140 targets slated for air strikes.
80. Frederick Kagan, Reza Jan, and Charlie Szrom, "The War in Waziristan: Operation Rah-e-Nijat—Phase 1 Analysis," *Critical Threats Report*, Nov. 18, 2009; Kagan, Jan, and Szrom, "The War in Waziristan: Week 1 Analysis of Operation Rah-e-Nijat," *Critical Threats Report*, Oct. 26, 2009.
81. Kagan et al., Oct. 26, 2009.
82. Eric Schmitt, "U.S. Quietly Speeds Aid to Pakistan to Fight Taliban," *New York Times*, Oct. 28, 2009.
83. BBC News, "Pakistan Taliban Offensive in S. Waziristan to 'Go On,'" Dec. 12, 2009.
84. Imtiaz Ali, "Military Victory in South Waziristan or Beginning of a Long War?" *Terrorism Monitor* (Jamestown Foundation), Vol. 7, No. 38, Dec. 15, 2009.
85. Yusufzai, 2009.
86. Ibid.; Alex Rodriguez, "Pakistan Taliban Regrouping Outside Waziristan," *Los Angeles Times*, Nov. 26, 2009; Saeed Shah, "Big Pakistan Offensive Has Failed to Nab Any Taliban Leaders," McClatchy Newspapers, Nov. 24, 2009. For updated data on suicide bombings and fatalities, see South Asia Terrorism Portal, "Suicide Attacks in Pakistan" database.
87. Javed Hussain, quoted in Shah, 2009.
88. Durrani, 2009; interview with a Pakistani analyst.
89. Resources emphasized by Durrani, 2009.
90. "Pakistan: Countering Militancy in FATA," International Crisis Group Report, No. 178, Oct. 21, 2009; Lt. Gen. Talat Masood, "Pakistan's Military Examines Its Options in North Waziristan," *Terrorism Monitor* (Jamestown Foundation), Vol. 8, No. 5, Feb. 4, 2010.
91. Reports suggest support is already declining to 51 percent. See Yusufzai, 2009; "Most Pakistanis Back War Against Militants," Reuters, Nov. 4, 2009.
92. Durrani, 2009; Johnson and Mason, 2008.
93. Johnson and Mason, 2008.
94. This includes views on extremist positions as Pew categorizes it, including support for suicide bombing and terrorism.
95. Pew Global Attitudes Project, "Key Indicators Database."
96. Syed Farooq Hasnat, "Pakistan's Strategic Interests, Afghanistan and the Fluctuating U.S. Strategy," *Journal of International Affairs*, Vol. 63, No. 1, Fall/Winter 2009, pp. 141–55.

97. C. Christine Fair, "Pakistan's Own War on Terror: What the Pakistani Public Thinks," *Journal of International Affairs*, Vol. 63, No. 1, Fall/Winter 2009, pp. 39–55.

98. "Survey of Pakistan Public Opinion," International Republican Institute, Oct. 1, 2009.

99. "Pakistan: State of the Nation," Al Jazeera/Gallup Pakistan Survey, Aug. 13, 2009, http://english.aljazeera.net/focus/2009/08/2009888238994769.html.

100. "Military Action in Waziristan: Opinion Poll," Gilani Poll/Gallup Pakistan, Nov. 3, 2009, http://www.gallup.com.pk/Polls/03-11-09.pdf. This finding was supported by other polls that found Pakistanis blaming the United States for instability in terrorism. In 2007, 73 percent of Pakistanis blamed the United States for unrest in South Asia (see Ijaz Shafi Gilani, *The Voice of the People*, Oxford University Press, 2010, p. 81), and in 2009 31 percent held U.S. agencies responsible for terrorist activities in Pakistan. See "30 Years of Polling on Crimes, Violence, Terrorism & Social Evils, 1980–2010," Pakistan Gallup and Gilani, Jan. 6, 2011, p. 46.

101. Jacob N. Shapiro and C. Christine Fair, "Understanding Support for Islamist Militancy in Pakistan," *International Security*, Vol. 34, No. 3, Winter 2009/10, pp. 79–118.

102. Ali, 2009.

103. Naveed Ahmad Shinwari, *Understanding FATA: 2011, Volume V*, Islamabad: Community Appraisal & Motivation Program, February 2012, p. 84.

104. Shinwari, *Understanding FATA: 2011*, pp. 74, 76, 78, 85–86.

105. A recent poll shows that even though Pakistani concern over terrorism remains high, economic issues still trump. When asked to identify the number one problem in Pakistan, 43 percent said inflation and 20 percent said unemployment, while 32 percent said terrorism. See "Economic Issues Perceived to Be Number One Problem of Pakistan," Gilani Poll/Gallup Pakistan, Feb. 15, 2010, http://www.gallup.com.pk/Polls/15-02-10.pdf.

106. As mentioned earlier, U.S. training of Pakistani forces for counterinsurgency has largely been limited to the Frontier Corps and not the regular army. This chapter suggests that public sentiment constrains the degree of public cooperation with the United States that the Pakistani military can embrace.

107. Even the recent changes in training and curriculum fall more under the concept "learning by doing" than a doctrinal shift. See Nawaz, 2011.

108. Fair and Jones, December 2009, p. 181.

109. Moeed Yusuf, "Rational Institutional Design, Perverse Incentives, and the US-Pakistan Partnership in post-9/11," *Defence Against Terrorism Review*, Vol. 2, No. 1, Spring 2009.

110. "A Great Deal of Ruin in a Nation," *Economist*, Mar. 31, 2011.

111. This figure is cited by Lt. Gen. Talat Masood, "Pakistan's Military Examines its Options in North Waziristan," *Terrorism Monitor* (Jamestown Foundation), Vol. 8, No. 5, Feb. 4, 2010. The figure was produced by Pakistani economist Dr. Shahid Hasan Siddiqui (chairman and chief executive, Research Institute

of Islamic Banking and Finance, Karachi; fellow, Institute of Bankers, Pakistan; and fellow, Institute of Islamic Banking and Insurance, London), who estimates the total cost to the Pakistani economy due to depressed growth rates has been $40 billion minus the $12 billion in aid provided by the United States. More important than the estimate itself, which may be credibly challenged by others, is the perceived costliness of the venture by the Pakistani strategic establishment, including respected generals such as Talat Masood.

112. Wajahat S. Khan, "The Ghosts That Haunt Kiyani," *Friday Times*, Vol. 23, No. 37, Oct. 28, 2011; Khalid Aziz, "Endgame in Afghanistan," *Dawn*, Sept. 30, 2011. Both authors come to this conclusion and Khan explains the rationale—with roughly 10 officers per battalion (nine hundred soldiers) and nine battalions to a division, the loss of 194 officers amounts to decapitation of nineteen battalions or two divisions.

113. See Masood, "Pakistan Military Examines Its Options," 2010.

114. Fair and Jones conclude similarly.

SEVEN

CIA Drone Strikes and the Taliban

Peter Bergen and Jennifer Rowland

O N JULY 1, 2012, a missile launched from a U.S. drone struck a house in Pakistan's remote tribal agency of North Waziristan, killing eight suspected militants, most of whom were loyal to the Pakistani Taliban commander Hafiz Gul Bahadur. Bahadur had reportedly overseen multiple attacks against NATO troops in Afghanistan.

Although the CIA drone war against al-Qaeda is well known and is even, on occasion, publicly acknowledged by senior Obama administration officials, the strike against Bahadur's fighters was part of a lesser-known campaign to target Pakistani militants who were generally unlikely to pose a threat to the U.S. homeland—an expansion of the drone program that occurred during the administration of President Barack Obama.[1]

In 2004, President George W. Bush authorized for the first time the covert lethal use of drones inside Pakistani territory. Forty-five drone strikes took place in the Federally Administered Tribal Areas (FATA) during Bush's tenure, but when Obama took office in January 2009, the drone program began to ramp up quickly, accelerating from an average of one strike every forty days to one every four days by mid-2011.

The 307 drone strikes launched by the United States in Pakistan between June 2004 and June 2012 killed an estimated 1,562 to 2,377 suspected militants, according to reliable news accounts. Of those 307 strikes, 70 percent have hit North Waziristan, home to factions of the Pakistani Taliban and the Haqqani Network. More than a third of these 307 strikes have reportedly targeted members of the Taliban, with at least ten of these killing senior Taliban commanders, as well as

Taliban Leaders Killed in Drone Strikes	
Date Killed	Name and Position
June 18, 2004	Nek Mohammad, Taliban leader
August 13, 2008	Abdul Rehman, Taliban commander in South Waziristan
October 26, 2008	Mohammad Omar, close associate of Nek Mohammad
August 5, 2009	Baitullah Mehsud, overall leader of the Pakistani Taliban
December 31, 2009	Haji Omar, a key Taliban commander in North Waziristan
January 2010 (exact date unknown)	Mahmud Mahdi Zeidan, Jordanian Taliban commander
February 24, 2010	Mohammad Qari Zafar, Taliban commander wanted in connection with a bombing in Karachi in 2006
December 17, 2010	Ibne Amin, Taliban commander in Swat
October 27, 2011	Khan Mohammad, deputy to Taliban commander Maulvi Nazir
March 13, 2012	Shamsullah and Amir Hamza Toji Khel, two of Maulvi Nazir's senior commanders

hundreds of lower-level fighters. The box on the preceding page lists the Taliban leaders who have been killed in the CIA drone campaign.

The aggressive drone campaign in Pakistan slowed considerably in 2011. There were 70 drone strikes in the tribal regions that year, down from 118 in 2010, which saw the peak number since the program began.

Figure 7.1 illustrates the changing frequency in drone attacks over the years.

The drop in drone strikes during 2011 was the result of a series of events that wore on the ever-fragile U.S.-Pakistan relationship. On January 27, 2011, an American citizen, Raymond Davis, shot and killed two Pakistanis who he said were attempting to rob him in the streets of Lahore. Despite U.S. claims of diplomatic immunity because of Davis's employment at the U.S. consulate in Lahore, he landed in jail, charged with a double murder and illegal weapons possession. Much of the Pakistani public was outraged when it was revealed that Davis was, in fact, a CIA contractor.[2]

As a result of the complex negotiations to get Davis out of Pakistani jail, there were just three CIA drone strikes in February 2011 and only nine in March 2011 while U.S. officials worked to settle the issue and finally bring Davis home. The day after Davis was finally released, a strike on March 17, 2011, killed a reported thirty-six people, including a top Taliban commander. Pakistani officials condemned the strike, and Pakistanis took to the streets to protest them.[3] The CIA suspended drone strikes for a month before resuming them again.

Less than a month after the drone strikes picked up again, on May 1, U.S. Navy SEALs secretly flew into Pakistani territory aboard stealth

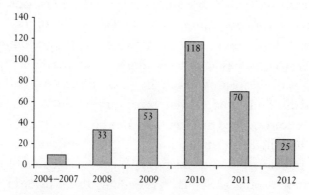

FIGURE 7.1 Number of U.S. Drone Strikes in Pakistan
Note: * as of June 28, 2012.

helicopters to capture or kill Osama bin Laden, who was living not far from the Pakistani capital, Islamabad. Pakistan's powerful military establishment was angry about the violation of its sovereignty, and relations between the U.S. and Pakistan sank further. For their part, many Americans were outraged that al-Qaeda's leader had been living for years in a sizable city in central Pakistan. The drone strikes were paused briefly, but then resumed.

At 2:00 a.m. on November 26, 2011, two Pakistani border posts about a half-kilometer from the Afghan border came under heavy fire from NATO helicopters that had strayed across the border into Pakistani airspace.[4] Pakistani officials immediately termed the attack, which killed twenty-four of their soldiers, a "deliberate act of aggression,"[5] while U.S. officials maintained that the Pakistani security officials had fired on the helicopters first.[6] Either way, the friendly fire incident was devastating, not least to the U.S. drone program in Pakistan's tribal regions, which was subsequently suspended for almost seven weeks, one of the longest pauses since the program started in 2004. Pakistan also ordered the United States to vacate Shamsi Air Base in Balochistan, from which many of the CIA drones were launched.[7]

***

The New America Foundation maintains a database of every reported drone strike in Pakistan's tribal regions since 2004. We monitor reports about the strikes from the top Western and Pakistani news sources, such as the *New York Times*, Associated Press, CNN, Reuters, *Express Tribune*, *Dawn*, and Geo TV. According to our data, 7 percent of the fatalities resulting from drone strikes in 2011 were civilians, up 2 percentage points from our figure in 2010. Over the life of the CIA drone program in Pakistan from June 2004 to June 2012, we found that the civilian casualty rate has been 16 percent (Figure 7.2).

Clearly, as the years progressed, the drone strikes have become more precise and discriminating. In March 2011, Pakistani Maj. Gen. Ghayur Mehmood acknowledged that fact when he said "the number of innocent people being killed is relatively low" and that "most of the targets are hard-core militants," the first such public acknowledgment by a senior Pakistani military officer.[8] Similarly, President Obama made his first public comments about the covert drone program when he told participants of a Google+ "hangout" on January 30, 2012, that the United States

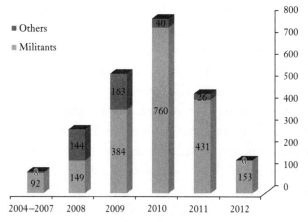

FIGURE 7.2 Militants and Civilians Killed in U.S. Drone Strikes in Pakistan

Note: * as of June 28, 2012.

conducts only "very precise precision strikes against al Qaeda and their affiliates, and we're very careful in terms of how it's been applied."[9]

Even if it is the case that there are relatively few civilians killed in the strikes, the drone program is quite unpopular in Pakistan. During the summer of 2010 the New America Foundation sponsored one of the few public opinion polls ever to be conducted in the FATA and found that almost 90 percent of the respondents opposed U.S. military operations in the region. The wider Pakistani public shares this sentiment, though to a lesser degree. A poll conducted by the Pew Research Center in June 2012 found that about three-quarters of the Pakistani public consider the drone campaign to be unnecessary.[10]

Aware of how unpopular the drone strikes were becoming in Pakistan, some top U.S. Defense and State Department officials behind the scenes pushed for more selective drone strikes, which the CIA opposed. The White House ordered an evaluation of the drone program during the summer of 2011.[11] The study found that the CIA was primarily killing low-level militants in its drone strikes. Those results prompted the government to implement new rules in November 2011 governing when and how specific drone strikes were authorized. The State Department was given a larger say in the decision-making process. Pakistani leaders were promised advance notification of some strikes, and the CIA pledged to refrain from conducting strikes during visits by Pakistani officials to the United States.[12]

However, on April 12, 2012, the Pakistani parliament unanimously approved a resolution on U.S.-Pakistan relations that included a demand for immediate cessation of drone strikes on Pakistani territory. This marked the first time the parliament had officially entered this sphere of Pakistan's foreign policy, and it formalized the elected officials' opposition to the U.S. drone program. Defense Secretary Leon Panetta said in an interview soon after the resolution was passed that the United States would continue to "defend itself under any circumstance." But in a sign of growing confidence, Pakistan's Foreign Ministry, too, joined the chorus of government officials speaking out against the strikes. The ministry released statements condemning the two drone strikes that occurred immediately after the parliamentary resolution was passed.

Despite their lack of popularity, the drone strikes may have contributed to a relative decrease in violence across Pakistan. There were forty-one suicide attacks in Pakistan in 2011, down from forty-nine in 2010 and a record high of eighty-seven in 2009.[13] The 118 drone strikes carried out in 2010 coincided with an almost 50 percent drop in suicide attacks across Pakistan. A 2012 study coauthored by RAND Corporation analyst Patrick Johnston found that as the frequency of drone strikes in Pakistan increased, the frequency of suicide bombings across the country decreased, indicating that drone strikes might help reduce the domestic threat of terrorism.[14]

The Pakistani military's own operations against the Taliban, particularly those in Swat and South Waziristan in 2009, have surely also contributed to this trend. Some sixteen hundred Taliban fighters were killed during Operation Rah-e-Rast in Swat between April 27 and June 30, 2009, while hundreds more surrendered to the government.[15]

Evidence of the drone strikes' impact can be found in the atmosphere of fear and distrust among members of al-Qaeda in Pakistan described by several European militants captured in late 2008.[16] David Rohde, the *New York Times* reporter who was held by the Taliban Haqqani Network for months in 2009,[17] called the drones "a terrifying presence" in South Waziristan. Key militant figures reportedly started sleeping outside under trees to avoid being targeted, and Taliban militants regularly executed suspected "spies" in Waziristan accused of providing information to the United States, suggesting they feared betrayal from within.[18] In June 2012, a top Taliban commander in South Waziristan, Mullah Nazir, halted all polio eradication efforts in the area for fear that the health workers were U.S. spies in disguise assisting the CIA drone program.[19]

The CIA drone attacks in Pakistan have undoubtedly hindered some of the Taliban's operations, killing hundreds of their low-level fighters and a number of their top commanders. But they have also slowed considerably since their peak in 2010 and have come under harsher scrutiny both in Pakistan and the West, rendering the program's future in the region uncertain.

Notes

1. Mark Mazzetti and Scott Shane, "Evidence Mounts for Taliban Role in Bomb Plot," *New York Times*, May 5, 2010, http://www.nytimes.com/2010/05/06/nyregion/06bomb.html?pagewanted=all.

2. Mark Mazzetti, Ashley Parker, Jane Perlez, and Eric Schmitt, "American Held in Pakistan Worked for CIA," *New York Times*, Feb. 21, 2011, http://www.nytimes.com/2011/02/22/world/asia/22pakistan.html.

3. Salman Masood and Pir Zubair Shah, "CIA Drones Kill Civilians in Pakistan," *New York Times*, March 17, 2011, http://www.nytimes.com/2011/03/18/world/asia/18pakistan.html.

4. Salman Masood and Eric Schmitt, "Tensions Flare Between U.S. and Pakistan After Strike," *New York Times*, Nov. 26, 2011, http://www.nytimes.com/2011/11/27/world/asia/pakistan-says-nato-helicopters-kill-dozens-of-soldiers.html?_r=1&pagewanted=1.

5. Chris Brummitt and Sebastian Abbot, "Pakistan Calls NATO Raid an 'Act of Aggression,'" Associated Press, Nov. 29, 2011.

6. "Pakistan Border Fire Provoked NATO Raid: Report," AFP, Nov. 28, 2011, http://tribune.com.pk/story/298827/pakistan-border-fire-provoked-nato-raid-reports/.

7. Tabassum Zakaria and Mark Hosenball, "U.S. Prepares to Vacate Pakistan Airbase," Reuters, Nov. 29, 2012, http://www.reuters.com/article/2011/11/29/us-pakistan-usa-idUSTRE7AS2M420111129.

8. "Pakistan Acknowledges U.S. Drone Strikes Targeting Militants," CNN, Mar. 10, 2011, http://articles.cnn.com/2011-03-10/world/pakistan.drone.attacks_1_drone-strikes-militants-on-pakistani-soil-north-waziristan?_s=PM:WORLD.

9. "Barack Obama Admits US Drone Strikes on Pakistan," *Telegraph*, Jan., 31, 2012, http://www.telegraph.co.uk/news/worldnews/northamerica/usa/9050993/Barack-Obama-admits-US-drone-strikes-on-Pakistan.html.

10. "Pakistani Public Opinion Ever More Critical of U.S." Pew Research Center, June 27, 2012, http://www.pewglobal.org/files/2012/06/Pew-Global-Attitudes-Project-Pakistan-Report-FINAL-Wednesday-June-27-2012.pdf.

11. Adam Entous, Siobhan Gorman, and Julian E. Barnes, "U.S. Tightens Drone Rules," *Wall Street Journal*, Nov. 4, 2011, http://online.wsj.com/article/SB10001424052970204621904577013982672973836.html.

12. Ken Dilanian, "U.S. Put New Restrictions on CIA Drone Strikes in Pakistan," *Los Angeles Times*, Nov. 7, 2011, http://articles.latimes.com/2011/nov/07/world/la-fg-cia-drones-20111108.

13. "Pakistan Security Report 2009," Pakistan Institute for Peace Studies, January 2010.

14. Patrick B. Johnston and Anoop Sarbahi, "The Impact of U.S. Drone Strikes on Terrorism in Pakistan," Working Paper, Feb. 25, 2012, http://patrickjohnston.info/materials/drones.pdf.

15. Dr. Noor Ul-Haq, "The Operation Rah-e-Rast," Islamabad Policy Research Institute FactFile, #111, June 2009, pg. http://ipripak.org/factfiles/ff111.pdf. Ghulam Farooq, "105 Taliban Surrender, 15 Killed in Swat Clashes," *Daily Times*, Sept. 2, 2009, http://www.dailytimes.com.pk/default.asp?page=2009\09\02\story_2-9-2009_pg7_6.

16. Jane Mayer, "The Predator War," *New Yorker*, Oct. 26, 2009, http://www.newyorker.com/reporting/2009/10/26/091026fa_fact_mayer?printable=true.

17. "David Rohde, Times Reporter, Escapes Taliban After 7 Months," *New York Times*, June 20, 2009, http://www.nytimes.com/2009/06/21/world/asia/21taliban.html.

18. David Rohde, "Held by the Taliban, Part Four—A Drone Strike and Dwindling Hope," *New York Times*, Oct. 20, 2009, http://www.nytimes.com/2009/10/21/world/asia/21hostage.html?pagewanted=print; Jason Burke, "On the Front Line in War on Pakistan's Taliban," *Guardian*, Nov. 16, 2008, "Taliban Kill Seven 'US Spies' in North Waziristan," *Dawn*, Jan. 24, 2010, http://www.dawn.com/wps/wcm/connect/dawn-contentlibrary/dawn/news/pakistan/04-taliban-kill-six-nwaziristan-qs-06; "Taliban Kill Two US 'Spies' in Miranshah," *Daily Times*, Jan. 31, 2010, http://www.dailytimes.com.pk/default.asp?page=2010\01\31\story_31-1-2010_pg1_3.

19. Jon Boone, "Taliban Leader Bans Polio Vaccinations in Protest at Drone Strikes," *Guardian*, June 26, 2012, http://www.guardian.co.uk/world/2012/jun/26/taliban-bans-polio-vaccinations?newsfeed=true.

EIGHT

The Drone War: View from the Ground

Pir Zubair Shah

"WE DON'T EVEN sit together to chat anymore," the Taliban fighter told me, his voice hoarse as he combed his beard with his fingers. We were talking in a safe house in Peshawar as the fighter and one of his comrades sketched a picture of life on the run in the borderlands of Waziristan. The deadly American drones buzzing overhead, the two men said, had changed everything for al-Qaeda and its local allies.

The whitewashed two-story villa bristled with activity. Down the hall from my Taliban sources sat an aggrieved tribal elder and his son in one room and two officers from Pakistan's powerful Inter-Services Intelligence (ISI) Directorate in another. I had gathered them all there to make sense of what was becoming the signature incident of the war in Afghanistan and Pakistan: an American drone strike, one of the first ordered on the watch of the new U.S. president, Barack Obama. The early-2009 strike had killed a local elder, along with his son, two nephews, and a guest in the South Waziristan town of Wana. Several sources told me the family was innocent, with no connections to the Taliban or al-Qaeda. But traveling to Waziristan was too dangerous even for me, a reporter who had grown up there. So instead I brought Waziristan to Peshawar, renting rooms for my sources in the guesthouse. I had just one night to try to figure out what had happened.

I spent the night running from room to room, assembling the story in pieces. On the first floor sat the dead elder's brother and nephew, who told me what little they knew of the incident. On the second floor, the ISI officers, over whiskey and lamb tikka, described their work helping U.S. intelligence agents sort out targets from among the images relayed back from the drones. Then there were the two Taliban fighters, whom I had first met in Waziristan in 2007. One was a fixer for the Haqqani Network, skilled at smuggling men and matériel from Pakistan into Afghanistan. The other drew a government salary as an employee of Pakistan's agriculture department but worked across the border as an explosives expert; he had lost a finger fighting the allied forces in Afghanistan. None of the men in the house knew the others were there.

The two fighters described how the militants were adapting to this new kind of warfare. The Taliban and al-Qaeda had stopped using electronic devices, they told me. They would no longer gather in huge numbers, even in mosques to pray, and spent their nights outside for safety; it was a life that was wearing thin. "We can't sleep in the jungle the whole of our lives," one told me. Gradually, a picture of a rare incident came into focus: a deadly strike that had mistakenly taken out a man with no connection to al-Qaeda or the Taliban.

This is how it has gone with the drone war, a beat I covered for six years, first for *Newsday* and then the *New York Times*. By the time I left Pakistan in the summer of 2010, the job was nearly impossible, though it was always a dauntingly difficult story to tell. The drone campaign is one of the U.S. government's most secret programs. Although the most authoritative study[1] on the subject, by the New America Foundation, calculated that almost three hundred drone strikes had occurred in the Afghanistan-Pakistan border region between 2004 and 2011, Obama never even publicly acknowledged them until January 2012. Making matters still more difficult, the targets are in one of the world's most inaccessible areas, traditionally out of bounds for outsiders and a place where the state of Pakistan has nominal governing authority or none. It is an environment in which accurate reporting is an often unattainable goal, where confusion, controversies, and myths proliferate.

Although the drone campaign has become the linchpin of the Obama administration's counterterrorism strategy in Central Asia—and one it is increasingly exporting to places such as Yemen and the Horn of Africa—we know virtually nothing about it. I spent more than half a decade tracking this most secret of wars across northern Pakistan, taking late-night calls from intelligence agents, sorting through missile fragments at attack sites, counting bodies and graves, interviewing militants and victims. I dodged bullets and, once, escaped an improvised explosive device. At various times I found myself imprisoned by the Taliban and detained by the Pakistani military. Yet even I can say very little for certain about what has happened.

The evening of June 18, 2004, was a sweltering one in South Waziristan, and the twenty-seven-year-old local Taliban leader, Nek Muhammad Wazir, had decided to eat dinner in the courtyard of his house in the village of Kari Kot, along with his two brothers and two bodyguards. Muhammad's satellite phone rang, and he picked it up. Moments later, a missile streaked through the compound and exploded, killing all five men.

At the time, no one in the Pakistani public or media knew that it was a drone. The government would say nothing, and everyone else attributed Muhammad's killing either to a Pakistani military operation—after all, soldiers had gone looking for him without success on six occasions—or to the work of U.S. forces across the border in Afghanistan. A Taliban fighter who was within earshot of the explosion told me later that the militants were totally taken by surprise. "There was a noise in the air before, and then we heard the explosion," he recalled. The villagers, however, supplied the explanation: they collected the fragments of the missile, on which was printed in black, "Made in USA."

Then, in late 2005, a similarly mysterious explosion killed Abu Hamza Rabia, a high-ranking Egyptian member of al-Qaeda, outside North Waziristan's capital city, Miram Shah. President Pervez Musharraf refused to explain what had happened, saying only that he was "200 percent"[2] sure Rabia was dead. But a local reporter named Hayatullah Khan, who lived in the next village over from where Rabia was killed, had gone to the site to sift through the rubble. Amid the debris were pieces of a Hellfire missile. He took pictures, which swiftly appeared in newspapers around the world.

The photographs directly contradicted the statements of Musharraf's government, which had variously claimed that Pakistani forces killed Rabia or that the militants blew themselves up by accident. The following month, Khan was abducted by gunmen. His body was found six months later near the Afghan border with handcuffs on his wrists; he had been shot in the back, apparently while trying to escape. When I visited his family in North Waziristan a year later, Khan's brother told me he blamed the ISI.

In January 2006, shortly after Khan's disappearance, I got an early-morning phone call at my home in Islamabad from a colleague at *Newsday*, where I was then working as a fixer and bureau manager. There had been another drone strike in the Bajaur tribal area, he told me; could I go investigate? I picked up a friend who worked for the BBC and drove north to Bajaur to see my first drone strike. It would be the first newspaper story to appear under my own byline—and my first experience covering the drone war.

As we drove into Damadola, a farming village sprawled across a wide valley, I spotted the bodies of a cow and a calf, splayed out underneath a tree with their eyes wide open. Nearby were the fresh ruins of three houses.

The drone's presumed target had been Osama bin Laden's deputy, Ayman al-Zawahiri, rumored to be in the area. I arrived on the scene ahead of most other reporters, and the families of the victims took me to see their newly dug graves. "All those killed, including women and children, are from this village," a villager told me as he showed me the burial site. "There were no foreigners here." Then I noticed something odd: although I counted thirteen graves, the locals would tell me the names only of seven women and children who had been killed. When it came to the men, they were silent. Later, a Pakistani official told me foreigners had indeed been present, including Zawahiri, though he had left some time before the missile hit. Drones were not yet common, but the fugitive al-Qaeda No. 2 was long since accustomed to moving quickly from place to place.

It was in September 2006 that I heard a drone for the first time, flying over the mud-walled village of Ali Khel, a couple of miles west of Miram Shah. It was a hot summer night, too hot in the house of the building-contractor friend with whom I was staying, so I had gone out to sleep in the open along with several laborers who worked for him.

The men were telling me about their travels in Afghanistan, how they would cross the border to fight for the Taliban and then return after a week or two to North Waziristan to work and make some money. Then I heard the buzzing, far above our heads—like a bee, but heavier and unceasing, drifting in and out of earshot. The laborers said nothing.

On the other side of the Tochi River, in the village of Khatai, lived a famous Taliban commander whom the Pakistani military had once tried to kill. The operation was a debacle; the military lost at least two senior officers, and hundreds of soldiers found themselves besieged not only by Taliban fighters but by the local villagers. But the small, lethal machine flying far overhead accomplished what the Pakistani soldiers could not. "Nowadays he doesn't live here all the time," my host that night said as he pointed toward the commander's nearby compound. "There are drones in the air now."

Taliban fighters speaking a Waziri dialect of Pashto call the drones *bhungana*, "the one that produces a bee-like sound." Their local adversaries call them *ababeel*, the name of a bird mentioned in the Quran, sent by God to defend the holy city of Mecca from an invading army by hurling small stones from its mouth. Over the several days I spent in Ali Khel, I became accustomed to their sound. It was there all the time. During the day it was mostly absorbed into the hum of daily life, but in the calm of night the buzzing was all you heard.

This kind of reporting trip, risky as it was, became increasingly necessary, given the cagey and outright confusing response by the Pakistani government to the escalating air war over its territory. When news of the early attacks got out, officials were evasive, suggesting that the militants had been killed while making explosives in their compounds. Then, after a drone strike took out a madrassa in the Bajaur tribal area in October 2006, killing more than eighty people, the government claimed that Pakistani bombers had done the job. Militants responded that November with a suicide bombing of a military barracks in the Dargai area of Malakand district, killing forty-two soldiers and wounding dozens more.

The government learned its lesson, retreating back into ambiguity. From that moment on, only the residents of the areas targeted by the drones would have a clear understanding of what was happening—but those areas were mostly beyond the reach of the media.

If the conduct of the drone war is mysterious, the terrain over which it is fought is not, at least to me; I have known it all my life. I was born in South Waziristan, to parents from two Pashtun tribes, in a town that was famous in the British colonial era for its gun and knife factories. My ancestors came from Afghanistan as preachers, and I took my first steps as a child in the Afghan city of Khost, just across the border, where my maternal grandfather lived.

After graduating from university in Islamabad in 2001, I returned to the tribal regions to prepare for my civil service exam. As unthinkable as it seems now, it was then the most peaceful, tranquil place I knew, and I spent my evenings in Bajaur studying with a college professor in preparation for a career in Pakistan's foreign service. During the days I would travel with my uncle, a government irrigation engineer, to villages in the area, meeting the residents and elders.

As the media poured into Afghanistan and Pakistan after the September 11 attacks, someone with my background and English-language skills was suddenly very much in demand, and I got my first job in *Newsday*'s Islamabad bureau. On my trips back to Waziristan, I saw the landscape of my childhood transforming into a war zone. By 2004, people I had known there in my youth were on all sides of the region's worsening conflict, in the Taliban and al-Qaeda, as well as the Pakistani military and intelligence services.

As the Pakistani military operations started to expand from one tribal area to the next, reporting on the ground went from difficult to impossible. I found myself working more and more over the phone, canvassing the contacts I had made during my travels in the region. When it came to the drone attacks, some of my sources would have access to the site of the strike and would tell me what really happened. I soon learned that the official version of the story was usually the least reliable. The military often had the same access problem I did and was itself relying on secondary sources.

The Taliban started adapting, too. The militants came to realize that the increasingly effective drone strikes made them look weak, and they began getting rid of the evidence as fast as they could. After every attack they would cordon off the area and remove the bodies of the dead, making it difficult to verify who and how many people had been killed. Going to the site of a drone attack became a futile exercise; only a very few local reporters known for their deference to the Taliban were given any meaningful access.

I made my last visit to Waziristan in June 2007. By then, people there knew I worked for an American newspaper; fearing for my safety, my family discouraged me from going. The military was turning away representatives of foreign news organizations, and the Taliban was increasingly paranoid—a fact I learned the hard way a year later.

It was a hot, sunny day in July 2008, and I set out from Peshawar with a photographer to report on the Taliban in the Mohmand tribal area, where the group had taken over a series of marble quarries.[3] After meeting up with a local guide, we arrived in the village of Ziarat and headed toward the local Taliban checkpoint. We had dressed in the traditional shalwar kameez and had worn hats in an effort to blend in. My photographer was from Karachi, though, and I worried that his presence would mark us as outsiders. I asked him to stay near the car while I ventured out to the checkpoint, where I interviewed a contractor working in the mines. As I was about to finish my interview, I saw my photographer approaching, so I wrapped up the conversation and hustled him back to the car. But it was too late. A bearded man shouted at us—he had seen the photographer's camera bag.

We were escorted away from the main road in our car, a Talib riding alongside us with a rifle. The Taliban held us in a prison in the base of a mountain, guarded by young volunteers from a nearby village. When we arrived, all our belongings, including our cell phones and money, were confiscated. But we were treated well—better, at any rate, than the prisoners we saw chained up in the neighboring rooms.

In the evening two Taliban came to our room. "Who is the Waziristani?" one of them asked. I said it was me, and I followed them into a half-destroyed room elsewhere in the compound. "Tell us who really you are," one of them said. They looked through the contacts in my cell phone, demanding to know why they included the commander of the Frontier Corps, the regional U.S.-trained paramilitary force the Taliban were fighting. The questioning went on for three days. I told them I was a reporter. My Waziristan connections were of some help, but they posed a risk too: I knew the local Taliban had recently attacked my family's village in the nearby district of Tank, killing more than a dozen of my relatives. I didn't want them to know that I knew.

Finally, Abdul Wali, the local Taliban leader, arrived and, satisfied that we were who we said we were, ordered our release. They had to be vigilant, he told us. "People come here under the guise of journalists and photographers, and they either take pictures of our locations and pass them on to the authorities or drop a SIM [card] to facilitate a drone strike," he said. "You never know who is a reporter and who is a spy."

Among Waziristan's residents, "I will drone you" has by now entered the vocabulary of day-to-day conversation as a morbid joke. The mysterious machines buzzing far overhead have become part of the local folklore. "I am looking for you like a drone, my love," goes a romantic Pashto verse I've often heard the locals recite. "You have become Osama; no one knows your whereabouts."

But it was only when WikiLeaks released its cache of U.S. State Department cables beginning in late 2010 that Pakistanis learned just how complicit their government has been in the drone campaign. A February 2008 cable[4] from the embassy in Islamabad reported that Pakistan's Army chief, Gen. Ashfaq Parvez Kayani, met with the U.S. CentCom commander, Adm. William Fallon, and asked the U.S. military for "continuous Predator coverage of the conflict area" in South Waziristan, where the Pakistani Army was fighting the militants at the time. "Kayani knows full well that the strikes have been precise (creating few civilian casualties) and targeted primarily at foreign fighters" in Waziristan, asserted a February 2009 cable[5] signed by Anne Patterson, then the U.S. ambassador.

In an August 2008 meeting with Patterson, Prime Minister Yousuf Raza Gilani—the same man who, after Navy SEALs dropped into Pakistan to raid bin Laden's compound last year, warned that "Pakistan reserves the right to retaliate with full force"—gave Patterson his go-ahead for a drone campaign in Pakistan's tribal regions. "I don't care if they do it as long as they get the right people," he told her, according to a U.S. cable.[6] "We'll protest in the National Assembly and then ignore it."

Eventually, the disclosures prompted a response: in March 2011, Pakistani Maj. Gen. Ghayur Mehmood, the commander in North Waziristan, appeared before reporters in Miram Shah and told them,[7] "Myths and rumors about U.S. Predator strikes and the casualty figures are many, but it's a reality that many of those being killed in these strikes are hard-core elements, a sizable number of them foreigners. Yes, there are a few civilian casualties in such precision strikes, but a majority of those eliminated are terrorists, including foreign terrorist elements." It was an unusually candid public statement on the drone strikes from a high-ranking Pakistani official. Mehmood also provided something else that had until then been missing: official numbers. According to the government's figures, he said, 164 drone strikes had taken place since 2007, killing 964 terrorists—793 locals and 171 foreigners. The dead included Arabs, Chechens, Filipinos, Moroccans, Tajiks, and Uzbeks. The figures also confirmed the dramatic escalation of the drone war. In 2007, the government said, a single drone strike had killed a single militant. In 2010, the strikes killed 423.

Some such admission was probably inevitable; the revelations in the WikiLeaks cables and Pakistan's obvious inability to stop the attacks put the government in a position where it had to say something. Arguing that the drones were killing real terrorists was the best option available (though a military spokesman still tried to distance the army from Mehmood's statements, saying they reflected only the general's opinion).

But it was also an acknowledgment of defeat: the secret war has become a lot less secret. At first, the tribal areas of Pakistan seemed to present the perfect testing ground for a remote-controlled military strategy; it is a land set apart from its own country and mostly inaccessible to the international media and human rights groups, a place where violations of international law and civilian casualties go mostly uninvestigated. It is, in short, a black hole. But even as the Obama administration was increasingly embracing the drones as an alternative to the boots-on-the-ground military actions inherited from its predecessor, the secret war was becoming as much a political liability as a precision weapon.

As the strikes continue, they give rise to a narrative that explains away the country's worsening radicalization and extremist violence as a product of the drones—a narrative that has served as a bargaining chip for Pakistani leaders in their dealings with the United States as they once again raise the price of Pakistan's cooperation in the war. (After a November 2011 incident in Mohmand district in which NATO forces mistakenly killed Pakistani soldiers, the first thing Pakistan demanded was evacuation of the Shamsi air base in Baluchistan province, being used by the Americans for launching drones over the tribal areas; pictures of the emptied base immediately flashed across the Pakistani media.) In reality, the country's worsening anti-Americanism is driven more by the portrayal of the drones in the Pakistani media, which paints them as a scourge targeting innocent civilians, than by the drones themselves. Few Pakistanis have actually visited the tribal areas or even know much about them. Until the United States and Pakistan come clean about the program, though, it is an image that will persist, worsening the frictions within Pakistan's already divided society and between the United States and Pakistan.

That's too bad, because in reality Pakistanis are deeply torn about the drones. For every anti-American rant they inspire—the recent meteoric rise of Imran Khan, the cricketer turned politician, owes a great deal to his strong opposition to the drone strikes—there is also recognition that these strikes from the sky have their purpose. At times, they have outright benefited the Pakistani state, as in the summer of 2009, when a drone attack killed Baitullah Mehsud, the leader of a militant alliance in Waziristan who was suspected of masterminding former Prime Minister Benazir Bhutto's 2007 assassination; he was Pakistan's Enemy Number One, but a villain of less consequence to the United States.

Residents of the tribal areas are similarly conflicted. Many favor the drone strikes over the alternatives, such as military operations or less-selective bombardments by Pakistani bombers and helicopter gunships. Better a few houses get vaporized than an entire village turned into refugees. Even the brother of the elder I brought to the Peshawar guesthouse said as much, allowing that "in our case, it might be faulty intelligence or mischief by someone" that had caused the strike that killed his brother. Regardless, he said, "I would always go for the drones."

Either way, they are now a fact of life in a secret war that is far from over. Once I called a source, a Taliban commander in one of the tribal areas. His brother picked up the phone and told me that the commander was asleep. It was noon, and I remarked that it was an odd time for a nap. "There are drones in the sky," the brother laughingly replied, "so he is not feeling well."

Notes

1. "The Year of the Drone," study by the New America Foundation, 2012, http://counterterrorism.newamerica.net/drones.
2. "Blast 'Kills al-Qaeda Commander,'" BBC News, March 2005, http://news.bbc.co.uk/2/hi/south_asia/4494428.stm.
3. Pir Zubair Shah and Jane Perlez, "Pakistan Marble Helps Taliban Stay in Business," *New York Times*, July 2008, http://www.pulitzer.org/archives/8320.
4. "Kayani Asked for 'Continuous Predator Coverage,' Dawn.com, June 2011, http://www.dawn.com/2011/05/20/kayani-asked-for-continuous-predator-coverage.html.
5. "Patterson's 'Scenesetter' for Gen Kayani's US Visit," Dawn.com, May 2011, http://www.dawn.com/2011/05/20/pattersons-scenesetter-for-gen-kayanis-us-visit.html.
6. "WikiLeaks: Gilani Open to Drone Strike on 'Right People,'" *Express Tribune*, December 2010, http://tribune.com.pk/story/84402/wikileaks-gilani-open-to-drone-strikes-on-right-people/.
7. Zahir Shah Sherazi, "Most of Those Killed in Drone Attacks Were Terrorists: Military," Dawn.com, March 2011, http://www.dawn.com/2011/03/09/most-of-those-killed-in-drone-attacks-were-terrorists-military.html.

NINE

Public Opinion in Pakistan's Tribal Regions

Ken Ballen, Peter Bergen, and Patrick Doherty

P AKISTAN'S FEDERALLY ADMINISTERED Tribal Areas (FATA) are home to the country's most dangerous militant groups, and consequently the site of all U.S. drone strikes on Pakistani territory. But they are also home to some three million civilians, whose voices are seldom heard in the clamor over the Pakistan Army's military operations, reconciliation with the Pakistani Taliban, CIA drone strikes, or domestic terrorist attacks. From June 30 to July 20, 2010, the New America Foundation and Terror Free Tomorrow conducted the first comprehensive public opinion survey covering sensitive political issues in FATA.

The unprecedented survey consisted of face-to-face interviews of one thousand residents age eighteen or older, across 120 villages and sampling points in all seven tribal agencies of FATA, and fieldwork by the locally based Community Appraisal and Motivation Programme. The poll was conducted before the large-scale floods that inundated Pakistan during the summer of 2010, and it has a margin of error of +/– 3 percent.[1]

The results of the study are telling, but not altogether surprising: FATA residents reject U.S. drone strikes and have highly negative

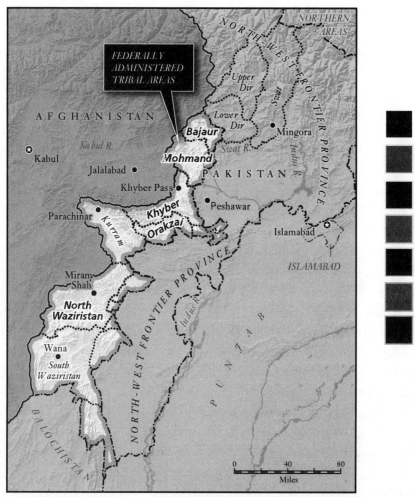

MAP BY GENE THORP OF CARTOGRAPHIC CONCEPTS, INC.

views of the U.S. military, but they also expressed their opposition to the Taliban and to al-Qaeda.

OPPOSITION TO THE U.S. MILITARY AND DRONE CAMPAIGN

Nearly nine out of every ten people in FATA oppose the U.S. military pursuing al-Qaeda and the Taliban in their region. Nearly 70 percent of FATA residents instead want the Pakistani military alone to fight Taliban and al-Qaeda militants in the tribal areas.

The intensity of opposition to the American military is high. Although only one in ten FATA residents think suicide attacks are often or sometimes justified against the Pakistani military and police, almost six in ten believe these attacks are justified against the U.S. military. (The United Nations has determined that many of the suicide attackers in Afghanistan hail from the Pakistani tribal regions.)[2]

More than three-quarters of FATA residents oppose American drone strikes. Indeed, only 16 percent think these strikes accurately target militants; 48 percent think they largely kill civilians and another 33 percent feel they kill both civilians and militants. Directed by the Central Intelligence Agency, missiles are launched from unmanned drone aircraft in the FATA region of Pakistan. President Obama dramatically ramped up the drone program when he took office in January 2009, authorizing 127 strikes through September 2010, more than double the number authorized by President George W. Bush during his entire eight years in office.[3] This may help account for why Obama is viewed unfavorably by 83 percent of FATA residents in our poll.

A plurality of FATA residents consider the United States to be the party most responsible for the violence that is occurring in their region today. Nearly 80 percent of the people in FATA also oppose the U.S.-led "war on terror," believing its real purpose is to weaken and divide the Islamic world, while ensuring American domination. Only 10 percent thought the U.S. was motivated to defeat al-Qaeda and its allies. Similarly, three-quarters of FATA residents thought that the continuing American occupation of Afghanistan was because of its larger war on Islam or part of an effort to secure oil and minerals in the region. Eleven percent said it was because of the September 11 attacks, and just 5 percent to prevent the Taliban from returning to power.

What is interesting about the findings, however, is that the intense opposition to the U.S. military and the drone program is *not* based on general anti-American feelings. Almost three-quarters of the people inside the tribal regions said that their opinion of the United States would improve if the U.S. increased visas for FATA residents and educational scholarships to America, withdrew the American military from Afghanistan, or brokered a comprehensive peace between Israelis and Palestinians. A majority even said their opinion of the U.S. would improve a great deal. Two-thirds said that policies such as American aid for education and medical care would improve their opinion as well.

This dramatic willingness to think better of America demonstrates a notable lack of deep-seated hostility. For many FATA residents, opposition to the U.S. is based on current American military policy, not any intractably held anti-American beliefs.

REJECTION OF AL-QAEDA AND THE TALIBAN

Opposition to American policies in the region does not mean, however, that the people of FATA embrace either al-Qaeda or the Taliban. More than three-quarters of FATA residents oppose the presence inside their region of al-Qaeda, and more than two-thirds the Pakistan Taliban (60 percent oppose the Afghan Taliban led by Mullah Omar). Indeed, if al-Qaeda or the Pakistani Taliban were on the ballot in an election, fewer than 1 percent of FATA residents said they would vote for either group.

Though the U.S. military, as well as Taliban and Al-Qaeda fighters, enjoy little popular support in the region, the people overwhelmingly support the Pakistani Army. Nearly 70 percent back the Pakistani military pursuing al-Qaeda and Taliban fighters in the Tribal Areas. By a significant margin, the most popular individual among the people of FATA is General Ashfaq Parvez Kayani, the Pakistani army chief of staff. And even though American drone attacks are strongly opposed, the public's approval of the drone program would actually split almost evenly if those attacks were to be carried out by the Pakistani military instead. Indeed, when asked how FATA should be governed, 79 percent said it should be governed by the Pakistani military, followed by FATA becoming a separate province of Pakistan (70 percent). Becoming part of Afghanistan was the most unpopular choice.

PRIORITIES: UNEMPLOYMENT AND EDUCATION

Unemployment is very high in FATA, with only 20 percent of respondents in our survey saying they were working full-time. Indeed, lack of jobs was chosen as the most important problem in the region by 95 percent of those surveyed. This was closely followed by lack of schools, good roads and security, poor health care, and corruption of local officials. Lesser problems to be addressed, in descending order of importance, were drone attacks, Taliban and foreign fighters, and issues involving refugees.

Despite the reputation that the people in FATA are socially conservative, nine out of ten identified lack of education and schools as their most important problem. Indeed, building new schools was chosen as a high priority for both boys and girls.

In terms of administering justice in the tribal regions, the least popular option was having justice delivered by the Taliban, with only 12 percent believing this to be very important. By contrast, nearly two-thirds chose to be governed by local tribal leaders.

CONCLUSION

Unsurprisingly for a region struggling to cope with a full-fledged insurgency, regular but impossibly unpredictable drone strikes, and searing poverty, the residents of FATA expressed a deep distaste for all the players involved in local conflicts. Opposition to U.S. policies and a fundamental misunderstanding of the purpose of U.S. security operations in the region highlight the difficulty of fighting a counterinsurgency war from afar. Despite rejecting insurgent groups such as al-Qaeda and the Taliban, a majority of residents agreed that suicide attacks against the U.S. military are often or sometimes justified.

Encouragingly, many in FATA are still supportive of the Pakistani military, which has carried out several campaigns to rid the agencies of militants. And like most impoverished populations, FATA residents simply want a stable, economically viable, well-educated community to call home.

CHARTS

The charts that follow illustrate the findings of the Terror Free Tomorrow/New America FATA survey.

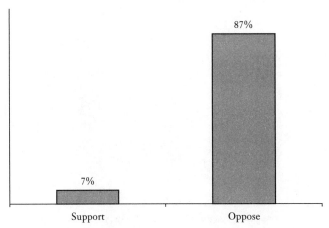

FIGURE 9.1 FATA Residents Who Support/Oppose U.S. Military
Action Against Al-Qaeda and Taliban in Their Region

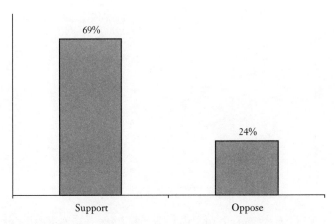

FIGURE 9.2 FATA Residents Who Support/Oppose Pakistani
Military Action Against al-Qaeda and Taliban in Their Region

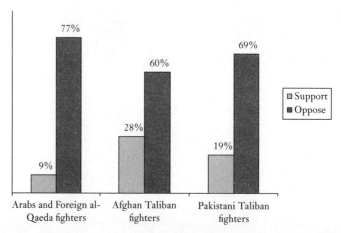

FIGURE 9.3 The Presence of FATA Residents Who Support/Oppose Inside FATA

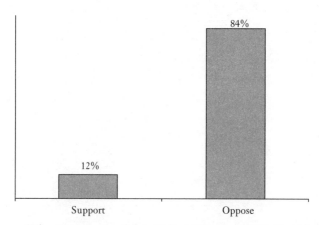

FIGURE 9.4 The Presence of the U.S. Military FATA Residents Who Support/Oppose Inside FATA

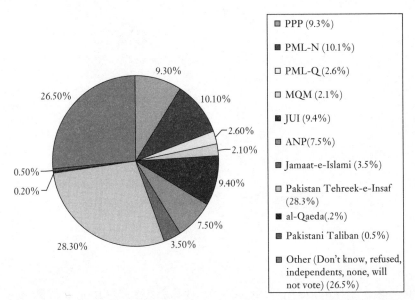

FIGURE 9.5 If You Could Vote for Any, Which Would You Vote For?

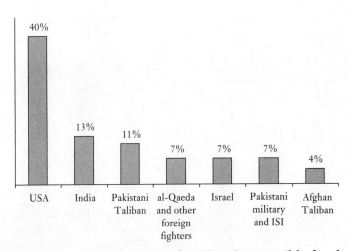

FIGURE 9.6 Whom Do You Consider Most Responsible for the Violence That Is Occurring Inside FATA Today?

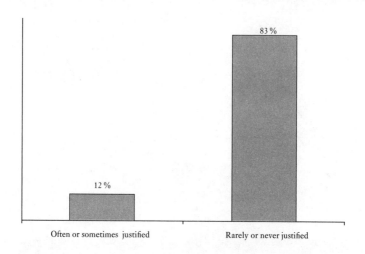

FIGURE 9.7 Suicide Bombings Against Pakistani Military and Police Are:

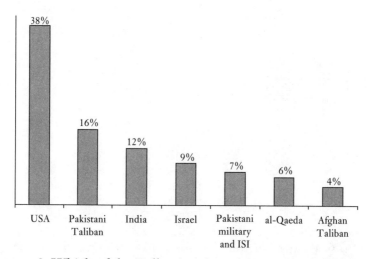

FIGURE 9.8 Which of the Following Countries or Groups Do You Think Pose the Greatest Threat to Your Personal Safety?

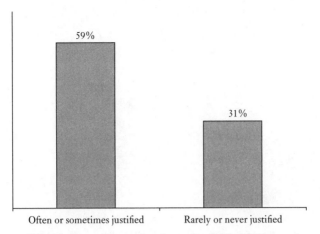

FIGURE 9.9 Suicide Bombings Against the U.S. Military Are:

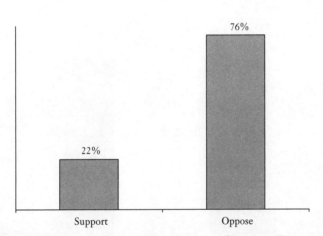

FIGURE 9.10 FATA Residents Who Support/Oppose Drone Attacks Inside FATA

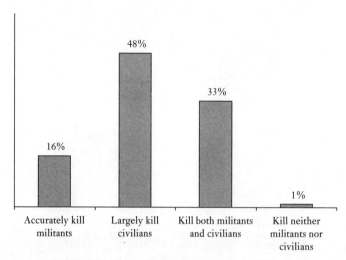

FIGURE 9.11 FATA Residents Think U.S. Drone Attacks:

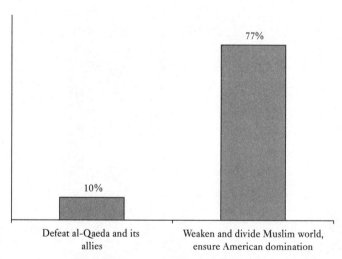

FIGURE 9.12 On Real Purpose of U.S.-Led War on Terror:

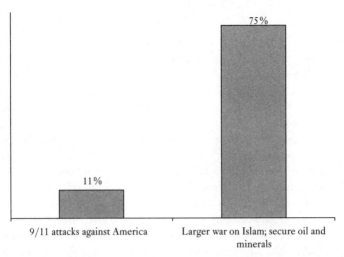

FIGURE 9.13 Why Does America Continue to Occupy Afghanistan?

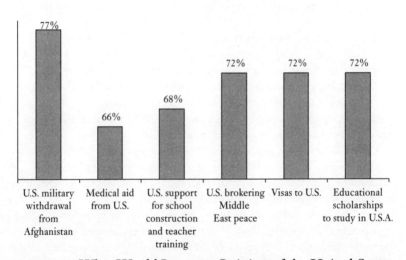

FIGURE 9.14 What Would Improve Opinion of the United States Among FATA Residents:

Notes

1. Methodology: This survey was jointly conducted by the New America Foundation (NAF) and Terror Free Tomorrow (TFT), with fieldwork in the Federally Administered Tribal Areas of Pakistan (FATA) by the Community Appraisal and Motivation Programme (CAMP), a Pakistani NGO operating in FATA and Khyber Pakhtunkhwa Province. Interviews were conducted face-to-face with one thousand FATA residents age eighteen or older across 120 villages or sampling points in all seven tribal agencies of FATA-Pakistan. The fieldwork was conducted from June 30 to July 20, 2010. NAF-TFT-CAMP also conducted two hundred separate interviews with local maliks and tribal elders. This study is held for future release. The conclusions in this report are based solely on the one-thousand-resident sample.

   The questionnaire consisted of forty-three substantive questions, nineteen demographic questions, and twenty-four quality-control questions. Respondents were selected using a multistage random stratified sampling methodology. During the course of fieldwork, there were 1,294 contact attempts made. There were 294 refusals, giving the study a net response rate of 77.3 percent. The poll has a +/- 3 percent margin of error at the 95 percent confidence interval.

   TFT, NAF, and CAMP used face-to-face research techniques in FATA. Interviews were conducted by twenty-two trained interviewers (male and female) and six field supervisors, all of whom are Pakistanis and residents of FATA.

   Before sending the interviewers and supervisors to the field, extensive project orientation and training workshops were conducted in Peshawar. During the training, interviewers and supervisors were briefed on a number of topics, including, but not limited to, the objective of the survey and its details, selection of respondents, the questionnaire (both asking of questions and recording of responses), timing and control issues, and usage of the questionnaire. Mock interviews and field testing were also conducted.

   Eleven survey teams were deployed, under the supervision of six supervisors. Each team was made responsible for interviewing respondents in their respective areas. Detailed field work-plan and list of villages were shared with the field teams before field deployment.

   Interviews were subjected to numerous quality-control procedures, including 54.1 percent direct supervision of interviews, 27.8 percent back-check in person by the supervisor, and back-check by telephonic call by supervisor or the central office.

   The survey was conducted in Federally Administered Tribal Areas (FATA). The target sample was a random selection of Pakistani nationals having FATA residence, both male and female, above the age of eighteen. The sample covered all seven tribal agencies, namely Khyber, Mohmand, Bajaur, Kurram, Orakzai, North Waziristan, and South Waziristan, with the number of sampling points chosen in proportion to the size of each agency's population. Following is the sample plan of the survey.

   The National Census data from 1998 are used as the universe for this sample. The national census classifies villages as the primary unit in the rural areas.

Agency	Proportionate Stratified Sample Size			
	Population	Sample	Leaders Sample	Total
Bajaur	595,227	202	40	242
Mohmand	334,453	114	23	137
Khyber	546,730	186	37	223
Orakzai	225,441	77	15	92
Kurram	448,310	152	31	183
North Waziristan	361,246	123	25	148
South Waziristan	429,841	146	29	175
TOTAL	**2,941,248**	**1,000**	**200**	**1,200**

We used a multistage random stratified sampling method and selected more than 120 primary sampling units, comprising villages in all the seven agencies of FATA. The completed primary sample contains 120 sampling points in which approximately eight interviews were carried out in households selected in each village using a random walk. A total of one thousand men and women from a scientific cross-section of FATA in terms of gender, age, and other socioeconomic characteristics are represented in the sample. For South and North Waziristan, however, local conditions permitted CAMP personnel to sample only men.

After selecting the villages, each village was divided into four hypothetical quarters. A starting point was selected in each quarter. Two starting points were selected for male respondents and two for female respondents. Three interviews were conducted around each starting point. Skipping of three households in Stratum I villages and skipping of three households in Stratum II villages was done after each successful interview. Male and female surveyors were used for male and females respondents respectively. For the selection of a household around a particular starting point, the Right Hand Rule (RHR) was used for female interviewees and the Left Hand Rule (LHR) was used for male respondents.

TFT's previous nationwide surveys of Pakistan can be accessed in the Polls section of www.terrorfreetomorrow.org. Additional findings, particularly the survey of local leaders, have been held for future release.

2. United Nations Assistance Mission to Afghanistan, "Suicide Attacks in Afghanistan," Sept. 9, 2007, http://www.unhcr.org/refworld/pdfid/49997b00d. pdf.

3. As of Sept. 30, 2010. Peter Bergen and Katherine Tiedemann, "The Year of the Drone," New America Foundation, Sept. 30, 2010, http://counterterrorism. newamerica.net/drones.

TEN

The Political Landscape of the Taliban Insurgency in Pakistan

Hassan Abbas

DESPITE COMPARATIVELY PROGRESSIVE forces taking control of Pakistan's Khyber Pakhtunkhwa Province (KPP)[1] after success in the February 2008 provincial elections, stability remains elusive and the law and order situation has gradually deteriorated, raising important questions about the correlation between politics in the province and the nature and extent of militancy there. This essay investigates how various political and religious forces have influenced the state of affairs in the province in recent years.

There has been a sharp rise in the number of terrorist attacks in KPP. In 2009, there were forty-nine suicide attacks targeting police, security forces, political figures, markets, and social and religious gatherings.[2] The number of similar attacks in 2010 was twenty-six, and in 2011 the figure was twenty-three. This pattern continues in 2012, with an increase in the number of terrorist attacks targeting police and areas that are sensitive because of sectarian factors. Many of the attacks have targeted Peshawar, the KPP capital, posing a serious challenge to the province's coalition government, led by the Awami National Party (ANP) and the Pakistan People's Party (PPP). Militants crossing into the KPP from the Federally Administered Tribal Areas (FATA) and fighters from South Punjab (where most sectarian and Kashmir-focused groups recruit) moving to the FATA through various KPP routes (especially via the districts of Dera Ismail Khan and Lakki Marwat) have made the province militarily dangerous.

The social and political dynamics in NWFP are also inextricably linked with the security environment in the ever-volatile tribal areas. Militancy in the FATA (widely known in Pakistan as *illaqa ghair*, "foreign area") has often negatively affected law and order in the adjacent KPP, especially since the 1980s. Likewise, political developments in the mainstream KPP (also called "settled areas") increasingly influence political dynamics in the FATA. Despite stark differences in the administrative and political systems of the two regions, the same political parties operate in both areas. According to Owais Ghani, former governor of KPP, there has been some government discussion about merging KPP and FATA to resolve the lingering crisis in the area, but such an undertaking will be very difficult to manage and can only be implemented in a step-by-step process provided all sides agree.[3] Lt. Gen. Tariq Khan, formerly inspector general of Frontier Corps and now a corps commander, however, insightfully argues that:

> if there were violent reactions to calling the province Pakhtunkhwa and Hazara wanted to separate then what do you think is going to happen if the FATA status changes through unilateral means and then it is forced to merge to Khyber Pakhtunkhwa? FATA is very proud of its tribal heritage, its unique independence and would go into a civil war situation if forced to give up these privileges without an autonomous standing i.e. separate provincial status.[4]

Pakistani security forces were slow to react to signs that militants were growing more aggressive from 2007 to 2009. Political instability played a major role in the government's inability to devise an effective counterterrorism policy, and the alliance of progressive political parties elected in February 2008 was overwhelmed by the Swat crisis, in which militants used brutality, violence, and political manipulation to conquer major swaths of the Swat Valley and adjoining areas. Belated but effective military action in 2009 reasserted government control in the region, but it will be some time before things return to normal in the Malakand division of the KPP, as the Swat, Malakand, Chitral, and Dir districts are known collectively.

The crisis situation in the KPP did not emerge overnight; the deterioration was a product of years of poor governance, regional tension, and economic distress, in addition to the gradual strengthening of militant forces, especially since the Taliban regime in neighboring Afghanistan fell in 2001. The prolonged presence of foreign troops in Afghanistan and overdependence on military means to defeat insurgents in the region also negatively affected the residents of KPP, and predictably so.

POLITICAL STRUCTURE

Pakistan is a federation and has a bicameral parliament, where a prime minister is elected by the majority party or coalition in the National Assembly, while the president is elected by the four provincial assemblies and parliament. The KPP is one of the four provinces of Pakistan, but there are a few regions that are governed according to special rules: the FATA, Frontier Regions in the NWFP, Gilgit-Baltistan (earlier known as Northern Areas), and Pakistani-controlled Azad Kashmir. Behind the well-developed state structure and democratic setup, Pakistan's army has extraordinary influence. Four periods of martial law, spanning more than thirty-two years in total, have entrenched the military's role in the country's security and foreign policy.[5] Additionally, the Pakistani constitution (as amended during military rule) provided the president with a variety of tools to suspend ordinary legislative processes and even dismiss governments without any accountability. These provisions were removed, however, through a package of reforms collectively known as the Eighteenth Amendment, which stripped the office of the president of the authority to dissolve parliament without the advice of the prime minister, impose unilateral emergency rule, and appoint judges, and especially the power to appoint chiefs of the armed forces of Pakistan.

POLITICS IN THE KPP

The History of the KPP

Often overlooked, the KPP's strategic location has influenced its politics and culture in significant ways. On one end is the Khyber Pass, Pakistan's link to Afghanistan; on the other end are the

Northern Areas, connecting Pakistan with China via the pictur-
esque route of the Karakoram highway. Although often hailed as
the land of Pashtuns, the KPP is diverse in its cultural and ethnic heritage and traditions and was the home of some of the great
Hindu and Buddhist empires. Very few cherish this history today,
in part because the Afghan jihad of the 1980s radically changed the
sociopolitical realities of the region.

The KPP is quite diverse. Chitralis- and Hindko-speaking communities in the Hazara division constitute about 30 percent of
the population.[6] Politics in the province, however, are dominated
by Pashtuns. In Urdu, the NWFP (the former name of the province) is also called *Sarhad*, meaning "border region," which suggests
it is ancillary to the core of Pakistan. This formulation has been
unsatisfactory to many Pashtuns, who are proud of their ethnic and
tribal identity. These ethno-nationalist sentiments are reflected
in the Pashtun-dominated ANP's effort to rename the province
Pakhtunkhwa.[7] The effort largely succeeded—with the compromise of adding the word Khyber—despite stiff opposition from
non-Pashtun areas, which are generally represented by the PML-N.
This debate over nomenclature delayed finalization of President
Asif Ali Zardari's constitutional amendment package.[8] Zardari's
PPP has been supportive of the ANP's position on Pakhtunkhwa
as a way of enhancing secular rather than religious identity in the
region. However, the name change has deeply troubled some segments of non-Pashtuns in the Hazara division of KPP, comprising
the Haripur, Mansehra, Battagram, Kohistan, and Abbottabad districts, even leading to violent protests.[9]

Tribal affiliations determine political association less in the KPP
than in the FATA. Unlike in the FATA, where tribes tend to have distinct geographic strongholds, tribes in the KPP are dispersed across
different districts, and urban and rural areas. Class identity is comparatively more important in shaping political outlooks in the KPP, and
religious and sectarian affiliations are increasingly relevant. Relative to
the FATA, the KPP (or "settled areas") is more mainstream and driven
by progressive political forces. Indeed, pro-Soviet leftist parties have
historically attracted strong support.

With better governance, the KPP could have developed a strong
economy and become self-sufficient. The area has many natural

resources, attractive tourist spots, and agricultural land. But the literacy rate is low, health care is scarce, and law enforcement capacity is weak. Illegal trade, smuggling, and inadequate infrastructure undermine the economy. The provincial Finance Department in 2010 described the economic conditions in stark terms:

> NWFP has a very limited tax base and relies for 92% of its revenues on the Federal Government. All the vital socio-economic indicators of the Province are lowest among the other Provinces. The Province is also confronted with war on terror, causing huge losses to human life, business and property.[10]

Since 2001, three factors have played critical roles in the destabilization and radicalization of KPP: first, the politics and performance of the MMA government from 2002 to 2007; second, the lack of reform in KPP's madrassas; and third, the insurgency in neighboring FATA, which is largely a consequence of decades of negligence on the part of the state and persistent conflict across the border in Afghanistan.

The MMA government was formed after an electoral victory in 2002, but swept out of office in 2008. It turned out to be a huge disappointment, even for its supporters. Corruption, nepotism, and incompetence were rampant under MMA rule—problems that the religious leaders and politicians in the MMA were supposed to eliminate.[11] The MMA failed to make good on its campaign promises to provide better access to fair justice and accountability for public servants. Instead, MMA policies restricted civil liberties, slowed progressive legal reforms, and undermined religious tolerance. Women's rights were set back, as was madrassa reform, which was to include teaching science and registering foreign students.[12] The MMA instead moved to "Islamize" the public education system in the province and banned music on public transportation. The KPP Assembly legislated that women could be treated only by a female doctor, which, given the lack of trained female health care professionals, would have been very dangerous, particularly in rural areas.[13]

The most significant development, however, was the Assembly's passage in July 2005 of the "Hisba Bill," which amounted to strict imposition of sharia, or Islamic law, as understood and interpreted by the MMA's leaders.[14] Despite major objections by opposition parties and even by the federal government in Islamabad, MMA leadership in the NWFP went ahead with the controversial sharia project. The most onerous provision of the law created new institutions in KPP in which clerics associated with the MMA religious alliance could be given government jobs equivalent to judgeships. The new position of *Mohtisib* (ombudsman) was tasked with investigating public corruption and monitoring individuals' moral behavior. Vigilante action, such as the blackening of billboards in Peshawar that featured female models, created an environment of fear in the province.

Though the Supreme Court of Pakistan declared various aspects of the law unconstitutional, the MMA government was able to defy that ruling indirectly by renaming provisions of the law and changing procedural rules, allowing it to bypass checks and balances.

President Pervez Musharraf ignored some of the MMA's excesses because he needed its votes to support his efforts to compel the national legislature to allow him to serve both as army chief and president. This behind-the-scenes alliance with Gen. Musharraf inspired critics to call the MMA government a "Mullah-Military Alliance." According to Afrasiyab Khattak, the former chair of Pakistan's Human Rights Commission and the current peace envoy of the KPP government, the MMA's "phenomenal rise in October 2002 elections was not just coincidental, but a part of the political plans of the military. Without the threat of religious extremism, the military would have lost its utility for Western powers."[15]

Another context to these developments is provided by writer Brian Cloughley, who argues: "Unfortunately Musharraf, as Byron had it, 'nursed the pinion that impelled the steel,' in that in 2002 he endorsed the election efforts of the religious crackpots in the interests of sidelining the two mainstream political parties."[16] Consequently, as one of the International Crisis Group's insightful reports maintains, "In return for helping Musharraf consolidate power, the MMA was allowed to pursue its Islamisation agenda in NWFP."[17]

The 2008 KPP election victory by the ANP and PPP was a public repudiation of controversial MMA policies, but the MMA's five-plus years in government had allowed it to institutionalize some of its policies. For instance, many bureaucrats with extremist religious views were given important positions and developed extensive connections within government departments.

The impact on madrassas was also important. These religious schools proliferated in the 1980s under the patronage of Gen. Zia's military government, and many were established in NWFP to recruit, groom, and train Afghan refugees for fighting in Afghanistan.[18] According to an International Crisis Group report, the madrassas run by JUI were instrumental in encouraging "Jihad culture" for religious as well as political ends in Pakistan's tribal belt.[19] The trend continued in the 1990s. A few halfhearted attempts to rein in the extremist madrassas were made in the last decade, but the MMA government (2002–2007) ensured that such efforts remained limited. According to a credible study of Pakistani law enforcement, some suicide bomber training camps in the Malakand division were destroyed only during 2009 military operations in the Swat area.[20] Most likely these were established during MMA years as militancy in the area gained momentum. Some madrassas in the KPP continue to create an environment conducive to religious bigotry and extremism.[21]

PREVAILING TRENDS IN KPP

The Growth of Militancy

The MMA's unwillingness to foster support for counterterrorism during the Musharraf presidency, especially between 2004 and 2007, allowed the Taliban to establish networks in the KPP.[22] The KPP government did not listen to political and social groups that favored strong action against extremism. As the Taliban groups strengthened, they attacked military and government infrastructure in the FATA. But in the KPP, the Taliban did not directly confront the government initially, instead focusing on ideological targets, such as girls' schools, ancient Buddhist shrines, women's rights activists, video and music shops, and barbershops (which shave beards against Islamist wishes).[23]

In the KPP, militants began warning women as early as 2005 not to appear in public without a veil. The movement started in the southern areas of KPP—Tank, Dera Ismail Khan, Lakki Marwat, and Bannu—that bordered South and North Waziristan, hotbeds of Taliban activity in the FATA. Later the activity spread north into Kohat, Charsadda, Mardan, Dir, Swat, and the provincial capital, Peshawar—areas bordering the Kurram, Orakzai, Khyber, and

Mohmand agencies in the FATA.[24] It was obvious that militant activity in NWFP was linked to developments in adjoining parts of the FATA. For example, the "peace deals" in Waziristan and the Khyber agency in 2004–2006 were followed by more aggressive actions taken by extremists in KPP.

The MMA government did not adopt defensive measures to monitor the movement of militants from FATA to KPP. The militants and the Islamist political parties in Pakistan share some ideas and social support. Component parties of MMA, especially Jamiat Ulema-e-Islam (both the Sami and Fazlur factions), run madrassas that provide recruits for militant training camps in FATA. Analyzing the situation in 2009, journalist Talat Farooq argued:

> After 9/11 the Taliban and Al-Qaeda elements, supported by their Pakistani sympathizers, crossed over into FATA as a result of Musharraf's two-faced policy that strengthened the Pakistani Taliban. This particular policy was never criticized by either the religious or the conservative parties…with the result that the militants have grown in power with the help of local criminals, drug mafia, arms dealers and foreign "hands" that have joined them along the way.[25]

Bureaucrats in the six transitional areas wedged between FATA and NWFP districts—collectively known as the Frontier Regions—also failed to alert national authorities about the growing militancy.[26] Both incompetence and sympathy with militants were at play.

The most serious problems in the KPP today are occurring in Peshawar and its suburbs, where the Taliban and associated militant groups target government buildings, law enforcement officials, and ANP and PPP officials at will. Attacks on schools in Peshawar and its suburbs, mostly since 2010, are a disturbing new trend.[27] KPP Chief Minister Amir Haider Khan Hoti aptly said in early 2011, "We are trying to put pens in the hands of students while terrorists are trying to equip them with guns to carry forward their agenda and push the region toward illiteracy."[28]

In the aftermath of the military offensive in South Waziristan in October 2009, 221 people were killed and nearly 500 were wounded in bombings from mid-October to mid-November.[29] Some of this violence was spillover from troubles in FATA's Khyber agency between

Lashkar-e-Islam, led by Mangal Bagh, and Ansar-ul-Islam.[30] But the Tehrik-e-Taliban Pakistan (TTP) is active as well and has claimed that many of the terrorist attacks in KPP were retaliatory. For instance, it declared that the June 2009 attack on Peshawar's luxury Pearl Continental Hotel was to avenge the attack on a madrassa in the FATA's Orakzai agency.[31] The TTP's activities are dependent on the strength of its logistical networks in a given area, and there is increasing evidence that terrorists who strike in Peshawar are based in adjacent Khyber agency.[32] Another potent reason behind TTP attacks in Peshawar is the emergence of local lashkars (militias) in suburban Peshawar through a jirga, or tribal assembly, in collaboration with the local police and the provincial administration, to fight Taliban encroachments.[33] Further, TTP also raise funds from kidnapping (for ransom) of members of wealthy families living in comparatively posh localities in Peshawar area. Even top TTP leadership acknowledges their involvement in kidnappings for ransom.[34]

Swat and the Army

Pakistan waited far too long before directly confronting Sufi Muhammad's militant Tehrik-i-Nifaz-i-Shariat-i-Mohammadi (TNSM) in the NWFP's Swat district. By the time security forces largely cleared the district in the second half of 2009, adjacent regions were convulsing from two million displaced people. This took the civilian government by surprise, though the military authorities had warned of such a possibility. The ad hoc response allowed some extremist groups to increase their influence among the internally displaced people (IDPs). For instance, Jamaat-e-Islami's Al-Khidmat organization and Jamaat-ud-Dawa's new incarnation, the Falah-i-Insaniat Foundation (FIF), established various charity camps in the Swat area to create goodwill and potentially attract future recruits.[35] Although most of their activities were humanitarian, the government's failure provided these militant groups with growth possibilities in the area.[36]

The government finally cracked down on the TNSM after the situation became untenable and U.S. pressure increased. Several thousand militants were reportedly killed, but the TNSM's military leader, Maulana Fazlullah, surprisingly escaped. Public and political support strengthened the military leadership's ability to take decisive action against the militants. Nonetheless, many questions about the Swat situation remain unanswered. For instance, why was Fazlullah's FM radio station, which he used for propaganda and communication with supporters, not disabled in 2007–08? He had used radio announcements to threaten teachers and students at girls' schools in the region.[37] Moreover, Fazlullah was seemingly allowed to escape after being surrounded by police in 2008. Some ascribe it to sheer incompetence, while others believe that Fazlullah cut a deal with elements in the security forces during the early phase of his militancy campaign.[38] Fazlullah is now hiding in Afghanistan, and according to Pakistani security experts he is involved in mounting attacks against the Pakistan army in the FATA area.[39]

The Pakistani army since then has focused more on enhancing its coordination with civilian law enforcement agencies and started training KPP police, with around five thousand officials educated in counterterrorism and combat techniques during the 2009–10 period.[40]

The Swat conflict was also influenced by the Panjpirs of Swabi district, adjacent to the Malakand division of KPP. The Panjpirs follow a localized version of Saudi Wahhabism that was introduced in Pakistan by Maulana Tahir, father of Major Amir, an ISI operative who allegedly helped topple Benazir Bhutto's first government.[41] The madrassa at Panjpir, administered by Maulana Tayyab, Major Amir's brother, is associated with a who's who of Pakistan's extremist leaders, including TNSM chief Sufi Muhammad, Bajaur Taliban commander Maulvi Faqir Muhammad (who recently split from TTP), and the Khyber agency's notorious militant leader Mangal Bagh. TNSM military chief Fazlullah also adhered to the Panjpir group.[42] This madrassa was an important recruitment camp that also performed the role of a think tank for strategic planning during the Afghan war of the 1980s.

ROLE AND STRENGTH OF POLITICAL
PARTIES IN KPP

Political dynamics in the KPP have changed rapidly since the 2002 general election was won by the MMA. The ANP's 2008 successes in Kohat, Hangu, Nowshera, and Peshawar, and the PPP's similar gains in Nowshera, D.I. Khan, Upper Dir, Lower Dir, and Swat, were very significant because those regions were considered strongholds of religious parties such as the JUI and JI.[43] However, voters rejected JUI and JI because they linked signs of Talibanization to the religious parties in power. According to Joshua White, an academic studying KPP politics, the MMA's defeat can also be attributed to the coalition's perceived failures in its education, health, and anticorruption policies and to an anti-incumbency trend in Pakistani politics.[44] The issues of bureaucratic corruption and incompetence, however, were widely covered by local media during the MMA rule.[45]

Public expectations were high when the ANP-PPP alliance took power in March 2008. But the euphoria was short-lived, as ANP almost immediately began negotiating with the TNSM leadership to stabilize Swat district. ANP leaders were facing an assassination campaign by the TTP in FATA and by the TNSM's allies in the Swat Valley.[46] ANP workers and legislators were systematically targeted, forcing many to disappear from the public arena altogether.[47] Such threats and attacks continue today.[48] The ANP explained its decision to negotiate with TNSM by arguing that if the "army is not interested in challenging the expanding writ of Taliban, why should we continue to sacrifice our lives?"[49] Interestingly, Asfandyar Wali Khan, the president of the ANP, secretly visited Washington in May 2008 to brief the U.S. government about the prospective deal.[50] ANP leaders ultimately cut a deal in 2008 with Sufi Muhammad, who was in prison at the time, thinking he might be able to moderate the fighters led by his son-in-law, Maulana Fazlullah.

Ameer Haider Khan Hoti, the ANP's chief minister of the KPP government, explained: "Our policy is political dialogue. That will eventually be the way out."[51] He also defended the decision to release Sufi Muhammad, saying it was on humanitarian grounds.[52] However, Sufi Muhammad violated the presumably "confidential" agreement with the ANP soon after his release and began expressing controversial views. For instance, he unequivocally said that democracy is un-Islamic.[53] He also declared that women should leave their homes only for Haj in Mecca and should not leave even for medical treatment.[54]

The severe public backlash from these statements altered the political dynamic in Pakistan and, together with mounting U.S. pressure, convinced the Zardari government and the Pakistani army to finally tackle the TNSM. Operation Rah-e-Rast (The Right Path) pushed the TNSM out of Swat and largely eliminated its ability to regain control over the area, though human rights groups claim the Pakistani Army committed violations during this campaign—which the Army denies.[55] In fact, the army also suffered a high number of casualties (including officers) in the operations. The entire episode, however, damaged the ANP's reputation, and fractures have appeared in its political support base. This raises the possibility that religious parties could regain some of the lost support in the next election.[56]

Whatever the political impact, anti-Taliban sentiment in KPP is on the rise. Terrorism in the Swat Valley in the 2008–09 time frame played a crucial role in this reassessment. According to a Gallup poll in November-December 2009, only 1 percent of NWFP residents said that the Taliban have a positive influence, down from 11 percent in June 2009.[57] Public frustration with suicide bombings in KPP has risen significantly, concurrent with an expansion of military operations. Still, in the absence of economic opportunities and development, the frustrated younger generation of the province (especially in districts bordering FATA) is susceptible to radicalization and joining militant groups rather than the religious political parties that are part of the country's political system. Critical perception about drone attacks also contributed to hardening of public opinion in FATA as well as KPP.

General Public Grievances

The Taliban play on a variety of grievances in the KPP in order to recruit. Many Pashtuns feel helpless in the face of what is perceived as an "attack on Pashtuns from all sides"—the Taliban, the Pakistani military, and the United States. Many Pashtuns are angry that other Pakistanis increasingly see them as pro-Taliban and habitually violent. These social concerns are compounded by economic concerns and the federal government's inability to respond to growing problems. According to Peshawar's Sarhad Chamber of Commerce, in early 2009 only 594 of the province's 2,500 "industrial units" were functional.[58] The situation hasn't changed much since then. Civilians are also angry that police and civilian law enforcement fail to provide adequate security, though security personnel tend to be a prime target of terrorists. There have been some improvements in police performance in KPP in the last couple of years thanks to increased funding and provision of better equipment, but serious weaknesses remain entrenched.

FUTURE PROSPECTS

The future of KPP will be determined by many factors, not just fluctuating support for various political parties. Quick and effective implementation of the political reforms proposed in 2009 for the FATA—which aim to increase political participation and limit collective judicial punishments—will be critical.[59] So will security operations in South Punjab, where many militants fled after military operations in South Waziristan in late 2009.[60] If those fighters are not neutralized, they are likely to stoke further militancy in the region. Moreover, government pressure in Punjab may push them back to the FATA and NWFP. Likewise, police reform in the KPP is critical for containing local militancy, as are the ongoing military campaigns in FATA.[61] Holding cleared areas and building trust are critical and will have a psychological impact in the KPP. And ultimately, economic development is vital.

Finally, distinguishing irreconcilable militant elements from those who can be co-opted will be crucial. As seen in Swat, many ordinary people joined or supported extremist elements when they felt they were at the total mercy of such groups. Empowering local leaders to help the disgruntled elements reimagine their future can reignite hope among the people. Hopelessness and frustration among Pashtuns must be treated through better governance and security before the state can realistically expect to engage reconcilable opposition groups. The Pashtuns' history is rife with internal conflicts and brutal tribal rivalries, but they would not have survived as an ethnic group if they were incapable of resolving their internal feuds through negotiations. However, for such negotiations to be effective, the writ of the state is critical.

Military action can only create a window of opportunity for civil society and political actors to take charge of the situation and start rebuilding. The Swat operation of 2009 and its aftermath must be analyzed thoroughly and dispassionately by leading political forces in KPP, so as to avoid repeating such a challenging and grave situation in any other part of the province.

Last but not least, it is important to recognize that many brave citizens of Khyber Pakhtunkhwa province also continue to defy Taliban and extremist elements. Two examples are worth mentioning here:

Farooq Khan, a progressive religious scholar, who was establishing an Islamic University in the Swat area, was tragically gunned down in late 2010 by pro-Taliban forces. But many of his students and supporters in KPP continue to pursue the goals he set.[62] He was aware of the challenges but never gave up his struggle. Bushra Gohar, another courageous Pushtun parliamentarian from KPP, also refuses to be harassed by Taliban who threatened her if she did not quit politics.[63] She remains a vocal critic of all things Taliban, keeping alive the hope that Pushtuns will reclaim their lost territory—in both the intellectual and the physical sense.

POLITICAL PARTIES IN PAKISTAN

Pakistan Muslim League (Nawaz)

The Pakistan Muslim League or PML-N[64] in essence was a product of Gen. Zia-ul-Haq's military rule (1977–1988). The original Muslim League was led by Pakistan's founding father, Quaid-i-Azam Mohammad Ali Jinnah, and played a critical role in the country's freedom movement, but the party almost fizzled out in the 1950s. Since then, almost every military dictator in the country has tried to resurrect this party—primarily to gather political orphans and supporters of military rule under one banner in order to earn political legitimacy. Zia's "Muslim League" was born in 1985 and split into two groups in 1988. One of these splinter groups, under Nawaz Sharif, emerged as PML-N in 1993.

Both in the early 1990s and during the 1997–1999 period, PML-N formed coalition governments in NWFP with ANP's support and participation. Gen. Pervez Musharraf's martial law in October 1999 removed Sharif as prime minister, and the PML-N split into two factions in 2001, when a group under Chaudhry Shujaat Hussain decided to break away and launch the Pakistan Muslim League Quaid-i-Azam (PML-Q) to support Musharraf.[65] PML-Q later decided to join the PPP alliance in Islamabad in 2011. Though a product of military rule and intelligence agencies, PML-N of today is an independent and important political force, especially in Punjab and KPP. In terms of ideology, it is a center-right party and its leadership is known for close relations with the government of Saudi Arabia.

Muttahida Majlis-e-Amal

Muttahida Majlis-e-Amal (MMA) is a coalition formed in 2002 of five religious political parties: the Deobandi-dominated Jamiat Ulema-e-Islam (JUI), Barelvi-oriented Jamiat Ulema-e-Pakistan, the traditionally Islamist Jamaat-e-Islami (JI) founded by Abul Ala Maududi, the Shiite Tehrik-e-Jafaria Pakistan, and the Wahhabi-inspired Jamiat Ahle Hadith.

The JUI was founded by Maulana Shabbir Ahmed Usmani in 1945. In the 1970s, it was revived by Mufti Mahmud, whose son Maulana Fazlur Rehman took over in the early 1980s. The party split into two factions in the mid-1980s—JUI-F, led by Fazlur Rehman, and JUI-S, led by Maulana Sami-ul-Haq—following disagreements over political strategy. JUI played an important role during the Afghan jihad of the 1980s, and many graduates of the religious schools, or madrassas, associated with both JUI factions joined Taliban forces in Afghanistan in 1990s. According to Ahmed Rashid, at least eight of the Taliban cabinet ministers in the Kabul regime in 1999 were graduates of Sami-ul-Haq's Darul Uloom Haqqania.[66] Both factions joined the MMA in 2002. As per JUI's official manifesto, the party is committed to the establishment of an Islamic state in Pakistan.

Though widely known as an umbrella group sponsored originally by Pakistan's Inter-Services Intelligence (ISI), MMA lost its relevance and was practically dismembered after the 2008 elections. JUI leader Fazlur Rahman also became part of the PPP-led coalition in Islamabad for a few years after 2008. His political stunts in the past indicate that he truly is a political animal and can join hands with any force at any given time depending upon his political interests. In early 2012, he made news headlines with his critical statements about Pakistan's intelligence services. While speaking to a major public gathering in late January 2012, he said: "The establishment has turned Pakistan into a security state. Pakistan's resources don't go to people but for the establishment's extravagances.... Over 60% of the budget still goes to the military."[67]

Awami National Party[68]

The Awami National Party, or ANP, is a secular and nationalist Pashtun party associated with the legendary Abdul Ghaffar Khan, also known as "Frontier Gandhi" for his political affinity and relationship with the renowned Mohandas Gandhi. Ghaffar Khan's son, Wali Khan, revived what had been the National Awami Party (NAP) from 1957 to 1975 (when it was outlawed by Zulfikar Ali Bhutto's government under controversial sedition charges) with a slightly different name, Awami National Party, in 1986; now his son, Asfandyar Wali Khan, leads the party.[69] NAP also had support in the former East Pakistan (now Bangladesh), and in the late 1960s and early 1970s it was deemed sympathetic to the Soviet Union. The party's leftist orientation and manifesto remained intact over the years, though NAP had a broader national support base than the ANP and garnered support from other provinces as well. Although ANP was part of coalition governments in KPP as well as in Islamabad during the late 1980s and 1990s, not until 2008 was it able to install a chief minister in KPP. In another first, in the 2008 elections ANP captured a couple of seats in the Sindh provincial assembly from Karachi, where large Pashtun pockets exist. These electoral successes came at a cost, however. ANP legislators and leaders were consistently targeted by militants all across the KPP since 2008, and ANP faced these challenges bravely. Its track record in governing the province effectively has not been that bright, though.

Pakistan People's Party

The Pakistan People's Party, also progressive, has roots and support all across Pakistan. Zulfikar Ali Bhutto, along with a group of intellectuals and socialist-minded activists, formed the PPP in 1967, and since then it has held power in Islamabad at various times. Bhutto became Pakistan's president in 1971 and, after the introduction of a new constitution, remained prime minister from 1973 to 1977. He was overthrown in July 1977 by Gen. Zia, who hanged him in 1979 under terms of a controversial court ruling. The party remained popular, and Bhutto's daughter, Benazir Bhutto, served as prime minister in 1988–1990 and 1993–1996. PPP also remained a major coalition partner in provincial governments in the KPP during these years. PPP again formed the central government in Islamabad in March 2008 (with ANP help) and joined hands with ANP to form a government in the KPP as well.[70] The ANP-PPP alliance remained stable during the 2008–2012 time frame; a change in the name of the province as per ANP's original demand helped this cooperation grow.

Led by renowned cricketer and philanthropist Imran Khan, the Pakistan Tehreek-e-Insaf (PTI) remained in oblivion since its inception in 1996. Credit goes to Imran Khan for raising the issue of need for an independent judiciary in Pakistan, but the party remained a one-man show till recently and could not garner wide public support. All of this changed in late 2011 when Imran Khan expanded his support base, especially in KPP to begin with, and addressed huge public gatherings across Pakistan—most notably in Lahore, Karachi, and some rural areas of Punjab and KPP. Many political stalwarts from other parties started joining him. His critics argue that he is too sympathetic to the Taliban and that Pakistan's ISI is helping him in his political campaign. There is likely some truth to these allegations, but the reality is that his public support has increased significantly over time and his credibility with people and integrity is well regarded. He argues that dialogue and negotiations with extremists and militants is needed for resolving the crisis. The national and provincial election, expected in late 2012 or early 2013, will be a big test for PTI. The party is generally expected to do well in KPP.

BACKGROUND: ETHNIC, TRIBAL, AND POLITICAL AFFILIATIONS OF THE TWENTY-FOUR DISTRICTS OF KPP

1. Abbottabad District[71]: Major ethnicities—locally called *biradaris*—in Abbottabad district include Sardars, Abbassis, Jadoons, Tanolis, Syeds, Awans, and Rajputs. Abbassis and Jadoons are the largest and most influential, and they play a decisive role as members of a biradari generally vote together. A few Christian and Sikh families reside in the area, but predominantly it is a Sunni area (with a large conservative Deobandi influence), with Shiite pockets in and around Abbottabad city. Prominent political figures include Amanullah Khan Jadoon, Air Marshal Asghar Khan, Sardar Mohammad Yaqub, Gohar Ayub, and Sardar Mehtab Khan. The PML-N is strong in the district; PML-N members won all three of its National Assembly (NA) seats in the 2008 elections. In response to the prospects of the province's name change to Pukhtunkhwa, a "Hazara province movement" centered in

Abbottabad began in April 2010.[72] The district also has the country's premier military training academy in the Kakul area and is also known for many well-reputed schools and colleges where students come from across the country. Abbottabad Public School and Burn Hall College are among the highest-rated educational institutions in the country.

2. Bannu District: Major Pashtun ethnic groups residing in the district are the Banochi, Wazir, Marwat, Bhittani, and Daur. Banochi tribesmen reside mostly in the city of Bannu, while Wazir inhabit the remote areas and the Bannu suburbs. Daur, who mostly live in the neighboring North Waziristan agency of the FATA, have also settled in the area and are involved in local businesses. The jirga, or tribal assembly, system is stronger in Bannu than in other districts of the NWFP, which is largely due to FATA influence. There are also small Christian, Hindu, and Ahmedi communities. JUI-F, ANP, and to a lesser degree PPP have strong support in the district. Baz Muhammad Khan (ANP) and Akram Khan Durrani (JUI-F: MMA) are two important political players in the district. In the 2008 elections, Maulana Fazlur Rehman of JUI-F won the NA seat from the area. This was the home constituency of MMA chief minister Akram Durrani (2002–2007) and hence received disproportionate development funds, making JUI-F victory easier.

3. Battagram District: The major ethnic groups of the district are Gujjar, Swati, Akhunkhel, and Medakhel. Swatis are the most influential in political activities, but the Akhunkhel tribe, residing in the Alai area, is also influential. Tribal divisions rather than political ideals determine voting patterns in the district. Darul Uloom Ishaatul Islam in Battagram, a madrassa led by Qari Mohammad Yusuf (associated with MMA), is known for its hard-line and conservative views. Among other politicians, Malang Khan and Yusuf Khan Taran are important. PML-Q has strong support in the area, and its candidate won the NA seat in 2008.

4. Buner District: Buner is mainly inhabited by the Yousafzai tribe. Other tribes and clans include Mandar, Syed, Gujjar, and Mohmand. Gujjars of the area are among the most impoverished, while Yousafzais are the most powerful (in both political and economic spheres). Buner is also the land of many great saints; the shrines of Pir Baba and Shalbandi Baba are famous among the locals. There are small Sikh and Hindu communities. The ANP and PPP are strong in the district. Important political leaders include Sher Akbar Khan, of a PPP splinter group (Sherpao); Abdul Mateen Khan (ANP); and Ali Sher Khan (PML-N). ANP won the NA seat from the area in 2008 elections.

5. Charsadda District: The important tribes in Charsadda are Mohmadzai, Mohmand, and Gigiani. The largest and most influential is Mohmadzai, followed by Mohmand. The jirga institution is effective in Charsadda society, and this is one of the few areas of KPP with a shrine to a female saint. It is also ANP's stronghold, from which members of Ghaffar Khan's family contest elections. However, the PPP (Sherpao) group also regularly performs well in elections from this district.

6. Chitral District: The general population is mainly the Kho ethnic group that speaks the Khowar or Chitrali language, which is also used in parts of Gilgit in the Northern Areas and Swat. Major clans include Adamzada and Arbabzada. Chitral is also home to the Kalash tribe that resides in three remote valleys southwest of the town of Chitral. The district is traditionally a PPP stronghold. Maulana Abdul Akbar Khan Chitrali (MMA) and Shahzada Ghulam Mahyuddin of PML-Q (who was earlier in PPP) are popular politicians. The latter won the 2008 NA election from the district.

7. Dera Ismail Khan District: The major ethnic groups of D.I. Khan are the Baloch, Muhajirs (immigrants from India in 1947), Jat, and Pashtuns (Mottani tribe). The majority language is Seraiki; however, Pashto and Urdu are also spoken widely. This is the only Seraiki-speaking district in KPP, and with it starts the Seraiki belt that stretches east into Punjab and south into Sindh. There is also a small Sikh community. The district is named after Ismail Khan, a Baloch tribesman. JUI's Maulana Fazlur Rehman and his brothers are politically well established here. Members of the Kundi tribe are challengers to JUI-F. In the 2008 national elections, PPP candidate Faisal Kundi, who is currently deputy speaker of the NA, defeated Fazlur Rehman (who contested seats in various regions, as is permitted under Pakistan's election laws).

8. Haripur District: As in Abbottabad, there are various biradaris well established in Haripur, including Jadoon, Tareen, Dilazaq,

Tanolis (a majority in the Ghazi area), Sardar, Awan, and Rajas. Members of the family of the late president Ayub Khan (his son and grandson), affiliated with PML-Q, are politically strong in the district. However, a PML-N candidate won the NA seat from the area in 2008.

9. Hangu District: In a district influenced greatly by the adjacent Kurram agency of FATA, the following tribes are dominant: Bangash, Orakzai, Khattak, Shinwari, and Afridi. Sectarian violence is common in the area. JUI-F (MMA) and ANP are the two strongest parties, but sectarian identities of the candidates also influence election results. Currently the NA seat from the area is occupied by ANP's Syed Haider Ali Shah.

10. Karak District: The district is predominantly populated by the Khattak tribe (subsect Barak), known throughout Pakistan for the traditional Khattak dance. Karak produces many senior military officers and civil servants. JI (MMA), ANP, and PPP are equally strong in the area. Afrasiyab Khattak, a human rights campaigner and ANP leader, is active in this district. In 2008, a JUI (MMA) member won the NA seat.

11. Kohat District: Kohat is divided between two important Pashtun tribes, the Bangash and the Khattak. The Bangash occupy the central, northern, and northwestern parts of the district. The Khattaks are divided into Teri, Akora, and Sagri Khattaks. The Akora Khattaks reside mostly in the district's northeast, but also in the adjoining parts of Peshawar. Kohat city is primarily a military town, with an air force base. Prominent politicians include Syed Iftikhar Hussain Gilani, Imtiaz Gilani, and Javed Ibrahim Paracha. Paracha is a former legislator from the PML-N known for his avowed respect for Taliban leader Mullah Omar and al-Qaeda chief Osama bin Laden. In an interesting political shift, an ANP candidate won the NA seat from the area in 2008.

12. Kohistan District: The tribes that are strong in the district are the Manzar, Money, Koka, Mankekhel, and Darramkhel. A very low literacy rate and difficult terrain partly explain why the district has poor political turnout. JUI-F (MMA) has developed strong political roots in the area, though there remains significant support for PPP, whose candidate won the NA seat in 2008. The district connects KPP to the Gilgit-Baltistan area, and targeted killing of Shiites in the district in early 2012 created tension in the region.

13. Lakki Marwat District: This is the land of the Pashtun Marwat, one of the four great subtribes of the Lohani tribe (also known as Speen Lohani, or white Lohanis). The word *Marwat* is derived from the Arabic *murrawat*, which means compassion and generosity. Marwat tribesmen are reputed to be strong, sturdy, and tall, with a fair complexion. Clan is often considered more important than political creed in the district, and the candidate supported by the Marwat tribe usually wins. PML-Q and JUI-F, however, also have independent political support in the area. Salim Saifullah Khan of the PML-Q and his brother Anwar Saifullah Khan are important political players in the area. JUI-F's Naseer Khan won a special election for the National Assembly from the area in February 2010 because of nearly complete support from the Marwat tribe.

14. Lower Dir District: Many Pashtun tribes and clans reside in the area, including Mashwani, Shinwari, Yousafzai, Shahkhel, Mastkkhel, Umerkhel, Dushkhel, Mayar, Anikhel, Sultankhel, and Aka Khel. There are also non-Pashtun Syed and Gujjar communities. Politically, it is a JI stronghold. Former JI chief Qazi Hussain Ahmed (though based in Nowshera district) contested elections in Lower Dir in 2002. ANP is the second most popular party in the area. Siraj ul Haq, a hard-line member of JI, and Zahid Khan, the central information secretary of ANP, are very active in the district as well as in provincial politics. However, in a surprise electoral shift, PPP won the NA seat from the district in 2008.

15. Malakand District: The main tribes in Malakand are Akozai Yousafzais (Khankhel, Baizai, and Ranizai) and Uthmankhel. Among non-Pashtuns, Syeds and Gujjars are strong in the area. The Baizai and Ranizai migrated from Afghanistan a few centuries ago and still maintain links there. Maulana Mohammad Inayatur Rehman of MMA (known for his sympathies for Taliban militants) and Lal Mohammad Khan of the PPP are strong in the area. PPP won the district's NA seat in 2008.

16. Mansehra District: Mansehra is home to a diverse group of ethnicities: Pashtuns, Hindkowans, Rajputs, and Punjabis. Among Hindkowans, Tanoli are predominant. Bukhari Syeds, Mashhadi Syeds, and Tirmizi Syeds are also well established. Muzammad Shah and Qasim Shah of Balakot, Wajihuzzaman and Azam Swati of Ogi, and Nawabzada Salahuddin, Zargul Khan, and Habib ur Rehman Tanoli of the Tanawal area are major political players. PML-Q and PML-N are strong in the district. JUI's win in by-polls in early 2010 indicates shifting trends, however.

17. Mardan District: Yousafzai, Khattak, and Mohmand are the dominant Pashtun tribes. The Yousafzai tribe and its clans are the most well established in the district, which is known as an ANP and PPP stronghold. Ameer Haider Khan Hoti of ANP, the present chief minister of NWFP, is from this district. The Hoti family is very influential in the area, but its support is divided between PPP and ANP. The district is also home to a few military training centers. In recent years, an increasing number of terrorist attacks in the district have worsened the overall law-and-order situation of the district.

18. Nowshera District: The Akora Khattak subtribe of the Khattak is the dominant tribe in the district. It is divided further into six clans: Akorkhels, Khwarra Khattak, Swera Khattak, Uryakhels, Samikhel, and Kakakhels (Miangan). The Gumriyani tribe is also based here; legend has it that this tribe came originally from Afghanistan to help the Pashtuns of the area, and then settled down. Other tribes include the Durrani, and among non-Pashtuns, Awan and Malyar. An important and controversial landmark in the district is Darul Uloom Haqqania at Akora Khattak, the seminary where many senior Taliban leaders received their religious education. ANP and PPP are strong in the district, and each succeeded in winning a seat in the 2008 NA elections. The district is also an important hub for local smugglers.

19. Peshawar District: Many Pashtun as well as non-Pashtun tribes live in the area. The prominent Pashtun tribes are Afridi, Khattak, Orakzai, Wazir, Mehsud, Mohmand, Daudzai, and Chamkani. Peshawar is more cosmopolitan and diverse than other areas of KPP. Residents of the city are known as Peshawari (who mostly speak Hindko). Politics in the district have been dominated by the Bilours, long affiliated with Khan Abdul Ghaffar Khan and ANP. The PPP traditionally is also strong, and the late Benazir Bhutto won elections in Peshawar in 1988. In the 2008 NA elections, the ANP and PPP split the district's four seats.

20. Shangla District: Almost the entire population of Shangla belongs to the Pashtun tribe Yousafzai (Azikhel and Babozai). Azikhel live mainly in Chakesar, Martung, and Shahpur, while Babozai live in the Puran area. Small non-Pashtun ethnic groups include Syed and Qureshis. MMA and PML-Q are strong in the area. PML-Q leader Ameer Muqam (who had originally won the 2002 elections under the MMA banner) won the 2008 NA election.

21. Swabi District: A majority of the district belongs to the Yousafzai tribe. Other tribes of the area include Jadoon, Razar, and Khattak. The largest Afghan refugee camp was established in this district. It is traditionally an ANP support base, though JUI-F (MMA) has gained influence. ANP did well in 2008 NA elections. Along with Mardan, this district is known for its tobacco products (including fake Marlboro!) throughout the region.

22. Swat District: The people of Swat are mainly Pashtuns belonging to the Yousafzai tribe. However, Kohistanis and Gujjars are also strong in the Kalam Valley area. Despite inroads made by the extremist TNSM, the people of Swat voted for ANP in the 2008 elections. Afzal Khan Lala of ANP is the most prominent politician; he had courageously stayed in the area when Fazlullah was the uncrowned king of the district in 2007–08. Both JUI factions and the JI are also active.

23. Tank District: Pashtuns and Seraiki-speaking people share this district with almost equal strength. Kattikhel (originally from Afghanistan) are strongest, however, as they ruled the area for many decades in the nineteenth and twentieth centuries. Among other tribes, Bhittani, Kundi, and Marwat are strong in the Gomal Valley. The Wazir and the Mehsud routinely quarrel in this area, claiming the district to be theirs. Tank is a JUI-F stronghold, and historically the area is known as a venue for negotiations to resolve local conflicts. Militants have also increased their presence here in recent years.

24. Upper Dir District: The district has a mixture of various Pashtun as well as non-Pashtun tribes: Kohistani, Yousafzai, Katami, Roghani, and Swati. PPP and JI are strong in the area; the PPP candidate won the NA seat in 2008. The area is known for timber smuggling, and the "timber mafia" is politically influential here.

Notes

1. The former and more widely known name of the province is North-West Frontier Province (NWFP).
2. For details about the suicide attacks and targets, see "Suicide Attacks in Khyber Pakhtunkhwa Province," South Asia Terrorism Portal, http://www.satp.org/satporgtp/countries/pakistan/nwfp/datasheet/suicideattack.htm.
3. Discussion with Owais Ghani, governor of KPP, Feb. 1, 2011, New York.
4. Quoted in Sabina Khan, "FATA's Political Status," *Strategic Insights*, Summer 2011, Volume 10, Issue 2, 42.
5. Some analysts sarcastically call the army the country's largest political party.
6. Since the late 1980s, the Nawaz Sharif–led faction of the Pakistan Muslim League (PML-N) has expanded its influence in these areas, and in the 2008 elections it did well in these districts. "PESHAWAR: PML-N Regains Lost Glory in Hazara Region," *Dawn Report*, Feb. 20, 2008, http://www.dawn.com/2008/02/20/local28.htm.
7. Pukhtun is an alternative spelling for Pashtun.
8. "EDITORIAL: 17th Amendment as safety valve?" *Daily Times*, Nov. 5, 2009.
9. For details, see Rashid Javed, "Violence in Abbottabad claims seven lives," *Dawn*, Apr. 13, 2010.
10. "White Paper 2009–10," Government of NWFP, Finance Department, June 17, 2009.
11. The public perception of MMA is evident from the views of a Peshawar shopkeeper expressed in 2007: "I voted for the mullahs last time but I won't vote for them this time…. They have done nothing for the people. They've just filled their own pockets."
12. For instance, according to official NWFP records (2006), out of an estimated total of 4,680 madrassas in NWFP, only 1,077 were registered—as the rest either refused to register or ignored government instructions to register. See Akhtar Amin, "Only 22% of NWFP Madrassas Registered," *Daily Times*, Mar. 24, 2006.
13. Isobel Coleman, "Gender Disparities, Economic Growth and Islamization in Pakistan," in Robert M. Hathaway and Wilson Lee (eds.), *Islamization and the Pakistan Economy*, Woodrow Wilson International Center for Scholars, Washington, DC, 2004. For a detailed context and impact of the changes introduced by MMA, see Anita M. Weiss, "Straddling CEDAW and the MMA," in Kenneth M. Cuno and Manisha Desai (eds.), *Family, Gender, and Law in a Globalizing Middle East and South Asia* (Syracuse University Press, 2009), 163–83.
14. For details, see "Text of Hisba Bill," *Dawn*, July 16, 2005.
15. Quoted in International Crisis Group, "Pakistan's Tribal Areas: Appeasing the Militants," *Asia Report*, 125, Dec. 11, 2006. Also see International Crisis Group, "Pakistan: The Mullah and the Military," *Asia Report*, 49, Mar. 20, 2003.
16. Brian Cloughley, *War, Coups and Terror: Pakistan's Army in Years of Turmoil* (New York: Skyhorse, 2008), 184.
17. International Crisis Group, "Pakistan: The Militant Jihadi Challenge," *Asia Report*, 164, Mar. 13, 2009.
18. For instance, see Hasan Askari Rizvi, "ANALYSIS: Madrassas and Militancy," *Daily Times*, Oct. 29, 2009.

19. "Pakistan: Madrassas, Extremism and the Military," *ICG Asia Report*, 36, July 29, 2002.

20. See S. H. Tajik, "Insight into a Suicide Bomber Training Camp in Waziristan," *CTC Sentinel*, Vol. 3, Issue 3, March 2010.

21. For a detailed and nuanced assessment of the issue, see C. Christine Fair, "The Madrassah Challenge: Militancy and Religious Education in Pakistan," Washington, DC: United States Institute of Peace Press, 2008.

22. Hasan Askari Rizvi, "VIEW: Counter-terrorism: The Missing Links," *Daily Times*, Mar. 4, 2007.

23. For instance, see references in Hassan Abbas, "From FATA to the NWFP: The Taliban Spread Their Grip in Pakistan," *CTC Sentinel*, 1, No. 10 (September 2008): 3–5.

24. Abubakr Siddique, "The Pace of 'Talibanization' Appears to Accelerate in Pakistani Tribal Areas," *Eurasia Insight*, Apr. 26, 2007.

25. Talat Farooq, "Politicians and Rah-e-Rast," *The News*, July 13, 2009.

26. The six Frontier Regions are FR Peshawar, FR Kohat, FR Bannu, FR Tank, FR D.I. Khan, and FR Lakki Marwat. These FRs are administered by the NWFP government through the district coordination officer (DCO) of the respective NWFP district, who exercises the powers of a political agent. (For example, the DCO of Tank administers FR Tank.)

27. "4 Schools Bombed in Peshawar, Bara," *The News*, Apr. 9, 2010.

28. Amir Mohammad Khan, "Khyber Pakhtunkhwa Education Under Attack," *Central Asia Online*, Jan. 15, 2011.

29. "Peshawar on Front Line of Country's War Against Terrorism," *Daily Times*, Dec. 14, 2009.

30. For details about militant rivalries in Khyber agency, see Mukhtar A. Khan, "Local Militants Struggle with Taliban Government for Control of Pakistan's Khyber Agency," *Terrorism Monitor*, Vol. 7, Issue 24, Aug. 6, 2009.

31. "TTP Claims Lahore, Nowshera Attacks," *Daily Times*, June 13, 2009.

32. This link was accepted by NWFP officials on various occasions. For instance, see Ijaz Kakakhel, "Foreign Hand Behind Peshawar Bombings: NWFP Minister," *Daily Times*, Nov. 25, 2009.

33. Khadim Hussain, "Militants Open a New Front," *Dawn*, Nov. 10, 2009.

34. Mushtaq Yusufzai, "No Halt to Fight Against Pakistani Forces: TTP," *The News*, Jan. 3, 2012.

35. For details, see "Pakistan's IDP Crisis: Challenges and Opportunities," International Crisis Group, Asia Briefing 93, June 3, 2009.

36. For instance, the FIF, led by Hafiz Abdur Rauf, a Lashkar-e-Taiba leader and formerly head of Jamaat-ud-Dawa's welfare wing, claimed that its roadside kitchens in the area had fed around fifty thousand people by mid-May 2009. It also claimed to have made available twenty-three minibuses and seven ambulances to transport residents and the injured to camps and hospitals. Ibid.

37. Yasmeen Hassan, "A War on Pakistan's Schoolgirls," *Washington Post*, Jan. 26, 2009.

38. Author interviews with locals and civilian law enforcement officials in NWFP, June 2009.

39. *Dawn* editorial: "Fazlullah in Afghanistan," Oct. 19, 2011.

40. Interview of Naveed Malik, NWFP inspector general, Dawn TV, Dec. 2, 2009.

41. Shahzad Raza, "Return of the 'Midnight Jackal'?" *Dawn*, Apr. 8, 2009.

42. Abdul Hai Kakar, "Same Militants, Different Aims," *Dawn*, Nov. 15, 2009.

43. For data about National Assembly seats, see http://www.na.gov.pk/nwfp.html, and for provincial assembly seats, see http://www.panwfp.gov.pk/index.php/members/bydistrict/en.

44. Briefing on "Security for a New Century: Study Group Report," Henry L. Stimson Center, Mar. 27, 2008.

45. For instance, see Ismail Khan, "MMA in the Dock," *Dawn*, Dec. 21, 2007.

46. For instance, see "Asfandyar Condemns ANP Leader's Killing," *Daily Times*, Feb. 7, 2008; "Taliban Abduct ANP Leader in Hangu," *Daily Times*, Dec. 26, 2008; "ANP Legislator Killed in Bomb Attack," *Daily Times*, Feb. 12, 2009; "Swat Taliban Summon Politicians to Sharia Court," *Daily Times*, Jan. 26, 2009.

47. According to a 2008 STRATFOR analysis: "There appears to be a trend in Pakistan's North-West Frontier Province of attacking members of the ANP, one of the only groups that poses a viable threat to radical Islamists' control in the area." See "Pakistan: A Suicide Bombing and a Potential U.S. Ally," STRATFOR, Oct. 2, 2008.

48. "3-member TTP Squad Formed to Kill ANP Leaders," *Daily Times*, Dec. 20, 2009.

49. Interview with a leading ANP leader, Peshawar, July 2008.

50. Delawar Jan, "NWFP Government, Swat Militant Strike Ceasefire," *The News*, May 10, 2008; "U.S. Silent on Visit of Asfandyar," *Dawn*, May 10, 2008.

51. "Hardtalk," *Daily Times*, Feb. 2, 2009.

52. Ibid.

53. "Hardtalk," *Daily Times*, Mar. 19, 2009.

54. To watch the interview on Geo TV, visit http://www.pakhtun.com/index.php/about-pashtuns/current-issues/sufi-muhammad-interview.

55. Kamran Bokhari and Fred Burton, "The Counterinsurgency in Pakistan," STRATFOR, Aug. 13, 2009; Human Rights Watch, "Pakistan: Military Undermines Government on Human Rights," Jan. 20, 2010, http://www.hrw.org/en/news/2010/01/20/pakistan-military-undermines-government-human-rights.

56. The PML-N (despite recently losing support in the province as per media polls) is expected to draw more support because it has not criticized religious and conservative elements in the KPP. The PPP may lose some seats because of anti-incumbency sentiment in KPP and Islamabad. The MMA's religious parties are unlikely to benefit from the ANP's decline because militants in the KPP (including TTP) have cut into the support base of these parties. In early 2010 the JUI-F surprisingly won a seat in Mansehra (a stronghold of PML-N), but analysts blamed it on PML-N's failure to field a strong candidate. JUI-F also won a seat in Lakki Marwat (where Taliban activity has been significant in recent months) with a big margin in February 2010, but in its stronghold Dera Ismail Khan it lost by-polls (late March 2010) to PPP. Rahimullah Yusufzai, "JUI-F Scores Remarkable Win in Mansehra By-election," *The News*, Jan. 30, 2010; and for details, see Ghulam M. Marwat, "JUI-F Wins Lakki By-poll,"

Nation, Feb. 11, 2010; "PML-N, PPP Win Gujrat, DI Khan By-polls," *The News*, Mar. 25, 2010.

57. Julie Ray and Rajesh Srinivasan, "Taliban Increasingly Unpopular in Pakistan," Gallup, Mar. 12, 2010.

58. Mubarak Zeb Khan, "Banks in NWFP Reluctant to Lend to Industry," *Dawn*, Jan. 30, 2009.

59. For details about reforms, see Syed Irfan Raza, "Far-reaching Fata Reforms Unveiled," *Dawn*, Aug. 14, 2009.

60. Nasir Jamal, "On Trail of Punjabi Taliban," *Dawn*, Oct. 17, 2009.

61. "The U.S. Provides $103.5 Million In Law Enforcement and Border Security Assistance," News Release, USAID, Oct. 29, 2009.

62. For details about Farooq Khan, see http://www.drfarooqkhan.com/; also see Ayesha Umar, "Dr Farooq: The Loss of an Intellectual," *Express Tribune* blog, Oct. 6, 2010.

63. Farangis Najibullah, Farkhanda Wazir, "Politics as Unusual for a Pakistani Woman Amid the Taliban," Radio Liberty, Oct. 3, 2011, http://www.rferl.org/content/pakistan_politicas_as_unusual_for_a_woman_amid_the_taliban/24347792.html

64. The official website of the PML-N is at http://www.pmln.org.pk/. The site provides no information about the party's genesis and history.

65. The official website of the PML-Q is at http://www.pml.org.pk/. This site provides details about the various splits that the party went through since the late 1980s under the category of PML History (accessible through link to "Manifesto" on main page), at http://www.pml.org.pk/details.aspx?id=10f35391-e34b-4527-a55b-2643035c9d53&cha=1&cat=9&subcat=9.

66. Ahmed Rashid, *Taliban: Islam, Oil and the New Great Game in Central Asia* (London: I. B. Tauris, 2000), 90.

67. Saba Imtiaz, "When Thousands Show Up to a Rally, It's Change Fazlur Rehman Wants You to Believe In," *Express Tribune*, Jan. 28, 2012.

68. ANP's official website is at http://www.awaminationalparty.org/.

69. For ANP background and the views of Asfandyar Wali, see Hassan Abbas, "Asfandyar Wali: Profile of a Progressive Pashtun Politician," *Terrorism Monitor*, Vol. 5 Issue 2, Feb. 21, 2007.

70. For more details, see PPP's official website, http://www.ppp.org.pk/.

71. District profiles were prepared by a group of students at Peshawar University under Sami Zaidi's guidance, 2009. Local websites used for information include www.malakand.8m.com/index.html; www.mardan.com; www.palasvalley.org; www.buner.gov.pk; www.chitraltoday.com; www.khyber.org/places/2007/TheWalledCity.shtml; and www.valleyswat.net. Profiles of various NWFP districts published by *Dawn* newspaper before the February 2008 elections are also a useful resource.

72. See "Movement for Hazara Province," *The News*, Apr. 12, 2010.

ELEVEN

The Taliban in Swat

Daud Khan Khattak

EXECUTIVE SUMMARY

Swat is one of the seven districts of the Malakand Division in Pakistan's Khyber-Pakhtunkhwa province.[1] This once-popular Hindu Kush tourist destination is located around 170 kilometers northeast of Peshawar, the provincial capital of Khyber-Pakhtunkhwa and the gateway to Afghanistan. Although Swat is known as the Switzerland of Asia because of its scenic beauty, the name became more familiar to many across the world following the emergence of the Taliban in the mid-2000s and the subsequent Pakistani military operations in the valley. Talibanization in Swat brought destruction to the otherwise peaceful area, and hundreds of people—anti-Taliban and bystanders—were gunned down, beheaded, kidnapped, or expelled from their homes.

These violent excesses and the reactions throughout Pakistan to them finally forced the Pakistani government to take serious action, which culminated in the launch of Operation Rah-e-Rast, or "Right Path," in April 2009. The offensive mostly quelled the militant movement in Swat, while killing nearly six hundred Taliban foot soldiers and some of their leaders. However, some 2.5 million people were displaced from the Malakand area following the launch

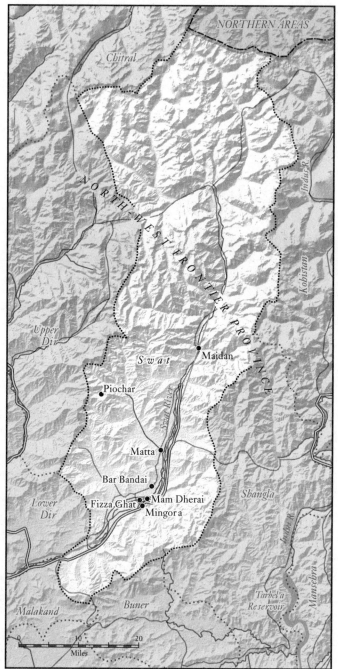

MAP BY GENE THORP OF CARTOGRAPHIC CONCEPTS, INC.

of the operation, scores of civilians were killed, and much property was destroyed by Pakistani military airpower and artillery shelling. Citizens of Swat were finally able to return in mid-July that year after the Taliban was routed, although occasional incidents continue today.

Although peace has been restored in Swat, the locals are not happy with the slow pace of reconstruction process in rebuilding roads, bridges, schools, hospitals, and other public and private property damaged by the Taliban. They are also complaining, though privately, about the presence of the military and reports about establishment of a permanent army cantonment in the valley.

GRIEVANCES OF THE POPULATION

Pakistan's slow, corrupt, and inefficient justice system in the Swat Valley played a large role in the rise of the Swat Taliban. Despite living for nearly forty years under the Pakistani government, many Swatis could recall the era of the last wali, whose rule was known for "easy and speedy" justice for all. Under the wali, the maximum period for resolving a serious case was one to two weeks, according to Miangul Aurangzeb, a member of the former royal family and ex-governor of Balochistan and (then) NWFP.[2] But the Pakistani judicial system could take years, if not decades, which allowed Sufi Muhammad and later Fazlullah to step in with promises of quick justice.[3]

"Prolonged legal procedures…, undue delay, heightened expenditure, bribery…and further deterioration…had already aggrieved most people of Swat…[and] resulted in an increased momentum for the TNSM movement in Swat," Sultan-i-Rome wrote in a critical analysis of Swat for an independent think tank based in New Delhi.[4] Instead of addressing the genuine demands of the people, ensuring easy and speedy justice, and providing them with civic facilities and job opportunities, the government further aggravated the situation by succumbing to the TNSM demands. "The government should have eliminated the TNSM by giving the facilities," added Shaukat Sharar, the Swat-based head of an NGO, while discussing the successive deals with the Taliban in Swat and the negative results.[5]

Not only was the judicial system corrupt and slow, but many Swatis were dismayed by the corruption of some civic officials. This dissatisfaction caused the people to seek other means of governance, including the Taliban. Additionally, social and educational facilities were not constructed in Swat after the rule of the wali as they had been under him; there were five upper secondary institutions for a population of two hundred thousand in Swat in 1969. Not a single public school has been constructed since then, while the population now exceeds two million.[6] Widespread unemployment and loss of land also caused frustration among Swatis, and the majority of Fazlullah's armed supporters were drawn from jobless, uneducated youths and landless tenants. They were either serving khans or struggling to find work.

Government neglect by the Pakistani intelligence agencies and the Muttahida Majlis-e-Amal, a coalition of Islamic parties then governing NWFP, further aided the rise of the Swat Taliban. The militants' growing influence and activities were mostly ignored before 2006, despite protests from Swatis.[7]

The government did acknowledge from time to time that the people of Swat had valid complaints, particularly regarding the justice system, employment, administrative discrepancies, and lack of proper civic amenities. Mian Iftikhar Hussain, information minister of the NWFP government, said in July 2009, during the Pakistani military operations in Swat, "The grievances of the people were just, but one should not take up arms to resolve that."[8]

THE STRUCTURE OF THE INSURGENCY IN SWAT

The roots of militancy in Malakand can be traced to the days when Swat was an independent state under a wali, or prince, and then its merger into Pakistan in 1969.[9] In 1949, Miangul Abdul Wadood handed over the reins of the state of Swat to his son Miangul Jahanzeb, who was known as the *Wali-e-Swat*; his rule is often viewed as the golden period in the history of the valley. Schools, hospitals, roads, and communication systems were constructed in that era, and there was generally peace and order in the valley.

Serious issues of justice were decided by the wali with the help of his ministers and a tribal assembly, or jirga, within days. However, after the merger of the state of Swat with Pakistan in 1969, there was little further development in the valley. Few schools, if any, were constructed, and the justice system, in which civil and criminal cases alike were delayed for years, caused frustration among the people. Although the Swat Valley is relatively close to the Afghan border, it was not much affected by the Afghan-Soviet war of the 1980s. When the Taliban came to power in Afghanistan, however, many Swatis were generally supportive, having viewed the Islamic militants as freedom fighters against the Soviets. This was an image reinforced during the fighting by Pakistani media, which highlighted the struggle, or jihad. Jihadist leaders would roam freely in Swat's cities and markets in pickup trucks carrying gunmen. This residual support for the Taliban in Afghanistan among the people of Swat Valley partially contributed to the rise of Sufi Muhammad.

Sufi Muhammad

Signs of trouble first appeared in the Swat Valley following the rise to power of the radical cleric Sufi Muhammad, a local leader of the Islamist party Jamaat-e-Islami[10] (JI) in the Maidan area of Lower Dir district, and his initial formation in 1989 of the Tehrik Nifaz-e-Shariat-e-Muhammadi (TNSM, or Movement for Implementation of Sharia of Muhammad).[11] Sufi Muhammad hails from the Kumbar area of Lower Dir, where he received his religious education at local seminaries. In 1985, he was elected as a local village councilor as a member of JI, in which he had become active earlier in the decade. After some time, however, he apparently became disillusioned with JI and returned to Maidan, center of Lower Dir, to lead prayers at a local mosque and teach at an Islamic school, or madrassa, while beginning to agitate for implementation of Islamic law, or sharia. Temperamentally, Sufi Muhammad is quiet and not particularly charismatic, but he is a smooth talker who, unlike other mullahs, does not deliver angry sermons.

During the early 1990s, Sufi Muhammad began a relatively peaceful campaign on a limited scale in favor of implementing sharia across the valley, but gradually the movement became more militant. His supporters, exasperated by the slow system of justice and corrupt public officials in Malakand, adopted the slogan *"shariat ya shahadat"* (sharia or martyrdom). In 1994, Sufi Muhammad and his followers, called *Tor Patkais* for their black turbans, started blockading roads after the Pakistani government was unresponsive to their campaign. The same tactic—blocking roads in an attempt to force the government to implement sharia in Malakand—was also used by JI's Qazi Hussain Ahmad, with whom Sufi Muhammad parted ways in the late 1980s to form the TNSM. The blockades led to fighting with Pakistani security forces. Eleven people were killed in Buner district on May 16, 1994, an early example of violence in Malakand by supporters of sharia.[12] There were other bloody clashes between Sufi Muhammad's followers and Pakistan's Frontier Corps, which had been deployed to combat the movement, and many from both sides were killed. The uprising ended in November 1994 following an agreement between the government and Sufi Muhammad that negotiated the Nizam-i-Adl Regulation, meaning "the implementation of a justice-based system," which authorized sharia in Malakand.[13] The agreement was viewed as a concession by the government and a victory for Sufi Muhammad's supporters, although his armed uprising was suppressed.

Sufi Muhammad's popularity in Swat and neighboring Dir sank to a low point during the late 1990s, because many locals had been killed during the uprising and Sufi Muhammad himself fled the area and then joined the government in talks. His supporters questioned why he led his fighters into a conflict and then went into hiding. But Sufi Muhammad worked hard to restore his image, aided by the popularity of the Taliban government in Afghanistan among Pashtuns living in Swat; Pakistan's sole official television station, PTV, regularly aired stories of Taliban victories across the border.

The September 11, 2001, terrorist attacks on the United States catapulted Sufi Muhammad into a renewed position of power, and he led a tribal militia, or lashkar, of some ten thousand volunteers from the Swat, Dir, Buner, and Shangla districts, and the Bajaur and Mohmand tribal agencies, to fight U.S. forces in Afghanistan.[14] The citizens of Dir and Swat, however, were not happy with Sufi Muhammad for leading their kinsmen into the Afghan morass and held him responsible for the deaths of their relatives. Pakistani security officials seemingly did the old man a favor by imprisoning him in Dera Ismail Khan for nearly seven years (for leading forces against American soldiers and crossing the border without proper documentation), a time span in which the anger of the people could recede.[15] The TNSM, meanwhile, was banned by the government.

Maulana Fazlullah

Sufi Muhammad's arrest in late 2001 left a vacuum in Swat's militant movement. Sufi Muhammad's son-in-law Fazle Hayat, who had fought with him in Afghanistan and spent about seventeen months in jail in Pakistan upon his return,[16] stepped into the void and started preaching at a small mosque in the Swati town of Mam Dheri, which he later renamed "Imam Dheri" to add a more Islamic touch.[17] Born in 1975 to a simple farming family in Mam Dheri near Fizza Ghat,[18] Fazle Hayat changed his name in the 1990s to Fazlullah in order to bolster his credentials as an Islamic leader, even though he had failed to receive full credentials from any religious institution.[19] Fazlullah, once an employee at a resort in Fizza Ghat, used to say he was not a religious scholar, but this did not stop him from advocating for imposition of sharia in Swat.[20]

Though Fazlullah initially taught the Quran to children at his Mam Dheri mosque, his preaching changed in tone from sermons to threats after he launched his unauthorized FM radio channel in 2004.[21] People started supporting him with men and material as he earned the nickname "Maulana Radio." Though Fazlullah at first addressed the people of Swat very generally, he soon gained supporters among the conservative Pashtuns of the area as well as erstwhile supporters of the jailed Sufi Muhammad, in addition to Pakistanis working abroad in Dubai and Saudi Arabia, whose families back in the country relayed Fazlullah's messages. Such was his influence that women of the valley even donated their earrings and bangle bracelets. While encouraging his listeners to pray five times a day and avoid sinning, Fazlullah also preached anti-Americanism, focusing on U.S. forces fighting the Taliban in Afghanistan. As his audience grew, he started discouraging parents from sending their girls to schools and spoke out against watching television or listening to music. He also criticized landlords who refused to make donations to his madrassa, according to local sources. Pakistan analyst Imtiaz Ali assessed, "A generation has grown up under the shadow of TNSM and its strict version of Islam, providing Fazlullah with a ready pool of fighters."[22] In 2007, after Fazlullah criticized the "evils of television," some local Swatis responded by setting fire to thousands of TV sets.[23]

Fazlullah's fiery speeches carried an appeal for virtually everyone, from household women and laborers to landowners. They came forward in large numbers to donate goods such as wheat flour, cooking oil, and sugar, as well as cement and bricks for construction work.[24] Fazlullah also promised social justice for the people of Swat, along with paradise in the life after death. Swatis, who were fed up with the inefficient Pakistani judicial system and recalled the days of their wali, saw a ray of hope for revival in Fazlullah's speeches. Fazlullah, and Sufi Muhammad before him, exploited this mentality among the Swatis—who according to analyst Mukhtar Khan were "more used to personal rule than democracy or any other form of governance"—by developing a "cult of personality around themselves."[25] For example, Fazlullah collected about 35 million rupees (around $600,000) from supporters to build a two-story madrassa complex; it was later destroyed by Pakistani security forces in the spring of 2009.[26]

A warning sign was Fazlullah's campaign to oppose polio vaccinations across Pakistan, which he called "a conspiracy of the Jews and Christians to stunt the population growth of Muslims."[27] In September 2007, Fazlullah's supporters also tried to destroy the centuries-old statues of Buddha and prehistoric rock carvings in the Swat Valley on the grounds that they were un-Islamic.[28] (The Afghan Taliban, despite international protests, had blown up two giant Buddha statues in Bamiyan in 2001.) According to Fazlullah himself, he burned TV sets, video equipment, computers, and digital cameras worth 20 million rupees because "these are the main sources of sin." He also said, in essence, "Now we have no other option but to re-organize our movement and work for a society purged of all types of evils including music, dancing and drinking alcohol."[29]

Like Sufi Muhammad before him, Fazlullah called for social parity, quick justice, provision of civic facilities, more jobs for Swatis, and redistribution of property.[30] The promise of land distribution attracted many followers for Fazlullah's movement in Swat, which started capturing the orchards, farms, and other land of the khans, or local leaders and landowners, who had abandoned the areas from late 2007 to late 2008 after Fazlullah's men carried out several targeted killings against them.

Most of the Swatis who supported Fazlullah did so only morally, but some took up arms after being inspired by his FM radio sermons; many of these recruits were disenchanted, poor, illiterate, and unemployed youth.[31] The Swat Taliban leader also appealed to the religious sentiments of the people by saying that alien forces were present in Afghanistan and that this was war between *kufr* (infidels) and Islam. Fazlullah also used his brother's death in a drone strike in Damadola, Bajaur, in early January 2006, to gain supporters, and he likewise exploited the inflamed passions following the deadly storming of Islamabad's Red Mosque by security forces in the summer of 2007.[32] In spite of Swatis' initial support for Fazlullah, however, his movement began to lose popularity: Fazlullah's armed brigades patrolled marketplaces across the valley, intimidating locals into keeping their daughters home from school and beheading local opponents. But the general population was unable to resist publicly, because by late 2007 Fazlullah had gained too much power.

Many Taliban recruits were criminals who pursued their livelihood by joining the movement. Others joined to settle personal scores with opponents of the Swat Taliban. The Taliban welcomed the criminals to increase its power against the Pakistani security forces as well as against some local khans, who had their own armed groups in Swat. The arrangement was mutually reinforcing. The Taliban needed support from the strong criminal gangs to terrorize people and raise money, while the criminals needed a cover to save their skins and continue their activities.[33]

Fazlullah's fighters in Swat totaled fewer than five thousand at their peak. His second-in-command was Shah Dauran, another cleric and erstwhile criminal who sold food items to children in the markets of Mingora, the main town in Swat, before joining Fazlullah and helping run his FM broadcasts.[34] Shah Dauran reportedly died of kidney failure in Bajaur in late 2009, and since the Taliban's organizational structure in the Swat Valley was more or less shattered, no one has stepped forward to replace him.[35] Another key man in the Swat Taliban was Muslim Khan, the movement's spokesman, who is now in the custody of Pakistani security forces. Fazlullah went underground following the Pakistani military operations in Swat in 2009 and was believed to be hiding with Maulvi Faqir Muhammad, the deputy leader of the Tehrik-i-Taliban Pakistan (TTP) in Bajaur.[36] Muhammad developed differences with the TTP high command following the killing of its chief, Baitullah Mehsud, in a drone strike in 2009 and was removed from the position of deputy TTP chief in March 2012.

Mullah Fazlullah, according to Pakistani officials, crossed the border into Afghanistan's Nuristan province from where his men launch attacks from time to time against the Pakistani security forces. The Afghan side, however, rejected the Pakistani allegations that they (Afghan government) are complacent about Fazlullah. According to locals (who talked to me), some of Fazlullah's commanders have taken refuge in the remote Tirah area of the Khyber tribal district.

Organizational Structure

Initially, the Taliban in Swat was not as organized as compatriots in Waziristan, because its mission was based first on achieving Islamic law in the region, not attacking Western targets. After coming to power in the mid-2000s, the group's leaders formed a council, or shura, with varied membership from time to time. The Swat Taliban's first spokesman was known as Sirajuddin, a resident of Swat who was involved with Jaish-e-Muhammad, a Kashmiri militant group. He was replaced for unknown reasons in late 2007 by Muslim Khan, who is currently in custody. Muslim Khan, a fifty-seven-year-old resident of Swat, reputedly speaks Pashto, Urdu, Arabic, English, and Japanese and was involved with the People's Students Federation, the student wing of the Pakistan People's Party, during his college life in the 1970s.[37] He was an active member of Sufi Muhammad's TNSM in the early 1990s and then went abroad, working for a British company as a sailor for several years before moving to Kuwait to look for a job, and later living in the United States and Japan. In the United States in 1999, he worked for a paint-producing company, later telling the BBC's Urdu service that "the U.S. government is rogue, but its people are civilized," and commenting that he liked the people of Japan the most because they were hard working.[38] After his return home to Pakistan after the September 11 attacks, he opened a pharmacy and supported Fazlullah when he came to power. Local sources say Muslim Khan provided some of the funding for Fazlullah to purchase his FM broadcast station.

Fazlullah headed the shura, which has between thirty and fifty members at any given time, and served as the movement's military commander. Shura members were responsible for particular areas and control

individual units of fighters, some of whom are designated as foot soldiers, suicide bombers, trainers, and other special commandos. In 2007,
Fazlullah announced his Shaheen Commando Force, with between four
thousand and five thousand fighters.[39] He also organized a force of moral
police to stop women from going into markets without veils, shut down
music shops, searched for musical instruments in transport, and closed
cinema houses and markets dealing in women's garments.[40]

The box shows the organizational structure of the Swat Taliban.

Chief: Mullah Fazlullah
Deputy chief: Shah Dauran (died in Bajaur of kidney disease; however, some local sources suggest he was killed in the operation)
Spokesman: Muslim Khan (in custody)
Shura members: Sirajuddin (also former spokesman for Fazlullah,
who disappeared after the military operation and reappeared only
last year; he called one of my colleagues in Prague to say he is alive
and they are reorganizing their group)

    Muslim Khan

    Mahmood Khan (in custody)

    Qari Mushtaq (resident of Swat; no word about him since
the operation in 2009)

    Nisar Khan (resident of Kooza Bandai area of Swat; no word
about him since the operation in 2009)

    Ibn-e-Amin (resident of Swat and said to be a leader of
Lashkar-e-Jhangvi; he was killed in a drone strike in Tirah area of
Khyber tribal district)

    Maulana Muhammad Alam Binori (FM channel manager,
killed March 1, 2010)

Quetta Shura and the Swat Taliban

The Quetta Shura, led by Mullah Omar, have no known links with
the Taliban currently led by Maulana Fazlullah in Swat. The Quetta
Shura interacts with the Taliban in Waziristan and the rest of the
tribal areas via the Haqqani Network, led by the aging insurgent

commander Jalaluddin Haqqani and his son Sirajuddin, who serves as the movement's operational commander.[41] While Sufi Muhammad's and Fazlullah's admiration for Mullah Omar and the Quetta Shura was clear in their FM broadcasts and speeches in the early 2000s, there are no operational or tactical links between the two groups. Sufi Muhammad's admiration for Mullah Omar was further demonstrated by the development of his ten-thousand-strong lashkar, which he led over the Afghan border to fight against the U.S. and NATO invasion in 2001, but there is no proof Sufi Muhammad has ever been in direct contact with Mullah Omar.

The "code of conduct" released by the Taliban in Afghanistan in the summer of 2009, similarly, has had no impact on fighters in Swat.[42] It was aimed specifically at the Taliban fighting in Afghanistan and to some extent those in Waziristan staging cross-border raids, but not the TNSM-inspired militants in the Swat Valley. A Quetta Shura Taliban spokesman jokingly said in an interview, "What kind of people are they?" referring to the destruction of schools and occasional beheadings of enemies by the Swat Taliban.[43]

Links Between al-Qaeda, the TTP, and the Swat Taliban

During the 2000s, as the Swat Taliban under Fazlullah ascended to power and spread over the valley, there was no al-Qaeda presence in Malakand. Though Pakistani troops claimed to have found caves full of arms and ammunition during the spring 2009 military operations, there was no trace of al-Qaeda involvement.

Sufi Muhammad's TNSM, formed around two decades ago, also has had no known operational links with the Tehrik-i-Taliban Pakistan as a whole, which was founded in December 2007 by Baitullah Mehsud to unite the various factions of Pakistani Taliban fighters under one umbrella.

However, the Swat Taliban under Fazlullah has been closely linked to the TTP, as Fazlullah and his Swat Taliban fighters declared their allegiance to Baitullah and to Mullah Omar, the chief of the Afghan Taliban, in the summer of 2007 following the Pakistani government's actions at the Red Mosque in Islamabad. In June 2009, the Pakistani army's media wing released an intercepted conversation in which Muslim Khan told a close aide of Baitullah Mehsud about the recently begun Pakistani military operations in Swat and asked for support. Baitullah's aide promised that the TTP would launch more attacks in cities across Pakistan and against government and military targets to divert attention from the operations in Swat. Suicide bombings in Pakistan escalated following this conversation.[44] But Fazlullah has no known role in decision making in the upper echelons of the TTP, which is run by leaders in Waziristan.

Some Uzbek and Arab fighters—their numbers in the dozens, but not in the hundreds—arrived in Swat from Waziristan in the summer of 2008 to support the Taliban against the impending Pakistani military operations in the Swat Valley, and their arrival coincided with an increase in targeted killings and beheadings in Swat. However, these foreign fighters fled Swat when more Pakistani military operations began in May 2009; they had few connections to the local Swati militants, who were closer operationally to their neighbors in Bajaur and Mohmand.

Financing

A variety of sources have funded the Swat Taliban. During the early days of his Quran-based FM broadcasts across the valley, Fazlullah usually depended on charitable donations from the people of Swat. However, after he gained more power and increased his radio audience, he started extorting money from the rich, taxing businessmen, and renting out shops and markets abandoned by the local khans. Additionally, the Taliban allowed contractors and commission agents from Swat and nearby areas to cut down precious trees and sell the wood in markets.[45] After capturing Mingora in 2008, the militants also seized control of its three emerald quarries, two of which were operational at that time, and leased them to contractors.[46] "I left the machinery and all the survey works causing losses worth millions. They captured the mine and then employed people to excavate the precious stones," said Hekmatullah Shinwari, a geologist who had leased one of the emerald mines in 2007.

Kidnapping for ransom has been another source of income for the Swat Taliban, as notorious gangs joined the movement.[47] Money from the Waziristan Taliban was also coming to the Swat Taliban in late 2008.[48]

RECENT PAKISTANI MILITARY OPERATIONS
IN SWAT

Pakistani military operations in Swat have been marked by uneven outcomes. Although the first several operations in the second half of the 2000s failed and the Pakistani government was eventually forced to make concessions to the Swat Taliban, the most recent major operations, in the spring of 2009, held off a resurgence of the militant movement.

Operation Rah-e-Haq (Just Path)

Despite the Swat Taliban's increasing militancy in the valley—including the razing of CD shops, forcing women to stay at home, and attempting to destroy the Buddha statues—the ruling coalition of religious parties in the (then) NWFP government, as well as the Pakistani central government, turned a blind eye to Swat in late 2006 and early 2007.[49] But the July 7, 2007, Pakistani military operations against a radical cleric and his students in Islamabad's Red Mosque brought Fazlullah new prominence and gave him a platform from which to fight against Pakistani security forces in Swat. During the next several months, Fazlullah's supporters carried out a series of suicide attacks on Pakistani security targets in the valley, and the Swat Taliban began warning women in Mingora to stop going out to markets.[50]

On October 24, 2007, the NWFP government announced the first operation in Swat to dislodge Fazlullah and his men from the fifty-nine villages of Matta, a subdistrict of Swat, where they had set up a parallel government and taken control of police stations, even installing signs reading "Taliban Police Station."[51] By October 31, security personnel claimed to have killed 130 militants in limited operations, but the Taliban overran a military post the next day and captured nearly fifty soldiers, who were disarmed and later freed. With Taliban fighters targeting them ruthlessly, Pakistani police started deserting their posts in early November, and almost all the police stations in Matta and the town of Khwazakhela were soon empty.[52]

The Pakistani army launched the first phase of the Operation Rah-e-Haq, or Just Path, in early November 2007.[53] Fighting between Pakistani forces and the Taliban continued throughout November, with the army employing heavy artillery shelling.[54] The militants vacated almost all of the government buildings, police stations, and other public places they had occupied—including those in Mam Dheri, the headquarters of Fazlullah—and by the end of December had retreated into the mountains.

Despite their retreat, the militants continued hit-and-run activities from the mountainous areas outside the Swat Valley until the spring of 2008, when a newly elected provincial government, led by the secular Awami National Party (ANP), took office. By then the violence had taken a heavy toll. An NWFP government report in February 2008 found that three hundred people, including eighty Pakistani security personnel, had been killed in the conflict with the militants since February 2007, and that nearly six hundred thousand people were affected directly or indirectly by the Talibanization and the military operations.[55]

After taking office, the ANP, a secular Pashtun nationalist party, started a dialogue with the militants and released Sufi Muhammad from prison in April as a goodwill gesture.[56] The two sides signed a sixteen-point agreement on May 21, 2008.[57] The gist of the pact was that in exchange for implementation of Islamic law in Swat, the Taliban would cease attacks on police, the army, and the Frontier Corps and would not destroy any more property.[58] The agreement also suggested that if the Taliban respected the agreement, the Pakistani government would release some Taliban prisoners. Representing Fazlullah in the several rounds of peace talks were Muslim Khan, Ali Bakht (a commander who was later killed), and Mahmood Khan, who was arrested in September 2009 along with Muslim Khan.[59] Several local ministers from the NWFP government represented the Pakistani government. Although both sides claimed victory—the Taliban for winning implementation of sharia, and the government for gaining peace—both proved to be losers, as neither peace nor sharia came to Swat.

On June 27, 2008, after disagreements over the sequencing of the truce terms—Fazlullah insisted that the Pakistani government withdraw troops from Swat before his fighters would lay down their arms, while the government wanted the Swat Taliban to disarm first—Fazlullah renounced the May 21 pact and ordered his armed volunteers to attack Pakistani security forces on suspicion that Pakistani intelligence services were spying on his fighters.[60] Taliban fighters killed two junior officers of the Inter-Services Intelligence agency in upper Swat, prompting the army to start new operations on June 29.[61]

Fierce clashes were reported in Kabal, Matta, Khwazakhela, Bara Bandai, Kooza Bandai, and other main towns in Swat. A few prominent Taliban leaders, among them Tor Mulla and Ali Bakht, were killed during the second phase, but in late June the militants blew up Pakistan's only ski resort, the beautiful PTDC Motel in the town of Malam Jabba, and accelerated their targeted killings and attacks on security forces.[62]

The second half of 2008 through the first few months of 2009 was the worst time in recent Swati history. Scores of schools were burned or bombed by the militants or destroyed in retaliatory military operations; music was banned; barbers were again forbidden to shave men's beards. Some two million Swatis fled the valley for Peshawar, Islamabad, and other cities, as eight thousand or more (later estimates were as high as twenty thousand) Pakistani troops battled between five thousand and six thousand Taliban fighters.[63] The Pakistani police were able to operate only in the town of Mingora, while the rest of Swat was controlled by the Taliban, which ran its own courts and frequently punished locals for alleged wrongdoing.

Per the demand of the cleric Sufi Muhammad, the NWFP government agreed to enforce the Nizam-i-Adl Regulation, a new act implementing sharia in Malakand, and another peace agreement was reached on February 15, 2009.[64] This move was difficult for the secular ANP, but the party apparently succumbed to pressure from militants and promised to implement Islamic law despite pressure from other secular groups, such as the Pakhtunkhwa Milli Awami Party and NATO, which sought to avoid renewed strengthening of the Taliban and an increase in attacks on their forces in Afghanistan.

Sufi Muhammad led a large rally on February 18 in the Grassy Ground meeting place of Mingora, where he promised lasting peace in the valley following the controversial agreement. Thousands joined the rally to express their support for peace efforts, and on the same day Fazlullah asked his followers to halt attacks on security forces.[65] Soon, however, Fazlullah and his commanders began complaining that their men were being unfairly stopped and searched by Pakistani soldiers. They also failed to honor the treaty terms compelling them to lay down their arms and abandon their check posts across the valley.[66] When Pakistani security forces tried to enforce the treaty, the militants continued killing government officials, while spreading the violence from Swat to other parts of Malakand. They killed a district police officer in Lower Dir in one attack and five policemen in Upper Dir in another.[67] Within two months of the peace deal, the Taliban also spread to Buner district, just seventy miles from Islamabad, with armed patrols in several areas, capturing the town of Daggar and some villages, in what is widely believed to have been the TNSM's moment of overreach.[68]

Operation Rah-e-Rast (Right Path)

After failing to persuade the Taliban to vacate Buner, Dir, and Swat, where the militants had consolidated control in the first several months of 2009,[69] the Pakistani army began another full-fledged series of military operations in late April. Local residents were asked beforehand to vacate their areas, and between May and mid-July nearly 2.5 million people arrived in Peshawar, Mardan, Swabi, Charsadda, Nowshera, and other Pakistani cities to live in camps, with relatives, or in rented houses.[70] Bands of Taliban fighters had taken over the key towns of Mingora in Swat and Daggar in Buner in the spring. This was not unexpected, despite the military and police actions in 2007 and 2008. Not only did those operations fail to remove the Taliban from control in Malakand, but the militant movement expanded its reach, at one point coming within seventy miles of the capital, Islamabad, causing alarm in Pakistan and across the world.[71]

During the months of fighting in 2009, many Taliban commanders were killed, and the Swat Taliban's spokesman, Muslim Khan, was arrested by security forces in September.[72] According to army figures, nearly thirteen hundred militants were killed in the 2009 operations in Swat, Dir, Buner, and Shangla districts, and hundreds more were arrested.[73] In July, army troops reached the Taliban stronghold of Piochar, where they said they discovered caves and huge caches of arms.

Pakistani troops claimed they were in full control of Swat as of July 2009[74]; the militants have been killed, fled the area, or gone into hiding. Since then, people in the valley have found bullet-riddled bodies of Taliban fighters in fields outside Mingora, Khwazakhela,

Kanjoo, Matta, Kalam, and Manglawar; presumably, the men were killed by government-supported lashkars, or tribal militias, as a message to would-be Taliban recruits. However, an atmosphere of fear has persisted in Swat. In November 2009, a suicide attack killed a local ANP leader and member of the NWFP assembly, Shamsher Ali Khan, at his house in Mingora.[75] (His brother, Rehmat Ali, took over the assembly seat after winning a special election lauded as peaceful and orderly.[76])

The Aftermath of Operations in Swat

Several factors distinguish the 2009 campaign from earlier Pakistani military efforts to rout the Taliban from the Swat Valley. First and most important, public opinion in Pakistan had turned almost totally against the Taliban, especially after the peaceful people of Swat were exposed to the militants' ruthless rule and saw beheadings, bombings, and other violence in the valley. Therefore, the population supported the full-scale military operations in 2009; one poll found that 86 percent of those surveyed in the NWFP (Khyber-Pakhtunkhwa) in May 2009 were sympathetic toward the government, while only 6 percent supported the "Pakistani Taliban."[77]

Second, previous military and police operations in Swat were half-hearted. Operations were launched, then stopped; the army went after the Taliban in some areas of Swat, but not others; troops would begin operations, and Taliban fighters would melt away into the mountains. The 2009 campaign, on the other hand, encompassed the entire valley after Swatis were given the opportunity to flee the fighting, showing the seriousness of the Pakistani military.

Third, the Awami National Party–led government of the NWFP (Khyber-Pakhtunkhwa), which had come to power in early 2008 promising peace, tried twice to resolve problems with the Swat Taliban and failed both times. This emboldened the militants, who staged more daring attacks on police targets, Frontier Corps personnel, and civilians. Thus the ANP government wanted the army to start a serious operation. In fact, the ANP, with the support of the central government, gave the military an ultimatum: undertake a major campaign, or the party would walk out of the provincial government and make a point of explaining why.[78]

Although the 2009 operation appears to have succeeded, problems remain. Dreaded commanders remain at large, as does Swat Taliban chief Fazlullah, who in November 2009 reportedly said from Afghanistan that he would relaunch a guerrilla war in Swat.[79]

However, the spring 2009 military offensive helped restore the confidence of Swatis. It brought calm back to the valley, ending the frequent bombing of girls' schools, hospitals, and police stations; beheadings of opponents and law enforcement personnel; and kidnappings and suicide bombings.[80] Many people in Swat are now relatively confident that security forces will not allow another Taliban resurgence; in any case, they feel prepared to meet this challenge if necessary. There are few people still clamoring for implementation of sharia, as Sufi Muhammad is back in jail, and several of Fazlullah's commanders have either been killed or disappeared.[81]

As the people of Swat gradually have returned home, the Pakistani government has done little to provide services. Schools are still dilapidated, forcing boys and girls to study in the open air. Although the government has tried to revive the police in Swat by inducting hundreds of recruits, Swatis want their local civil administration to take charge of all work from army officials and let them have their say in the area's political affairs. With the local economy shattered by years of fighting, residents are in dire need of jobs; they do want federal government support to help revive their businesses, particularly the once-thriving tourism industry.

While the people were yet to resettle in their areas and rebuild their damaged property and establish their businesses, another calamity hit Swat—the July 2010 devastating floods that destroyed whatever was left standing by the Taliban—roads, bridges, schools, health facilities, orchards, farms, and hotels. The people are yet to recover from the double shock—Taliban and the natural calamity. In spite of government assurances that the Swat Valley has been cleared of militants, the current status of Maulana Fazlullah and some of his top commanders is unclear, and several suicide bombings in Mingora, the center of Swat, in the past suggest that the Valley still simmers. There is calm in the valley, but not peace.

A few attacks from across the border in the adjacent Dir and Chitral regions and claims by Mullah Fazlullah in 2011 once again spread fear among Swatis of the return of Taliban. It is because of this fear that investors are not stepping in with full confidence in the Swat Valley, once known to be a magnet for the hotel industry and tourists from all over Pakistan and abroad. Business activity could have increased employment opportunities for otherwise jobless youths.

The reconstruction process, despite promises by the civil administration, is slow and causing disappointment among the people, who suffered heavily during the years of Taliban presence in the Valley.

The presence of army troops in the main center Mingora and plans to establish a permanent army cantonment in the valley are being seen as a conspiracy to evict the locals from their land.

TRIBAL STRUCTURE OF SWAT

The Swat Valley is dominated by ethnic Pashtuns of the Yousafzai tribe, but other ethnic groups live there as well, mostly in the more remote and mountainous areas.

Following is a list of the three major ethnic groups and where they live.

Gujjars and Kohistanis make up fewer than 15 percent of the population of Swat. Important Pashtun tribal elders in Swat are Afzal Khan Lala (who controls the area of Khwazakhela), Shujaat Ali Khan, and Bakht Bedar Khan (who was killed in 2008, but his family remains powerful in the valley). Shujaat Ali Khan was one of the first to flee the area for fear of the militants, leaving in early 2007 for Islamabad and Peshawar. His lands were occupied by Taliban, who redistributed some of it. Afzal Khan Lala was attacked many times by Taliban fighters in Swat, was injured, and lost many relatives, but he stayed in the valley. To many Swatis he is a symbol of resistance to the Taliban.

TABLE 11.1 Geographical distribution of Swat tribes

Ethnicity	Area	Language
Pashtuns	Whole of Swat and Malakand Division	Pashto
Gujjars	Scattered but mostly in Matta subdistrict of Swat	Gujri
Kohistanis	Mostly in Bahrain and Kalam areas of Swat	Kohistani

Although Sufi Muhammad's support was based among Pashtuns in Swat, the emergence of his son-in-law Fazlullah's popular FM channel in 2004 led some in the Gujjar community to back the younger preacher. Most of the Pashtuns and Gujjars who supported Fazlullah were poor; they were inspired by his fiery broadcasts advocating social justice and stirring up resentment against the powerful landlords, or khans. Peasants who worked the khans' lands and sought equality also backed Fazlullah's efforts. Finally, Fazlullah garnered support among Pashtuns seeking to settle scores. Revenge is a part of Pashtun life, but for those who could not themselves take revenge against their rich and powerful enemies, joining Fazlullah's movement provided an opportunity.

Notes

1. Previously known as North-West Frontier Province, or NWFP.
2. Carol Grisanti, "Former Swat Ruler: 'Revenge' Motivates Taliban," MSNBC, Aug. 14, 2009, http://worldblog.msnbc.msn.com/archive/2009/08/14/2031724. aspx.
3. Waqar Ahmad Khan, a member of NWFP assembly from Swat, told me in an interview in Peshawar in June 2009 that his family was involved in a land dispute case with a court in Swat when he was a child, and now he is forty and the case remains unresolved.
4. Sultan-i-Rome, "Swat: A Critical Analysis," Institute of Peace and Conflict Studies, New Delhi, January 2009, http://www.ipcs.org/pdf_file/issue/1542140255RP18-Rome-Swat.pdf.
5. Shaukat Sharar, Swat-based architect and head of the nongovernmental organization Disaster Response Network (DR-Net), interview, October 2009, Mingora.
6. Ibid.
7. Zahid Khan, president, All Swat Hotels Association, interview, October 2009, Mingora.
8. Mian Iftikhar Hussain, interview, July 2009, Peshawar.
9. Sultan-i-Rome, "Swat: A Critical Analysis," Institute of Peace and Conflict Studies, New Delhi, January 2009, http://www.ipcs.org/pdf_file/issue/1542140255RP18-Rome-Swat.pdf. As an example of nascent extremism in Swat under the wali, allow me to recount an old but little-known Swati story. There was a mullah in the early twentieth century named Sandaki Mulla, who helped the new wali establish his rule in the valley with the aim of creating an Islamic ministate. After the wali's power was secured, Sandaki Mula and some

of his followers approached the wali's palace to ask about implementation of Islamic law, or sharia. The wali told Sandaki Mula to bring all of his followers to court, which he did. The wali promptly had the mullah and the followers killed at a secret location to preemptively quell opposition to his rule.

10. Christine Fair, "Pakistan Loses Swat to Local Taliban," Jamestown Terrorism Focus, Nov. 13, 2007, http://www.jamestown.org/single/?no_cache=1&tx_ttnews[tt_news]=4537.

11. Sayyad Ali Shah, *Da Shariat Karwan: Manzal ba Manzal*, Lahore, Mukhtar Ahmad Khan Swati, 1995.

12. Sultan-i-Rome, "Swat: A Critical Analysis."

13. Ibid.

14. Shaheen Sardar Ali, "Is Sharia the Answer?" *Dawn*, Feb. 17, 2009.

15. Zahid Khan (president of All Swat Hotel Associations), interview, Nov. 21, 2009, Mingora.

16. Rahimullah Yousufzai, Nov. 6, 2007, http://www.valleyswat.net/.

17. Khurshid Khan, "Exclusive: An Interview with Maulana Fazlullah," Swat, Apr. 21, 2007, http://www.valleyswat.net.

18. Afzal Khan, "Revolt in Pakistan's NWFP: A Profile of Maulana Fazlullah of Swat," Jamestown Terrorism Focus, Nov. 20, 2007, http://www.jamestown.org/single/?no_cache=1&tx_ttnews[tt_news]=4555.

19. Ibid.

20. Mukhtar A. Khan, "A Profile of Militant Groups in Bajaur Tribal Agency," *Jamestown Terrorism Monitor*, Mar. 3, 2009, http://www.jamestown.org/programs/gta/single/?tx_ttnews[tt_news]=34729&tx_ttnews[backPid]=26&cHash=cce9e6a8f9.

21. Afzal Khan, "Revolt in Pakistan's NWFP."

22. Imtiaz Ali, "Pakistan's Military Offensive in Swat May Be Start of Long Campaign," Jamestown Terrorism Focus, Dec. 7, 2007, http://www.jamestown.org/single/?no_cache=1&tx_ttnews[tt_news]=4586.

23. Griff Witte and Imtiaz Ali, "Musharraf's Army Losing Ground in Insurgent Areas," *Washington Post*, Nov. 13, 2007, http://www.washingtonpost.com/wp-dyn/content/article/2007/11/12/AR2007111202043.html.

24. Ziauddin Yousafza (Swat-based educator), interview, October 2009, Mingora.

25. Mukhtar A. Khan, "The Return of Shari'a Law to Pakistan's Swat Region," *Jamestown Terrorism Monitor*, Mar. 3, 2009, http://www.jamestown.org/single/?no_cache=1&tx_ttnews[tt_news]=34576&tx_ttnews[backPid]=7&cHash=081b812552.

26. Musa Khankhel and Mushtaq Yusufzai, "30 FC Men Die in Swat Blast," *News International*, Oct. 26, 2007, http://www.thenews.com.pk/top_story_detail.asp?Id=10817.

27. Ashfaq Yusufzai, "Impotence Fears Hit Polio Drive," BBC, Jan. 25, 2007, http://news.bbc.co.uk/2/hi/south_asia/6299325.stm.

28. "Pakistan Militants Try to Blow Up Buddha Statue," Associated Press, Sept. 12, 2007, http://www.usatoday.com/news/world/2007-09-12-pakistan-buddha_N.htm.

29. Fazlullah, interview with Freemuse radio, February 2008, http://www.freemuse.org/sw24746.asp.

30. Shaukat Sharar, Swat-based architect and head of the nongovernmental organization Disaster Response Network (DR-Net), interview, October 2009, Mingora.

31. Shamim Shahid, "Baitullah Rival Shot Dead," *Nation*, June 24, 2009, http://www.nation.com.pk/pakistan-news-newspaper-daily-english-online/Politics/24-Jun-2009/Baitullah-rival-shot-dead.

32. In the video "Swat Volume III," released by the Taliban, many young boys mention the operation against the Red Mosque and the adjacent Jamia Hafsa madrassa as the reason for their becoming suicide bombers, to avenge the killing of young girls and boys.

33. Malak Naveed Khan, inspector general of the NWFP Police, interview, October 2009, Peshawar.

34. Locals who claim they knew him before he joined the Taliban said he was a criminal, involved in petty theft, robbery, and land grabbing.

35. "Swat Taliban 'Commander' Dies of Kidney Failure," *Dawn*, Dec. 27, 2009, http://www.dawn.com/wps/wcm/connect/dawn-content-library/dawn/the-newspaper/front-page/19-swat-taliban-commander-dies-of-kidney-failure-729-hh-05.

36. Abdul Hayee Kakar, BBC Urdu Service, in Peshawar, http://www.bbc.co.uk/urdu/pakistan/2009/11/091117_fazlullah_afg_rh.shtml.

37. BBC Urdu Service, in Peshawar, http://www.bbc.co.uk/urdu/pakistan/story/2008/10/081018_muslim_khan.shtml.

38. Ibid.

39. Javid Aziz Khan, "Forces Launch Operation in Swat," *News International*, Oct. 25, 2007, http://server.kbri-islamabad.go.id/index2.php?option=com_content&task=view&id=2529&pop=1&page=0&Itemid=45.

40. *The News on Sunday*, Dilawar Jan Banori, Sept. 16, 2007.

41. Anand Gopal, Mansur Khan Mahsud, and Brian Fishman, "The Battle for Pakistan; Militancy and Conflict in North Waziristan," New America Foundation, April 2010.

42. CNN, "Translated Excerpts from the Taliban Code of Conduct," July 30, 2009, http://www.cnn.com/2009/WORLD/asiapcf/07/30/taliban.code.excerpt/index.html.

43. Qari Yousaf Ahmadi, interview by author, telephone, 2009.

44. The conversation was released by the Pakistani army's publicity wing ISPR during a news conference in Islamabad in August 2009.

45. Wajid Ali Khan, NWFP minister for forests and environment, interview, October 2009, Peshawar. Timber smuggling has long been a part of gray and black markets in Swat.

46. Hekmatullah Shinwari, a geologist who got the Shamozai emerald mine on lease for thirty years in 2007, interview, October 2009, Peshawar.

47. Malak Naveed Khan, interview, October 2009, Peshawar.

48. Governor Ali Jan Orakzai, quoted by Swat-based Urdu daily *Azadi*; Swat based-journalist interview, Peshawar.

49. *The News on Sunday*, Dilawar Jan Banori, Sept. 16, 2007.

50. Hameedullah Khan, "Swat Cleric 'Ends' Peace Deal," *Dawn*, Sept. 22, 2007, http://www.dawn.com/2007/09/22/top9.htm.

51. Javid Aziz Khan, "Forces Launch Operation in Swat," *News International*, Oct. 25, 2007, http://server.kbri-islamabad.go.id/index2.php?option=com_content&

task=view&id=2529&pop=1&page=0&Itemid=45; Khalid Qayum and Khaleeq Ahmed, "Pakistan Deploys Troops in Swat to Curb Militants," Bloomberg, Oct. 25, 2007, http://www.bloomberg.com/apps/news?pid=20601102&sid=akTcKrCt bmWE&refer=uk.

52. Swat-based newspapers *Chand* and *Shamal*, March 2009–May 15, 2009; Musa Khankhel and Mushtaq Yusufza, "Army Joins Swat Operation," *News International*, Oct. 28, 2007, http://www.thenews.com.pk/top_story_detail. asp?Id=10857.

53. Akhtar Amin, "Army Troops Moved into Swat," *Daily Times*, Nov. 11, 2007.

54. Hameedullah Khan, "'Cantonment in Matta Planned,'" *Dawn*, Dec. 5, 2007, http://www.dawn.com/2007/12/05/top12.htm.

55. *Daily Times*, Feb. 9, 2008.

56. "Top Pakistani Militant Released," BBC, Apr. 21, 2008, http://news.bbc.co.uk/2/ hi/south_asia/7359523.stm.

57. Daud Khattak, "Govt, Swat Taliban Sign Peace Deal," *Daily Times*, May 22, 2008, http://www.dailytimes.com.pk/default.asp?date=5%2F22%2F2008.

58. Ibid.

59. Jane Perlez and Pir Zubair Shah, "Pakistan Says It Has Seized Taliban Spokesman," *New York Times*, Sept. 12, 2009, http://www.nytimes. com/2009/09/12/world/asia/12pstan-.html?_r=2.

60. "Militants Pull Out of Talks in Swat," *Dawn*, June 30, 2008, http://www.dawn. com/2008/06/30/top2.htm.

61. Ibid.

62. Hameedullah Khan, "Malam Jabba Motel Set on Fire," June 27, 2008, http:// www.dawn.com/2008/06/27/top2.htm.

63. Omar Waraich, "Refugees Head Home After Army Scatters the Taliban," *Independent*, Aug. 3, 2009, http://www.independent.co.uk/news/world/asia/ refugees-head-home-after-army-scatters-the-taliban-1766564.html.

64. Daud Khattak, "Govt, TNSM Agree on Nizam-e-Adl in Malakand," *Daily Times*, Feb. 16, 2009, http://www.dailytimes.com.pk/default.asp?page=2009/02/16/ story_16-2-2009_pg1_1; "Pakistan Agrees Sharia Law Deal," BBC, Feb. 16, 2009, http://news.bbc.co.uk/2/hi/south_asia/7891955.stm.

65. Delawar Jan, "Swat Taliban Declare Permanent Ceasefire," *News International*, Feb. 25, 2009.

66. Author observations, Feb. 18, 2009, Mingora, Swat.

67. Delawar Jan, "DPO Among Five Killed in Lower Dir," *News International*, Mar. 30, 2009.

68. Hamid Mir, "Secret of Details of Swat Peace Deal," *News International*, Apr. 11, 2009, http://www.thenews.com.pk/top_story_detail.asp?Id=21455; Jane Perlez, "Taliban Seize Vital Area Closer to the Capital," *New York Times*, Apr. 22, 2009, http://www.nytimes.com/2009/04/23/world/asia/23buner.html.

69. "Pakistan to Allow Sharia in Swat," *Al-Jazeera English*, Feb. 17, 2009, http:// english.aljazeera.net/news/asia/2009/02/200921611102341o105.html.

70. "Swat Taliban Pull Out of Buner," *Dawn*, Apr. 25, 2009, http://www.dawn.com/ wps/wcm/connect/dawn-content-library/dawn/news/pakistan/nwfp/troops-man- buner-police-stations-official-ss.

71. Jane Perlez, "Taliban Seize Vital Pakistan Area Closer to the Capital," *New York Times*, Apr. 23, 2009,http://www.nytimes.com/2009/04/23/world/asia/23buner.html.

72. Ismail Khan, "Swat Taliban Mouthpiece, Top Commander Captured," *Dawn*, Sept. 12, 2009, http://www.dawn.com/wps/wcm/connect/dawn-content-library/dawn/news/pakistan/04-muslim-khan-arrested-qs-03.

73. Pakistan army spokesman Maj. General Athar Abbas, in his regular media briefings in Islamabad throughout June, July, August, and September 2009.

74. Qurat ul ain Siddiqui, "2009 in Broad Strokes," *Dawn*, Dec. 30, 2009, http://www.dawn.com/wps/wcm/connect/dawn-content-library/dawn/news/pakistan/04-2009-in-broad-strokes-qs-01.

75. Hameedullah Khan, "Suicide Bomber Kills ANP Lawmaker," *Dawn*, Dec. 1, 2009, http://www.dawn.com/wps/wcm/connect/dawn-content-library/dawn/news/pakistan/03-anp-mpa-killed-in-suicide-attack-ss-05.

76. Hameedullah Khan, "Rehmat Ali of ANP Wins Swat Seat," *Dawn*, Jan. 29, 2010, http://www.dawn.com/wps/wcm/connect/dawn-content-library/dawn/the-newspaper/national/12-rehmat-ali-of-anp-wins-swat-seat-910 – bi-07.

77. Christine Fair, "Islamist Militancy in Pakistan: A View from the Provinces," WorldPublicOpinion.org, July 10, 2009, http://www.worldpublicopinion.org/pipa/pdf/jul09/PakProvinces_Jul09_rpt.pdf.

78. Provincial government official, interview, undated.

79. Abdul Hayee Kakar, BBC Urdu Service, in Peshawar, http://www.bbc.co.uk/urdu/pakistan/2009/11/091117_fazlullah_afg_rh.shtml.

80. Muhammad Rome, professor at Jehanzeb College Swat, interview, Nov. 21, 2009, Swat.

81. "Swat Deal Broker Cleric 'Charged,'" BBC, Aug. 2, 2009, http://news.bbc.co.uk/2/hi/south_asia/8180607.stm.

TWELVE

The Taliban in Bajaur

Rahmanullah

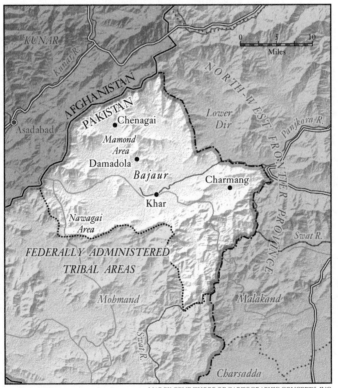

MAP BY GENE THORP OF CARTOGRAPHIC CONCEPTS, INC.

BAJAUR IS THE smallest of the seven administrative units of the Federally Administered Tribal Areas (FATA) of northwest Pakistan, a relatively inaccessible agency known for its hilly terrain. It borders Afghanistan's Kunar province and Pakistan's Dir district, a gateway to the Swat Valley in the North-West Frontier Province (NWFP), making it of strategic importance to Pakistan and the region.[1] The current population of Bajaur is more than one million, and the agency's administrative headquarters is the town of Khar.

As a hub of Taliban and al-Qaeda activities, the Afghan province of Kunar has greatly influenced the conservative and traditional Pashtun tribesmen of Bajaur. After the fall of the Taliban regime in Afghanistan in 2001, fleeing militants crossed the border into Bajaur and exploited the tribal code of Pashtunwali, which requires hospitality and the giving of shelter. Bajauris treated the Afghan Taliban and al-Qaeda fighters as guests.[2] Bajaur still functions as a logistical base for the Taliban on both sides of the Durand Line, which divides Afghanistan and Pakistan. The agency's significance in terrorists' operational planning is illustrated by the fact that plots targeting London and Barcelona were linked to al-Qaeda operatives based in Bajaur.[3] Additionally, a senior member of al-Qaeda, Abu Faraj al-Libbi, who was involved in attempts to assassinate Gen. Pervez Musharraf, then Pakistan's president, told interrogators after his arrest in 2005 that he had lived in Bajaur for some time.[4]

THE STRUCTURE OF THE INSURGENCY
IN BAJAUR

Although the founder of the militant group Tehrik-i-Nifaz-i-Shariat-i-Mohammadi (TNSM), Sufi Muhammad, was agitating for institution of sharia, or Islamic law, in the neighboring Malakand district as early as 1989, the Taliban movement did not truly emerge in Bajaur until the Taliban fell in 2001. Exploiting the fury felt by local Pashtuns at the U.S. invasion of Afghanistan, Sufi Muhammad set up a recruiting camp for the nascent Taliban in Mamond tehsil (subdivision) in Bajaur. He was assisted by Maulvi Faqir Muhammad, who was then the commander of the Taliban in Bajaur and *naib amir*, or vice chief, of the TNSM.

In late 2001, Sufi Muhammad led a contingent of around ten thousand fighters to battle coalition forces across the border in Afghanistan, and hundreds of Bajauri militants were killed or captured; there are some reports that many still have not returned to Bajaur and are perhaps being held in Afghan jails.[5] A local journalist who accompanied Sufi Muhammad's forces to Afghanistan says that half returned and half are still missing, either killed or imprisoned. Anwarullah, the journalist, said that Sufi Muhammad's supporters entered Kunar in eastern Afghanistan via the pass at Ghahi, some thirty kilometers (about twenty miles) northwest of Khar, the main town in Bajaur.[6]

After Musharraf, Pakistan's president, allied himself with the U.S. anti-Taliban efforts in Afghanistan, the Pakistani army's image was tarnished in the tribal areas. This, combined with the desire for revenge against the invading Americans, provided some of the basis for the Talibanization of Bajaur.

After Sufi Muhammad's return to Pakistan in early 2002, he and his son-in-law Maulana Fazlullah were arrested for raising a force against the Americans, further angering the populations of Bajaur and Swat. This anger helped unite Bajauri militants under the leadership of Maulvi Faqir Muhammad, whose supporters called over loudspeakers for donations and volunteers. After a slow start, Maulvi Faqir gradually built up a force of about four to five thousand fighters in 2002 in the Mamond and Nawagai tehsils of Bajaur.[7] The local Taliban gave shelter to the Afghan and foreign fighters fleeing the conflict in Afghanistan and at times incorporated the outsiders into their families via marriage.

However, as the war in Afghanistan continued and more Bajauris lost family members to the fighting, support for Sufi Muhammad's Taliban began to dwindle; he had left thousands of his fighters behind upon his return to Pakistan. But this disappointment was not enough to overcome Bajauris' dislike of the Afghan Northern Alliance and U.S. troops in Afghanistan, and fleeing Taliban fighters were able to regroup in Bajaur in the early 2000s.[8]

Maulvi Faqir Muhammad and the TTP

Born in 1970 in Sewai, a village in Bajaur's Mamond tehsil near the Afghan border, Maulvi Faqir Muhammad belongs to the locally popular and powerful Mamond tribe. He fought against the Soviet occupation in Afghanistan in the 1980s and alongside the Taliban in Afghanistan during the 1990s.[9] Raised in a religious family, he started his education at a local madrassa, where his teacher was the widely respected Maulana Abdus Salam, who belonged to the Deobandi sect of Islam but was not involved in politics or militancy, according to researcher Sohail Abdul Nasir. Under Abdus Salam, Maulvi Faqir achieved the *Dars-e-Nizami*, which is equal to graduation, in the 1990s. He also studied the Quran at the Darul-Uloom Panjpir, a seminary in the Swabi district of the NWFP,[10] which promotes a Wahhabist ideology similar to that followed in Saudi Arabia.[11]

Physically, Maulvi Faqir is tall and well built and wears a long, Taliban-style black beard. He has only one wife, but his family is large and nearly everyone associated with him is allegedly involved with his militant activities.[12] Before he became involved with the TNSM in 1993 or 1994 after being mentored by TNSM founder Sufi Muhammad, Maulvi Faqir was a local leader of Jamaat-e-Islami, an Islamist political party popular in the tribal areas. After joining the TNSM, he accompanied Sufi Muhammad in his disastrous attempt in late 2001 to reinforce the Afghan Taliban with Pakistani fighters to battle the Americans.

In 2009, Maulvi Faqir commanded around six thousand fighters,[13] including about five hundred Afghans and about a hundred other foreign fighters, mostly Arabs and Chechens. Uzbek fighters are present in the Charmang area of Bajaur's Nawagai tehsil, commanded by Qari Zia ur-Rehman, who according to security sources also trains other foreign fighters.[14] Maulvi Faqir was one of the founders of the Tehrik-e-Taliban Pakistan (TTP), the umbrella organization formed in December 2007 to unite the various factions of the Pakistani Taliban, first headed by Baitullah Mehsud.

As Baitullah's right-hand man, Maulvi Faqir repeatedly pledged his loyalty to the head of the Quetta Shura Taliban, Mullah Omar, showing that he believes the Afghan and Pakistani Taliban movements are two sides of the same coin. According to a local Mehsud khan, or landowner, Maulvi Faqir told a large gathering in Sewai in 2008, "We think of Mullah Omar and Osama bin Laden as our supreme leaders, though Osama has not spent a night with me. But if he comes, we will welcome him."[15] Another local, Imran Khan, heard Maulvi Faqir announce his support for Mullah Omar and Osama bin Laden during a broadcast on his FM radio station, saying, "We and Maulvi Omar are one; there is no difference in our movements."[16]

The Quetta Shura Taliban have no known operational links with militant groups in Bajaur, however. The Taliban groups in Bajaur primarily target the Pakistani state, while the Taliban in Afghanistan—those fighters led by the Quetta Shura and Mullah Omar—focus mainly on hostilities against U.S. and NATO forces. In fact, some Taliban in Afghanistan don't want the Taliban fighters in Pakistan to use the term "Taliban" because it may damage the group's popular support. The "code of conduct"[17] released by the Taliban in Afghanistan in the summer of 2009, similarly, has had no effect on the Taliban in Bajaur.[18]

Maulvi Faqir has also expressed his support for al-Qaeda, come out in favor of the TTP's targeting of U.S. and NATO forces in Afghanistan, and commented about the September 11, 2001, attacks on the United States,[19] "Things have changed for the better [after September 11], it has sustained this struggle. It has awakened Muslims, and the *Ummah* [community] has come to know who their enemy is. If the attack had taken place earlier, many Muslim lands would be free from foreign occupation by now." The Pakistani government has offered a reward of 15 million rupees ($180,000) for his capture.[20]

Like Sufi Muhammad and his son-in-law Maulana Fazlullah in the Swat Valley, Maulvi Faqir seems to understand the importance of radio outreach. His sermons on his illegal FM channel can be heard across Bajaur. Because his broadcasting equipment is easily assembled and mobile, Pakistani security forces have been unable to stop his propagandizing. Maulvi Faqir has also made himself available to the news media, giving occasional interviews and claiming to local journalists that he was the interim chief of the TTP after news of Baitullah Mehsud's death swirled in late August 2009.[21]

Besides Afghans and some other foreigners, followers of Islamist groups such as the banned Jaish-e-Muhammad and the TNSM are also attached to Maulvi Faqir. The Taliban commander and these groups run combined courts in Bajaur, mete out similar punishments for alleged spies, and hold joint jirgas or assemblies to discuss matters critical to the militancy in Bajaur. "Their names are different, but there is no apparent difference between them," said a local senior journalist, Haji Babibullah Khan.[22] Maulvi Faqir is also suspected to have close ties with al-Qaeda's number two leader, Ayman al-Zawahiri, and is believed to have hosted a dinner for the terrorist leader in Damadola in January 2006 that was targeted by a U.S. drone strike.[23] In early March

2010, Maulvi Faqir was reported killed by a Pakistani air strike in the Mohmand tribal agency, but a Reuters reporter received a phone call later in which a man who identified himself as Maulvi Faqir said he was fine and called reports of his death "propaganda"; the reporter said he recognized the voice.[24] Maulvi Faqir later phoned the BBC's Peshawar office and confirmed that he and his fighters were safe.[25]

There have been reports that Maulvi Faqir was replaced as the Taliban leader in Bajaur by Jamal ud-Din Dadullah, the TTP's vice amir in the agency, because Maulvi Faqir ordered his followers not to fight Pakistani forces during the 2010 military operations in Bajaur, thus irritating prominent Taliban leaders who continuously target the Pakistani state.[26] Jamal ud-Din Dadullah hails from the Markhano Zangal Wara Mamond tehsil, northwest of Khar, and has some religious education from the Pamjpeer seminary, but not much else is known about him. Maulvi Faqir denies being replaced but acknowledges ongoing conflicts with other Taliban leaders in Bajaur.[27]

On March 5, 2012, Maulvi Faqir was reportedly demoted from his position as deputy commander, a sign of splits in the Pakistani Taliban's leadership, according to some analysts. Maulvi Faqir later gave an interview to Pakistan's *The News*, saying he had not been informed about his removal and learned about it through the media like everyone else. He also reiterated his support for peace talks with the government, which may have been the reason behind Hakimullah Mehsud's decision that there was "no longer a need" for the deputy commander post.

Other Militant Groups in Bajaur

Though the TTP and the TNSM are the major militant groups in Bajaur, several other jihadist groups also operate there. Jaish-i-Islami is headed by Qari Ali Rehman, a militant from the Yusuf Khel tribe of the Loi Mamond tehsil,[28] and is active in Loi Mamond tehsil. Before becoming the head of Jaish-i-Islami in 2008, he was a high-ranking security guard for Maulvi Faqir.[29] Jaish-i-Islami was upset when Maulvi Faqir did not react to the Pakistani army offensive in Bajaur and accused him of collusion with the government, so there is some tension in their relationship.[30]

Harkatul Jihad-ul Islami (HUJI), a Punjabi outfit of militants once headed by Qari Saifullah Akhtar, is also active in Bajaur. Pakistani intelligence claims that Akhtar and the HUJI were involved in the September 2008 suicide attack on the Marriott Hotel in Islamabad as well as other suicide bombings across the country, including the attack on former prime minister Benazir Bhutto's convoy when she arrived in Karachi on October 18, 2007.[31]

Two Uzbek groups, the Islamic Movement of Uzbekistan and a splinter group, the Islamic Jihad Union, also have some roots in Bajaur and neighboring Kunar in Afghanistan, though they are not believed to have more than a hundred or so fighters.[32] Additionally, there are Arab militants in Bajaur, most of whom crossed into the agency after the fall of the Taliban government in Afghanistan in 2001.[33] Maulvi Faqir is skilled at uniting the various jihadist groups in Bajaur, and his support for Mullah Omar and Osama bin Laden is a good indicator that some of these Arabs in Bajaur may be al-Qaeda fighters.[34]

In addition to Maulvi Faqir, there are a handful of other important Taliban commanders in Bajaur: Pervez, who goes by one name, controls Nawagai tehsil, west of Khar; Zia ur-Rehman, an Afghan, administers the area of Charmang along the border with Kunar; Maulana Ismail supervises the Taliban in Chenagai and Damadola; Maulvi Abdullah heads the movement in the Banda region in Salarzai tehsil; and Wali ur-Rehman controls the Irab area of Loi Mamond tehsil. These commanders have a very strong communications system and seek direction from Maulvi Faqir when possible. However, during military operations, when contact is limited because of security concerns, each of these local leaders has sole authority for militant activities in his region.[35]

Bordering Afghanistan's Kunar province, a stronghold of insurgent commander Gulbuddin Hekmatyar, many of the Afghan refugees who fled to Bajaur after the fall of the Taliban government in 2001 were supportive of Gulbuddin. However, most of these refugees left the agency after the Pakistani Army launched its operations in Bajaur in the summer of 2008. A small number of Afghan refugees still living in Bajaur support the religious political party Jamiat-i-Islami, which has strong links with Hizb-i-Islami, Gulbuddin's insurgent group. However, Hizb-i-Islami Gulbuddin has no known links with local anti-Pakistan militants, as Gulbuddin has ties with the Pakistani government and Taliban fighters in Bajaur have been attacking the Pakistani state.[36]

Training Camps

The Taliban in Bajaur run a network of mobile training camps in forests, at the bottom of hills, and in religious schools abandoned by the Pakistani government. Some of the camps are located in Ambar, about seventy kilometers (forty-three miles) south of Khar on the border with Mohmand, and in Charmang, near the Mohmand and Afghan borders.[37] Additionally, militants have captured some individual homes in Loi Sam, about twelve kilometers (seven miles) west of Khar, to use as camps. Other locations, according to local officials, include the Malasaid and Banda areas of Salarzai, the Kaga area of Mamond, and the Damadola area. The Pakistani army asserts it has now cleared the Damadola area and advanced to other areas.[38] At the camps, which are moved frequently because of security concerns, newly recruited militants are given training in firing rocket launchers and in making and defusing bombs. Most of the bombs and suicide vests are homemade, with components including cooking oil, ball bearings, nuts and bolts, and nails. The Taliban in Bajaur also retain a number of weapons used by their forerunners in Afghanistan against the Soviets in the 1980s. In general, recruits don't need much training with firearms, as they have been accustomed to using Kalashnikov assault rifles since childhood.

Financing

Many Pakistani officials believe the Taliban in Pakistan have access to foreign funds, and Owais Ahmed Ghani, the governor of North-West Frontier Province, has frequently said that Afghanistan's "narcomafia" contributes funds to the Pakistani Taliban.[39] In February 2010, he estimated that the TTP spends nearly 3.6 billion rupees (about $4.3 million) on fifteen thousand fighters in Pakistan, citing the opium trade as a main source of income.[40] Though Bajaur is not directly involved in Afghanistan's opium traffic, its border with the country ensures that it is affected. Taliban militants in Bajaur also engage in timber smuggling, collection of funds from local mosques, *bahtta* (forced taxes on local citizens), and kidnapping for ransom to support the movement.

Tactics: Suicide Bombings

Suicide bombings in the FATA overall are masterminded by TTP commander Qari Hussain, who is based in South Waziristan and was the right-hand man of the late Baitullah Mehsud, but suicide attackers are also trained and deployed in Bajaur. Qari Hussain has the ability to send suicide attackers anywhere in the FATA, including Bajaur.[41] Meanwhile, the efforts of Maulana Fazlullah to encourage suicide attacks against Pakistani government and military targets in the Swat Valley have spread to Bajaur. The Swat Taliban leader said in July 2007, "Through suicide bombings, Muslim youths are showing the world they can use their bones and flesh as bullets to strike the infidels."[42] Locals have heard Maulvi Faqir tell gatherings in various towns of Bajaur that the TTP has several suicide bombers. He claimed that the fighters feel honored to become *fidayeen* (the term used for suicide bombers by the Taliban). Locals have also heard him say that even women now want to become suicide bombers.[43]

In his frequent speeches during 2008 and 2009 across Bajaur, Maulvi Faqir also boasted of having large numbers of suicide bombers and recruits at his disposal, claiming that suicide attackers are highly revered, both by the Taliban before their missions and in heaven. A Taliban suicide bomber attacked a police checkpoint in Khar on January 31, 2010, killing at least seventeen and illustrating that even after a series of Pakistani military operations the movement retains its ability to strike in the heart of Bajaur.

MILITARY OPERATIONS IN BAJAUR

Drone Strikes

In mid-January 2006, a U.S. drone strike destroyed a house in Damadola, a hamlet in northern Bajaur northwest of Khar, killing as many as twenty-two people in an attack believed to have targeted al-Qaeda deputy leader Ayman al-Zawahiri at a dinner celebrating Eid.[44] Though al-Zawahiri escaped, his son-in-law, who was reputedly involved with al-Qaeda's media arm, and Abu Obaidah al-Masri, al-Qaeda operations chief for Afghanistan's Kunar province, were among those killed.[45]

An attack in late October 2006 demolished a madrassa a few kilometers away in Chenagai, a village in the Mamond area. Although the strike was reportedly carried out by Pakistani forces with helicopters, some local sources claimed it was a drone strike, again likely targeting al-Zawahiri.[46] More than eighty suspected militants were killed in the attack, though villagers claimed the dead were students in the madrassa, and the TNSM leader of the religious school, Maulana Liaqat, also died. The October attack came two days after some three thousand militants held a rally in Sadiq Abad, about five kilometers west of Khar, chanting slogans of support for Osama bin Laden and Mullah Omar.[47]

Maulvi Faqir was outraged at the casualties. He addressed a crowd of gunmen and supporters in the rubble of the building, saying, "May Allah protect Sheikh Osama. May Allah protect Mullah Omar," and melodramatically claiming that he wished he too had been martyred.[48]

The two air strikes in 2006 roused the sentiments of Bajauris against the Pakistani government and the United States, and Maulvi Faqir's fiery speeches helped mobilize support for the Taliban in Bajaur. Just over a week after the second strike, Taliban fighters carried out a suicide attack on a Pakistani army base in Dargai, a hundred kilometers (sixty-two miles) north of Peshawar in Malakand, specifically to avenge the madrassa attack.[49] It was the deadliest such attack to date against the Pakistani military, killing at least forty soldiers and wounding twenty-two. A military spokesman, Maj. Gen. Shaukat Sultan, said, "We strongly suspect the attack on the army center was done by the people trained in Bajaur in the madrassa run by al-Qaeda facilitators Maulvi Liaqat and Maulvi Faqir."[50]

Maulvi Faqir launched a large-scale recruitment drive for his Taliban group, and by 2006 he had amassed thousands of fighters under his command. By early 2007, Bajaur was largely under Taliban control; between that summer and August 2008, Taliban fighters captured about 150 Pakistani military outposts in the agency.[51]

U.S. drones have reportedly struck Bajaur at least two more times. One attack, in May 2008 in Damadola, killed al-Qaeda planner Abu Sulayman al-Jazairi, an Algerian believed to have been plotting attacks against the West, and about a dozen others.[52] Another reported strike, in late October 2009, targeted Maulvi Faqir, who just minutes earlier had left the house that was destroyed; about thirty people were killed, including Maulvi Faqir's nephew and son-in-law.[53] The strike apparently was aimed at a meeting of a Taliban shura, or council, in Bajaur.

Pakistani Military Offensives in Bajaur

After the ill-equipped and undertrained Frontier Corps failed to flush out Taliban fighters under the leadership of Maulvi Faqir Muhammad, the Pakistani army was sent to Bajaur in the summer of 2008. The intent was to clear the area of Taliban militants, who had established a parallel government in the agency and were controlling local market prices, forbidding barbers to shave beards, and opposing polio vaccination campaigns. Operation Sherdil ("Lion's Heart"), begun in early August 2008, was also intended to slow the flow of militants across the border into Afghanistan's Kunar province.[54] Local officials claim that more than twenty thousand troops, including Bajaur conscripts and Army soldiers backed by helicopter gunships, tanks, and artillery, were fighting against twenty-five hundred to three thousand Taliban in Bajaur.[55] However, other estimates put the number of Pakistani troops at around eight thousand.[56]

During the first few months of fighting, the army did not have much success, as it seemed to underestimate the strength of the Bajaur Taliban and possessed weak intelligence on the ground.[57] Security forces were also apparently unaware of the long tunnels dug by the Taliban for storing weapons and for protection from Pakistani jets. Habibullah Khan, a top official in the FATA Secretariat, said in September 2008, "These tunnels are called *asmasta* and some of them are about half a mile, and insurgents can stay there a long time to protect themselves from security forces' shelling."[58]

On September 20, 2008, the offensive in Bajaur assumed increased significance as a suicide truck bomber detonated his explosives outside the five-star Marriott Hotel in Islamabad, killing more than fifty and wounding at least 250[59] in the deadliest attack in the Pakistani capital to date.[60] Pakistani officials claimed the hotel was targeted because the speaker of the National Assembly, Fahmida Mirza, was to host a dinner there for Prime Minister Yousaf Raza Gilani and President Asif Ali Zardari, who had just given his first speech to Parliament,[61] though the administration denied the hotel had been booked in advance.[62] (Pakistani officials claimed they had inquired about rates for using the hotel's space but never officially booked it.[63]) Suspicion eventually landed on HUJI, which has its roots in Bajaur, and Muhammad Qari Zafar, a Punjabi Taliban leader with ties to the al-Qaeda-linked Lashkar-e-Jhangvi; he was the suspected mastermind of the attack.[64] Zardari condemned the "cowardly attack," and Pakistan intensified its military operations in Bajaur.[65]

The dean of Western reporters in South Asia, Carlotta Gall, wrote about six weeks into Operation Sherdil that, after Waziristan, "Bajaur is perhaps the most significant stronghold of militants from the Taliban and Al Qaeda who have entrenched themselves in the tribal areas." She and co-author Ismail Khan quoted officials as saying that the militants were using everything they had to hold their ground. The officials also expressed surprise at the level of resistance and the sophistication of the militants' tactics, weapons, and communications.[66] "Even the sniper rifles they use are better than some of ours," one official said. "Their tactics are mind-boggling and they have defenses that would take us days to build. It does not look as though we are fighting a rag-tag militia. They are fighting like an organized force."

As the Pakistani military operations continued in the fall of 2008, however, the Taliban's communications systems were slowly dismantled and the militants ceased patrolling in broad daylight in Mamond and Salarzai.[67] Security forces also shut down the Taliban's illegal FM channel and destroyed several Taliban training camps. By late September, Pakistani authorities claimed that more than a thousand militants had been killed in the Bajaur operations.[68]

Meanwhile, informal tribal lashkars, or militias, were being mobilized in Bajaur in frustration over the Pakistani government's inconsistent response to the militant threat in the region.[69] Though the lashkars were not formally used until 2008, some pro-government maliks and their supporters had been targeted by the Taliban as early as 2007: hundreds[70] of influential tribal elders and lashkar followers were killed by Taliban attacks in Pakistan's seven tribal agencies and in the settled areas of Dir, Swat, and Buner districts of the NWFP. The tribal militias were attacked almost immediately by Taliban fighters, who came by the hundreds under the command of Qari Zia ur-Rehman.[71]

One area of Bajaur where the lashkars have had more success is Salarzai, because the Taliban never had strong roots there.[72] A Salarzai elder said his tribe was annoyed that the Pakistani government was unable to provide security for Bajauris, hence the formation of tribal lashkars.[73] Some members of the Salarzai tribe believe the targeted killings of lashkar leaders were the work of the Inter-Services Intelligence agency, attempting to keep the Taliban's influence as a hedge against the U.S. and NATO presence in Afghanistan.[74] However, there is no evidence of this.

After months of pitched battles that displaced half a million Pakistanis and destroyed nearly five thousand homes,[75] Maulvi Faqir declared a unilateral cease-fire in late February 2009, saying in a thirty-minute radio address, "We don't want to fight the army, but some elements have been creating misunderstandings between us....Pakistan is our country and the Pakistan army is our army."[76] Four days later, the army suspended its operations in Bajaur.[77] In early March, the army declared victory over the militants in Bajaur and the government signed a twenty-eight-point agreement with the leading Mamond tribe, and later the Tarkani and Utman Khel, that required the tribe to surrender key TTP figures to Pakistani authorities, lay down arms, and stop supporting militants.[78] In the past, however, such agreements have provided the Taliban with a chance to regroup; this seems to have occurred in the summer and fall of 2009.[79]

Pro-government forces in Bajaur had prominent success in August 2009 with the capture of Taliban spokesman Maulvi Omar, a deputy of Maulvi Faqir who had reputedly orchestrated several suicide blasts and attacks on security forces. He was arrested by local fighters of an anti-Taliban lashkar in neighboring Mohmand.[80]

In late January 2010, the Pakistani military began another series of operations in Bajaur, involving some four thousand troops, including Tochi scouts, Bajaur scouts, the 25th Punjab Regiment, and the 14th Punjab Regiment. The troops, backed by helicopter gunships, faced about two thousand Taliban fighters in the battle.[81] After about a week of fighting, several dozen militants surrendered to security forces, who were able to take control of strategically important Damadola, Maulvi Faqir's home town.[82]

Among those who surrendered was Masud Salar, Taliban commander in the Kas area of Mamond.[83] In mid-March, a prominent commander called Khalifa surrendered along with nearly forty of his men in Khar, promising never to take up arms again.[84] After claiming full control of Damadola, the army hoisted the Pakistani flag. "We have completely defeated the Taliban," Maj. Gen. Tariq Hayat, inspector general of the Frontier Corps, told reporters.[85] A Pakistani army spokesman, Maj. Gen. Athar Abbas, asserted that the army had taken control of 90–95 percent of Bajaur and killed fifty to sixty militants, while losing ten security personnel.[86]

The people of Mamond welcomed the military operation, believing that this time the army was serious about eradicating militants from Bajaur. A Bajauri named Bakhtawar Shah said the people showed full support for the army, as they hoped it would restore peace in the area.[87] Additionally, locals said they were pleased to see the Pakistani flag flying over Damadola and were not giving shelter to fleeing Taliban fighters.[88] An elder of the Salarzai tribe, Malak Manasib, said the local militias will continue to cooperate with the government to clear Bajaur of militants. The Salarzais have announced that they will fine those cooperating with the Taliban 2 million rupees and burn their houses.[89]

GRIEVANCES OF THE POPULATION

Poverty, a low literacy rate, deficient health facilities, and unemployment are major issues in all seven agencies of the FATA and have been generally ignored by Pakistan's central government for years. The pervasive poverty—about 60 percent of FATA residents live below the poverty line—is often mentioned as a possible factor contributing to the militancy of the region.[90] Naveed Ahmad Shinwari, a researcher in the FATA, observed:

> Natural resources are under-exploited in the FATA and the majority of the local population depends on agriculture, transport, arms manufacturing and trade, drug-trafficking, cross border trade (or so called smuggling) and shop-keeping....Entire families often depend on a single person's income. In the absence of any employment opportunities, the temptation for young people...to get involved in other activities—including crime and religious extremism—is strong.[91]

Researcher Safiya Aftab wrote for the Pak Institute for Peace Studies in 2008 that "poverty and a lack of job prospects may very well be strong contributing factors" behind militancy in the FATA, but "poverty is endemic across Pakistan, and employment prospects are at best highly variable."[92] Pakistani Interior Minister Rehman Malik has repeatedly told both Pakistani and international media that the Taliban pay handsome salaries to their fighters. "It is clear that the country's enemies and the hired killers of the Taliban want to continue their activities to keep their masters happy. In all these activities which we investigated, all roads lead to South Waziristan," Malik told reporters outside Parliament in October 2009.[93] South Waziristan is considered a safe haven for al-Qaeda, the Taliban, and foreign fighters, and significant militant commanders such as TTP chief Baitullah Mehsud have been killed there by drone strikes.

There are a total of seventeen health clinics[94] in Bajaur and one general hospital in the agency's administrative center of Khar—not nearly enough to meet the needs of Bajaur's million-plus residents. Similarly, the 615 schools in Bajaur, frequently targeted by suspected Taliban militants opposed to education, are not enough for the ninety thousand students in the agency.[95]

Abdul Qayum, a resident of Bai Cheena in Khar tehsil, said: "There are meager health facilities in Bajaur, but there is almost no concept of shifting women to dispensaries during delivery times, as our women cannot get good treatment at these dispensaries." According to Hanifullah, a resident of Nawakaly in Khar tehsil, "We have no objection to the army operation, but the government should provide us jobs, as military operations cannot fill our stomachs."[96]

There is also little infrastructure in Bajaur, such as paved roads. Ahmad Khan, a farmer in the Doda area of Nawagai tehsil, said, "We cannot ship our produce to market in time due to a lack of roads, so most of our crops rot, at a great loss for us. And we don't know our sin, for which the government has punished us for over sixty years."[97]

Additionally, local tribal elders are wary of both the Pakistani army and the Taliban, as neither has brought peace to Bajaur.[98] Malik Abdul Nasir of Salarzai tehsil commented, "We assist security forces to maintain peace and tranquility in our area, as the lashkar fighters and security forces have common foes." Another tribal elder, of the Tali area of Salarzai tehsil, said:

Our fighters and security forces do joint patrolling to clean the area of militants, as security forces are not well aware of the area's traditions. We help provide them secret information and also help them in open fighting against the militants. There is no question of leaving us alone at the needed hours, as we fight for a common cause—that is, to eliminate Taliban from Bajaur.[99]

As many as half a million Bajauris were displaced from the agency during the Pakistani military operations in the fall of 2008, causing great frustration among residents with both the state and the Taliban. Some of these displaced people have since returned home from shelters in the NWFP areas of Mardan, Swabi, and Peshawar, but many still live in Jalozai, Nowshera, and camps outside Peshawar, the provincial capital.[100] A resident of the Jalozai camp commented, "If there were no Taliban, there would be no army," expressing his rage at both while asserting that Pakistani helicopters caused unnecessary civilian casualties during the Bajaur operations.[101]

TRIBAL STRUCTURE OF BAJAUR

Tarkani and Utman Khel are the two major tribes in Bajaur. They are subdivided as shown below.[102]

Tarkani

- Salarzai
- Mamond (Salarzai, Kakazi)
- Chamarkand
- Charmang
- Nawagai
- Khar

Utman Khel

- Aseel
- Shamozai
- Mandal
- Lar-tras

- Bar-tras
- Arang
- Ali Zai

The Tarkanis, in whom the extremists have their roots, have about half a million members and live in five of the seven tehsils in Bajaur: Mamond, Chamarkand, Charmang, Salarzai, and Nawagai. Maulvi Faqir, former TTP spokesman Maulvi Omar, and the head of Bajaur's Taliban courts, Mufti Bashir, are all Tarkanis. He is commonly known as Bashir in the area and hails from Mamond. In the Utman Khel tribe, the important elders are Mian Masud Jan of the Chenagai area, Haji Qadir Khan of the Alizo area, Malik Naushad of the Batai area, and Haji Bismullah Khan of the Nawagai area. In general, the Taliban are unable to exercise control over these powerful tribal leaders, who have established anti-Taliban lashkars in their areas.[103]

Notes

1. The NWFP has been renamed Khyber-Pukhtunkhwa.
2. Bahaudin (local journalist), interview, Sept. 13, 2009, Peshawar.
3. Claudio Franco, "The Tehrik-e-Taliban Pakistan: The Bajaur Case," NEFA Foundation, July 2009, http://www.nefafoundation.org/miscellaneous/FeaturedDocs/nefa_ttp0709part1.pdf.
4. "The Guantanamo Docket: Abu Faraj al Libbi," *New York Times*, n.d., http://projects.nytimes.com/guantanamo/detainees/10017-abu-faraj-al-libbi; Ismail Khan, "'Zawahiri Was Not Here,'" *Dawn*, Jan. 15, 2006, http://www.dawn.com/2006/01/15/top3.htm.
5. Ishtiaq Ahmad, "The Valley of Death," *Pak Tribune*, Nov. 7, 2007, http://www.paktribune.com/news/print.php?id=193997.
6. Anwarullah (local journalist), interview, Feb. 22, 2010, Peshawar.
7. Ibid.
8. Haji Habibullah (local senior journalist), telephone interview, Mar. 19, 2010.
9. Mukhtar A. Khan, "A Profile of Militant Groups in Bajaur Tribal Agency," *Jamestown Terrorism Monitor*, Mar. 19, 2009, http://www.jamestown.org/single/?no_cache=1&tx_ttnews[tt_news]=34729&tx_ttnews[backPid]=7&cHash=a3e8ad5b5f.
10. The NWFP has recently been renamed Khyber-Pukhtunkhwa.
11. Khadim Hussein, interview, Feb. 25, 2010, Peshawar.
12. Sohail Abdul Nasir, "Al-Zawahiri's Pakistani Ally: Profile of Maulana Faqir Mohammed," *Jamestown Terrorism Monitor*, Feb. 9, 2006, http://www.jamestown.org/single/?no_cache=1&tx_ttnews%5Btt_news%5D=641.

13. Bahaudin (local journalist), interview, Sept. 13, 2009, Peshawar.

14. "Foreign Militants Target of Bajaur Operation: Hoti," *Daily Times*, Aug. 15, 2008, http://www.dailytimes.com.pk/default.asp?page=2008\08\15\story_15-8-2008_pg7_34.

15. Mehsud Khan, telephone interview, Feb. 24, 2010.

16. Imran Khan, telephone interview, Feb. 24, 2010.

17. CNN, "Translated Excerpts from the Taliban Code of Conduct," July 30, 2009, http://www.cnn.com/2009/WORLD/asiapcf/07/30/taliban.code.excerpt/index.html.

18. Interview with Rustam Shah Momand, political analyst and former ambassador of Pakistan to Kabul, Peshawar, Apr. 10, 2010.

19. Claudio Franco, "Part III of a Special NEFA Report: Militant Groups Active in the Bajaur Region," August 2009, http://www.nefafoundation.org/miscellaneous/FeaturedDocs/nefa_ttp0809part3.pdf.

20. Mukhtar Khan, op. cit.

21. "Maulvi Faqir Claims Taking Over TTP Leadership," *Dawn*, Aug. 20, 2009, http://www.dawn.com/wps/wcm/connect/dawn-content-library/dawn/the-newspaper/front-page/maulvi-faqir-claims-taking-over-ttp-leadership-089.

22. Haji Babibullah Khan (local senior journalist and analyst), interview, Mar. 18, 2010.

23. Christina Lamb, "Airstrike Misses Al-Qaeda Chief," *Sunday Times*, Jan. 15, 2006, http://www.timesonline.co.uk/tol/news/world/article788673.ece; Khan, op. cit.

24. Katherine Tiedemann, "A Guide to Recent Militant Arrests and Deaths in Afghanistan and Pakistan," AfPak Channel, *Foreign Policy*, Mar. 10, 2010, http://afpak.foreignpolicy.com/posts/2010/03/08/a_guide_to_recent_militant_arrests_and_deaths_in_afghanistan_and_pakistan.

25. "Maulvi Fakir Alive," BBC Urdu, Mar. 11, 2010, http://www.bbc.co.uk/urdu/pakistan/2010/03/100311_maulvi_fakir_alive_rh.shtml.

26. Hisbanullah (local journalist), telephone interview, Mar. 17, 2010.

27. "No Resistance: Maulvi Faqir and the Army in Bajaur," BBC Urdu, Feb. 10, 2010, http://www.bbc.co.uk/urdu/pakistan/2010/02/100210_bajaur_army_fakir.shtml.

28. Haji Babibullah Khan (local senior journalist and analyst), interview, Mar. 18, 2010.

29. Anwarullah (local journalist), interview, Feb. 22, 2010, Peshawar.

30. Mushtaq Yusufzai, interview, Mar. 16, 2010, Peshawar.

31. Amir Mir, "HUJI Chief Still at Large," *The News*, Sept. 23, 2008, http://www.thenews.com.pk/top_story_detail.asp?Id=17449.

32. Dr. Khadim Hussein, interview, Feb. 25, 2010, Peshawar.

33. Mushtaq Yusufzai, interview, Mar. 16, 2010, Peshawar.

34. Dr. Khadim Hussein, interview, Feb. 25, 2010, Peshawar.

35. Bahaudin (local journalist), interview, Sept. 13, 2009, Peshawar; Anwarullah (local journalist), interview, Feb. 22, 2010, Peshawar.

36. Interview with Tahir Khan, BBC correspondent in Islamabad, Apr. 9, 2010, Peshawar. Tahir Khan has closely observed functions of Hizb-i-Islami in Pakistan and Afghanistan.

37. Hisbanullah (local journalist), telephone interview, Mar. 17, 2010.
38. General Tariq Hayat, interview with GeoTV, Sept. 12, 2009.
39. "Narco Mafia in Afghan Govt Funding Militants: Ghani," *Daily Times*, Aug. 25, 2008, http://www.dailytimes.com.pk/default.asp?page=2008\08\25\story_25-8-2008_pg7_42.
40. "'TTP Spending Rs. 3.6 Billion on Its Fighters,'" *Dawn*, Feb. 6, 2010, http://www.dawn.com/wps/wcm/connect/dawn-content-library/dawn/news/pakistan/03-ttp-spending-rs3–6-billion-on-its-fighters-ss-06.
41. Dilawar Wazir, interview, Oct. 7, 2009, Peshawar.
42. Rahmanullah, "Fiery Radio Speeches Make Islamic Faithful Toe the Line," *San Francisco Chronicle*, July 3, 2007, http://www.sfgate.com/cgi-bin/article.cgi?f=/c/a/2007/07/03/MNGS8QPQ7R1.DTL&hw=rahmanullah&sn=001&sc=1000).
43. Mehsud Khan, telephone interview, Feb. 24, 2010.
44. Christina Lamb, op. cit.; Rahimullah Yusufzai, "80 Die in Air Attack on Bajaur Seminary," *News International*, Oct. 31, 2006, http://www.thenews.com.pk/top_story_detail.asp?Id=3945.
45. Ismail Khan, "Two Senior Al Qaeda Men Killed in Bajaur Raid," *Dawn*, Jan. 19, 2006, http://www.dawn.com/2006/01/19/top4.htm.
46. Anwarullah Khan, "Pakistan Army Kills up to 80 at Qaeda-linked School," Reuters AlertNet, Oct. 30, 2006, http://www.alertnet.org/thenews/newsdesk/ISL72506.htm; "Pakistan Madrassa Raid 'Kills 80,'" BBC News, Oct. 30, 2006, http://news.bbc.co.uk/2/hi/south_asia/6097636.stm; Rahimullah Yusufzai, op. cit.
47. Anwarullah Khan, op. cit.
48. Ibid.; Rahimullah Yusufzai, op. cit.
49. Ismail Khan, "Suicide Attack on Army Base: 40 Troops Dead; Search on for Bomber's Aide," *Dawn*, Nov. 9, 2006, http://www.dawn.com/2006/11/09/top1.htm.
50. Ismail Khan, op. cit.
51. Jane Perlez and Pir Zubair Shah, "Pakistani Taliban Repel Government Offensive," *New York Times*, Aug. 10, 2008, http://www.nytimes.com/2008/08/11/world/asia/11pstan.html?_r=1&ref=asia.
52. "Key Qaeda Figure Died in Bajaur Strike," *Daily Times*, May 25, 2008, http://www.dailytimes.com.pk/default.asp?page=2008\05\25\story_25-5-2008_pg7_1; Anwar Iqbal, "Drones Killed High-value Targets, US Tells Pakistan," *Dawn*, Feb. 9, 2009, http://www.dawn.com/2009/02/09/top4.htm; Josh Meyer and Sebastian Rotella, "U.S. Believes Strike in Pakistan Killed Key Terrorist," *Los Angeles Times*, May 24, 2008, http://articles.latimes.com/2008/may/24/world/fg-militant24.
53. Ivan Watson, Samson Desta, and Nasir Habib, "Helicopter Crash in Pakistan Kills 3," CNN, Oct. 25, 2009, http://edition.cnn.com/2009/WORLD/asiapcf/10/25/pakistan.helicopter.crash/; Kamran Haider, "Suspecte [*sic*] U.S. Drone Kills 10 in Pakistan's Bajaur," Reuters India, Oct. 24, 2009, http://in.reuters.com/article/worldNews/idINIndia-43405420091024; Hasbanullah Khan, "22 Killed as Drone Targets Taliban Shura Meeting in Bajaur," *Daily Times*, Oct. 25, 2009, http://www.dailytimes.com.pk/default.asp?page=2009\10\25\story_25-10-2009_pg1_3; "Death Toll Rises to 27 in Bajaur Drone Attack," *Nation*, Oct. 24, 2009, http://www.nation.com.pk/pakistan-news-newspaper-daily-english-online/Regional/

Islamabad/24-Oct-2009/Death-toll-rises-to-27-in-Bajaur-drone-attack; "Bajaur Agency Drone Strike Toll Rises to 33," *News International*, Oct. 26, 2009, http://www.thenews.com.pk/print1.asp?id=205112; Anwarullah Khan, "US Drone Strike Kills 24 in Bajaur," *Dawn*, Oct. 25, 2009, http://www.dawn.com/wps/wcm/connect/dawn-content-library/dawn/news/pakistan/04-suspected-us-drone-attack-in-bajaur-qs-09.

54. Irfanullah (local journalist), telephone interview, Oct. 17, 2009. Perlez and Zubair Shah, op. cit.; Ismail Khan and Carlotta Gall, "Battle of Bajaur: A Critical Test for Pakistan's Military," *New York Times*, Sept. 23, 2008, http://www.nytimes.com/2008/09/23/world/asia/23iht-23assess.16388481.html?pagewanted=print.

55. Pakistani Army official involved in operations in Bajaur, interview, Feb. 21, 2010, Peshawar.

56. Zahid Hussain, "8,000 Pakistani Soldiers Take on al-Qaeda in Volatile Tribal Region," *Times*, Sept. 27, 2008, http://www.timesonline.co.uk/tol/news/world/asia/article4834396.ece.

57. Sami Yusufzai, interview, Oct. 17, 2009.

58. Habibullah Khan, interview, Sept. 2008, Peshawar.

59. "Survivors Sought in Wake of Pakistan Hotel Blast," *USA Today*, Sept. 21, 2008, http://www.usatoday.com/news/world/2008-09-20-pakistan-blast_N.htm.

60. "FACTBOX—Questions About Blast at Pakistan's Marriott Hotel," Reuters UK, Sept. 23, 2008, http://uk.reuters.com/article/idUKTRE48M33420080923.

61. "Survivors Sought in Wake of Pakistan Hotel Blast."

62. "Editorial: Interpreting Zardari's US Visit," *Daily Times*, Sept. 25, 2008, http://www.dailytimes.com.pk/default.asp?page=2008/09/25/story_25-9-2008_pg3_1

63. Ibid.

64. Amir Mir, *The News*, Sept. 22, 2008; "Pakistani Taliban Confirm Death of Qari Zafar," *Dawn*, Mar. 2, 2010.

65. Stephen Graham and Nahal Toosi, "40 Dead in Pakistan Hotel Bombing," *Spartanburg Herald-Journal*, Sept. 21, 2008, http://news.google.com/newspapers?nid=1876&dat=20080921&id=nwgqAAAAIBAJ&sjid=vdAEAAAAIBAJ&pg=6802,1262003.

66. Ismail Khan and Carlotta Gall, "Battle of Bajaur: A Critical Test for Pakistan's Military," *New York Times*, Sept. 23, 2008, http://www.nytimes.com/2008/09/23/world/asia/23iht-23assess.16388481.html?pagewanted=print.

67. Brigadier Saad Mohammad (ret.), interview, Mar. 16, 2010, Peshawar.

68. Zahid Hussain, "8,000 Pakistani Soldiers Take on al-Qaeda in Volatile Tribal Region," *Times*, Sept. 27, 2008, http://www.timesonline.co.uk/tol/news/world/asia/article4834396.ece.

69. Farah Taj, interview with the BBC Pashto Service program "Staso Nary," September 2009.

70. *News International*, Oct. 26, 2009.

71. Jane Perlez and Pir Zubair Shah, "Pakistan Uses Tribal Militias in Taliban War," *New York Times*, Oct. 24, 2008, http://www.nytimes.com/2008/10/24/world/asia/24militia.html?pagewanted=print.

72. Ibid.

73. Malak Manasib of Salarzai tribe, interview, Mar. 18, 2010.

74. Farhat Taj, "The Taliban and Salarzais," *News International*, Sept. 27, 2009, http://
    thenews.jang.com.pk/daily_detail.asp?id=200309.

75. Fazal Rahim Marwat, professor at Area Study Center, University of Peshawar,
    interview, Oct. 17, 2009, Peshawar; Shafir Ullah Khan, political administrator of
    Bajaur, interview with the BBC, Mar. 9, 2009.

76. "Pakistan Taleban in Bajaur Truce," BBC News, Feb. 23, 2009, http://news.bbc.
    co.uk/2/hi/south_asia/7906592.stm?lss.

77. Anwarullah Khan, "Four-day Truce Sparks Jubilation in Bajaur," *Dawn*, Feb. 25,
    2009, http://www.dawn.com/2009/02/25/top2.htm.

78. Ismail Khan and Anwarullah Khan, "Bajaur Tribe Pledges to End Militancy,
    Respect Govt Writ," *Dawn*, Mar. 10, 2009, http://www.dawn.com/wps/
    wcm/connect/dawn-content-library/dawn/the-newspaper/front-page/
    bajaur-tribe-pledges-to-end-militancy,-respect-govt-writ.

79. Abdul Latif Afridi (lawyer and analyst), interview, Feb. 26, 2010, Peshawar.

80. Mushtaq Yusufzai, Shah Nawaz, and Shakirullah, "Taliban Spokesman Maulvi
    Omar Captured," *News International*, Aug. 19, 2009, http://www.thenews.com.pk/
    top_story_detail.asp?Id=23945.

81. Mohammad Saleem (local journalist), interview, Mar. 15, 2010, Peshawar.

82. Hisbanullah (local journalist) interview, Mar. 19, 2010, telephone; Anwarullah
    Khan, "Troops Wrest Damadola from Taliban," *Dawn*, Feb. 7, 2010, http://www.
    dawn.com/wps/wcm/connect/dawn-content-library/dawn/news/pakistan/03-
    security-forces-seize-control-of-damadola-ss-10.

83. Irfanullah (local journalist with Voice of America Deewa Radio), telephone
    interview, Mar. 2, 2010.

84. "38 Taliban Surrender in Bajaur," *Daily Times*, Mar. 17, 2010, http://www.
    dailytimes.com.pk/default.asp?page=2010\03\17\story_17-3-2010_pg7_11.

85. *Daily Times*, Mar. 3, 2010.

86. "Forces Regain Control of Bajaur," *News International*, Mar. 3, 2010, http://www.
    thenews.com.pk/top_story_detail.asp?Id=27582.

87. Bakhtawar Shah, interview, Mar. 20, 2010.

88. Akhtar Munir, interview, Mar. 20, 2010; Sanaullah Khan, interview, Mar. 20,
    2010.

89. Malak Manasib of Salarzai tribe, interview, Mar. 18, 2010.

90. Safiya Aftab, "Poverty and Militancy," *Pips Journal of Conflict and Peace Studies*,
    October–December 2008, http://docs.google.com/viewer?a=v&q=cache:7Dt238
    daMLwJ:san-pips.com/download.php%3Ff%3D20.pdf+Safiya+Aftab,+Poverty+a
    nd+Militancy.&hl=en&gl=us&pid=bl&srcid=ADGEEShRaTQM6SpZpm3Gs99
    bjbVTFjRR8Tnev__g7tHsvotF_
    7tDdK9823hGqV1yOZaQ1VONpZgtEyyokvGU8tmyM72udFgBgraU
    UXSroovVtXFF9gBk9bWZ7u1DSYELVJSqsgupy6RE&sig=AHIEtb
    TOrf7oN3aiBwOxIoRGbAFVfRzk7A.

91. Naveed Ahmad Shinwari, "Understanding FATA," http://www.understandingfata.
    org/u-f-v-1/Acknowledgement.pdf.

92. Safiya Aftab, op. cit.

93. "50 Killed in Bomb Blast in Peshawar," *Deccan Herald*, Oct. 9, 2009.

94. Dr. Jehanzeb, agency surgeon at Khar (Bajaur), telephone interview, Sept. 4,
    2009.

95. Haji Gul Rahman, agency education officer (AEO) at Khar, telephone interview, Apr. 1, 2010.
96. Residents of Bajaur, telephone interview, Oct. 8, 2009.
97. Ahmad Khan, telephone interview, Oct. 8, 2009.
98. Yusuf Ali (local journalist in Peshawar who has done thorough reporting on Bajaur), telephone interview, Feb. 28, 2010.
99. Tribal elders, interview, Oct. 13, 2009, Bajaur.
100. Mushtaq Yusufzai, interview, Mar. 16, 2010, Peshawar.
101. Gul Jan, interview, Mar. 21, 2010, Jalozai camp.
102. "Historical and Administrative Profile of the Bajaur Agency," http://www.fata.gov.pk/subpages/bajaur.php.
103. Hisbanullah (local journalist), telephone interview, Mar. 17, 2010.

THIRTEEN

The Taliban in Pakistan: An Overview

Brian Fishman

THE UNIVERSE OF militants in Pakistan's Federally Administered Tribal Areas (FATA) and Khyber-Pukhtunkhwa (KPP) is far more diverse than commonly understood. Although there are important ideological and historical commonalities among the fighters, militant groups have very different backgrounds, tribal affiliations, and strategic concepts. The oft-used terminology dividing "Afghan" Taliban from "Pakistani" Taliban is inadequate for describing this complex milieu. A more effective analysis requires understanding the unique histories of specific militant groups, their social roots, and strategic outlook.

There are, of course, commonalities among militants in the FATA. In many areas, the Pakistani government's shortsighted peace deals with militants bolstered fighters, while the government's July 2007 military operation against the Lal Masjid (Red Mosque) in Islamabad was a critical catalyst for militancy across the region. FATA-based militants operate widely in Afghanistan, most prominently in the east, and work through groups that control the local area, most notably the Haqqani Network. The southern Afghanistan heartland of Mullah Omar's

Quetta Shura is hundreds of miles from the FATA and is thus rarely a battlefield for FATA-based militants. Taliban across the FATA have garnered support by promising to replace the Pakistani governance and judicial system, which is widely viewed as corrupt and unjust.

Divisions between Taliban groups are important as well. Some militants, inspired by the Lal Masjid incident, have brutally attacked the Pakistani government, and in doing so they have abandoned the traditional Haqqani and Quetta Shura strategy of conciliation with the Pakistani state while conducting military operations inside Afghanistan. Many of the anti-Pakistan militants organize under a broad umbrella called the Tehrik-i-Taliban Pakistan (TTP), though local leadership commands day-to-day operations. al-Qaeda and other foreign militants support the TTP's agenda, and al-Qaeda in particular used its propaganda arm to support the anti-Pakistan cause in the wake of the Lal Masjid incident. But not all militants in the FATA support the TTP's anti-Pakistan agenda, and anti-Pakistan violence has ebbed since 2010. Some militants even collaborate with the Pakistani state against other fighters while continuing to fight U.S. and NATO forces in Afghanistan. Other militant networks are essentially criminals in Islamist garb. al-Qaeda has been substantially degraded in Pakistan, notably by American drone strikes and the U.S. raid on Osama bin Laden's hideout in Abbottabad.

This chapter suggests that observers can improve their understanding of militant groups in the FATA by asking six questions: (1) Does the militant group attack government and civilian targets in Pakistan? (2) What are the militant group's tribal and social roots? (3) What are the militant group's relationships with foreign (not Afghan) militants? (4) How aggressively does the militant group target U.S. and NATO forces in Afghanistan? (5) Does the militant group engage in or support attacks on nonmilitary Western targets? (6) Does the militant group take strategic or operational direction from Mullah Omar?

The answers to these questions cannot on their own determine which groups pose the greatest threat to U.S. or South Asian interests, but they provide a substantially more accurate framework than the analytically fragile "Afghan Taliban" and "Pakistani Taliban" terminology. A more useful lexicon should identify between militants affiliated with specific groups, Mullah Omar's Quetta Shura, the Haqqani Network, and the Tehrik-i-Taliban Pakistan.

The chapter has five sections. The first addresses the crosscutting background issues that shape militancy in the region. The second analyzes the importance of Mullah Omar, the TTP, al-Qaeda, and drone strikes in the FATA. The third addresses the idioms and concepts used to understand the militant actors in the FATA. The fourth summarizes militancy in each FATA agency and Swat. The fifth is a brief conclusion.

***

CROSSCUTTING ISSUES FOR FATA'S MILITANTS

Geography and War

Militants in the FATA come from a patchwork of tribes and political backgrounds, but they almost universally oppose the U.S. and NATO presence in Afghanistan and work with Afghan militants against the foreign troops.[1] Operationally, the FATA militants rely on older militant networks with extensive infrastructure in Afghanistan. South Waziristan-based Mullah Nazir has explained that FATA-based militants fight under the leadership of local commanders when they are in Afghanistan.[2]

There are three basic geographic zones of violence straddling the Afghanistan-Pakistan border.[3] South of the FATA, Mullah Omar's Quetta Shura directs militants centered in Afghanistan's Helmand and Kandahar provinces, which are across the border from the Pakistani province of Baluchistan. Farther north, the Haqqani-directed Miram Shah Shura manages the insurrection in Afghanistan's Paktika, Paktiya, and Khost provinces (known collectively as Loya Paktiya) from Pakistan's South Waziristan and North Waziristan, home of the FATA's most powerful militant groups.[4] In the FATA's north, a messy collection of militants, including Gulbuddin Hekmatyar's Hizb-e-Islami, operates in Nangarhar and Kunar provinces, which are supported from bases in the FATA's Mohmand and Bajaur agencies.

Geography, terrain, and proximity influence militant coalitions and the operational cooperation they can foster. The Taliban strongholds in Kandahar and Helmand provinces of Afghanistan, which are generally controlled by Mullah Omar's Quetta Shura, are hundreds of miles from the FATA. The FATA adjoins Loya Paktiya, Logar, Nangarhar, and Kunar provinces of Afghanistan, and so such regions are where the FATA-based militants—including al-Qaeda—are most active.[5] Location has empowered the Haqqani Network militarily and politically because of the proximity between its bases in North Waziristan, where it shares ground with a wide variety of other militants, and its operating areas in Loya Paktiya. This geography affects al-Qaeda as well, since its leadership is in the FATA rubbing elbows with the Haqqanis, rather than Mullah Omar and the Quetta Shura, who are based farther south.

The Fall of the Taliban Government in Kabul

The FATA was an important source of support for the Taliban in Afghanistan before the attacks of September 11, 2001, but it became a critical base after the fall of the Taliban government in November 2001. The southern FATA (North and South Waziristan, Kurram) saw a slew of foreign militants, including Taliban fighters from the displaced Afghan government, Arab al-Qaeda members, and Central Asian fighters, cross the border from Afghanistan seeking shelter from the U.S. bombardment. One reason so many fighters crossed into the southern FATA is that Taliban and foreign fighters in Afghanistan coalesced in Kandahar before Mullah Omar gave the order to retreat across the Pakistani border to prepare for guerrilla war.[6] Although the influx must have been a burden for many tribes, they followed the ancient *Pashtunwali* code and embraced the refugees.

The northern FATA witnessed an influx of fighters from Afghanistan as well, but not in the same numbers. There, an existing militant network linked to the Tehrik-i-Nifaz-i-Shariat-i Mohammadi (TNSM) was dominant. Sufi Muhammad, the *amir* or leader of the TNSM movement, led a hastily recruited would-be army into Afghanistan after the U.S. invasion, where it was promptly destroyed on the battlefield.[7]

The continued presence of U.S. and NATO forces in Afghanistan is a grievance for militants across the FATA. For many, the occupation of a Muslim country by non-Muslim troops is fundamentally unjust and demands violent resistance, much as it did when the Soviet Union occupied Afghanistan in the 1980s.

North-West Frontier Province

Since Pakistan's independence in 1947, violence, religio-political activism, and tribal autonomy have been features of its political landscape. Moreover, the scope of political activity considered "legitimate" is much wider in the frontier regions of Pakistan than in the West. Violent activism and imprisonment do not necessarily delegitimize political leaders.[8] Judicial process is often subservient to political expediency, which means the line between political activism and illegitimate militancy often blurs.

The influx of militants from Afghanistan following the Taliban government's demise emboldened tribal and religious groups in Pakistan already chafing at Pakistan's often-dysfunctional democracy and corruption-riddled governance structures in the FATA and NWFP.[9] Indeed, some of the FATA and NWFP militants are disillusioned members of mainstream Pakistani religio-political parties, the Jamaat-e-Islami (JI) and Jamiat Ulema-e-Islam-Fazul (JUI).[10] A coalition led by JI and JUI called Muttahida Majlis-e-Amal (MMA) dramatically won NWFP provincial elections in 2002 and subsequently failed to aggressively challenge growing militancy in either the NWFP or the FATA.[11]

In the NWFP, the MMA tried to balance its sympathy toward some of the social positions espoused by militants with an institutional commitment to democratic process.[12] But MMA rule proved just as inefficient and corrupt as that of previous governments and it was swept out of power in 2008, replaced by a secular coalition between the Pakistan People's Party and the Pashtun-nationalist Awami National Party (ANP).[13] The change did not immediately strengthen counterterrorism efforts in Pakistan. After taking office in March 2008, the ANP submitted to some militant demands, including the imposition of a form of Islamic law, or *sharia*.[14] The ANP has taken a stiffer line against militants since early 2009, largely in conjunction with successful Pakistani military operations in Swat and Buner districts of the NWFP.[15]

Although militant groups in the FATA and NWFP tend to traverse administrative boundaries, Pakistani responses to that militancy are affected by the differences between administrative and political structures in the FATA and NWFP. The NWFP operates like other provinces in Pakistan and is governed by a provincial assembly based in

Peshawar.[16] The NWFP is divided into twenty-four districts, each of which is governed by a district coordination officer. Pakistani political parties participate fully in NWFP politics, running public campaigns and vying for control of a government that imposes taxes and provides regular services.

Federally Administered Tribal Areas

The Federally Administered Tribal Areas are administered very differently. The seven agencies in the FATA are each governed by a political agent who reports to the NWFP governor, who is appointed directly by Pakistan's president.[17] The political agents have few bureaucratic tools; they exert authority by coordinating with tribal leaders, known as maliks, who use tribal resources to maintain law and order and provide services. Although there are representatives from the FATA in Pakistan's parliament, nonreligious political parties were historically banned from organizing.[18] A package of reforms to allow nonreligious political parties to fully participate in elections and alter the Frontier Crimes Regulation, which allows collective punishment, was finally signed in August 2011.[19]

Before the arrival of the Taliban in 2001, Pakistan's political agents in the FATA often treated their respective agencies as personal fiefdoms, doling out money and resources to the wealthy and well-connected. The government was perceived as corrupt, tribal judicial processes as unfair and too slow. The Taliban's strict interpretation of sharia did not appeal to everyone in the tribal agencies, but its promises of fairness and swift dispute resolution appealed to many. Unlike Pakistani civil institutions, Taliban courts delivered justice quickly and could implement punishments immediately. The process was initially successful; Taliban courts resolved disputes between tribes and clans that had dragged on for decades. The Taliban even limited corruption among some political agents. Its efforts were initially rewarded with broad-based political support from everyday people in the FATA.[20]

But popular support for the Taliban has waned since they organized in the FATA after the U.S. and NATO invasion of Afghanistan. After taking control in various areas, Taliban groups began brutal crackdowns on behavior considered "un-Islamic," while simultaneously enlisting criminals into their ranks. Employment opportunities were limited because of violence between the Taliban and Pakistani security forces, a problem that curtailed trade along traditional routes. Even in periods of relative calm, roads were often closed because of government curfews.

Taliban governance proved to be brutal, especially in the way it challenged traditional tribal structures. Taliban militants have systematically undermined the tribal system, which serves as a social organizing principle and the primary system of governance in the FATA. The most overt method has been to kill the tribal elders who serve as interlocutors between the political agent and locals.[21] The assassinations served the dual purpose of intimidating local tribes and eliminating the tenuous links between Pakistan's central government and tribes in the FATA. Such killings have angered locals, but the elimination of maliks has destroyed the most likely nodes of resistance to Taliban control.[22] Nonetheless, tribal opposition to Taliban rule has grown across much of the FATA. Uprisings by tribal militias (*lashkars*) are common, though tribes are still loath to take on the Taliban without assured support from the Pakistani government.[23]

FRIENDS, ALLIES, AND ENEMIES: MULLAH OMAR, THE TTP, AL-QAEDA, AMERICAN DRONES, AND THE PAKISTANI ARMY

Friends But Not Allies: Mullah Omar and the Tehrik-i-Taliban Pakistan

Mullah Omar's role among FATA militants is ambiguous. He is widely acknowledged as the *Amir ul-Mumineen* (Commander of the Faithful) by militants in the FATA, a powerful honorific that reflects authority worthy of a leader who commanded the Taliban state in Afghanistan, but the extent of his actual control over militant fighters operating in the FATA is limited. The Haqqani Network, al-Qaeda, and many members of the TTP publicly defer to his leadership; Ayman al-Zawahiri's first public statement as the amir of al-Qaeda made sure to swear allegiance to Mullah Omar. But the Quetta Shura seems to have the most direct influence in its traditional bastions in southern Afghanistan, not in Afghanistan's east or in the FATA; this was the case even during Mullah Omar's reign in Kabul.[24] Despite these limitations Mullah Omar has reportedly intervened in FATA tribal politics to bolster leaders he favored, including the now-dead Baitullah Mehsud and Mullah Nazir in South Waziristan.[25]

Most militant groups in the FATA organized independently, but in December 2007 many rallied together in a coalition called the Tehrik-i-Taliban Pakistan (TTP). The alliance was formed to unite militants to attack the Pakistani state, not just U.S. and NATO forces in Afghanistan. The group attracted support from militants across the FATA and Malakand division of the NWFP by arguing that Pakistan's support for the U.S. and NATO effort in Afghanistan made the government illegitimate. Momentum for the TTP was bolstered by the Lal Masjid (Red Mosque) incident in July 2007, in which Pakistani security forces raided an Islamabad mosque known as a center for religious militancy. The incident excited militants in the FATA, NWFP, and Punjab, who viewed the Lal Masjid and its two leaders, Abdul Aziz Ghazi and Abdul Rashid Ghazi, as righteous defenders of the faith. Militant groups with very different histories began to discover that they had a lot in common.

The TTP was organized around a forty-person council, or *shura*, with representatives from all seven tribal agencies of the FATA and several districts of the NWFP.[26] Baitullah Mehsud, a militant leader from South Waziristan, was named amir, Hafiz Gul Bahadur, from North Waziristan, was named his deputy, and Maulvi Faqir Muhammad from Bajaur was appointed third in command.[27] Despite limited command-and-control infrastructure, the TTP united militants dedicated to the risky strategy of attacking the Pakistani state. The coalition created some strange bedfellows, including a slew of Punjabi fighters who work with Pashtun allies to strike at targets in Pakistan's major cities.[28]

But the TTP's early military successes papered over disagreements between groups within the militant coalition. Hafiz Gul Bahadur backed out of the alliance in early 2008 and began a collaboration with Mullah Nazir in opposition to the Mehsud tribe, and by default the TTP. According to some reports, Mullah Omar and Haqqani Network leaders prodded Bahadur to leave the TTP because of its anti-Pakistan stance.[29] The TTP weakened further when its first amir, Baitullah Mehsud, was killed by an American drone strike in mid-2009, which brought Hakimullah Mehsud into power as head of the TTP.[30]

Outside of South Waziristan, the TTP has been most influential in North Waziristan and Orakzai, which suffered serious sectarian violence long before 9/11. Following the example of al-Qaeda and keen to build relations with sectarian militants in Pakistan's heartland, the TTP incorporated anti-Shia arguments into its core ideology. Hakimullah

Mehsud initially led TTP operations in Orakzai, perhaps because of his deep disdain for Shia; the agency has a major Shia population and thus the fight attracted sectarian activists from across Pakistan.[31] In general, the writ of the TTP is firmer in the southern FATA, closer to the South Waziristan homeland of the Mehsud tribe that generated the coalition's first two amirs.

The TTP's anti-Pakistan operations conflict with Quetta Shura and Haqqani Network efforts to accommodate the Pakistani state while organizing attacks inside Afghanistan. Whereas the Haqqanis and the Quetta Shura remain dedicated to war in Afghanistan and comity with Pakistan—a perspective generally consistent with Pakistan's historic national security strategy—the TTP, along with al-Qaeda, rejects the fundamental legitimacy of the Pakistani state. In general, however, the TTP's insurrection against the Pakistani state has waned since the death of Baitullah Mehsud. Aggressive Pakistani military actions, the defection of constituent groups, and stepped-up U.S. drone strikes against TTP officers seem to have weakened the TTP overall.

Some analysts doubt claims of disagreement between Mullah Omar and the TTP, noting the networks' cooperation in Afghanistan and interpersonal connections among leaders.[32] No doubt such relationships exist, and there is a shared sense of grievance and purpose between the TTP and Quetta Shura. But operational cooperation should not obscure the serious strategic differences between Mullah Omar's Quetta Shura—which has actively and tacitly cooperated with the Pakistani state since the mid-1990s—and the TTP, which considers the Pakistani state fundamentally illegitimate. Indeed, Mullah Omar's statements emphasize his nationalist agenda in Afghanistan, likely in an effort to reassure Pakistani authorities. In a September 2009 Eid al-Fitr statement, he said the Taliban "wants to maintain good and positive relations with all neighbors based on mutual respect...[and wants to] assure all countries that the Islamic Emirate of Afghanistan...will not extend its hand to jeopardize others."[33]

The Influence of al-Qaeda

al-Qaeda continues to operate in the FATA, though it is much diminished and is likely to be less influential after the death of Osama bin Laden. al-Qaeda uses the region, especially North Waziristan, to train operatives for attacks in the West and to propagandize. But it has also built an important niche in the Pakistani militant milieu, providing training and ideological justification for its allies' activities in the region.

al-Qaeda's presence in Pakistan's tribal areas is visible in several ways. First, there are numerous reports of Westerners traveling to the region for training, then telling their stories upon capture when they return home.[34] Indeed, more than half of the "serious" *jihadist* plots in the West since 2004 were directed from Pakistan, and al-Qaeda had direct operational ties to 38 percent of the overall number.[35] Many of al-Qaeda's most senior commanders are believed to be in the tribal regions, though bin Laden's presence in Abbottabad, in a major city of the NWFP, suggests they may be more widely dispersed. Most important among living commanders today are Ayman al-Zawahiri, Abu Yahya al-Libi, and Adnan Shukrijumah.[36] Despite increasingly effective drone strikes that have disrupted al-Qaeda operations in the region, the group has adapted and still has the capability to organize threats to the West.[37]

al-Qaeda's propaganda provides important evidence of its presence in and focus on the FATA. In 2009, 46 percent of the group's propaganda videos focused on events in Afghanistan or Pakistan rather than al-Qaeda's historical heartland in the Arab Middle East.[38] Much of al-Qaeda's infrastructure in the FATA appears to be concentrated in North Waziristan. A review of al-Qaeda's battle footage from the region released online from 2005 to 2009 suggests that the group is most active in Loya Paktiya (the Afghan provinces of Paktika, Khost, and Paktiya), just across the border from North Waziristan.[39] Loya Paktiya and North Waziristan are controlled by the Haqqani Network, which is headed by Jalaluddin Haqqani, a legendary mujahideen commander and old ally of Osama bin Laden from the 1980s, and his son Sirajuddin, who directs day-to-day operations.[40]

al-Qaeda does contribute directly to the militant groups operating from the FATA. It has provided suicide bombers for the Haqqani Network and helped arrange special operations against U.S. targets, including the Jordanian suicide bomber who killed seven Americans at a CIA base in Afghanistan's Khost province in December 2009.[41]

But al-Qaeda's most important role in the tribal areas since 2007 has been to provide ideological support for groups that have decided

to confront the Pakistani state militarily. After the Lal Masjid incident in July 2007, al-Qaeda ramped up condemnations of the Pakistani
state in its media and has not relented since. Just four days after the
mosque was raided by Pakistani troops, Ayman al-Zawahiri released
a statement condemning the action and urging the Pakistani people
to attack their government.[42] In a brief three-month period from July
to September 2007, Osama bin Laden, Ayman al-Zawahiri, and Abu
Yahya al-Libi all released major statements urging violence against
the Pakistani state.[43] al-Qaeda's focus on Pakistan has continued since;
27 percent of al-Qaeda's geographically focused propaganda releases
in 2009 focused on Pakistan.[44]

al-Qaeda initially championed the argument that Pakistan's army
is essentially a foreign infidel force because of the Pakistani government's collaboration with U.S. and NATO forces in Afghanistan.
Accordingly, resisting the army's incursions into the FATA is portrayed
as an obligatory "Defensive Jihad," an argument now echoed by TTP
propaganda.[45,46] al-Qaeda's support for the TTP's anti-Pakistan stance
has created rhetorical tension between it and Mullah Omar's Quetta
Shura, which opposes attacks on Pakistan.[47]

In the years since the Lal Masjid incident, al-Qaeda's denunciation
of Pakistan has grown more dangerous, and it now aims to delegitimize
the Pakistani state at its most fundamental level by rejecting the prem-
ise, accepted widely among pro-Pakistan militants, that Pakistan was
founded as an Islamic state.[48] In December 2009, Ayman al-Zawahiri
wrote a long critique of the Pakistani constitution in which he argued
that it was fundamentally un-Islamic:

> Shari'ah is not the supreme authority in Pakistan, rather the
> supreme authority is the will of the majority in the Parliament,
> which they claim...reflects the will and power of the people.
> Whether their claims are right or false, what is certain is that
> the authority in Pakistan does not belong to the Shari'ah law, the
> Koran or the righteous Sunnah. It rather belongs to other pow-
> ers that detour Pakistan from the Path of Islam, and manipulate
> its destiny according to their whims.[49]

Al-Zawahiri's argument is important because al-Qaeda is advocating attacks on Pakistan whether or not it supports the U.S. and NATO
presence in Afghanistan. The argument may be remembered as a

strategic mistake by al-Qaeda because it leaves Pakistan little option but to crack down harshly on al-Qaeda allies in the FATA—offensives that took place in the years following the Lal Masjid incident. Islamist sympathizers in the Pakistani bureaucracy can no longer credibly argue that militant attacks in Pakistan will cease if the United States withdraws from Afghanistan.

Although al-Qaeda has stepped into contentious disputes in the FATA, it has been much more successful than its Uzbek allies at avoiding deadly intra-Taliban conflict. Uzbeks from the Islamic Movement of Uzbekistan (IMU) and Islamic Jihad Union (IJU) have angered tribal leaders by running their own court systems and taking sides in tribal disputes.[50] al-Qaeda has avoided such activities, preferring instead to support efforts by local militant groups rather than establish its own governance systems.[51] This strategy is very different from al-Qaeda's efforts in Iraq, where it tried to seize and govern territory, irrespective of local tribal and militant concerns.[52] A number of al-Qaeda members have also married into local tribes in the FATA.[53] al-Qaeda's FATA strategy is far less likely to prompt a backlash from local militants and means that the group's position in the FATA is stabler than it ever was in Iraq.[54]

Pakistani Military Offensives and Peace Deals

Pakistani military offensives against militants in the FATA have sometimes been halfhearted, and militants have been bolstered by peace agreements made in the wake of conflict. Pakistan's track record of offensives in South Waziristan is illustrative of its overall approach.[55]

The first major Pakistani offensive was a 2004 campaign against Nek Muhammad in South Waziristan. After several weeks of staunch resistance from Wazir tribal fighters, Pakistan signed the Shakai agreement, in which Pakistan agreed to compensate Muhammad for his material and personnel losses and in exchange Muhammad promised to register foreigners in the area and cease his violence. Nek Muhammad did neither; the agreement bolstered his standing in South Waziristan and set a low standard for Pakistan's future negotiations with militants.[56]

Later Pakistani offensives did not go much better. In 2006, the Pakistani army made a similar agreement with Baitullah Mehsud after suffering serious casualties trying to root out foreign militants from

Mehsud territory. This agreement, reportedly brokered by Sirajuddin Haqqani, also conferred legitimacy on Baitullah's control over much of South Waziristan.[57] A 2008 offensive ended much the same way. Pakistan launched similarly feeble offensives across the FATA during those years.

But Pakistani military operations since 2009 have been more effective. In February 2009, Maulvi Faqir Muhammad, the TTP leader in Bajaur, renounced attacks on the Pakistani army after almost a year of military operations against him. Later that spring the Pakistani military launched operations against the TNSM in Swat, which largely ended the reign of terror of the militants there. Then, after having suffered three defeats in South Waziristan over the preceding five years, in October 2009 the Pakistani army went into Waziristan with a force of at least thirty thousand troops, following several months of bombing of Taliban positions.[58] The South Waziristan operation was relatively successful, though it was focused on fighters associated with the TTP rather than militants who adopted the Haqqani and Quetta Shura strategy of accommodation with the Pakistani state.

Effects of Drone Attacks

The United States has used unmanned drones to target militant groups in the FATA since 2004. The attacks have killed numerous militant leaders and severely disrupted movement and communications among fighters in the tribal areas.[59] Pakistani leaders often publicly condemn the attacks, but there is evidence suggesting coordination between the United States and Pakistan regarding them: after twenty-six U.S. drone strikes in South Waziristan in 2009, the attacks stopped cold after the October 2009 initiation of Pakistan's ground operations in the agency.

Drone strikes killed between 1,778 and 2,764 people in Pakistan from 2004 until March 13, 2012, approximately two-thirds of whom were "described as militants" in "reliable press reports."[60] The attacks increased dramatically after President Barack Obama entered the White House. There were 43 strikes from 2004 to 2008, and 241 from 2009 to the end of 2011.[61] The vast majority have occurred in either North Waziristan or South Waziristan, home to the most virulently pro-al-Qaeda militants in the FATA and the Haqqani Network.[62]

The drone strikes have killed important militants in the FATA, including Baitullah Mehsud (amir of the TTP) and numerous al-Qaeda figures, ranging from Abu Laith al-Libi to Saleh al-Somali.[63] Moreover, the threat from drones has forced militants to alter their operations. David Rohde, the *New York Times* reporter held captive by the Haqqani Network in North Waziristan in 2009, has described the fear that the overhead buzz of a drone—locals call them *machay* (wasps) because of the noise—reveals in the militants.[64] Fighters regularly change their location, and senior figures rarely spend multiple nights in the same place.[65] Taliban fighters avoid using phones and wireless for passing messages; they now exchange information only through trusted couriers.

But the drones have serious political costs as well. Numerous TTP spokesmen and both Hafiz Gul Bahadur of North Waziristan and Mullah Nazir of South Waziristan have cited the drones as the reason for their bouts of violence against the Pakistani state.[66] And Faisal Shahzad, who attempted to detonate an improvised explosive device in New York's Times Square, referenced the drone strikes as a key grievance.[67] Indeed, the drones are extraordinarily unpopular in Pakistan as a whole. A 2009 al-Jazeera-Gallup poll found that 64 percent of Pakistanis oppose U.S. drone strikes in the FATA.[68] There is little reliable information on public opinion regarding drones in the FATA itself, but it is notable that only 12.5 percent of respondents in a 2009 poll in the FATA had a positive image of the U.S. government.[69]

Strategic Mistakes?

By 2009 there were signs that the Taliban in the FATA may have made a critical mistake by attacking Pakistani government and civilian targets. Militant attacks on Pakistan increased nearly 800 percent from 2005 to 2009, and suicide attacks increased *twentyfold*.[70] Suicide bombers managed, for instance, to strike in three places in Pakistan in just one twenty-four-hour period in April 2009.[71] The cumulative weight of the assassination of Benazir Bhutto, the bombing of the Marriott Hotel in Islamabad in 2008, the widely circulated video images of the Taliban flogging a seventeen-year-old girl, and the twenty-hour Taliban attack in October 2009 on Pakistan's equivalent of the Pentagon provoked revulsion and fear among the Pakistani public.[72] Where once the Taliban enjoyed something of a religious Robin Hood image among ordinary Pakistanis, its members were increasingly seen as just thugs.

The Taliban's decision to take up positions in Buner district of the NWFP, only sixty miles from Islamabad, galvanized the sclerotic Pakistani state to confront the jihadist monster it had helped to create. When the Taliban fighters were largely confined to Pakistan's tribal regions (known in Urdu as "foreign area"[73]), the Pakistani government and military could more or less live with them, but when they attacked in major cities, the Pakistani establishment began to see the Taliban as a real threat. Pakistani military offensives against militants in 2009 were conducted with the support of the Pakistani public, which did not see them, in contrast to previous military operations, as being done solely for the benefit of the United States.[74]

The Pakistani government's changing perception helps explain Mullah Omar's repeated efforts to reassert his Afghan national-ist focus and distinguish himself from anti-Pakistan elements of the Taliban movement. Ultimately, however, the TTP's repeated attacks on Pakistani military infrastructure and civilians have all the hallmarks of a classic jihadist overreach. Just as jihadists in Algeria and Iraq ulti-mately provoked a backlash from superior local forces, the TTP may have done the same by attacking the Pakistani state.

Two questions stand out regarding the Pakistani counterattack against Taliban militants. The first is whether the Pakistani army will suppress all Taliban militants, even those who focus attacks solely in Afghanistan rather than Pakistan. The second is whether the military offensive will be backed by sustainable political and economic reforms that will improve governance in the FATA and bring about a stabler peace. The Pakistani government's traditional balancing strategy— attacking anti-Pakistan militants but allowing others to operate—is inadequate because they all host al-Qaeda, which has proven again and again that it is able to radicalize its hosts.[75] The TTP overreach was a strategic mistake, but the Pakistani establishment will make one of its own if it does not use the current momentum to radically change the governance dynamics in the FATA. The government's support for political organizing in the FATA is a positive development, but imple-mentation remains a question mark.

CONCEPTUALIZING MILITANCY IN PAKISTAN: LANGUAGE, IDEAS, AND GEOGRAPHY

Unhelpful Idioms: "Pakistani Taliban" and "Afghan Taliban"

The border between Afghanistan and Pakistan means more in Washington, Islamabad, and Kabul than in Miram Shah, Khost, or the Tirah Valley. Tribes straddle the border seamlessly, and trading relationships that have existed for millennia shape local cultural and political sensibilities more so than the vagaries of internationally accepted maps. This is one main reason that distinguishing between "Afghan Taliban" and "Pakistani Taliban" is misleading, even if it is useful shorthand. The leaders of the former Taliban government of Afghanistan are now called the Quetta Shura after the *Pakistani* city where they are based, and Mullah Omar's deputy, Mullah Baradar, was captured in the *Pakistani* city of Karachi, 350 miles from the Afghan border.[76] Likewise, the Haqqani Network, often considered "Afghan Taliban" because of its tribal roots and operational capacity in Afghanistan, has deep roots in Pakistani territory. The network's current operational leader, Sirajuddin Haqqani, was raised outside of Miram Shah in Pakistan's North Waziristan tribal agency and studied at a *madrassa*, or religious school, outside Peshawar. His father, Jalaluddin, had decided at a meeting in Miram Shah in 1978 to fight the Soviet-backed communist government in Afghanistan.[77] More recently, Sirajuddin has intervened in Pakistani tribal squabbles to prevent militants from being distracted from the fight in Afghanistan.[78]

The third group often called "Afghan Taliban" is Gulbuddin Hekmatyar's Hizb-i-Islami (HIG).[79] The HIG remains an important player in stoking cross-border violence in Afghanistan and Pakistan, but lumping it into the same category as the Quetta Shura and Haqqani Network is misleading. Hekmatyar was exiled from Afghanistan during the Taliban's reign in Kabul, and despite long ties to al-Qaeda and reconciliation with Mullah Omar since September 11, he now seems more focused on political reconciliation than violence.[80] The HIG does not have a major presence in the FATA, though it has extensive bases in Afghan refugee camps in the NWFP outside of Peshawar.[81]

In an environment where all of the major Taliban groups are headquartered in Pakistan and virtually all of them cooperate to support operations in Afghanistan, the distinction between "Afghan Taliban" and "Pakistani Taliban" is unhelpful. Moreover, the terminology reinforces the counterproductive fiction perpetrated by some in Pakistan that the Pakistani state is responsible for countering only certain elements of the Taliban—those with the "Pakistani" designation. In practice, the term "Pakistani Taliban" is often used interchangeably with Tehrik-i-Taliban Pakistan (TTP), the pan-FATA militant coalition that engages in brutal violence against the Pakistani state. The terminology usefully distinguishes such anti-Pakistan fighters from the Quetta Shura and Haqqani Network—"Afghan Taliban"—that avoid confrontation with Pakistan. But delineating this strategic difference in geographic terms enables those in the Pakistani establishment who support using militants against Pakistan's enemies to excuse their behavior by arguing that they are fighting against the "Pakistani Taliban" and that the "Afghan Taliban" are someone else's problem. When critical policy decisions are being made in Washington and Islamabad, the terminology favors those who do not want to take comprehensive action against militants in the FATA.

Throughout its existence, the TTP has also supported violence in Afghanistan and provided suicide bombers to bolster Haqqani Network and Quetta Shura operations there. Likewise, there are a host of FATA-based militants, including Mullah Nazir in South Waziristan and Hafiz Gul Bahadur in North Waziristan, who have not embraced the TTP's anti-Pakistan ideology and occasionally have clashed violently with the group. The terminology also obscures geographic and strategic differences *within* the TTP itself. For example, the TNSM movement in Swat is grounded in religious politics, not the tribal structures that guide the Mehsud fighters from South Waziristan.

Some might counter that the "Afghan" and "Pakistani" distinction is really a function of the tribal background of various militant groups. After all, the Haqqanis are from the Zadran tribe, which lives primarily in Afghanistan's Paktika province. But the Haqqani Network, Quetta Shura, and TTP all cross tribal boundaries, and the TTP in particular has aggressively sought to destroy tribal hierarchies in favor of ideological association. In any case, the blunt "Afghan" and "Pakistani" terminology simply fails to capture the complexity of these movements.

Muddying important differences with imprecise terminology leads to imprecise analysis and imprecise policy.

Six Questions for FATA's Militants

A useful assessment of Pakistan's militants must capture each group's social geography, religious and political outlook, and strategy. Physical geography is insufficient. The six questions that follow offer a more nuanced way to assess militants in the FATA rather than lumping them into two broad categories, "Afghan Taliban" and "Pakistani Taliban."

1. Does the Militant Group Attack Pakistan?

The most divisive strategic decision facing militant groups in the FATA is whether to attack Pakistani targets, either military or civilian. Doing so distinguishes them from the Quetta Shura and the Haqqanis—who oppose such attacks—but aligns them with al-Qaeda, which supports assaults on the state. Groups that attack Pakistan are also much more likely to be targeted by the Pakistani military, regardless of their activities against U.S. and NATO troops in Afghanistan.

2. What Are the Group's Tribal and Social Roots?

Understanding a group's tribal and social history is a good way to understand its strengths, weaknesses, and enemies. In the FATA, many militant groups are based on tribal relationships and the influx of Taliban members from Afghanistan in 2001. Others were formed when individuals or groups returned from travel abroad or are essentially groups that splintered from mainstream political movements.

3. What Are the Militant Group's Relationships with Foreign (Not Afghan) Militants?

A militant group's interaction with foreign jihadists offers insight into its ideology and strategy. In the FATA, Afghan and Pakistani militants interact with numerous foreign militant groups. al-Qaeda remains a largely Arab organization, though it continues to train Westerners. The Arab fighters have integrated themselves reasonably well into local society. Uzbek fighters are also common, but they have a reputation for being extremely violent and have contentious relations with many local militants.

4. How Aggressively Does the Militant Group Target U.S. and NATO Forces in Afghanistan?

All militant groups in the FATA oppose U.S. and NATO forces in Afghanistan, but not all of them use violence to express that anger, most notably the group led by Mangal Bagh in Khyber agency. Several other groups are focused on religious or political reform in their environs; still others are essentially criminals masquerading as mujahideen. Other armed bands are actually tribal lashkars (militias) with essentially local concerns. They may even be targeting anti-American militants.

5. Does the Militant Group Engage in or Support Attacks on Nonmilitary Western Targets?

Most militants in the FATA support attacks on U.S. and NATO troops in Afghanistan, but far fewer support attacks on civilians inside or outside of South Asia. Some, like the Haqqanis—allies of al-Qaeda for twenty years—have attacked civilians in Afghanistan but claim they have no interest in attacks abroad.[82]

6. Does the Militant Group Take Strategic or Operational Direction from Mullah Omar?

Virtually all militants in the FATA treat Mullah Omar with reverence, but many flout the Quetta Shura's strategy of nonconfrontation with the Pakistani state, and very few have direct operational links to the Quetta Shura.

MILITANCY SUMMARIES BY AGENCY

South Waziristan

South Waziristan is home to the TTP's historical leadership, leading elements in the Mehsud tribe. The TTP's anti-Pakistan stance is quite controversial among militants in the agency, which was already divided by tribal animosities. The Mehsud's tribal rivals, mostly in the Wazir tribe, have intermittently worked with the Pakistani government against the group, even as they supported anti-NATO attacks in Afghanistan. The Pakistani military did not take strong military action in South Waziristan until October 2009, when it began an operation that has forced TTP leaders to flee the agency.

The two most important tribal groups in South Waziristan are the Mehsuds, who tend to live in the mountains near the Afghan border, and the Ahmadzai Wazirs, who tend to live closer to the agency's head-quarters in Wana.[83] The Mehsud militant group that became the heart of the TTP was led first by Baitullah Mehsud and then Hakimullah Mehsud.[84] The most important Wazir commander is Mullah Nazir.[85] A third tribal group, the Bhittanis, is smaller than the Mehsuds or Wazirs but is important because its stronghold straddles the main road into South Waziristan from the NWFP.[86] Relations between the Wazirs and the Mehsuds are historically contentious, and the mistrust has a major impact on militancy in the agency today. The Wazirs tend to view the Mehsuds as robbers and brigands, whereas the Mehsuds look down on Wazirs, whom they view as weak.[87]

All of the militants in South Waziristan favor jihad in Afghanistan, but recent militancy in the agency has been shaped dramatically by the influx of Taliban, Arab, and Uzbek fighters after the U.S.-led invasion of Afghanistan in 2001. The newcomers were initially welcomed by South Waziristan's tribes, which formed militias to wage war against the U.S. and NATO forces in Afghanistan.[88] Despite their shared animosity toward the U.S. and NATO presence in Afghanistan, the militant groups in South Waziristan were divided over leadership, strategy, and what to do with the militant refugees from Afghanistan. Tribal groups continue to fight one another despite the shared Western enemy.

After the flood of militant refugees arrived from Afghanistan in the early 2000s, Baitullah Mehsud and Mullah Nazir vied with their fellow tribesmen for control over their respective tribal militias. Baitullah asserted his authority as a Taliban commander in 2004 by collaborating with a more senior leader named Abdullah Mehsud, who had spent time in the Guantánamo Bay prison, to overcome resistance within the Mehsud tribe to anti-Pakistan activities.[89] Baitullah was ultimately bolstered in early 2005 by signing a peace deal with the government that affirmed his authority in the region and allowed him to organize more openly.[90]

Mullah Nazir established himself in 2004 as well, but he had to compete with the legendary Wazir tribal figure Nek Muhammad to lead the local Taliban. The two commanders cooperated against

Pakistani military operations in 2004 but competed for funds provided by al-Qaeda militants sheltering near Wana.[91] Mullah Nazir was eventually arrested by Pakistani authorities but released following Nek Muhammad's assassination by a U.S. drone in June 2004. Mullah Omar himself reportedly supported Mullah Nazir's selection as amir of the Wazir Taliban following Nek Muhammad's death.[92] Mullah Nazir had a strong relationship with Taliban veterans of the fighting in Afghanistan.[93] He had worked with Gulbuddin Hekmatyar during the anti-Soviet jihad and claimed to own a home in Afghanistan's Paktika province and land in Kandahar.[94] The Pakistani military used its relationship with Mullah Nazir to facilitate a 2005 offensive against Baitullah Mehsud.

In 2006 and 2007, the Mehsud and Wazir coalitions fought over the role of Uzbek militants in South Waziristan and the appropriate policy toward the Pakistani state. Mullah Nazir expelled refugee militants associated with the IMU, led by Tahir Yuldashev, from his stronghold near Wana.[95] He acknowledged some Pakistani government support for the operation but argued that the Uzbeks had ceased to act as guests and were instead thieves.[96] The Mehsud militants not only supported the Uzbeks but took an increasingly confrontational approach toward the Pakistani state. Despite the Mehsud support, the Uzbeks were expelled from Wana and, according to Mullah Nazir, fled to Afghanistan or the town of Mir Ali in North Waziristan.[97] The tribal tensions were serious enough that when Baitullah Mehsud formed the TTP in late 2007, Mullah Nazir did not participate.

As the TTP grew stronger, Baitullah Mehsud became known as the most virulent and powerful militant in the FATA. His two most trusted aides were Wali ur Rehman and Qari Hussain, the most prolific trainer of suicide bombers in the FATA.[98] The group held at bay a third Pakistani military offensive into South Waziristan in February 2008.[99] The fighting, however, forced two hundred thousand people from their homes and was halted only after the intervention of Sirajuddin Haqqani, who mediated between Mehsud forces and the Pakistani government.[100]

Sirajuddin intervened in South Waziristan again after Baitullah Mehsud was killed by a U.S. drone strike on August 5, 2009.[101] With Sirajuddin's support, Hakimullah Mehsud was chosen as amir over Wali ur Rehman and Maulvi Faqir Muhammad. Hakimullah had deep deep ties with the Haqqanis; his first combat experience was a raid in

Mehsud Group (Tehrik-i-Taliban Pakistan)

1. Attacks Pakistani military and civilian targets?

Yes, very aggressively.

2. Social roots?

The Mehsud tribe, assisted by foreign militants.

3. Relations with foreign militants?

Military support from Uzbeks. Ideological and propaganda support from al-Qaeda.

4. Targets U.S. forces in Afghanistan?

Yes, but focused on attacking Pakistan since 2007.

5. Targets Western civilians?

Yes, in Pakistan, along with a 2008 plot in Barcelona and a 2010 attempt to bomb Times Square in New York City.

6. Takes strategic or operational direction from Mullah Omar?

It supports Mullah Omar rhetorically but has diverged from his instruction to avoid conflict with Pakistan.

Afghanistan's Khost province that was jointly led by Baitullah Mehsud and Mullah Sangin, a Haqqani commander.[102]

Hakimullah's ascension to power followed something of a détente between the Mehsuds and Wazirs in South Waziristan. In February 2009, Mullah Nazir, Baitullah Mehsud, and North Waziristan's Hafiz Gul Bahadur created a short-lived alliance called the Shura Ittihad-ul Mujahideen (SIM). Although the alliance fell apart in a matter of months, Mullah Nazir publicly condemned the Pakistani government and praised Osama bin Laden in a video recorded by al-Qaeda's as-Sahab media organization. He explained that drone strikes in South Waziristan were an important reason he had turned on the Pakistani government.[103]

The episode illustrates the potential for drone strikes to unify militants in the FATA, as well as the obstacles that prevent such alliances from being durable. Mullah Nazir's accord with al-Qaeda also indicates that the Arab group can skillfully maintain productive relationships with tribal militants who have conflicts with other foreign militants, such as the Uzbeks. Tribal support for or rejection of these foreign groups has less to do with the foreigners' global aspirations and strategy and more to do with their local behavior.

Mullah Nazir Group

1. Attacks Pakistani military and civilian targets?
Rarely. Cooperates with Pakistani military.
2. Social roots?
The Wazir tribe near Wana.
3. Relations with foreign militants?
Hostile toward Uzbeks. Cooperative with al-Qaeda.
4. Targets U.S. forces in Afghanistan?
Yes.
5. Targets Western civilians?
No.
6. Takes strategic or operational direction from Mullah Omar?
Partially. The group maintains good relations with the Haqqani Network and Quetta Shura and abides Mullah Omar's conciliatory position toward the Pakistani state.

The failure of the SIM alliance opened the door for renewed Pakistani army offensives against Mehsud militants in South Waziristan, which were initiated in October 2009. When those operations began, U.S. drone strikes stopped in South Waziristan. However, the combination of drones and military offensives has severely affected the Mehsud tribe and the TTP.[104] Despite notable TTP operations, including the suicide bombing by a Jordanian double agent of a CIA base in Khost, Afghanistan, on December 30, 2009, many in the movement have been forced to flee South Waziristan. Despite numerous attempts to kill him, Hakimullah Mehsud remained the TTP amir in early 2012, but he faced a leadership crisis over a predictable issue: the relationship with the Pakistani state. Hakimullah's deputy, Maulvi Faqir Muhammad, sought negotiations with the state after losing territory to government troops, a proposal rejected by Hakimullah Mehsud.[105]

North Waziristan

With the notable exception of American drone strikes, North Waziristan has been a relatively comfortable safe haven for militants. The agency's most important militant leaders are Hafiz Gul Bahadur and Sirajuddin

Haqqani, the operational commander of the Haqqani Network, one of the most active militant groups in Afghanistan. North Waziristan also hosts a variety of foreign militants, including al-Qaeda. Despite U.S. attention and al-Qaeda's presence, the Pakistani military has not aggressively targeted militants in North Waziristan, in part because of its long-standing relations with the Haqqani Network.

Geography explains much of North Waziristan's utility as a militant safe haven. It is remote, mountainous, and pressed against Afghanistan's Loya Paktiya—Khost, Paktiya, and Paktika provinces—home of the Haqqanis. The Haqqani Network is still nominally led by Jalaluddin Haqqani, a legendary militant from the anti-Soviet jihad and acquaintance of Osama bin Laden.[106] Jalaluddin used North Waziristan for strategic depth during the anti-Soviet jihad, while aggressively courting Arab fighters in the region and building relationships with Pakistan's Inter-Services Intelligence and the CIA.[107] Jalaluddin's son Sirajuddin was raised in North Waziristan's Miram Shah, and he replaced his father as the network's operational commander after September 11.[108] He quickly established himself as an effective leader, planning daring raids into the heart of Kabul and mediating disputes between various militant commanders in Pakistan.[109] Among other instances, Sirajuddin bolstered Mullah Nazir's legitimacy in 2006, smoothed relations between Mullah Nazir and Baitullah Mehsud in 2007, facilitated the move of Uzbek fighters to North Waziristan, and helped determine who would succeed Baitullah Mehsud as head of the TTP.[110]

Hafiz Gul Bahadur is an important Haqqani ally in North Waziristan, in part because he has a tribal base among the local Uthmanzai Wazirs that the Haqqanis do not.[111] Bahadur's deputy, Maulana Sadiq Noor, directed the Mamba-ul-Uloom madrassa in Miram Shah, an institution founded by Jalaluddin Haqqani.[112] Bahadur's tribal base near Miram Shah covers many of the approaches to Afghanistan, which offers him

---

Haqqani Network

1. Attacks Pakistani military and civilian targets?
No; long time allies of the Pakistani ISI.

2. Social roots?
The Zadran tribe, based in Afghanistan's Khost province. Widely respected as powerful mujahideen.

3. Relations with foreign militants?
Good, cooperative relations with al-Qaeda and Uzbeks.

4. Targets U.S. forces in Afghanistan?
Yes.

5. Targets Western civilians?
Rarely, and only inside Afghanistan.

6. Takes strategic or operational direction from Mullah Omar?
Close political ties. Has representatives in the Quetta Shura, but military operations are independent.

---

leverage over other fighters in the agency. Like the Haqqanis, Bahadur has balanced support for anti-Pakistan militant coalitions such as the TTP with avoidance of direct confrontation with Pakistani troops.[113]

Bahadur's stronghold is near Miram Shah, headquarters of North Waziristan. The second most important town is Mir Ali, which has a reputation as a haven for foreign militants, particularly Uzbeks. Arab militants from al-Qaeda have used the remote Shawal Valley on the border between North and South Waziristan as a safe haven since 2004.[114]

Two of the more independent militant leaders in North Waziristan are Rasool Khan Daur and an Iraqi named Abu Kasha, both of whom are based near Mir Ali. Gul Bahadur appointed Rasool Khan to manage the bazaar in Mir Ali but attempted to remove him in 2009 after allegations of corruption and other criminal activity.[115] Rasul Khan's militants are some of the very few in North Waziristan who do not engage in the fight against NATO troops in Afghanistan, leading many to believe that they are little more than a criminal gang.[116]

Abu Kasha is a different story. An Arab who settled in Mir Ali in 2002, he quit al-Qaeda in 2005 to protest the increasingly prominent role played by Egyptians in the group, particularly Ayman al-Zawahiri.[117] Although Abu Kasha retains relations with al-Qaeda, he finds his base of support among Central Asian fighters linked to the IMU and its offshoot, the Islamic Jihad Union (IJU), as well as local Daur tribesmen. Abu Kasha has worked hard to ingratiate himself with locals around Mir Ali and is known for attending every funeral and wedding in the area.

Kurram

Unlike other tribal agencies, militancy in Kurram is driven by the sectarian tension between Sunni and Shia (40 percent of Kurram's population is Shia, the most of any tribal agency). The Afghan-Soviet war of the 1980s exacerbated those tensions by introducing a host of new weapons into a simmering conflict.

The problem was worsened by the Taliban regime in Kabul, which prompted some in Kurram to emulate its anti-Shia practices.[118] The large Shia population, which al-Qaeda condemns, means that Kurram has not historically served as a haven for foreign militants, but it is a crossroads for the TTP and Punjabi sectarian groups such as

Gul Bahadur Group

1. Attacks Pakistani military and civilian targets?
Rarely, but sometimes fights Pakistan army troops in North Waziristan.

2. Social roots?
The Wazir and Daur tribes in North Waziristan, especially near Miram Shah.

3. Relations with foreign militants?
Incomplete information, but al-Qaeda and Uzbeks are common in North Waziristan.

4. Targets U.S. forces in Afghanistan?
Yes.

5. Targets Western civilians?
No.

6. Takes strategic or operational direction from Mullah Omar?
Implicit political allies, though little direct operational control.

Sources for North Waziristan text boxes: Anand Gopal, Brian Fishman, and Mansur Khan Mehsud, "The Battle for Pakistan: Militancy and Conflict in North Waziristan," New America Foundation, Apr. 19, 2010; Carlotta Gall, "Pakistan and Afghan Taliban Close Ranks," *New York Times*, Mar. 26, 2009; Mustafa Hamid (Abu Walid al-Masri), "Jalal al-Din Haqqani, a Legend in the History of the Afghanistan Jihad," *Al-Sumud* magazine in English, http://www.ansar1.info/showthread.php?t=20201, accessed Mar. 15, 2010.

Lashkar-e-Jhangvi. The number of foreign militants in Kurram seems to have grown since 2010, leading to an increase in American drone strikes in the agency.[119]

Militants from South and North Waziristan increasingly used Kurram in late 2007, reportedly as a way to circumvent provisions of a peace agreement with the government stating that fighters could not cross into Afghanistan from North or South Waziristan.[120] But such efforts were blocked by Shia Turi tribes in Kurram, who feared that TTP influence would bring destructive Pakistani military operations into the area. Baitullah Mehsud

Tehrik-i-Taliban Pakistan (Kurram)

1. Attacks Pakistani military or civilians?
Yes.

2. Social roots?
Based outside Kurram; feeds off sectarian tension in the agency.

3. Relations with foreign militants?
There are few reports of foreign militants in Kurram.

4. Targets U.S. forces in Afghanistan?
Yes.

5. Targets Western civilians?
Unknown.

6. Takes strategic or operational control from Mullah Omar?
Rhetorically supports Mullah Omar, but its focus is sectarian and anti-Pakistan, the latter of which conflicts with Mullah Omar's strategy.

Sources for Kurram text box: Mansur Khan Mehsud, "The Battle for Pakistan: Militancy and Conflict in Kurram," New America Foundation, Apr. 19, 2010; Mariam Abou Zahab, "Unholy Nexus: Talibanism and Sectarianism in Pakistan's Tribal Areas," CERI-SciencesPo, http://www.ceri-sciencespo.com/archive/2009/juin/dossier/art_mz.pdf, accessed Apr. 10, 2010.

ultimately ordered successive waves of fighters into Kurram to dislocate the Shia obstructionists.[121] The fighting was extremely brutal. Hakimullah Mehsud's designated commander in Kurram, Faqir Alam Mehsud, personally beheaded seventy Shia and was ultimately removed from his post over allegations of mental instability.[122]

Since 2008, waves of Taliban militants have traveled to Kurram to fight the Shia, including contingents from groups that are generally rivals, such as Mangal Bagh's Lashkar-e-Islam and Ansar-ul-Islam in Khyber. The repeated incursions by outside militants have angered even Sunnis from Kurram, who have occasionally raised local lashkars of their own to repel the intruders.[123]

Most Shia live in Upper Kurram, centered on the agency's headquarters in Parachinar, which is near the Afghan border. Parachinar is a relatively modern city for the FATA. The educational system is comparable to that in Pakistan's largest cities and includes a college for women. But the geography creates a variety of difficulties for Shia, most notably that they cannot reach the Pakistani heartland without traveling through very dangerous Taliban-controlled territory.[124] The Pakistani government has done little to control the sectarian violence in Kurram, prompting many Shia to accuse it of intentionally stoking the violence. In late 2009, however, the Frontier Corps began arresting Taliban fighters, which has raised hopes among Shia that the government will finally assert control in the agency.[125]

Orakzai

Orakzai is the only tribal agency that does not abut Afghanistan, but it has nonetheless served as a base for TTP operations. Sectarian violence between Sunnis and Shia (10 percent of the population) provides fertile ground for recruitment and a shared sense of purpose for TTP members and sectarian Punjabi militants, like those of Lashkar-e-Jhangvi (LeJ) from Pakistan's heartland cities. Hakimullah Mehsud helped build those relationships as amir of the TTP in Orakzai before taking over the entire group in August 2009.[126] Orakzai is poorly equipped to counter such militants; it is the only tribal agency that does not have a Frontier Corps presence.[127] Orakzai has become even more important since October 2009, when a Pakistani military operation in South Waziristan pushed many fighters into the agency.

Sectarian tensions in Orakzai are exacerbated by a built-in economic grievance against the minority Shia. Shia-dominated regions tend to be more fertile, and thus Shia in the area tend to be comparatively wealthy.[128] Sectarian violence in Orakzai goes back to at least 1927, when protests by Sunnis and Shia over a shrine to a local saint grew violent, and is heavily influenced by sectarian fighting in Kurram.[129]

The first Taliban group in Orakzai was founded in the late 1990s by Mullah Muhammad Rehmin. The group, named the Tehrik-e Tulaba Movement (TTM), was heavily influenced by the TNSM in the neighboring Malakand division of the NWFP. Indeed, Mullah Rehmin led hundreds of men from Orakzai to join Sufi Muhammad's ill-fated expedition to Afghanistan after the U.S. invasion in 2001.

Tehrik-i-Taliban Pakistan (Orakzai)

1. Attacks Pakistani military and civilians?
Yes, both civilians and military.
2. Social roots?
Based outside Orakzai; feeds off sectarian tension in the agency.
3. Relations with foreign militants?
Likely.
4. Targets U.S. forces in Afghanistan?
Yes, though Orakzai is not a prime staging area for attacks in Afghanistan.
5. Targets Western civilians?
Yes, in Pakistan.
6. Takes strategic or operational control from Mullah Omar?
Rhetorical support. Attacks on NATO-bound supplies in Khyber consistent with (but not directed by) Mullah Omar; attacks on Pakistan are not.

The TTM's initial focus was social reform rather than political revolution.

The fall of the Taliban regime in Kabul did not immediately affect Orakzai, but post–September 11 developments eventually had a major impact in the agency. Insurgents from South Waziristan began using Orakzai as a safe haven in 2004, and the TTP found the area useful as a base for attacks against urban targets in Pakistan.[130]

The TTP was founded in December 2007 and Hakimullah Mehsud was named the commander for Orakzai, Kurram, and Khyber agencies in 2008. He built strong relationships with LeJ, targeted local maliks, and used his proximity to the Khyber Pass to pressure U.S. and NATO supply lines.[131] The links to groups such as LeJ were particularly important because they gave the Pashtun TTP access to organizational infrastructure in Pakistan's Punjabi heartland, a capacity that seems to have facilitated deadly attacks.

In December 2008, the TTP officially imposed sharia in Orakzai, completely banning television, music, and women from visiting bazaars.

Lashkar-e-Jhangvi

1. Attacks Pakistani military and civilians?

Yes, both civilians and military.

2. Social roots?

Anti-Shia militant group from Punjab.

3. Relations with foreign militants?

Yes; ideologically and operationally supported by al-Qaeda.

4. Targets U.S. forces in Afghanistan?

No.

5. Targets Western civilians?

Yes, in Pakistan.

6. Takes strategic or operational control from Mullah Omar?

Historical links, but LeJ's anti-Pakistan focus is now at odds with Mullah Omar's strategy.

Sources for Orakzai text boxes: Raheel Khan, "The Battle for Pakistan: Militancy and Conflict in Orakzai Agency," New America Foundation, Apr. 19, 2010; Rahimullah Yusufzai, "Hakimullah Unveils Himself to the Media," *The News*, Nov. 30, 2008; Hassan Abbas, "Defining the Punjabi Taliban Network," *CTC Sentinel*, Apr. 2009, 2(4); Ahmed Rashid, *Taliban: Militant Islam, Oil and Fundamentalism in Central Asia* (Yale University Press, New Haven, 2000).

Hakimullah even imposed the *jizya* (a tax on non-Muslims) on Sikh families that had lived in Orakzai for a century.[132]

Despite the TTP's expansion in Orakzai, reporters who met with Hakimullah Mehsud in the agency in 2008 suggested that the core TTP organization was composed of Mehsud tribesmen from South Waziristan rather than Orakzai natives, many of whom were compelled to support the TTP after a brutal campaign against tribal leaders.[133]

Leaders from Orakzai have grown increasingly important in the TTP movement since Baitullah Mehsud's death in August 2009. Not only did Hakimullah take over as the overall TTP amir until his death in early 2010, but one of Hakimullah's commanders from Orakzai, Malik Noor Jamal, known by his nom de guerre Mullah Toofan, has been mentioned as a potential successor to Hakimullah as TTP amir. Saeed

Hafiz is a senior TTP commander in the agency. Maulvi Haider currently serves as a spokesman, and Aslam Farooqi and Tariq Afridi support TTP operations but seem to have fundamentally sectarian goals. On February 6, 2010, Mullah Saeed Khan claimed to be the new TTP amir in Orakzai, a claim that could not be independently confirmed.[134]

Pakistan dramatically increased its military efforts against insurgents in the FATA in 2009. Operations in South Waziristan pushed fighters north into Orakzai in early 2010, a move that has prompted Pakistani intervention on the ground, especially in an effort to disrupt the distribution of suicide bombers from the agency to major Pakistani cities.[135]

Khyber

Khyber agency is named after the famous mountain pass connecting Afghanistan and Pakistan, a geographical feature that makes it strategically critical as well. Khyber also abuts the capital of the NWFP, Peshawar, and because of its proximity to that urban center it has a reputation as being relatively modern and well developed.[136] Khyber agency is plagued by multiple Islamist militant groups, though the most potent, the Mangal Bagh-led Lashkar-e-Islam (LeI), has rebuffed TTP efforts to cooperate. TTP-affiliated groups nonetheless operate in Khyber, where they often attack Afghanistan-bound supply trucks in the Khyber Pass. The most dominant tribe in the agency is the Afridi, followed by the Shinwari. Afridis dominate the Tirah Valley, which is a traditional haven for criminals but is used by Islamist militants as well.[137]

The relationship between Bagh's LeI and the TTP is complex. LeI shares many of the TTP's religious and political ideas, but it has local roots and opposes attacks on American, NATO, or Pakistani forces. The groundwork for LeI was laid by a local tribesman named Haji Namdar, who in 2003 established a local group called Amr Bil Maroof Wa Nahi Anil Munkar (Invitation to Virtue and Negation of Vice) patterned on the former Taliban regime in Kabul.[138] The group banned music, and it forced men to grow beards and women to wear veils. Punishments were meted out in prisons named "Abu Ghraib" and "Guantanamo."[139] Haji Namdar also set up a bootleg FM radio channel and hired a virulently anti-Shia preacher named Mufti Munir Shakir to broadcast sermons.[140]

Mufti Shakir became the voice of violent activism in Khyber. A strict Deobandi preacher from Karak district in the NWFP, Mufti

---
Lashkar-e-Islam

1. Attacks Pakistani military and civilians?
Attacks civilians, but avoids confrontation with the Pakistani Army.

2. Social roots?
Deobandis.

3. Relations with foreign militants?
Unclear, but unlikely.

4. Targets U.S. forces in Afghanistan?
No.

5. Targets Western civilians?
No.

6. Takes strategic or operational control from Mullah Omar?
No, though it honors him as a good Muslim leader.

Ansar-ul-Islam

1. Attacks Pakistani military and civilians?
No.

2. Social roots?
Moderate Deobandis and Barelvis.

3. Relations with foreign militants?
No.

4. Targets U.S. forces in Afghanistan?
Yes.

5. Targets Western civilians?
No.

6. Takes strategic or operational control from Mullah Omar?
No.

Shakir had already been expelled from Kurram agency for preaching violence.[141] He established LeI in 2005 and preached that violence was necessary to achieve the group's goals.

The opposition to Mufti Shakir's Deobandi activism in Khyber was led by Pir Saif ur-Rehman, a preacher from the Barelvi school of Sunni Islam.[142,143] Pir Rehman had the support of several Afridi tribes and set up his own illegal FM radio station. The two clerics hurled religious and ideological invective at each other until November 2005, when supporters clashed violently in Bara.[144]

In February 2006, the government finally pushed Pir Rehman and Mufti Shakir out of Khyber. But their departure did not end the violence. In July 2006, a group of ideological moderates created an armed group called Ansar-ul-Islam (AuI) to oppose LeI.[145]

Mufti Shakir's departure opened the door for the rise of Mangal Bagh, LeI's current amir and the most important militant operating in Khyber agency. Mangal Bagh hails from the Sepah clan of the Afridi tribe, a relatively poor and politically disenfranchised group. Bagh is a savvy political operator who uses legitimate political processes and violence to pursue his Islamist ideas.[146] Bagh emphasizes law and order

---

Tehrik-i-Taliban Pakistan (Khyber)

1. Attacks Pakistani military and civilians?
Yes, both civilians and military.
2. Social roots?
Many from outside Khyber, directed from TTP in Orakzai.
3. Relations with foreign militants?
Yes.
4. Targets U.S. forces in Afghanistan?
Yes.
5. Targets Western civilians?
Yes, particularly in Pakistan.
6. Takes strategic or operational control from Mullah Omar?
No, though it supports him rhetorically. Attacks on NATO-bound supplies are in line with Mullah Omar's Afghan-focused strategy.
Sources for Khyber text boxes: Raheel Khan, "The Battle for Pakistan: Militancy and Conflict in Khyber Agency," New America Foundation, Apr. 19, 2010; Syed Saleem Shahzad, "Taliban Bitten by a Snake in the Grass," *Asia Times*, Apr. 26, 2008; Rahimullah Yusufzai, "A Who's Who of the Insurgency in Pakistan's North-West Frontier Province: Part 2—FATA Excluding North and South Waziristan," *Terrorism Monitor*, 7(4).

and has challenged the traditional tribal malik system in the FATA. Like Haji Namdar, he has imposed a variety of social regulations and enforces fines as punishment. Bagh has not joined the anti-Pakistan TTP and urges his followers not to attack government troops in Khyber. In 2008, however, TTP representatives approached Haji Namdar about striking NATO-bound supplies plying the highway toward Afghanistan.[147] Haji Namdar initially agreed and the TTP established a local command led by an Afghan named Kamran Mustafa Hijrat.[148]

The Pakistani military attacked TTP forces in June 2008, forcing them back from the outskirts of Peshawar.[149] The government also seems to have co-opted Haji Namdar, who provided information on TTP safe houses throughout Khyber agency in 2008.[150] The TTP ultimately killed Haji Namdar. Hakimullah Mehsud, then amir of the TTP in neighboring Orakzai agency, organized a series of assassination attempts that culminated in a successful shooting inside a Bara mosque.[151]

The TTP maintains a presence in Khyber, and LeI continues to fight AuI.[152] The most powerful commander in Khyber, Mangal Bagh, still has not joined the TTP or refocused attacks into Afghanistan. He has said: "While the Americans are in Afghanistan, there is no way to bring peace and prosperity, over there and here. We don't want to kill the Americans, we just want to make them Muslims."[153]

Mohmand

Despite being considered relatively well integrated into Pakistani society, Mohmand has an active Taliban insurgency led by Omar Khalid. Khalid volunteered in Kashmir before September 11 and led tribal fighters in Afghanistan after the U.S. invasion. He became a major commander in 2007 when he captured a local shrine to protest the Lal Masjid incident in Islamabad. Khalid has joined the TTP and supports violence in Afghanistan and against Pakistani security forces in Mohmand, Bajaur, and nearby Peshawar.

Mohmand hosted thousands of Afghan refugees in the 1980s and was a recruiting ground for TNSM, which was centered in Bajaur agency and Malakand division of the NWFP. In 1985, Jamil al-Rahman, of the Safi tribe, split from Gulbuddin Hekmatyar's Hizb-e-Islami to found Jamaat al-Dawa, a Salafi party that attracted both Arab fighters and a slew of money from private Saudi and Kuwaiti sources.[154] Jamaat al-Dawa grew very strong in Afghanistan's Kunar River Valley but adopted several brutal doctrines, including the practice of treating any civilian living in government-controlled territory as an unbeliever, which meant that males could be killed, women and children enslaved.[155] Al-Rahman's brutality ultimately made him very unpopular, and he was assassinated by an Egyptian gunman in 1991. His failure, like that of jihadis in Algeria in the mid-1980s, is still used as a warning by jihadis concerned that fundamentalism will alienate local populations. Indeed, Ayman al-Zawahiri cited Jamil al-Rahman's failure in his famous 2005 letter urging Abu Mus'ab al-Zarqawi to moderate his behavior in Iraq.[156]

But whereas some jihadis take Jamil al-Rahman as a lesson of failure, Omar Khalid, also of al-Rahman's Safi tribe, seems to have taken him for inspiration. In 2007, Khalid stepped to the forefront of the militant movement in Mohmand by seizing the shrine of a famous anti-colonialist fighter in the village of Ghazi Abad and renaming it "Lal Masjid" in a show of solidarity with besieged Islamists in Islamabad.[157] Shortly thereafter, he joined the pan-FATA TTP and began to impose his own brutal rule in Mohmand.

Omar Khalid's deputy is Qari Shakeel and his spokesman is known as Dr. Asad. The organization has subcommanders for each of Mohmand's seven administrative divisions, or tehsils.[158] Omar Khalid claims to lead about twenty-five hundred militants in Mohmand and is reportedly dominant in three tehsils, Khawezai-Baizai, Lakaro, and Ambar.[159] The militants and tribes in northern Mohmand have close relations with militants in Bajaur agency and have been targeted by the Pakistani military for harboring fighters who cross into Mohmand from the north.[160] Although Khalid's organization joined the TTP and accepts guidance from the umbrella group, it operates independently and has not been weakened by the Pakistani army offensives against TTP strongholds in South Waziristan.

The Pakistani military has had poor showings in Mohmand. As in other tribal agencies, it signed peace agreements with the militants that essentially legitimized their authority in the area.[161] The government has grown more aggressive since late 2009, however, and Pakistani officials suggest that a recent series of attacks in Peshawar on Awami National Party offices and the U.S. Consulate may have been organized from Mohmand.[162]

Bajaur

Bajaur is a hotbed for militancy in large measure because of its proximity to Afghanistan's Kunar province. Militants fleeing Afghanistan established themselves in Bajaur in 2001, including some al-Qaeda members, who made the agency their most important safe haven in the FATA outside of North or South Waziristan.[163] The Taliban in Bajaur today is led by Maulvi Faqir Muhammad, once a senior leader in the TTP who has now moderated his stance toward the Pakistani state.

Militant rumblings in Bajaur started in 1994 when a group named the Tehrik-i-Nifaz-i-Shariat-i-Mohammadi (TNSM), led by Sufi Muhammad, began organizing protests in the nearby Malakand division of the NWFP. The movement did not progress, however, until after 2001, when Sufi Muhammad led thousands of fighters into Afghanistan to battle U.S. and NATO forces. The expedition was a failure, but Sufi Muhammad's subsequent arrest by Pakistani forces was manipulated by Maulvi Faqir Muhammad to build support for his movement. Maulvi Faqir was born and raised in Bajaur and as a teenager fought against the Soviets in Afghanistan before studying at the Darul-Uloom Panjpeer, a Wahhabi madrassa.[164]

Maulvi Faqir organized a militia of around six thousand men and aligned himself closely with the TTP, while publicly expressing support for Mullah Omar and Osama bin Laden.[165] Maulvi Faqir had some relationship with al-Qaeda; Ayman al-Zawahiri was to attend a dinner he hosted that was targeted by a U.S. drone strike.[166] Al-Zawahiri left the house shortly before the drone attacked.[167]

al-Qaeda has continued to use Bajaur as an important safe haven. Captured al-Qaeda leader Abu Faraj al-Libbi may have lived there, and al-Qaeda battle videos indicate that the group is often active in Afghanistan's Kunar province, which abuts Bajaur.[168] The al-Qaeda presence explains three of the four U.S. drone strikes in the agency.[169] The last one, in October 2009, appears to have targeted Maulvi Faqir himself.[170]

Drone strikes and Pakistani military operations may have altered Maulvi Faqir's strategic thinking. In 2008, a Pakistani offensive killed

---

Maulvi Faqir Muhammad

1. Attacks Pakistani military and civilians?
Not since early 2009.

2. Social roots?
TNSM social activists.

3. Relations with foreign militants?
Yes, especially al-Qaeda.

4. Targets U.S. forces in Afghanistan?
Yes.

5. Targets Western civilians?
Supported TTP until 2009.

6. Takes strategic or operational control from Mullah Omar?
Offers strong rhetorical support. Past attacks on Pakistan conflict with Mullah Omar's strategy. Minimal operational linkages.

Sources for Bajaur text box: Rahmanullah, "The Battle for Pakistan: Militancy and Conflict in Bajaur," New America Foundation, Apr. 19, 2010; Anne Stenersen, "Al-Qaeda's Allies in the FATA" New America Foundation, Apr. 19, 2010.

---

more than a thousand militants.[171] The fighting continued until February 2009, when Maulvi Faqir ordered a unilateral cease-fire, declaring, "Pakistan is our country and the Pakistan army is our army," which was an implicit rejection of the TTP's ideology.[172] Such statements have complicated Maulvi Faqir's leadership position. He has squabbled with other militants, including Hakimullah Mehsud, who want him to take a harder line against the Pakistani military.[173]

Maulvi Faqir's group is not the only militant outfit in Bajaur. Kashmir-focused Harakat-ul Jihad-ul Islami (HUJI) has roots in Bajaur, and Uzbek groups have used the territory and neighboring Kunar province for transit since shortly after 2001.[174]

Swat

The Swat district of Malakand division in the NWFP was not affected by the anti-Soviet jihad in Afghanistan to the same degree as agencies in the FATA, but it has a unique history of militancy that has made it a central front in Pakistan's fight against Taliban militants. Militancy in Swat centers on the TNSM, a fundamentalist group founded by Sufi Muhammad in 1989, before the rise of Mullah Omar's Taliban movement in Afghanistan. Pakistani politics plays a central role in determining the nature of militancy in Swat, which participates in the national electoral system, unlike areas of the FATA that are administered outside the main political system. Thus, both militant strategy and counterinsurgency operations are deeply influenced by popular and political opinion in the district; likewise, militant and counterinsurgency operations are often designed to influence the mainstream political process in Swat.[175]

Sufi Muhammad began his rise to prominence as a local leader in the Jamaat-e-Islami (JI) religious political party.[176] Originally from Lower Dir district, the cleric was trained and taught in local madrassas until founding the TNSM with the stated goal of implementing sharia in Malakand division.[177] TNSM's initial campaigns in the early 1990s were relatively peaceful but became ever more confrontational. The group adopted the slogan "sharia or martyrdom" (*shariat ya shahadat*) and in 1994 began blockading roads in Malakand division.[178] On May 16, 1994, eleven people were killed in Swat's neighboring district of Buner.[179] The crisis was resolved in November 1994 when the

Pakistani government agreed to implement the Nifaz-i-Nizam-i-Adl Regulation, which established a form of sharia.

Sufi Muhammad mustered opposition to the Pakistani state by pointing out the weaknesses of Pakistan's administration in the district, but his controversial tactics and oscillation between confrontation and negotiation with the government alienated many in Swat. After the 1994 violence, the cleric was forced out of Swat amid a shower of complaints that he had gotten supporters killed without taking personal risks and then had negotiated with the government.[180]

Sufi Muhammad's career and the fortunes of the TNSM were bolstered by the U.S. and NATO invasion of Afghanistan in late 2001. Returning to Swat shortly after the September 11 attacks, he rallied a tribal lashkar rumored to be ten thousand strong to oppose the U.S.-led invasion.[181] The operation was a disaster. Untold numbers of Pakistanis were killed, and locals in Swat and elsewhere in Malakand division blamed Sufi Muhammad for the carnage. Pakistani security forces arrested the cleric in 2002.

Sufi Muhammad's arrest opened the way for his son-in-law, Fazlullah, to take a leadership role in TNSM. Combining religious appeals, anti-Americanism, and condemnations of traditional class hierarchies protected by corrupt Pakistani governance, Fazlullah built a broad audience.[182] By 2007, his militia was a dominant force in Swat, prohibiting education for girls and enforcing moral codes outside of the government's authority. His shura had forty to fifty members and a strong organizational structure.[183]

When Pakistani troops raided the Lal Masjid in July 2007, Fazlullah used the incident as a pretext for aggressive operations against Pakistani security forces in Swat. The initial Pakistani counteroffensive, entitled Rah-e-Haq (Just Path), was launched in October 2007 but proved ineffective because it lacked political and popular support. The NWFP provincial government at the time was led by the Muttahida Majlis-e-Amal (MMA) coalition of religious parties, which opposed a harsh crackdown on Islamist militants.[184] Many expected that to change in 2008, when a political coalition led by the secular and anti-Taliban Awami National Party (ANP) won provincial elections, but party members—threatened with death by the Taliban—began to negotiate with the TNSM almost immediately. Negotiations with Fazlullah failed, and eventually Sufi Muhammad was released from prison as a goodwill gesture. Ultimately an agreement with Sufi Muhammad was reached on February 15, 2009, stipulating that the government would extend sharia in the district.[185]

The Pakistani government finally launched a persistent counterattack on the militants in April 2009.[186] Although Fazlullah was not captured and the violence drove nearly 2.5 million people from their homes, the Pakistani offensive removed TNSM from power in Swat, and many of the displaced have since returned home. The TNSM leaders may find safe haven elsewhere in the NWFP or FATA, as the group does coordinate with the TTP. The Pakistani government has released tapes purportedly showing TNSM spokesman Muslim Khan discussing strategy with the late Baitullah Mehsud.[187]

CONCLUSIONS

The Future of Militancy in the FATA

Militant groups in the FATA will be shaped by tradition, ideology, the Pakistani political environment, international context, and the peculiar and very dangerous influence of al-Qaeda. The overriding question for all of these militants is whether the Pakistani military will continue to calculate that independently operating militias in the tribal regions provide the Pakistani state strategic depth and leverage with which to counter internal and international threats, most notably from India. If it does, they will continue to adapt to changing political and military conditions. If it determines they are a threat, then these groups are very vulnerable to Pakistani military and political pressure.

The Pakistani military establishment has been slow to respond to the al-Qaeda-influenced Taliban in the post–September 11 era, but its offensives from 2009 forward in Swat, South Waziristan, and Bajaur suggest it has finally recognized the danger of religious militants bent on social and political revolution in Pakistan. The danger is that the Pakistani establishment will continue to distinguish between obvious threats such as those in the TTP and the looming danger of well-armed religious radicals in other networks. Pakistan deserves credit for increasingly aggressive operations against militants in the FATA since the beginning of 2009, but the scope of Pakistan's targets are still limited to anti-Pakistan fighters generally grouped under the TTP umbrella.

Pakistan's approach to militancy in the FATA remains inadequate. It has strengthened military operations against militants threatening it today but failed to implement a strategy to prevent militants from attacking it tomorrow. For Pakistan, the great strategic lesson of the last decade should be not just that anti-Pakistan militants must be dealt with promptly but that the radicalism of al-Qaeda and its ilk is a metastasizing cancer that will infect and co-opt militant groups that have served Pakistan's interests in the past. The lesson of Osama bin Laden being discovered and killed a half-mile from the Pakistani military academy must be that Pakistan's government cannot be relied on to challenge al-Qaeda, because of either weakness or unwillingness. al-Qaeda's proven ability to co-opt such groups is its most dangerous feature. The Pakistani establishment is loath to cut ties with militants, and concerned that the United States will withdraw from the region and leave it to confront these problems alone. But al-Qaeda now argues that the Pakistani state is fundamentally corrupt and deserves to be overthrown whether or not it supports a Western effort in Afghanistan. Pakistani policy essentially aims to return to a *status quo ante*, wherein it limits the risk from anti-Pakistan militants and foreign threats by supporting militants in the FATA that attack outside of Pakistan. This approach is increasingly inconsistent and shortsighted because many groups that currently operate outside Pakistan nonetheless have active relationships with al-Qaeda, which has repeatedly demonstrated its ability to convert groups to its radical way of thinking.

Military action against militants is inadequate for securing the FATA over the long run. Pakistan's counterinsurgency operations have improved since 2009, but they must be complemented by substantive political reform in the FATA. Reforms to allow political parties to compete in Pakistani elections, thus increasing political participation, and reform colonial-era judicial processes that condone collective punishment and arbitrary detention are critical for the future of the region. They must be not only law but practice in the FATA.

There are important structural limits to how much the United States can achieve unilaterally in the FATA. Drone strikes against al-Qaeda leaders and other militants are a valuable tool, but they cannot provide security for the United States, Afghanistan, or Pakistan over the long run. Rather, the complex U.S. diplomatic effort to persuade Pakistan to take determined military and political action in the FATA, as well as U.S. support of such action, is critical.

Three Militant Coalitions in the FATA

The militant universe in Pakistan's FATA is tremendously complex. Alliances constantly shift, and any typology of militants there is necessarily incomplete and destined to become outdated. In practice, militants in the FATA are a series of relatively localized groups that coalesce into strategic and operational alliances on the basis of shared purpose, common history, and operational compatibility. There are three of these coalitions of militants in the FATA: the Tehrik-i-Taliban Pakistan, the Haqqani Network, and the Quetta Shura. Importantly, however, not all militant groups in the FATA operate in one of these alliances; not surprisingly groups with particularly localized and parochial interests tend to steer clear of the larger coalitions. We should simply refer to these alliances—and their constituent groups—by their proper names rather than apply geographic monikers, such as "Pakistani Taliban" and "Afghan Taliban," that imply false analytical and practical distinctions.

The TTP, once the most important militant coalition in the FATA, has declined substantially since 2010, mostly because of effective Pakistani military action. Maulvi Faqir Muhammad in Bajaur has essentially renounced attacks on the Pakistani state, and the remaining coalition is divided. Nonetheless, the TTP represents a dangerous faction because of its willingness to attack the Pakistani state and collaborate directly with foreign militants for attacks outside of South Asia.

The Haqqani Network coalition is led from North Waziristan by Jalaluddin and Sirajuddin Haqqani, but it includes Gul Bahadur aligned groups and Mullah Nazir from South Waziristan. Haqqani Network affiliated groups tend to focus on attacks in Afghanistan and generally have good relations with Arab al-Qaeda members, though its constituent groups have squabbled with Uzbek militants and one another. Importantly, the Haqqani Network groups have all negotiated with the Pakistani establishment since 2001 and, in general, have avoided confrontation with the Pakistani state. To date, Haqqani Network strongholds in North Waziristan have been relatively immune from Pakistani military operations, despite the extensive presence of al-Qaeda members in the region.

The last coalition is Mullah Omar's Quetta Shura, which must be mentioned despite its limited influence in the FATA itself. The Quetta Shura exerts direct operational control in southern Afghanistan, but it is based far from the FATA and seems to have limited strategic or operational influence in the FATA because of that distance. In general, FATA-based militants are careful to demonstrate their respect for Mullah Omar, but the Haqqani-affiliated groups are the only ones that seem to take specific direction, and then only sometimes. The TTP groups have rejected Mullah Omar's exhortation not to attack Pakistan, and the hints of Mullah Omar's manipulation of political alignments between militant groups, especially improving the relationship between the Mehsud tribe and the Wazir tribe in North and South Waziristan, have been limited.

There are many militants in the FATA who do not fall into any of these coalitions but are nonetheless important players in the region. Mangal Bagh's Lashkar-e Islam and its competitor Ansar-ul Islam are very important in Khyber agency, and there are a variety of independent fighters in North Waziristan. One might even consider Maulvi Faqir Muhammad of Bajaur as independent now that he has renounced violence against the Pakistani state. It makes little sense to consider him part of the TTP alliance if he truly now rejects its central strategic tenet, which is to attack targets in Pakistan.

The decline of al-Qaeda may reduce American interest in FATA-based militancy, but ignoring the militants there will not make them go away. Militancy in the FATA remains vibrant and will continue to have a negative impact on U.S. national security.

Notes

1. See the collection of essays "The Battle for Pakistan" published by the New America Foundation, Apr. 19, 2010.
2. "An Interview with the Amir of Mujahidin in South Waziristan—Mullah Nazir Ahmed," As-Sahab, Apr. 7, 2009.
3. Stanley McChrystal, "Commander's Initial Assessment," Aug. 30, 2009, pp. 2–6.
4. Anand Gopal, Brian Fishman, and Saifullah Khan Mehsud, "The Battle for Pakistan: Militancy and Conflict in North Waziristan," New America Foundation, Apr. 19, 2010.
5. For al-Qaeda, see Anne Stenersen, "Al-Qaeda's Allies in the FATA," New America Foundation, Apr. 19, 2010.
6. "'No More Retreat' Taliban Troops Told," BBC News, Nov. 13, 2001.
7. Daud Khattak, "The Battle for Pakistan: Militancy and Conflict in Swat" New America Foundation, Apr. 19, 2010.
8. For example, see Sufi Muhammad's turns in and out of prison. Zulqifar Ali, "Sufi Muhammad, Two Sons Held in Peshawar," Dawn, July 27, 2009.
9. Hassan Abbas, "The Battle for Pakistan: Politics and Militancy in the Northwest Frontier Province," New America Foundation, Apr. 19, 2010.
10. For example, Sufi Muhammad, Hafez Gul Bahadur, and the Ansar-ul Islam movement in Khyber Agency.
11. Abbas (2010).
12. Josh White, "Pakistan's Islamist Frontier: Islamic Politics and U.S. Policy in Pakistan's North-West Frontier," Religion and Security Monograph Series, no. 1 (Arlington, VA: Center on Faith and International Affairs, 2008).
13. Ibid.; Abbas (2010).
14. Abbas (2010).
15. Ibid.
16. Descriptions of political organization in the NWFP and FATA draw heavily on White (2008).
17. Ibid.
18. Salman Masood, "Pakistan Lifts Longtime Ban on Political Activities in Restive Tribal Areas," New York Times, Aug. 14, 2009.

19. "Frontier Crimes Regulation Amended," *Daily Times*, Aug. 13, 2011, http://dailytimes.com.pk/default.asp?page=2011\08\13\story_13-8-2011_pg1_1.

20. Raheel Khan interview with Asif Khan Daur, local journalist and resident of Mir Ali area in North Waziristan Agency, conducted on Aug. 12, 2009, in Peshawar.

21. For example, Abdul Salam, "Militants Kill Seven Tribal Elders," *Dawn*, Sept. 25, 2009.

22. Dexter Filkins, "Right at the Edge," *New York Times Magazine*, Sept. 5, 2008.

23. Khan, interview with Asif Khan Daur.

24. For the Haqqanis, see Gopal, Fishman, and Khan Mehsud, "The Battle for Pakistan"; for al-Qaeda, see Daniel Kimmage, "al-Qaeda Central and the Internet," New America Foundation, February 2010; for TTP leaders, see Rahmanullah, "The Battle for Pakistan: Militancy and Conflict in Bajaur," New America Foundation, Apr. 19, 2010.

25. For Baitullah Mehsud, see Claudio Franco, "The Tehrik-i-Taliban Pakistan," in Antonio Giustozzi, *Decoding the New Taliban* (Columbia University Press, New York, 2009); for Mullah Nazir, see Mansur Khan Mehsud, "The Battle for Pakistan: Militancy and Conflict in South Waziristan," New America Foundation, Apr. 19, 2010.

26. Hassan Abbas, "A Profile of Tehrik-Taliban Pakistan," *CTC Sentinel*, 1(2), January 2008.

27. Ibid.

28. Hassan Abbas, "Defining the Punjabi Taliban Network," *CTC Sentinel*, April 2009, 2(4).

29. Syed Saleem Shahzad, "Taliban Wield the Axe Ahead of New Battle," *Asia Times*, Jan. 24, 2008, http://www.atimes.com/atimes/South_Asia/JA24Df03.html, accessed Feb. 8, 2010.

30. Declan Walsh, "Airstrike Kills Taliban Leader Baitullah Mehsud," *Guardian*, Aug. 7, 2009.

31. Raheel Khan, "Militancy and Conflict in Orakzai Agency," Apr. 19, 2010.

32. Claudio Franco, "The Tehrik-i-Taliban Pakistan," in Antonio Giustozzi, *Decoding the New Taliban* (New York: Columbia University Press, 2009).

33. Mullah Omar, "Eid al-Fitr Statement," Sept. 21, 2009, http://www.jihadica.com/wp-content/uploads/2009/10/10-21-09-mullah-omar-eid-message.pdf; Vahid Brown, "Al-Qa'ida and the Afghan Taliban: 'Diametrically Opposed,'" *Jihadica*, Oct. 21, 2009; see also "Mullah Omar Gets on Message with Speech Aimed at the West," *Nation*, Nov. 26, 2009; Mehlaqa Samdani, "Mullah Omar and al-Qaida: Things Fall Apart?" *CSIS*, Dec. 11, 2009.

34. Paul Cruickshank, "The Militant Pipeline," New America Foundation, February 2010.

35. Ibid.

36. Barbara Sude, "Al-Qaeda Central," New America Foundation, February 2010.

37. Cruickshank, "The Militant Pipeline"; Sude, "Al-Qaeda Central."

38. Daniel Kimmage, "al-Qaeda Central and the Internet."

39. Anne Stenersen, "Al-Qaeda's Allies in the FATA," New America Foundation, Apr. 19, 2010.

40. Mustafa Hamid (Abu Walid al-Masri), "Jalal al-Din Haqqani, a Legend in the History of the Afghanistan Jihad," *Al-Sumud* magazine in English, http://www.ansar1.info/showthread.php?t=20201, accessed Mar. 15, 2010.

41. Mark Hosenball, "CIA Investigators Believe Suicide Bomber Was Qaeda Plant from the Outset," *Newsweek Declassified*, Mar. 5, 2010.

42. Ayman al-Zawahiri, "The Aggression Against the Lal Masjid," As-Sahab, July 11, 2007.

43. Abu Yahya al-Libi, "The Masters of the Martyrs," As-Sahab, July 31, 2007; "Interview with Abu Yahya al-Libi," As-Sahab, August 2007; Osama bin Laden, "A Speech to the People of Pakistan," As-Sahab, Sept. 20, 2007; "The Power of Truth," As-Sahab, Sept. 20, 2007.

44. Kimmage, February 2010.

45. This ideological context is crucial for understanding the importance of nonmainstream statements by TTP commanders, such Maulvi Faqir Muhammad of Bajaur, who in 2009 called the Pakistani military "our army."

46. For example, see Ayman al-Zawahiri, "The Morning and the Lamp," As-Sahab, Dec. 16, 2009. Interestingly, Abu Yahya al-Libi seems to have taken much of the rhetorical lead condemning the Pakistani state and justifying violence against it; Thomas Hegghammer, "Justifying Jihad Against Pakistan," *Jihadica*, Feb. 19, 2010.

47. For an argument that al-Qaeda's relationship with Mullah Omar has always been weak and is fraying even more, see Vahid Brown, "Al-Qaeda and the Afghan Taliban: 'Diametrically Opposed?'" *Jihadica*, Oct. 21, 2009; Vahid Brown, "The Façade of Allegiance: Bin Ladin's Dubious Pledge to Mullah Omar," *CTC Sentinel*, January 2010, 3(1).

48. Mariam Abou Zahab and Olivier Roy, *Islamist Networks: The Afghan-Pakistan Connection* (Columbia University Press, New York, 2004); Ayman al-Zawahiri, "The Morning and the Lamp," As-Sahab, December 2009.

49. Al-Zawahiri, "The Morning and the Lamp."

50. Sadia Sulaiman, "Empowering 'Soft' Taliban over 'Hard' Taliban: Pakistan's Counter-Terrorism Strategy," *Terrorism Monitor*, July 25, 2008.

51. Stenersen, Apr. 19, 2010.

52. Brian Fishman and Joseph Felter, "Bombers, Bank Accounts, and Bleedout: Al-Qa'ida's Road in and out of Iraq," Combating Terrorism Center at West Point, July 2008; Brian Fishman, "Dysfunction and Decline: Lessons Learned from Inside al-Qa'ida in Iraq," Combating Terrorism Center at West Point, March 2009.

53. Stenersen, Apr. 19, 2010.

54. See Brian Fishman, "All al-Qaeda's Are Not Created Equal," *AfPak Channel*, Oct. 14, 2009.

55. For a more detailed discussion of Pakistan's counterinsurgency operations, see Sameer Lalwani, "Pakistan's COIN Flip," New America Foundation, Apr. 19, 2010.

56. Mansur Mahsud, "South Waziristan's Militants," New America Foundation, Apr. 19, 2010.

57. Sohail Abdul Nasir, "Baitullah Mehsud: South Waziristan's Unofficial Amir," *Terrorism Focus*, July 9, 2006.

58. "At least 30,000 troops": Karin Bruillard, "Pakistan Launches Full-scale Offensive," *Washington Post*, Oct. 18, 2009, http://www.washingtonpost.com/wp-dyn/content/article/2009/10/17/AR2009101700673.html.

59. David Rohde, "Held by the Taliban—Part Three," *New York Times*, Oct. 19, 2009.

60. Peter Bergen and Jennifer Rowland, "The Year of the Drone," New America Foundation, http://counterterrorism.newamerica.net/drones.

61. Ibid.

62. Ibid.

63. There is still some uncertainty about whether Hakimullah Mehsud was killed, but he has not been seen or heard from in public since a drone strike in the village of Shaktoi on Jan. 14, 2010.

64. Rohde, "Held by the Taliban—Part Three" (2009); Jane Mayer, "The Predator War," *New Yorker*, Oct. 26, 2009.

65. Rohde (2009).

66. "An Interview with the Amir of Mujahidin in South Waziristan—Mullah Nazir Ahmed," As-Sahab, Apr. 7, 2009.

67. Mark Mazzetti and Scott Shane, "Evidence Mounts for Taliban Role in Bomb Plot," *New York Times*, May 5, 2010.

68. "Pakistan: State of the Nation," Al Jazeera-Gallup International Poll conducted July 26–27, 2009, http://english.aljazeera.net/focus/2009/08/2009888238994769.html.

69. "Poll: Understanding FATA Vol. 3," Community Appraisal and Motivation Programme, 2009.

70. "Had grown exponentially": Pak Institute for Peace Studies, Security Report, 2009.

71. "Strike in three different places": Jane Perlez and Pir Zubair Shah, "Day of Suicide Attacks Displays Strength of Pakistani Taliban," *New York Times*, Apr. 5, 2009, http://www.nytimes.com/2009/04/06/world/asia/06pstan.html.

72. "20-hour Taliban attack": "10 Dead in Attack on Pakistani Military HQ," CBS/AP, Oct. 10, 2009, http://www.cbsnews.com/stories/2009/10/10/world/main5375901.shtml.

73. "Foreign area": Ilaqa ghair is often used in Urdu to refer to the FATA, meaning generally "no-go area." I. A. Rehman, "FATA Priorities," *Dawn*, June 25, 2009.

74. For an account of those operations, see Sameer Lalwani, "The Pakistani Military's Adaptation to Counterinsurgency in 2009," *CTC Sentinel*, January 2010, and for Pakistani public support of these operations see "Military Action in Waziristan: Opinion Poll," Gilani Poll/Gallup Pakistan, Nov. 3, 2009, www.gallup.com.pk/Polls/03-11-09.pdf.

75. For more, see Brian Fishman, "Pakistan's Failing War on Terror," *Foreign Policy*, Dec. 1, 2009.

76. Mark Mazzetti and Dexter Filkins, "Secret Joint Raid Captures Taliban's Top Commander," *New York Times*, Feb. 15, 2010.

77. Mustafa Hamid, "Jalal al-Din Haqqani: A Legend in the History of the Afghanistan Jihad," *Al-Sumud* magazine in English, http://www.ansar1.info/showthread.php?t=20201.

78. Gopal, Fishman, and Khan Mehsud, "The Battle for Pakistan."

79. McChrystal, "Commander's Initial Assessment," Aug. 30, 2009.

80. "Support bases": see Omid Marzban, "Shamshatoo Refugee Camp: A Base of Support for Gulbuddin Hekmatyar," *Terrorism Monitor*, May 24, 2007; "exiled from Afghanistan": see Ahmed Rashid Taliban, *Militant Islam, Oil and Fundamentalism in Central Asia* (New Haven: Yale University Press, 2000), pp. 26–27; "reconciliation with Mullah Omar": see "Hekmatyar's Hizb-e Islami Expresses Solidarity with Taliban," *Afghan Islamic Press*, Apr. 1, 2005; "focused on political reconciliation": see "Gulbuddin Hekmatyar: Ruthless Warlord, Karzai Ally, or Both," *Voice of America*, Mar. 24, 2010.

81. Omid Mazban, "Shamshatoo Refugee Camp."

82. Gopal, Fishman, and Khan Mehsud, "The Battle for Pakistan," Apr. 19, 2010.

83. Iqbal Khattak, "Mehsud-Wazir Tension Grows After Power Cut," *Daily Times*, Jan. 17, 2008.

84. Ismail Khan, "Mehsuds Watch Bid to Isolate Baitullah from the Fence," *Dawn*, June 16, 2009; for more on Baitullah Mehsud's rise to power, particularly his relationship with Abdallah Mehsud, see Syed Manzar Abbas Zaidi, "A Profile of Baitullah Mehsud," *Long War Journal*, http://www. longwarjournal.org/multimedia/Baitullah-profile-Manzar-LWJ-09302008. pdf.

85. Mansur Khan Mehsud, "The Battle for Pakistan: Militancy and Conflict in South Waziristan," New America Foundation, Apr. 19, 2010.

86. Ibid.

87. "The Last Frontier," *Economist*, Jan. 2–8, 2010, 394(8663).

88. Khan Mehsud (2010).

89. "Tense Calm Prevails in SWA," *The News*, Aug. 9, 2004.

90. Sailab Mehsud, "Baitullah Offered Amnesty for Renouncing Militancy," *The News*, Feb. 1, 2005; he may also have been assisted by Taliban elements from Afghanistan, including Mullah Dadullah, a commander working for Mullah Omar, although this claim is not well sourced. See Claudio Franco, "The Tehrik-i-Taliban Pakistan," in Antonio Giustozzi, *Decoding the New Taliban* (New York: Columbia University Press, 2009).

91. M. Ilyas Khan, "With a Little Help from His Friends," *Karachi Herald*, June 2004.

92. Iqbal Khattak, "Who Is Maulvi Nazir?" *Friday Times*, Mar. 30, 2007.

93. Khattak (2007).

94. Alamgir Bitani, "Pakistani Taliban Militant Offers Refuge to bin Laden," *Reuters*, Apr. 20, 2007.

95. Javed Afridi and Mushtaq Yusufazi, "Tribal Leader Willing to Give Shelter to Osama, Denies Any Knowledge of Al-Qa'ida Leaders' Whereabouts," *The News*, Apr. 21, 2007.

96. Afridi and Yusufzai, Apr. 21, 2007.

97. Ibid.

98. Mansur Khan Mehsud, Apr. 19, 2010.

99. Ibid.

100. Ibid.

101. Ismail Khan, "Baitullah Mehsud Is Dead," *Dawn*, Aug. 8, 2009.

102. Khan Mehsud, translation of Hakimullah Mehsud's Handwritten Autobiographical Notes, NEFA, Oct. 3, 2009, http://www.nefafoundation.org/ miscellaneous/Hakimullahnotetranslation.pdf.

103. "An Interview with the Amir of Mujahidin in South Waziristan—Mullah Nazir Ahmed," As-Sahab, Apr. 7, 2009.

104. Peter Bergen and Katherine Tiedemann, "The Year of the Drone," New America Foundation, Feb. 24, 2010, http://counterterrorism.newamerica.net/ drones.

105. Declan Walsh, "Leadership Rift Emerges in Pakistani Taliban," *New York Times*, Mar. 5, 2012.

106. Mustafa Hamid (Abu Walid al-Masri), "Jalal al-Din Haqqani, a Legend in the History of the Afghanistan Jihad," *Al-Sumud* magazine in English, http://www.ansar1.info/showthread.php?t=20201, accessed Mar. 15, 2010.

107. Steve Coll, *Ghost Wars* (Penguin Books, New York, 2004), pp. 157, 202, 237.

108. Gopal, Fishman, and Khan Mehsud, "The Battle for Pakistan."

109. Ibid.

110. Hassan Abbas, "South Waziristan's Maulvi Nazir: The New Face of the Taliban," *Terrorism Monitor*, 5(9); Rahimullah Yusufzai, "Jirga Brokered Truce Holds in South Waziristan," *The News*, Mar. 24, 2007; Gopal, Fishman, and Khan Mehsud, Apr. 19, 2010; "Today with Kamran Khan," Geo TV News, Aug. 11, 2009.

111. Gopal, Fishman, and Khan Mehsud, "The Battle for Pakistan."

112. Ibid.

113. Bahadur was named the deputy amir of the anti-Pakistan TTP at its founding in December 2007 but signed a treaty with the Pakistani military shortly afterward to keep troops out of North Waziristan. In July 2008, Bahadur formed an alliance with Mullah Nazir of South Waziristan to oppose TTP-style violence in Pakistan (Gopal, Fishman, and Khan Mehsud, "The Battle for Pakistan"). In February 2009, that alliance gave way to the Shura Ittihad-ul Mujahideen (SIM), a Haqqani-negotiated alliance among Bahadur, Mullah Nazir, and Baitullah Mehsud designed to end their skirmishing. Carlotta Gall, "Pakistan and Afghan Taliban Close Ranks," *New York Times*, Mar. 26, 2009.

114. Gopal, Fishman, and Khan Mehsud, "The Battle for Pakistan."

115. Ibid.

116. Ibid.

117. Ibid.

118. Mansur Khan Mehsud, "The Battle for Pakistan: Militancy and Conflict in Kurram," New America Foundation, Apr. 19, 2010.

119. Zahir Shah Zerazi, "Identity of al-Qaeda Militant Killed in Kurram Revealed," *Dawn*, Feb. 4, 2012.

120. Khan Mehsud, "Kurram," Apr. 19, 2010.

121. Ibid.

122. Ibid.

123. Ibid.

124. Ibid.

125. Ibid.

126. Ibid.

127. Asad Munir, "Taliban & Orakzai," *The News*, June 13, 2009.

128. Raheel Khan, "The Battle for Pakistan: Militancy and Conflict in Orakzai Agency," New America Foundation, Apr. 19, 2010.

129. Mariam Abou Zahab, "Unholy Nexus: Talibanism and Sectarianism in Pakistan's Tribal Areas," CERI-SciencesPo, http://www.ceri-sciencespo.com/archive/2009/juin/dossier/art_mz.pdf, accessed Apr. 10, 2010.

130. Ibid.

131. Khan, "The Battle for Pakistan."

132. Khan, "Militancy and Conflict in Orakzai Agency."

133. Rahimullah Yusufzai, "Hakimullah Unveils Himself to the Media," *The News*, Nov. 30, 2008.

134. Khan, "Orakzai."

135. Ibid.

136. Raheel Khan, "Khyber Agency," New American Foundation, Apr. 19, 2010.

137. Ibid.

138. Ibid.

139. Ibid.

140. Ibid.

141. Ibid.

142. Barelvis believe in saints and ascribe divine powers to the prophet Muhammad. Deobandis eschew saints and believe that the prophet was simply a man led by God.

143. Khan, "Khyber Agency."

144. Ibid.

145. Ibid.

146. Bagh even joined the secular Awami National Party (ANP) to bolster a campaign to become secretary of the Bara Transportation Association.

147. Syed Saleem Shahzad, "Taliban Bitten by a Snake in the Grass," *Asia Times*, Apr. 26, 2008.

148. Rahimullah Yusufzai, "A Who's Who of the Insurgency in Pakistan's Northwest Frontier Province: Part 2—FATA Excluding North and South Waziristan," *Terrorism Monitor*, 7(4).

149. Ashfaq Yusufzai, "Taliban Move in on Peshawar?" ISPNews, July 21, 2008.

150. Shahzad (2008).

151. Ibrahim Shinwari, "Bara Boy Kills Militant Leader," *Dawn*, Aug. 4, 2008.

152. Khan, "Khyber Agency."

153. Saeed Shah, "U.S. Afghan Supply Lines Depend on Islamic Militant," McClatchy Newspapers, Apr. 25, 2008.

154. Barnett Rubin, *The Fragmentation of Afghanistan* (Yale University Press, New Haven, 2002).

155. Ibid.

156. Ayman al-Zawahiri, "Letter to Abu Mus'ab al-Zarqawi," http://www.globalsecurity.org/security/library/report/2005/zawahiri-zarqawi-letter_9jul2005.htm, accessed Apr. 16, 2010; Shmuel Bar and Yair Minzili, "The Zawahiri Letter and the Strategy of al-Qaeda," *Current Trends in Islamist Ideology*, vol. 3, February 2006.

157. Raza Khan, Apr. 19, 2010.

158. Ibid.

159. Ibid.

160. Fauzee Khan Mohmand, "Major Offensive in Mohmand," *Dawn*, Jan. 21, 2009.

161. Raza Khan, Apr. 19, 2010.

162. Imtiaz Gul, "Motives Behind the Attack on the U.S. Consulate in Peshawar," AfPak Channel, Apr. 5, 2010.

163. See Rahmanullah, "The Battle for Pakistan: Militancy and Conflict in Bajaur," New America Foundation, Apr. 19, 2010; Stenersen, Apr. 19, 2010.

164. Rahmanullah, Apr. 19, 2010.

165. Ibid.

166. Christina Lamb, "Airstrike Misses al-Qaeda Chief," *The Times*, Jan. 15, 2010; Rahmanullah, Apr. 19, 2010.

167. Rahmanullah, Apr. 19, 2010; for Abu Khabab's survival, see Craig Whitlock, "The New al-Qaeda Central," *Washington Post*, Sept. 9, 2007.
168. For Abu Faraj al-Libi, see Rahmanullah, Apr. 19, 2010; and Ismail Khan, "'Zawahiri Was Not Here,'" *Dawn*, Jan. 15, 2006. For al-Qaeda videos, see Stenersen, Apr. 19, 2010.
169. Bergen and Tiedemann, "The Year of the Drone."
170. Ibid.
171. Rahmanullah, Apr. 19, 2010.
172. Ibid.; "Pakistan Taliban in Bajaur Truce," BBC News, Feb. 23, 2009.
173. Rahmanullah, Apr. 19, 2010.
174. Ibid.
175. Hassan Abbas, "The Battle for Pakistan: Politics and Militancy in the Northwest Frontier Province," New America Foundation, Apr. 19, 2010.
176. Daud Khattak, "The Battle for Pakistan: Militancy and Conflict in Swat District," New America Foundation, Apr. 19, 2010.
177. Ibid.
178. Ibid.
179. Ibid.
180. Ibid.
181. "Tehreek-e-Nafaz-e Shariati-Muhammadi," South Asian Terrorism Portal, http://www.satp.org/satporgtp/countries/pakistan/terroristoutfits/TNSM.htm, accessed Apr. 6, 2010.
182. Khattak, Apr. 19, 2010; Jane Perlez, "Taliban Exploit Class Rift in Pakistan," *New York Times*, Apr. 16, 2009.
183. Khattak (2010).
184. Abbas, Apr. 19, 2010.
185. Ibid.
186. Khattak, Apr. 19, 2010.
187. Ibid.

FOURTEEN

The 80 Percent Solution: The Strategic Defeat of bin Laden's Al-Qaeda and Implications for South Asian Security

Thomas F. Lynch III

EXECUTIVE SUMMARY

With the death of Osama bin Laden in May 2011, the United States and Western governments scored a major but still underappreciated victory in the nearly decade-and-a-half-old war against al-Qaeda. Bin Laden's death did not eliminate all of the features of al-Qaeda that make it dangerous as a factor in terrorism internationally. Its role in assisting regional jihadist groups in strikes against local governments and by inspiring "lone wolf" would-be martyrs in acts of violence will remain with us for many years. Yet the manner in which U.S. intelligence and military operatives found and eliminated bin Laden in Abbottabad, Pakistan, was devastating to three of the five most critical features of al-Qaeda:

- Its legitimacy as a core organization capable of choreographing catastrophic global terrorist events
- Its brand-name rights as the ultimate victor should any of its loosely affiliated Salafi jihadist regional movements ever achieve success in a local insurgency
- Its ability to claim that it was the base for certain victory—much less one able to reestablish a credible unfettered training area for global jihad—in the area most critical to its own mystical lore: Afghanistan and western Pakistan

Bin Laden's demise also degraded by half—but did not eliminate—the fourth and fifth elements of al-Qaeda's essence: its role as a "vanguard" of a wider network of Sunni Salafi groups, and its ability to serve as a key point of inspiration for lone-wolf terrorists around the globe. As a consequence, the death of Osama bin Laden has produced an 80 percent solution to the problems that this unique terrorist organization poses for Western policy makers.

This 80 percent solution has multiple, important implications. Globally, it means that al-Qaeda's growing isolation from alternative, nonviolent approaches to political change in the Muslim world must be reinforced—and is best reinforced—with a deliberate and visible reduction in the U.S. military footprint in Islamic countries worldwide. Washington can best isolate al-Qaeda and limit its ability to reclaim relevance in the struggle for reform in the Islamic world by quietly enabling security forces in Muslim states to counter al-Qaeda affiliates while simultaneously providing judicious and enduring support for Muslim voices for nonviolent political change.

Yet the most immediate implications of the historic development of May 2, 2011, matter to the trajectory of U.S. policy in South Asia. Bin Laden's demise fundamentally alters the current framework of U.S. and coalition strategy in Afghanistan, and it challenges the underpinnings of U.S. policy toward Pakistan. Bin Laden's unique and pivotal role in grafting al-Qaeda's aspirations onto the regional and local aims of the Afghan Taliban and extremist groups in Pakistan means that the U.S. understanding of the major security risks in South Asia must change in the wake of his death. Absent bin Laden, the risks of al-Qaeda's return to unfettered sanctuary in Afghanistan or western Pakistan have dropped dramatically, while the risks of a devastating proxy war between India and Pakistan over their relative positions in Afghanistan continue to grow. The United States and its Afghan coalition partners must better appreciate this altered risk calculus and reframe diplomatic, military, and economic plans accordingly. The United States must reduce its present focus on killing off every last al-Qaeda affiliated leader or midlevel Haqqani Network operative[1] in Pakistan and pay far more attention to the factors necessary to inhibit proxy war in Afghanistan: an enduring relationship with Pakistan and diplomatic engagement with Pakistan and India on an acceptable political and security framework for Afghanistan into the next decade.

PART ONE: DEFEATING AL-QAEDA

October 2011 was the ten-year anniversary of U.S. military action against al-Qaeda and its Taliban allies in Afghanistan. Yet there remains much popular confusion and too little consensus on the appropriate definition of al-Qaeda. This confusion is unwarranted. al-Qaeda is best understood in the manner most serious scholars of the group have defined it for almost a decade—along five critical dimensions:

- A core organization dedicated to planning, recruiting and training for, and organizing catastrophic global terrorist events against "American, Western, and Zionist crusader" targets, especially in their homelands
- A vanguard for organizing and coordinating regionally focused jihadist groups toward acts of violence against "American and Zionist crusaders" in the Muslim lands where their presence is believed to defile Islam, and in their homelands
- An inspiration to disaffected individual lone-wolf Muslims worldwide to act on their frustrations through violence against the symbols of perceived oppression of Islam
- A brand name representing the ideology of successful violence against so-called crusader governments and officials, in which the most senior leaders of the jihad remain free from serious punishment, penalty, or harm from their acts of terrorism
- The base for certain conquest of Afghanistan (and western Pakistan) in the name of global jihad

These five dimensions stand out in the substantive analytical writings about al-Qaeda since at least 2002.[2]

First, it is a small, core organization wedded to the pursuit of spectacular, catastrophic attacks against Western targets. This is the al-Qaeda dimension conceived by bin Laden and focused in the mid-1990s by bin Laden and his deputy, Ayman al-Zawahiri, on the primary mission of cataclysmic attacks against America and Western states. The goal: to drive them from Muslim lands, much as the mujahideen drove the Soviet Union from Afghanistan.[3] It is also the feature of al-Qaeda that motivated the post–September 11 U.S. policy responses in Afghanistan and subsequently in Iraq and Pakistan.[4] Second, al-Qaeda is the vanguard of a wider network of affiliated Sunni Salafi jihadist[5] groups with origins and deep roots in local and regional struggles to topple standing governments perceived as insufficiently Muslim. These are groups that al-Qaeda's core leaders have attempted, with varying degrees of success, to co-opt into its agenda of catastrophic global terrorism.[6] Third, al-Qaeda is the inspiration for a broad variety of Sunni Muslim malcontents around the world who harbor personal or religiously generated resentment against their specific governments. These individuals might be inspired to act independently and violently on their frustrations through Internet or social media contact with al-Qaeda's core, or more recently some of its loosely affiliated jihadist groups.[7]

Fourth, since September 11, 2001, al-Qaeda has evolved into a global brand, as observed by al-Qaeda chronicler and author Steve Coll during his January 2010 testimony before the U.S. House Armed Services Committee.[8]

al-Qaeda's spectacular success that day, with its attacks on the World Trade Center and the Pentagon, allowed it to ride a wave of popular support across the wider Islamic world for several years. Its popularity in opinion polls among Muslims waned only after 2005, when its ever-widening affiliation with violence against Muslims—from Saudi Arabia to Indonesia—began to wear poorly. Despite this decline, al-Qaeda's relevance as the premier jihadist "brand" lived on in the personas of bin Laden and al-Zawahiri. Both remained folk heroes thanks to their ability to survive for years beyond the reach of vigorous efforts by the United States and other Western governments to capture or kill them. The al-Qaeda brand also retained value through dissemination of prolific video, audio, and Internet messages—the former through the group's modern media production arm, known as *As-Sahab* (translated from Arabic as The Cloud), and the latter in a more recent Internet media center known as *Al-Fajr* (translated from Arabic as The Dawn). These public outreach efforts were also propelled by other affiliated or sympathetic media outlets. Abetted by other spokesmen in recent years, bin Laden and Zawahiri led a personality-driven media and Internet campaign aimed at inspiring violent activity and taking credit for even the most loosely affiliated acts of global terrorism, so long as the violence might be seen as part of the jihadist struggle against outside anti-Islam forces.

Taken together, the core, vanguard, and brand name elements of al-Qaeda made it unique and exceptional within the Salafi jihadist movement. Bin Laden and Zawahiri consciously organized al-Qaeda as an anchor point for their radical ideology. They channeled a minority, reactionary viewpoint into an often acrimonious debate among Muslims about how to harness the frustration unleashed across the Islamic world by modernization and globalization into a movement to violently remake the world order.[9] The individual leadership talents and unique personalities of bin Laden and Zawahiri mattered greatly to the exceptional characteristics of al-Qaeda. Men of vision, organization, and action, they became to Salafi jihadism's world relevance what Lenin and Trotsky became to what was a diffuse and faltering communist cause in the early 1900s.[10] A proper accounting of the lethality and trajectory of al-Qaeda must acknowledge the historically rare and exceedingly important role that bin Laden and Zawahiri played within a movement that saw itself as "the base" of a global revolution and the organizational cadre for that violent revolt.

A fifth and final critical aspect of al-Qaeda has been its mystical affiliation with Afghanistan and western Pakistan. As global terrorism expert Rohan Gunaratna wrote in 2002, al-Qaeda's earliest conception of itself—developed in the late 1980s—included the bedrock function of serving as the base for continuing guerrilla warfare in Afghanistan.[11] Its largely Arab and Egyptian core leadership shared a bond forged in the fight against the Soviet Union and felt the victory over the Soviets in Afghanistan to be of Allah's will and making. Though veterans from that victory tried and failed during the early 1990s to topple what they saw as insufficiently Islamic regimes in Algeria, Azerbaijan, Egypt, Libya, Saudi Arabia, and Tunisia, it was in Afghanistan that groups with mujahideen origins—relying on critical support from

Pakistan's intelligence services—succeeded in establishing a fundamentalist Salafi Sunni state. Claiming this singular jihadist success as their own, al-Qaeda's senior leaders returned from Sudan first to Peshawar, Pakistan, and then to south and southeastern Afghanistan in the late 1990s, making this their base for planning, recruiting, and training international cadres for global catastrophic terrorism. Bin Laden extended his close mujahideen-based personal ties with Afghan Taliban cabinet-level leaders Gulbuddin Hekmatyar, Younis Khalis, and Jalaluddin Haqqani in the form of a personal oath (or *bay'a*) to the Taliban leader of Afghanistan, Mullah Omar.[12] A growing body of literature now demonstrates that al-Qaeda's relationship with Afghanistan's Taliban leadership was punctuated by tensions and misapprehensions, that bin Laden frequently worked around Mullah Omar when making some of his most important decisions and declarations about global jihad, and that bin Laden relied on personal connections in the Afghan mujahideen alumni (unparalleled among his fellow Arabs) to overcome the reluctance of Omar and the wider Afghan Taliban to support his extraregional, global jihadist agenda.[13] It is important to understand the historical importance of Afghanistan and western Pakistan in terms of the legacy of the mujahideen fight, and in the context of the personal relationships among bin Laden, Mullah Omar, and a select number of other Afghan Taliban veterans of the war against the Soviets.

Although bin Laden's death affects each of al-Qaeda's five essential features, his passing is most damaging to al-Qaeda's core, brand name, and base for certain Afghanistan conquest, collapsing al-Qaeda's long-standing dominance in these dimensions. Coupled with the reduction in al-Qaeda's effectiveness as a vanguard and inspiration to Salafi jihadist groups and individuals, the death of bin Laden has produced an 80 percent solution to the more-than-decade-old U.S. quest to defeat al-Qaeda. These underappreciated achievements require a comprehensive reconsideration of U.S. counterinsurgency and counterterrorism strategy for South Asia.

al-Qaeda's Diminished Vanguard Role

Although bin Laden's death will certainly continue the decline in al-Qaeda's relevance to the constellation of Salafi jihadist groups across the Muslim world, it is unlikely to have an immediate discernible impact on the activity of these groups. Since 2002, a few have retained—or regained—their formal affiliation with al-Qaeda's core organization, but most of them have been in decline since shortly after September 11. So too has the capability of peripheral groups to participate regularly or relevantly in al-Qaeda's catastrophic global terrorism aims. In the past decade, al-Qaeda affiliates from Indonesia to the Philippines and Saudi Arabia have lost their leadership and seen an end to unfettered access to al-Qaeda's once-unparalleled training camps that formerly infested eastern Afghanistan and western Pakistan. Gone are the days of the late 1990s and early 2000s when a host of al-Qaeda affiliates were carrying out sophisticated international terrorist attacks. The affiliate group in Yemen (al-Qaeda in the Arabian Peninsula, or AQAP) appears to be the exception; it is still capable of preparing attacks with global import, but not sophisticated or even successful ones.[14]

The cases of Jemaah Islamiyah (JI) in Indonesia and the Abu Sayyaf group in the Philippines stand as prime examples of al-Qaeda's withered reach as an international terrorist vanguard well before bin Laden's death.[15] From the mid-1990s, JI and Abu Sayyaf collaborated closely on national and international terrorist objectives. In 1994 and 1995, JI and Abu Sayyaf facilitated the movement of key al-Qaeda operational leader Khalid Sheikh Mohammed (KSM) as he tested bombs that killed passengers and narrowly missed bringing down a commercial airliner originating from Manila.[16] JI members who ran camps in the Philippines built bombs in 2002 that blew apart Bali, Indonesia, nightclubs and killed more than two hundred people, including many Australian tourists. JI and Abu Sayyaf jointly operated terrorist training camps in Mindanao, a southern Philippines province with islands near Malaysia and Indonesia.

Since 2002, counterterrorism operations carried out by the governments in Jakarta and Manila, along with American, Australian, and other international partners, captured or killed the major leaders of these jihadist groups—terminating long-standing relationships between their senior leaders and those in al-Qaeda's core organization. JI has not been eradicated in Indonesia, but its threat to the Indonesian government is minor and its external operations are believed to be nonexistent. JI's latest leader, an American-educated Malaysian engineer known as Marwan, is the most wanted terrorist in the Philippines. Abu Sayyaf, however, still poses some threat to the government of the Philippines and its military. In July 2011, Abu Sayyaf killed seven Philippine marines and wounded twenty-three in an ambush, and the group's leader, Radullan Sahiron, is believed to have participated in the attack and escaped. Interviewed in the fall of 2011, Rohan Gunaratna, head of the International Centre for Political Violence and Terrorism Research in Singapore, said, "What is crucial for us to understand is the security situation has vastly improved in the southern Philippines, and that improvement is largely from the collaboration between the U.S. and the Armed Forces of the Philippines."[17]

Jemaah Islamiyah is still interested in international terrorism and could regroup, but its major operatives are on the run. Indeed, Umar Patek, a member of JI and the alleged mastermind of the 2002 Bali nightclub bombings, was arrested with his Filipino wife in January in Abbottabad, Pakistan, just months before bin Laden was killed there.

Other groups still generate their own pull, some using western Pakistan as a mixing bowl for interaction with would-be jihadists from non-Muslim countries. The Islamic Movement of Uzbekistan (IMU) poses a conspicuous example in its relationships with disaffected Muslims from Germany. A prominent case of this was documented in 2010 after the capture of German-Afghan Ahmad Wali Siddiqui and his accomplices by NATO-ISAF forces in Afghanistan.[18] The details in this case also reveal that the Pakistani intelligence services are acutely concerned with monitoring and disrupting foreign national activities that might lead to major international terrorism events.

Some of what has been made available in the public domain from the haul of information found in bin Laden's Abbottabad compound seems to underscore the difficulty experienced by al-Qaeda's core leadership in performing its vanguard role in recent years. Information shared by U.S. counterterrorism officials in the open press shows bin Laden himself to have been heavily focused in recent years on corralling and redirecting fragile relationships with regional and national Salafi jihadist groups more oriented toward their own local agendas than the one most important to al-Qaeda.[19]

Despite this ongoing struggle to remain the prominent revolutionary vanguard, al-Qaeda's greatest prospect for successful terrorism today—and into the foreseeable future—rests with the violence promulgated by those in Salafi jihadist regional and national-level networks. British terrorism expert Paul Cruickshank's early-2010 review of the twenty-one most serious terrorism plots against the West from 2004 to 2009 revealed that only six received operational direction and tactical training from al-Qaeda operatives in Pakistan. The fifteen other cases, including the one plotted by AQAP involving an underwear bomb device targeting a Detroit-bound U.S. airliner in December 2009, were either homegrown or developed by autonomous Salafi jihadist groups in Muslim states.[20] A subsequent study of major international terrorism plots in 2010 revealed that three of the twenty plots recorded against Western nations and two of the six planned against the United States originated from regional "franchise" groups.[21] Compared to the aspirations of core al-Qaeda's plots in earlier years, the regionally and locally developed plots of 2009 and 2010 paled in ambition and potential consequence—an underwear bomber in a single airplane and two bombs placed in ink cartridges in a cargo aircraft versus a half-dozen simultaneous airliner explosions or a massive bomb blast geared to collapse a major bridge or tunnel during an urban center rush hour.

In addition, these regional networks may be al-Qaeda-inspired or ideologically aligned, but few have been directly linked to al-Qaeda in terms of interactive planning or operational direction. Those with like-minded ideologies are most concentrated today in the Afghanistan-Pakistan region, Yemen, and Somalia. This is a far cry from the extensive networking in 2000–01 among groups with both regional and global terror aspirations that had critical nodes in locations stretching from the Philippines to Indonesia, Pakistan, Uzbekistan, Saudi Arabia, Yemen, and Sudan.

The formal linkages among these groups waned long before bin Laden's death, and from its inception al-Qaeda has struggled to orchestrate, much less control, the activities of affiliated Salafi jihadist movements.[22] Yet without direct interaction with al-Qaeda's long-standing hierarchy, none have focused on catastrophic terrorist actions against Western targets as a first priority.[23]

There is evidence that the Tehrik-i-Taliban Pakistan (TTP), or Pakistani Taliban, promised to attack American targets as revenge for U.S. targeting of its leadership, notably Baitullah Mehsud, who was killed in a 2009 U.S. drone strike in the Federally Administered Tribal Areas (FATA).[24]

There is also evidence that the peculiar combination in AQAP of original al-Qaeda leaders who had been confined at Guantánamo Bay and American-born militant Anwar al-Awlaki undertook amateurish, failed, and relatively small-scale efforts to down single Western airliners, and that Awlaki, who was killed in a September 2011 drone attack, interacted with American servicemen already inclined to act out violently against U.S. military targets. In addition, there is some evidence that al-Shabaab operatives in Somalia have worked with American expatriates in the hope they might repatriate to the United States and conduct terrorism here.

al-Qaeda's Inspirational Role

Long before the death of bin Laden, al-Qaeda and other jihadist groups worked to inspire grassroots operatives or lone wolves such as U.S. Army Major Nidal Malik Hasan, the Fort Hood shooter. This trend has been increasing and is likely to continue without bin Laden. His persona was generally supportive of but never a direct catalyst for Salafi jihadist radicalization of individuals or small groups toward violence in non-Muslim countries.

In 2010, this type of Salafi jihadist-incited grassroots terrorism accounted for fifteen of the twenty major events or plots recorded.[25] al-Qaeda's role in encouraging this kind of plotting has a long history, but the organization was not directly involved in these specific plots. The growing prevalence of Salafi jihadist social media and Internet sites inciting lone-wolf or grassroots terrorism is both bad news and good news. The bad news is that grassroots operatives can be hard to identify, especially if they operate alone. The good news is twofold. First, their activities tend to be sporadic, as Dennis Blair, then U.S. director of national intelligence, observed in early 2010 in congressional testimony:

> Thus far, however, US Intelligence Community and law enforcement agencies with a domestic mandate assess that violence from homegrown jihadists probably will persist, but will be sporadic. A handful of individuals and small, discrete cells will seek to mount attacks each year, with only a small portion of that activity materializing into violence against the Homeland.[26]

Second, these small groups and individuals tend to be far less capable than well-trained, more "professional" terrorist operatives. And this means they are more likely to make critical mistakes that will allow their attacks to be detected and thwarted. Phrased in a slightly different manner, by analysts Daniel Byman and Christine Fair in summer 2010:

> The difference between a sophisticated killer like Mohamed Atta and so many of his hapless successors lies in training and inherent aptitude. Atta spent months learning his trade in Afghanistan and had the help of al-Qaeda's senior leadership—a fact that underscores the importance of rooting out al-Qaeda havens in Pakistan.[27]

The ascendance of grassroots terrorism posed a threat before bin Laden's death, but it is more evident now. The challenge is that some terrorist attacks must eventually succeed. Terrorism is a tactic; as long as the jihadist ideology—with its emphasis on acting out in violence— survives, its adherents will pose a terrorist threat. But when these plots devolve into relatively simple ones, rather than those of a far more complex and spectacular September 11–style operation, do they constitute a *casus belli* for expansive bureaucracies, extended encroachment on civil liberties, and lavish expense? If the public recognizes that terrorist attacks are part of the human condition, like cancer or hurricanes, it can take steps to deny the practitioners of terrorism the ability to terrorize.[28]

al-Qaeda's Reduced Core

The enormous influence of bin Laden and Zawahiri on al-Qaeda's core function amplifies the impact of bin Laden's death on this dimension of al-Qaeda, especially when compared to its function as a vanguard or an inspiration.

The reorientation of al-Qaeda's 1998 core organization for the practice of serious and credible international terrorism was owed entirely to the mid-1990s combination of bin Laden's charisma and financial connections with Zawahiri's cadre of well-practiced and capable Egyptian and Libyan refugee terror practitioners from the Salafi jihadist group known as Egyptian Islamic Jihad (EIJ).

This combination led to al-Qaeda's rapid ascent as an organization uniquely capable of planning, funding, training for, and launching truly catastrophic global terrorist events. Although it remains relevant in promulgating Salafi jihadist ideology and inspiring groups and individuals already keen on using terrorism against what they see as insufficiently Muslim governments and agencies, al-Qaeda's core has been marginalized on the physical battlefield for a couple of years. Bin Laden's critical role in hatching plots, attaining financial support, and attempting to incite catastrophic global terrorist activities wasn't easy to detect during recent years. Early insights from the material taken by U.S. forces from his compound in Abbottabad indicate that bin Laden was vital in this role until the very end—albeit with very limited payoff.[29]

Bin Laden's death puts al-Qaeda's core group firmly on the ropes. His demise pushes its central organization past the "tipping point" described by many U.S. government intelligence figures in recent years and cogently summarized by the director of national intelligence in early 2010:

> Counterterrorism efforts against al-Qa'ida have put the organization in one of its most difficult positions since the early days of Operation Enduring Freedom in late 2001. However, while these efforts have slowed the pace of anti-US planning and hindered progress on new external operations, they have not been sufficient to stop them....We assess that at least until Usama Bin Ladin and Ayman al-Zawahiri are dead or captured, al-Qa'ida will retain its resolute intent to strike the Homeland. We assess that until counterterrorism pressure on al-Qa'ida's place of refuge, key lieutenants, and operative cadre outpaces the group's ability to recover, al-Qa'ida will retain its capability to mount an attack.[30]

Proof of this trend—even before the death of bin Laden—was evident throughout the year that began with this testimony. Only one of the twenty major terrorist plots against American and Western targets in 2010 could be traced back to al-Qaeda's core leadership in western Pakistan.[31] We should expect this trend to hold true in the final statistics compiled for 2011 and for the global terrorism patterns to come in 2012 and beyond. Save for Ayman al-Zawahiri—the lone remaining *essential* core al-Qaeda leader—none of the central group's remaining leaders poses a credible threat to reorganizing the core mission (see the Appendix). Then again, as CIA Director David Petraeus testified on September 13, 2011, even Zawahiri is no bin Laden:

> Bin Laden's longtime deputy, Ayman al-Zawahiri, succeeded him in June, but much of al-Qa'ida's support base finds Zawahiri less compelling as a leader. We thus assess that he will have more difficulty than did Usama Bin Ladin in maintaining the group's cohesion and its collective motivation in the face of continued pressure.[32]

What's left of the core group simply does not have the operational capability to travel abroad and transfer money that it had prior to September 11. al-Qaeda has been doing its utmost to attack the United States and has not pulled any punches. But it largely failed before bin Laden's death, and it should be expected to fail consistently now that he is dead.[33] Thus, even as al-Qaeda's leadership continues to project an image of being in control, its operatives in Pakistan resemble a driver holding a steering wheel that is no longer attached to the car.[34]

al-Qaeda's Brand-Name Resonance

al-Qaeda's brand-name resonance since September 11 has emanated from two critical factors, both of which have withered in recent years.

First, al-Qaeda's ability to plan and execute a spectacular strike against prominent American targets on U.S. soil gave its core leadership iconic status. Although a majority of Muslims around the world were appalled by the orgy of violence represented by al-Qaeda's attacks in September 2001, many of those who felt disempowered or repressed by domestic or regional leadership—which they long suspected was somehow benefiting from American policy support—suddenly felt empowered. The scope of the September 11 strike set al-Qaeda's core apart from the many regionally based and focused Sunni jihadist organizations. From 2002 to 2005, al-Qaeda operatives planned, executed, or claimed credit for spectacular strikes against Western targets in Bali, Madrid, and London. Yet al-Qaeda's run of truly dramatic successes against the "far enemy" subsequently stagnated. Foiled strikes against airliners flying out of Britain's Heathrow Airport in 2006 and against U.S. military bases in Germany in 2007, New York bridges in 2009, and a Danish newspaper office in 2010—each of which originated with al-Qaeda's central cell in western Pakistan[35]—diminished al-Qaeda's predominance in executing its chief calling card. Subsequent international media attention to planned (and often failed) acts of international terrorism sponsored by regional Salafi jihadist groups from Yemen and Somalia further eroded the exclusivity of al-Qaeda's branding on spectacular attacks (the kind that pose a true strategic threat).

al-Qaeda's brand remained strong despite this declining capacity for large-scale strikes against the United States and other Western nations thanks to the survivability of bin Laden (and to a lesser extent Zawahiri) in the face of an intense global manhunt. The two leaders remained beyond the reach of powerful American and Western forces seeking their demise—adding an aura of impunity to the al-Qaeda brand. This came to a crashing end on May 2, 2011. The swiftness and finality of bin Laden's demise reverberated sharply across the Muslim world. Denials and conspiracy theories remain—and will likely endure—but for most of his longtime admirers, bin Laden's dramatic end exploded this myth of invincibility and impunity.

al-Qaeda's Afghan Fascination

Despite the fact that al-Qaeda's antecedents lie in the Islamist extremist movements that formed to fight against the autocratic, oppressive regimes of Egypt, Saudi Arabia, and Algeria,[36] Afghanistan has held a special fascination. This fascination is derivative of al-Qaeda's peculiar history and its unique aspirations. al-Qaeda was founded in eastern Afghanistan by bin Laden's longtime Palestinian mentor, Abdullah Azzam, and set up shop in Peshawar, Pakistan, in 1988. Before his 1989 assassination, Azzam, with the assistance of bin Laden and other Arab members of the mujahideen, ensured that al-Qaeda's organizing cadre of mujahideen received more than its fair share of credit across the Muslim world for the defeat of the Soviet empire in Afghanistan and tied this victory into a narrative asserting the power of violent jihad to fully remake the Islamic world. The mujahideen database originally created by bin Laden for tracking the martyred and the missing in the anti-Soviet jihad provided the springboard for global al-Qaeda recruiting. When bin Laden and Zawahiri were forced from Sudan in the mid-1990s, their return to refuge in Taliban-led Afghanistan allowed al-Qaeda to develop the planning, training, and management capabilities to become the general headquarters for international Islamist terrorism. Since late 2001, al-Qaeda has shared with the Afghan Taliban a view that Pakistan is the natural location for vital efforts to free Afghanistan from foreign rule—to validate the victory over the Soviet Union in Afghanistan by another successful guerrilla war.[37] Born, inspired, reborn, and steeled in Afghanistan for global jihad, al-Qaeda sees success there as an unparalleled bellwether.

At the same time, the Afghan Taliban and al-Qaeda's core leadership diverge in many goals and aspirations. The divergence has been present since the relationship between the two groups began to evolve in the late 1990s. First, the Taliban remains a provincially oriented movement. Its focus has been to control Afghanistan as an Islamic emirate. al-Qaeda has been a globally oriented, anti-imperialist movement. Many Taliban leaders, including Mullah Omar, have expressed frustration with al-Qaeda's expansive aspirations, seeing them as recklessly risking consolidation of the Taliban's more limited goals in Afghanistan. Second, al-Qaeda's core leadership is largely bereft of ethnic Afghans and South Asian Pashtuns. Long-standing leaders of the Afghan Taliban have associations with al-Qaeda leaders going back to the anti-Soviet jihad, but none are among the key cadre of core al-Qaeda leaders.[38] Related to both points is the curious divergence in how each group describes Afghanistan. The Afghan Taliban calls it the "Islamic Emirate of Afghanistan" and believes it is a unique, distinct entity with a government-in-exile awaiting return to Kabul under the rightful leadership of Mullah Omar. al-Qaeda's core leadership refers to Afghanistan as but a part of the "Islamic Emirate of Khorasan (or Khoristan)," a territory including Afghanistan, eastern Iran, and western Pakistan, without reference to Mullah Omar as the rightful emir. al-Qaeda has even appointed its own Arab and North African–born leaders of this Emirate of Khorasan since 2007.[39] The fact that it has appointed no such parallel emir for Iraq, North Africa, or the Arabian Peninsula appears to be at least circumstantial evidence of important ideological and philosophical differences.

These differences were papered over by the personal history between bin Laden and key Afghan Taliban figures and the mystical history attached by bin Laden to Afghanistan as the cradle for an Islamic emirate and caliphate.[40] Two critical factors discussed by regional experts, including bin Laden's Pakistani biographer, Hamid Mir,[41] diminished the policy relevance of these fissures. First, deposed emir Mullah Omar steadfastly refused to renounce ties to bin Laden or the al-Qaeda core vision of global jihad, despite the fact that his September 2001 refusal to hand over bin Laden to the United States led to precisely what a majority of his fellow Afghan Taliban leaders feared: the toppling of the Taliban emirate in Afghanistan by a U.S.-led invasion.

Second, bin Laden remained at large, with a hyperinflated aura of invincibility and an intact personal bay'a to Mullah Omar. For these reasons, bin Laden alone was uniquely critical to aligning an Afghan Taliban movement most focused on its nationalist agenda with his al-Qaeda movement focused on a globally oriented jihad.

With bin Laden's death, the glue that papered over these fissures is gone. His bay'a to Mullah Omar has no analog with Zawahiri or the cohort of Egyptians and Libyans at the helm of al-Qaeda's remaining core elements in Pakistan. It has absolutely no relevance to al-Qaeda's major leaders elsewhere around the globe. Bin Laden's long-standing ties to the late Younis Khalis and Jalaluddin Haqqani, cut with the death of Khalis in 2006, are now totally severed in the aftermath of the Abbottabad raid.[42] The Haqqani Network has been recognized recently as the successor to Hizb-i-Islami-Khalis in facilitating al-Qaeda's global propaganda, which has clashed with Mullah Omar's Afghanistan-focused jihad. But that role can best be understood as fundamentally altered since May 2, 2011. With bin Laden and his closest Pakistani couriers gone, the Haqqanis now, more than ever, need to adhere to the wishes of the Pakistani Inter-Services Intelligence agency (ISI). And the ISI's wishes—since at least late 2008—are that its Islamic proxy militias not be engaged in activities construed as extraregional global jihad.[43]

al-Qaeda may continue to drape itself in the Taliban flag and proclaim allegiance to Mullah Omar (although this remains to be seen), but with bin Laden's death the Afghan Taliban faces one stark certainty. Though it shares a loose but important Salafi jihadist credo with al-Qaeda, it remains dependent on all manner of support for its insurgency from elements within and beholden to the Pakistani security services. Mullah Omar, Haqqani, and even Gulbuddin Hekmatyar must calculate their futures on the basis of this dominant reality. As they do, al-Qaeda's ability to repeat its propaganda performance following the Soviet withdrawal from Afghanistan—taking credit for any (unlikely) defeat of the United States or any important role in the (more likely) successes the Taliban may have in carving out political space in the country—will wither rapidly. More important, there will be less risk that al-Qaeda will find a serious safe haven in Afghanistan in the near to mid-term future for plotting and conducting training for catastrophic global terrorism.[44] Absent the onset of a stark proxy war between Afghanistan and Pakistan in Afghanistan, Pakistan's military and intelligence leadership will have very little interest in seeing al-Qaeda again set up shop from which to wage a bloody campaign of international terrorism, and it will use the tools at its disposal to constrain this possibility.[45]

PART TWO: THE CURRENT POLITICAL LANDSCAPE IN SOUTH ASIA

The present circumstances are fundamentally different from those at the middle of the last decade—a time when, as critics rightly point out, far too many officials in the U.S. government prematurely declared that al-Qaeda was either dead or terminally on the run.[46] Then, America's distractions in Iraq clouded proper judgment about the degree to which al-Qaeda remained a vibrant and evolving organization in western Pakistan, obfuscated the critical manner in which bin Laden was able to bring together disparate local jihadist groups, and generated intemperate claims of victory. The three elements of al-Qaeda most affected by Laden's death were all alive and well at that time.[47]

In 2005–2008, al-Qaeda's planning for large-scale terrorist attacks—its core function—was on the rebound. The core had unfettered sanctuary in Pakistan's western frontier, where a critical mass of its main surviving pre–September 11 alumni had gathered and were actively plotting, training operatives, and sending them off for spectacular, though ultimately unsuccessful, attacks in Germany, the United Kingdom, and the United States.[48] Bin Laden's reputation as the greatest escape artist since Harry Houdini remained intact.

Moreover, bin Laden's personal pledge, or bay'a, to Mullah Omar left al-Qaeda well poised to capitalize on an apparent rising torrent of Afghan Taliban and Haqqani Network insurgency successes against an underresourced NATO military operation and an inept and corrupt Karzai government in Kabul.

It took the focused attention of significant U.S. military and intelligence activities from late 2008 through 2011 to arrest these negative trends and establish a serious network of agents and operatives necessary to severely erode al-Qaeda's key core elements in western Pakistan and kill bin Laden, thus eliminating his irreplaceable import in three of al-Qaeda's five critical elements and his important role in the two others.

This critical American counterterrorism achievement cannot be overstated. However, it can be misappreciated and fumbled if not put in proper context of the long-standing—and now unambiguously more dominant—challenges inherent in South Asian security. Bin Laden's demise represents a substantial solution to the challenges to the West from global terrorism and is the critical element in disentangling core al-Qaeda's aims from those of the Afghan Taliban insurgency. The regional dynamics of the Afghan Taliban insurgency and metastasizing Islamist radicalism in Pakistan—some of it under the control of Pakistan's intelligence agencies and some of it not—remain at work and are now more important than ever.

The Danger of Proxy War in South Asia

The war in Afghanistan has long been viewed by American leaders as a struggle to empower a government in Kabul that could resist any return of al-Qaeda's core group of global jihadists. In the aftermath of bin Laden's death, the war is best reconsidered as it has always been viewed in Afghan, Pakistani, and Indian circles, that is, as a Pakistani-supported Pashtun rebellion against a Tajik, Uzbek, and Hazara-dominated Government of the Islamic Republic of Afghanistan with links to New Delhi and Tehran, and only a fig leaf of Pashtun representation in the form of President Hamid Karzai, who is completely mistrusted in Pakistan as too cozy with India. Bin Laden's demise should encourage a more sober American and coalition revisiting of the narrative that matters most in the region: one in which Western forces are seen as having taken sides since 2001 in a regional proxy war between India and Pakistan. The United States has placed itself in the middle of a conflict that began long before the Afghan war, with the collapse of the Najibullah regime in 1992, by favoring northern Afghans with Indian ties in opposition to southern Afghan Pashtuns viewed in Islamabad as a buffer against Hindu encroachment. Furthermore, the United States has failed to provide sufficient political or military guarantees in Afghanistan that those conservative, largely rural Pashtuns were not discriminated against by a political construct that allowed for too little regional representation and too much Indian encroachment.

As they have for more than thirty years, Pakistan's intelligence services retain the critical, even if far from omnipotent, role in guiding the multiple factions of the Pashtun-dominated Afghan Taliban insurgency. Pakistan's aims in sponsoring the Afghan Taliban do not align—and have never aligned—completely with those of the Taliban itself. First and foremost, Pakistan aims to neuter Indian influence in Afghanistan and prevent what Islamabad fears would be hegemonic encirclement by New Delhi in league with the government in Kabul. Pakistani military and intelligence services view the Afghan Taliban as the most effective agent to secure this objective, with certain martial groups like the Haqqani Network possessing conspicuous talent in perpetrating acts of targeted violence. Pakistan also supports the constellation of Afghan Taliban groups as it seeks to effectively manage the dangerous undertones present in Pashtun nationalism—trying to ensure that militant Pashtun groups do not coalesce around any vision for a "Greater Pashtunistan" that would threaten a move toward autonomy in the almost 50 percent of Pakistani territory where Pashtuns constitute the majority ethnic group.[49]

With bin Laden dead and the critical mass of the al-Qaeda core in western Pakistan eliminated or severely compromised, the essential dynamics of the Afghanistan war are those with regional, rather than international, import. Fundamentally, the war in Afghanistan is an Indo-Pakistan proxy war—between nations that have fought three shooting wars and indulged in several other martial crises since 1947— layered atop the ethnic cleavages unique to Afghanistan. In this proxy war, NATO counterinsurgency forces are bit players, and America's counterterrorism activities are perceived as tilting in favor of northern Afghan ethnic groups and Indian long-term interests. America's ability to help wind down the violence will amount to little without a sober evaluation of how its enhanced diplomatic presence and a steady but well-managed reduction in Western military forces must be used to dampen prospects for a rapidly accelerating proxy war between these historical South Asian antagonists.

Islamabad believes that India has established increasingly effective political and economic influence in Afghanistan by leveraging American naiveté, the long-standing hatred of Pakistan among non-Pashtuns in northern Afghanistan,[50] and economic assistance amounting to some $1.4 billion, with another $500 million promised.[51] Pakistan's perceptions persist—and are growing—despite the fact that Indian sources report, and many outside observers confirm, that fewer than thirty-six hundred Indians live or work in Afghanistan, and almost all of them are businessmen or contract workers. Also, there are only four Indian consulates in Afghanistan in addition to its Kabul embassy, precisely the same number that Pakistan maintains.[52] Yet the fear of being squeezed in an Indian nutcracker has led Pakistan's intelligence services to keep the Afghan Taliban in play and its leadership under the ISI's watch and patronage at various locations across western Pakistan.[53]

The high degree of ISI influence over these groups has long been suspected, but it became clear in the past couple of years as outside civilian researchers and Western intelligence services gained access to corroborating information. Important 2010 reports by Matt Waldman at the Carr Center for Human Rights Policy at Harvard; Anand Gopal, Mansur Khan Mahsud, and Brian Fishman at the New America Foundation (NAF); and Jeffrey Dressler at the Institute for the Study of War (ISW) chronicled these intimate relationships in some detail.[54] Waldman's work, based on his interviews with ten midlevel Afghan Taliban commanders from south and east Afghanistan, established that they all understood the role of Pakistan's ISI as indispensable to their insurgency, a role termed "as clear as the sun in the sky."[55] One of the commanders explained why this pervasive role was not more widely appreciated by outsiders for such a long time:

> Every commander knows about the involvement of the ISI in the leadership but we do not discuss it because we do not trust each other, and they are much stronger than us. They are afraid that if they say anything against the Taliban or ISI it would be

reported to the higher ranks—and they may be removed or assassinated....[56]

These commanders also told Waldman that the leadership of the ISI is in the hands of the Taliban, or the Taliban would not be able to receive the medical, munitions, or family support they receive consistently in Pakistan.[57]

The NAF work by Gopal and coauthors, along with that by ISW's Dressler, established the especially important role of the Haqqani Network in advancing Pakistani interests against Indian "agents and provocateurs" in Afghanistan, making the Haqqani Network one of Pakistan's favored Afghan insurgent groups.[58]

This is not to suggest that Afghan Taliban leaders don't resent ISI manipulation. Waldman's interviews confirm reports by Michael Semple and others with contacts in the Afghan Taliban that its leadership deeply resents ISI pressure. This is largely because Pakistan's second critical security aim in managing Afghan insurgent groups is to constrain Taliban abilities to effect any independent "Greater Pashtunistan" or "Greater Afghanistan" that could usurp Pakistani territory west of the Indus River—endangering the very construct of Pakistan since 1971.

Here, Pakistani management techniques exploit Taliban fissures and favor those Pashtun subgroups deemed less likely to pursue agendas contrary to Pakistani security interests.[59]

Waldman's interviews with Haqqani Network leaders apprehended in Afghanistan during 2009 indicated that they had been trained by the ISI, with one of his subjects claiming, "The ISI is hard to recognise; we could tell, but we kept it secret."[60] An increasing body of evidence confirms that although the ISI remains active with a constellation of Pashtun militants and Afghan Taliban groups astride eastern and northeastern Afghanistan, it has designated the Haqqani Network as a preferred "strategic asset," affording its operatives discreet but special assistance.[61] The network has moved beyond its reputation for local antigovernment operations in the Paktia, Paktika, and Khowst provinces of eastern Afghanistan to successful high-profile strikes such as the July 2008 and October 2009 attacks on the Indian Embassy compound in Kabul, coordination of the September 2011 suicide truck bombing in Wardak province that killed five Afghan civilians and injured seventy-seven U.S. troops, another strike that month in Kabul that included a twenty-hour commando-style attack on International Security Assistance Force (ISAF) headquarters and the U.S. Embassy, and a suicide car bombing in the capital in October that killed thirteen U.S. personnel.[62] The increasing pace and audacity of Haqqani Network operations reveals the extent to which Afghan militants play a key role in Pakistan's security strategy for Afghanistan, as well as how the ISI and parts of the Pakistani military play an essential role in sustaining the viability and relative fortunes of Afghan Taliban groups.

These groups serve as Pakistan's proxy against Indian agents and influence in Afghanistan, but also against those viewed as too cozy with Indian interests—including the Karzai government and the NATO/ ISAF military forces and Western governments supporting it. As NATO/ISAF military operations since 2009 in southern Afghanistan eroded Mullah Omar's Afghan Taliban as a prominent proxy for Pakistani interests, Pakistan's intelligence and military activities have helped offset these losses, enabling the Haqqani Network to make a wide and growing reach into Afghanistan.[63] Properly understood, this disturbing certainty makes it clear that real progress against the Afghan insurgency, or toward political engagement with it, requires Pakistani support.

PART THREE: POLICY OPTIONS FOR THE FUTURE

Washington's conflict resolution strategy for Afghanistan and Pakistan is much overdue for a rethinking. A sober approach to future policy must look beyond Afghanistan, and even Afghanistan-Pakistan, to focus on the core dynamics of the South Asian security dilemma.

The Afghanistan Context

With its links to al-Qaeda largely broken by the death of bin Laden, the Afghan Taliban must be reconsidered for what it is in terms of a dangerous proxy war in Afghanistan: a repugnant but resilient insurgent constellation with unwavering Pakistani support, but also in many ways an authentic voice for conservative rural Pashtuns who remain severely disenfranchised from the Kabul government along social, economic, justice, and political lines.[64] In this light, a critical mass of the Afghan Taliban must be better integrated into Afghanistan's fledgling polity in a manner that overcomes its present political isolation without accelerating a decline toward proxy-funded civil war.

American diplomats need to sponsor quiet but serious talks between Pakistani and Indian representatives to craft a set of mutually acceptable rules for enfranchisement of the Taliban, bringing it into an Afghan polity. India is unlikely to ever accept a prominent role at the national level of Afghan governance for the senior Taliban leaders who led the country from 1996 to 2001. Pakistan will certainly want a prominent role for conservative Afghan Pashtuns along its immediate border region even if those provincial leaders are not the same ones who led Afghanistan in the late 1990s. Within this broad construct, there appears room for painstaking but essential negotiations between the two antagonists most likely to nudge Afghanistan toward a more federal governance structure, in which Islamabad and New Delhi realize their minimal security needs, not their ultimate security wants. American and NATO force planners must devise processes to draw down to the residual U.S./coalition forces or U.N. military stabilization forces necessary to stay on for the rest of the decade, enforce this essential Indo-Pakistani framework agreement, and serve as a buttress against points of friction or violence that could descend into the chaos of a new conflict.

On June 17, 2011, in a major step forward, the U.N. Security Council accepted a U.S. request to treat al-Qaeda and the Taliban separately, dividing their members into two lists from a single list of global terrorists the United Nations has maintained since 1998.[65] Despite its understandable reservations, India acquiesced to this change. With the two separate lists, U.N. sanctions on core al-Qaeda members will not necessarily apply to the Afghan Taliban. As Pakistani journalist Ahmed Rashid noted shortly after the change, this will be a major boost for the Afghan political reconciliation process.[66] However, more work must be done to craft a durable political reconciliation process that militates against the most critical risk of future proxy war in Afghanistan. The Bonn II discussions of December 2011 failed in this regard. Bonn II began before proper preconditions were set for a more federal system of governance in Afghanistan, and the last-minute Pakistani boycott negated serious discussion of the critical conditions to be met by the most critical actor outside of Afghanistan.

The eventual establishment of a Taliban political office in Doha, Qatar, is another necessary positive step, but one that will take time to mature.[67] It must become a complement with—for it will never be a substitute for—necessary discussions between Pakistan's military-intelligence establishment, the Indian government, and Afghanistan coalition partners on the future shape of an Afghanistan that is stabler and less violent.

Led by the United States, the coalition in Afghanistan must now shepherd reconciliation talks among the Afghan government, the Taliban, and representatives from Pakistan's military and intelligence services to show how a more federal system in Afghanistan can meet Pakistani and Taliban aims while preserving the basic framework of an Afghan republic. Most important, the United States must quietly encourage talks between Pakistan and India that lead to a framework for national governance and security in Afghanistan that each can live with and that outside parties can help enforce. The requirement for such talks is certain and the need to get them started is vital. Without an Indo-Pakistani framework for the future in Afghanistan, Pakistan's military-intelligence leadership will continue to hedge on the certainty of a U.S. troop departure, worry that India will be the main benefactor from the future orientation of Afghan National Security Forces, and continue to interfere with the security situation in Afghanistan as a result.

The Pakistani Context

Much as bin Laden's demise opened the door to better American understanding of the fundamental South Asian security situation that U.S. policy must address, it also requires a revisiting of the issue most critical to U.S.-Pakistan relations. Pakistan's failure to seriously pursue bin Laden within its borders for most of a decade brought it well-deserved scrutiny in the wake of the Abbottabad raid. This raid complemented—indeed capped off—the necessary and highly successful American-dominated efforts since late 2008 to kill al-Qaeda core leaders and disrupt al-Qaeda operations across Pakistan.

Since the May 2011 raid, American policy toward Pakistan has featured a single-minded focus on unilateral counterterrorist actions geared to "break the back" of al-Qaeda's core leadership in that country.[68] Despite a late-2011 halt on counterterrorism drone strikes in Pakistan after the November 26 cross-border incident that killed twenty-four Pakistani soldiers, this U.S. policy emphasis remains dominant, even though two factors suggest it lacks proper focus or reasonable prospect for success. First, the remaining al-Qaeda leaders in Pakistan—with the exception of Ayman al-Zawahiri—appear ill-suited for consideration as credible core leaders for al-Qaeda's future.[69] Despite his reputation for divisiveness, Zawahiri's qualifications as a proven thinker, organizer, and catalyst of international terrorist activities dwarf those of anyone else believed to be in Pakistan. Among those left there, only Abu Yahya al-Libi and Sulaiman Abu Ghaith have résumés with anything resembling the kind of vision, organizational skill, and leadership quality necessary to resuscitate a badly shattered al-Qaeda core program driving global catastrophic terrorism (see the Appendix). Second, the documented success of the American-driven drone program in the FATA makes it unlikely that Zawahiri would risk staying there. He is far more likely to be in and out of asylum near urban areas in Pakistan, where drone strikes pose an unacceptable risk of collateral damage to a large number of innocent civilians, and where his apprehension or elimination would require an important level of Pakistani cooperation.

Thus, it appears a quixotic venture to continue a single-minded, unilateral U.S. counterterrorism tactic in Pakistan led by unending drone strikes that are unlikely to eliminate the prime al-Qaeda target and that have become the universal symbol in Pakistan of American disrespect for Pakistani sovereignty and disregard for innocent Pakistani life.[70] The aggressive drone strikes from the May 2011 death of bin Laden to the November 2011 cross-border U.S./NATO-on-Pakistani-military firing incident played directly into a Pakistani narrative of American hubris and unworthiness as a moral arbiter as much as they appear to be a self-defeating tactic. Each additional strike stirred up an ever-more-critical mass of animosity toward America across Pakistani society in a fashion now encouraging what David Kilcullen described as "accidental guerrillas."[71] More young Pakistani males, ordinarily content to remain detached from violence, are becoming charged with participatory zeal to join a fight in Afghanistan that they believe is a righteous jihad to avenge innocent Muslim victims of drone strikes.[72]

Pakistani animus toward unilateral U.S. action has huge implications for America's counterterrorism aspirations in the country, and for the many other security challenges active in Pakistan. First, Ayman al-Zawahiri's death or apprehension will likely require Pakistani cooperation. It would be both prudent and necessary for the United States to pressure Pakistan to focus on the hunt for the most dangerous residual al-Qaeda figure. Second, Pakistan's reported August 2011 dressing-down by Beijing, which allegedly links a Muslim terrorist attack in the western Chinese province of Xinjiang and terrorist organizations in western Pakistan, provides the United States with an opportunity to parallel the Chinese pressure with more of its own.[73] Third, Pakistan's internal challenges from Islamist militants, including the growing incidence of militant-inspired violence against mosques and government facilities,[74] though not threatening an imminent takeover, will continue for some time and require Pakistan's military and intelligence services to seek outside assistance to make up for their obvious deficiencies. Finally, Pakistan's growing nuclear arsenal—much of this growth focusing on smaller, more accurate, and shorter-range weapons—may eventually play into a crisis between Pakistan and nuclear-armed India that will require U.S. diplomatic or even military intervention.[75]

Indeed, the potential for India-focused Islamic militant groups in Pakistan, with or without clandestine collaboration by Pakistani security forces, to carry out a strike in India that exceeds the November 2008 Mumbai attack is one of the most serious and growing threats to U.S. interests in South Asia.[76] All four of these critical security scenarios require more, not less, open lines of communication and coordination between Islamabad and Washington. Single-minded American pursuit of technologically driven strikes against lesser al-Qaeda figures and middling Afghan Taliban insurgents puts these frustrating, but essential, American-Pakistani lines of communication at risk, setting up an undesirable long-term future of isolation and miscommunication. A multifaceted, forward-looking American policy toward Pakistan must assess the risk-reward outcomes from a failure to think beyond the anti-al-Qaeda, anti–Afghan Taliban framework that has come to largely overwhelm the other critical security dynamics in this critical bilateral relationship.

CONCLUSION

In a strategic or global sense, one can make the case—as many senior U.S. leaders began to do in the summer of 2011—that al-Qaeda seems well along in a process of defeating itself. Its accelerating political isolation in the Muslim world during the mid-2000s was accompanied by a successful post-2007 effort by the United States and allied governments to largely destroy central al-Qaeda's leadership along the Afghanistan-Pakistan border. The May 2011 death of Osama bin Laden has brought an end to the destabilizing pattern of hunt-and-escape that elevated the terrorist leader's reputation (and to a lesser extent, that of Ayman al-Zawahiri) to living legend status for so long. Indeed, bin Laden's demise has provided a substantial—80 percent—solution to the most critical international security challenges posed by al-Qaeda.

Now, it is important to allow al-Qaeda's increasing self-isolation from alternative, nonviolent Muslim approaches toward political change in the Islamic world to better inform the framework for U.S. counterterrorism policy in general and America's policy approach to Afghanistan, Pakistan, and South Asia in particular.

To prevail in Afghanistan on the timetable announced by the Obama administration and minimize the more serious risk of a larger conflict breaking out, American policy must change tack in the wake of bin Laden's death. We need to understand that the risks of devastating proxy war between India and Pakistan now dwarf the risks of al-Qaeda's return to unfettered sanctuary and recalibrate our diplomatic energies and military priorities accordingly. This will require earnest and difficult negotiations with the Pakistanis, Indians, Afghan Taliban, and northern ethnic groups in Afghanistan.

In Pakistan, we must eschew the intemperate approach of unilaterally attacking al-Qaeda's remaining core leaders or midlevel Afghan Taliban figures to their last breath. Instead, we must work to recalibrate the always difficult but supremely important relationship with Pakistan so that Islamabad will do more in a bilateral effort to eliminate the international terrorist presence from the country. In addition, we must help Pakistan work quietly with India to find the necessary accommodation in Afghanistan that will inhibit the possibility of a reckless proxy war between two nuclear-armed states that could seriously threaten a calamity of global import.

APPENDIX

Major al-Qaeda Core Terrorist Figures Status 2007–2011

This list was compiled using information from the following sources: U.N. Security Council Resolutions 1267 (1999) and 1989 (2011) concerning al-Qaeda and associated individuals and entities, available at http://www.un.org/sc/committees/1267/aq_sanctions_list.shtml; the 2009 compilation on the Long War Journal website found at http://www.longwarjournal.org/al-qaeda-leaders.php#ixzz1WlmckeWX; the Global Security website page of al-Qaeda senior leader lists, found at http://www.globalsecurity.org/security/profiles/generate_members.php?name=Al-Qaeda and at http://www.globalsecurity.org/security/profiles/al-qaeda_leadership_losses.htm; and Rohan Gunaratna, *Inside Al Qaeda: Global Network of Terror* (New York: Columbia University Press, 2002), pp. 56–58.

Core Leaders Believed to Be in Pakistan/Afghanistan

Estimated sixteen out of thirty-two at large; one *essential*** and two *key** figures remain alive. **Bold** denotes a leader who has been captured or killed.

- Abu Faraj al-Yemeni
- **Abu Haris—killed in Pakistan, September 2008 (former Pakistani Jaish-e-Mohammad head)**
- **Abu Ihklas al-Masri—captured in Kunar, Afghanistan, April 2011**
- Abu Kasha al-Iraqi
- Abu Khabab al-Masri*—killed in Pakistan, July 2008
- **Abu Obaidah al-Masri—deceased in Pakistan, spring 2008**
- **Abu Turab al-Urduni* [Jordanian]—son-in-law of Zawahiri, multiple reports say killed in 2001 or 2010**
- Abu Yahya al-Libi*—reported killed in Pakistan, December 2009; later rescinded
- Adam Gadahn (ne: Adam Pearlman) [U.S.]
- **Atiyah Abd al-Rahman—killed in Pakistan, August 2011**
- Ayman al-Zawahiri** [Egyptian]
- Amin al-Haq [Afghan]—Osama bin Laden's security coordinator, captured/released by Pakistanis in January 2008

- Hamza bin Laden [Saudi]
- **Ilyas Kashmiri*—reported killed (for a second time) in Pakistan, June 2011, awaiting firm confirmation**
- **Marwan al-Suri [Syrian]—reported killed in gun battle with Pakistani authorities, April 2006; later doubts**
- Matiur Rehman [Pakistani]
- Mohamed Abul Khair [Saudi]—bin Laden bodyguard
- **Mohamad Usman—killed in Pakistan, fall 2010**
- **Mustafa al-Jaziri—killed in Pakistan, May 2010**
- **Osama al-Kini—killed in Pakistan, January 2009**
- **Qari Mohammad Zafar—former head of Pakistan's Lahskar-e-Jhangvi, reported killed in Pakistan, March 2010**
- Qari Saifullah Akhtar [Pakistani—HUJI]—reportedly wounded in Pakistan, August 2010
- **Qari Zia Rahman [Pakistani]—reported killed by Pakistani forces, April 2010; later doubts**
- Rashid Rauf [U.K. of Pakistani origin]—reported killed in Pakistan, November 2008; later retracted
- Saad al-Sharif [Saudi]
- **Sa'ad bin Laden*—killed in Afghanistan/Pakistan, spring 2009**
- **Saleh al-Somali—killed in Pakistan, winter 2009**
- **Sheikh Sa'id al-Masri (aka Mustafa Abu Yazid)*—killed in Pakistan, May 2010**
- Sulaiman Abu Ghaith* [Kuwaiti]—reportedly released by Iran in prisoner exchange, September 2010
- Thirwat Saleh Shihata [Egyptian]
- Younis al-Mauritani*—reported detained in Pakistan, September 2011

Core Leaders Believed to Be in Yemen

Estimated six of ten at large, 1 *key** figure remains alive. **Bold** denotes a leader who has been captured or killed.

- **Anwar al-Awlaki [dual U.S.-Yemeni]—killed in Yemen, September 2011**
- Fahd al-Quso [Yemeni]—USS *Cole* conspirator, falsely reported killed, October 2009

- **Hamza Ali Saleh al-Dhayani [Yemeni]—surrendered to Yemeni authorities, June 2010**
- Ibrahim Hassan al-Asiri [Saudi]—known as key bomb maker
- Ibrahim Suleiman al-Rubaish [Saudi]—2006 GTMO (Guantánamo Bay) release and failed Saudi rehabilitation program
- **Mohammed al-Awfi [Saudi]—2007 GTMO release, failed Saudi reprogramming, AQAP cofounder; surrendered to Saudi Arabia, 2010**
- Nasser al-Wuhayshi* [Yemeni]—bin Laden bodyguard, 2006 Sanaa jailbreak, and AQAP cofounder
- Othman al-Ghamdi [Saudi]—2006 GTMO release and failed Saudi rehabilitation program
- Said Ali al-Shihri [Saudi]—released to Saudi Arabia from Guantánamo in 2007
- **Youssef al-Shihri [Saudi]—2006 GTMO release, failed reprogramming—killed in Saudi Arabia, October 2009**

Note: eleven former Guantánamo terrorism detainees. The relationship between AQAP figures such as al-Wuhayshi and al-Rubaish and bin Laden helps explain why AQAP has been the franchise jihadist group that is the closest ideologically to the al-Qaeda core and its global terror aspirations if not in its capability to achieve catastrophic terrorism.

Core Leaders Believed to Be in Iran

Estimated seven at-large core figures, 1 *key** figure. None have been captured or killed. In addition, Saudi Arabia claims forty of its most wanted are there.

- Abdullah Ahmed Abdullah [Egyptian]
- Abdullah al-Qarawi [Saudi]—may have joined AQAP in Yemen during 2010
- Ali Sayyid Muhamed Mustafa al-Bakri (aka Abd al Aziz al-Masri) [Egyptian]
- Ali Saleh Husain [Yemeni]
- Muhammad Rab'a al Sayid al-Bahtiti [Egyptian]
- Mustafa Hamid [Egyptian]
- Saif al-Adel* [Egyptian]

Core Leaders, Whereabouts Unknown/Uncertain

Estimated five of seven at large, 2 *key** figures. **Bold** denotes a leader who has been captured or killed.

- Abu Khalaf—killed in Mosul, Iraq, January 2010
- **Abu Ayyub al-Masri—al-Qaeda emir in Iraq, killed there, April 2010**
- Abu Mus'ab al-Suri* [Syrian]—believed in Syria since 2006
- Adnan G. el Shukrijumah* [U.S. of Saudi ancestry]—may be in Pakistan or North Africa
- **Fazul Abdullah Mohammed—killed in Somalia, summer 2011**
- Mafouz Ould Walid (aka Abu Hafs al-Mauritani)—in Iran or North Africa
- Sheikh Issa al-Masri (Abu 'Amr 'Abd al-Hakim) [Syrian]—suspected to be in Syria since 2009

Core Leaders Believed Held at Guantánamo Bay

Six *key** figures of 171 remaining detainees. All **bolded** because captured and in detention.

- **Abd al-Rahim al-Nashiri* [Saudi]—apprehended in UAE, 2002**
- **Abu Faraj al-Libi*—arrested in Pakistan 2005, to GTMO in 2006; Pearl killing, suspect in Musharraf assassination plots and 2006 airliner plot**
- **Abu Zubaydah* [Saudi]—arrested in Pakistan, 2002**
- **Hambali* [Indonesian]—arrested in Thailand, 2003**
- **Khalid Sheikh Mohammed* [Pakistani]—arrested in Pakistan, 2003**
- **Walid bin Attash* [Yemeni]—arrested in Pakistan, 2003**

Notes

1. This is not to say that al-Qaeda and the Haqqani Network are the same entity. American policy treats them as different entities and targets each for specific reasons. However, I will assert in this monograph that the intense American policy focus from mid-2011 on attacking these terrorists and radicals in

Pakistan harms far more important, long-term policy interests in Pakistan and Afghanistan.

2. Among the early works best defining the true nature of al-Qaeda and the policy implications is *Defeating the Jihadis: A Blueprint for Action*, Century Foundation, 2004. The Century Foundation task force responsible for this report referred to al-Qaeda's three critical elements in a construct of nested concentric circles. The small, interior "core" circle is the core organization of al-Qaeda's vanguard with some four hundred to two thousand people; the next circle, affiliated Salafi jihadist movements, includes an estimated fifty thousand to two hundred thousand people; and the third ring features Muslim sympathizers to the al-Qaeda message of jihad against those perceived as oppressing Muslims, perhaps some two hundred to five hundred million people, all nested in the wider world of 1.5 billion Muslims. See especially pp. 14–20. For a similar construct, see Special Report: *Jihadism in 2011: A Persistent Grassroots Threat*, STRATFOR, Jan. 24, 2011, especially pp. 2–4. For most of the past half-decade, analyses of al-Qaeda by the Congressional Research Service (CRS) have used a similar trilateral taxonomy featuring references to an al-Qaeda core, global jihadist affiliates, and unaffiliated adherents. For a recent example, see John Rollins, *Osama bin Laden's Death: Implications and Considerations*, Congressional Research Service Report 7-5700, May 5, 2011.

3. For a review of the genesis of this crucial dimension of al-Qaeda, see Steve Coll's Pulitzer Prize–winning *Ghost Wars: The Secret History of the CIA, Afghanistan, and Bin Laden, from the Soviet Invasion to September 10, 2001* (New York: Penguin Press, 2004). For a detailed discussion of this aspect of al-Qaeda as its central, most critical dimension, see Bruce Hoffman, "The Myth of Grassroots Terrorism: Why bin Laden Still Matters," *Foreign Affairs*, May/June 2008, pp. 133–38.

4. This holistic response, codified formally in early 2003, featured an approach anchored in four counterterrorism principles aimed at taking the fight to the core of al-Qaeda: "Defeat, Deny, Diminish, Defend." In this sense, it was the offensive policy to complement the defensive National Strategy for Homeland Security published in July 2002. See *National Strategy for Combating Terrorism*, Washington, DC: Government Printing Office (GPO), February 2003; and a comparative analysis of it found in *Combating Terrorism: Observations on National Strategies Related to Terrorism; Statement of GAO Defense Capabilities and Management Director, Raymond J. Decker*, GAO Publication released on Mar. 3, 2003, and accessed at http://www.gao.gov/new.items/d03519t.pdf, especially pp. 6–12.

5. The term *Salafi* is used to describe a particular type of fundamentalist thought in Sunni Islam. In Arabic, the word is a reference to the first three generations of Muslims venerated as "the forefathers" and best generations in the history of Islam. Contemporary Sunni Muslim groups that are Salafi in orientation believe that imitation of the behavior of the Prophet Muhammad and his closest followers and descendants should be the basis of modern social order. Wahhabi Islam, practiced predominantly in Saudi Arabia and Qatar, is a variant of Salafism, but not its sole manifestation. Many Salafis are zealous in their beliefs, but few pursue violence as the principal means to achieve their aims.

Salafi jihadists are a small minority of Salafis who believe that violence and terrorism are essential to purge the Muslim world of nonbelieving Westerners and correct those of the Muslim faith who insufficiently practice fundamentalist Islam in their daily lives or in the management of Islamic communities. al-Qaeda is the most notorious of the many small but deadly Salafi jihadist groups in the Muslim world. For a more detailed discussion of Salafism and Salafi jihadists, see Quintan Wiktorowicz, "A Genealogy of Radical Islam," in Russell D. Howard, Reid L. Sawyer, and Natasha E. Bajema, eds., *Terrorism and CounterTerrorism: Understanding the New Security Environment*, 3rd ed. (New York: McGraw-Hill Higher Education, 2009), pp. 225–44.

6. Also see Michael Scott Doran, "Somebody Else's Civil War," *Foreign Affairs*, January/February 2002, http://www.foreignaffairs.com/articles/57618/michael-scott-doran/somebody-elses-civil-war.

7. This is the aspect of al-Qaeda advanced most vigorously by Marc Sageman in *Leaderless Jihad: Terror Networks in the Twenty-First Century* (Philadelphia: University of Pennsylvania Press, 2008) and defended by Sageman in his debate with Bruce Hoffman in "Does Osama Still Call the Shots: Debating the Containment of al-Qaeda's Leadership," *Foreign Affairs*, July/August 2008, pp. 163–68.

8. In this testimony, Coll argued that al-Qaeda was several things at once: an organization, a network, an ideological movement, and a brand name. See Steve Coll, "House Testimony: The Paradoxes of al-Qaeda," posted on "Think Tank," in *The New Yorker*, http://www.newyorker.com/online/blogs/stevecoll/steve-coll/2010/01.

9. For a more detailed discussion of how al-Qaeda corralled the disparate focus of Salafi jihadist ideology into a historically rare—and exceptionally dangerous—radical global ideology, see Mark Stout, T. X. Hammes, and Thomas Lynch, "Chapter 6: Transnational Movements and Terrorism," in *Global Strategic Assessment 2009: America's Security Role in a Changing World*, International Institute for Strategic Studies, National Defense University [NDU-INSS] (Washington, DC: NDU Press, Spring 2009), pp. 119–32.

10. For a more detailed explanation of radical ideologies and the role of critical personalities in launching these violent movements into serious global threats, see Thomas F. Lynch, "Foundations of Radicalism," in *Understanding International Relations*, 2nd ed., Daniel J. Kaufman et al., eds. (New York: McGraw-Hill, 1993), pp. 884–900.

11. Gunaratna wrote that al-Qaeda's founding charter was anchored in four elements: a "core group" to facilitate strategic and tactical terror direction, action by that group as a "vanguard" to inspire an ever-widening global terrorist network, activity to loosely coordinate transnational Sunni terrorist groups, and serving as a base for continuing guerrilla warfare in Afghanistan. See Rohan Gunaratna, *Inside Al-Qaeda: Global Network of Terror* (New York: Columbia University Press, 2002), p. 57. Also see Peter L. Bergen, *The Osama bin Laden I Know* (2006), pp. 73–76 and 82–85; Coll, *Ghost Wars* (2004), p. 204; and Bruce Reidel, *The Search for Al-Qaeda: Its Leadership, Ideology and Future* (Washington, DC: Brookings Institution, 2008), pp. 45 and 122–24. For a more recent discussion of both the importance of Afghanistan and the long-exaggerated role

of "Afghan Arabs" in the defeat of the Soviet Union there, see Michael Semple, "Osama bin Laden's Death Gives Peace a Chance in Afghanistan," *Guardian (UK)*, May 7, 2011, http://www.guardian.co.uk/commentisfree/2011/may/07/ osama-bin-laden-death-peace-afghanistan.

12. For a review of bin Laden's personal relationships with Hekmatyar, Khalis, and Haqqani and the oath taken with Omar, see Coll, *Ghost Wars* (2004), pp. 327–28; and Reidel, *The Search for Al-Qaeda* (2009), pp. 42–46. For a more detailed discussion of the bay'a between bin Laden and Mullah Omar and some of the controversy associated with the precise nature of that oath, see Vahid Brown, "The Façade of Allegiance: Bin Laden's Dubious Pledge to bin Laden," *Sentinel* (West Point, NY: Combating Terrorism Center, Jan. 13, 2010), p. 1, http:// www.ctc.usma.edu/posts/the-facade-of-allegiance-bin-ladin%E2%80% 99s-dubious-pledge-to-mullah-omar.

13. See Vahid Brown and Don Rassler, *The Haqqani Nexus and the Evolution of al-Qa'ida* (West Point, NY: Combating Terrorism Center, Harmony Program, July 14, 2011); Michael Semple, *Reconciliation in Afghanistan* (Washington, DC: United States Institute of Peace, September 2009); and Henry McDonald, "We Can Persuade Taliban to Be Peaceful—Expelled EU Man," *Guardian [UK]*, Feb.16, 2008. As I will discuss later, although I find the Brown-Rassler scholarship to provide an important understanding of the tensions between bin Laden, Mullah Omar, and many of the Afghan Taliban senior leaders during the period 1996–2001, with the death of bin Laden I now align more with Michael Semple in arguing against their conclusions of intimate coupling between the Haqqani Network and al-Qaeda beyond bin Laden. As a consequence, I reject their conclusion that U.S. policy should treat the Haqqanis as an extension of al-Qaeda's global agenda, believing it based upon incomplete analysis of the Younis Khalis–bin Laden relationship and the Haqqani-Pakistani ISI relationship and an incomplete assessment of the relative importance of Pakistani military-intelligence manipulation to the choices made by the Afghan Taliban. For a discussion of the weak connection of Ayman al-Zawahiri and his Egyptian followers with the Afghan Taliban leadership, including their refusal to consider a bay'a to Mullah Omar during discussions between al-Qaeda leaders on this topic, see Brown, "The Façade of Allegiance" (2010), p. 1.

14. For an insightful characterization of the failed underwear bomber (or jihadist jockstrap) plot generated by al-Qaeda of the Arabian Peninsula (AQAP), in which Nigerian Umar Farouk Abdulmutallab was to destroy a Detroit-bound airliner in December 2009, see Daniel Byman and Christine Fair, "The Case for Calling Them Nitwits," *Atlantic* (July/August 2010), http://www.theatlantic.com/ magazine/archive/2010/07/the-case-for-calling-them-nitwits/8130/.

15. New CIA Director David Petraeus specifically referenced the decline of JI as a force for regional, much less global, terrorism in his Sept. 13, 2011, testimony before Congress on the topic of the terrorist threat ten years after September 11. See *Statement by the Director of the Central Intelligence Agency David H. Petraeus to Congress on the Terrorist Threat Ten Years After 9/11*, https://www.cia. gov/news-information/speeches-testimony/speeches-testimony-archive-2011/ statement-on-the-terrorist-threat-after-9–11.html.

16. Although KSM's bombs didn't down the commercial airliner targeted in the operation, the rigorous study of lessons learned from the mission allowed al-Qaeda to improve its planning and execution of subsequent commercial airliner attacks. See Anonymous (ne: Michael Scheuer), *Through Our Enemy's Eyes: Osama bin Laden, Radical Islam, and the Future of America* (Dulles, VA: Brasseys, 2004), pp. 24–29.

17. Travis J. Tritten, "Are We Finished in the Philippines? Fight Against Terrorism Threat in Country Deemed a Success, But the Way out Is Unclear," *Stars and Stripes*, Sept. 3, 2011.

18. See Ali K. Chishti, "EU Plot, German Jihadis and the Waziristan Connection," *Daily Times [Pakistan]*, Oct. 5, 2010, http://www.dailytimes.com.pk/default.asp?page=2010%5C10%5C05%5Cstory_5-10-2010_pg7_34. Also see "German-Afghan Charged over Qaeda Links," *Daily Times [Pakistan]*, Nov. 11, 2011, http://www.dailytimes.com.pk/default.asp?page=2011%5C11%5C11%5Cstory_11-11-2011_pg7_6.

19. See Mark Mazzetti and Scott Shane, "Data Show Bin Laden Plots; C.I.A. Hid Near Raided House," *New York Times*, May 5, 2011, http://www.nytimes.com/2011/05/06/world/asia/06intel.html; and "Secrets of the Squalid Lair: Bin Laden WAS Still Directing Al Qaeda Terror Attacks up Until His Death, Claims U.S.," *Mail Online [UK]*, May 8, 2011, http://www.dailymail.co.uk/news/article-1384596/Osama-bin-Laden-directing-al-Qaeda-operations-right-death.html. Also see reference to bin Laden's critical role in directing al-Qaeda's international operations and strategy in *Statement by the Director of the Central Intelligence Agency David H. Petraeus to Congress on the Terrorist Threat Ten Years After 9/11*.

20. See the table and analysis from pp. 3–7 in Paul Cruickshank, "The Militant Pipeline: Between the Afghanistan-Pakistan Border Region and the West," Counterterrorism Strategy Initiative Policy Paper, New America Foundation, February 2010, http://counterterrorism.newamerica.net/sites/newamerica.net/files/policydocs/cruickshank.pdf.

21. See "Annual Jihadism Review: 2011," STRATFOR Global Intelligence, Jan. 24, 2011.

22. For a discussion of the long-standing and often vexing challenges presented to al-Qaeda's efforts to co-opt "classic" (or local) jihadist groups into its version of global jihad, see Vahid Brown, "Classical and Global Jihad: Al Qa'ida Franchising Frustrations," in *Fault Lines in Global Jihad: Organizational, Strategic, and Ideological Fissures*, Assaf Moghadam and Brian Fishman, eds. (London: Routledge, 2011), pp. 88–116.

23. For a conspicuous example of the local aims of even those al-Qaeda affiliates most recently tied to international terrorism plots, see the detailed discussion of the names and the primarily anti-Saudi, not anti-Western, motives of key members of al-Qaeda in the Arabian Peninsula (AQAP) in Christopher Boucek, "Carnegie Guide to the Saudi Eleven," http://carnegieendowment.org/2011/09/07/carnegie-guide-to-the-saudi-eleven/519s.

24. It is now understood that this revenge motive inspired the documented interaction between failed May 2010 Times Square bomber Faisal Shahzad and some members of TTP near Peshawar in western Pakistan sometime in

late 2009. For evidence of the revenge threat made by TTP after Baitullah's 2009 death, see Lehaz Ali, "Pakistan Taliban Chief Baitullah Mehsud Dead: Militants," Agence France-Presse, Aug. 25, 2009, http://www.google.com/ hostednews/afp/article/ALeqM5hslzq5SB_vZ392DU2-n7M8WWo5cw; and for the Faisal Shahzad links to this motivation, see Sami Yousafzai and Ron Moreau, "Pakistan Taliban Source: Times Square Bombing Attempt Was 'Revenge Against America,'" *Newsweek*, May 6, 2010, http://www.thedailybeast.com/ newsweek/blogs/declassified/2010/05/06/pakistan-taliban-source-times-square-bombing-attempt-was-revenge-against-america.html. Shahzad's truncated time in the FATA and his limited training there were not enough to get him beyond construction of a crude bomb and a quickly fizzled plot. For a discussion of the symptom of undertraining, see Byman and Fair, "The Case for Calling Them Nitwits," *Atlantic Monthly* (July/August 2010), http://www. theatlantic.com/magazine/archive/2010/07/the-case-for-calling-them-nitwi ts/8130/. TTP's most recent threats against U.S. targets outside of Pakistan also feature a motive of revenge for American military action taken within Pakistan—this time against bin Laden. See "Tehrik-e-Taliban Pakistan Vow to Attack American Targets," translation of a statement by Mohmand agency TTP commander Omar Khalid Khorasani in the Pakistani *Express Tribune*, June 6, 2011, http://tribune.com.pk/story/183467/tehrik-e-taliban-pakistan-vow-to-attack-american-targets.

25. See "Annual Jihadism Review: 2011," STRATFOR Global Intelligence, Jan. 24, 2011.

26. Dennis C. Blair, *Annual Threat Assessment of the US Intelligence Community, Testimony Before the Senate Select Committee on Intelligence*, Feb. 2, 2010, p. 12, http://www.dni.gov/testimonies/20100202_testimony.pdf.

27. See Byman and Fair, "The Case for Calling Them Nitwits" (2010).

28. For a similar argument, see Scott Stewart, "Why al-Qaeda Is Unlikely to Execute Another 9/11," STRATFOR, Sept. 1, 2011, http://www.stratfor.com/ weekly/20110831-why-al-qaeda-unlikely-execute-another-911?ip_auth_redirect=1.

29. For discussion of this emerging evidence, see "Secrets of the Squalid Lair: Bin Laden Was Still Directing Al Qaeda Terror Attacks up Until His Death, Claims U.S.," *Mail Online [UK]*, May 8, 2011, http://www.dailymail.co.uk/news/ article-1384596/Osama-bin-Laden-directing-al-Qaeda-operations-right-death. html; and "7/7 London Bombings 'Were Osama bin Laden's Last Successful Operation,'" *Guardian [UK]*, July 13, 2011, http://www.guardian.co.uk/uk/2011/ jul/13/7-july-bin-laden-last-operation.

30. Dennis C. Blair, *Annual Threat Assessment of the US Intelligence Community, Testimony Before the Senate Select Committee on Intelligence* (2010), p. 9.

31. See "Annual Jihadism Review: 2011," STRATFOR Global Intelligence, Jan. 24, 2011.

32. See *Statement by the Director of the Central Intelligence Agency David H. Petraeus to Congress on the Terrorist Threat Ten Years After 9/11*, Sept. 13, 2011.

33. For this reason, I think it justifiable to agree with the thrust of the mid-summer 2011 assertion by Defense Undersecretary for Intelligence Michael Vickers that there are perhaps four important al-Qaeda leaders left in Pakistan, and ten to twenty leaders overall in Pakistan, Yemen, and Somalia, while simultaneously

questioning as a bit overly cautious his conclusion that even if the United States kills them all in drone strikes, "You still have al-Qaeda, the idea…. You're never going to eradicate that, but you want to take away their ability to be this global threat…. So yes, it is possible. It will take time." Vickers, as quoted in Elisabeth Bumiller, "Soldier, Thinker, Hunter, Spy: Drawing a Bead on Al Qaeda," *New York Times*, Sept. 3, 2011, http://www.nytimes.com/2011/09/04/world/04vickers.html?_r=1&ref=elisabethbumiller.

34. This image drawn from Mark Mazzetti, "Al-Qaeda Affiliates Growing Independent," *New York Times*, Aug. 29, 2011, http://www.nytimes.com/2011/08/30/world/asia/30qaeda.html?_r=1&ref=osamabinladen.

35. Refer again to Paul Cruickshank, "The Militant Pipeline: Between the Afghanistan-Pakistan Border Region and the West," pp. 3–7.

36. For a similar assessment, see Rohan Gunaratna, *Inside Al Qaeda: Global Network of Terror* (New York: Berkley Books, 2003), pp. 72–76.

37. Gunaratna, *Inside Al Qaeda* (2003), especially pp. 287–91.

38. For a discussion of these prominent differences, see Barnett Rubin and Ahmed Rashid, "From Great Game to Grand Bargain: Ending Chaos in Afghanistan and Pakistan," *Foreign Affairs* (November/December 2008). Also see Ron Synovitz, "Taliban and Al-Qaeda—Provincial vs. Global," Radio Free Europe/Radio Liberty, Aug. 25, 2004, http://www.rferl.org/content/article/1054493.html.

39. See Mark E. Stout, Thomas F. Lynch III, and T. X. Hammes, "Transnational Movements and Terrorism," *Joint Forces Quarterly*, April 2009. Also see the reference to al-Qaeda's affiliation with Lashkar-e-Khorasan as a entity separate from the Afghan Taliban in Hamza Ameer, "New Leader Plans Attacks on Pakistan," *Asia Times Online*, Aug. 31, 2011.

40. See Michael Semple, "Osama bin Laden's Death Gives Peace a Chance in Afghanistan" (May 2011), http://www.guardian.co.uk/commentisfree/2011/may/07/osama-bin-laden-death-peace-afghanistan.

41. See Peter Bergen's account of Hamid Mir on the tense relations between many in the Afghan Taliban and bin Laden. Bergen, *The Osama bin Laden I Know* (New York: Free Press, 2006), p. 236.

42. For a discussion of Younis Khalis, leader of the Hizb-i-Islami-Khalis; his patriarchal control of mujahideen and Taliban factions in North Waziristan, Paktia, Paktika, and Khowst provinces from the early 1980s to his death in 2006; his mentor role with Mullah Omar during the anti-Soviet mujahideen fight; and his featured role in facilitating bin Laden's return to Afghanistan in 1996 and enabling many of bin Laden's major moments in pre–September 11 global jihad, see Bergen, *The Osama bin Laden I Know* (2006), pp. 105 and 158–59; Coll, *Ghost Wars* (2004), p. 288; and Brown and Rassler, *The Haqqani Nexus* (2011), pp. 14–17. For Khalis's important personal role in calling for jihad against U.S.-led foreign forces in Afghanistan in October 2003, see Anonymous (ne: Michael Scheuer), *Imperial Hubris: Why the West Is Losing the War on Terror* (Dulles, VA: Brasseys, 2004), p. 45. The reader will note that I take issue with Brown and Rassler's conclusion about the dangers of the Haqqani Network's role in present and future global jihad. Although their paper makes a strong case for the relative importance of Younis Khalis and Jalaluddin Haqqani in facilitating bin Laden's global terrorism agenda when compared to the role of Mullah Omar

or Gulbuddin Hekmatyar, it doesn't account for three important factors that matter to Western policy moving forward: (1) Neither Khalis nor Haqqani ever personally endorsed bin Laden's "far enemy" priorities for jihad; (2) Khalis's death cut the most personal ties with bin Laden and bin Laden's death severs the ties with Jalaluddin Haqqani; and most important (3) the Haqqani Network's parallel but increasing position as a favorite irregular militia group for use by the Pakistani ISI against Indian interests in Afghanistan is of crucial and rising importance to the resilience and capability of the Haqqanis; at the same time, it critically constrains the degree to which the Haqqani leadership can or would actively support, much less assertively practice, acts of international terrorism that would be of grave concern to their Pakistani handlers.

43. For a good general overview of the close linkage between Pakistan's ISI S Wing (the "S" roughly translates to special actions) and the Afghan Taliban, see Mark Mazzetti and Eric Schmitt, "Afghan Strikes by Taliban Get Pakistan Help, U.S. Aides Say," *New York Times*, Mar. 25, 2009. For reference to the intense U.S. pressure on the ISI (and Pakistan's government) to contain if not eliminate plots for jihad emanating from militant groups operating in its territory, see "[Ambassador] Haqqani Rejects Reports of U.S. Pressure," *Express Tribune*, May 27, 2010, http://tribune.com.pk/story/16587/haqqani-rejects-reports-of-us-pressure/.

44. In the aftermath of bin Laden's death, I believe it is now objectively viable to share this assessment as made by Vahid Brown in a piece he wrote a year before the Abbottabad raid. See Brown, "The Façade of Allegiance" (2010), p. 1.

45. Pakistan continues selective cooperation with the intelligence and law enforcement agencies of the United States and other Western countries against al-Qaeda operatives within its borders. There are many examples of this cooperation, including during the darkest moments of the U.S.-Pakistan relationship in 2011. Among them, the early September 2011 collaborative effort that led to the capture in Quetta of Younis al-Mauritani, the newly named al-Qaeda external operations chief, stands out as a prime example. Armed with American intelligence that Mauritani was in Baluchistan and keen not to be seen as harboring an al-Qaeda leader who might be responsible for September 11 anniversary attacks against Western targets, Pakistan's ISI and Frontier Corps paramilitary forces rounded up Mauritani and provided U.S. officials access to key information on potential threats connected to the anniversary. See Baqir Sajjad Syed, "Al Qaeda's 'Foreign Minister' Captured," Dawn.com (Sept. 6, 2011), accessed at http://www.dawn.com/2011/09/06/al-qaedas-foreign-minister-captured.html; and Eli Lake, "America's Shadow State in Pakistan," *Daily Beast* (Dec. 5, 2011), http://www.thedailybeast.com/articles/2011/12/05/america-s-shadow-state-in-pakistan.html.

46. See the relevant cautions thrown out in early 2008 by Daveed Gartenstein-Ross and Kyle Dabruzzi in "Is Al-Qaeda's Central Leadership Still Relevant?" *Middle East Quarterly*, Spring 2008, pp. 27–36, http://www.meforum.org/1875/is-al-qaedas-central-leadership-still-relevant. Also, the degree to which more focused, publicly unavailable intelligence was exploding the myth of al-Qaeda core irrelevance on the basis of its ongoing activities in western Pakistan became well known after U.S. intelligence officials such as Mike McConnell (DNI)

and Michael V. Hayden (CIA director) began to render public accounts of al-Qaeda's rebound there during congressional testimony in early 2008, see Mark Mazzetti, "Intelligence Chief Cites Qaeda Threat to U.S.," *New York Times*, Feb. 6, 2008, http://www.nytimes.com/2008/02/06/washington/06intel.html?n=Top/Reference/Times%20Topics/People/M/McConnell,%20John%20Michael?ref=johnmichaelmcconnell.

47. These three elements are al-Qaeda's core organization, its unique brand name, and its role as a base for certain conquest in Afghanistan. They are addressed in the following paragraph.

48. For a short overview of the degree to which al-Qaeda was regrouped in western Pakistan by 2007, see Stout, Lynch, and Hammes, "Transnational Movements and Terrorism," *Joint Forces Quarterly* (2009). For a summary of these plots and a reminder of the degree to which U.S. hyperbole about the imminent demise of al-Qaeda's core was exposed as false by this confluence, see Daveed Gartenstein-Ross, "Al-Qaeda on the Brink: The Intelligence Assessments Have Been Wrong Before," *National Review Online*, July 28, 2011, http://www.nationalreview.com/articles/272920/al-Qaeda-brink-daveed-gartenstein-ross.

49. For evidence of the historical ISI role in aligning against Pashtun groups oriented toward a "Greater Pashtunistan" or "Greater Afghanistan," see Husain Haqqani, *Pakistan: Between Mosque and Military* (Washington, DC: Carnegie Endowment for International Peace, 2005), pp. 172–75. Also reference the text "But ISI also has another vital mission. Preventing Pakistan's Pashtun, 15–20% of the population of 165 million, from rekindling the old 'Greater Pashtunistan' movement calling for union of the Pashtun tribes of Pakistan and Afghanistan into a new Pashtun nation. The Pashtun have never recognized the Durand Line (today's Pakistan-Afghan border) drawn by British imperialists to sunder the world's largest tribal people. Greater Pashtunistan would tear apart Pakistan and invite Indian military intervention," as found in the article entitled "Pakistan's ISI" at the Pashtun Foundation Organization website, http://en.pashtunfoundation.org/bodytext.php?request=724.

50. Many Afghan Pashtuns also express hatred for Pakistan. Indeed, the Taliban commanders interviewed by Matt Waldman in 2009 told him that the only people they hated more than American occupiers in Afghanistan were Pakistan ISI agents. See Waldman, *The Sun in the Sky: The Relationship Between Pakistan's ISI and Afghan Insurgents*, Crisis States Research Centre Discussion Papers, London School of Economics, June 2010, pp. 4–6. Nonetheless, Pakistan's military-intelligence apparatus has a history of defining this as mainly misguided thinking and not as threatening as the enmity found in the non-Pashtun tribes of Afghanistan.

51. See "$500m Indian Aid to Afghanistan," *Khaama Press*, May 13, 2011, http://www.khaama.com/500m-indian-aid-to-afghanistan.

52. The deep historical ties between Afghans and Indians, along with the extensive travel by Afghans to India, strikes many observers as fair explanation for the number of consulates that India maintains in Afghanistan. By way of comparison: Pakistan maintains four consulates and an embassy in Afghanistan and the United States maintains two consulates and three forward-based consular agents along with its Kabul embassy. The Iranians, Swedes, Spanish, and Italians each

have one consulate and an embassy in Afghanistan. See http://pakistan.visahq.com/embassy/Afghanistan/, http://www.dawatfreemedia.org/english/index.php?mod=article&cat=News&article=34, http://embassy.goabroad.com/embassies-in/afghanistan#, and http://iranianvisa.com/emb1.htm.

53. See Blair, *Annual Threat Assessment of the US Intelligence Community, Testimony Before the Senate Select Committee on Intelligence* (2010), p. 19; and William Dalrymple, "Why the Taliban Are Winning in Afghanistan," *New Statesman [UK]*, June 22, 2010, http://www.newstatesman.com/international-politics/2010/06/british-afghanistan-government.

54. See Matthew Waldman, *The Sun in the Sky: The Relationship Between Pakistan's ISI and Afghan Insurgents*, Crisis States Research Centre Discussion Papers, London School of Economics, June 2010; Anand Gopal, Mansur Khan Mahsud, and Brian Fishman, *The Battle for Pakistan: Militancy and Conflict in North Waziristan* (Washington, DC: New American Foundation, April 2010); and Jeffrey Dressler, *The Haqqani Network: From Pakistan to Afghanistan*, Afghanistan Report 6 (Washington, DC: Institute for the Study of War, 2010).

55. Waldman, *The Sun in the Sky* (2010), p. 4.

56. Ibid., p. 6.

57. Ibid., pp. 6, 13–16.

58. See Gopal et al., *Militancy and Conflict in North Waziristan* (2010), pp. 12–13; and Dressler, *The Haqqani Network*, pp. 33–35.

59. ISI managers have a record of bias against Afghanistan's southern Popalzai Durrani subtribes due to the Popalzai history of support for the idea of "Greater Pashtunistan," as well as the fact that President Karzai is a Popalzai. Mullah Baradar, a Popalzai and longtime member of the Afghan Taliban Quetta Shura, or governing council, was rounded up by Pakistani security services in early 2010 when rumors of his possible outreach to Karzai began to circulate. Baradar remains under house arrest. Conversely, a competitor Pashtun tribe, the Panjpai Durrani, seemingly has benefited from ISI preferences. Its subtribe, the Alizai, has been favored with two Quetta Shura Taliban members of rising stature, Mullah Zakir and Mullah Raof, even as Mullah Baradar's long-standing role in that Taliban hierarchy has been severely constrained. Increasing Panjpai Durrani representation on the Quetta Shura helps to strengthen the authority of the movement, given Afghanistan's long tradition of Durrani rulers, and gives Pakistan more leverage in any possible Afghanistan peace negotiations. See Waldman, *The Sun in the Sky* (2010), p. 10. For additional evidence of Pakistani ISI mistrust of the Durrani Pashtuns of Afghanistan, see the discussion of ISI preferences in the 1990s found in Coll, *Ghost Wars* (2004), pp. 280–82.

60. Waldman, *The Sun in the Sky* (2010), p. 10. Again, Waldman's interviews corroborated long-standing Pakistani ISI Pashtun subtribal preferences dating back decades. For a discussion of Pakistani military and intelligence special care and feeding of the madrassa Haqqania that began during the anti-Soviet jihad in Afghanistan and got another boost during the mid-1990s, see Coll, *Ghost Wars* (2004), pp. 284–85. It is important to note that Waldman's interviews with Haqqani commanders suggested that their trainers were all Pakistan ISI. The training was in military tactics: attacks, ambushes, and improvised explosive devices, but not suicide bombings. They reported that this suicide training was

separate, very specialized, and under the tutelage of outside groups like Arabs and Chechens apparently preying on uneducated boys thirteen to fifteen years old. Also see Anthony Loyd, "Terror Link Alleged as Saudi Millions Flow into Afghanistan War Zone," *Times [UK]*, May 31, 2010.

61. For a discussion of then-Pakistani President Musharraf's reference to Jalaluddin Haqqani as a "strategic asset," see Catherine Philp, "Pervez Musharraf Was Playing 'Double Game' with U.S.," *Times [UK]*, Feb. 17, 2009.

62. For a review of these Haqqani Network attacks, see Bill Roggio, "Suicide Attack Kills 17 Outside Indian Embassy in Kabul," *Long War Journal* (Oct. 8, 2009), http://www.longwarjournal.org/archives/2009/10/suicide_attack_kills_2.php; David Alexander, "Haqqani Network Behind Afghan Truck Blast: Pentagon," Reuters (Sept. 12, 2011), http://en.infoanda.com/link.php?lh=BlkGVF9TA1BW; "U.S. Blames Haqqani Network for Kabul Attacks," *Al Jazeera English Online* (Sept. 14, 2011), http://www.aljazeera.com/news/asia/2011/09/2011914184333835511.html; and Sami Yousafzai and Ron Moreau, "Taliban Boast of Kabul Embassy Attack," *Daily Beast* (Sept. 14, 2011) http://www.thedailybeast.com/articles/2011/09/14/taliban-embassy-attack-in-kabul-afghan-insurgents-tell-of-secret-war-room-haqqani-alliance.html.

63. See Jeffrey Dressler, "Pakistan's Kurram Offensive—Implications for Afghanistan," *Institute for the Study of War: Backgrounder* (Aug.18, 2011), http://www.understandingwar.org/backgrounder/pakistans-kurram-offensive-implications-afghanistan; and Jeffrey Dressler, "The Haqqani Network and the Threat to Afghanistan: Why the Terrorist Syndicate Is the Biggest Threat to South Asia," *Foreign Affairs Online* (Nov. 11, 2011), http://www.foreignaffairs.com/articles/136661/jeffrey-dressler/the-haqqani-network-and-the-threat-to-afghanistan. Although I agree with Dressler's evidence and argument that the Haqqani Network has become the favored proxy for Pakistan's ISI over the past two to three years, I disagree with his extension of this argument to suggest that this bodes well for al-Qaeda's aspirations in the region, much less globally. As I argue throughout this chapter, the death of bin Laden makes it ever more certain that all Afghan Taliban elements must dance to the tune of the Pakistani ISI, not that of al-Qaeda international, and Pakistan's tune is not one of global Salafi jihad. Also see Anindya Batabyal, "Pakistan and the Haqqani Network," Article #3482, *Institute of Peace and Conflict Studies—India* (Nov. 2, 2011), http://www.ipcs.org/article/india/pakistan-and-the-haqqani-network-3482.html.

64. Dalrymple, "Why the Taliban Are Winning in Afghanistan," *New Statesman [UK]* (2010); and Semple, *Reconciliation in Afghanistan* (2009).

65. See U.N. Security Council press release of July 7, 2011, announcing the split of UNSCR 1267 (1999) al-Qaeda listing into UNSCR 1988 (2011), an Afghan Taliban listing, and UNSCR 1989 (2011), an al-Qaeda listing, http://www.un.org/News/Press/docs//2011/sc10312.doc.htm. Then see UNSCR 1989, reissued on July 1, 2011, http://www.un.org/ga/search/view_doc.asp?symbol=S/RES/1989 (2011), and UNSCR 1988 (2011).

66. Ahmed Rashid, "The Truth Behind America's Taliban Talks," *Financial Times Online*, June 29, 2011.

67. See Ron Moreau, Sami Yousafzai, and Tara McKelvey, "U.S. Officials Holding Secret Talks with the Taliban in Qatar," *Daily Beast*, Dec. 31, 2011, http://www.

thedailybeast.com/articles/2011/12/31/u-s-officials-holding-secret-talks-with-the-taliban-in-qatar.html.

68. This view that the United States is "within reach" of defeating al-Qaeda and is targeting ten to twenty leaders who are the key to the terrorist network's survival is derived from statements by Defense Secretary (and former CIA Director) Leon Panetta and Gen. David Petraeus, now CIA director, in July 2011 and later Undersecretary of Defense Michael Vickers. See Craig Whitlock, "Panetta: U.S. 'Within Reach' of Defeating al-Qaeda," *Washington Post*, July 9, 2011, http://www.washingtonpost.com/world/panetta-us-within-reach-of-defeating-al-qaeda/2011/07/09/gIQAvPpG5H_story.html; and Bumiller, "Soldier, Thinker, Hunter, Spy" (Sept. 3, 2011).

69. Indeed, new CIA Director Petraeus has properly made this point in his early public appearances. See especially *Statement by the Director of the Central Intelligence Agency David H. Petraeus to Congress on the Terrorist Threat Ten Years After 9/11*, Sept. 13, 2011.

70. This assessment is in marked contrast to the interview comments made by White House Counterterrorism Director John Brennan in Kimberly Dozier, "U.S. Counterterror Chief: Al Qaida Now on the Ropes," Associated Press (Sept. 1, 2011).

71. The universality of Pakistani disdain for America's drone strike policy was confirmed in author interviews with Pakistani political, military, media, and religious figures in Islamabad during July 2011. Pakistani public approval of drone strikes fell sharply from 2009 to 2010, remaining negative in 2011. This change paralleled a statistically significant increase in favorable Pakistani views of the Afghan Taliban and popular support for suicide strikes against coalition forces in Afghanistan as part of defensive jihad. See *Pakistani Public Opinion: Growing Concerns About Extremism, Continuing Discontent with U.S.*, Pew Global Attitudes Project, Aug. 13, 2009; *America's Image Remains Poor: Concern About Extremist Threat Slips in Pakistan*, Pew Global Attitudes Project, July 29, 2010; and *Support for Campaign Against Extremists Wanes: U.S. Image in Pakistan Falls No Further Following bin Laden Killing*, Pew Global Attitudes Project, June 21, 2011. All accessed at http://www.pewglobal.org/2011/06/21/u-s-image-in-pakistan-falls-no-further-following-bin-laden-killing/. These general trends for all of Pakistan are refined for localized belief in the FATA in the mid-2010 New America Foundation (NAF) survey of the seven tribal agencies there; see http://pakistansurvey.org/. For an articulation of the construct whereby otherwise nonviolent, ideologically disinclined individuals turn to violence to avenge perceived violent wrongs done to them or their primary association group, see David Kilcullen, *The Accidental Guerrilla: Fighting Small Wars in the Midst of a Big One* (London: Oxford University Press, 2009).

72. The omnipresence of Pakistani press reporting of civilian casualties caused by "unilateral, sovereignty violating" U.S. drone strikes in the FATA and the growing outrage this generates in young Pakistani males contemplating jihad was conveyed to the author in multiple interviews with press reporters and Pakistani think tank officials during a trip to Islamabad during July 2011. These interviews confirmed the early 2011 assessment of Peter Bergen and Katherine Tiedemann of the New America Foundation about the counterproductive impact of drone

strikes resulting in their becoming a recruiting tool for extremist groups across Pakistan. See Peter Bergen and Katherine Tiedemann, "Washington's Phantom War: The Effects of the U.S. Drone Program in Pakistan," *Foreign Affairs* (July/August 2011). For other recent independent reporting on the manner in which popular Pakistani outrage with U.S. drone activity assists Taliban and Islamic militant recruiting across Pakistan, see Shuja Nawaz, "Drone Attacks Inside Pakistan: Wayang or Willing Suspension of Disbelief," *Conflict and Security* (Summer/Fall 2011), pp. 82–83, and Kathy Gannon, "Pakistani Taliban splintering into factions," Associated Press (Dec. 3, 2011).

73. On China's growing frustration with Pakistan's inability to control Islamic extremists training there for attacks in China's western regions, see "Xinjiang Attack Masterminded by Terrorists Trained in Pakistan," *Dawn [Pakistan]* (Aug. 1, 2011), http://www.dawn.com/2011/08/01/xinjiang-attack-masterminded-by-terrorists-trained-in-pakistan-china.html. One must be careful to recognize that this frustration doesn't mean Beijing will exert clear and consistent pressure on Pakistan to halt relationships with Islamic militant groups, much less collaborate with Washington or other international actors to goad Pakistan in this direction. China's concerns about militants remain dwarfed by the common Chinese-Pakistani strategic cause against India and China's more pressing security issues with nations such as the United States, Russia, and India. This unique approach toward policy with Pakistan greatly constrains Beijing's willingness to partner with regional or international efforts to pressure Islamabad. For a useful review of these limitations, see Andrew Small, "China's Caution on Afghanistan-Pakistan," *Washington Quarterly* (July 2010), pp. 86–87; and Isaac B. Kardon, *China and Pakistan: Emerging Strains in the Entente Cordiale* (Washington, DC: Project 2049 Institute, March 2011).

74. From mid-2007 to mid-2011, Pakistan ranked second behind Iraq (and ahead of Afghanistan) as the country most affected by catastrophic terrorism, with 256 attacks and 4,825 recorded deaths over a forty-five-month period. See the last table in *Crises in South Asia: Trends and Potential Consequences*, Michael Krepon and Nathan Cohn, eds. (Washington, DC: Stimson Center, September 2011), p. 111, with data corroborated at www.nctc.gov.

75. Since 1998, India has joined Pakistan in a consistent ability to walk up to the line of catastrophic interstate war while simultaneously beckoning U.S. diplomatic intervention to hold the clash short of conflagration. In large measure, this increasingly unstable brinksmanship has relied for resolution on America's unique diplomatic access in both Islamabad and New Delhi—access that could be compromised in Islamabad should U.S. counterterrorism policy fully alienate the regime. For a review of this pattern of U.S.-focused brinksmanship, see Samuel Black, "The Structure of South Asian Crises from Brasstacks to Mumbai," in *Crises in South Asia*, Krepon and Cohn, eds., pp. 38–70.

76. For a discussion of this and related growing security risks inherent in the exceedingly tense and nuclear arms–fueled rivalry between Pakistan and India, see *Crises in South Asia*, Krepon and Cohn, eds., pp. 35–38 and 77–99; and Coll, "House Testimony: The Paradoxes of al-Qaeda" (2010).

FIFTEEN

Negotiations with the Taliban

Thomas Ruttig

EXECUTIVE SUMMARY

This chapter analyzes the debate over "reconciliation" with the Taliban. The first section provides an overview of the context and clarifies the language of the current debate in order to avoid misunderstandings and shed light on the "public diplomacy" spin that aims to show progress where there is little. The second and third sections detail and weigh the reported initial contacts between insurgents and the Afghan government. The fourth section describes the motivations of the main actors, discusses the aspects of a negotiated settlement in Afghanistan—principles, obstacles, and possible steps and mechanisms—and explores the likelihood of such a process being initiated. The chapter concludes with recommendations and suggestions on where to begin and what needs to be changed for the process to have a chance of success. The reconciliation process is only in a very early stage, and many questions remain unanswered, involving details about how meaningful negotiations can be structured, both at the Afghan level and internationally.

What was really new in the developments concerning "reconciliation" with the Taliban from 2010 forward? For the first time, the Kabul government affirmed that there were contacts with Taliban leaders. At the same time, it played them down as unsubstantial and without results. No doubt contacts between the Karzai government and individual insurgents exist, but they have not been systematized and there is still no comprehensive strategy for going forward on talks or even negotiations on reconciliation.

Second, NATO confirmed that it has facilitated these talks technically, and by implicitly giving security guarantees for interlocutors. At the same, the new U.S. strategy, including a kill-and-capture program targeting Taliban commanders, does not point toward reconciliation; rather, it has given the upper hand to Taliban hardliners who oppose any talks. This could lead to the ascent of a younger, more radicalized generation of Taliban commanders to replace those killed, who were better known and might have included some inclined toward a political solution.

Third, a High Peace Council with seventy members has been established by the Afghan government as the sole body authorized to pursue reconciliation. Because President Hamid Karzai nominated its members, however, it is seen as a governmental body that will not be able to conduct meaningful negotiations since the Taliban, and many Afghans, do not consider it a neutral party.

The fourth new point is that Pakistani authorities have dropped their line of denying all support for and control over the Taliban. For the first time, they admitted openly that they are able to "deliver" Taliban leaders for talks. The arrest of Mullah Abdul Ghani Baradar, deputy to Taliban leader Mullah Muhammad Omar, was a statement of intent: talks with the Afghan Taliban are possible, but not without a key Pakistani role. At the same time, new research asserted that even though the Taliban accept Pakistani support, many of their commanders nevertheless do not appreciate Pakistani influence on Afghan politics.[1]

These developments have created a growing fear among important social, political, and ethnic groups in Afghanistan that Karzai might go for a deal with the Taliban, or with certain elements of the movement. This is seen by many Afghans as a Pashtun solution, at the expense of other ethnic minorities and women. It has increased polarization and mistrust and undermines the still-weak Afghan institutions.

CONTEXT AND MAIN DEVELOPMENTS IN 2010

In a significant development in 2010, Pakistan, as the main protector of various insurgent groups, claimed a key position in any political initiative by making clear—with the public arrest of Taliban deputy leader Mullah Baradar in early February 2010[2]—that no talks could be held without its consent. Baradar, the Taliban movement's de facto chief of operations, reportedly had attempted to open a separate channel of talks with the Kabul government, using channels in the Karzai family, both in Kabul and in Kandahar and trying to act independently from the Taliban supporters (and minders) in Pakistan's military establishment.[3] According to some unofficial reports, the meetings took place in Spin Boldak, a border town inside Afghanistan, included relatives of President Karzai, and did not focus on political matters but on business-related issues. At the time of his arrest, Baradar headed the Taliban's second-highest authority, the Leadership Council (the Rahbari Shura, also known as the Quetta Shura), and was the highest-ranking Talib still able to operate; only Mullah Omar, as the Taliban's spiritual leader, or *amir ul-mo'menin*, has a higher position. Omar, however, is in hiding and being kept isolated from much of the movement, and he is reported not to be in favor of talks.[4]

Pakistan also moved on from sending mixed messages about whether or not the Taliban are using safe havens on its territory to openly and unequivocally admitting that it is able to influence them. In February 2010, Gen. Ashfaq Parvez Kayani, the head of Pakistan's military, told NATO that his country would be ready to open communication channels with the Taliban.[5] Around the same time, a high-ranking official of Islamabad's Ministry of Foreign Affairs spoke of Pakistan's "considerable influence on the Taliban."[6]

On the Afghan domestic stage, in 2010 President Karzai, under pressure from the Western plan to hand over lead security responsibility to Afghan security forces by 2014, confirmed for the first time that his government has maintained "long-lasting" contacts with the Taliban on different levels. At the same time, he played down their significance as still "in a nascent stage" and "little more than the exchange of desires for peace."[7] There were also several Kabul government contacts with Hizb-i-Islami Gulbuddin (HIG), the second-largest insurgent group operating in Afghanistan.[8] Two HIG deputy leaders were received by Karzai and held talks in Kabul, which ended without clear results.

On the administrative side, the Karzai government in late September 2010 established a seventy-member High Peace Council, which is supposed to open channels and create a mechanism for talks with insurgents. This followed a National Consultative Peace Jirga in Kabul in June, after which the Afghan government claimed it had achieved a national consensus on "reconciliation."[9] In July 2010, it submitted the Afghanistan Peace and Reintegration Program (APRP) to the international Kabul Conference on the country's future, where the program was endorsed by the international community.

In contrast, the international dimension of the conflict—in particular Pakistan's support for the insurgency—has not yet been sufficiently addressed, by the Afghan or the U.S. government. Although Kabul's relationship with Islamabad has been going through a roller coaster of accusations and rapprochement since 2001, the U.S. government is stuck between recognizing the necessity to exert pressure on Pakistan, in order to curb Afghan insurgent infrastructure and stop Pakistani political support for them (while fighting its own Taliban), and fearing that Pakistan might become the larger problem compared with Afghanistan if there is state failure or an Islamist takeover that puts the country's nuclear arsenal into the hands of radicals possibly linked to al-Qaeda. Apart from bilateral U.S.-Pakistani and Afghan-Pakistani channels as well as the Afghan-Pakistani-ISAF (International Security Assistance Force) Tripartite Commission, which is a military body, no mechanisms exist to address this purpose.

In late November 2010, controversy erupted when it was discovered that a man involved in secret meetings with top Afghan leaders, who claimed to be Mullah Akhtar Muhammad Mansour, the current Taliban's number two and minister for civil aviation during their regime in the 1990s, was actually an impostor.[10] This significantly discredited the current approach to reconciliation among the public and signified the complexity of the process when even basic information is missing that would have allowed positive identification of possible high-ranking Taliban interlocutors.

Following Gen. Stanley McChrystal's replacement in June 2010 as commander of the U.S.-led forces in Afghanistan, there was another shift in U.S. strategy. Under his successor, Gen. David Petraeus, a two-pronged approach was adopted: talking to the insurgents while continuing to decimate them. This was based on President Barack Obama's intention to "disrupt" al-Qaeda and "degrade" the Taliban[11] to a level where they would not be able to return to power. It was widely read as an attempt to weaken the Taliban militarily and ultimately force them to the negotiating table. A wave of reports on alleged "talks" between high-ranking insurgents and the Afghan government created the impression that significant progress had been made in the fall of 2010, but this soon died down.[12]

The U.S. strategy, however, has in effect undermined the chances for negotiations rather than improving them. The Taliban leadership—along with large parts of the Afghan population, including the political class—does not believe that the United States is really committed to "reconciliation." Conspicuously, there was no reference to the subject of reconciliation in the final document of the NATO summit in Lisbon in November 2010. Despite the significant number of casualties the Taliban have suffered, including among commanders, there is no sign that their momentum has been stopped, in spite of U.S. military assertions to the contrary. Instead, their geographic reach, ethnic inclusiveness, and potential for intimidation seem to be growing. This has been confirmed for the three major regions of the insurgency's influence, in Afghanistan's south, southeast, and north; there also is an escalation of fighting in the eastern region.[13] In fact, the U.S. dual strategy has pushed the Taliban further away from any readiness to enter into talks.

Particularly important are new tendencies—since their successful expansion into the Afghan north and northeast beginning in 2008—indicating the Taliban's growing ability to cross ethnic boundaries between Pashtuns and non-Pashtuns. In the first phase of this expansion, former Tajik mujahideen groups in Herat province joined the fight against the "foreign occupation" in 2008. The Tajik groups were organizationally still independent of the Taliban, but they adopted the Taliban's rhetoric and modus operandi.[14] Farther east, in Faryab, Balkh, and Kunduz, the Taliban initially used Pashtun minority pockets as door openers but have been recruiting non-Pashtun commanders and fighters since at least 2009. One recent report points to an "increasing number of non-Pashtun fighters" all over northern Afghanistan, among them "Uzbeks, Turkmen, Aimaqs and to a lesser extent, Tajiks...in significant numbers." Another one that looked at twenty provinces pointed to "Afghans of Uzbek, Nuristani, Pashai, Gujar, Aimaq, Baluch and Tajik ethnicity participating in the insurgency."[15] In southern Afghanistan, Baluch smuggling networks are cooperating with the Taliban. Giustozzi and Reuter point to the role of the Islamic clergy in recruitment that cuts across ethnic lines.[16] This indicates that although the Taliban have never seen themselves as a Pashtun-only movement, they are increasingly able to show this on the ground.

The Taliban leadership has also shifted its rhetoric—and possibly its position—with regard to the Shia minority in Afghanistan in the past few years. Even though Taliban fighters committed a number of massacres against Shia Hazara during the movement's rule in the 1990s, in his October 2006 message on the eve of the Eid holiday Taliban leader Mullah Omar for the first time appealed to his fighters "not to go for sectarian hatred. All Muslims of different schools of thought are brothers and there is no difference among them."[17] This was an attempt to make overtures to former Shia mujahideen commanders. Although the majority of Taliban fighters still are Pashtuns, the movement has started to redefine itself as a nationalist-Islamist one, emphasizing the message that it fights a foreign occupation and wants to restore Afghanistan's independence.[18]

On the other hand, the Taliban's expansion into new ethnic and social environments is hampered by the movement's symbiosis with the country's drug economy and a surge of armed criminal groups using the Taliban label, which limits its appeal to large portions of the Afghan population. Among the Hazara and other Shia groups, in particular, the Taliban's rhetoric of inclusiveness has not met with much sympathy.

Apart from these shifts, the U.S. strategy is also leading to the rise of a new generation of younger, more radical Taliban commanders who are replacing those killed or captured by the U.S. forces. If they move up in the hierarchy, a real neo-Taliban movement could emerge. Those young-generation neo-Taliban could turn out to be more "jihadist-internationalist" than the current one. It even could split off the original Taliban and reject a political deal agreed to by the current old guard leaders. Educated in radical madrassas in Pakistan and much more dependent on the ISI, since they lack the contact with rural society within Afghanistan that the old guard still commands, such a movement would be under much stronger Pakistani influence than the current one. It could serve as a pro-Pakistani proxy "reserve force" for the period after the anticipated Western withdrawal, in case the insurgency continues or a full-scale civil war breaks out.

Language: Reconciliation vs. "Reconciliation"

The Afghan, and even more the international, debate over "reconciliation" is polluted by imprecise or euphemistic language that needs to be clarified. The term *reconciliation* is widely used as a synonym for "talks with the Taliban" aimed at ending armed hostilities and reaching a political accommodation in Afghanistan. But conceptually, this definition is much too narrow, first because a political deal would not automatically end the current conflict. Similarly, an end to the fighting would not be the same as "peace."

Many Afghans, particularly in the Pashtun-dominated south, see reconciliation first as the need for an accommodation between alienated tribal (or other) groups and the national government and its local representatives. This would end the monopoly of power wielded by some tribes that are closely linked with the central government and would reintegrate the alienated groups—that is, create tribally broad-based administrations in the provinces again. For others, reconciliation should also involve the failure to address the war crimes and human rights abuses committed during the Soviet invasion, Afghanistan's civil war, and the Taliban's rule.

In this chapter, therefore, "reconciliation" refers to a broad societal process of addressing and healing wounds suffered by Afghans during more than thirty years of war with all its accompanying features, notably gross human rights violations, war crimes, the disintegration of the social fabric of Afghanistan, and the emergence of a culture of violence—including the spread of terrorism—that still dominates relations in Afghanistan's society and state institutions. Contacts with the Taliban and other insurgent groups—ranging from initial exploratory talks to possible future negotiations—would be just one part of this broader agenda. If talks with the Taliban proceed without being embedded in a broader social process, they might even run counter to genuine reconciliation, particularly if a limited political deal between armed factions or political cliques not based on a broad political consensus leaves out and is imposed on those who are not a party to it.

For example, negotiations leading to a possible power-sharing arrangement including the Karzai camp in Kabul (essentially a patronage network based on economic power reinforced by quasi-militias) on one hand and any insurgent group (or faction of it) on the other would very likely not result in an end to the fighting. Rather, it would be a rearrangement of how the spoils are distributed. This option is often described as a "thieves' pact."[19] More importantly, it would not remove the major causes of the insurgency, among them widespread political and economic exclusion, predatory behavior by government representatives, corruption, and impunity.

Parts of the insurgency might decide to continue fighting, in particular if they have continued backing from outside powers—as in the case of a potential Pakistani-backed neo-Taliban movement. Armed factions from the Afghan north that were not included in a deal, or are opposed to it, might continue to rearm themselves and take to the mountains again. Civil society, and social and political groups, might start a campaign of civil protests against such a deal.

In general, the terms used with regard to policies and institutions meant to bring forward reconciliation, and created in the follow-up to the latest international Afghanistan conferences, have a strong whiff of euphemism about them. The separation, in the officially used terminology and in the design of programs, between "reconciliation" (now replaced by "peace" in the APRP's language; it is widely used for a power-sharing agreement between the current Kabul government and parts of the insurgents) and "reintegration" (aiming at "peeling off" insurgents individually with the help of material incentives) is artificial. It is driven by the politically correct language of an "Afghan lead" in this process, which does not exist in reality, treats the insurgency mainly as a technical problem, and supposes that many Taliban can be won over by economic and social incentives—thereby underestimating the political motives that drive the Taliban insurgency, including its foot soldiers.

In this constellation, the West needs to rethink its position. As a party to the conflict, it cannot claim to act as the "reconciler," i.e., a neutral referee—not in the eyes of the majority of Afghans who initially supported the post–September 11 intervention, in both military and civilian incarnations, and not in the eyes of the insurgents. The West lost this position exactly because it did not behave as a neutral actor in the immediate post-Taliban Afghan political arena: first by integrating the delegitimized warlords into the new political setup while providing them with impunity; second by unconditionally supporting a central government that largely behaved like just another faction instead of unifying the country, and thus increasingly lost legitimacy; and third by not reacting to Taliban overtures to join the new system.[20]

INITIAL CONTACTS BETWEEN THE AFGHAN GOVERNMENT AND THE INSURGENTS

Post–September 11 and the Fall of the Taliban

The events of 2010 were certainly not the first attempts at talking to the Taliban or including them in the post-2001 political setup. According to journalist Anand Gopal, on the Taliban's part the first effort was reportedly made by a group of "Mullah Omar's chief lieutenants [who] secretly gathered and decided to surrender to the forces of Hamid Karzai" in late 2001, claiming to have permission from the Taliban leader to surrender. This group included Mullah Omar's chief of office during the Taliban regime, Tayyeb Agha; the movement's number two after the collapse of the Taliban regime, then already a powerful commander, Mullah Baradar; the Taliban regime's defense minister, Mullah Obaidullah[21]; and its interior minister, Mullah Abdul Razzaq—all still relevant actors today. In a letter delivered to Karzai, they "accepted Karzai's recent selection at the Bonn Conference as the country's interim leader and acknowledged that the Islamic Emirate [the official name of the Taliban government] had no chance of surviving." The group's main request "was to be given immunity from arrest in exchange for agreeing to abstain from political life....Some members even saw the new government as Islamic and legitimate....But Karzai...ignored the overtures—largely due to pressures from the United States and the Northern Alliance, the Taliban's erstwhile enemy." As a result of continuing intimidation and harassment by the Afghan government, most of the involved Taliban leaders slipped back into Pakistan and became leading figures in the movement's resurgence.[22]

Simultaneously in late 2001, a group of ex-Talibs established a political party in Pakistan called Jamiat-e Khuddam ul-Furqan, which presented itself as the moderate Taliban group. But in those days, the U.S. strategy of mopping up "Taliban remnants" was accompanied by the "we do not talk to terrorists" doctrine, and the group's overture to the Kabul government was rejected under this influence. Its members were allowed to return and settle in Kabul in 2004 but were basically left alone in a guesthouse for some years without any political role. Only recently, and much too late, were they finally incorporated into the High Peace Council.[23] But it can be assumed that the years of neglect sent a clear message to Taliban on the other side who would have been willing to join the process—namely, if you do so, you will end up in oblivion.

Former Taliban also took part as individuals in the Emergency Loya Jirga, or grand assembly, in 2002. One of them was Abdul Hakim Munib,[24] who even served as governor of Uruzgan province for about a year in 2006 and 2007. Since he was not deleted from the U.N. sanctions list, even Western countries active in this province—the Netherlands with their PRT as well as the U.S. and Australia—were unable to officially support him in this role and create a positive example of what political reintegration could look like.

The First Saudi Initiative

During 2007 and 2008, a relatively strong current within the Kandahari mainstream of the Taliban realized that they were not able to achieve victory (i.e., reestablish the Islamic Emirate) by military means and that this would be too costly in human lives, recognizing that civilian casualties could result in a loss of support among the Afghan population. These elements, called "pious Taliban" by some Afghans, particularly considered the contemporary wave of suicide attacks as "un-Islamic" and reacted to it by issuing the layha (the code of conduct for Taliban fighters, a revised edition of which was published in mid-2010), which provides for more consideration of civilians during such attacks.[25] These Taliban also might have had a role—by supplying inside information—in the May 2007 killing of Mullah Dadullah, the most notorious proponent of the Taliban's terrorist tendencies, who had copied the methods used by Abu Musab al-Zarqawi in Iraq and was considered out of control by the Taliban's leadership body, the Quetta Shura. This Taliban current had been discussing the usefulness of a political solution that would involve talks with the Afghan government and its foreign allies and reached out to individual Afghan politicians. This was the pre-surge phase, and according to a report referring to one key player in such contacts—London-based Abdullah Anas, an Algerian who had fought with the mujahideen and was later close to Osama bin Laden—Mullah Omar had "given the green light to talks" before Saudi-sponsored talks in October 2008 and "for the first time, there [was] a language of peace [used] on both sides."[26]

Qudratullah Jamal, the former Taliban minister for information and culture, has often been cited as open to and involved in negotiations. He is said to have played a leading role in Taliban contacts with Kabul as early as 2004 and also recently, in fall 2010.[27] According to one newspaper report, Jamal was appointed by the Taliban leadership council in early 2009 as a liaison officer for "well-wishers and friends throughout the world," something like an ambassador-at-large.[28] This would make him a possible go-between for Arab and other governments.

The first serious attempt at direct contacts was undertaken when the Saudi king invited a delegation of Afghan government officials, legislators, and former but now "reconciled" Taliban officials to Mecca in October 2008. During the holy month of Ramadan, they met with "Afghans close to the Quetta-based Taliban leadership"[29] and envoys sent by HIG.[30] Abdullah Anas, reportedly also has made efforts "supported by Mr. Karzai" to lobby "influential Muslim clerics and international leaders of jihads in an attempt to draw the Taliban away from Al Qaeda and to bring peace to Afghanistan" since 2006.[31] High-ranking Saudi officials have recently stated, however, that they will not pursue the peace process until the Taliban agree to sever links with al-Qaeda.[32]

The UAE Role

Various other contacts, involving also the United Nations, were made in or financed by the United Arab Emirates. These included meetings in Dubai in spring 2009 and early 2010 between Kai Eide, then U.N. special representative for Afghanistan, and Taliban envoys who—according to some sources with insight into these issues—were authorized by Mullah Omar and included the current head of the Taliban's political committee, Tayyeb Agha, a confidant of the Taliban leader. This was before the arrest of Taliban second-in-command Mullah Baradar in February 2010. In early October 2010, a second round of meetings of the so-called Abu Dhabi process was held in Kabul, funded by the emirate of Abu Dhabi through the U.S.-based East-West Institute. Hekmat Karzai, President Karzai's cousin and head of the Kabul-based Centre for Conflict and Peace Studies, is a senior fellow at the institute. But no "serving" Taliban took part in these meetings, just some "reconciled" ones, including Mullah Abdul Salam Zaeef and former foreign minister Wakil Ahmed Mutawakil. These meetings, however, represent exploratory attempts involving people who are perceived to be close to—but not necessarily representing or speaking for—the Taliban.

Gulbuddin Hekmatyar

A more focused attempt was undertaken by the Kabul government with HIG, starting in late 2008. These contacts were expedited by the availability of many possible go-betweens. Already in 2003, there were more than two hundred former high- or midranking Hezb cadres working in governmental institutions. Today, there is a growing number of Hezb-affiliated provincial and district governors and a Hezb wing officially operating as a registered political party (though its reluctantly declared break with Gulbuddin Hekmatyar is doubted by many Afghan observers).[33] Before the 2010 elections, there was an unofficial Hezb faction of some thirty-five in the lower house of parliament, likely the biggest one there.[34] Furthermore, Hezb has been the natural political orientation for many otherwise unaffiliated Pashtun intellectuals who are not able to identify with more traditional, conservative outlets such as Hezb-e Islami (Khalis) or Islamic Party, Khales faction; Harakat-e Inqilab-e Islami (Movement for an Islamic Revolution); or the Wahhabi Dawat-e Islami (formerly Ittehad-e Islami; Islamic Call/Islamic Unity), led by former warlord Abdul Rabb Rassul Sayyaf, now a member of the Afghan lower house.[35]

For the first time, HIG leader Gulbuddin Hekmatyar signaled readiness for conditional peace talks—at least publicly—in late 2006, a move preceded by general offers for reconciliation by President Karzai. In May 2008, reports about an exchange of letters between Hekmatyar and Karzai leaked into the Afghan media, and in October 2008 the

HIG conditions for talks were reported for the first time.[36] One of Hekmatyar's sons-in-law, Ghairat Bahir, a deputy leader of HIG, was released from a Kabul jail in May 2008; he was immediately received by President Karzai[37] and U.N. Special Representative Kai Eide. This was followed by the release of Hekmatyar's brother Shahabuddin by the Pakistani authorities in January 2009 after five months of custody. In January 2010, the party's other deputy leader, Qutbuddin Hellal, led an HIG delegation to Kabul, where it handed over a peace proposal including the demand for a timetable for the withdrawal of all Western troops from Afghanistan as a prerequisite for any negotiations.[38] Although the talks were called unsuccessful by HIG,[39] they seem to have resulted in a softening of the party's position vis-à-vis the September 2010 parliamentary elections; at least this was the perception of the Taliban, who openly criticized this position and became more confrontational with HIG in various areas of Afghanistan.[40] In October 2010, Bahir was quoted as saying that HIG still had "regular contacts" with the Kabul government but that the process was "at an early stage."[41]

In a parallel but less influential development, a series of talks in the Maldives since at least January 2010[42] involved a number of Afghan parliamentarians and HIG figures—among them Hekmatyar's son Firuz and son-in-law Humayun Jarir—as well as religious scholars close to the Taliban.

The releases of Bahir and Shahabuddin signal that Pakistan is again diversifying its options within the Afghan insurgency. It is not focusing entirely on the Taliban anymore but bringing HIG, which relied more on Iranian support in past years, back into the political arena.[43] Ever since, HIG has become more visible militarily in eastern and northeastern Afghanistan.

Of late, Pakistan and some Saudi officials have been promoting the idea that the Haqqani network needs to be included in a possible "reconciliation" because it represented a "moderate strand" in the insurgency.[44] Behind these attempts, there is one main motivation: Pakistan is interested in implanting its proxy, the Haqqani Network, known to be close to the Pakistani intelligence service and not directly involved in the Pakistani Taliban's insurgency against the government in Islamabad. If implemented, this would give the Pakistani establishment a more direct say in Afghan affairs.

President Karzai has long advocated political accommodation with the Taliban and the HIG.[45] He has repeatedly called them "disaffected brothers" and urged their leaders personally to return to the political process, only to be rebuffed by the U.S. government—which, like the United Nations, the European Union, and individual countries, has kept many of them on its sanctions list, branded as terrorists. Such rhetorical forays by Karzai have also been opposed by a large variety of Afghan political and social groups, from segments of the non-Pashtun former mujahideen to pro-democracy parties and organized women.

A first attempt to entice Taliban foot soldiers to switch sides with financial incentives—the so-called PTS, Dari for "Program for Strengthening Peace"—ended in complete failure and was called "financially and morally corrupt."[46] Assessments have shown that among "all 4,634 individuals who had entered the program by October 2007...there had been almost no previously known [insurgency-related] individuals,"[47] let alone members of the Taliban or HIG leaderships. Nevertheless, the program was never officially dissolved, and President Karzai contemplated for some time appointing its head, Sebghatullah Mojaddedi, the chairman of the Afghan Senate, also as chairman of the High Peace Council established in September 2010. He ultimately chose former President Burhanuddin Rabbani instead.

RECONCILIATION IN 2010

The Arrest of Mullah Baradar

Baradar's arrest in early 2010 was accompanied by a wave of arrests or summonses (some reported, some unreported) of at least half a dozen high-ranking Talibs by the Pakistani intelligence service, the ISI.[48] Among the names mentioned:

- Former Taliban deputy and acting "prime minister" Maulvi Kabir[49]
- Former head of the "commission"[50] and former Zabul governor Maulvi Muhammad Yunos

- Former Kandahar governor Mullah Muhammad Hassan Rahmani
- Former Herat and Kabul corps commander Mullah Abdul Ra'uf
- Mullah Abdul Qayyum Zaker, now one of Baradar's two successors
- Mullah Omar's close advisers Seyyed Tayyeb Agha and Jehangirwal
- Agha Jan Mutassem, a former Taliban finance minister said to be Mullah Omar's son-in-law who also was head of the Taliban's political committee until early 2009
- The Taliban "shadow" provincial governors of Kunduz and Baghlan
- Sirajuddin Haqqani and Anwar-ul-Haq Mujahed, the leaders of two semiautonomous networks associated with the Taliban.[51]

This list includes almost everyone with key positions in the Taliban movement and reflects Pakistan's enormous control over the Taliban leadership on its territory. With these measures, the Pakistani military de facto claimed a veto on all negotiations with the Taliban and therefore on Afghanistan's political future.

Meanwhile, the U.S. and NATO commander in Afghanistan, Gen. David Petraeus, essentially dropped the population-centered counterinsurgency (COIN) approach he initially developed in favor of a primarily antiterrorism approach, and he has replaced the more qualitative criteria for measuring progress in Afghanistan with quantitative measures. Although his new strategy has been described as a two-pronged approach of "shooting and talking,"[52] its emphasis is on killing and capturing insurgents.

This strategy resulted in a large number of Taliban commanders being taken out of action by U.S. forces in 2010. Between mid-May and mid-August alone, 350 midlevel commanders reportedly were killed or captured, with (by the end of October) fifteen "shadow" governors among them; at the same point, the U.S. military had registered an 11 percent increase in civilian deaths, compared with the previous year.[53]

In the regions where the insurgency is strongest, however, this has not resulted in a decrease in insurgent activity. In southern and southeastern Afghanistan, the number of insurgent attacks is rising further, in the southeast more rapidly than in the south. The Taliban's recruitment drive is also reportedly unhampered. NATO operations in the south, such as in Marjah and around Kandahar, resulted in only limited success. In the southeast, the Haqqani Network has set up permanent bases on Afghan territory for the first time and now is establishing structures of a shadow government as in the south. Even according to some U.S. military sources—against the backdrop of a well-resourced U.S. and NATO public information campaign that has tried to spin the narrative in the opposite direction—the Taliban remain able to compensate for their losses and maintain their command-and-control structure.[54]

At the same time, reports from various areas of Afghanistan indicate that the commanders replacing the killed and captured leaders are younger and more radical than their predecessors. The generational change at the top of the more centralized Haqqani Network in the southeast is only one example. There, the transition from the charismatic, tribally grounded, but ailing mujahideen leader Jalaluddin Haqqani to his son, the less experienced but radical Sirajuddin Haqqani, who already has assumed responsibility for the network's day-to-day military operations, is almost complete. Haqqani the son was too young to fight in the anti-Soviet jihad and received a Wahhabi religious education in Saudi Arabia during that time. Therefore, he is more weakly rooted in the Zadran tribe—the network's core basis—than his father.[55]

Altogether, the U.S. military and political practice on the ground does not seem to indicate that the United States is really interested in pursuing a political solution with the Taliban at the present. Negotiations seem to be a Plan B only—with the mentality, Why negotiate when the adversaries are weak? The emphasis seems rather to be on "degrading"[56] or even militarily destroying the movement. This approach might have been encouraged by events in Colombia and Sri Lanka, where long-term insurgencies were crushed or at least heavily weakened by military means.

The New Wave of Contacts

The 2010 U.S. strategy shift under Gen. Petraeus was accompanied by a wave of reports about alleged high-level contacts between insurgents and the Kabul government, ostensibly indicating acceleration toward a political solution in Afghanistan.

It started when al-Jazeera reported on a shuttle mission of Haqqani Network emissaries to Kabul. On June 27, 2010, the Qatar-based TV channel reported that President Karzai "has met Sirajuddin Haqqani, leader of a major anti-government faction, in face-to-face talks" and that the younger Haqqani "is reported to have been accompanied by Pakistan's army chief and the head of its intelligence services."[57] This raised observers' eyebrows, as the Haqqanis are the primary target of U.S. drone strikes in the Pakistani tribal areas. Taliban specialist Michael Semple, contacted by al-Jazeera for comment on the same day, hung the story a bit lower but might have been closer to the truth: "Afghans that I talk to…passed along stories of shuttle diplomacy between Ibrahim Haqqani [brother of Jalaluddin Haqqani] and Karzai's government. They claimed Haqqani would travel between Islamabad, Kabul, and Miranshah."[58] (Ibrahim Haqqani uses Omari as his second name; Haqqani is often ascribed to him to show his family relationship with the network's leaders.) It is possible, though, Ibrahim Omari/Haqqani did not himself travel.

In the event that these reports have some element of truth, this raises the question of whether Omari/Haqqani was talking on behalf of Jalaluddin Haqqani, the aging founder of the network, or Sirajuddin, the son who leads the movement operationally, and if the latter, whether he also talked on behalf of the Taliban leadership. Sirajuddin Haqqani has made it clear he does not consider his network to be a separate entity from the Taliban movement and its Quetta Shura leadership council.[59]

The "Haqqani overture" was followed by a systematic press briefing campaign in autumn 2010. In late September, Gen. Petraeus told a newspaper that there were "very high-level Taliban leaders who have sought to reach out to the highest levels of the Afghan government and, indeed, have done that."[60] This followed the June 2010 Peace Jirga and establishment of the Afghan government's High Peace Council in September. On September 30, U.N. special envoy to Afghanistan Staffan de Mistura announced optimistically in a speech at a New York–based think tank that he reckoned the reconciliation process with the Taliban could be completed by July 2011, the date set by President Obama for the beginning of the U.S. withdrawal, and would lead to a peace settlement because he believed the Taliban had concluded they could not win the war militarily.[61]

On October 6, 2010, the Associated Press reported that

> several Pakistanis and Afghans insist that CIA officials have held clandestine meetings with top Taliban leaders, some at the level of the Taliban's shadow Cabinet ministers. At least two rounds of meetings were held in Pakistan's Khyber Pakhtunkhwa province bordering Afghanistan, according to a former Taliban member who spoke on condition of anonymity because of fears for his own safety. He said the talks were held in the area between the towns of Peshawar and Mardan and included Qudratullah Jamal, the former Taliban information minister.

The report did not say when these supposed talks occurred, and the CIA denied that any such meetings took place.[62]

One day later, the British *Independent*, citing diplomatic sources, reported that

> secret high-level negotiations between the Afghan government and the Taliban leadership aimed at ending the war have begun....Meetings which included delegates of the Quetta Shura, the Taliban's Pakistan-based governing body which is overseen by Mullah Mohammed Omar, are believed to have taken place in Dubai....Talks have also taken place in Kabul with "indirect representatives" of the insurgency.[63]

On October 19, the *New York Times* cited an Afghan official "with knowledge of the talks" as saying that

> in at least one case, Taliban leaders crossed the border and boarded a NATO aircraft bound for Kabul....In other cases, NATO troops have secured roads to allow Taliban officials to reach Afghan- and NATO-controlled areas so they can take part in discussions. Most of the discussions have taken place outside of Kabul.

This followed a *Times* report from Brussels in which a NATO official confirmed that "personnel from NATO nations in Afghanistan 'have indeed facilitated to various degrees the contacts' by allowing Taliban leaders to travel to the Afghan capital."[64]

The *Independent* reported on October 18 that it had "learned that there are six sets of negotiations, some more viable than others, taking place with the aim of arriving at a cease-fire and paving the way for Western forces to pull out of the conflict."[65]

On October 31, the AP's Kathy Gannon reported that "three Taliban figures met secretly with Afghanistan's president two weeks ago." According to a former Afghan official cited as the source for the report, the group included Maulvi Abdul Kabir, who is from the same Zadran tribe as the leaders of the Haqqani Network and had served as governor of Nangarhar province and deputy (and later acting) prime minister during the Taliban rule. The two others were identified as Mullah Sadre Azam and Anwar-ul-Haq Mujahed, the latter "credited with helping Osama bin Laden escape the U.S. assault on Tora Bora in 2001."[66] The report said the men "were brought by helicopter from Peshawar and spent two nights in a luxury Kabul hotel before returning to Pakistan." According to the story, these talks were "an effort by the Afghan government to weaken the U.S.-led coalition's most vicious enemy...the Haqqani network." U.S. and Afghan officials, the report said, "hope that if Kabir agrees to quit the insurgency, it could split the Zadran tribe and undercut the pool of recruits from which the Haqqanis currently draw fighters" and thus "help shift the power balance in eastern provinces where the network poses a major threat."[67]

Kabir is the case that most clearly demonstrates how Pakistan's intelligence service, the ISI, is handling leading Taliban figures and how it might facilitate talks with the movement: when reportedly arrested as one of a number of Taliban leaders in early 2009 by the Pakistani authorities, Kabir was not active at the front anymore. Instead, he reportedly led a life of relative luxury—with "a beautiful house close to the Pakistani town of Nowshera in the North West Frontier Province [now renamed Khyber Pakhtunkhwa] and placidly driving around in a posh SUV with a diplomatic number plate."[68] In other words, Pakistan has relatively easy ways to "deliver" leading Taliban for negotiations with Kabul. It is just a matter of political will and interest.

Although many of the reports of contacts have been published by respected media and journalists, they are difficult to verify. They are often based on anonymous sources (Afghan, U.S., or "Western"), and they may well be part of a psychological warfare operation to sow mistrust in insurgent ranks or even an attempt to undermine genuine negotiations. In a serious process, such contacts do not belong in the public realm, at least in their initial phases, as this could jeopardize those on the insurgents' side who participate, apart from a general necessity for confidentiality.

There have always been contacts and talks with the Taliban. This is ingrained in the network-based nature of Afghan society. But it is important to look at their substance. Martine van Bijlert explains how this works:

> Adversaries tend to stay in touch with each other as much as they can. Seeming opponents share tribal ties, years in the trenches, histories as former classmates, neighbours, business partners, brothers-in-arms....Much of the talk is simply to keep channels of communication open. A fair share of it is focused on practical issues, most prominently the release of detainees and property, safe access to the wounded and dead on a shared battlefield, and safe passage in general. These are largely low- or mid-level contacts and much of it is done without explicit authorisation or high-level backing on both sides (although it is unlikely to be done without any). However, given the nature of Afghan patronage politics, petitioners will go as high up the chain as they possibly can—on both sides—to get their requests granted and to establish contacts that may prove useful in the future. This means that even relatively minor issues can involve quite high-level contacts. [The current contacts are] mainly aimed at figuring out what was on the table and whether the talk of talks...was serious and was taking place at the right level.[69]

This was confirmed by "Pakistanis and Afghans familiar with the process" who insisted that "all contacts have been limited to indirect message exchanges, using mediators who include former Taliban members" and were "exploratory, with all sides trying to assess the other's positions."[70]

Afghan and Western officials tried to play down the reported contacts—or, according to another interpretation, put them to the right level. President Karzai stated in an interview with the *Washington Post* that he held "one or two" meetings with Taliban leaders but they were not much more than "the exchange of desires for peace."[71]

He previously described such meetings as "rather unofficial personal contacts." NATO's civilian representative in Kabul, Mark Sedwill, saw the contacts as being at an "embryonic stage." The late Richard

Holbrooke, then the special U.S. envoy, stated that "there's less here than meets the eye," adding that "I know the difference between talks, negotiations, talks about talks, and we're not even at that stage."[72] This was followed by the disclosure that the man who was purportedly the highest-ranking Taliban contact so far was in fact an impostor.[73]

A Wrong Start: The Peace Jirga and the High Peace Council

Starting with the January 2010 London conference on the future of Afghanistan, the Karzai government has ostensibly taken the lead on "reconciliation" matters. The political basis is the Afghanistan Peace and Reintegration Program (APRP), which looks more like a project-and-funding proposal than a full-fledged strategy. The substantial budget submitted with it will surely create perverse incentives.

The bodies established on the basis of the London conference—the Peace Jirga and the HPC—have significant shortcomings. The major one is that they do not represent a national consensus on talks and reconciliation. The Peace Jirga delegates, as well as those of the HPC, were handpicked by presidential allies and then decorated with a "woman quota"—which, by the way, is substantially lower in the HPC than in parliament.

The Peace Jirga was a déjà vu of big tent "democracy" as experienced during the 2002 and 2003 Loya Jirgas, when there was relatively lively discussion but key decision making was top-down, prearranged and imposed by former mujahideen leaders and Karzai allies such as Sayyaf and Shia Pashtun former mujahideen leader Sheikh Muhammad Asef Mohseni from the podium. The same happened at the Peace Jirga: there were pluralistic voices during the initial working group phase, although the selection of the jirga deputies was highly controlled (with some fig-leaf participation from civil society that was more vocal than expected by the organizers). But control over key procedures, such as the composition of discussion groups and the choice of chairpersons and rapporteurs (and note that only one group was led by a woman) made sure that no dissent was passed upward. In the final plenary session, the jirga chairman announced that "we unanimously support [the] government's peace plan" (i.e., the APRP), without it being discussed in the working groups or the final plenary session, or the document even being distributed among everyone.

The HPC is largely made up of heavyweight former jihadi and anti-Taliban leaders, several regional strongmen, leaders of the above ground Hezb-e Islami wing and some of the jihadi splinter groups, various "reconciled Taliban," and a large number of regular Karzai loyalists (some of these categories overlap). There is also a sprinkling of women and one nonaffiliated "urban intellectual." Absent are members of the top rank of the political opposition (or at least that remaining part of it, led by Dr. Abdullah, Yunus Qanuni, and the family of the late mujahideen leader Ahmad Shah Massoud), civil society, representatives of the moderate or pro-democratic political parties, independent businesspeople, and the NGO community that delivers aid and medical services in insurgency-influenced areas. Also absent are media personalities who can bridge the divides between urban and rural settings and between tribal and civil society, people with experience in the Najibullah-led reconciliation efforts between 1986 and his fall in 1992, and politicians or local leaders who have earned a reputation of speaking up for their communities or for mediating conflicts, a capacity close to social reality. There is also not a single representative of the royal family with its diverse branches.

The High Peace Council is not a group of people chosen for their contacts or mediation skills. It is a confirmation of where the armed—and increasingly, economic—power lies and where it will remain; that is, among the kind of people trusted by "the palace." In particular, the council features the same figures at its top (as demonstrated by the members' list with its consecutive numbers[74]) who are already in Karzai's informal advisory council of "jihadi" (former mujahideen) leaders or in his kitchen cabinet in the presidential office. From that point of view, the HPC is more of a status-quo-preserving body than one that might open up the process and integrate newcomers on terms not already established. This raises the bigger question of whether the Karzai government and the former jihadi leaders on the HPC are really ready to reconcile with other actors—that is, to share power, particularly with a movement like the Taliban that, at least in parts, is known for its anticorruption attitude, coupled with crude methods to implement it.

However, even these policies and structures might still serve as a starting point if their conceptual scope and inclusiveness can be substantially expanded, and if they are coupled with some proper checks and balances provided by representatives of those concerned about where a hasty, unconditional "reconciliation" could lead the country.

Several Afghan civil society umbrella groups called on October 4, 2010, for the replacement of HPC members accused of human rights violations or suspected of war crimes "with experts and those with greater experience in conflict resolution, mediation and reconciliation" and for the involvement of civil society organizations "in all decision making."[75] It is unlikely, however, that these demands will be met. Possible alternatives include expanding the HPC or establishing a "shadow HPC" with representatives from civil society and other underrepresented groups. In both options, members should include second- and third-tier politicians and civil society figures with good reputations and proven negotiation skills who are not too close to the government. If members are added to the HPC, they should equal the number already on the council. If a shadow HPC is formed, it should be mandatory for the government to consult it on equal terms with the HPC.

Also, greater presence of former Taliban with insight into processes among insurgents would be a step in the right direction if used properly, in particular given that this group submitted its own seven-point plan for negotiations to major domestic and international actors in Kabul in mid-2008 under the self-explanatory title *"Sola gam pe gam"* (Peace Step by Step):

1. That the Afghan government convince the international military forces that the war cannot be won militarily;
2. Starting initial contacts between all involved parties on confidence-building measures, including that the "armed opposition" stop destroying civilian infrastructure, Kabul release "some" Taliban prisoners, and the international forces stop all operations not approved by the Afghan government (including house searches and arrests);
3. A jirga of mutually acceptable Afghans contacts the parties who will be tasked with working out a peace plan;
4. The jirga informs all relevant Afghan forces about the procedure of the peace process, and secures U.N. and Islamic Conference support for roundtable talks, including security guarantees for the Taliban participants;

5. The Taliban leaders are de-blacklisted, bounties on their heads lifted, and a cease-fire called;
6. A commission is established to organize a Loya Jirga;
7. This Loya Jirga votes on the decisions taken in the roundtable discussions and proceeds to end the war.[76]

This plan has strongly influenced initial steps taken by the HPC where some of its authors, notably former Taliban minister (and now Senator) Arsala Rahmani, are among the most active and vocal.

AIMS AND OBSTACLES

The Afghan Actors' Aims

The political aims of the major Afghan actors involved are not clear-cut. With it still unclear whether there will ever be a negotiations process (and how it would be conducted), everyone keeps as many options open as possible, such as being on board with any new initiative in case it really takes off. The actors include the Taliban, Hezb-e Islami Gulbuddin, the Haqqani Network, the Afghan government, and the political opposition.

The Taliban

The Taliban seem to be in the best starting position for any political process. Although they are under strong military pressure, the West's timeline for a 2014 withdrawal of troops gives them a silver lining on the horizon. In their view, they can wait out the withdrawal and hope that power will simply fall into their hands when the Karzai government collapses—particularly if Pakistan keeps the movement as its strategic card for the next (regional) round of the power play in Afghanistan. Even if they come to a power-sharing agreement, the Taliban gain by peacefully reentering the country's political institutions. And even if they do not regain power, merely remaining as a political force beyond a U.S. withdrawal would be seen as a Taliban victory over a powerful adversary.

Their political program for a future Afghanistan remains opaque, however.[77] With Islam being both their program and their ideology, the Taliban never published a political manifesto. In practice, the one-point agenda during their ascent in the 1990s needed no printing and was sufficient to appeal to Afghans who had tired of the political chaos: to establish a "truly Islamic order" by disarming all other groups that had "betrayed" Islam. (The Taliban considered themselves neutral in the interfactional fighting.) Their understanding of politics and society became manifest only after they began taking power in Kandahar in 1994, where they established their headquarters; and Kabul in 1996, through the rejection of any pluralism—religious or political—and the exclusion of women from the public sphere. Details were to be decided after the end of the civil war by Islamic scholars (*ulema*).

Since then, statements of Taliban leaders about their political aims have not become much clearer. In his latest Eid message, dated November 15, 2010, Mullah Omar called for the "establishment of a true Islamic and independent system in the country." He added that

> the Islamic Emirate of Afghanistan has [a] comprehensive policy for the efficiency of the future government of Afghanistan about true security, Islamic justice, education, economic progress, national unity and a foreign policy based on norms to protect itself from the harm of others and convince the world that the future Afghanistan will not harm them.[78]

In a 2009 interview, deputy leader Mullah Baradar listed the Taliban's aims in more detail: regaining "freedom, authority and…Islamic Sovereignty" for "our Muslim nation" (Afghanistan) through "complete and unconditional withdrawal" of all Western forces; the establishment of a "truly representative Islamic Afghan administration based on the consent of our people"; and "a policy of mutual respect and non-interference with all countries of the world." He said the Taliban would give "special attention to education as our financial resources permit us."[79] Mullah Mutassim, then head of the Taliban political committee, earlier that year rejected any political power sharing: "The Islamic Emirate demands to rule the country so as to establish an…Islamic system in it." Somewhat contradictorily, however, he said that "an Afghan strategy" for the future of the country should be determined "in consultation with all the Afghan groups."[80]

From those statements, it follows that the Taliban leadership's current main political aim is to reestablish the Islamic Emirate. To achieve this, they are attempting to coerce international forces to withdraw and the Kabul government to collapse by curbing its access to a growing area of the country. Additionally, they try to build political pressure on the governments of the troop-providing countries by influencing public opinion, which, in many European countries and increasingly in North America, already has turned against the Western engagement in Afghanistan. By these means, they are effectively blocking the physical and institutional reconstruction process and creating permanent instability.

At the same time, the Taliban have gradually changed attitudes on a series of contentious issues such as education, health services, the role of the media, and their infamous dress code. Although these changes are not systematic and it is not clear to what extent they are accepted by field commanders and the rank and file, they do signal that the Taliban are able to change and respond in particular to negative attitudes in the population caused by their zealotry. In a number of areas under Taliban control or influence, educational and health facilities are operating, female staff is accepted, and women and girls have access—although this varies locally, always under Taliban-set conditions.[81] The same goes for access by journalists and NGOs. This reflects the Taliban's attempt to present itself as a government-in-waiting that expects to return to the official political arena.

The Haqqani Network

The political aims of the Haqqani Network are even more unclear. The network can best be described as a semiautonomous part of the Taliban movement, with its ability to take its own decisions hampered by two sets of dependencies. On one hand, it has put itself under the leadership—religious or moral, at least—of Mullah Omar and the Taliban's Quetta Shura; at the same time, it makes decisions about daily military affairs and the shadow administrations in areas under its influence. Second, it is the part of the Afghan insurgency that is most strictly controlled by the ISI[82] and most closely linked to Arab jihadists, given the independent links to Arab funding of Jalaluddin Haqqani and the Wahhabi upbringing of his son Sirajuddin in Saudi Arabia. Jalaluddin Haqqani is described as harboring only vague political ideas, centered on "sharia rule"; Sirajuddin Haqqani has not articulated his program.

The network has put much less emphasis on developing structures of a parallel government in its areas and seems to be motivated mainly by old conflicts and recent grievances, mainly caused by corrupt and predatory behavior of local government representatives that often causes violent ethnic or intertribal conflict and—given the lack of viable political alternatives—often leaves open only the way "into the mountains" for its victims.

Hezb-e Islami Gulbuddin (HIG)

Hezb-e Islami published a peace plan in March 2010. Although it is very detailed about an interim period during and after a quick withdrawal of foreign troops, it is vague about what a future Afghanistan would look like. It stipulates only that the first new elected parliament will revise the constitution. Apart from the establishment of Islamic courts to try war criminals and corrupt officials, there is not even the standard reference to an Islamic system of government; apparently, that goes without saying.

The plan foresees a withdrawal of foreign forces from populated areas and their concentration in military bases without the right to conduct operations on their own. The Afghan security forces are supposed to come under the control of a new seven-member National Security Council, composed of all important Afghan factions and based in a province without a foreign troop presence. A cease-fire would be in force and all political prisoners released. The current government and parliament would continue their duties until the withdrawal was completed; presidential, parliamentary, and provincial council elections would then be held on a party basis. The new cabinet would be an all-party body, with parties receiving seats according to the percentage of votes received. In the second elections, only those parties that received at least 10 percent of the vote in the first elections could participate.[83]

The plan, however, should be taken with a grain of salt. HIG and its undisputed leader, Hekmatyar, are known for political opportunism. The group would probably accept any political deal that gives it a foothold in the Kabul government. This would be extremely dangerous, as HIG is known for its historical inability to share power and for its ruthless approach to any competitors. It could try to neutralize competitors much better from inside. On the other hand, HIG's comparative "flexibility" vis-à-vis Kabul, including the attempts to open direct negotiations described above, has led to increased tensions with the Taliban. The latter accuse HIG of giving up the principles of the insurgency.[84]

The Afghan Government and Political Opposition

Both the Karzai camp and the political opposition—the mujahideen "parties" that emerged from the Northern Alliance, the Taliban's main pre-2001 adversary—have the least to gain from a political deal that ends in power sharing with insurgents. Not used to sharing but prone to monopolizing power and resources, they would definitely have to give up positions if other actors were added to the current setup. Their respective positions vis-à-vis the Taliban have additionally been undermined by loss of the moral high ground and political legitimacy. In the case of the mujahideen, they lost the moral clout gained during their anti-Soviet resistance, when they proved to be unable to properly govern Afghanistan after the fall of the Najibullah regime in 1992—when, instead, they caused another round of interfactional war. Furthermore, they were not able to present a unity candidate during the 2004 and 2009 presidential elections (with some of its leaders choosing an alliance with Karzai) as well as strong lists during the 2005 and 2010 parliamentary elections. Although Karzai won both presidential elections, his own political legitimacy was undermined as a result of the massive electoral fraud committed during the second electoral cycle of 2009–10, when between one-fifth and one-fourth of all votes had to be disqualified. Both the Karzai and the opposition camps have to particularly fear the Taliban, whose leaders still can be expected, at least partially, to implement strict moral standards and could fight corruption and the drug trade once back in power, to the detriment of the two camps, whose ties to economic networks that are linked to illicit sectors of the economy make them particularly vulnerable to anti-corruption campaigns.

Officially, the Afghan government has adopted the "red lines" developed by the West for dealing with the insurgents: that they sever all ties with al-Qaeda, lay down arms, and recognize the current constitution. However, its track record on respecting the Afghan constitution, including enshrined rights and freedoms, is ambivalent at best. The government is dominated ideologically by Islamists and religious conservatives who enjoy significant influence over the president. At the same time, the moderating effect of individual reformers and democrats has all but disappeared. In recent meetings with foreign visitors, high-ranking officials have presented their own version of the red lines: national unity and integrity, the Islamic character of the state, and "basic" human rights. Though there is little dissent from anyone on the first two issues, from the Taliban to the former mujahideen and even many of the democrats, the last point opens the doors wide for a watered-down compromise. What constitutes "basic" will be defined by those in power, and the likely outcome of a Karzai-Taliban agreement is some "Taliban lite" version of the state. It would be vehemently opposed by the democrats, the minorities, and the marginalized.

Apart from these two forces—the Karzai camp and the opposition—in the Afghan state's current political setup, there is a fragmented but ever more vocal spectrum of civil society forces in the broader sense, from non-Islamist tribal leaders to pro-democratic parties, human rights groups, and the women's movement. These forces strive to safeguard the democratic freedoms and individual rights enshrined in the constitution and partially implemented since 2001, but they have been neglected as genuine political partners by the West as a result of its single-minded focus on the person of Karzai.

Parts of the political opposition, primarily the non-Pashtun elements, share the fears of the pro-democratic forces that the Taliban and Hezb-e Islami will return and dominate a future political setup. However, the opposition also could become part of the problem rather than the solution; the major parties' pasts are tainted, they are often still armed and lacking internal democratic procedures, and they waver between an opposition role and partaking in the spoils of government. This does not make them a counterweight to the Taliban. Among neither these nor the other parties is there any political force that can attract significant parts of the Pashtun population. Because of their ideological closeness, based on varieties of Islamism, even a new alliance between the Taliban and parts of the current ex-mujahideen opposition is possible—in particular when there is no or less Western presence that still bolsters pro-democratic and pro–human rights political forces. The result could be a government based on a broad alliance of multiethnic Islamist forces.

PRECONDITIONS AND RED LINES

As is to be expected early in a process of talking, there are a number of preconditions or "red lines" in the way of meaningful talks. These positions, however, are not necessarily unchangeable. For a first step, meaningful channels should be opened to sound out each other's positions. In this sense, contacts as recently reported make sense. However, a coordinated approach among the Afghan government, the HPC, and other Afghan actors, as well as their foreign allies, must be adopted to avoid making this a free-for-all that would create a cacophony of voices and allow involved actors to be played against one another.

The Taliban's public position is that they want all Western troops out of the country first before entering into structured talks. HIG has been more nuanced on this point; it instead demands a timetable for withdrawal as a prerequisite for any talks. It also suggests redeploying the Western troops to specified bases until the withdrawal. Such a change of position might be expected from the Taliban, too, at some point in a quid pro quo.

The existence of U.S. bases on Afghan territory and Washington's interest in keeping them after the handover of security responsibilities to the Afghan government, envisaged for 2014, also might become a stumbling block. From the U.S. point of view, an agreement to retain such bases is a core prerequisite for its antiterrorism policy, mainly with an eye toward the Pakistan-Afghanistan border regions that serve as staging areas for a variety of militant Islamist and terrorist groups and a possible takeover of Pakistan (including its nuclear arsenal). It is hard to imagine, though, that the Taliban, whose raison d'être has increasingly become to fight a "foreign occupation," might accept such installations in the long run, and some close to the movement have already expressed such views.[85]

The same goes for a rebranded "training" mission. Most of the political opposition also would like to see the international troops depart, and members have pushed for a status of forces agreement in the meantime, as a number of initiatives in the 2005–2010 Wolesi Jirga (the lower house of parliament) showed. Both the Karzai camp and the pro-democratic forces, meanwhile, see the presence of the troops as insurance for the ability to maintain power or for the continuation of freedom and rights. Common among all of them and the Taliban, with gradual differences, is the demand for a modus operandi respecting Afghans and a growing dislike of the current U.S. military approach of "kinetic" and Special Forces operations.

With regard to Afghanistan's future political setup, the Taliban demand the reestablishment of the Islamic Emirate on the basis of sharia, or Islamic law. However, their leaders also have made statements that include the possibility of "consultations" with other groups about the future state structure. HIG, in contrast, favors an elected, party-based parliamentarian system with high hurdles that, in effect, would limit inclusiveness significantly. The Karzai camp, the political opposition, and the pro-democratic forces are not unified on this subject. Although the first camp prefers maintaining the current, strongly centralized presidential system, the opposition favors transitioning to a parliamentary system, with some elements supporting a federal system that would allow devolution of power either to the provinces or larger regions.[86] The weak and disunited pro-democratic forces favor a system as open as possible and would, therefore, line up with these forces in favor of the parliamentary option, but necessarily toward more provincial and regional autonomy.[87] Most political forces, with the exception of the supporters of a federal state, prefer a unitary centralized state.

As for the future of the main insurgent organizations' leaders, a proposal has been floated that would result in the Taliban's Mullah Omar and the HIG's Hekmatyar going into exile in Saudi Arabia or another Islamic country "with protection and treatment as a former head of state."[88]

However, it is hard to believe that either organization would accept this, given the key role both leaders play, and in Mullah Omar's case his symbolic role as the embodiment of unity in the various Taliban networks. Dropping Mullah Omar would basically jeopardize the movement's very coherence. This should not be confused with the floated proposal that Mullah Omar not directly participate in negotiations (which also would be a question of personal security) and that in particular the Taliban need an "address" outside or inside Afghanistan.

On the other hand, the West has established its own preconditions that the Taliban must meet to enter any official talks: accepting the current Afghan constitution (including a broad set of international norms and standards, human and women's rights, freedom of media and speech, etc.), stopping violence and laying down arms, and severing all links with al-Qaeda. Secretary of State Hillary Clinton, however, seems to have recently reinterpreted these "red lines" from preconditions to enter talks to "necessary outcomes of any negotiation," that is, parts of a desired end state of a political process.[89]

Speaking practically, the last point—severing links with al-Qaeda—does not seem to be out of range; the Kandahari mainstream of the Taliban,[90] represented by the "Quetta Shura," have repeatedly made clear that they do not share the international jihadist agenda of al-Qaeda; nor are they organizationally linked to the group. Although Mullah Omar refused to denounce Osama bin Laden before the terrorist attacks of September 11, 2011, and to distance himself and his organization from al-Qaeda afterward, there are signs of a growing pragmatism—and even realism—on this particular point. In a key 2009 interview, Taliban spokesman Zabihullah Mujahid declared that "we [the Taliban] are one thing and al-Qaeda is another. They are global[,] we are just in the region."[91] Despite Mullah Omar's stubborn insistence on not withdrawing "hospitality" from the al-Qaeda leader, the Taliban have at times kept themselves away from al-Qaeda organizationally: the group did not join the "World Islamic Front for Jihad against Jews and Crusaders" set up by Osama bin Laden in February 1998 in Afghanistan with groups from Bangladesh, Egypt, and Pakistan. Over the recent years, the Taliban also have become less dependent on al-Qaeda financially and logistically because they managed to diversify their funding base, with income from "taxes" raised by their shadow structures—among other issues on reconstruction and even military contracts—becoming more and more important. To expect an open Taliban *declaration* of a break with al-Qaeda under current circumstances is premature; it should correctly be made a target of negotiations. This will also be true for the Haqqani Network, whether it acts on its own or under its allegiance with the Taliban leadership: its special links with al-Qaeda and other Arab elements are driven more by history and family links than by ideology at this point.[92]

Laying down arms, however—coupled with "reintegration"—will be unacceptable for the Taliban because they perceive this as a demand for surrender. So far, only local fringe groups of insurgents have accepted that offer—and often under pressure from rival groups, as was the case when HIG fighters lost a fight for domination in the north of Baghlan province in mid-2010 against the Taliban[93]—and decided to "reconcile" with the government. Such groups can easily cross back to the front line again if the reason they change sides disappears, or if incentives are more attractive elsewhere. (The Soviet-Afghan attempts at reconciliation in the 1980s and 1990s proved that an incentives-based approach is highly problematic and not sustainable. It creates perverse incentives and encourages multiple side switching; in this period the Soviet-backed Kabul government was almost in a competition to pay off mujahideen groups.)[94]

The current Afghan constitution clashes with the Taliban demand for the reestablishment of the Islamic Emirate and the predominance of sharia. Implicit in the West's red line referring to the constitution are guaranteed rights and freedoms. However, it cannot be taken for granted that both the West and the Karzai government (already under strong Islamist influence from within) will stick to them. And ideally, negotiations need to involve give-and-take and end in compromise. This includes increasing the pressure on the Taliban that they will not renege on some of their post-2011 shifts of position on some major political issues that were contentious for the pre-2001 Taliban—such as education, health services, the role of the media and NGOs, and their dress code—and make them their officially recognized policies. Such statements of their leadership are still missing on every single one of the issues. But they represent attractive incentives for a movement that traditionally has sought official recognition by the world and that currently aims at presenting itself as a political force and even a kind of government-in-waiting.

Obstacles

The Taliban's ability to negotiate is hampered by the lack of a political arm similar to the IRA's Sinn Féin in Northern Ireland, the ETA's Herri Batasuna in Spain, or the FARC's Unión Patriotica in Colombia. The Taliban's political committee is too dependent on the movement's leaders and has neither the autonomy to act nor—at least currently, in contrast to 2007–08—the authority to negotiate. More important, it is not clear whether there is a continuing discussion among the committee members about civilian casualties and the need for a political solution since the U.S. surge beginning in early 2009, which was perceived by the Taliban as a declaration of war—in short, whether there still is a pragmatic faction of "doves."

Therefore, it is more useful to differentiate between two unstructured currents, one being the pragmatic, politically thinking, pro-talks Taliban who understand that a political solution is desirable but who are still conservative Islamists; and the other being those who favor a purely military approach, often combined with excessive use of terrorist means. Both groups compete for the allegiance of foot soldiers who have joined the insurgency because of marginalization or exclusion by the current regime—the *majburi* (forced) and *na-raz* (disappointed)— and who are originally nonpolitical (although there is a radicalization process going on among them).[95]

But with the Taliban still extending their reach, their operational scope unstopped, and the hard-liners still dominating, they might have no appetite to negotiate and may prefer to wait out the expected withdrawal of Western troops.

The West's ability to negotiate is also hampered by the currently predominant strategy of "shooting and talking," which boils down to an attempt to weaken the Taliban and gain a position of strength before entering any meaningful negotiations. However, the failure to make substantial military gains against the insurgency, the insurgency's growing geographical and ethnic scope, and the eroding mistrust of the coalition among the population show that this strategy is not working. Therefore, a redefinition of "position of strength" is necessary, from military strength to moral and political strength. This must include, for example, practical steps to show that the statement that there can be "no military solution" is more than lip service. There also must be steps to remove obstacles to a political solution, and above all to push for governance and institutional reform on the "Kabul side" of things. Giving up on state (or institution) building leads in the wrong direction. As the "ripeness" theory of negotiations suggests, the best conditions for negotiations are when both sides believe neither can escalate to victory or a significantly stronger position.[96]

This would require that both sides—the United States and International Security Assistance Force, and the Taliban leadership— make the human security of Afghans and the protection of the civilian population their most relevant target, not, in the first case, force protection and in the second, the power to intimidate.

Also extremely helpful for a negotiated settlement would be for the West to redefine its timelines for engagement in Afghanistan—beyond the military drawdown scheduled to be completed by 2014—and to genuinely commit to further engagement, including investment in Afghan institutions, aid, and development.[97] The lethal "logic" that a military drawdown will also pull away most civilian resources from Afghanistan needs to be reversed.

Confidence-Building Measures

Apart from opening meaningful channels—including through track II and similar processes—there is a need for confidence-building measures to facilitate reconciliation processes in Afghanistan. This means first continuing what already is under way, officially and unofficially, including the removal of politically minded insurgent leaders from sanctions and terrorism lists, vetted and lawful release of prisoners, and local cease-fires. The last can provide a bridge to the establishment of "calm zones" (without fighting) and more formal demilitarized zones. Ceasing to label insurgents as terrorists on the part of the Afghan government and the international community might also be such a step—not least because that description of them is too narrow.

The Afghan government, through the High Peace Council, and its external allies should scrutinize whether a sufficiently extensive area inside Afghanistan could be designed as a demilitarized hub, without compromising national sovereignty. It would be a place where the Taliban leadership could relocate without fear of attack or where negotiations could be conducted, as was done (although finally unsuccessfully) in Colombia. It could also take advantage of the fact that the insurgents already virtually control large swaths of Afghan territory. Most important, this could "liberate" the Taliban leadership from the undue influence of Pakistan and contribute to "Afghanizing" the conflict. (Such a step would require, however, that the insurgents subscribe to a set of obligations as well, such as not using this hub as a staging area for attacks.) Supplying the population of an area with aid and development assistance, and regulating traffic in and out, would also serve to build confidence. However, this plan would require a measure of trust on the part of the insurgents (who would give up their safe havens in Pakistan), which currently seems utopian. Therefore, such an option should be considered for an advanced stage of the process.

The value of such confidence-building measures in general depends on "whether they are part of a structured dialogue and are reciprocal."[98]

The demands for reciprocity on the part of the insurgents should focus on the needs of the Afghan civilian population, not primarily on the Western troops. It could include the release of kidnapped persons, an agreement to halt attacks on civilians and civilian facilities such as health clinics and schools, and allowing access for NGOs and government workers. Furthermore, the Afghan government (which often remains surprisingly quiet about Taliban atrocities) and its international backers should demand that the Taliban stick to their own code of conduct, the *layha*, which is implemented very randomly at best when it comes to protection of civilians. This would also encourage the Afghan media and other societal groups to join in holding the Taliban to account for disregarding civilian casualties.

Confidence-building measures also need to consider those political and social forces in Afghanistan that fear to lose out in a possible political deal with the Taliban—notably women, ethnic and other minorities, and the pro-democratic forces. Foremost, there must be transparency in the approach to contacts and future negotiations. Among the most controversial issues is amnesty for insurgents, either in a pre-talks process or as a result of talks. Most Afghans are not in favor of an amnesty for the people who were politically responsible for mass human rights violations or war crimes committed up to the end of the Taliban regime in 2001,[99] or for those who were politically responsible for such actions. On the other hand, there is a de facto amnesty for the civil war parties linked to the current setup in Kabul, the so-called amnesty bill passed by the Afghan parliament in 2007 but enforced only in late 2009.[100] The amnesty in the bill covers the post-2001 insurgents by implication as well. Although this form of law is de facto a form of collective impunity, reconciliation would demand an approach based on individual accountability.

The way the members of the Peace Jirga and the HPC were handpicked set a negative example, despite the symbolic presence of some women and civil society actors. It also has exacerbated the fears of those groups that were excluded or still feel sidelined from the "reconciliation" process as it has played out. Here, the international community can play a central role by helping the Afghan government start nationwide consultations and a public debate about reconciliation issues, and to open up the space for it, including a guarantee of media freedom and the protection of critical voices.

Ideally, any negotiation process should be based on a joint strategy agreed between the Afghan government (from a consensus reached in truly nationwide consultations) and its international allies. On the U.S. side, in particular, unity of command and policy needs to be established. Among other steps, the Special Forces need to be brought under ISAF command in practice, and their central role needs to be relinquished. Basically, it is the decision between a military approach to the insurgency or a political-diplomatic one.

These steps, taken by the strongest actor, would help to reestablish the international community's ability to find its way back to a neutral role in Afghanistan as during the immediate post-Taliban period, with the Bonn Conference and the U.N. lead. This way, it would be able to provide the "credible external guarantees," and the ability to exert political pressure when needed, "required to underwrite and support any agreement."[101]

The Pakistan Factor

The Taliban and their associated networks, as well as HIG, can rely on a system of extensive relations in Pakistan. These include the local tribal populations, parts of the Pakistani government (primarily in the armed forces, the ISI, and the Frontier Corps), and the various Islamist parties and terrorist groups in the Federally Administered Tribal Areas and beyond. The logistical and political backing the insurgents enjoy in and from Pakistan clearly belongs to their infrastructure. This Pakistani approach—denied for many years but now claimed with much self-assuredness by the Pakistanis[102]—stems from the tense relationship between Afghanistan and Pakistan since the 1947 partition of British-ruled India and the establishment of Pakistan.[103]

In this new Great Game, officially retired ISI officers, open proponents of an Islamist and anti-Western agenda, are likely one outsourced political instrument that provides the Pakistani military "plausible deniability" in cases where it is accused of aiding the Taliban while officially following a line that supports peace talks between Kabul and the insurgents. Following from this, the Haqqani Network seems to enjoy most-favored status currently. Those links and structures are vital for the Taliban. It also can be safely assumed that Taliban leaders who have been flown to Kabul for talks—if indeed this is true—traveled with Pakistan's consent, or even under its orders.

As long as Islamabad stays entangled in such a game, and India and Pakistan do not allow at least a degree of moderation in their own conflict, a solution in Afghanistan will remain extremely difficult. Therefore, steps toward detente between India and Pakistan are vital for stabilization in Afghanistan. This would provide for a realistic redefinition of both countries' national security interests in the region.

CONCLUSION: SOME ELEMENTS FOR A RECONCILIATION FRAMEWORK

The current situation—with the West's timetable for a 2014 withdrawal and a resilient and growing insurgency—leaves two main options on reconciliation: to approach it as a broad societal process, or to go for a quick fix.

In the first case, the core causes of the Afghan conflicts[104] would be addressed in all its dimensions over the long run. This would include the development of an increasingly efficient, transparent, and legitimate government, as well as Afghan mechanisms to discuss the country's future political course, including possible constitutional and institutional reforms. During this process, the lead would be transferred to Afghan institutions—but only when they are ready for the job, that is, when they are recognized by most Afghans as sufficiently impartial, uncorrupted, and effective. Ways to achieve this would be determined in a process involving a broad variety of Afghan players interacting on a level playing field, "escorted" and guaranteed by the international community—which is to say, within a democratic and participative framework. Talks with insurgents, direct or indirect, would be only one part of the overall reconciliation process, which would be aimed at reaching an initial political settlement to end violence, creating transitional institutions to pursue the process, and providing a mechanism for constitutional and institutional reform.

This would also mean redefining the role of the West—the United States as its strongest actor, the U.N. as its most representative one—away from being parties to the conflict and toward being (more) neutral actors again. What could be honestly called the "international community" with regard to Afghanistan needs to be revived. This would require the West to step back from its currently monopolistic role and bring in non-NATO countries such as China and Russia on terms that reflect their respective weight. At the same time, the West should not withdraw from the political responsibility it accepted at the 2001 Bonn conference, which has been magnified by the failures of the post-2001 political process in Afghanistan.

This will not occur without a real (and not only gradual) strategic shift on the part of the United States that commits fully to a political solution in Afghanistan. Instead of the current double strategy of "shooting and talking" at the same time, it should concentrate on "talking instead of shooting." This means turning the tanker around, not steering it a bit more to the east or west. It would redefine the current understanding of "position of strength" away from strictly military terms to political and moral terms. In this framework, military means would be used only for self-defense (which includes defending Afghan institutions and their officials) as well as the work of political reform. Such a shift in the military approach would also significantly remove a major recruitment factor for the insurgents: civilian casualties. On the U.S. side, this would require implementing full unity of command within the military, including a stop to any independent action by special operations forces as well as an approach that is unified between civilian and military actors. A transparent status-of-forces agreement for U.S. troops needs to be concluded, with involvement by the Afghan parliament.

In this framework, the international community should urge the Afghan government to start genuine nationwide consultations and a public debate about reconciliation-related issues, based on the lessons of 2001 to 2010, to avoid a repetition of governmental failure. It needs to ensure that open space for this process exists; media freedom and protection for critical voices are essential.

As a first step, existing "reconciliation" bodies such as the High Peace Council and its secretariat should be reformed by broadening participation. Checks and balances must be added, either by expanding the existing HPC with the addition of civil society representatives and experts on mediation, or by creating another council to shadow it. In the latter case, the two groups should be on equal terms, both in numbers and with the same rights; that is, a shadow HPC should be consulted as intensively as the original HPC. These bodies could tie together existing contacts with insurgents, both at the institutional level (via presidential diplomacy, the HPC, and so on) and at the personal level, namely, relations between political leaders at all levels and even individuals who know insurgent commanders or fighters personally or are related to them and maintain personal links, characteristic of Afghan society. They could ensure that each side has the ability to sound out the other's current positions on a political solution. This would require a joint strategy agreed on by the Afghan government (and based on a consensus reached in truly national consultations) and its international allies. A proliferation of "talking" actors should be avoided, such as different governments developing their own channels.

Current confidence-building measures such as dropping U.N. sanctions against conciliatory insurgent leaders and releases of political prisoners (done in a transparent way, based on clear criteria) should be continued and expanded. They should be grounded in reciprocity and focused on the needs of the Afghan civilian population and the aid community; force protection should not be the defining factor. New measures can be explored, such as local cease-fires and the establishment of a neutral zone where the Taliban leadership can reside, without fear of attack, for the purpose of negotiations. Supplying the population of such an area with aid and services, and arranging for humanitarian providers to cross the front lines of the area, would also build confidence.

Confidence-building measures also need to consider those political and social forces in Afghanistan that fear to lose out in a possible political deal with the Taliban; this could be addressed mainly through transparency and inclusion.

Inclusive regional mechanisms of consultation need to be reestablished immediately, so that neighboring nations and other interested countries buy into a political solution. The issue of post-2014 U.S. bases on Afghan territory is central: alternative and collective options to defend against terrorist threats in the region should be explored and developed. The "Pakistan factor" also needs to be part of such regional mechanisms. This would be best supported by separate initiatives aimed at easing tensions between Pakistan and India, and with Iran.

The other alternative—a quick fix power-sharing agreement between the current unreformed Kabul government and elements of the insurgents—would only paper over the causes of the current conflicts. It would redistribute the cards in the current game of resource capture for a while, but in fact it would perpetuate the conflicts, increasing the danger of a new round of civil war. It would lead to more years of muddling through until the end of 2014, and then possibly force the international community, against its desire, to return to Afghanistan at some point in the future. Only a push for better governance and institutional reform, as well as regional mechanisms for further stability, will create a chance to win back the Afghan population's declining support for the current form of international involvement in their country—and that of their neighboring Muslim countries. Finally, it will be the mass of ordinary Afghans who will decide the success or failure of any political solution—just by opting for one side or the other.

This chapter was originally written in late 2010. Since then, significant first steps toward substantial negotiations about a political solution to the current insurgency in Afghanistan have been made, and backlashes registered.

In 2011, for the first time a direct U.S. channel to the Taliban leadership was opened that is real[105] and promising, with the help of the German government and intelligence as well as that of the government of Qatar. This is a new situation because for the first time, as Michael Semple, an expert on Taliban affairs, explains, "the Taliban movement, its leadership, have officially committed themselves to engaging in a political process....Few people appreciate how rapidly the debate inside the Taliban has changed over even the past few weeks."[106] In January 2012 it transpired—after the Taliban officially acknowledged it—that an agreement had been reached between their leadership and the governments of the United States and Qatar over the opening of a Taliban office in Qatar,[107] although there are contradictory reports about the exact "term of reference" of the Qatar office itself and whether it has already been inaugurated or is functioning. Former Taliban officials residing in Kabul reported in late January 2012 that "four to eight Taliban representatives had travelled to Qatar from Pakistan" already.

Practically, however, it did not matter much whether the office was opened or not. Meetings had been held in Qatar anyway already and, according to media reports, these talks were "fairly advanced," focusing on a prisoner exchange as well as on the removal of some Taliban members from NATO's "kill or capture" lists.[108]

The backlash came in mid-March 2012. On March 15, the Taliban suspended the talks with the U.S. government, accusing Washington of a "shaky, erratic and vague" approach to the talks and of breaching a memorandum of understanding that both sides had previously arrived at. The U.S. government, meanwhile, reiterated its commitment to an "Afghan peace process" in general and told the Taliban that they cannot contribute to one by walking away from the negotiating table. The Taliban decision is not necessarily the end of the peace process. It leaves the door open for later resumption of the contacts, while putting the ball in the U.S. court, but it also indicates how difficult it will be to achieve a peaceful solution for Afghanistan.[109]

Most of the previous progress was achieved without the Kabul government's participation, and often against its resistance.[110] The agreement on the Qatar office has even led to a diplomatic crisis between Afghanistan and Qatar that has not been fully settled yet. Moreover, this controversy has created potential new hurdles for meaningful talks. President Karzai has announced the start of an "other effort" to talk with the Taliban, through Saudi Arabia, "before the [official] establishment of a Taliban office in Qatar."[111] Although the Taliban so far reject direct talks with the Karzai government, which they consider a "Western puppet," this announcement can be read as a sign of Karzai's remaining anger with Qatar and the United States, as an attempt to counter, or even undermine, the Qatar channel not controlled by him and to play on tensions between Saudi Arabia and Qatar.

Earlier, in spring 2011, elements in the Afghan government came close to sabotaging the contacts facilitated by Germany and Qatar for the first time by leaking the name of the leader of the Taliban contact team to the media.[112] The interlocutor was forced underground—temporarily. The reason for this step was Kabul's insistence on its own lead in any Taliban contacts, an approach to which Western governments officially had subscribed during the international conference on Afghanistan in London in early 2010, where they endorsed the Afghanistan Peace and Reconciliation Programme, the Kabul government's political document on negotiations with the insurgent groups.[113]

In autumn 2011, another blow to the talks came with the assassination of the chairman of the High Peace Council (HPC) and former Afghan president, Burhanuddin Rabbani, in Kabul. On closer look, however, it was mainly opposition politicians and some government members who had been opposed to negotiations with the Taliban for a long time who declared the talks with the Taliban dead after the murder.

The assassination was overinterpreted as a reflection of the Taliban movement's unwillingness—in its entirety—to talk, as later events proved. (It is also still not clear who committed the crime.) This discussion about the murder also often overlooked the question of whether the HPC had been rather ineffective so far. Despite claims to the contrary by some HPC members, there is no proof that it has been able to open a single meaningful channel to the insurgents. In general, there was not much of a "peace process" going on that needed to be stopped.

The debate about "reconciliation" between Taliban insurgents and the Afghan government started moving again in 2010. Substantive talks, however, have clearly not gotten under way yet. All the contacts with the Taliban were preliminary and exploratory to that time, as all sides involved—including the Taliban—stressed. They had not reached the "negotiations" stage. This means that both sides favored exploring a political solution as one option while continuing to fight at the same time.

Notes

1. Matt Waldman, *The Sun in the Sky: The Relationship Between Pakistan's ISI and Afghan Insurgents*, London School of Economics, Crisis States Research Centre, Discussion Paper No. 18, June 2010.
2. A nom de guerre; his real name is Abdul Ghani. The exact date of his arrest is unknown. The *New York Times*, the original source of the report of the arrest, said it had learned about the operation on February 11 and that Baradar had been arrested almost a week earlier. Mark Mazzetti and Dexter Filkins, "Secret Joint Raid Captures Taliban's Top Commander," *New York Times*, Feb. 15, 2010, http://www.nytimes.com/2010/02/16/world/asia/16intel.html?ref=asia.

3. Dean Nelson/Ben Farmer, "Hamid Karzai Held Secret Talks with Mullah Baradar in Afghanistan," *Daily Telegraph*, Mar. 16, 2010, http://www.telegraph.co.uk/news/worldnews/asia/afghanistan/7457861/Hamid-Karzai-held-secret-talks-with-Mullah-Baradar-in-Afghanistan.html; personal interview, sources close to the Taliban, March 2010.

4. "Taliban Chief Mullah Omar Rules out Afghan Peace Talks," BBC, Nov. 15, 2010, http://www.bbc.co.uk/news/world-south-asia-11760383.

5. Jane Perlez, "Pakistan Is Said to Pursue Role in U.S.-Afghan Talks," *New York Times*, Feb. 9, 2010, http://www.nytimes.com/2010/02/10/world/asia/10pstan.html.

6. Willi Germund, "Pakistan lässt Taliban-Chef auffliegen," *Salzburger Nachrichten*, Feb. 17, 2010, http://www.salzburg.com/online/nachrichten/newsletter/Pakistan-laesst-Taliban-Chef-auffliegen.html?article=eGMmOI8VfD9DlwoTcrgfrICcm bnCwxLPomzO3cn&img=&text=&mode=.

7. Joshua Partlow, "Karzai Wants U.S. to Reduce Military Operations in Afghanistan," *Washington Post*, Nov. 14, 2010, http://www.washingtonpost.com/wp-dyn/content/story/2010/11/13/ST2010111305091.html?sid=ST2010111305091.

8. I do not consider the Haqqani Network an independent organization but a semiautonomous entity within the Taliban movement. See Thomas Ruttig, "Loya Paktia's Insurgency: The Haqqani Network as an Autonomous Entity in the Taliban Universe," in Antonio Giustozzi (ed.), *Decoding the New Taliban: Insights from the Afghan Field* (New York: Columbia University Press, 2009), pp. 57–88.

9. Both, however, were convened by President Karzai, who—mainly through close advisors—handpicked mainly allies for both bodies. See Martine van Bijlert and Thomas Ruttig, "Warlords' Peace Council," *AAN blog*, Sept. 28, 2010, http://www.aan-afghanistan.org/index.asp?id=1175; Thomas Ruttig, "The Big Karzai Show," *AAN blog*, June 2, 2010, http://www.aan-afghanistan.org/index.asp?id=790.

10. Dexter Filkins and Carlotta Gall, "Taliban Leader in Secret Talks Was an Impostor," *New York Times*, Nov. 22, 2010, http://www.nytimes.com/2010/11/23/world/asia/23kabul.html?_r=1&nl=todaysheadlines&emc=a2.

11. "President Obama's Final Orders for Afghanistan Pakistan Strategy, or Terms Sheet," in Bob Woodward, *Obama's Wars* (New York: Simon & Schuster, 2010), p. 385.

12. Martine van Bijlert, "Are Talks with the Taliban Snow-Balling?" *AAN blog*, Oct. 20, 2010, http://www.aan-afghanistan.org/index.asp?id=1241.

13. Here the traditional Afghan regional terminology is used: south for the provinces around Kandahar, southeast for greater Paktia and Ghazni, east for the provinces around Jalalabad. For the trends in the political and security situation, see, for the south: Anand Gopal, *The Battle for Afghanistan: Militancy and Conflict in Kandahar*, New America Foundation Policy Paper, Washington, Nov. 9, 2010; and for the north Antonio Giustozzi and Christoph Reuter, *The Insurgents of the North: The Rise of the Taliban, the Self-Abandonment of the Afghan Government and the Effects of ISAF's "Capture-and-Kill Campaign,"* Afghanistan Analysts Network, Berlin/Kabul, forthcoming. For the southeast, this was

confirmed by various local observers during the author's trip to the region in
early December 2010.

14. Shapoor Saber, "Rebel Chief Defies Coalition Forces," Institute for War and
Peace Reporting (Kabul), Afghan Recovery Report No. 313, Feb. 18, 2009.

15. *TLO Reflections on the Afghanistan Study Group Report*, Liaison Office, Kabul, Sept.
30, 2010, S. 2; Antonio Giustozzi and Christoph Reuter, *The Northern Front: The
Afghan Insurgency Spreading Beyond the Pashtuns*, AAN Briefing Paper 03/2010,
Kabul/Berlin, June 2010, p. 4.

16. Giustozzi and Reuter, *The Northern Front*, p. 1.

17. "Mullah Omar Eid message," Afghan Islamic Press (Peshawar), Oct. 21, 2006.

18. See a more detailed discussion of this development: Thomas Ruttig, *How Tribal
Are the Taliban? Afghanistan's Largest Insurgent Movement Between Its Tribal Roots
and Islamist Ideology*, AAN Thematic Report 04/2010, June 2010, Kabul/Berlin,
pp. 15–16.

19. Matt Waldman, *Dangerous Liaisons with the Afghan Taliban: The Feasibility and
Risks of Negotiations*, USIP Special Report 256, Oct. 10, 2010, p. 15.

20. On Taliban overtures, see Gopal, *The Battle for Afghanistan*, p. 6; Michael Semple,
Reconciliation in Afghanistan, USIP Perspectives Series, Washington, 2009, pp.
39–42.

21. Announced dead by the Pakistani authorities in early 2012, confirmed by a
Taliban statement: http://alemaral.com/index.php?option=com_content&view=
article&id=22059:2012-02-13-06-10-57&catid=6:officiale-statmenst&Itemid=7.

22. Anand Gopal, "Missed Opportunities in Kandahar," *Foreign Policy, AfPak Channel
blog*, Nov. 10, 2010.

23. Thomas Ruttig: *The Ex-Taliban on the High Peace Council: A New Role for the
Khuddam ul-Furqan?*, AAN Discussion Paper 04/2010, Kabul/Berlin, October
2010.

24. This author participated in the ELJ's organization and was present during its
proceedings.

25. The author is in possession of a full original copy in Pashto. That a new layha
was issued by the Taliban had also been mentioned by a number of media; see,
for example, Amir Shah and Deb Riechmann, Associated Press, Aug. 3 2010,
http://abcnews.go.com/International/wireStory?id=11310793.

26. Christina Lamb, "Taliban Chief Backs Afghan Peace Talks," *The Times*, Mar.
15, 2009, http://www.timesonline.co.uk/tol/news/world/asia/article5908498.
ece. Recently leaked U.S. embassy cables confirm that Abdullah Anas was
instrumental in setting up the Saudi channel together with Qayum Karzai,
the president's brother (also see below); "US Embassy Cables: Hamid
Karzai's Brother on Preliminary Taliban Peace Talks," *Guardian*, Dec. 2,
2010.

27. Kathy Gannon, "Afghan Taliban Threaten Death to All Talking Peace,"
Associated Press, Nov. 5, 2010.

28. Shamim Shahid, "Quetta-based Taliban Move to Karachi," *Nation* (Pakistan),
Apr. 30, 2009, http://www.nation.com.pk/pakistan-news-newspaper-daily-
english-online/Politics/30-Apr-2009/Quettabased-Taliban-move-to-Karachi.

29. Semple, *Reconciliation in Afghanistan*, p. 76. This was also confirmed by a recently
leaked U.S. cable that refers to "the Quetta participants." "US Embassy Cables:

Hamid Karzai's Brother on Preliminary Taliban Peace Talks," *Guardian*, Dec. 2, 2010.

30. Matthew Rosenberg, "Karzai, in Saudi Arabia, Pursues Taliban Talks," *Wall Street Journal*, Feb. 2, 2010; on the "reconciled" Taliban, see Ruttig, *The Ex-Taliban on the High Peace Council: A New Role for the Khuddam ul-Furqan?* AAN Discussion Paper 04/2010, Kabul/Berlin, October 2010, pp. 3, 7.

31. Carlotta Gall, "Afghanistan Tests Waters for Overture to Taliban," *New York Times*, Oct. 30, 2008.

32. Kathy Gannon, "Taliban Sets Preconditions for Formal Peace Talks," Associated Press, Oct. 6, 2010.

33. Based on a number of informal interviews by the author in Afghanistan, among them with former HIG members, over the past years.

34. Interviews with former Hezb members, Kabul 2003. The Hezb parliamentary faction was reduced in numbers in the 2010 parliamentary elections; its unofficial 2005–2010 chairman, Ataullah Ludin, is now one of the three vice chairmen of the High Peace Council.

35. These groups belonged to the seven main Sunni mujahideen groups during the fight against the Soviet occupation (1979–1989) and are now registered as official political parties.

36. "Hekmatyar Shows Readiness for Conditional Peace Talks," *Pajhwok Afghan News*, Kabul, Oct. 28, 2006; "No Talks Between Afghan Government, Fugitive Leader: UN," Tolo TV, Kabul, May 12, 2008; Janullah Hashimzada, "Hekmatyar Offers Conditions for Talks," *Pajhwok Afghan News*, Kabul, Oct. 14, 2008.

37. "Son-in-law of Hekmatyar Freed in Kabul," *The News* (Pakistan), June 1, 2008. Bahir was arrested by the Pakistani authorities in 2002 as a leader of an Afghan insurgent organization and was transferred to Kabul later.

38. A short version of its main content was published for the first time by Afghan Islamic Press (Peshawar) on Oct. 14, 2008. For the full proposal, see Thomas Ruttig, "Gulbuddin Ante Portas—Again," *AAN blog*, Mar. 22, 2010, http://www.aan-afghanistan.org/index.asp?id=706.

39. "Rebel Group Says [It] Will Never Accept Afghan Government's Peace Talks Conditions," Afghan Islamic Press (Peshawar), Apr. 10, 2010.

40. The strongest fighting took place in Baghlan and Wardak, but there were also some armed skirmishes and the expulsion of HIG representatives from Taliban-controlled areas in the southeast. Author's interviews with local analysts in Gardez and Kabul, September, October, and December 2010.

41. Rob Crilly and Ben Farmer, "Taliban Makes Demands in Afghan Peace Talks," *Daily Telegraph*, Oct. 29, 2010.

42. Julian Borger, "UN in Secret Peace Talks with Taliban," *Guardian*, Jan. 28, 2010.

43. Hekmatyar lived in Iran under house arrest after the Taliban took Kabul in 1996 but was released following President George W. Bush's "axis of evil" speech in 2002. His family resides in Tehran. Bahir visited Britain in early 2009, and there were HIG contacts with the team led by U.S. envoy Richard Holbrooke in early spring 2009. The latter was confirmed by Hekmatyar in an interview with German TV, a transcript of which is at http://www.heute.de/ZDFheute/download/0,6741,7018647,00.pdf.

44. "Jalaluddin Haqqani is 'someone who could be reached out to…to negotiate and bring [the Taliban] into the fold,' Prince Turki, the former Saudi ambassador to the U.S., told a group of about 80 government and business leaders and journalists over dinner in Washington." Jon Ward, "Saudi Prince Says Taliban Leader Could Be U.S. ally," *Washington Times*, Apr. 27, 2009, http://www. washingtontimes.com/weblogs/potus-notes/2009/apr/27/saudi-prince-says-taliban-leader-could-be-us-ally/. See also "Pakistan Plans to Broker Afghan Deal," Agence France-Presse, June 16, 2010, http://www.google.com/hostednews/afp/article/ALeqM5iCQ35TNlzjhFUxn_ugUlfXB1b2mA.

45. All other "organizations," such as the Haqqani, Mansour, and other networks, are parts of the Taliban movement, recognizing Mullah Omar as their spiritual leader, or have become so of late, as with the hitherto independent Wahhabi groups in Kunar and Nuristan in early 2010. For details on the relationships between the insurgent groups and with the mainstream Taliban, see Thomas Ruttig, *The Other Side: Dimensions of the Afghan Insurgency: Causes, Actors and Approaches to "Talks,"* AAN Thematic Report 01/2009, Kabul/Berlin, July 2009.

46. Internal U.N. document seen by the author. Parallel to PTS, the U.S. military started an allegiance program for Taliban fighters who wished to lay down their arms, "requiring them to take an oath of allegiance to the Afghan government and giving them an identification card to guarantee their safety." Carlotta Gall, "Taliban Trek Rocky Road Back to Afghanistan," *New York Times*, Mar. 20, 2005, http://www.nytimes.com/2005/03/20/international/asia/20afghan.html.

47. Semple, *Reconciliation in Afghanistan*, p. 55.

48. Various sources (both media reports and individuals with links to the Taliban interviewed by the author in Kabul in March and November 2010) differed about who was arrested and "summoned" or not. See, for example, Anand Gopal, "Half of Afghanistan Taliban Leadership Arrested in Pakistan," *Christian Science Monitor*, Feb. 24, 2010, http://www.csmonitor.com/World/Asia-South-Central/2010/0224/Half-of-Afghanistan-Taliban-leadership-arrested-in-Pakistan; Deb Riechmann and Munir Ahmad, "Pakistani Officials: Nearly 15 Top Taliban Held," Associated Press, Feb. 25, 2010, http://www.washingtonpost.com/wp-dyn/content/article/2010/02/25/AR2010022501502.html; Tolo TV (Kabul), news in Dari, Feb. 28, 2010, cited in BBC Monitoring Service (Afghanistan) Mar. 1, 2010; "Pakistan: Key Taliban Leader 'Held in Karachi.'" AKI news agency, Mar. 4, 2010, http://www.adnkronos.com/AKI/English/Security/?id=3.1.79935520.

49. Some observers believe he is a member of the Quetta Shura under the nom de guerre Mullah Qaher.

50. The "commission" was a Taliban body that traveled through various provinces to question the Afghan population about the behavior of local Taliban commanders. This happened after the publication of the *layha*, the third edition of the code of conduct for Taliban fighters issued in the name of Mullah Omar in mid-2009. On the commission, see also Thomas Ruttig, *The Other Side*, pp. 17–18.

51. Thomas Ruttig, "The Taliban Arrest Wave in Pakistan: Reasserting Strategic Depth?" *CTC Sentinel*, March 2010, vol. 3, issue 3, pp. 14–16. Mujahed is the leader of the Tora Bora Jehad Front (*De Tora Bora Jehadi Mahaz*) in Nangrahar province (eastern Afghanistan), which is based on remnants of the former mujahideen organization Hezb-e Eslami (Khales).

52. David Ignatius wrote: "He is shooting more, increasing special-operations raids and bombings on Taliban commanders. But he is also talking more—endorsing President Hamid Karzai's reconciliation talks with Taliban officials," in "Diplomacy with a Punch," *Washington Post*, Oct. 19, 2010.

53. David S. Cloud, "Afghan Civilian Deaths Caused by Allied Forces Rise," *Los Angeles Times*, Nov. 1, 2010, referring to "internal U.S. military statistics."

54. See: Greg Miller, "U.S. Military Campaign to Topple Resilient Taliban Hasn't Succeeded," *Washington Post*, Oct. 27, 2010. This was confirmed to the author by Afghan and international observers for the Haqqani Network in southeastern Afghanistan (September and December 2010).

55. See also Tom Gregg, "Talk to the Haqqanis, Before It's Too Late," *Foreign Policy*, *AfPak Channel*, Sept. 22, 2010, http://afpak.foreignpolicy.com/posts/2010/09/22/talk_to_the_haqqanis_before_its_too_late.

56. President Obama's Final Orders, in *Obama's Wars*, p. 385.

57. Zeina Khodr, "Karzai 'Holds Talks' with Haqqani," al-Jazeera, June 27, 2010, http://english.aljazeera.net/news/asia/2010/06/20106277582708497.html.

58. Greg Carlstrom, "Afghan Talks Raise Speculation," al-Jazeera, June 27, 2010, http://english.aljazeera.net/news/asia/2010/06/2010627202528829196.html.

59. "The Haqqani Group or the Haqqani Network Group is not an official name or a name we chose. This name is used by the enemies in order to divide the Mujahideen. We are under the highly capable Emirate of the Amir of the Faithful Mullah Umar, may Allah protect him, and we wage Jihad in the path of Allah. The name of Islamic Emirate is the official name for us and all the Mujahideen in Afghanistan." Ansar al-Mujahideen Forum Q&A with Sirajuddin Haqqani, June 11, 2010, English translation released on June 11, 2010, by the NEFA Foundation, http://www.nefafoundation.org/miscellaneous/NEFA_Sirajuddin_6102010.pdf.

60. Alissa J. Rubin, "Petraeus Says Taliban Have Reached out to Karzai," *New York Times*, Sept. 28, 2010.

61. Reported in the *Huffington Post*, Oct. 1, 2010, http://www.huffingtonpost.com/stephen-schlesinger/the-un-thinks-the-end-is_b_747555.html.

62. Gannon, "Taliban Set Preconditions."

63. Kim Sengupta and Julius Cavendish, "Taliban's High Command in Secret Talks to End War in Afghanistan," *Independent*, Oct. 7, 2010.

64. Dexter Filkins, "Taliban Elite, Aided by NATO, Join Talks for Afghan Peace," *New York Times*, Oct. 19, 2010; Thom Shanker, David E. Sanger, and Eric Schmitt, "U.S. Aids Taliban to Attend Talks on Making Peace," *New York Times*, Oct. 13, 2010.

65. Kim Sengupta, "Nato Launches Major Offensive to Clear Taliban Heartland," *Independent*, Oct. 18, 2010.

66. Anwar ul-Haq Mujahed is the son of the deceased Maulvi Yunes Khales, leader of Hezb-e Islami (Khales), one of the seven major Sunni and Pakistan-based mujahideen "parties" in the 1980s. This party has split into two wings: one is now allied with Karzai, and the other, under Anwar ul-Haq, opposes the Karzai government. Anwar ul-Haq Mujahed, aka "khalifa," the son, established the so-called Tora Bora Military Front in early 2007 as an insurgent outfit operating in the southern Nangarhar home area of the Khugiani tribe.

67. Kathy Gannon, "Taliban Hold Secret Talks with Afghan President," Associated Press, Oct. 31, 2010.

68. Willi Germund, "Finding Kabir," *AAN blog*, Mar. 2, 2010, http://www.aan-afghanistan.org/index.asp?id=688.

69. Martine van Bijlert, "Are Talks with the Taliban Snow-Balling?" http://www.aan-afghanistan.org/index.asp?id=1241.

70. Gannon, "Taliban Set Preconditions."

71. Joshua Partlow, "Karzai Wants U.S. to Reduce Military Operations in Afghanistan," *Washington Post*, Nov. 14, 2010.

72. Partlow, "Karzai Wants"; "Afghan President Karzai Confirms Taliban 'Contacts,'" BBC, Oct. 11, 2010; "Taliban Contacts Still at Embryonic Stage: NATO Envoy," Reuters, Sept. 28, 2010; "'Less Than Meets the Eye' on Taliban Talks: US Envoy," Agence France-Presse, Oct. 29, 2010.

73. Dexter Filkins and Carlotta Gall, "Taliban Leader"; "Taliban Chief Mullah Omar Rules Out Afghan Peace Talks," BBC, Nov. 15, 2010.

74. Van Bijlert and Ruttig, "Warlords' Peace Council."

75. Civil Society Resolution, Oct. 4, 2010, http://www.reliefweb.int/rw/rwb.nsf/db900SID/VVOS-89WJSX?OpenDocument.

76. For more details, see Ruttig, *The Ex-Taliban*, p. 4.

77. The following part is an updated version from Ruttig, *The Other Side*, pp. 19–20.

78. "Message of Felicitation of the Esteemed Amir-ol-Momineen on the Occasion of Eid-ul-Odha," Nov. 15, 2010, translated by the NEFA Foundation.

79. "Text of Interview of the Esteemed Mullah Beradar Akhund, Deputy Ameerul Mo'mineen of the Islamic Emirate of Afghanistan with the 'SARK' Magazine," June 23, 2009, http://alemarah1.org/english/marki-23-06-2009.html (accessed July 1, 2009. The link no longer works, but the author has a downloaded copy. The magazine's name is misspelled and should read *Srak*, Pashto for beam of light).

80. Sayed Salahuddin, "Taliban Say Want Peace with Afghans, NATO Troops Out," Reuters, Feb. 26, 2009.

81. See, for example, Yaroslav Trofimov and Habib Khan Totakhil, "Aid Groups Seek Safety Pacts with Taliban," *Wall Street Journal*, Nov. 22, 2010, http://online.wsj.com/article/SB10001424052748704756804575608440626421822.html; Thomas Ruttig, "The Air Is Getting Thicker in Paktia," *AAN blog*, Dec. 8, 2010, http://www.aan-afghanistan.org/index.asp?id=1372.

82. Its ailing leader, Jalaluddin Haqqani, is reportedly hospitalized in Rawalpindi, most likely under strict ISI supervision.

83. Ruttig, "Gulbuddin Ante Portas—Again."

84. Author's interviews, local observers in Gardez, September, October, and December 2010.

85. Author's interview with a high-ranking Talib released from a Kabul jail, March 2010.

86. Here, one should have no illusions: as long as those political forces are still armed, federalism would transfer the current undemocratic system into the regions. Instead of one clientele system, there would a number of subnational systems.

87. Almost all political parties opted to replace the current Single Non-Transferable Vote (SNTV) election system with a combined party-based, single-seat constituency system before the 2005 parliamentary elections, and many reiterated this position before the 2010 elections although, in contrast to 2005, there was no consultation with them when the new election law was composed.

88. Gannon, "Taliban Set Preconditions."

89. In her Inaugural Holbrooke Lecture at the Asia Society in New York, Feb. 18, 2011.

90. This should also be the case with the Haqqani Network, which considers itself a part of the Taliban movement, not a separate organization. Although the Haqqani Network has closer (and historically longer) relations with al-Qaeda, this does not necessarily mean that it shares its Jihadist ideas.

91. Transcript: Afghan Taliban spokesman discusses war, *CNN* (online), May 5, 2009.

92. This might change, however, once the transition from Haqqani the Elder, who is more of a tribal leader, to the younger Serajuddin Haqqani, who has been educated as a Wahhabi in Saudi Arabia, is final. Much depends on whether Riyad is willing to use its influence on him.

93. See, for example, Thomas Ruttig, "Another Militia Creation Gone Wrong," Afghanistan Analysts Network, Oct. 18, 2010, http://aan-afghanistan.com/index.asp?id=1234.

94. The author was a witness to the Soviet-Afghan policy of "national reconciliation" in 1988–89 as a political officer at the GDR Embassy in Kabul.

95. My AAN colleague Martine van Bijlert has introduced these local Afghan terms into the literature: *majburi* (forced) and *na-raz* (discontent) Taliban. See "Unruly Commanders and Violent Power Struggles: Taliban Networks in Uruzgan," in Giustozzi, *Decoding the New Taliban*, pp. 160–161.

96. See Matt Waldman, *Navigating Negotiations in Afghanistan*, USIP Peace Brief 52, Sept. 13, 2010, pp. 2–3.

97. See media reports about the lack of progress in building up local government—for example, Josh Boak, "In Afghanistan, U.S. 'Civilian Surge' Falls Short in Building Local Government," *Washington Post*, Mar. 8, 2011, http://www.washingtonpost.com/wp-dyn/content/article/2011/03/08/AR2011030805351.html.

98. Waldman, *Navigating Negotiations*, p. 3.

99. See the most comprehensive poll on this issue so far, Afghan Independent Human Rights Commission, *A Call for Justice*, Kabul 2005. There has been no similar research on post-Taliban regime crimes published yet.

100. Officially called the National Reconciliation, General Amnesty and National Stability Law, it was passed and approved by President Karzai in March 2007 but was not published (and therefore did not become law) until December 2009. See Sari Kouvo, "After Two Years in Legal Limbo: A First Glance at the Approved 'Amnesty Law,'" *AAN blog*, Feb. 22, 2010.

101. Waldman, *Navigating Negotiations*, p. 4.

102. Pakistan's military chief, Gen. Ashfaq Parvez Kayani, has told NATO that his country would be ready to open communication channels with the Taliban. See Jane Perlez, "Pakistan Is Said to Pursue Role in U.S.-Afghan Talks," *New York Times*, Feb. 9, 2010. A high-ranking official of Islamabad's foreign office was blunter: "We have considerable influence on the Taliban and will play our role in securing peace in Afghanistan." See Willi Germund, "Pakistan lässt Taliban-Chef auffliegen," *Salzburger Nachrichten*, Feb. 17, 2010.

103. Afghanistan and Pakistan have witnessed tense bilateral relations since Pakistan became independent after the 1947 partition of India. This was mainly caused by the incorporation of Pashtun areas of former British India into Pakistan against Afghanistan's will and Afghanistan, as a result, opposing the U.N. accession of its new neighbor. Both countries mutually supported armed insurgencies on the other side of the border and imposed trade blockades on the other side during various periods over the past sixty-three years. The biggest problem is that most of the common border, the so-called Durand Line—seen as British-imposed by Kabul—remains without recognition.

104. These causes include the insurgency against the Karzai government and its external allies, and also grave differences among various actors about the political system in Afghanistan, questions of justice for wrongs committed during three decades of war, as well as many conflicts about local resources that have become politicized over the past three decades and consequently escalated while traditional mechanisms of resolution have been undermined.

105. Earlier, there had been some imposters who showed up in Kabul claiming to speak for the Quetta Shura, fooling the U.S. and British intelligence as well as the Kabul government. Tragically, the killing of Rabbani itself was such a case. More details in Kate Clark, "Death of Rabbani (5): Where Is the Evidence?" *Afghanistan Analysts Network blog*, 13 Oct. 13, 2011, http://www.aan-afghanistan.org/index. asp?id=2158.

106. Renee Montagne, "Taliban's New Political Office Is a 'Game-Changer,'" interview with Michael Semple, National Public Radio, Jan. 18, 2012, http://www.npr.org/2012/01/18/145384414/ exploring-peace-talks-with-the-taliban.

107. See http://www.washingtonpost.com/world/asia-pacific/afghan-police-suicide-attack-in-southern-kandahar-city-kills-5-including-policeman/2012/01/03/gIQATUHiXP_story.html.

108. Alissa J Rubin, "Former Taliban Officials Say U.S. Talks Started," *New York Times*, Jan. 28, 2012, http://www.nytimes.com/2012/01/29/world/ asia/taliban-have-begun-talks-with-us-former-taliban-aides-say.html; Quentin Sommerville and Bilal Sarwary, "Afghan President Hamid

Karzai 'Plans Talks with Taliban,'" BBC News, Jan. 29, 2012, http://www.bbc.co.uk/news/world-asia-16779547.

109. The full text of the Taliban statement and further details on this latest development are in Kate Clark, "The End of the Affair? Taliban Suspend Talks," Afghanistan Analysts Network (AAN) blog, Mar. 15, 2012, http://www.aan-afghanistan.org/index.asp?id=2610.

110. There are contradictory statements by President Karzai as to whether he has been briefed about these contacts or not. Ahmed Rashid reports, though, that "Mr. Karzai has been fully briefed after each round and has unstintingly supported the Taliban's desire to hold separate talks with the Americans." Ahmed Rashid, "Talks with Taliban Must Be Secret to Be Successful," *The Globe and Mail*, July 1, 2011, http://www.theglobeandmail.com/news/world/asia-pacific/talks-with-taliban-must-be-secret-to-be-successful/article2084159/.

111. The Afghan government denies that the Taliban office has officially been inaugurated. See also Thomas Ruttig, "Talks on Two Channels? The Qatar office and Karzai's Saudi option," *AAN blog*, Jan. 29, 2012, http://www.aan-afghanistan.org/index.asp?id=2474.

112. His name is Tayyeb Agha, a very close confidant of Mulla Omar who also, during the Taliban regime, was Mulla Omar's "head of office" in Kandahar. For a while, in 1999–2000, he also worked at the Taliban embassy in Islamabad, which might have acquainted him not only with the ISI but also with Western diplomats. "Taliban Have Recently Twice Held Talks with Americans Under Leadership of Taib Agha," *Weesa*, Kabul, Mar. 20, 2011, quoted from BBC Monitoring.

113. For an assessment of the APRP, see Kate Clark, "New Bureaucracies to Welcome 'Upset Brothers,'" AAN blog, May 14, 2010, http://www.aan-afghanistan.org/index.asp?id=751.

A Note on Spelling

We have used standard English spellings of Middle Eastern and South Asian names and words throughout the text—for instance, al-Qaeda, Osama bin Laden, Mullah Omar, Taliban, and mujahideen.

A Note on the Notes

Although there is a possibility of links in endnotes no longer being active or otherwise problematic, please be assured that the chapter authors and volume editors gave their best effort to capture source information at the time of manuscript completion, in an online landscape that is sometimes as volatile and changing as the terrain and status of Talibanistan itself.

Index